Fortran 90
Programming

INTERNATIONAL COMPUTER SCIENCE SERIES

Consulting Editor   **A D McGettrick**   University of Strathclyde

SELECTED TITLES IN THE SERIES

Fortran 90
Programming

T.M.R. ELLIS *University of Oxford*

IVOR R. PHILIPS *Boeing Computer Services*

THOMAS M. LAHEY *Lahey Computer Systems, Inc.*

Addison-Wesley

Harlow, England • Reading, Massachusetts • Menlo Park, California
New York • Don Mills, Ontario • Amsterdam • Bonn • Sydney • Singapore
Tokyo • Madrid • San Juan • Milan • Mexico City • Seoul • Taipei

© 1994 Addison-Wesley Publishers Ltd.
© 1994 Addison-Wesley Publishing Company Inc.

Addison Wesley Longman Limited
Edinburgh Gate
Harlow
Essex, CM20 2JE
England

The programs in this book have been included for their instructional value. They have been tested with care but are not guaranteed for any particular purpose. The publisher does not offer any warranties or representations, nor does it accept any liabilities with respect to the programs.

Many of the designations used by manufacturers and sellers to distinguish their products are claimed as trademarks. Addison-Wesley has made every attempt to supply trademark information about manufacturers and their products mentioned in this book. A list of the trademark designations and their owners appears on p. xviii.

Cover designed by Viva Design Limited, Henley-on-Thames incorporating photograph © Michael Short, reproduced courtesy the Robert Harding Picture Library
Text designed by Lesley Stewart
Typeset by CRB Associates, Norwich
Printed in The United States of America

First printed 1994. Reprinted 1995 and 1996.

ISBN 0-201-54446-6

British Library Cataloguing in Publication Data
A catalogue record for this book is available from the British Library.

Library of Congress Cataloging in Publication Data
Ellis, T.M.R., date
    Fortran 90 programming / T.M.R. Ellis, Ivor R. Philips, Thomas M. Lahey.
        p.   cm. -- (International computer science series)
    Includes bibliographical references and index.
    ISBN 0-201-54446-6
    1. FORTRAN 90 (Computer program language)   I. Philips, Ivor R.
II. Lahey, Thomas M.   III. Title.   IV. Series.
QA76.73.F25E435   1994
005. 13'3--dc20   94-3153
                                                      CIP

Preface

Fortran 90 is the latest version of the world's oldest and most widely used scientific programming language, and was accepted as an international standard language in the summer of 1991 after a twelve year development process involving experts from around the world. The major development work was carried out by the American Fortran Standards Committee (X3J3), of which all three of us are long-standing members, with the final stages being directed by the International Organization for Standardization's Fortran Working Group (WG5), of which we are also all active members.

Fortran dates from 1954, when the first FORmula TRANslation system was developed at IBM by a team led by John Backus. Since those early days there have been a number of definitive stages in the development of Fortran — FORTRAN II, FORTRAN IV, FORTRAN 66, FORTRAN 77 and now Fortran 90. This latest step is, in many ways, the most important of all, for it marks the full emergence of Fortran as a modern programming language, with many new features based on the experience gained with similar concepts in other languages, and others which provide Fortran's own contribution to the development of new programming concepts.

This book is primarily intended for college students who are learning how to program in Fortran 90, and is a natural successor to the similar book written by one of us (TMRE) about FORTRAN 77 programming. We have therefore written it in such a way as to encourage readers to utilize fully the power and flexibility of Fortran 90 from the outset, while also making them aware of important older constructs which remain in the language for compatibility with earlier versions. These older constructs will often be found in existing programs, or in programs written by Fortran programmers who learned their programming in an earlier age and have not yet fully adapted to the current style and capability of Fortran 90.

Every chapter of the book follows a similar structure, and is introduced by a short overview of the topic covered in that chapter, with an emphasis on the class of problems that it helps to solve and the key techniques that are being introduced. At several points within each chapter there are short **self-test exercises** which should be used to check and to reinforce the material covered thus far. Every chapter also includes a number of worked examples which illustrate both the features of the language that have most recently been introduced and, equally importantly, a recommended approach to the design and development of programs. Finally, at the end of each chapter, before the programming exercises for that chapter, there is a brief checklist of the main features of the chapter, together with a summary of all new syntax introduced.

It seems appropriate here to emphasize that the programming community has, since the very beginning, consisted of both men and women, although in recent years there seems to have been an unfortunate reduction in the number of women entering it. We, therefore, very much hope that people of both sexes will be reading this book. We believe that men and women make equally good programmers, and will, wherever possible, avoid the use of words such as 'he' or 'she' throughout the book.

An important message for experienced Fortran programmers

The book is also suitable for experienced FORTRAN 77 programmers who wish to update their knowledge to take advantage of the new features of Fortran 90. Although such readers will, inevitably, be tempted to simply dip into the book in order to find out how a particular feature works, we would strongly urge them to try to resist this temptation and to read the book from the beginning – although they could omit Chapter 1 if they wish. The reason for this advice is that, although Fortran 90 contains all of FORTRAN 77 within it and could, therefore, be considered to be little more than FORTRAN 77 plus a set of additional features to be incorporated in programs as and when appropriate, some of the new features, notably **modules** and the new **array processing** features, will have a profound effect on the way in which Fortran programs are designed and written in the future. In order to appreciate our recommended approach to writing Fortran 90 programs, therefore, even experienced Fortran programmers should read the book from the beginning to the end, and not jump about at random (as we are all tempted to do with, for example, the manual accompanying a new item of software!).

How to use this book

Fortran 90 is a large language, partly because it contains many features which are included for compatibility with earlier versions of the language – some of which should never be used in new programs. We have, therefore, defined a smaller language, which we shall refer to as the **core language**, and have concentrated the bulk of the book on this pure Fortran 90 language.

In line with our overall philosophy of learning through experience, the book is structured in two parts. The first part covers many of the main features of Fortran 90, and it is possible to write programs to solve a very high proportion of problems by using only these features. Each chapter contains a number of worked examples, as well as self-test exercises and a substantial number of programming exercises; sample solutions to a small proportion of the programming exercises will be found at the end of the book, and sample solutions to many more can be obtained by teachers from the publishers, both in printed form in the accompanying *Instructor's Guide* and in electronic form on disk. The eight chapters which make up Part I, together with the introductory Chapter 1, can easily, therefore, form the basis of an introductory course in Fortran programming.

Part II develops most of the topics covered in Part I to make the student aware of other possibilities which will both help to solve most remaining problems and introduce alternative, or better, ways of dealing with the more straightforward ones. However, unlike Part I, it is not essential that the student covers all the material. Although the order of presentation creates a logical development, and will frequently utilize material that has been introduced in an earlier chapter, it is feasible to omit certain chapters, or combinations of chapters, for certain categories of students. The *Instructor's Guide* discusses this topic in more detail for those involved in planning courses for particular categories of students.

As already mentioned, every chapter contains several groups of self-test exercises, as well as a set of programming exercises. We strongly recommend that you should attempt all the self-test exercises, and check your answers with those included at the back of the book before proceeding. You should also carefully study the worked examples in each chapter, as these illustrate not only how to code a solution to a particular problem but, more importantly, how to design a program to meet the requirements of the problem.

Once you have completed the chapter you should always attempt some of the programming exercises, *and run your solutions on a computer*, before proceeding to the next chapter. Experience is even more important than theoretical knowledge in programming. Sample solutions to one or two of these exercises are included at the end of the book; more are included in the *Instructor's Guide*. Your programs will, almost certainly, differ from these sample solutions. If the difference is substantial then it is worth comparing them in order to establish why they differ and how one of them might have been improved; differences as a result of individual programming styles are, however, unimportant.

We have already mentioned that Fortran 90 contains all the features of FORTRAN 77, although many of these features are not recommended for new programs. The Fortran 90 standard identifies a small number of features which are obsolete and which are candidates for removal from the formal definition of the language at the next revision (or the one after!). However, language features cannot be removed from the defining standard until some time after they have ceased to be used in practice, and there are a number of other features of

Fortran 90 which we believe should not be used, since much better alternatives exist elsewhere in the language. Most of these are gathered together in Appendix E, but are not discussed elsewhere in the book, while the remainder are identified as obsolescent features when referred to in the appropriate chapter of the book, and are not otherwise discussed. All of these features, which fall outside our core language, are printed in a smaller font, identical to that used for this sentence, as a visual reminder that this feature is not recommended for new programs. When discussing Fortran 90 features for which older, obsolescent, alternatives are described in Appendix E, a special symbol will be found in the margin to identify that fact; an example is shown on this page adjacent to this sentence.

It is strongly recommended that new programs should never use any of these obsolescent features of Fortran 90.

There is one major exception to this philosophy, namely the whole area of **storage association**, and in particular **COMMON** blocks and **EQUIVALENCE** statements. Although Fortran 90's new module facility eliminates the need for **COMMON** as a means of providing global access to data, the concept of **COMMON** data is so fundamental to all existing Fortran programs that we feel that it deserves a more thorough treatment than would otherwise be given to an obsolete feature. Chapter 17 therefore discusses this topic in some detail, although it must be emphasized that we do not believe that this concept should be used in new programs.

To the teacher

Since this book follows quite soon after the second edition of *FORTRAN 77 Programming* (by T.M.R. Ellis), it will come as no surprise to find that it shares many of the same concepts as that book. Indeed, the FORTRAN 77 book was quite deliberately written in the expectation that it would be followed quite shortly by a Fortran 90 one, and the time lapse of over three years between the two is mainly due to delays in the final processing of the Fortran 90 standard, which was completed only in the summer of 1991 – almost a year later than had been anticipated when the FORTRAN 77 book was being completed. Like that book, therefore, this book contains a wealth of worked examples, all of which have been fully tested, and a large number of programming exercises at the end of each chapter. Sample solutions to some of these exercises will be found at the end of the book, while sample solutions to a great many more are included in the accompanying *Instructor's Guide*. In addition, each chapter contains several self-test exercises by means of which students can assess their progress and understanding; solutions to all the self-test exercises are provided at the end of the book.

The Computing Teaching Centre (CTC) at the University of Oxford, of which TMRE had the privilege to be the Director throughout its all-too-short life of only eight years, was a central service department which taught courses about all aspects of computing to students of all disciplines, both on a vocational basis and through courses organized in conjunction with their own academic departments. This gave the teaching staff of the CTC a unique perspective of the problems found by widely differing types of student on different types of courses, and we spent a great deal of time developing new approaches to teaching in order to obtain the best results. In particular, we discovered that there are very few textbooks *for any language* which introduce the features of the language in what we had established to be the best order. The second edition of TMRE's widely used textbook used this experience to create what was seen by some as a radically new approach, but which was in reality simply a formalization of the methods already developed at the CTC.

This book continues with this approach, with the added benefit that Fortran 90 contains all the modern features necessary to enable programs to be properly designed and written – which FORTRAN 77 did not. However, the most important aspect of the ordering of the previous book was probably its early treatment of procedures, and this practice is further developed in this book, in which both procedures and modules are introduced at a very early stage, before there is any discussion of control structures or, indeed, of anything other than simple assignment and list-directed input/output. This means that procedures are treated as a basic programming block, and that modules are seen as a natural way of grouping similar entities, with the result that students learn to develop programs in a modular fashion from the outset. The CTC experience was that students have far less trouble with procedures and modules if they are introduced at this early stage than if they are left until most of the other features of the language have been met and the students' own programming styles have begun to form.

Programming is nowadays recognized to be an engineering discipline (**information engineering**), and as such it draws on both art and science. As with any other branch of engineering it involves both the learning of the theory and the incorporation of that theory into practical work. In particular, it is impossible to learn to write programs without plenty of practical experience, and it is also impossible to learn to write *good* programs without the opportunity to see and examine other people's programs.

This book uses the concept of an English language **structure plan** as an aid to program design, and from their first introduction in Chapter 2 structure plans are developed for all the worked examples throughout the remainder of the book. There are 51 such worked examples and a total of over 139 complete programs and subprograms in this book, of which 107 are in the main text of the book and the remainder are included as example solutions to some of the programming exercises. *All of these have been fully tested on an 80486-based PC using either the Lahey Fortran 90 compiler or the Salford Software Fortran 90 compiler.* Since many of these programs, subroutines and functions may be of more general use there is a special index to them at the end of the book, before the general index.

Each chapter contains two types of exercise for the student. The first type are **self-test exercises** which do not require the writing of complete programs, and are designed to enable students to verify their understanding of the material covered in the chapter, or in part of it. Every chapter has a set of these exercises at the end, while some also contain a set in the middle of the chapter. Answers, with explanations where appropriate, to all of these exercises are included at the end of the book. The second type of exercises, which only appear at the end of a chapter, are programming exercises for students to write *and test on a computer*. Example solutions to some of these are also included at the end of the book.

Because students from many different subject areas need to learn Fortran, great care has been taken to avoid any bias towards particular scientific or engineering concepts in the worked examples. The purpose of these examples is to help students to understand how to use particular programming concepts and how to develop well-structured programs using these concepts. Many of these worked examples are, therefore, intended to solve quite general and non-scientific problems which will be understood by students of any background. One particular group of examples is, however, worthy of special mention here.

One of the many improvements of Fortran 90 over FORTRAN 77 is its ability to define new data types and the operators to enable them to be fully integrated into the language. This provides the means for greater data abstraction and the design of application-oriented data structures. As an example of this, one of the worked examples in Chapter 3 creates two data types, for points and lines, and a program to calculate the line joining two points. In subsequent chapters, other two-dimensional geometric data types are added and a small library of procedures is built up to solve certain types of interaction. In addition, several of the programming exercises are also related to this topic. By the end of the book a complete geometric module has been developed which could be used in simple computer-aided design programs. This gradual development both illustrates the various techniques being learned and also demontrates how a complex program, procedure library or module can be developed in stages.

The 208 programming exercises are mainly drawn from a range of different scientific and engineering disciplines, although there are a few more general ones which do not assume any particular prior scientific knowledge. In this way, students can be directed to those programming exercises that are most appropriate for their specific background, while ensuring that students with a different background can attempt a different set of exercises.

Mention has already been made of the accompanying *Instructor's Guide*. This contains a short summary of the major points involved in each chapter, with a note of any particular areas where experience shows that students may have problems. The *Instructor's Guide* also contains example solutions to all of the 176 programming exercises for which solutions are not included in this book. A disk containing all the programs in this book and in the *Instructor's Guide* is also available from your local Addison-Wesley office.

The programs in the book, but not those in the *Instructor's Guide*, are also available on the Internet by anonymous FTP. In order to obtain the programs in this way, you should type **ftp aw.com** on a computer which is connected to the Internet and login as **anonymous**, giving your email address as a password.

You should then change to the appropriate directory by first typing `cd aw.computer.science`, followed by `cd Ellis.F90`. The file **README** contains further information about the files in this directory. Note that case *is* significant in typing these directory and file names. If you are not familiar with using FTP to transfer files from remote computers, you should first consult your local computer advisor.

Acknowledgements

This book has been developed from the experience which we have collectively gathered over the last 25 years in teaching, using and implementing various dialects of Fortran – a total of over 80 years' Fortran experience between the three of us! During that time we have all benefited from the advice, assistance and encouragement of a great many people who must, of necessity, remain anonymous. We should, nevertheless, wish to record our thanks to all those who have helped us in so many different ways over the years.

There are, however, several people whose help has been directly related to the writing of this book and we should like to acknowledge their assistance in a more personal manner: Marilyn Philips, who typed all the chapters written by her husband, Ivor; Connie Peake, who looked after much of the day-to-day management of the Educational Technology Resources Centre at the University of Oxford while Miles Ellis was preparing the final draft of this book, as well as typing the Glossary when he broke his arm at a critical juncture; and last, but by no means least, the anonymous reviewers of an early draft whose encouraging comments and constructive criticisms were of great help in the final phases of writing.

We must also thank the many staff of Addison-Wesley who have been involved in the production of this book, especially Sheila Chatten, our production editor, who successfully guided the book through the production process, despite occasional tantrums from the authors, Stephen Bishop, and Ian Kingston who undertook the onerous task of copy-editing our manuscript.

Finally, we owe a great debt of gratitude to our wives, Maggie, Marilyn and Kathy, for putting up with our destruction of evenings and weekends when the pressure on meeting deadlines was at its greatest, and with the general disruption of normal activities which seems to be an inevitable result of the writing process. In Miles' case, this gratitude must also be extended to his children David, Sarah and Richard for putting up with a 'non-existent dad' for weeks at a time.

The bridge

On a lighter note, we must finish with a few words about the bridge on the cover of this book.

Those familiar with TMRE's earlier books on FORTRAN 77 programming will be familiar with his penchant for bridges. The first edition of that book showed the famous Iron Bridge in Shropshire, England — the first bridge in the world to be built entirely of cast iron. As the preface records, 'You can read whatever you like into this — building bridges, developing structures, elegance, style, permanence, etc. — but at least it makes a change from abstract patterns and punched cards!' The second edition showed the two Forth Bridges near Edinburgh, Scotland, and the preface to that edition records that 'the old Forth railway bridge in the foreground symbolizes old "brute force" technology that has stood the test of time, while the more recent Forth road bridge in the distance symbolizes newer, more elegant technology and the fact that this complements but does not supersede its predecessor'. It also noted that the railway bridge celebrated its centenary the year that the book was published and that the road bridge was opened only a few days before the author wrote his first Fortran program in 1964! It concluded by wondering 'which bridge we shall use for Fortran 90?'.

This question did give rise to considerable thought, and we hope that you approve of the result! This bridge is, like the language described in this book, much newer than those in the earlier books. It is the Fatih Sultan Mehmet Bridge, which crosses the Bosporus just north of Istanbul, and was opened in 1988, the same year that the technical content of Fortran 90 was finally agreed by the two committees involved, X3J3 and WG5. It is the second longest suspension bridge in the world, and one of only two bridges to link two continents, Europe and Asia — the other being a few miles to the south; furthermore, it crosses the Bosporus close to the point at which King Darius of Persia crossed it with half a million men using a bridge of boats in 514 BC.

In the same spirit of whimsy that was reflected in the earlier covers, we note that Fortran is the second most widely used programming language in the world, that its parameterized data types allow it to be equally applicable in different environments through its ability to process text in many character sets and numbers of many precisions, and that it has grown from an old, historical, foundation to the modern language of today. We also think that it is a very elegant bridge!

Finally, since everyone who has seen a draft of the cover has asked the same question: the red stripe is a Turkish flag, blowing in the breeze!

Miles Ellis
Oxford, England

Ivor Philips
Bellevue, Washington, USA

Tom Lahey
Incline Village, Nevada, USA

March 1994

Contents

Trademark notice

Cray X-MP^{TM} is a trademark of Cray Research, Inc.
Digital^{TM} and VAX^{TM} are trademarks of Digital Equipment Corporation
IBM^{TM} and IBM PS/2^{TM} are trademarks of International Business Machines Corporation
Apple^{TM} and Macintosh^{TM} are trademarks of Apple Computer, Inc.

Introduction – Six key questions

Computers are today used to solve an almost unimaginable range of problems, and yet their basic structure has hardly changed in 40 years. They have become faster and more powerful, as well as smaller and cheaper, but the key to this change in the role that they play is due almost entirely to the developments in the programming languages which control their every action.

Fortran 90 is the latest version of the world's oldest high-level programming language, and is designed to provide better facilities for the solution of scientific and technological problems and to provide a firm base for further developments to meet the needs of the last years of the 20th century and of the early 21st.

This chapter explains the background to both Fortran 90 and its predecessor, FORTRAN 77, and emphasizes the importance of the new language for the future development of scientific, technological and numerical computation. It also establishes certain fundamental concepts, common to all computers, which will provide the basis for further discussion in later chapters.

1.1 What is Fortran 90? Why is it important?

Computers first moved out of the research laboratory into industry and commerce in the early 1950s. In many ways their basic design has not changed significantly since then – they have got very much faster, very much more powerful, very much smaller, and, paradoxically, very much cheaper. But, when you get down to details, they work in much the same way now as they did then. Where the massive changes *have* come, however, is in the problems to which computers are applied, and the methods that are used in the solution of these problems. The key to making better and more effective use of computers lies in the **programming languages** which are used to define the problem and to specify the method of its solution in terms that can be understood by a computer system.

Note the use of the expression *computer system*, for nowadays we should not simply think of a computer – which is a collection of electronic and electromechanical components and devices – but also of the many computer programs without which it remains simply an inanimate collection of bits and pieces. For many years the actual computer has been referred to as the **hardware**, while the programs that control it make up the **software**. There are many different items of software on all computers, but whether a computer is a large multi-million dollar supercomputer or a small hand-held notebook computer, every single item of software has been written in one of a number of programming languages.

A question that is often asked is 'why are there so many different programming languages?', and in an ideal world it is possible that one such language might be sufficient. However, just as there are thousands of natural languages which have evolved over many centuries in different parts of the world, so there are hundreds of programming languages which have evolved over a mere 50 years. Many of these are little used, but there are a small number which are very widely used throughout the world and have been standardized (either through formal international processes or as a result of *de facto* widespread acceptance) to encourage their continuing use. Most of these major languages are particularly suited to a particular class of problems, although this class is often very wide. Fortran is one such language, and is particularly well suited for almost all scientific and technological problems, as well as to a wide range of other problem areas – especially those with a significant numerical or computational content.

Fortran 90 is the latest version of the Fortran language and provides a great many more features than its predecessors to assist the programmer in writing programs to solve problems of a scientific, technological or computational nature. Furthermore, because of Fortran's pre-eminent position in these areas, programs written in Fortran 90 can readily be transferred to run, and run *correctly*, on other types of computers in a way that is not always possible when they are written in other languages.

Nowadays, almost everyone in the developed world, and a great many outside it, have at some time used a computer and believe that they are familiar with the basic concepts. Frequently, however, this knowledge only relates to a small aspect of the whole computer system, and people are either completely unaware of extremely important concepts or, at best, only partially understand them. Before we start to examine the features of Fortran 90 and the ways in which we can use them to solve problems, therefore, we should step back slightly and establish (or even re-establish) some of the basic concepts to which we shall return from time to time throughout the remainder of this book.

1.2   What do we mean by 'a computer'?

There cannot be any aspect of modern 20th century life that is not touched by computers, and it is sometimes difficult to believe that they have only existed in anything like their present form for about 50 years. It is hard to accept that the $1000 notebook computer that can be purchased today in thousands of retail outlets is more powerful than any computer that existed 40 years ago, and that, furthermore, the most powerful computers in existence then cost well over 1000 times as much, and occupied at least 10,000 times as much space. Nevertheless, in their essential characteristics such disparate machines are essentially the same − as are virtually all computers anywhere in the world today.

However, even though computers have existed in essentially their modern form for over 50 years, it is only since the early 1980s that they have moved from the realm of the specialist into everyday use in schools, offices and homes throughout the developed world, and there can be little doubt that most of the people who use computers every day do not have any real idea of what a computer actually is.

This book is not going to answer that question, other than to emphasize that, essentially, a computer is merely an inanimate collection of electronic circuits and devices with, usually, a certain amount of electromechanical equipment attached to it. What sets a computer apart from other machines which may be built from similar (or even identical) component parts is its ability to *remember* a sequence of instructions and to *obey* these instructions at a predetermined point in time. Such a sequence of instructions is called a **program**, and what we usually refer to as a computer is more correctly called a **stored-program computer**. How we write a program to instruct the computer to perform the task(s) that we require of it is the subject of this book.

Although we do not need to know exactly how a computer works in order to use it, it is useful to create a conceptual model of a computer which will enable us to understand more easily exactly what we are doing when we write a program.

We have already referred to a computer's ability to remember a sequence of instructions and, not unreasonably, that part of a computer in which such information is stored is known as the **memory**. In fact there are two main types of information stored in a computer's memory, namely a **program** − instructions which the computer is to obey – and **data** – values (numbers, words etc.) which the computer is to process in a way defined by a program.

This processing is carried out by the **central processing unit** (CPU) which consists of (at least) two quite separate parts – a **control unit**, which fetches instructions, decodes them and initiates appropriate action, and an **arithmetic unit**, which carries out arithmetic and other types of operation on items of data.

These two parts – the CPU and the memory – could be said to constitute the computer, but there are other essential parts of the system still to be discussed. To be of any practical use a computer must be able to communicate its results to the outside world, and this calls for some form of **output device**, such as a display or a printer. Similarly, there must be some way of getting both the program and any variable data it requires into the computer, and therefore an **input device** is needed, such as a keyboard or, on some older computers, a card reader or a paper tape reader. Modern computers may have a wide range of input and output devices attached, including those which interface with instruments or other computers, but the essential concepts remain the same.

Finally, there is the question of large and/or long-term data storage. The devices used to form the memory of a computer are normally transient devices – when the power is switched off they lose the information stored in them and are thus of no use for storage of information other than during the running of a program. In addition, if the computer is to be able to access the information in the memory rapidly it can only be of a relatively small size (typically of the order of a few million characters). A memory of more than this size would place unacceptable burdens on both power requirements and physical space. However, magnetic media, such as disks or tapes coated with a fine magnetic oxide (similar to that used on tapes for domestic cassette or videotape recorders), and optical media, such as a disk whose surface is covered with tiny pits that can be detected by a reflected laser beam, can be used to store very large amounts of information easily and economically, although at the cost of slower access time. Virtually all computers use magnetic media as a **file store**, enabling programs and data to be stored in a permanent fashion within the overall computer system, while the use of optical, or magneto-optical, media is becoming increasingly popular due to the enormously greater amounts of data that can be stored in these ways compared to purely magnetic methods. A single unit of program or data is called a **file**.

Thus a computer can be represented by a simple diagram as shown in Figure 1.1.

The memory and central processor are usually electronic; however, the input, output and file store devices usually also contain mechanical components, with the result that the speed of transfer of information between them and the central processor is many times slower than that between the memory and the central processor. Because of this disparity in speed, most computers arrange for transfers between the central processor and input, output and file store devices to proceed semi-autonomously – and in many cases bypass the central processor

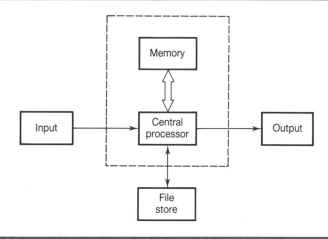

Figure 1.1   An idealized computer.

and transfer information directly to or from the memory. As a result of this, and because in earlier computers they were usually physically separated from the CPU, these types of device are often referred to as **peripheral devices** – a distinction which has been emphasized in Figure 1.1 by enclosing the memory and central processor in a dashed box.

This idealized structure applies to all computers, although a modern supercomputer may be more elaborate and have thousands of processing units in order to perform many simultaneous calculations; however, the underlying design concepts are still the same. In recent years, however, the development of the **microcomputer** has changed many people's perception of computers, for whereas large computers such as a Cray X-MP supercomputer or a Digital Equipment VAX 11-780 can easily be seen to consist of a number of discrete parts, microcomputers such as an IBM PS/2 or an Apple Macintosh take up only a few square inches of desk space and appear to consist of little more than a television monitor, a keyboard and a small box, while in a **notebook computer** everything is contained in a single, battery-powered box about the same size as a rather thick pad of paper. Nevertheless, the keyboard is the main input device, the monitor or screen is the main output device, and the small box contains a faster CPU, more memory, and more file store than all but a handful of the most powerful supercomputers of ten years ago!

Let us now return to the memory and consider its mode of operation. Conceptually, we can use an analogy with a large number of glass boxes, each containing a single ball on which is written a number, or a word, or any other single item that we may wish to store. To distinguish one box from another each has a label attached with an identifying name (see Figure 1.2). Clearly we can find out what is in any of the boxes simply by looking at it, as long as we have the name of the box. Equally clearly, if we wish to put another value in a box we shall

Figure 1.2   A storage model.

first have to remove (or otherwise get rid of) the ball which is already there so as to leave room for the new one. This is exactly the way in which a computer's memory works – if we wish to find out what is stored in a particular location the process does not affect what is stored there, whereas if we store a new value in some location then whatever was stored there is destroyed and lost.

Now consider the names on the boxes, **a**, **x** and **p**, in Figure 1.2. It is quite clear that these are the names of the *boxes* and not their contents, for if we were to store a new ball with the value 6 in box **a** we would not alter its name, and if we now looked at box **a** we would find that it contained the value 6 (Figure 1.3). We shall come back to this when we start to write programs, but it is important to realize from the outset that the names that are used to refer to storage locations in the memory always identify the *location* and not the value that is stored there.

The boxes have, by implication, been open so that the current value may be removed and a new one inserted. To complete the analogy with the computer's memory we must have a rule that says that a box is never left empty; every box must contain a ball, even if it is a blank one or one with the value zero. Because such boxes, or rather the corresponding storage locations in the memory, can have their contents changed at will they are referred to as variable storage locations, or **variables**. Boxes which are identical with these except that they

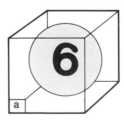

Figure 1.3   An altered storage model.

have a sealed lid can have their contents looked at, but it is not possible to replace the contents by a new value. Such storage locations are called constant storage locations, or **constants**.

1.3 Where did Fortran come from? How has it evolved?

We have already emphasized that the key feature of a computer is its ability to store a program, or sequence of instructions, and then to obey these instructions in order to solve a particular problem. In the very early days of computing such programs consisted of strings of 0s and 1s known as **machine code** and were unique to a particular type of computer, as well as being almost totally incomprehensible to a human being. It was not long, therefore, before a more compact form was devised in which each group of three **binary digits** (or **bits**) was replaced by a single number in the range 0–7 (the **octal** equivalent of the 3-bit binary number). Thus the binary sequence

```
010100011 010 000 010111
```

would be replaced by the octal sequence

```
243 2 0 27
```

This was still a matter for a specialist, although, as there were only a handful of computers in the world at that time, that in itself was of no great importance. Even for a specialist, however, it was difficult to remember which code number represented which operation, and where each data value was kept in the computer's memory. The next development, therefore, was the creation of a mnemonic form for the instructions, and the use of names to identify memory locations. For example

```
LDA 2 X
```

meant *load a special location in the CPU (register 2) with the contents of memory location X*. This is known as **assembly language** programming, and the principles have survived almost unchanged to the present day.

Towards the end of 1953, John Backus proposed to his employers, the International Business Machines Corporation (IBM), that it would be beneficial if a small research group were to be set up to develop a more efficient and economical method of programming their 704 computer than the assembly language used at that time. The proposal was accepted and the group started work almost at once. By mid-1954 an initial specification had been produced for a **programming language** of considerable power and flexibility. This language

was to be called the *IBM Mathematical FORmula TRANslation System,
FORTRAN*. The project was initially intended purely for use by IBM on a
single computer; however, soon after the preliminary report on the language was
produced word got out to some of IBM's customers, with the result that the
decision was made to make it available to anyone purchasing a 704 computer.

Although, as its name implied, FORTRAN was initially seen as a means of
converting mathematical formulae into a machine code or assembly language
form that the computer could use, it also embodied several other extremely
important concepts. By far the most important of these was that the program was
formulated in the *user's* terms, and not in those of the computer, as a result of
using an algebraic method of expressing formulae and a 'pidgin English' method
of describing the other (non-mathematical) operations. The resulting program was
subsequently said to use a **high-level language**, since the method enabled a
programmer to write programs without needing to know much about the details
of the computer itself.

Since a computer can only understand its own machine code, before a
high-level program can be obeyed by a computer it must be **translated** into the
appropriate machine code for that computer. A special program (a **compiler**) is
used to translate the high-level language program into a machine code program
for a specific computer in such a way that the machine code may be kept for use
on subsequent occasions. Since the compiler can only translate correct high-level
program statements, an important part of its task is to check the syntax (the
grammar or the structure) of each statement and to produce **diagnostic**
information to help the programmer to correct any errors.

The first *Programmer's Reference Manual* for the FORTRAN language was
released in October 1956 and the compiler was finally delivered to customers in
April 1957. This was followed twelve months later by FORTRAN II – an
improved version of the system with a considerably enhanced diagnostic
capability and a number of significant extensions to the language. Despite initial
resistance on the grounds that the compiled programs were not as efficient as
hand-coded ones, the language soon caught on, and by 1960 IBM had released
versions of FORTRAN for their 709, 650, 1620 and 7070 computers. The most
important development, however, was that other manufacturers started to write
compilers for FORTRAN and by 1963 there were over 40 different FORTRAN
compilers in existence! This led to a completely unexpected development of
enormous importance, namely program **portability**, since once a program had
been written for one computer in a high-level language such as FORTRAN it
could be easily moved to another computer with little or no change. This
development can, with the benefit of hindsight, be seen to have been the single
most important factor in the development of the computer age, for it led to large
gains in productivity and, moreover, to the possibility of developing programs
which were intended from the outset to be run on a wide range of computers.

One problem that was encountered by these early pioneers, however, was
that IBM FORTRAN used specific features of the 704 computer's instruction set
and, when they could, the other FORTRAN compilers tended to do likewise. In

addition, the advantages to be gained by having a standard language were not fully appreciated, and there were incompatibilities between different compilers, even between those written by the same manufacturer. As a result of pressure from their users as early as 1961, IBM set about developing a still further improved FORTRAN which did away with the machine-dependent features of FORTRAN II. This new system, FORTRAN IV, was released for the IBM 7030 (Stretch) computer in 1962, and later for the IBM 7090/7094 machines. Because programs written in FORTRAN IV were almost totally independent of the computer on which they were to be run, such programs could easily be transferred to a quite different computer, as long as that computer had a FORTRAN IV compiler, thus paving the way for the development of programs which were not directed at any particular type of computer, and which could therefore be used by a much larger community of users than had ever been possible before.

Perhaps the most significant development of all, however, was the decision of the American Standards Association (now the American National Standards Institute, ANSI) to set up a committee in May 1962 to develop an American Standard FORTRAN. This committee, in fact, defined two languages — FORTRAN, based largely on FORTRAN IV, and Basic FORTRAN, which was based on FORTRAN II but without the machine-dependent features. These standards were ratified in March 1966.

The existence of an officially defined standard (ANSI, 1966), which was also effectively an international standard, meant that further development of the language had a firm and well-defined base from which to work. The 1960s and early 1970s saw computers becoming established in all areas of society, and this dramatic growth led, among other things, to a proliferation of different programming languages. Many of these were oriented towards specific application areas, but a substantial proportion were intended to be **general-purpose languages**. Most noteworthy among these were ALGOL 60, ALGOL 68, BASIC, COBOL, Pascal and PL/I.

In the midst of all this language research and development FORTRAN did not remain static. Computer manufacturers wrote compilers which accepted considerable extensions to the standard FORTRAN, while in 1969 ANSI set up a working committee to revise the 1966 standard. Partly because of the many changes in the philosophy and practice of programming during this period, a draft standard did not appear until some seven years had elapsed. During 1977 this draft was the subject of worldwide discussion and comment before a revised version was approved as the new standard in April 1978 (ANSI, 1978); this was subsequently ratified as an international standard in 1980.

The new (1977) standard FORTRAN replaced both the older (1966) FORTRAN and Basic FORTRAN. In order to distinguish the new standard language from the old one, the standard suggested that the new language should be called **FORTRAN 77**.

Although the first FORTRAN 77 compiler (written largely by one of the authors of this book, TML) was available even before the standard had been approved, it was several years before compilers became widely available, and it was not until the mid-1980s that it could truly be thought of as the 'universal' FORTRAN. In the meantime, however, the computing world had not stood still and many new programming concepts were being developed, as well as many new languages, such as Ada, C and Modula-2. A new ANSI committee, X3J3, was therefore set up in 1980 to develop the *next* FORTRAN standard under delegated authority from the International Organization for Standardization's Fortran Working Group, WG5. These committees (of which the authors are all members) had originally hoped to produce a new standard by 1986 but underestimated the technical difficulties involved. Nevertheless, the new international standard was finally published in August 1991 (ISO/IEC, 1991), and, as on the previous occasion, the standard suggests an informal name for the new language to distinguish it from its predecessor; that name is **Fortran 90**.

Note, incidentally, that the defining standard uses lower case letters to spell Fortran 90, unlike the upper case letters used, officially, for FORTRAN 77 and its predecessors. In this book we shall use lower case letters whenever referring to Fortran, unless we are specifically referring to FORTRAN 77.

One extremely important aspect of the work of the two committees involved in the development of Fortran 90 (X3J3 and WG5) was that it should be fully compatible with FORTRAN 77, in order that programs written in FORTRAN 77 should function correctly when processed by a Fortran 90 processor. It is, however, important that the meaning of this commitment to full FORTRAN 77 compatibility is properly understood.

The FORTRAN 77 standard was an extremely permissive standard, in the sense that for a FORTRAN 77 processor to conform to the standard it had merely to process any standard FORTRAN 77 program correctly. However, the standard made no requirements on the processor regarding what it did with any non-conforming programs. In particular, this meant that a fully standard conforming processor could allow *extensions* to the language. Over the 12 years since the FORTRAN 77 standard was issued the art of programming has developed very considerably and, as a result, most, if not all, FORTRAN 77 compilers allowed a wide variety of extensions to the standard language.

Some of these extensions have been provided in the same way by many different compilers, notably those which were specified in the US Military Standard MIL STD 1753, but others have been done differently, if at all, in different systems. The Fortran 90 standard only claims upward compatibility with *standard* FORTRAN 77 programs; it would have been impossible to ensure that all the myriad extensions were also standardized.

Any standard FORTRAN 77 program or procedure is therefore a valid Fortran 90 program or procedure, and should behave in an identical manner – apart from one minor problem area that is discussed in Chapter 4. Thus all the wealth of existing Fortran code, written in accord with the FORTRAN 77 standard, can continue to be utilized for as long as necessary without the need for modification. Indeed, it is precisely this care for the protection of existing investment that explains why Fortran, which is the oldest of all current programming languages, is still by far the most widely used language for scientific programming.

1.4   Why learn Fortran 90?

As we have seen, there are, today, a very great many programming languages available throughout the world, some widely available, some not so widely, and some only in one place. However, two languages stand head and shoulders above the others in terms of their total usage. These languages are COBOL (first released in 1960) and Fortran (first released in 1957).

COBOL is used for business data processing and it has been estimated that over 70% of all programming carried out in 1990 used COBOL! Fortran programs probably constitute around 60% of the remainder, with all the other languages trailing far behind.

Fortran was originally designed with scientific and engineering users in mind, and during its first 30 years it has completely dominated this area of programming. For example, most of the analysis of the air flow past a modern aircraft or the path of a NASA lunar capsule is performed by a Fortran program. The dies which are used in pressing the body shells of virtually all mass-produced motor vehicles are also made by machines controlled by Fortran programs. The control of experiments investigating the sub-atomic particles which constitute the matter of our universe and the analysis of the results of these experiments are mainly carried out by Fortran programs. The structural analysis of bridges or skyscrapers, the calculation of stresses in chemical plant piping systems, the design of electric generators, and the analysis of the flow of molten glass are all usually carried out using computer programs written in Fortran.

Fortran has also been the dominant computer language for engineering and scientific applications in academic circles and has been widely used in other, less obvious, areas, such as musicology, for example. One of the most widely used programs in both British and American Universities is SPSS (Statistical Package for the Social Sciences) which enables social scientists to analyse survey or other research data (SPSS, 1988); SPSS is written in FORTRAN 77. Indeed, because of the extremely widespread use of Fortran in higher education and industry, many standard **libraries** have been written in Fortran in order to enable programmers to utilize the experience and expertise of others when writing their own Fortran programs. Two notable examples are the IMSL and NAG libraries (Visual Numerics, 1992; NAG, 1988; Hopkins and Phillips, 1988), both of which are large and extremely comprehensive collections of **subprograms** for numerical analysis applications, to which we shall refer in Chapters 10 and 18 when discussing numerical methods in Fortran 90 programs. Thus, because of the widespread use of Fortran over a period of more than 30 years, a vast body of experience is available in the form of existing Fortran programs. Fortran 90 allows access to all this experience, while adding new and more powerful facilities to the Fortran language.

Fortran has evolved over 35 years in what has often been a pragmatic fashion, but always with the emphasis on efficiency and ease of use. However, FORTRAN 77 did not have many of the features which programmers using other, newer, languages had come to find invaluable. Fortran 90, therefore, rectifies this situation by adding a considerable number of very powerful new features *while retaining all of FORTRAN 77*. In particular, many of the new features that are present in Fortran 90 will enable Fortran programs to be written more easily, more safely and more portably.

Fortran 90 has, therefore, given a new lease of life to the oldest of all programming languages, and is already being used as the base from which still more versions of the language are being developed, for example to take advantage of some of the new types of computers, such as **massively parallel computers**, which are being developed as the 20th century draws to a close. The ability to write programs in Fortran 90 will undoubtedly, therefore, be a major requirement for a high proportion of scientific and technological computing in the future, just as the ability to use FORTRAN 77, and before that FORTRAN IV, was in the past.

This book introduces the Fortran 90 language in a way that will encourage embryo programmers to develop a good style of programming and a sound approach to the design of their programs. It must, however, be emphasized that programming is a practical skill, and that to develop this skill it is essential that as many programs as possible are written and tested on a computer. The exercises at the end of each chapter will help here, but it should always be realized that to write fluent, precise and well-structured programs requires both planning and experience – and there are no short-cuts to gaining experience in any walk of life!

PART I

Fundamental Principles

First steps in Fortran 90 programming

The most important aspect of programming is undoubtedly its design, while the next most important is the thorough testing of the program. The actual coding of the program, important though it is, is relatively straightforward by comparison.

This chapter discusses some of the most important principles of program design and introduces a technique, known as a structure plan, for helping to create well-designed programs. This technique is illustrated by reference to a simple problem, a Fortran 90 solution for which is used to introduce some of the fundamental concepts of Fortran 90 programs.

Some of the key aspects of program testing are also briefly discussed, although space does not permit a full coverage of this important aspect of programming. We will return to this topic in the Intermission between Parts I and II of this book.

Finally, the difference between the old fixed form way of writing Fortran programs, which owed its origin to punched cards, and the alternative free form approach introduced in Fortran 90 is presented. Only the new form will be used in this book, but the older form is also perfectly acceptable, although not very desirable in new programs.

2.1 From problem to program in three basic steps

It has been claimed that programming is both an art (Knuth, 1969) and a science (Gries, 1991). In fact, it contains elements of both art and science, but in reality it is an **engineering discipline**, and as such it is governed by rules of procedure – albeit rules which contain a large element of pragmatism.

The reason for writing a program, *any program*, is to cause a computer to solve a specified problem. The nature of that problem may vary from manipulating text, which will subsequently be printed on some form of printer attached to the computer (**word processing**), to landing a spacecraft on a far-off planet; it can vary from controlling the traffic lights in a large city centre to analysing baseball statistics or cricket averages; it can vary from **compiling** a Fortran 90 program to controlling all aspects of the computer system on which the Fortran 90 compiler is running (the **operating system**). It should never be forgotten that *programming is not an end in itself*.

The task of writing a program to solve a particular problem can be broken down into three basic steps:

(1) Specify the problem clearly

(2) Analyse the problem and break it down into its fundamental elements

(3) Code the program according to the plan developed at step 2

There is also a fourth step which, as we shall see, is often the most difficult of all:

(4) Test the program exhaustively, and repeat steps 2 and 3 as necessary until the program works correctly in all situations that you can envisage

We shall discuss the testing of programs briefly later in this chapter, and also in the Intermission between Parts I and II of this book, but will, for reasons of clarity and space, generally omit any reference to testing elsewhere in the book. It is a vitally important part of programming, however, since no-one can guarantee to write any program of any sophistication perfectly the first time, and no-one would ever claim that a really complex program could be written in such a way that all possible situations have been anticipated and dealt with correctly from the outset.

Equally, it is important that the problem to be solved is specified clearly and unambiguously from the outset. If you are not absolutely clear about what is required it is extremely unlikely that your program will do exactly what was wanted! Specifying exactly the problem that a computer program is to solve is not always easy, but it is not the subject of this book. In all the examples and exercises in this book the problem will be clearly defined at the outset; in real-life programming, however, the problems will frequently not be so clearly defined and you will have to spend a significant amount of effort establishing exactly what is required before starting to develop any programs.

Throughout this book, therefore, we shall concentrate on steps 2 and 3 – especially in the numerous example programs which we shall use to illustrate the concepts being explained. As an example of the approach that we shall use, Example 2.1 illustrates how a simple problem can be converted into a Fortran 90 program.

■ **EXAMPLE 2.1**

1 Problem

Write a program which will ask the user for the x and y coordinates of three points and which will calculate the equation of the circle passing through those three points, namely

$$(x - a)^2 + (y - b)^2 = r^2$$

and then display the coordinates (a, b) of the centre of the circle and its radius, r.

2 Analysis

There are a number of methods of analysing problems for which programming solutions are required, both formal and informal. The approach that we shall use throughout this book is a refinement of the one that was developed by one of us (TMRE) for teaching Fortran 77, and which has been used with considerable success to teach many thousands of Fortran programmers for more than a decade. It involves creating a **structure plan** of successive levels of refinement until a point is reached where the programmer can readily code the individual steps without the need for further analysis. This **top-down** approach is universally recognized as being the ideal model for developing programs although, as we shall see, there are situations when it is necessary to also look at the problem from the other direction (**bottom-up**).

In this example we shall start by listing the major steps required.

(1) Read three sets of coordinates $(x1, y1)$, $(x2, y2)$ and $(x3, y3)$
(2) Calculate the equation of the circle $(x - a)^2 + (y - b)^2 = r^2$
(3) Display the coordinates (a, b) and the radius r

Now the first and last of these steps are fairly straightforward (once we know something about input and output in Fortran 90), but the second step is more complicated and might need further analysis. However we can defer that work until later, or can even delegate it to someone else, by writing this part of the program as a **procedure** or **subprogram**. We shall not discuss this concept any further at this stage, but will simply modify our structure plan to reflect the fact that step 2 will be carried out in a procedure which we shall call *calculate_circle*.

Our structure plan now looks like this:

> 1   Read three sets of coordinates $(x1, y1)$, $(x2, y2)$ and $(x3, y3)$
>
> 2   Calculate the equation of the circle $(x - a)^2 + (y - b)^2 = r^2$ using the procedure *calculate_circle*
>
> 3   Display the values a, b and r

There is, however, one major potential problem which we have ignored, namely what will happen if there is no solution possible. This might occur if, for example, the points lie on a straight line, or nearly on a straight line, since this will cause the equations which are to be solved to be **ill-conditioned** — a concept that we shall examine further in Chapter 10. For the present we shall ignore this problem in the name of simplicity, but it is an important one, and a proposed solution should always be examined for potential problems before coding is started, and appropriate recovery mechanisms devised. In this case, for example, it would not be too difficult to check for the two situations mentioned before attempting to solve the equations, and to print an appropriate message to the user.

3 Solution

A Fortran 90 program to implement this structure might look as follows:

```
PROGRAM circle
   IMPLICIT NONE

   ! This program calculates the equation of a circle passing
   ! through three points

   ! Variable declarations
   REAL :: x1,y1,x2,y2,x3,y3,a,b,r

   ! Step 1
   PRINT *,"Please type the coordinates of three points"
   PRINT *,"in the order x1,y1,x2,y2,x3,y3"
   READ *,x1,y1,x2,y2,x3,y3        ! Read the three points

   ! Step 2
   CALL calculate_circle(x1,y1,x2,y2,x3,y3,a,b,r)

   ! Step 3
   PRINT *,"The centre of the circle through these points is &
         &(",a,",",b,")"
   PRINT *,"Its radius is ",r

END PROGRAM circle
```

```
Please type the coordinates of three points
in the order x1,y1,x2,y2,x3,y3
4.71 4.71
6.39 0.63
0.63 3.03
The centre of the circle through these points is ( 3.510, 1.830)
Its radius is  3.120
```

Figure 2.1 The result of running the solution to Example 2.1.

We shall examine this program in some detail in Section 2.2, but even without any knowledge of Fortran 90 it is relatively easy to see that this program does reflect the structure plan that we had previously developed. Figure 2.1 shows how the screen might appear after running this program.

2.2 Some basic Fortran 90 concepts

The program written in Example 2.1 is a very simple one, but it does contain many of the basic building blocks and concepts which apply to all Fortran 90 programs. We shall therefore examine it carefully line by line to establish these concepts before we move on to look at the language itself in any detail. Before doing so, however, we must emphasize that the code shown in Example 2.1 is not the whole program, since the procedure **calculate_circle** is also part of the same program. What is shown is simply the **main program** or, more correctly, the **main program unit**. We shall have more to say about the other types of program unit later.

The first line of our program reads

PROGRAM circle

Every main program unit must start with a **PROGRAM** statement which consists of the word **PROGRAM** followed by the name of the program. This name must follow the rules which apply to all Fortran 90 names, namely

- It must begin with a letter — either upper or lower case
- It may only contain the letters A–Z and a–z, the digits 0–9, and the underscore character _
- It must consist of a maximum of 31 characters

In Fortran 90 names and keywords, upper and lower case letters are treated as identical, but can be used by the programmer to assist in the readability of the program. In this book we shall use upper case for all words which have a special meaning in Fortran, known as **keywords**, and will use lower case for names created by the programmer.

The name of the program should be chosen to indicate what the program does and should be different from any other names used for other purposes elsewhere in the program.

Note also that the blank (or space) between the word `PROGRAM` and the name `circle` is included, as in normal English, to make the program easier to read. There may be any number of blanks between successive words in a Fortran 90 statement, as long as there is at least one, but they will be treated as though there was only one by the compiler when it is analysing the program. It is not necessary to include blanks between successive items in a list separated by commas or other punctuation characters, although they may be included if desired to make the program easier to read. However, it is not permitted to include spaces within a Fortran keyword or a user-specified name, except when using the older fixed form style of programming which is described in Section 2.6.

```
IMPLICIT NONE
```

This is a special statement which is used to inhibit a particularly undesirable feature of Fortran which is carried over from earlier versions of Fortran. We shall explain its meaning in full in Chapter 3; for the present we shall merely state that it should *always* be placed immediately after the `PROGRAM` statement.

```
! This program calculates the equation of a circle passing
! through three points
```

These two lines are **comments**.

A comment is a line, or part of a line, which is included purely for information for the programmer or anyone else reading the program; it is ignored by the compiler. A comment line is a line whose first non-blank character is an exclamation mark, !; alternatively, a comment, preceded by an exclamation mark, may follow any Fortran statement or statements on a line, as can be seen later in this program. We shall normally use comment lines in example programs, but will also use trailing comments where these are more appropriate.

You should always use comments liberally in your programs to explain anything which is not obvious from the code itself. You should always err on the side of caution, since what is clear to you may not be clear to someone else who has to read your program. Indeed, it may not even be clear to you six months after the code was written!

```
! Variable declarations
REAL :: x1,y1,x2,y2,x3,y3,a,b,r
```

The first of these lines is a comment which indicates that the line following contains one or more **variable declarations**. It is not obligatory, but such comments help a reader to follow the program more easily.

The next line is a **specification statement** and provides important information about the program to the compiler. In this case it specifies that the nine names **x1**, **y1**, ..., **r** are the names of variables which will be used to hold numeric information. As we shall see in Chapter 3, there are several ways in which numeric information may be stored in a computer, but the most common type is known as a **real number**. We shall examine the detailed syntax of variable declarations in Chapter 3.

```
! Step 1
PRINT *,"Please type the coordinates of three points"
PRINT *,"in the order x1,y1,x2,y2,x3,y3"
```

The next block of statements is preceded by the comment **Step 1**, simply to indicate that these statements correspond to step 1 of our structure plan.

The following two statements are the first statements to be obeyed during the *execution* of the program, and are called **executable statements**. These particular executable statements are known as **list-directed output statements** and will cause the text contained between the quotation marks (or *quotes*) to be displayed on your computer's default output device, probably the screen. We shall examine the way in which these statements work in Chapter 3.

```
READ *,x1,y1,x2,y2,x3,y3        ! Read the three points
```

This statement is clearly closely related to the previous two statements and has a very similar structure. It is called a **list-directed input statement** and will *read* information from the keyboard, or other default input device. It will be discussed in detail in Chapter 3. Note the use of a trailing comment.

```
! Step 2
CALL calculate_circle(x1,y1,x2,y2,x3,y3,a,b,r)
```

We now move on to step 2 of the structure plan. The **CALL** statement causes the processing of the main program unit to be interrupted and processing to continue with the procedure, or **subroutine**, whose name is given in the statement. Thus, as we anticipated in our structure plan, we do not need to know at this stage (or perhaps ever, if someone else writes it!) how the procedure will calculate the coefficients of the equation which defines the required circle. The items enclosed in parentheses following the procedure name are known as **arguments** and are used to transmit information between the main program and the procedure; in this case the relevant information required by the procedure is the coordinates supplied by the user, while the information returned by the procedure will be the coordinates of the centre of the circle and its radius. We shall investigate the way in which procedures are used and written in Chapter 4, as soon as we have learned about the various types of data that Fortran can process.

```
! Step 3
PRINT *,"The centre of the circle through these points is &
      &(",a,",",b,")"
PRINT *,"Its radius is ",r
```

Step 3 of the structure plan relates to the display of the required results. The first **PRINT** statement, however, incorporates a new concept – that of a **continuation line**. If the last non-blank character of a line is an ampersand, **&**, then this is an indication that the statement is continued on the next line.

There are two cases here. If, as in this case, the ampersand occurs in a **character context**, that is, in the middle of a character string enclosed in quotation marks (or one enclosed in apostrophes), then the first non-blank character on the next line must also be an ampersand, and the character string continues from the character after that ampersand. Thus the two lines above are identical to the single line

```
PRINT *,"The centre of the circle through these points is (",a,",",b,")"
```

(where the smaller type is used here solely to fit the whole statement on a single line).

The other situation is where the first ampersand does not occur within a character string enclosed in quotes or apostrophes. In this case there are two possibilities. The first is that, as in the character string case, the first non-blank character of the next line is an ampersand, in which case the effect is just as before. However if the first non-blank character on the next line is not an ampersand then the effect is as if the whole of that line follows the previous one (excluding the ampersand). Thus, for example, the statement discussed earlier, representing step 2 of the structure plan could also be written

```
CALL calculate_circle(x1,y1,x2,y2,x3,y3,&
            &a,b,r)
```

which would be identical, as far as the compiler was concerned, with the original version, or

```
CALL calculate_circle(x1,y1,x2,y2,x3,y3,&
            a,b,r)
```

which would be treated as though there were a number of spaces before **a**, although, as those spaces come between items in the list of arguments, they do not matter.

These two **PRINT** statements are different from the earlier ones in that they will print variable information as well as constant character strings. It should be obvious to the reader that they will print, or display, the appropriate text followed by the value of the specified variable or variables, as calculated by the procedure `calculate_circle`. This extended use will be described in detail in Chapter 3.

```
END PROGRAM circle
```

The final statement of a program must be an **END** statement. In this context it can take three forms:

```
END
```

```
END PROGRAM
```

or

```
END PROGRAM name
```

where name, if present, must be the same as the name on the corresponding **PROGRAM** statement. In general it is both good practice, and makes the program easier to follow, to use the third, full, form of the statement, as we shall do in all the examples in this book.

As might be expected, execution of the **END** statement brings the execution of the program to an end, and control is returned to the computer's operating system.

The overall structure of a Fortran 90 main program unit is shown in Figure 2.2.

```
PROGRAM name
    Specification statements
    .
    .
    .
    Executable statements
    .
    .
    .
END PROGRAM name          .
```

Figure 2.2 The structure of a main program unit.

SELF-TEST EXERCISES 2.1

Attempt all the following tests and then check your answers with the solutions at the end of the book. If you do not get them correct, and you are not sure why your answer is wrong, you should re-read the first two sections of this chapter before proceeding.

1   What are the three steps involved in writing a program?

2   What is usually the most difficult part of the programming process?

3   What are the rules for Fortran names?

4   What must be the first statement of a Fortran main program? And the last?

5   How is a Fortran statement continued onto a second line?

6   Why are comments important? Give two ways of including comments in your programs.

2.3   Running Fortran programs on a computer

In the preceding sections we have considered a Fortran program in isolation, with little reference to the method by which the program is input to the computer, compiled and executed. This omission is deliberate and is due to the fact that whereas the Fortran language is standardized the computer's **operating system** is not. We shall, therefore, digress slightly at this point and look at the broad principles of the overall computer system before returning to discuss the Fortran 90 language in detail.

In the early days of computing, programmers had to do everything themselves. They would load their programs (probably written in an assembly language or even machine code) and press the appropriate buttons on the machine to get it to work. When a program required data they would either type it in or, more probably, load some data cards. When a program wanted to print results, programmers would ensure that the printer (or other output device) was ready. Before long, the computers developed in two directions – first, magnetic tapes (and later disks) were added to provide backing store, and second, high-level languages such as Fortran became available. Now programmers had to load the compiler first and get it to input their programs as data (of a special kind). The compiled program (possibly on binary punched cards produced by the compiler) would then be input as before. In addition, if any file storage was required, programmers had to load the correct tapes. In some cases a full-time operator was employed to carry out all these tasks, but this of course meant that detailed instructions were required to ensure that the job was processed correctly, and so many programmers still preferred to run their programs themselves.

A major change was heralded by the development at the University of Manchester, in Britain, of the **multiprogramming** system for the Atlas computer. This took advantage of the high speed of a computer's arithmetic and logical functions compared with its input/output functions to process several programs apparently simultaneously. The effect is similar to that experienced by amateur chess-players when facing a chess master in a simultaneous display, where the master plays against a number of opponents at the same time. In fact, of course, the master moves from one board to another, but, because of his or her much greater ability and speed in assessing the positions of the pieces, the master appears to each opponent to be devoting most of the time to them. The Atlas system took advantage of the (relatively) long delays during input or output of even a single number to leave that program (whose input/output could proceed autonomously) and start to process another.

The next major development took place more or less at the same time at both Dartmouth College and the Massachusetts Institute of Technology in the USA, and led to the concept of **time-sharing**, which placed the user at a terminal through which most input/output took place, with each user having a small **slice** of time in turn. The much slower speed of a terminal allowed more programs to run at once, but, because users were communicating directly with the computer, their work was processed much more quickly in this new **interactive** mode of operation than was possible with **batch** working.

The advent of first multiprogramming and then time-sharing meant that it was no longer possible for a programmer, or even a full-time operator, to carry out all the routine tasks associated with loading and executing a program; too many things were happening in different jobs at the same time. Since the computer was now doing several things at once it was natural that it should be given the additional task of organizing its own work. Special programs were therefore written, called **operating systems**, which enabled a programmer to define what was required in the form of special instructions, and caused the computer to carry out these instructions. What gradually emerged were new languages (**job control languages**) with which programmers instructed the computer how to run their jobs.

With the advent of microcomputers and personal workstations in the 1980s the situation changed again, and although some form of operating system language always exists it is frequently hidden from users, who simply type a single command on their keyboards or select an appropriate symbol with a mouse.

Nevertheless, some action is required to run a Fortran program on a particular computer and to identify any specific requirements, and this action will be specific to the particular computer system and compiler being used. Throughout the rest of this book we shall ignore this aspect of running programs, and concentrate on the programs themselves. However, before any programs are actually compiled and executed it will be necessary for the reader to establish exactly how to input the program, and then to compile and execute it, on the particular computer system being used.

2.4   Errors in programs

It is an unfortunate fact that programs often (one might even say usually) contain errors. These fall into two distinct groups – syntactic (or grammatical) errors and semantic (or logical) errors. Before we examine how these two types of errors may occur in Fortran programs, and in order to emphasize the difference between them, we shall consider how they might occur in natural English by considering the well-known saying (among those just starting to read and write) to the effect that

> The cat sat on the mat

If this sentence was being analysed by some automatic device (a robot, perhaps?) which had a good knowledge of English grammar and of the meaning of words, but had no intuition or other means of interpreting what might have been intended by the author, then the mis-typed sentence

> The dat sat on the mat

would have no meaning. This is a *syntactic* error, since the word 'dat' does not exist in the English language, and our robot would diagnose it as such. On the other hand, the statement

> The cat sat the on mat

contains only valid English words, but the grammar is incorrect since a preposition ('on') cannot appear between the definite article ('the') and a noun ('mat'). Once again, therefore, our robot would indicate that there was a syntactic error in the sentence.

However, the sentence

> 'The mat sat on the cat

satisfies all the rules of grammar, and all the words are valid English words. Our robot will, therefore, move to the next stage and try to understand what the sentence means. Here it may have a problem! This is, therefore, an example of a *semantic* error, for there is nothing wrong grammatically (or syntactically) with the sentence; it just doesn't make any logical sense.

Notice, incidentally, that a typing mistake will not necessarily lead to a syntactic error. For example the following sentences each have a single typing error, but they are all syntactically correct, and even make sense – though not the sense that was intended:

The cat spat on the mat
The cot sat on the mat
The cat sat on the man

We can see from these examples that a syntactic, or grammatical, error is relatively easy to detect, and a Fortran compiler will always detect any such errors in a program. On the other hand, a semantic, or logical, error may result in a nonsensical meaning, or it may result in a reasonable, but incorrect meaning. In programming terms, a semantic error may result in the program failing during execution, or it may simply result in incorrect answers.

Returning to consideration of Fortran programs, therefore, an example of a syntactic error would be the omission of the asterisk in the first **PRINT** statement of the program written in Example 2.1:

```
PRINT "Please type the co-ordinates of three points"
```

When the compiler is translating this statement it finds that it does not match any of the valid forms of **PRINT** statement (there are several more, as we shall see in Chapters 3 and 8), and the appropriate machine code cannot be generated. It will therefore produce an error message such as

```
***   Syntax error
```

or probably a more helpful one such as

```
***   PRINT not followed by asterisk or format reference
```

although you should note that, since error messages are not standardized, the actual message that will be produced will vary from machine to machine.

Since a program may contain more than one error, a compiler will usually continue to check the rest of the program (although in some cases other apparent errors may be caused which will disappear when the first one is corrected). However, no machine code will be produced, and no loading or execution will take place (if these would have been automatically initiated). An **editor** will then normally be used by the programmer to correct the program before it is re-submitted to the compiler.

Errors detected by the compiler (called **compilation errors**) are no great problem. That they are there indicates a degree of carelessness on the part of the programmer, but they can be easily corrected and the program recompiled.

Semantic errors are far more serious, since they indicate that there is an error in the logic of the program. Occasionally this may lead to a compilation error, but usually it will lead either to an error during the execution of the program (an **execution error**), resulting in an abnormal end or in the program producing incorrect answers. For example, if one number was accidentally divided by zero, leading to a theoretical answer of infinity, this would result in an execution error. On the other hand, if the **READ** statement in our program had inadvertently been written as

```
READ *,x1,x2,x3,y1,y2,y3
```

then execution of the program would have led to the procedure being asked to determine the circle passing through the points $(x1, x2)$, $(x3, y1)$ and $(y2, y3)$ rather than the one passing through the points $(x1, y1)$, $(x2, y2)$ and $(x3, y3)$ as intended.

This latter example is a type of error with which the computer can give no help, since the program is syntactically correct and runs without causing a failure. It produces an incorrect answer because the logic was incorrect and only a thinking human being can detect and correct it. You should never forget that computers have no intelligence; they will only do what you tell them to do – no matter how silly that may be – rather than what you intended them to do.

Because errors in the logic of a program are often quite difficult to find (the trivial error in a very simple program shown above is hardly typical!) it is very important that programs are planned carefully in advance and not rushed. This discussion of errors underlines the importance of a planned structure to programs and programming such as that already introduced in Example 2.1, and you should get into the habit of developing structure plans before starting to code even the simplest programs.

2.5 The design and testing of programs

In the subsequent chapters of this book we shall meet the full range of Fortran 90 statements and facilities, and will begin to appreciate the richness of the language which is the basis of its ability to enable the Fortran programmer to solve an enormously wide range of problems easily and efficiently. The exercises and examples that will be used to illustrate that richness will, however, necessarily be brief, so that their complexity will not get in the way of the points that they are trying to make. Real programs will almost always be substantially larger than those that you will find in this book.

Although all the worked examples will develop the program's design by means of structure plans, it may sometimes seem that this is making the process unnecessarily difficult. *Such an attitude could not be more wrong!*

Computer programming is an activity that is extremely interesting, and one which can often exert a very considerable fascination upon those involved. It is so interesting because it requires a careful blend of knowledge from several different areas, and because the programmer is involved in a creative process which has almost no constraints, beyond the necessity to be logically consistent and obey the syntax and semantics of the language being used. In this, it has similarities with both pure mathematics and with the fine arts. As a consequence of this freedom, the programmer is free to be very creative, but abuse of this freedom will inevitably lead to poor programs.

In mathematics, a correct but ugly proof makes mathematicians uneasy, and they will strive to find an elegant proof to replace it. The same is true for computer programs, and a correct but ugly program will make people want to redesign and rewrite it. It is important to emphasize that this is not just aesthetics coming into play, for there are sound, very practical, reasons for writing elegant programs.

- The first of these is that an ugly program is almost synonymous with poor design, and with coding that was begun before the program was well thought out. This results in programs that can only be made to work correctly with considerable difficulty. Indeed, if a program is badly enough constructed, even after it has solved several test cases correctly the writer may have an uneasy feeling that it is not really reliable.

   The experience of many people over many years has shown that the time spent in careful initial design, before writing any code, is more than regained during the process of verification (often called debugging). The larger the project the more this principle comes into play. However, this does not mean that small projects do not benefit from some initial planning. Careful initial design always pays off, even on the smallest project.

- A second issue, and to many people of even more importance than the initial development of a program, is that of **maintainability** of programs. Programs need maintenance for several reasons. If a programming project goes beyond a certain small size, it will almost certainly, at some point during its lifetime, be found to have errors in special circumstances that were not thought of, or were incorrectly handled, during the initial design. Programs often have an unexpectedly long life (sometimes to the embarrassment of their authors!). Almost inevitably, most programs will, therefore, be subsequently extended to deal with new problems not in the original requirements. As a result, it is quite normal for more time and effort to be spent in extending and maintaining a program than was spent in originally developing it. The phrase 'write once and read many times' is a truism in programming.

- Finally, if you have written a program of more than parochial interest, you will undoubtedly receive requests from friends and colleagues for copies. The world is full of different types of computers. Imagine your colleagues' distress if they cannot readily compile and execute your program on their machines! You may also find that the computer on which a program was originally developed is being replaced with a new one – a circumstance that seems to be happening with ever-increasing frequency. Therefore, writing **portable programs** is important. Only for well-considered reasons should non-standard or obsolescent features of Fortran be used.

In summary, programs should be well designed before they are begun. This will lead to reliable, efficient, easily maintained, portable programs that are enjoyable to create and to work with.

There are many elements that go into good program design, and many approaches that have been developed to assist programmers to develop well-designed programs. However, regardless of the detailed approach that is used, there are a number of underlying principles that must always be incorporated in the design of any program, of which the following are the most important:

- Completely understand what the program is supposed to accomplish. What are the inputs and outputs supposed to be? This sounds too trivial to be worth mentioning, but it is not. It is all too easy not to have all the facts clearly understood before starting programming. This will lead to much painful and expensive redesign at a later stage.

- Make the input and output clear to understand for the program *user*. Make the input form as easy as possible and the output form as clear and useful as possible.

- Have a clear design for the method to be used to solve the problem. Write it down. We have already introduced one way to do this and will expand on this in later chapters. However, there are other approaches, and you should choose one that you feel comfortable with. It is surprising how often this stage has to be reworked until a correct solution is found.

- Look to see what functionality you can find in existing procedure libraries. We shall have more to say about this in Chapter 4, but we have already seen in Example 2.1 how a subroutine can be used to avoid the need to write all the program oneself. Reinventing the wheel is not an economical use of your time!

- When writing the program use a modular design. We shall discuss this topic in some detail in Chapter 4 and so will not say more here, except to point out that a good rule of thumb is that no single block of code (or *procedure*, see Chapter 4) should be longer than about 50 lines, excluding any comments.

- Use descriptive names for variables and program units and be lavish with comments. Code with few or no comments is usually impossible for even the author to understand once a few weeks have passed since its creation.

- Perform as much error checking on the input as is possible. Moreover, perform checks on the success of the internal stages of a calculation. Include, as part of the output, any problems the program detects and how the accuracy of the answer is being affected. This is actually a somewhat complicated topic and only a few introductory comments can be made here.

  For input error checking, try to catch, and report clearly back to the user, every error that the input data might contain. For example, if one of the data items is the number of items to be processed, this number should be checked to see that it is not negative, and should also be checked to see that it is not so large that the capacity of the program will be exceeded. This is an obvious type of check to make. A less obvious class of checks is on the self-consistency of the data. For example, if a program is supposed to take three points as input and calculate the radius and centre of the circle passing through them, the points should be checked to see that they do not lie on a straight line. If they are exactly collinear the radius is infinite and the coordinates of the centre have become indeterminate. Another check is to test that all the points are distinct. If they are not, then there are an infinite number of solutions.

  For errors that can be detected while the program is executing, consider checks on how many iterations are being performed in trying to converge to a solution. If this becomes too large, the user should be informed and given an option to terminate the process.

  Returning to the problem of determining the circle through three points, suppose the points are almost collinear or almost coincident. This is more difficult to detect than exact collinearity or coincidence. What does 'almost' mean here? How can a precise numerical value be given for 'almost'? There is a solution. The centre of the circle can be determined as the result of solving a pair of simultaneous linear equations. There are well established mathematical techniques, which are, however, outside the scope of this book, for estimating the *condition number* of such linear systems of equations. This analysis will detect near linearity or coincidence of points and can be used to report back to the user how many digits, if any, of the answer are accurate.

- Finally, test the program by using cases that execute *every* part of the program, including your input error tests and calculation problem tests. Although it may sound obvious, ensure that you know what the correct answer should be for those tests which are designed to run to completion. Just because your program produces an answer doesn't mean that it is the correct one!

These techniques do not take the interest and challenge out of programming, making it a mechanical process. Instead, they make a program easier to develop and maintain, thereby making the process more interesting and less painful. All of us have, at some time in our lives, been faced with the problem of trying to find the error in a badly written and badly documented program (written by someone else, of course!) and we do not recommend it to anyone.

We shall return to the question of testing programs in the Intermission between Parts I and II of this book, but we cannot overemphasize what a vitally important part of the programming process it is. Even with apparently simple programs, such as those which you will write in response to the exercises in the first part of this book, you should always thoroughly test them to ensure that they produce the correct answers from valid data, and react in a predictable and useful manner when presented with invalid data.

2.6 The old and new Fortran 90 source forms

The short program written as part of Example 2.1, and discussed in detail in Section 2.2, is written in a free form, in which the statements may be written anywhere on the line, thus enabling the programmer to arrange the layout of a program to suit any particular style preferences. There are relatively few constraints on programs written in this way, namely:

- Blank characters are significant and *must* be used to separate names, constants or statement labels from other names, constants or statement labels, and from Fortran keywords
- Comment lines are identified by having an exclamation mark as their first non-blank character
- Any characters following an exclamation mark, unless this is part of a character string, form a trailing comment
- A line may contain a maximum of 132 characters
- A line may contain more than one statement, in which case a semicolon separates each pair of successive statements
- A trailing ampersand indicates that the statement is continued on the next line; if it occurs in a character context, then the first non-blank character of the next line must also be an ampersand, and the character string continues from immediately after that ampersand
- A statement may have a maximum of 39 continuation lines
- A statement label, if required, consists of up to five consecutive digits representing a number in the range 1 to 99999, which precedes the statement, and is separated from it by at least one blank

Note, incidentally, that statement labels are rarely needed in Fortran 90, although they were much more common in earlier versions of Fortran; we shall meet them briefly in Sections 6.5 and 8.4.

```
      PROGRAM circle
C  This program calculates the equation of a circle passing
C  through three points

C  Variable declarations

C  Step 1
      PRINT *,"Please type the coordinates of three points"
      PRINT *,"in the order x1,y1,x2,y2,x3,y3"
      READ *,x1,y1,x2,y2,x3,y3

C  Step 2
      CALL calculate_coeffs(x1,y1,x2,y2,x3,y3,a,b,r)

C  Step 3
      PRINT *,"The centre of the circle through these points is",
     *        " (",a,",",b,")"
      PRINT *,"Its radius is ",r

      END PROGRAM circle
```

Figure 2.3 A fixed form version of the solution for Example 2.1.

All previous versions of Fortran used a quite different statement format, which was originally defined as part of the first FORTRAN system in 1954, when the only means of getting information into a computer was to punch it on special **punched cards**. These cards would hold a maximum of 80 characters – which is why, to this day, most computer terminals have 80 characters per line as the default size for their screens. Because it was easy to drop (and hence scramble the order of) a deck of punched cards, the last eight character positions were reserved for a sequence number, thus limiting the number of usable characters to 72. This older form of program layout is also available in Fortran 90 for compatibility with older, FORTRAN 77, programs, but it is not recommended that any new programs should use it.

In order to distinguish the two **source forms**, the old one is known as **fixed form** while the new, Fortran 90, source form is known as **free form**. This book will only use free form source, other than in Figure 2.3 which shows how the program written in Example 2.1 would look in fixed form, but the rules governing fixed form are summarized below:

- A Fortran statement is written in columns 7 to 72 only, with columns 1 to 6 being kept for special purposes, as detailed below

- Blanks have no significance (except in a character context), and may be used freely anywhere, even in the middle of words, or may be totally omitted

- The character C or the character * in the first character position of a line (column 1) indicates that the line is a comment line; an exclamation mark may also be used to initiate comments in Fortran 90, but not in FORTRAN 77, in the same way as in free form

- Columns 7 to 72 of a line may contain more than one statement in Fortran 90, separated by semicolons, although this is not allowed in Fortran 77
- A statement which is blank in columns 1 to 5, and contains any character other than zero in column 6, is treated as a continuation of the previous non-comment line
- A statement may include a maximum of 19 continuation lines
- Any statement labels must be written in columns 1 to 5 and consist, as in free form, of up to five digits representing a number in the range 1 to 99999

SELF-TEST EXERCISES 2.2

1   What is the difference between a syntactic error and a semantic error? Into which category do (a) compilation errors and (b) execution errors fall?

2   Give three reasons for the importance of well-designed programs.

3   Give four issues that should be considered *before* starting on the detailed design of a program.

4   Give four issues that should be considered *during* the testing of a program.

5   What is the maximum number of characters that may occur in one line of a Fortran program?

6   What is the maximum number of lines that a Fortran statement may be spread over?

7   What is the maximum number of Fortran statements that may appear on a single line? How are they separated?

SUMMARY

- Programming is an engineering discipline.
- The four basic steps involved in programming are *specification*, *analysis and design*, *coding* and *testing*.
- A structure plan is a method for assisting in the design of a program.
- Top-down design involves refining the problem into successively greater levels of detail.
- The programming of sub-problems identified during top-down design can be deferred by specifying a subprogram for the purpose.

- A Fortran name consists of up to 31 characters, and may be made up from any combination of the 26 upper case letters A–Z, the 26 lower case letters a–z, the ten digits 0–9, and the underscore character _ ; the first character must be a letter. Upper and lower case letters are considered to be identical in this context.

- Blank characters are significant and must not appear in names; at least one blank must be used to separate names from each other, and from numbers.

- Keywords are Fortran names which have a special meaning in the Fortran language; other names are called identifiers.

- Upper case and lower case letters are treated as identical in both Fortran keywords and identifiers.

- Every main program unit must start with a PROGRAM statement, and end with an END or END PROGRAM statement.

- An IMPLICIT NONE statement should always immediately follow a PROGRAM statement.

- A comment line is a line whose first non-blank character is an exclamation mark, !; a trailing comment is a comment whose initial ! follows the last statement on a line. Comments are ignored by the compiler.

- Specification statements provide information about the program to the compiler.

- Execution statements are obeyed by the computer during the execution of the program.

- A list-directed input statement is used to obtain information from the user of a program during execution.

- A list-directed output statement is used to give information to the user of a program during execution.

- A CALL statement is used to transfer processing to a subroutine, using information passed to the subroutine by means of arguments, enclosed in parentheses.

- There is an older fixed form method of writing programs which has slightly different rules.

- Fortran 90 syntax introduced in Chapter 2:

Initial statement	PROGRAM *name*
End statement	END PROGRAM *name* END PROGRAM END
Implicit type specification statement	IMPLICIT NONE
Variable declaration statement	REAL :: *list of names*

List-directed input and output statements	**READ** *, *list of names* **PRINT** *, *list of names and/or values*
Subroutine call	**CALL** *subroutine_name* (*argument1, argument2, . . .*)

PROGRAMMING EXERCISES

Exercises whose numbers are preceded by an asterisk (for example, 2.2 and 2.3) have sample solutions at the end of this book.

2.1 Find out how to use the editor on your computer to type and correct a Fortran program. Also find out how to submit your program for compiling and execution.

*2.2 The following simple program contains a number of errors. Identify them and produce a corrected version.

```
PROGRAM exercise 2.2
   IMPLICIT NONE
REAL : number
! This program contains a number of errors &
   is not a good example of Fortran 90 at all!
   PRINT *,"This &              ! Trailing
           &is a silly          ! comments!
           &program
   PRINT *,"Type a number"
   READ *,"number"
   PRINT "Thank you.  &
           Your number was" number

END exercise
```

Run the corrected program on your computer to check that it does indeed work. If it still does not work, then keep correcting it until it does!

*2.3 Enter the following program *exactly* as shown:

```
PROGRAM test
   ! This program contains four major errors &
   & and three examples of bad programming style
   PRINT *,Please type a number
   READ * numbr
   PRINT *,"The number you typed was ",number
END
```

The program contains four errors, only three of which will probably be detected by the compiler. There are also three additional mistakes in the program which, although not errors, are very poor programming practice. Can you find all seven? Now compile the program, correct only those errors detected by the compiler, and run it again, typing the value **123** when requested. Was the answer that was printed correct? If not, why not?

How could you improve this program so that the compiler found more of the errors?

2.4   How many mistakes can you find in the following program?

```
PROGRAM final test
! This program contains several errors
   IMPLICIT :: NONE
   REAL :: var-1,var 2,var_3,var4

   PRINT "Please type four numbers &
         separated by commas"
   READ var-1,var 2,var_3,var4

   ! Now print the numbers to check that they were
   ! input correctly
   PRINT *,"The numbers you typed were:
   PRINT *,var-1,var 2,var_3,var4
   PRINT *,"That's all for now. &
         & "How many errors did you find?"
END PROGRAM final_test
```

2.5   Write a Fortran 90 program that prints the following message when it is run:

Hello World!

Now modify your program so that it prints a message similar to the following:

Hello World!

My name is Natasha Rudikova, and this is my first program.
It won't be my last one, though!

Au revoir!

2.6   Write a program that expects three numbers to be entered, but only uses one READ statement, and then prints them out so that you can check that they have been input correctly.

When typing in the numbers at the keyboard try typing them all on one line

(a)   separated by spaces
(b)   separated by commas
(c)   separated by semicolons

Then run the program again, but type each of the three numbers on a separate line, followed by RETURN (or ENTER).

This exercise should help you to appreciate how a Fortran program expects input to a list of variables.

2.7   Write a program that asks for the time in the form **hh, mm** and then prints that time as a message in the following form:

The time is mm minutes after hh

What do you notice about the result of running this program?

Essential data handling

3

There are two fundamental types of numbers in both mathematics and programming – namely those which are whole numbers, and those which are not. In Fortran these are known as integers and real numbers, respectively, and the difference between them is of vital importance in all programming languages. A third fundamental data type allows character information to be stored and manipulated.

This chapter discusses these three basic data types, the ways in which they may be used in calculations or other types of expressions, and the facilities contained within Fortran for the input and output of numeric and textual information.

Finally, an important feature of Fortran 90 is its ability to allow programmers to create their own data types, so that they may more readily express problems in their own terms, rather than in an arbitrary set of more basic functions. This is an important new development in Fortran 90, and one which will be developed further in subsequent chapters.

3.1 The two fundamental types of numbers

When the first FORTRAN processor was developed in 1954 it introduced two, quite different, ways of storing numbers and of carrying out arithmetic. These have remained essentially unaltered in Fortran since that time, and before proceeding any further we must establish what they are and how they differ.

An **integer** is a whole number and is stored in the computer's memory without any decimal (or fractional) part. However, because of the way in which it is stored, there are always limits to its size. These limits vary from one computer to another and depend upon the physical design of the computer's memory. We can illustrate this by considering a hypothetical computer which (for ease of comprehension!) stores its data in decimal form instead of the binary (base 2) system used by almost all computers. This means that a single digit will be recorded by means of some device which has 10 states (corresponding to the 10 digits) instead of one with two states (for instance, on and off) as required for binary numbers. Each location in the memory used for storing integers will consist of a fixed number of these devices, say eight for the purposes of illustration, which will impose a limit on the size of the number – in this case up to 99 999 999. There remains the question of the sign of the numbers.

Suppose that the device which stored the integer was an electronic equivalent of a milometer or odometer, such as that fitted to a car to record the distance travelled (see Figure 3.1). If the reading is 00 000 000 and the car moves forward 2 miles (that is, adds 2) the milometer will read 00 000 002. However, if the car now reverses for 3 miles (that is, subtracts 3) the reading will successively go to 00 000 001, 00 000 000 and finally 99 999 999. Thus the same reading is obtained for a value of −1 as for + 99 999 999, and adding 1 to 99 999 999 will give zero. We could therefore adopt a convention which says that readings from 1 to 49 999 999 will be considered to be positive, whereas 50 000 000 to 99 999 999 will be considered to be negative, and equivalent to −50 000 000

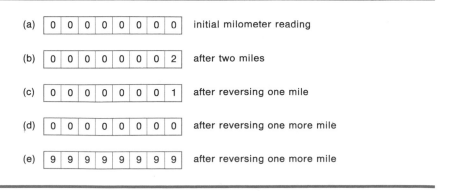

Figure 3.1 Milometer readings during travel.

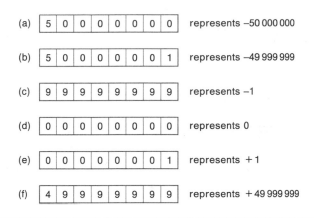

Figure 3.2 Storage of 8-digit integers.

to −1 respectively. Almost all computers work in a similar manner to this, although when using the binary system the effect is that if the first binary digit (or **bit**) is a one then the number is negative, while if it is zero the number is positive.

Using the convention just described our eight-digit memory location can hold a whole number in the range −50 000 000 to +49 999 999, as shown in Figure 3.2.

The other type of number is called a **real number**. A real number can be regarded as consisting of an integer part and a string of digits representing the fractional part, and clearly one way of storing such a number in an eight-digit memory location would be to assume that, for example, the first four digits come before the decimal point and the second four after it. However this would mean that the numbers could only lie between −5000.0 and +4999.9999, using the same convention as before regarding the sign, and that all numbers would be stored with exactly four decimal places. Clearly this is too restrictive and another way must be found. One solution might be to allow more digits, but the problem with this approach is that a large number of them will be wasted on many occasions. For example if 16 digits were allowed, so as to give the same range as for integers, but with eight places of decimals, then on the one hand a number such as 100 000 000.0 cannot be stored because it needs nine digits before the decimal place, even though none of those after it are needed, while on the other a number such as 0.000 000 004 would have to be treated as zero because it needs nine decimal places even though none of the eight before the decimal point are needed.

One solution for our hypothetical computer would be to consider any non-zero real number as a fraction lying between 0.1 and 1.0, called the *mantissa*, which is multiplied or divided by 10 a certain number of times, where this number is called the *exponent*. Thus 100 000 000.0 would be the same as 0.1×10^9, and 0.000 000 004 would be the same as $0.4 \div 10^8$, or 0.4×10^{-8}.

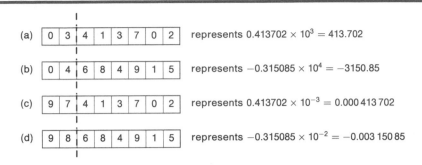

Figure 3.3 Floating-point numbers.

Using this approach, we could define a method of representation which says, for example, that the last six digits represent the mantissa as a fraction to six decimal places (with the first being non-zero), while the first two represent the exponent; that is, the number of times that the fraction is to be multiplied or divided by 10. The same technique as was used for integers to distinguish positive and negative numbers will be used for *both* the mantissa and the exponent. Figure 3.3 illustrates this method, which is known as **floating-point** representation.

This method of representation has two main implications. The first is that all numbers, whatever their size, are held to the same degree of accuracy. In the example being used they will all be stored to an accuracy of six significant digits. Thus the problem of wasted digits does not arise. The second implication is that the limits for the size of the numbers are very much greater than was the case for integers. In our hypothetical computer, for example, real numbers can lie anywhere in the range from -5×10^{48} to $+4.99999 \times 10^{48}$, and at the same time the smallest number that can be differentiated from zero is 0.1×10^{-50} (i.e. 10^{-51}).

In our hypothetical computer, therefore, the number 03413702 represents the real value 413.702 or the integer value 3413702, depending upon whether it is interpreted as a floating point number or as an integer. Note that there is nothing in the number 03413702 itself to indicate which of these two is intended; in this hypothetical example it would be the programmer's responsibility to remember which was intended.

In a real computer exactly the same situation arises and it is essential that the two methods of number representation are clearly defined; we shall see in the next section how to instruct the computer which method to use. We can already see, however, that it is extremely important that the difference between an integer and a real number is thoroughly appreciated:

- An integer is a whole number, is always held *exactly* in the computer's memory, and has a (relatively) limited range (between about -2×10^9 and $+2 \times 10^9$ on a typical 32-bit computer).

- A real number, on the other hand, is stored as a floating-point number, is held as an *approximation* to a fixed number of significant digits and has a very large range (typically between about -10^{38} and $+10^{38}$ to seven or eight significant digits on the same 32-bit computer).

3.2   REAL and INTEGER variables

The whole question of storage of different types of information in a computer can become quite complicated, and we shall return to this topic several times as we develop a fuller understanding of the power and flexibility of the Fortran language. In the last section we saw the importance of informing the computer what type of information is to be processed, and the main way in which we do this is by means of a *variable declaration*. At its simplest this takes the form

> *TYPE* :: *name*

where *TYPE* specifies the **data type** for which memory space is to be reserved, and *name* is a name chosen by the programmer with which to refer to the **variable** that has been declared.

In Chapter 1 we used an analogy with a series of glass boxes to represent the memory of a computer, and we can extend this analogy so that the box now contains two identifying symbols (see Figure 3.4), one of which is the *name* used in the earlier example, while the other identifies the *type* of information which may be stored in the box.

In general, there will be more than one variable of the same type being declared and so a list of names may be given:

> *TYPE* :: *name1*,*name2*,...

Thus we may declare three real variables by a statement such as

> `REAL :: a,b,c`

or

> `REAL :: first_real_variable,second_real_variable,  &`
> `        third_real_variable`

Note that real values are represented as floating-point numbers.

Figure 3.4 A typed storage model.

In a similar way, integer variables are declared as follows:

```
INTEGER :: first_integer,second_integer
```

We have already met the rules for Fortran names in Section 2.2, and in this book we have adopted the widely used convention that upper case will be used for Fortran keywords, such as **REAL** and **INTEGER**, while lower case will be used for names created by the programmer, such as **first_real_variable** etc.

There is, however, one rather serious problem which arises because of the age of the Fortran language, and the need to retain compatibility with earlier versions of the language. This is known as **implicit declaration**.

In the early days of programming, many programmers resented having to declare their variables before using them and so Fortran provided an alternative form of determining the type of a variable based on its initial letter. In Fortran 90, therefore, if you omit to declare a variable it will not normally lead to an error when it is first used; instead it will be implicitly declared to be an integer if the first letter of its name lies in the range I–N, and will be implicitly declared to be a real variable otherwise. *This is extremely dangerous, and should be avoided at all costs.*

Fortunately, Fortran 90 provides the means to avoid this problem by instructing the compiler that all variables *must* be declared before use, and that implicit declaration is not to be allowed. This is achieved by including the statement

```
IMPLICIT NONE
```

as the first statement after the initial **PROGRAM** statement.

It is extremely important that this statement appears at the beginning of every program in order that implicit declarations of variables are forbidden. There are a great many stories, some apocryphal and some true, about major catastrophes in Fortran programs that would never have happened had implicit declaration not masked a programming error.

3.3   Arithmetic expressions and assignment

Once we have declared one or more variables then we can start to use them to solve problems. First, however, we must establish how particular values are stored in the memory locations associated with the specified variables.

In fact, there are only two ways in which a variable can be given a value during the execution of a program – by **assignment** or by a **READ** statement. We met the **READ** statement in Chapter 2, and will discuss it in some detail in the next section; however, by far the most common means of giving a value to a variable is through an **assignment statement**. This takes the form

name **=** *expression*

where *name* is the name of a variable, and *expression* is an arithmetic, or other, expression which will be evaluated by the computer to calculate the value to be assigned to the variable *name*. Thus the statement

```
a = b + c
```

takes the value currently stored in **b**, adds to it the value currently stored in **c**, and stores the resulting value in **a**.

If **a**, **b** and **c** are all real variables, and the values in **b** and **c** were 2.8 and 3.72 before the statement was obeyed then the value assigned to **a** would be 6.52 – or rather it would be a very close approximation to 6.52, remembering that real arithmetic is always an approximation. Similarly, if **a**, **b** and **c** are all integer variables, and the values in **b** and **c** were 17 and 391 before the statement was obeyed then the value assigned to **a** would be 408; in this case the answer would, of course, be exact.

Figures 3.5 and 3.6 illustrate what has happened, by reference to the storage model used earlier, but what about the situation shown in Figure 3.7? In

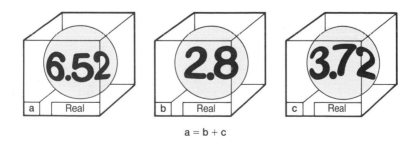

a = b + c

Figure 3.5   Real arithmetic and assignment.

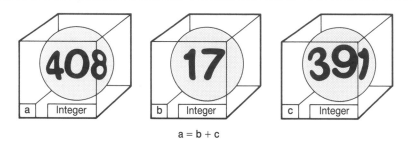

a = b + c

Figure 3.6   Integer arithmetic and assignment.

this example, the expression uses two real variables, and so the result is clearly real. However the variable **a** is an integer and so cannot hold a real value.

In this situation the result of the expression is **truncated** to an integer by, in effect, throwing away the fractional part, or, more formally, by rounding towards zero. Thus, if the values in **b** and **c** were 2.8 and 3.72 before the statement was obeyed, as before, then the value of the expression would be 6.52, which would be truncated to 6 before being assigned to **a**.

In the reverse case, where the value of the expression is an integer but the variable to be assigned the value is real, there is less of a problem since the integer result can easily be converted to its real equivalent without any loss of accuracy unless it is so large that it has more precision than a floating-point number can provide. For example, using the hypothetical computer used in Section 3.1 the integer number 12345678 has eight digits of precision and would need to be converted to 0.123457×10^8 (or 12345700.0).

A related problem occurs when not all of the entities making up the expression are of the same type, for example if **b** were real, while **c** were integer. In this case the rule is quite simple, namely that the integer is converted to real before the calculation is carried out. (This is an oversimplification, to which we shall return shortly, but it is sufficiently accurate for the present.)

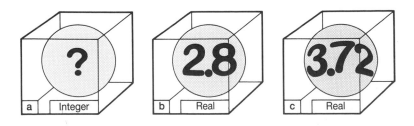

Figure 3.7   Mixed-mode assignment.

Operator	Meaning
+	addition
-	subtraction
*	multiplication
/	division
**	exponentiation (or 'raising to the power of')

Figure 3.8 Arithmetic operators in Fortran.

We must now examine the form of an arithmetic expression in more detail. As in mathematics, an arithmetic expression is created by use of the five primary arithmetic operations – addition, subtraction, multiplication, division and exponentiation (or 'raising one number to the power of another'). Although the addition and subtraction operators use the conventional mathematical operators + and -, it is not possible to express the other three operations in quite the same way as in conventional mathematics. Figure 3.8 shows the symbols used in Fortran.

We may create expressions of arbitrary complexity, subject to the limit on the length of a statement, by means of these operators, such as

```
a = b+c*d/e-f**g/h+i*j+k
```

However it is not at all obvious, at first sight, how the above expression will be evaluated!

In this situation, Fortran assigns the same priorities to operators as does mathematics, namely that exponentiation is carried out first, followed by multiplication and division, followed by addition and subtraction, as shown in Figure 3.9.

Within the same level of priority, addition and subtraction or multiplication and division, evaluation will proceed from left to right, except in

Operator	Priority
**	High
* and /	Medium
+ and -	Low

Figure 3.9 Arithmetic operator priorities.

the case of exponentiation, where evaluation proceeds from right to left. Thus the evaluation of the above expression proceeds as follows:

(1)   Calculate `f**g` and save it in `temp_1`

(2)   Calculate `c*d` and save it in `temp_2`

(3)   Calculate `temp_2/e` and save it in `temp_3`

(4)   Calculate `temp_1/h` and save it in `temp_4`

(5)   Calculate `i*j` and save it in `temp_5`

(6)   Calculate `b+temp_3` and save it in `temp_6`

(7)   Calculate `temp_6-temp_4` and save it in `temp_7`

(8)   Calculate `temp_7+temp_5` and save it in `temp_8`

(9)   Calculate `temp_8+k` and store it in `a`

In practice, many of the temporary variables `temp_1` ... `temp_8` will not actually be used as the computer will keep the intermediate results in special high-speed memory locations (called *registers*) to speed up the calculation, but the principle is correct − namely that the calculation proceeds step by step with each step consisting of the evaluation of a sub-expression consisting of one operator having two operands.

This leads us to a refinement of the earlier statement regarding what happens in a **mixed-mode expression**, where not all the operands are of the same type. The evaluation of the expression proceeds as already defined until a sub-expression is to be evaluated which has two operands of different types. At this point, and not before, the integer value is converted to real. The importance of this can be seen by considering the evaluation of the statement

`a = b*c/d`

where **b** is a real variable whose value is 100.0, while **c** and **d** are integers having the values 9 and 10, respectively.

Following the rules that have been already described, the value of **b*c** is first evaluated, with the value of **c** being first converted to the real value 9.0, to give an intermediate result of 900.0, after which the value of **d** is converted to its real equivalent before the division is carried out, to give a result to be assigned to **a** of 90.0.

Now consider what would have happened if the expression had been written in the different, but mathematically identical, way

`a = c/d*b`

Now, when the first operation is carried out both the operands are integers and so the sub-expression `c/d` is evaluated as an integer operation. Since integers can have no fractional parts the same procedure is carried out as was described for assignment, namely the mathematical result (0.9) is *truncated* to give an intermediate result of zero. This is then converted to its real equivalent (0.0!) before being multiplied by the real value of **b**, but it is already too late, and the result that will be assigned to **a** is also zero.

This phenomenon, known as **integer division** for obvious reasons, has caught out many a programmer (including all of the authors at some time in their careers!). In general, integer division is to be avoided except in situations where programmers know exactly what they are doing and wish to take advantage of the automatic truncation. Normally, however, it is preferable to carry out this type of arithmetic using real arithmetic and then deal with the result as required at the end of the calculation.

The reader should not assume, however, that the order of evaluation does not matter in real arithmetic, for consider the following statement:

```
w = x-y+z
```

where **x**, **y** and **z** all have the values 5.678. Clearly the correct value for assignment to **w** is also 5.678, and with the expression written as above this is, indeed, the result. However, consider what might happen if the statement was written in the mathematically identical form

```
w = x+z-y
```

and the program was executed on a computer which only held real numbers to four significant digits. In this case the first operation (5.678 + 5.678) would result in a 'true' value of 11.356 which would be saved (to four significant digits) as 11.36 before the subtraction took place leading to a result of 5.682 – an error of 0.004, or 0.07% on a simple addition and subtraction!

In practice, because modern computers carry out their arithmetic in special areas of memory capable of much greater precision than the main memory, this particular example would present no difficulty, but the principle that order of evaluation matters is an important one which will be taken up in more detail in Chapter 10.

We have seen that long expressions can become difficult to read and that the order of evaluation is often important; there are, however, two steps that can be taken to improve matters.

The first of these involves the use of parentheses which, just as in mathematics, alter the order of evaluation. Thus the statement

```
w = x*(z-y)
```

will result in the evaluation of the sub-expression **z-y** first, with the result being multiplied by **x** to obtain the value to be assigned to **w**.

The other thing that can be done is purely cosmetic and involves the use of spaces to make expressions more readable. For example, the expression used earlier in this section could be made easier to read and understand by writing it as

```
a = b + c*d/e - (f**g)/h + i*j + k
```

The spaces are purely for the human reader and are ignored by the Fortran compiler. In this instance, the parentheses are also only for the benefit of the human reader since the exponentiation would, in any case, be carried out first. We shall use spaces around the lowest priority operators in this way in most of the programs in the remainder of this book, but it must be emphasized that this is merely the authors' own style; programmers will develop their own styles as their experience grows.

There are two remaining points to be made at this stage concerning arithmetic expressions.

The first of these concerns the addition and subtraction operators. All five operators have been presented as **binary operators** thus far; that is they have always had two operands. This is always true of the multiplication, division and exponentiation operators, but the addition and subtraction operators can also be used as **unary operators**, having only one argument:

```
p = -q
x = +y
```

The meaning of these unary operators is obvious and the result is identical to the binary case if a zero were placed before the operator.

The other point to be made concerns **constants**. In Chapter 1, when discussing the concept of a variable by analogy with a glass box containing a ball representing a value, we mentioned that if the box was sealed so that its value could not be changed then it was called a constant. Such constants may have names like variables, as we shall see in Section 3.6, or they may simply appear in a Fortran statement by writing their value. In this latter case they are called **literal constants** because every digit of the numbers is specified *literally*. We shall see later that there are other ways of specifying constants.

All the program examples that have been presented in this section have only used variables, but in most expressions there are also some constant items. Numeric literal constants are usually written in the normal way, and the presence or absence of a decimal point defines the type of the constant.

Thus these are integer constants:

```
123
1000000
-981
0
```

while the following are real constants:

```
1.23
1000.0
-9.81
0.0
```

There is one exception to the rule that real constants must have a decimal point, namely the **exponential form**. This is typically used for very small or very large numbers and takes the form

$$m\mathrm{E}e$$

where m is called the **mantissa** and e is the **exponent**. The mantissa may be written either with or without a decimal point, whereas the exponent must take the form of an integer. Thus the value 0.000 001, or 10^{-6}, may be written in any of the following ways:

```
1E-6
100E-8
0.1E-5
```

etc.

3.4   List-directed input and output of numeric data

We have already met the **list-directed input/output statements** in Chapter 2, and with our new knowledge about variables and the real and integer data types it is now appropriate to define the format of these statements in more detail. In the form that we shall use them at present they have an almost identical syntax, as follows:

```
READ *,var_1,var_2, ...

PRINT *,item_1,item_2, ...
```

The main difference between them is that the list of items in a **READ** statement may only contain variable names, whereas the list in a **PRINT** statement may also contain constants or expressions. These lists of names and/or other items are referred to as an **input list** and an **output list**, respectively. The asterisk following the **READ** or **PRINT** indicates that **list-directed formatting** is to take place. We shall see in Chapter 8 how other forms of input and output formatting may be defined, but the list-directed form is more than adequate for the present.

The list-directed **READ** statement will take its input from a processor-defined input unit known as the **default input unit**, while the list-directed **PRINT** statement will send its output to a processor-defined unit known as the **default output unit**. In most systems, such as workstations or personal computers, these default units will be the keyboard and display, respectively; we shall see in Chapter 8 how to specify other input or output units where necessary.

The statement

```
READ *, real_var1,real_var2,int_var
```

will therefore read three values from the default input unit, normally the keyboard, and store them in the three variables **real_var1**, **real_var2** and **int_var**. A value that is input to a real variable may contain a decimal point, or the decimal point may be omitted, in which case it is treated as though the integer value read were followed by a decimal point. A value that is to be input to an integer variable must not contain a decimal point, and the occurrence of one will cause an error.

The term 'list-directed' is thus used because the interpretation of the data input, or the representation of the data output, is determined by the list of items in the input or output statement. We shall see in Chapter 8 how to specify our own formatting instead of the default one supplied by the Fortran processor.

One important point that must be considered with list-directed input concerns the **termination** of each data value being input. The rule is that each number, or other item, must be followed by a **value separator** consisting of a comma, a space, a slash (/) or the end of the line; any of these value separators may be preceded or followed by any number of consecutive blanks (or spaces). If there are two consecutive commas, then the effect is to read a **null value**, which results in the value of the corresponding variable in the input list being left unchanged. Note that a common cause of error is to believe that the value will be set to zero!

If the terminating character is a slash then no more data items are read, and processing of the input statement is ended. If there are any remaining items in the input list then the result is as though null values had been input to them; in other words, their values remain unchanged.

We can illustrate how this works by considering the following short program:

```
PROGRAM list_directed_input_example
  IMPLICIT NONE

  INTEGER :: int_1,int_2,int_3
  REAL :: real_1,real_2,real_3

! Initialize all variables to zero
  int_1 = 0;  int_2 = 0;  int_3 = 0
  real_1 = 0.0;  real_2 = 0.0;  real_3 = 0.0
```

```
!  Read data
   READ *,int_1,real_1,int_2,real_2,int_3,real_3

!  Print new values
   PRINT *,int_1,real_1,int_2,real_2,int_3,real_3

END PROGRAM list_directed_input_example
```

Figure 3.10 shows the result of reading several different sets of data with this program. Note that the number of decimal places printed is not defined and will vary according to the Fortran 90 system being used.

It is also permitted to include special data items of the form *n*c* or *n** where *n* is an unsigned non-zero integer constant and *c* is a real or integer data item. The first of these two forms represents *n* consecutive occurrences of the data item *c*, while the second represents *n* consecutive occurrences of a null value. These can be useful where it is required to read a large number of identical values.

We have already used the list-directed PRINT statement, and the statement

```
PRINT *,  entity_1,entity_2,entity_3
```

will output the values of *entity_1*, *entity_2* and *entity_3* to the default output unit, normally the display, where each of the three items in the output list may be a variable name, a constant or an expression. The only point to mention here concerns the layout, or **format**, of the results. On output, list-directed formatting causes the processor to use an appropriate format for the values being printed. Exactly what form this takes is processor-dependent, but it is usually perfectly adequate for simple programs and for initial testing. In general, however, more

Data	Printed result					
1,2.0,3,4.0,5,6.0	1	2.000	3	4.000	5	6.000
1 2.0 3 4.0 5 6.0	1	2.000	3	4.000	5	6.000
1 2.0 3 4.0 5 6.0	1	2.000	3	4.000	5	6.000
1,,,4.0,,6.0	1	0.000	0	4.000	0	6.000
1 , , 3 ,, ,6.0	1	0.000	3	0.000	0	6.000
1, 3, 5,6.0	1	0.000	3	0.000	5	6.000
1,2.0,3,4.0/	1	2.000	3	4.000	0	0.000
/	0	0.000	0	0.000	0	0.000

Figure 3.10 Examples of list-directed input.

control is required over the layout of results and we shall see in Chapter 8 how this may be achieved.

We have already discussed the form of integer and real constants in the context of arithmetic expressions and assignment, and they may, of course, be included within an output list if appropriate. Far more useful, however, is the ability to use character constants in output statements to provide textual information. Thus the program that was introduced in Chapter 2 contained a statement of the form

```
PRINT *,"The centre of the circle is (",a,",",b,")"
```

which causes five items to be printed (or displayed), namely

(1)   The character string: **The centre of the circle is (**
(2)   The value of the variable **a**
(3)   The character string: **,**
(4)   The value of the variable **b**
(5)   The character string: **)**

It can easily be deduced from this example that a character literal constant consists of a string of characters chosen from those available to the user on the computer system being used, enclosed between double quotation marks.

There is, however, an alternative form in which the character string is enclosed between apostrophes:

```
PRINT *,'This is a character literal constant', &
        " and so is this"
```

As long as the same character is used at the beginning and the end it does not matter which is used. One situation where the choice is important is where it is required to include an apostrophe or a quote within a character string:

```
PRINT *,"This string's got an apostrophe in it", &
        ' and this includes a "quotation"!'
```

If it is not possible to do this then two consecutive apostrophes in a character constant delimited by apostrophes, or two consecutive quotes in a character string delimited by quotes, are treated as a single one:

```
PRINT *,'This string''s got an apostrophe in it', &
        " and this includes a ""quotation""!"
```

In FORTRAN 77 only apostrophes could be used to delimit character constants and so the problem was a serious one. In Fortran 90 the need for this double apostrophe, or double quote, is much rarer.

■ **EXAMPLE 3.1**

1 Problem

Write a program to read a Centigrade temperature and convert it to Fahrenheit, using the formula

$$F = \frac{9C}{5} + 32$$

2 Analysis

This is a very simple problem (the classic 'first program'!) and can probably be written down without much difficulty. Nevertheless, we shall write a structure plan first.

> 1 Read Centigrade temperature (*temp_c*)
> 2 Convert to Fahrenheit (*temp_f*)
> 3 Print both temperatures

3 Solution

```
PROGRAM centigrade_to_fahrenheit
   IMPLICIT NONE

   ! A program to convert a Centigrade temperature to Fahrenheit

   ! Variable declarations
   REAL :: temp_c,temp_f

   ! Ask for Centigrade temperature
   PRINT *,"What is the Centigrade temperature? "
   READ *,temp_c

   ! Convert it to Fahrenheit
   temp_f = 9.0*temp_c/5.0 + 32.0

   ! Print both temperatures
   PRINT *,temp_c,"C = ",temp_f,"F"

END PROGRAM centigrade_to_fahrenheit
```

Note that some of the lines in the above program are printed in blue. In every worked example in this book some of the program statements will utilize features that have been discussed in the current chapter, and these will be highlighted in this way. Notice also that the program name and the names of the two variables have been chosen so as to indicate what their purpose is. We could have chosen any names of up to 31 characters which satisfy the Fortran 90 naming rules, but it is usually sensible to keep variable names somewhat less than this maximum in order to minimize typing and to make the program easier to read. A statement such as

```
fahrenheit_temperature = 9.0*centigrade_temperature/5.0 &
                       + 32.0
```

is perfectly valid, but is much too verbose – to the extent that it would not fit on one line!

The only exception to this is that the name of the main program, which only appears on the **PROGRAM** and **END PROGRAM** statements, is often rather longer in order to describe the purpose of the program.

Note also that we have written the calculation in a form that avoids any mixed-mode expression. As we have already seen, it would be perfectly acceptable to write

```
temp_f = 9*temp_c/5 + 32
```

and allow the processor to convert the three integer constants to their real equivalents before carrying out the calculation. However, this is rather lazy programming and can easily lead to mistakes such as writing the mathematically equivalent form

```
temp_f = 9/5*temp_c + 32
```

which causes an integer division to take place, with the result that the statement is effectively reduced to

```
temp_f = temp_c + 32
```

which is clearly wrong!

Of course, the best way to write this statement is actually

```
temp_f = 1.8*temp_c + 32.0
```

since this eliminates a division operation. However this is less clearly related to the formula, and it might be preferable, therefore, to include a comment to elaborate:

```
! Use the formula F=9C/5+32 (i.e. F=1.8C+32)
temp_f = 1.8*temp_c + 32.0
```

Finally, note that, since we can include expressions in an output list, we could have replaced the last two statements, and their associated comments by

```
! Use the formula F=9C/5+32 (i.e. F=1.8C+32)
! and print both temperatures
PRINT *,temp_c,"C = ",1.8*temp_c+32.0,"F"
```

We can also, of course, now remove the declaration of the variable `temp_f` from the program.

SELF-TEST EXERCISES 3.1

1   What is the difference between an integer and a real number?

2   What is the primary advantage of an integer over a real number?

3   What are two advantages of a real number over an integer?

4   What is a declaration statement?

5   Write declaration statements for variables which are to be used for the following purposes:

   (a)   to store the number of men, women and children living in a community, and the ratio of adults to children;
   (b)   to store the dimensions, in feet and inches, of a rectangular box;
   (c)   to store the dimensions, in metres and centimetres, of a rectangular box;
   (d)   to store the number of seconds that an experiment lasts, and the number of photons detected by a piece of experimental apparatus during that time.

6   What is implicit declaration? How can it be prevented? Why?

7   What is an assignment statement?

8   What are Fortran's five arithmetic operators? What are their respective priorities?

9   Write a statement to calculate the average of two numbers. Include the declaration of any necessary variables.

10   What will be printed by the following program?

```
PROGRAM test3_1_10
  IMPLICIT NONE
  REAL :: a,b,p,q,r
  INTEGER :: x,y,z
  a = 2.5
  b = 4.0
  p = a+b
  x = a+b
  q = a*b
```

```
      y = a*b
      r = p/q
      z = x/y
      PRINT *,p,q,r
      PRINT *,x,y,z
END PROGRAM test3_1_10
```

11 Give four different ways of typing the data so that the statement

```
READ *,a,b,c,d
```

will cause the real variables **a**, **b**, **c** and **d** to take the values 1.2, 3.456, 7.89 and 42.0.

3.5 Handling CHARACTER data

Having used **CHARACTER** constants in some of our **PRINT** statements it is now appropriate to consider how we may declare **CHARACTER** variables and manipulate **CHARACTER** data within a program. First, however, we must emphasize that characters and numbers are stored very differently in any computer.

As we have already seen, **REAL** and **INTEGER** variables can hold a wide range of numbers in a single variable. We must now introduce the concept of a **numeric storage unit**, which is that part of the memory of the computer in which a single **REAL** or **INTEGER** number can be stored. On most modern computers a numeric storage unit will consist of a contiguous area of memory capable of storing 16, 32, 48 or 64 **bits**, or binary digits. A 32-bit numeric storage unit is capable of storing integers in the range from about -2×10^9 to $+2 \times 10^9$, or real numbers in the range -10^{38} to $+10^{38}$ to an accuracy of about seven significant digits.

Characters, on the other hand, are stored in **character storage units**, typically occupying 8 or 16 bits, each of which can hold exactly one character in a coded form. A **character variable** consists of a sequence of one or more consecutive character storage units. There is no assumption about the relationship, if any, between numeric and character storage units, although, in practice, most computers will use the same physical memory devices for both types so that, for example, four 8-bit character storage units may be kept together in what would otherwise be a single 32-bit numeric storage unit.

Programs in the Fortran language are written using characters taken from the **Fortran Character Set**, which consists of the 26 letters of the Latin alphabet, the ten decimal digits, the underscore character and 21 additional special characters. These 58 characters are shown in Figure 3.11. Note that lower case letters are treated as identical to upper case letters when they appear in Fortran keywords or identifiers, although they are, of course, treated as different in data or in a character string.

```
A B C D E F G H I J K L M N O P Q R S T U V W X Y Z
0 1 2 3 4 5 6 7 8 9
♦ = + - * / ( ) , . ' : ! " % & ; < > ? $
```

(where ♦ represents the space, or blank, character)

Figure 3.11 The Fortran Character Set.

However, any particular implementation will almost certainly have codes for other characters and these may be used as part of a character constant, may be stored in character variables, may be input or output, and may appear in comments, although such a program may not then work on a different computer. The processor may, indeed, support several different families of characters, as we shall see in Chapter 14. For the present, however, we shall only concern ourselves with the **default character set**, which is that set of characters normally available on the computer system being used without any special action on the part of the user.

A character variable is declared in a very similar manner to that used for integer and real numbers, with the important difference that it is necessary to specify how many characters the variable is to be capable of storing. The declaration statement can take a number of similar forms, of which the fundamental one is as follows:

CHARACTER(LEN=*length*) :: *name1*,*name2*, ...

This declares one or more **CHARACTER** variables, each of which has a **length** of *length*. This means that each of the variables declared will hold exactly *length* characters.

There are two additional ways of writing this statement:

CHARACTER(*length*) :: *name1*,*name2*, ...
CHARACTER**length* :: *name1*,*name2*, ...

Although both of these are slightly shorter, we recommend, for the sake of greater clarity, that you use the full form of the declaration statement in your programs, as we shall do in this book.

If no length specification is provided, then the length is taken to be one.

Of course it is frequently the case that not all the character variables in a program are required to have the same length, and it is permitted to attach a length specification directly to the variable names in any of the above forms of declaration:

CHARACTER(LEN=*length*) :: *name1*,*name2**len_2,*name3**len_3, ...

In this example the variable *name1* is of length *length*, as are any other variables in the list without a specific length specification. *name2*, however, has a length of *len_2* while *name3* has a length of *len_3*. However, it is clearer, and less prone to error, to write separate declarations for character variables of different lengths, and we strongly recommend that you should adopt this approach.

The length specification may be either a positive integer constant or an integer constant **expression**; in the latter case it must be enclosed in parentheses if it is attached to a variable name. Thus the following three sets of declarations have an identical effect:

(1) `CHARACTER(LEN=6) :: a,b,c`

(2) `CHARACTER(LEN=12-6) :: a,b,c`

(3) `CHARACTER :: a*6,b*(8-2),c*(2*3)`

The fact that character variables always hold a specified number of characters leads to a number of potential problems when carrying out assignment or input. For example, what will be stored in the three variables **a**, **b** and **c** by the following program?

```
PROGRAM character_example
   IMPLICIT NONE
   CHARACTER(LEN=3) :: string_1
   CHARACTER(LEN=4) :: string_2,string_3
   string_1 = "End"
   string_2 = string_1
   string_3 = "Final"
END PROGRAM character_example
```

Here we have three character variables declared, two of length four, and one (**string_1**) of length three. The first assignment statement assigns the character constant **End** to **string_1**. We can readily see that the value to be assigned (the constant) has a length of three and so it exactly occupies the three storage units which constitute the variable **string_1**, and all is well.

The next assignment statement is, however, more of a problem. **string_1** has a length of 3 and contains the three characters **End**; **string_2**, however, has a length of 4, so what will be stored in the four storage units?

The answer is that if a character string has a shorter length than the length of the variable to which it is to be assigned then it is extended to the right with blank (or space) characters until it is the correct length. In this case, therefore, the contents of **string_1** will have a single blank character added after the letter **d**, thus making a length of four, before being assigned to **string_2**.

The third assignment statement poses the opposite problem. Here the character constant to be assigned has a length of 5, whereas the variable, **string_3**, only has a length of 4. In this case the string is truncated from the right to the correct length (4) before assignment.

At the end of this program, therefore, the three variables **string_1**, **string_2** and **string_3** contain the character strings **End**, **End♦** and **Fina**, respectively, where ♦ represents a blank, or space, character.

The importance of this extension and truncation makes it desirable that we restate these rules more formally:

- When assigning a character string to a character variable whose length is not the same as that of the string, the string stored in the variable is extended on the right with blanks, or truncated from the right, so as to exactly fill the character variable to which it is being assigned.

A similar situation can arise during the input of character data by a **READ** statement if the number of characters which form the input data is different from the length of the variable into which they are being read. Before discussing this in detail, however, we must examine the way in which character data is input and output by list-directed input/output statements.

The form of any character data to be read by a list-directed **READ** statement is normally the same as that of a character constant. In other words it must be delimited by either quotation marks or by apostrophes. There are some exceptions to this rule, however, in order to cater for common situations where the need for the apostrophes or quotes would be annoying. The delimiting characters are not required if *all* of the following conditions are met:

(1) the character data does not contain any blanks, any commas or any slashes (that is, it does not contain any of the value separators discussed earlier);

(2) the character data is all contained within a single record or line;

(3) the first non-blank character is not a quotation mark or an apostrophe, since this would be taken as a delimiting character;

(4) the leading characters are not numeric followed by an asterisk, since this would be confused with the multiple data item form ($n*c$).

In this case the character constant is terminated by any of the value separators which will terminate a numeric data item (blank, comma, slash or end of record), and it may be repeated by means of a multiple data item of the form $n*c$.

If the character data which is read by a list-directed **READ** statement is too long or too short for the variable concerned then it is truncated or extended on the right in exactly the same way as for assignment.

The output situation is rather simpler, and a list-directed **PRINT** statement will output exactly what is stored in a character variable or constant, including any trailing blanks, without any delimiting apostrophes or quotation marks.

Thus we could modify our earlier program to print the values of the three variables as follows:

```
PROGRAM character_example
  IMPLICIT NONE
  CHARACTER(LEN=3) :: string_1
  CHARACTER(LEN=4) :: string_2,string_3
  string_1 = "End"
  string_2 = string_1
  string_3 = "Final"
  PRINT *,string_1,string_2,string_3
END PROGRAM character_example
```

The result of running this program would be the following line of text:

EndEnd Fina

The ability to assign a character literal constant, or the string stored in a character variable, or to input and output character data, does not in itself take us very far. Just as we can write arithmetic expressions, therefore, so we can also create character expressions. The major difference between character expressions and the other types of expressions, however, is that there are very few things we can actually do with strings of characters!

One thing that we can do, though, is combine two strings to form a third, composite, string. This process is called **concatenation** and is carried out by means of the **concatenation operator**, consisting of two consecutive slashes:

```
char = "Fred"//"die"
```

The composite string will, of course, have a length equal to the sum of the lengths of the two strings which were concatenated to form it, and the variable **char** will contain the string **Freddie**, as long as it has a length of at least 7.

This is the only operator provided in Fortran for use with character strings; Fortran does, however, include one important additional capability, namely the identification of substrings. This is achieved by following the character variable name or character constant by two integer expressions separated by a colon and enclosed in parentheses. The two integer values represent the positions in the character variable or constant of the first and last characters of the substring. Either may be omitted, but not both, in which case the first or last character position is assumed, as appropriate.

Thus the substring **"rhubarb"(2:4)** specifies a substring consisting of the three characters **hub** taken from positions 2 to 4 of the character constant. In a similar way **alpha(5:7)** represents a three character substring of the value of the character variable **alpha**, while **beta(4:)** represents a substring starting at the fourth character of the value of **beta** and continuing to the last character, and **gamma(:6)** represents a substring consisting of the first six characters of the value of **gamma**.

It is also permitted to assign a value to a substring without altering the rest of the variable. Thus the following program fragment will result in the variable **ch** having the value **Alpine♦♦**, where, as before, ♦ represents a space:

```
PROGRAM substring
   IMPLICIT NONE
   CHARACTER(LEN=8) :: ch
   ch = "Alphabet"
   ch(4:) = "ine"
    .
    .
    .
```

It is instructive to examine this in detail.

The substring `ch(4:)` is the substring from character 4 to the end of `ch` — a total of five characters. The character constant `"ine"` only has a length of 3 so it is extended by adding two blank characters before being assigned to `ch(4:)`. The assignment means that the old substring value (`"habet"`) is replaced by the new value (`"ine♦♦"`), leaving the rest of `ch` unchanged. The final result, therefore, is that `ch` contains `"Alpine "`.

■ **EXAMPLE 3.2**

1 Problem

Write a program which asks the user for her title, first name and last name, and then prints a welcome message using both the full name and first name.

2 Analysis

This program is simply an exercise in simple character manipulation. However, there are some slight difficulties in combining the title, first and last names in a form which will avoid multiple spaces within the composite name. For example, if variables with a length of 12 characters were chosen, then the name **Kathy** would be followed by seven spaces.

In Chapter 2 we pointed out that many of the detailed aspects of programs can often be carried out in *procedures* which can be written later, or can be written by someone else, or which may already exist somewhere else. The Fortran language contains a large number of special procedures, known as **intrinsic procedures**, which provide a great many useful additional features. We shall examine this topic in some detail in Chapter 4, but for the present we shall simply note that there are several intrinsic procedures whose purpose is to assist in the manipulation of character strings. A list of all the intrinsic procedures in Fortran 90 will be found in Appendix A.

The most useful intrinsic procedure, for our present purpose, is **TRIM**, which removes any trailing blanks from the character string provided as its argument. There would still be a difficulty if the user types one or more blanks before the name, but we shall assume that this does not happen and ignore the problem for the present — although there is another intrinsic procedure that could be used to deal with it.

Armed with this intrinsic procedure we can develop our structure plan:

1 Read title, first name and last name

2 Concatenate the resulting strings together, using **TRIM** to remove trailing blanks from the title and first name

3 Print a welcome message using the formal address, and another using just the first name

③ Solution

```
PROGRAM welcome
   IMPLICIT NONE

   ! This program manipulates character strings to produce a
   ! properly formatted welcome message

   ! Variable declarations
   CHARACTER(LEN=20) :: title,first_name,last_name
   CHARACTER(LEN=40) :: full_name

   ! Ask for name, etc
   PRINT *,"Please give your full name in the form requested"
   PRINT *,"Title (Mr./Mrs./Ms./Professor/etc: "
   READ *,title

   PRINT *,"First name: "
   READ *,first_name

   PRINT *,"Last name: "
   READ *,last_name

   ! Create full name
   full_name = TRIM(title)//" "//TRIM(first_name)//" "//last_name

   ! Print messages
   PRINT *,"Welcome ",full_name
   PRINT *,"May I call you ",TRIM(first_name),"?"

END PROGRAM welcome
```

Notice that **TRIM** has been used in the second **PRINT** statement to ensure that the question mark at the end of the question comes immediately after the name, and not separated from it by several spaces.

SELF-TEST EXERCISES 3.2

1   What is the difference between the *Fortran Character Set* and the *default character set*?

2   What is the most obvious difference between the declaration of an integer or real variable and the declaration of a character variable?

3   Write declaration statements for six character variables, of which four are to contain character strings of up to 20 characters, one is to contain only a single character, and one is to contain the month of the year.

4   Write a single declaration statement for the same variables as in Question 3.

5   What will be printed by the following program?

```
PROGRAM test3_2_5
   IMPLICIT NONE
   CHARACTER(LEN=16) :: a,b,c,d
   a = "A kindly giant"
   b = "A small man"
   c = b(:8)//"step"
   d = "for a"//b(8:)
   b = " "//d(:4)//b(9:11)//a(3:6)
   a = a(:2)//a(10:15)//"leap"
   PRINT *,c(:13),d
   PRINT *,TRIM(a(:12)),b
END PROGRAM test3_2_5
```

3.6   Initial values and constants

There is one other method of giving a value to a variable, namely to provide an *initial value* for a variable as part of the declaration of the variable. This is achieved quite simply by following the name of the variable by an equals sign and the initial value:

```
REAL :: a=0.0, b=1.5, c, d, e=1E-6
INTEGER :: max = 100
CHARACTER(LEN=10) :: name="Undefined"
```

These initial values will be assigned to the variables by the Fortran processor before the execution of the program commences, thus avoiding the need, when the program is executed, either to obey a series of initial assignments or to read an initial set of values. By separating the initialization of the variables from any assignment during execution it is also easier to keep these two phases of a program more clearly delineated.

Any initial value specified must either be a literal constant or a **constant expression**, that is an expression whose component parts are all constants.

A related issue concerns creating and giving names to constants.

Frequently, a program will use certain constant values in many places, and it is not necessarily obvious what a particular constant represents. For example, it might be required to establish a maximum number of items that could appear in some data set, but using the same literal constant in all the places where it must be referred to is prone to error both when typing the program and, even more, when subsequently modifying it, and is less readable than would be the case if a name were used. Furthermore, there are a great many occasions when physical or natural constants, such as the value of π, are required in programs, and there is clearly no intention for these to be altered. Fortran allows us a convenient method of dealing with these situations by defining what are called **named constants** by use of the **parameter attribute** in a declaration statement:

```
REAL, PARAMETER :: pi=3.1415926, pi_by_2=pi/2.0
INTEGER, PARAMETER :: max_cases = 100
```

In this example **pi** is defined to be a constant, and then **pi_by_2** is defined by means of a constant expression involving **pi**. Since the statement is processed from left to right this is acceptable; if the two constants were listed in the opposite order then there would be an error. There will never be any need to change the values of these two constants, and their definition is purely to make the program easier to read and to avoid errors in typing long constants since, instead of writing, for example

```
area = 3.1415926*r*r
```

we can write

```
area = pi*r*r
```

On the other hand, the integer constant **max_cases** might need to be changed if the size of problem being processed were to change. This is a case where there might be many places where the constant value of 100 appears, not all of which refer to the maximum number of cases. Modifying the program to change the maximum would then be highly prone to error. By making the maximum value a named constant the program is easier to read and any change subsequently required need only be made in one place.

Finally, we note that, since the whole reason for giving an entity the parameter attribute is to declare a named constant, it is not permitted to attempt to change its value at a subsequent point in the program. The only way that its value can be changed is by modifying the declaration statement accordingly, and recompiling the program.

3.7   Creating your own data types

We have now met the three major types of data that can be processed by Fortran programs, although there are three more that we shall meet later. These six data types are called **intrinsic data types**, and were the only data types in all earlier versions of Fortran. However, Fortran 90 also includes the capability for programmers to create their own data types to supplement the intrinsic types provided within the Fortran language. Because these new data types must be derived from the intrinsic data types and/or previously defined new data types they are called **derived types**.

A derived type is defined by a special sequence of statements, which in their simplest form are as follows:

```
TYPE new_type
     component_definition
     .
     .
     .
END TYPE new_type
```

There may be as many component definitions as required, and each takes the same form as a variable declaration. The concept is best illustrated by an example.

Let us imagine that a particular program is being used to collect data about individuals, and that each individual is identified by their name (first name, middle initial, last name), their age, their sex and their social security number. We could define a new data type called **person** which would contain all this information:

```
TYPE person
     CHARACTER(LEN=12) :: first_name, middle_initial*1, &
                          last_name
     INTEGER :: age
     CHARACTER :: sex      ! M or F
     CHARACTER(LEN=11) :: social_security
END TYPE person
```

Once we have defined a new type then we may declare variables of that type in a similar way to that used for intrinsic types, except that the type name is enclosed in parentheses and preceded by the keyword **TYPE**:

```
TYPE(person) :: jack, jill
```

A constant value of a derived type is written as a sequence of constants corresponding to the components of the derived type, enclosed in parentheses and preceded by the type name:

```
jack = person("Jack","R","Hagenbach",47,"M","123-45-6789")
jill = person("Jill","M","Smith",39,"F","987-65-4321")
```

This form of defining a constant value for a derived type is called a **structure constructor**. Note that it is quite different from the form of a constant for any of the intrinsic types.

In a similar fashion, a **READ** statement will expect a sequence of data values which matches the components in both type and order, while a **PRINT** statement will output the value of a derived type variable as a sequence of its component parts.

We may refer directly to a component of a derived type variable by following the variable by a percentage sign and the name of the component. Thus the following statement changes the last name of **jill** to that of **jack**, for example, if she had agreed to follow the common practice in many cultures following their marriage!

```
jill%last_name = jack%last_name
```

We may also, of course, use a previously defined derived type in the definition of another derived type:

```
TYPE employee
   TYPE(person) :: employee
   CHARACTER(LEN=20) :: department
   REAL :: salary
END TYPE employee
```

Note that it is permissible for a component name of a derived type to be the same as the name of the derived type itself, although it will usually be clearer if the names are kept distinct.

If **pat** is a variable of type **employee** whose sex had been incorrectly coded, it could be changed by a statement of the form

```
pat%employee%sex = "F"
```

■ EXAMPLE 3.3

1 Problem

Define two data types, one to represent a point by means of its coordinates (in two-dimensional space only) and the other to represent a line (also in two-dimensional space) by the coefficients of its defining equation. Write a program which reads the coordinates of two distinct points and which then calculates the line joining them, printing the equation of the line.

2 Analysis

This is the first of a set of examples which will develop a geometric sub-system for use in such areas as computer-aided design and geometric modelling. Many of the subsequent chapters of this book will contain examples and/or programming exercises which will, together, provide many of the components of this sub-system. Although each of these examples and exercises is complete in itself, the whole set will illustrate how large programming projects can be tackled in a modular fashion in a series of interrelated stages. In order that they can be more easily identified, all the examples and exercises of this type have an identifying symbol in the margin.

We must first establish the format of the two derived types – **point** and **line**.

The first of these is easy, as it will consist of two real components, representing the x and y coordinates, respectively.

The representation of a straight line is, however, slightly more difficult. A straight line is defined by an equation of the form

$$ax + by + c = 0$$

and at first sight we could simply use the three coefficients of this equation as the representation of a line. However, these three coefficients are not unique, since, for example, the equations

$$5x - 4y + 7 = 0$$

and

$$10x - 8y + 14 = 0$$

are identical apart from the fact that all the coefficients of the second equation are twice those of the first, and they both, therefore, represent the same line. This will, however, not cause any problems in the use of this data type as long as it is remembered that any non-zero multiple of a, b and c represents the same line. Simple algebra (see Figure 3.12) then leads us to the conclusion that

$$a = y_2 - y_1$$
$$b = x_1 - x_2$$
$$c = y_1x_2 - y_2x_1$$

We shall therefore define a line as having three coefficients.

Finally, we should note that our program should check that the two points input are not coincident, since in that event it is impossible to define a line joining them. We do not yet have the tools to make this check, but will return to this problem in Chapter 5. We shall ignore this problem here, therefore, and assume that the user does not supply two identical points.

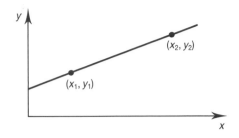

The equation of the line is $ax + by + c = 0$.

The slope of the line is $(y_2 - y_1)/(x_2 - x_1)$ if $x_1 \neq x_2$.

At any point (x, y), other than (x_1, y_1), the slope is $(y - y_1)/(x - x_1)$.

Therefore

$$\frac{y - y_1}{x - x_1} = \frac{y_2 - y_1}{x_2 - x_1} \text{ for } x_1 \neq x_2, \ x \neq x_1, \ y \neq y_1$$

Therefore

$$(x_2 - x_1)(y - y_1) = (y_2 - y_1)(x - x_1) \tag{1}$$

Now, the point (x_1, y_1) also satisfies equation (1) in this form, so we can drop the prohibition that $(x, y) \neq (x_1, y_1)$.

Also, if $x_1 = x_2$ the equation becomes

$$(y_2 - y_1)(x - x_1) = 0 \tag{2}$$

In this case, $y_1 \neq y_2$, since if it did the two points (x_1, y_1) and (x_2, y_2) would coincide and, hence, would not define a straight line. Consequently, we can divide equation (2) by $(y_2 - y_1)$ and obtain

$$x - x_1 = 0$$

In the case where $x_1 = x_2$, this is the equation of the line joining the two points.

Thus, in all cases, equation (1) is the equation of the straight line joining the two (distinct) points. Rearranging (1), we have

$$(y_2 - y_1)x + (x_1 - x_2)y - y_2x_1 + y_1x_1 + y_1x_2 - y_1x_1 = 0$$

or

$$(y_2 - y_1)x + (x_1 - x_2)y + y_1x_2 - y_2x_1 = 0$$

Therefore

$$a = y_2 - y_1$$
$$b = x_1 - x_2$$
$$c = y_1x_2 - y_2x_1$$

Figure 3.12 Calculation of the equation of a line joining two points.

We can now develop our structure plan:

---

1 Define data types for points and lines
2 Read coordinates of two points
3 Calculate the coefficients of the line joining the points
4 Print equation of line

---

3 Solution

```
PROGRAM geometry
   IMPLICIT NONE

   ! A program to use derived types for two-dimensional
   ! geometric calculations

   ! Type definitions
   TYPE point
      REAL :: x,y      ! Cartesian coordinates of the point
   END TYPE point

   TYPE line
      REAL :: a,b,c   ! coefficients of defining equation
   END TYPE line

   ! Variable declarations
   TYPE(point) :: p1,p2
   TYPE(line) :: p1_to_p2

   ! Read data
   PRINT *,"Please type co-ordinates of first point"
   READ *,p1
   PRINT *,"Please type co-ordinates of second point"
   READ *,p2

   ! Calculate coefficients of equation representing the line
   p1_to_p2%a = p2%y - p1%y
   p1_to_p2%b = p1%x - p2%x
   p1_to_p2%c = p1%y*p2%x - p2%y*p1%x

   ! Print result
   PRINT *,"The equation of the line joining these two points is"
   PRINT *,"ax + by + c = 0"
   PRINT *,"where a = ",p1_to_p2%a
   PRINT *,"      b = ",p1_to_p2%b
   PRINT *,"      c = ",p1_to_p2%c

END PROGRAM geometry
```

■ **EXAMPLE 3.4**

1 Problem

Define a data type which can be used to represent complex numbers, and then use it in a program which reads two complex numbers and calculates and prints their sum, their difference and their product.

2 Analysis

Complex numbers are used mainly by electrical engineers and by mathematicians, and consist of two parts – a real part and an imaginary part. A complex number is mathematically equivalent to $x + jy$, where x is the real part, y is the imaginary part, and j represents the square root of -1. It is often written in the form (x, y).

The rules for addition and subtraction are very simply derived:

$$(x_1 + jy_1) + (x_2 + jy_2) = ((x_1 + x_2) + j(y_1 + y_2))$$
$$(x_1 + jy_1) - (x_2 + jy_2) = ((x_1 - x_2) + j(y_1 - y_2))$$

while that for multiplication is not much more difficult (as long as we remember that j^2 is equal to -1):

$$(x_1 + jy_1) \times (x_2 + jy_2) = ((x_1 \times x_2 - y_1 \times y_2) + j(x_1 \times y_2 + x_2 \times y_1))$$

Division is more difficult to work out – which is why we are not bothering with it in this example!

We can express these rules using the parenthesized form of representation as

$$(x_1, y_1) + (x_2, y_2) = (x_1 + x_2, y_1 + y_2)$$
$$(x_1, y_1) - (x_2, y_2) = (x_1 - x_2, y_1 - y_2)$$
$$(x_1, y_1) \times (x_2, y_2) = (x_1 \times x_2 - y_1 \times y_2, x_1 \times y_2 + x_2 \times y_1)$$

We can now write a structure plan:

1   Define a data type for complex numbers
2   Read two complex numbers
3   Calculate their sum, difference and product
4   Print results

3 Solution

```
PROGRAM complex_arithmetic
    IMPLICIT NONE

    ! A program to illustrate the use of a derived type to perform
    ! complex arithmetic

    ! Type definition
    TYPE complex_number
        REAL :: real_part,imaginary_part
    END TYPE complex_number

    ! Variable definitions
    TYPE(complex_number) :: c1,c2,sum,diff,prod

    ! Read data
    PRINT *,"Please supply two complex numbers"
    PRINT *,"Each complex number should be typed as two numbers,"
    PRINT *,"representing the real and imaginary parts &
            &of the number"
    READ *,c1,c2

    ! Calculate sum, difference and product
    sum%real_part = c1%real_part + c2%real_part
    sum%imaginary_part = c1%imaginary_part + c2%imaginary_part

    diff%real_part = c1%real_part - c2%real_part
    diff%imaginary_part = c1%imaginary_part - c2%imaginary_part

    prod%real_part = c1%real_part*c2%real_part - &
                    c1%imaginary_part*c2%imaginary_part
    prod%imaginary_part = c1%real_part*c2%imaginary_part + &
                    c1%imaginary_part*c2%real_part

    ! Print results
    PRINT *,"The sum of the two numbers is ",sum
    PRINT *,"The difference between the two numbers is ",diff
    PRINT *,"The product of the two numbers is ",prod

END PROGRAM complex_arithmetic
```

Figure 3.13 shows the result of running this program, and it can be seen that a slight improvement would be to print out the three result as parenthesized pairs using statements such as

```
PRINT *,"The sum of the two numbers is (",sum%real_part, &
        ", ",sum%imaginary_part,")"
```

This example illustrates a common dilemma when reading and writing derived data types, namely that in order to properly control the layout of results, or even of data, it is necessary to work at the component level, whereas one of the

```
Please supply two complex numbers
Each complex number should be typed as two numbers,
representing the real and imaginary parts of the number
12.5 8.4
6.5 9.6
The sum of the two numbers is     19.0000   18.0000
The difference between the two numbers is     6.0000     -1.2000
The product of the two numbers is      0.6100  174.6000
```

Figure 3.13   Results produced by the program written for Example 3.4.

advantages, as we shall see later, of using derived types is that the underlying data structure can be ignored. We shall demonstrate how to resolve this dilemma in Chapter 12.

Note, incidentally, that Fortran does contain an intrinsic **COMPLEX** type which we shall meet in Chapter 14. Nevertheless, we shall continue to explore the development of our own **complex_number** derived type in future chapters as a readily comprehensible use of derived types.

3.8   Obsolete forms of declaration, initialization and constant definition

Before Fortran 90, variable declarations did not contain a double colon:

```
INTEGER first_integer,second_integer
```

Although this form is perfectly adequate for the simple case shown here, the newer form, with the double colon, is the only form of declaration which can be used when making use of many of the new features in Fortran 90 that will be met in subsequent chapters. Indeed, we have already met two new features which are not available when using the obsolete form of variable declaration, namely the inclusion of initial values in the declaration and the use of the **PARAMETER** attribute to define a named constant.

In earlier versions of Fortran, initial values were assigned by means of a separate **DATA** statement, while constants were declared in a **PARAMETER** statement. Both of these statements are now redundant and should not be used in new programs. They are briefly described in Appendix E, together with other obsolete features of Fortran 90 which readers may come across in older programs that they are having to maintain or modify.

SELF-TEST EXERCISES 3.3

1   What is the difference between giving an initial value to an entity and giving it the **PARAMETER** attribute?

2   What is a derived type? From what is it derived?

3   Why are derived types useful?

4   Define a type to store a typical domestic address in your country's standard form.

5   Write a declaration for a variable of the type defined in Question 4, and a single assignment statement to assign your own address to this variable.

6   Define a type to store a person's name and address and the necessary statement or statements to read the user's name and address into a variable of this type.

SUMMARY

- Variables are locations in the computer's memory in which variable information may be stored; constants are locations in which information is stored which cannot be altered during the execution of the program.

- An integer is a whole number; its representation in a computer is always exact.

- A real number may have a fractional part; it is represented in a computer as a floating-point number which is a close approximation to its true value.

- Integers and real numbers are both stored in numeric storage units.

- All Fortran processors support the 58 characters which constitute the Fortran Character Set; most processors also support a number of other characters as part of their default character set.

- Characters in the default character set may be used to form character strings; each character is stored in a separate character storage unit.

- All variables should be declared in a type declaration statement before their first use; a character variable must have its length declared.

- An IMPLICIT NONE statement should always be placed immediately after the initial statement of the main program unit to force the compiler to require that all variables appear in a type declaration statement.

- A variable declaration may include the specification of an initial value.

- A named constant declaration takes the same form as a variable declaration specifying an initial value, except that the name has the PARAMETER attribute.

- The priority of arithmetic operators in an arithmetic expression is the same as in mathematics; evaluation of the expression proceeds from left to right, within a priority level, except for exponentiation which is carried out from right to left, but may be altered by the use of parentheses.

- If one of the operands of an arithmetic operator is real, then the evaluation of that operation is carried out using real arithmetic, with any integer operand being converted to real.

- If an integer value is assigned to a real variable it is converted to its real equivalent before assignment; if a real value is assigned to an integer variable it is truncated before conversion to integer, and any fractional part is lost.

- Character strings may be concatenated to form a longer character string.

- Character substrings may be used wherever the character variables or character constants of which they are substrings may be used.

- Character strings are extended with blanks to the right, or truncated from the right, before assignment to make them the same length as the variable they are being assigned to.

- A list-directed READ statement takes its data from the default input unit, and a list-directed PRINT statement sends its results to the default output unit.

- A derived type is a user-defined data type, each of whose components is either an intrinsic type or a previously defined derived type.

- Derived type literal constants are specified by means of structure constructors.

- Input and output of derived type objects takes place component by component.

- Fortran 90 syntax introduced in Chapter 3:

Derived type definition	TYPE type_name *1st_component_declaration* *2nd_component_declaration* . . . END TYPE *type_name*
Variable declarations	REAL :: *list of variable names* INTEGER :: *list of variable names* CHARACTER(LEN=*length*) :: *list of variable names* TYPE(*derived_type_name*) :: *list of variable names*
Initial value specification	*type* :: *name=initial_value*, ...
Named constant declaration	*type*, PARAMETER :: *name=initial_value*, ...
Assignment statement	*variable_name* = *expression*
Character substring specification	*name*(*first_position*:*last_position*) *name*(*first_position*:) *name*(:*last_position*)
Arithmetic operators	**, *, /, +, −
Character operator	//

PROGRAMMING EXERCISES

*3.1   Write and run a program which will read 10 numbers and find their sum. Test the program with several sets of data, including the following:

  1, 5, 17.3, 9, -23.714, 12.9647, 0.0005, -2974, 3951.44899, -1000

Were the answers what you expected?

3.2   The following program is intended to swap the values of **var_1** and **var_2**:

```
PROGRAM swap
   IMPLICIT NONE
   REAL :: var_1=111.111,var_2=222.222

   ! Exchange values
   var_2 = var_1
   var_1 = var_2

   ! Print swapped values
   PRINT *,var_1,var_2

END PROGRAM swap
```

The program contains an error, however, and will not print the correct values. Determine the error and correct it so that it works properly. -

Now modify the corrected program so that you can enter the two numbers from the keyboard.

3.3   Write a program to input a number x and print the values of $x - 1$, $x + 2$ and $x^2 + x - 2$.

3.4   The reduced mass of a diatomic molecule is given by the expression

$$\mu = \frac{m_a m_b}{m_a + m_b}$$

Write a program that calculates μ, where you enter m_a and m_b from the keyboard.

*3.5   Write a program to print a list of the characters in the Fortran character set, followed by their internal representation on your computer.

3.6   Write a program that reads a six word sentence, one word at a time, into six variables, and then prints the sentence formed by concatenating the six variables.

3.7   Write a program that reads a six word sentence into a single variable. The program should then read the number of characters in each of the six words and use this information to store each word in a separate variable. Finally, the program should list these six words, one to a line.

3.8   When visitors come to dinner at his home in Copenhagen, Mr Schmidt always makes them Danish Apple Cake. For four people this requires the following ingredients:

675 g of apples
75 g of butter
150 g of sugar
100 g of breadcrumbs
150 ml of cream

Write a program which inputs the number of people coming to dinner, and then prints the amount of each ingredient required.

3.9 Write a program that contains two derived types. The first of these should contain relevant details for an individual, such as first name, middle initial, last name, sex, age, occupation, and anything else you think relevant. The second should contain an address in an appropriate form for your environment.

Use a structure constructor to store your own details, or those of a friend, in variables of these types and then print a message giving these details in a format similar to that below:

```
My name is James D Smith
I am a 23 year-old male student, and I live at
871 rue de la Triomphe
Montmartre
Paris
France
```

3.10 A woman wishes to build a brick wall 4 ft high along one side of her garden. The bricks are 9 in long, $4\frac{1}{2}$ in wide, and 3 in high, and there should be $\frac{1}{2}$ in of mortar between bricks. Write a program to calculate how many bricks she will need if the wall is to be 23 ft 6 in long, and then use this program to calculate the number of bricks needed for walls of different heights and lengths.

3.11 A small business wishes to use a computer program to calculate how to make up the pay packets for its employees. The program should read the total amount to be paid, and print the number of £20, £10 and £5 notes required, and the number of £1, 50p, 20p, 10p, 5p, 2p and 1p coins needed. It is a requirement that every pay packet should contain at least 40p in coins, and at least one £5 note. Subject to this restriction, the pay packet should contain as few coins and notes as possible. Note that £1 = 100p.

Write a program to provide the required information, and test it with a wide variety of cases, including those with a total pay of £125.39 and £65.40.

3.12 The equation of a circle can be written as

$$(x - x_0)^2 + (y - y_0)^2 = r^2$$

where the point (x_0, y_0) is the centre of the circle, and its radius is r.

Define a derived type, along similar lines to those used in Example 3.3, which can be used to represent a circle by its name, the coordinates of its centre, and its radius. Use this derived type in a program which requests the user to provide the coordinates of the centre of the circle, and of a point on its circumference, and calculates the radius of the circle from this information. Finally, the program should print the coefficients of the equation that defines the circle in the form

$$ax^2 + by^2 + cx + dy + e = 0$$

3.13 Using the two derived types that were defined for Exercise 3.9, create a third derived type, called **family**, which contains the names of the father, mother, son and daughter of a 'typical' four-person family, together with their home address. Use this in a program which requests the relevant details for each member of the family, and where they live, and then prints a summary of the family in a form similar to that shown below:

```
The Addison family live in Reading, MA
Wesley is 53
His wife Sheila is 47
Their daughter Lynne is 21 and their son Stephen is 24
```

3.14 A body that experiences a uniform acceleration moves a distance s in a time t, where s is given by the formula

$$s = \tfrac{1}{2}at^2 + ut$$

where a is the acceleration in metres/sec^2, and u is the initial velocity in metres/sec.

A body falling freely under gravity is in such a situation, with $a = g = 9.81$ metres/sec^2.

Write a program that asks the user for the body's initial velocity (in metres/sec) and time of flight (in seconds). The program should then calculate and print the height from which the body fell.

3.15 Calculate the Coulomb potential at a distance r from a particle with a charge of z. The required formula is

$$\phi(r) = \frac{ze}{4\pi\epsilon r}$$

where $e = 1.6 \times 10^{-19}$ C, $\epsilon = 8.86 \times 10^{-12}$ F/m, and $\pi = 3.1416$. r is specified in metres (m) and z is an integer number.

Basic building blocks

In all walks of life, the easiest way to solve most problems is to break them down into smaller sub-problems and deal with each of these in turn, further subdividing these sub-problems as necessary.

This chapter introduces the concept of a procedure to assist in the solution of such sub-problems, and shows how Fortran's two types of procedures, functions and subroutines, are used as the primary building blocks in well-designed programs.

A further encapsulation facility, known as a module, is also introduced in this chapter as a means of providing controlled access to global data, and is also shown to be an essential tool in the use of derived (or user-defined) datatypes. Modules are also recommended as a means of packaging groups of related procedures, for ease of manipulation, as a means of providing additional security and to simplify the use of some of the powerful features of Fortran 90 that will be met in subsequent chapters.

4.1 Procedures, subprograms and functions

The statements that we met in the last chapter enable us to write programs consisting of a number of lines of instructions that will be obeyed in sequence in order to cause the required actions to take place. However this is not always the way we do things in real life. For example, look at Figure 4.1. This is a note such as might be left to instruct someone how to prepare the evening meal. It is a sequence of instructions but with one important difference – *not all the instructions are there*. The main part of the preparation is covered in a cookery book (*The Silver Palate Cookbook*, by Julee Rosso and Sheila Lukins), so, instead of writing it all down, the writer simply referred to the appropriate page of the book. There was no point in either copying it out or describing what to do in different words; it was much easier to make use of what had already been written by the authors of the book.

Figure 4.2 shows part of the actual recipe for Raspberry Chicken referred to in the note in Figure 4.1, and we can see that even here the whole recipe is not included. In this case the details of how to prepare the Chicken Stock and the Crème Fraîche are to be found elsewhere in the book, on pages 342 and 339, respectively, and it would be wasteful to keep repeating them in the many recipes that use either or both. A cross-reference to the other recipes, therefore, saves space and, incidentally, also keeps the main recipe less cluttered and thus easier to follow.

Both of these situations (use of standard procedures and avoidance of duplication with consequent structural improvements) appear in programming as well. A special section of program which is, in some way, referred to whenever required is known as a **procedure**.

Procedures fall into two broad categories, namely those which are written by the programmer (or by some other person who then allows the programmer to use them) and those which are part of the Fortran language. There is a further categorization, based upon their mode of use, into what are called **subroutines** and **functions**. Almost all of the procedures which are part of the Fortran 90 language are functions and are referred to as **intrinsic functions**. There are also five **intrinsic subroutines**.

Miles,
    I thought we might have Raspberry Chicken tonight (see page 87 of the Silver Palate cookbook). I'll be a bit late home, so could you make a start please?
    Love
        Maggie

Figure 4.1 An example of the use of a standard cooking procedure.

RASPBERRY CHICKEN

Boneless chicken breasts are quick and economical to serve but often dull to eat. In this recipe, ready in minutes, raspberry vinegar lends a bit of welcome tartness, mellowed by chicken stock and heavy cream. A handful of fresh raspberries, poached briefly in the sauce just before serving, adds an elegant note. Wild rice and a simple sautéed green vegetable would be good accompaniments.

2 whole boneless, skinless chicken breasts, about 2 pounds
2 tablespoons sweet butter
¼ cup finely chopped yellow onion
4 tablespoons raspberry vinegar*
¼ cup Chicken Stock (see page 342), or canned chicken broth
¼ cup heavy cream, or Crème Fraîche (see page 339)
1 tablespoon canned crushed tomatoes
16 fresh raspberries (optional)

1. Cut each chicken breast into halves along the breastbone line. Remove the filet mignon, the finger-size muscle on the back of each half, and reserve for another use. Flatten each breast half or *suprême* by pressing it gently with the palm of your hand.
2. Melt the butter in a large skillet. Bring the heat, add the *suprêmes*, and cook for abou

Figure 4.2 Using cross-referencing to avoid duplication (reproduced with permission from *The Silver Palate Cookbook*, by Julee Rosso and Sheila Lukins, published by Workman Publishing, New York, 1982).

The purpose of a function is to take one or more values (or **arguments**) and create a single result, and Fortran, for example, contains a number of intrinsic functions for elementary mathematical functions, such as

`SIN(x)` which calculates the value of $\sin x$ (where **x** is in radians)
`LOG(x)` which calculates the value of $\log_e x$
`SQRT(x)` which calculates the value of $\sqrt{x}$

As can be seen from these examples a function reference takes the general form

name (*argument*)

or, where there are two or more arguments

name (*arg1*, *arg2*, ...)

A function is used simply by referring to it in an expression in place of a variable or constant. Thus

```
a+b*LOG(c)
```

will first calculate $\log_e c$, then $b \times \log_e c$, and finally add this to **a**. Similarly

```
-b + SQRT(b*b - 4.0*a*c)
```

will first calculate (**b*b - 4.0*a*c**), then use the function **SQRT** to find its square root, and finally add this to **-b**.

There are 108 intrinsic functions available in Fortran 90, more than twice as many as in Fortran 77; some of these are concerned with standard mathematical functions such as those illustrated above, but many deal with other matters. We shall introduce the intrinsic functions, or families of related intrinsic functions, at appropriate stages as we increase our knowledge and understanding of the Fortran 90 language. A full list can be found in Appendix A for reference.

Many of these functions can have arguments of more than one type, in which case the type of the result will usually (though not always) be of the same type as the arguments. Thus

```
REAL :: x,y
     .
     .
     .
y = ABS(x)
```

will produce the absolute value of the real variable **x** (that is the value ignoring the sign) as a real value and assign it to the real variable **y**, whereas

```
INTEGER :: x,y
     .
     .
     .
y = ABS(x)
```

will produce the absolute value of the integer variable **x** as an integer value and assign it to the integer variable **y**.

Those functions which exhibit this quality are referred to as **generic functions**, since their name really refers to a group of functions, the appropriate one of which will be selected by the compiler depending upon the types of the arguments.

It is also possible to refer directly to the actual function instead of using its generic name (for example, **IABS(x)**), although this is only to provide compatibility with earlier versions of Fortran which had no generic capability; this practice is not recommended.

■ EXAMPLE 4.1

1 Problem

A farmer has a triangular field which he wishes to sow with wheat. Write a program that reads the lengths of the three sides of the field (in metres), and the sowing density (in grams per square metre). Print the number of 10 kilo bags of wheat he must purchase in order to sow the whole field.

2 Analysis

The key to the solution of this problem is the equation

$$area = \sqrt{s(s - a)(s - b)(s - c)}$$

for the area of a triangle whose sides have lengths a, b and c, where $2s = a + b + c$. (This is known as Heron's formula, and dates from the first century AD.)

Our structure plan is then quite simple:

> 1   Read lengths of the sides of the field (a, b and c)
> 2   Calculate the area of the field
> 3   Read the sowing density
> 4   Calculate the quantity of wheat seed required
> 5   Calculate the number of 10 kilo bags this represents

Step 5 is the only one of these which may cause some slight difficulty. The solution can, however, be easily obtained by considering what will happen if we simply divide the quantity of wheat (in grams) by 10 000 to obtain the number of 10 kilo bags. Unless the result of step 4 was an exact multiple of 10 000 (and remember that real arithmetic is, anyway, only an approximation), then there will be some fractional part in the answer. We may decide that if this is less than 0.1 (one kilo) then we will ignore it, but that if it is more than that then we shall need an extra bag – even though we shall not use all of that bag. If we add 0.9 to the result of this division, therefore, the resulting figure will be the number of bags required, probably plus a fractional part. This fractional part will be lost through truncation when the result is assigned to an integer – which is, of course, what the number of bags should be represented as since it has to be a whole number. We can therefore modify step 5 as follows:

    5   Calculate the number of 10 kilo bags as $0.0001 \times$ quantity $+ 0.9$ (to allow for a partly used bag)

3 Solution

```fortran
PROGRAM wheat_sowing
   IMPLICIT NONE

   ! A program to calculate the quantity of wheat required to
   ! sow a triangular field

   ! Variable declarations
   REAL :: a,b,c,s,area,density,quantity
   INTEGER :: num_bags

   ! Read the lengths of the sides of the field
   PRINT *,"Type the lengths of the three sides of the field &
         &in metres: "
   READ *,a,b,c

   ! Calculate the area of the field
   s = 0.5*(a+b+c)
   area = SQRT(s*(s-a)*(s-b)*(s-c))

   ! Read sowing density
   PRINT *,"What is the sowing density (gm/sq.m.)? "
   READ *,density

   ! Calculate quantity of wheat and the number of 10 kg bags
   quantity = density*area
   num_bags = 0.0001*quantity + 0.9  ! Round up more than 1kg

   ! Print results
   PRINT *,"The area of the field is ",area," sq. metres"
   PRINT *,"and ",num_bags," 10 kilo bags will be required"

END PROGRAM wheat_sowing
```

4.2 Programs and program units

In the previous section we stated that a procedure may be part of the Fortran language, in which case it is called an intrinsic procedure, or it may be provided by the programmer. In the latter case it is normally implemented by means of a Fortran **subprogram**.

PROGRAM *name*

.
.
.

Specification statements etc.

.
.
.

Executable statements

.
.
.

END PROGRAM *name*

Figure 4.3   A main program unit.

Up to this point we have not concerned ourselves with subprograms and have considered our programs to consist of a sequence of statements starting with a **PROGRAM** statement and finishing with an **END PROGRAM** statement, as shown in Figure 4.3. Between these two statements there are two main groups of statements, namely **specification statements**, of which declaration statements are the only ones we have met so far, and **executable statements**. The purpose of the specification statements is primarily to provide information to the Fortran processor about the nature of the program, and we shall introduce several more specification statements in subsequent chapters, as well as extending the specification of those we have already discussed. Executable statements, on the other hand, are the statements which cause the computer to carry out some specified action during the execution of the program. All the specification statements must precede the executable statements.

We have already used the term **main program unit**, and we must now briefly introduce the four other types of program units. They all have the same broad structure, consisting of an **initial statement**, any specification statements, any executable statements and an **END** statement. These four program units are two types of **external subprograms**, known as **function subprograms** and **subroutine subprograms**, **modules** and **block data program units** (see Figures 4.4–4.7). We shall discuss the first three of these in this chapter, while the block data program unit will be introduced in Chapter 17.

A program will normally consist of a number of different program units, of which exactly one must be a main program unit. Execution of the program will start at the beginning of the main program unit.

There may be any number of subprogram units in a complete program and one of the most important concepts of Fortran is that *one program unit need never be aware of the internal details of any other program unit*. The only link between one program unit and a subsidiary program unit is through the **interface** of the subsidiary program unit, which consists of the name of the program unit and

```
FUNCTION name(arg,...)
   .
   .
   .
Specification statements etc.
   .
   .
   .
Executable statements
   .
   .
   .
END FUNCTION name
```

Figure 4.4 A function subprogram unit.

```
SUBROUTINE name(arg,...)
   .
   .
   .
Specification statements etc.
   .
   .
   .
Executable statements
   .
   .
   .
END SUBROUTINE name
```

Figure 4.5 A subroutine subprogram unit.

```
MODULE name
   .
   .
   .
Specification statements etc.
   .
   .
   .
Executable statements
   .
   .
   .
END MODULE name
```

Figure 4.6 A module program unit.

BLOCK DATA *name*

.

.

.

Specification statements etc.

.

.

.

END BLOCK DATA *name*

Figure 4.7   A block data program unit.

certain other **public** entities of the program unit. This very important principle means that it is possible to write subprograms totally independently of the main program, and of each other. This feature opens up the way for **libraries** of subprograms: collections of subprograms that can be used by more than one program. It also permits large projects to use more than one programmer; all the programmers need to communicate to each other is the information about the interfaces of their procedures.

4.3   External functions

The intrinsic functions available as part of the Fortran 90 language cover many of the major mathematical functions, as well as meeting other common requirements. However, when developing a program it is often necessary to write our own **function subprograms**, frequently referred to as **external functions** to distinguish them from the intrinsic functions.

An external function takes a very similar form to the programs we have written so far, except that the first statement of the function is not a PROGRAM statement but is a special FUNCTION statement which takes the form

type FUNCTION *name(d1,d2, ...)*

where *d1, d2, ...* are **dummy arguments** which represent the **actual arguments** which will be used when the function is used (or **referenced**), and *type* is the type of the result of the function. For example, we could write a function to calculate the cube root of a positive real number as follows:

```
REAL FUNCTION cube_root(x)
   IMPLICIT NONE
```

```
! Function to calculate the cube root of a positive
! real number

! Dummy argument declaration
REAL, INTENT(IN) :: x

! Local variable declaration
REAL :: log_x

! Calculate cube root by using logs
log_x = LOG(x)
cube_root = EXP(log_x/3.0)

END FUNCTION cube_root
```

This function will only work for positive values of **x** because the method involves taking the log of **x**. In Chapter 5 we shall see how we can extend this function to handle negative or zero values of **x** successfully.

There are four very important points to notice about this function.

The first is that the variable **log_x** is not accessible from outside the function. It is called an **internal variable** (of the function in which it is declared), or a **local variable**, and has no existence outside the function. Thus the main program, or another procedure, could use the name **log_x** for any purpose it wished with no fear of the two uses of the same name being confused with each other. It is this isolation of the inside of a procedure from the outside that makes procedures such powerful tools in the writing of large or complicated programs.

The second point is that the declaration of the dummy argument **x** takes a slightly different form from the declarations that we have used up to now, namely the inclusion of the phrase **INTENT(IN)** after the type, **REAL**. This is the second *attribute* that we have met so far (**PARAMETER** was the other), and like all attributes appears in a declaration statement in order to provide additional information about the object being declared. In this case it informs the compiler that the dummy argument **x** may not be changed by the function **cube_root**. We shall discuss this attribute in detail in Section 4.5 when we discuss the relationship between actual arguments and dummy arguments; for the present we shall simply note that dummy arguments to functions should *always* be declared with **INTENT(IN)**.

The third point to note is that although the dummy argument **x** and the variable **log_x** have been declared, there is, apparently, one further variable called **cube_root** which has not been declared. Furthermore, this variable has the same name as the function, in an apparent direct contradiction of the rule we established in Chapter 1 for the name of the program.

In fact this is a special variable, known as the **result variable**, and is the means by which a function returns its value. Every function *must* contain a variable having the same name as the function, and this variable *must* be assigned, or otherwise given, a value to return as the value of the function before an exit is made from the function.

Now, of course, this special result variable must have a type, like any other variable, but because it is also the name of the function it is permitted either to declare its type as part of the **FUNCTION** statement, or to declare it by means of a conventional type declaration statement. For example, it would also have been permissible to write

```
FUNCTION cube_root(x)
   IMPLICIT NONE
   REAL :: cube_root
   .
   .
   .
```

In the simple case shown here the first form is probably more satisfactory, but we shall meet cases later where it is essential to use the second form.

The other important point concerns the last statement of the procedure. As was the case with the **END** statement at the end of the main program unit, it is not obligatory to include the function name, and any of the following are acceptable:

```
END FUNCTION cube_root
END FUNCTION
END
```

We would, however, strongly recommend that the first form always be used, as this helps to make the structure of the program clearer. It is, of course, a requirement that the name included in this form of the **END FUNCTION** statement matches the name on the initial **FUNCTION** statement!

When the **END** statement is obeyed, in whatever form it is written, it causes execution of the program to return to the point in the calling procedure at which the function was referenced as though a variable had been inserted in the code at that point, having as its value the value calculated by the function. Thus the statement

```
a = b*cube_root(c)+d
```

will cause the cube root of **c** to be calculated by the function, multiplied by **b**, have **d** added, and the result to be stored in **a**. Note, however, that the function **cube_root** must be declared in the calling program unit in a conventional declaration statement in order that the Fortran processor is aware of its type, and any other relevant information:

```
REAL :: cube_root
```

Although it is not necessary, it is possible to add an **EXTERNAL** attribute specification to such a declaration by writing

```
REAL,EXTERNAL :: cube_root
```

The addition of this attribute informs the compiler that the name is that of a real function and not of a real variable. Although this should be readily deducible from the context in which the name **cube_root** occurs, it is a valuable security check, and we recommend that this attribute is always included in the declaration of external functions.

In Section 4.2 we said that only the interface of a subprogram was known to any other program units, and in the case of a function subprogram this interface consists of the name and type of the function (**cube_root** and real in this example), and the number and type of its dummy arguments (one real dummy argument in this case). We shall meet other items that may be part of the interface in Chapter 11.

Before leaving discussion of this function we should briefly mention the situation where we wish to write a function which has no arguments. In this situation we must still include the parentheses around the non-existent argument when declaring the function, and also when using the function, as the presence of the parentheses is one of the ways in which Fortran compilers recognize a function reference. For example, we could define a function which prompts the user to type a number and which then delivers this number to the program:

```
INTEGER FUNCTION next_int()
   IMPLICIT NONE

   ! This function requests an integer from the keyboard

   ! Get number
   PRINT *,"Please type an integer"
   READ *,next_int

END FUNCTION next_int
```

This function could be used in the following program:

```
PROGRAM next_int_test
   IMPLICIT NONE

   ! This program displays the product of two numbers which are
   ! typed at the keyboard

   ! External function declaration
   INTEGER, EXTERNAL :: next_int
```

```
Please type an integer
17
Please type an integer
23
Their product is    391
```

Figure 4.8 Results produced by the program product using the function **next_int**.

```
! Variable declaration
INTEGER :: product

product = next_int()*next_int()

PRINT *,"The product is ",product

END PROGRAM next_int_test
```

When the first executable statement is executed, the first function reference **next_item()** will cause the request for a number to be displayed, and when one has been typed and control returned to the main program the second function reference will repeat the process. Now that two values are available the product can be calculated and the assignment carried out. The result of running this program is shown in Figure 4.8.

Finally, we must emphasize that, although all the example functions shown in this section have all been referenced in the main program, they can equally well be referenced in another function or, as we shall see in the next section, subroutine. However, a very important point is that a function must not refer to itself, either directly or indirectly (for example, through referencing another procedure which, in turn, references the original function). This is known as **recursion** and is not allowed unless we take special action to permit it. This will be discussed in Chapter 11.

4.4 Subroutines

In Section 4.1 we mentioned that there were two types of procedures in Fortran — functions and subroutines. It is now time to examine how a subroutine differs from a function.

The difference lies in how a subroutine is referenced and how the results, if any, are returned.

A function, as we have seen, is referenced in the same way as a variable simply by writing its name, followed by any arguments it may have enclosed in parentheses; such a function reference causes a **transfer of control** so that, instead of continuing to process the current statement, the computer executes the statements contained within the function. The execution of the function utilizes the values provided as arguments to calculate a single value (the **function value**) which is available as the value of the function reference, just as writing the name of a variable in an expression provides a value – the value stored in a particular memory location. A **function reference**, therefore, is not a complete statement but is part of an expression, and may appear anywhere that an expression may appear (for example, on the right-hand side of an assignment statement, in an output list, as an argument in a function reference, etc.). We have already used a number of intrinsic functions, which are defined within the Fortran language, and external functions which we wrote ourselves, but both types are referenced in the same way:

```
var = fun(arg1, arg2, ...)
PRINT *,fun1(arg1, arg2, ...)
var = fun2(a1, fun3(arg1, arg2, ...), a2, a3, ...)
```

etc.

A subroutine, on the other hand, as we saw in Example 2.1, is accessed by means of a **CALL** statement, which gives the name of the subroutine and a list of arguments which will be used to transmit information between the calling program unit and the subroutine:

```
CALL name(arg1,arg2, ...)
```

The **CALL** statement causes a transfer of control so that, instead of executing the next statement in the program, the computer executes the statements contained within the subroutine *name*. When the subroutine has completed its task it returns to the calling program unit and execution continues with the next statement.

Unlike a function, which always returns the result of its execution as the value of the function, a subroutine need not return anything to the calling program unit; however, if it does return any values then they are returned by means of one or more of its arguments.

We can see how this works by writing a subroutine, **roots**, which calculates the square root, the cube root, the fourth root and the fifth root of a positive real number. This is, clearly, somewhat similar to the function **cube_root** developed in the last section, but will return four results instead of one; it must, therefore, be written as a subroutine:

```
SUBROUTINE roots(x,square_root,cube_root,fourth_root,fifth_root)
   IMPLICIT NONE

   ! Subroutine to calculate various roots of a positive real
   ! number supplied as the first argument, and return it in
   ! the second to fifth arguments
```

```
! Dummy argument declarations
REAL, INTENT(IN) :: x
REAL, INTENT(OUT) :: square_root,cube_root,fourth_root,    &
                     fifth_root

! Local variable declaration
REAL :: log_x

! Calculate square root using intrinsic SQRT
square_root = SQRT(x)

! Calculate other roots by using logs
log_x = LOG(x)
cube_root = EXP(log_x/3.0)
fourth_root = EXP(log_x/4.0)
fifth_root = EXP(log_x/5.0)

END SUBROUTINE roots
```

Note that, although the code is very similar to that written for the corresponding function, in this case the results of executing the subroutine are assigned to variables which are themselves dummy arguments. Notice, also, that these dummy arguments have been given an **INTENT(OUT)** attribute, to indicate that they are to be used to transfer information from the subroutine back to the calling program. We shall discuss the use of the **INTENT** attribute with subroutines in Section 4.5, when we discuss the relationship between dummy arguments and actual arguments in rather more detail. In the calling program unit the corresponding actual argument will contain the results on return from the subroutine:

```
PROGRAM subroutine_demo
   IMPLICIT NONE

   ! A program to demonstrate the use of the subroutine roots

   ! Variable declarations
   REAL :: pos_num,root_2,root_3,root_4,root_5

   ! Get positive number from user
   PRINT *,"Please type a positive real number: "
   READ *,pos_num

   ! Obtain roots
   CALL roots(pos_num,root_2,root_3,root_4,root_5)

   ! Display number and its roots
   PRINT *,"The square root of ",pos_num," is ",root_2
   PRINT *,"The cube root of ",pos_num," is ",root_3
   PRINT *,"The fourth root of ",pos_num," is ",root_4
   PRINT *,"The fifth root of ",pos_num," is ",root_5

END PROGRAM subroutine_demo
```

Since the name of a subroutine is simply a means of identification and does not have any type, the interface for a subroutine is the name of the subroutine, together with the number and type of any dummy arguments.

If a subroutine has no arguments then the **CALL** statement takes the form

CALL *sub*

or

CALL *sub*()

although we recommend the simpler form without any parentheses.

Finally, as was the case for functions, a subroutine may call other subroutines or reference functions, but it must not call itself, either directly or indirectly (for example, through referencing another procedure which, in turn, references the original subroutine). As with functions, such recursive calls are only allowed if specific steps are taken to permit it, as will be discussed in Chapter 11.

4.5   Actual arguments, dummy arguments and local variables

We have seen that, when a function or subroutine is referenced, information is passed to it through its arguments; in the case of a subroutine, information may also be returned to the calling program unit through its arguments. The relationship between the **actual arguments** in the calling program unit and the dummy arguments in the subroutine or function is of vital importance in this process.

The actual mechanism used is unimportant, and may vary from one computer system to another; the important thing to realize is that the dummy arguments do not exist as independent entities – they are a simply a means by which the procedure can identify the actual arguments in the calling program unit.

One very important point to stress is that *the order and types of the actual arguments must correspond exactly with the order and types of the corresponding dummy arguments.*

In Chapter 3 we refined a model that had first been introduced in Chapter 1 so that variables were represented by glass boxes, their values by balls stored in the boxes, and their names and types by labels on the boxes (Figure 4.9). We may extend this model by the addition of a noticeboard for each procedure, with a section for each dummy argument. When the procedure (function or subroutine) is called from some other program unit we can imagine that a message is pinned up for each dummy argument identifying the corresponding actual argument, as shown in Figures 4.10 and 4.11. Whenever a reference is made to one of these dummy arguments in the procedure the noticeboard will be used to show to

Figure 4.9 A storage model.

which *actual* location in the memory (one of the actual arguments) reference is
being made.

For example, if the only executable statement in the subroutine was

```
x = y + z
```

then the effect of the call in Figure 4.10 would be as if it was replaced in the
calling program unit by the statement

```
a = c + d
```

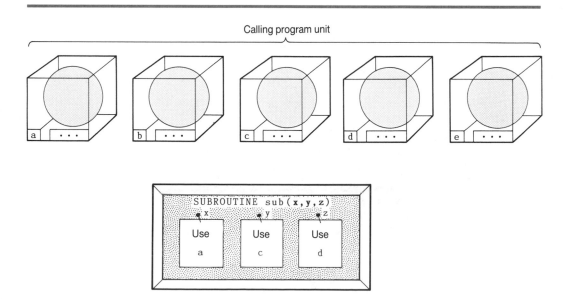

Figure 4.10 A representation of `CALL sub(a,c,d)`.

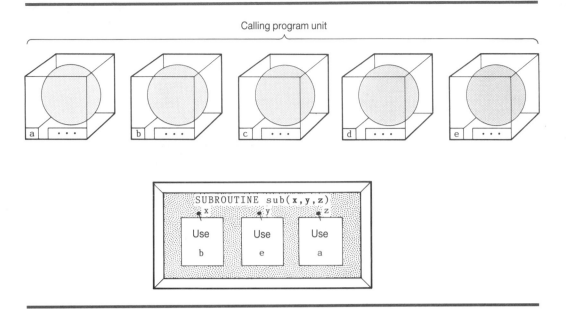

Figure 4.11 A representation of CALL sub(b,e,a).

whereas the effect of the call in Figure 4.11 would be as if it was replaced by the statement

```
b = e + a
```

It follows from this model that whereas an actual argument may be a variable or an expression (an open box), or a constant (a closed and sealed box), a dummy argument is a pseudo-variable, in the sense that the corresponding area of the noticeboard may have different notices pinned on it; in the procedure that defines it, it can be used just like any other variable in the procedure. However, it has no existence outside the procedure; whenever it is used it is always in the context of the actual argument being substituted for it.

Because the arguments of a subroutine can be used to transmit information from the calling program to the subroutine, or from the subroutine to the calling program, or for both purposes, it is important that the distinction between dummy arguments which are being used for these different purposes is recognized. This is achieved, as has been already mentioned, by use of the **INTENT** attribute, and it is now appropriate to examine this in more detail.

The **INTENT** attribute is one of a number of attributes that may follow the type in a declaration statement using the double colon, but which may not be used in the older form of declaration statement which does not use a double colon; note, however, that the **INTENT** attribute may only be used in the declaration of a dummy argument. It can take one of the following three forms:

- **INTENT(IN)** which informs the processor that this dummy argument is used only to provide information to the procedure, and the procedure will not be allowed to alter its value in any way;

- **INTENT(OUT)** which informs the processor that this dummy argument will only be used to return information from the pro-cedure to the calling program. Its value will be undefined on entry to the procedure and it must be given a value by some means before being used in an expression, or being otherwise referred to in a context which will require its value to be evaluated;

- **INTENT(INOUT)** which informs the processor that this dummy argument may be used for transmission of information in both directions.

As we have already indicated, a subroutine's arguments may have all three forms of **INTENT** attribute. In the case of a function, however, the arguments should only be used for giving information to the function, with the result of the function always being returned through its result variable; the dummy arguments in a function should always, therefore, be declared with **INTENT(IN)**.

To illustrate the importance of always specifying the **INTENT** attribute for dummy arguments let us examine the short program shown in Figure 4.12. The subroutine **problem_sub** appears to be perfectly straightforward and simply performs some simple arithmetic on its arguments. However, the description of the subroutine contained in the initial commentary indicates that there is a typing error in the assignment statement which should have read

```
arg3 = arg1*arg2
```

and not as shown. Since this statement is syntactically correct the program will compile without error. When the program is executed, however, the first call to the subroutine will cause the values of the two dummy arguments **arg2** and **arg3**, which correspond to the actual arguments **b** and **c**, to be multiplied together and the result stored in the dummy argument **arg1**. Thus the value 12 will be assigned to **arg1**. However, **arg1** corresponds to the actual argument **a**, which is a named constant! This may cause an error, but not all systems will detect it, and exactly what will happen is somewhat indeterminate; on some processors, however, reference to the literal constant 2 later in the program may result in the value 12 being used!

```
PROGRAM intent_demonstration
  IMPLICIT NONE

  INTEGER, PARAMETER :: a=2
  INTEGER :: b=3,c=4,d

  CALL problem_sub(a,b,c)
  CALL problem_sub(b,c,d)
  PRINT *,"a = ",a," and b = ",b

END PROGRAM intent_demonstration

SUBROUTINE problem_sub(arg1,arg2,arg3)
  IMPLICIT NONE

  ! This subroutine returns the product of its first two
  ! arguments via the third argument

  INTEGER :: arg1,arg2,arg3

  arg1 = arg2*arg3

END SUBROUTINE problem_sub
```

Figure 4.12 An example of confusion about the **INTENT** of dummy arguments.

Finally, if no execution error is caused by this attempt to change the value of a constant the second call to the subroutine will probably do so. In this case the third dummy argument, **arg3**, will take the value of the corresponding actual argument, **d**. However, **d** has not been assigned any value at the time of the call to the subroutine and its value is therefore undefined. Once again, the processor is not required to detect this error (although most will), but if it does not then the result of the calculation is obviously indeterminate!

If the declarations in the subroutine had read

```
INTEGER, INTENT(IN) :: arg1,arg2
INTEGER, INTENT(OUT) :: arg3
```

then the following assignment statement would have led to an error during compilation because of the attempt to change the value of an **INTENT(IN)** dummy argument. On the other hand, if it was the comment that was wrong, and the assignment was correct, then the declarations should have been

```
INTEGER, INTENT(OUT) :: arg1
INTEGER, INTENT(IN) :: arg2,arg3
```

In this situation, since the first argument has the **INTENT(OUT)** attribute, the attempted assignment to a constant will lead to an execution error. Ideally this error would be detected at compilation time, but since often nothing is known about any procedures that are called by another program unit during compilation, this is not possible unless special steps are taken. For the same reason, it is not normally possible to detect the attempted use of the undefined actual argument **d** during the program's compilation. There is, however, one very useful technique which can be used to provide this additional security, as well as being mandatory in other situations that we shall meet in later chapters. We shall discuss this in Section 4.9, when we have introduced the additional concept required for this purpose.

Returning to the noticeboard model that we used to illustrate the way in which actual and dummy arguments are related, we find that even this simple model highlights two further difficulties. All the examples that we have used so far have involved either real or integer arguments, but not character or derived type ones. Let us briefly examine how arguments of these types differ from numeric arguments.

The problem with character arguments concerns the length of the arguments, and can most easily be demonstrated by an example.

■ EXAMPLE 4.2

1 Problem

Write a procedure which will take two character arguments as input arguments, containing two names (a 'first name' and a 'family name', respectively), and which will return a string containing the two names with exactly one space separating them.

2 Analysis

This problem is similar to that presented in Example 3.2, but with two refinements.

The first, and major, difficulty is that the procedure, regardless of whether it is a function or a subroutine, cannot know the length that will be declared for each of the two names, so how can the corresponding dummy arguments be declared?

As might be expected, this is such a common problem that Fortran provides a solution – an **assumed-length character declaration**. This can only be used for declaring a dummy argument and involves replacing the length specifier by an asterisk:

```
CHARACTER(LEN=*) :: character_dummy_arg
```

This is called an assumed-length dummy argument because it *assumes* its length from the corresponding actual argument when the procedure is executed. If the correspondence between actual and dummy argument is carried out in a way analogous to the noticeboard used above then this is clearly no problem, as no extra storage is required.

The second difficulty is concerned with removing any redundant spaces at the beginning or the end of the two names and then inserting exactly one between them. In Example 3.2 we met the **TRIM** intrinsic function, which removes any trailing blanks from its argument. A second intrinsic function, **ADJUSTL**, which moves its argument enough spaces to the left to remove any leading blanks, will enable us to deal with the (unlikely) case that either of the arguments contains leading blanks.

Although the solution to this problem could be written as either a subroutine or a function, its purpose is to deliver a single result based on its arguments, and so a function is more appropriate:

Function *full_name*(*first_name,last_name*)
full_name, *first_name* and *last_name* are all **CHARACTER(LEN=*)**.

1   Concatenate names, using **ADJUSTL** to remove leading blanks from both names, and **TRIM** to remove trailing blanks from *first_name*

[3] **Solution**

```
CHARACTER(LEN=*) FUNCTION full_name(first_name,last_name)
   IMPLICIT NONE

   ! Function to join two names to form a full name with a
   ! single space between the first and last names

   ! Dummy argument declarations
   CHARACTER(LEN=*), INTENT(IN) :: first_name,last_name

   ! Use ADJUSTL to remove redundant leading blanks, and TRIM
   ! to remove redundant blanks at the end of first_name
   full_name = TRIM(ADJUSTL(first_name)) // " " //   &
               ADJUSTL(last_name)

END FUNCTION full_name
```

Note that the result variable **(full_name)** is declared to be of assumed length. In order for the processor to know what actual length to assume when the function is referenced, the function name *must* appear in a declaration statement in any program unit that references the function, and that declaration must specify the length of the function:

```
CHARACTER(LEN=30), EXTERNAL :: full_name
```

When the function is referenced the length of the result will be set at the declared length of the function; that is, 30 in the example just given. If this is longer than the result of the concatenation then the resulting full name will be extended on the right with blanks in the usual way. If it is shorter then the result of the concatenation will be truncated to the appropriate length. Because of this, there is no point in causing the function to remove any extra blanks at the end of the second name.

Note also that the result of the **ADJUSTL** function reference has been used as an argument to **TRIM**. The first function, **ADJUSTL**, therefore moves its argument, **first_name**, to the left to eliminate any leading blanks, and the second, **TRIM**, takes the result and removes any trailing blanks, including any that were introduced by **ADJUSTL**. Strictly speaking, it is not necessary to remove any leading spaces from **first_name** since they do not affect the main problem, which is ensuring that there is only one space between the two names, but while we are tidying up we may as well do everything properly!

Another approach, which avoids the nested intrinsic function references, is to declare two local variables and assign the two names, without leading blanks, to them. There is an apparent difficulty with determining the length for these variables, but once again an intrinsic function comes to our aid. **LEN**(*character_string*) returns the length of its argument, and can be used in the declaration of other character variables:

```
CHARACTER(LEN=*) FUNCTION full_name(first_name,last_name)
   IMPLICIT NONE

   ! Function to join two names to form a full name with a
   ! single space between the first and last names

   ! Dummy argument declarations
   CHARACTER(LEN=*), INTENT(IN) :: first_name,last_name

   ! Local variables
   CHARACTER(LEN=LEN(first_name)) :: new_first_name
   CHARACTER(LEN=LEN(last_name)) :: new_last_name

   ! Use ADJUSTL to remove redundant leading blanks
   new_first_name = ADJUSTL(first_name)
   new_last_name = ADJUSTL(last_name)

   ! Use TRIM to remove blanks at the end of new_first_name
   full_name = TRIM(new_first_name) // " " // new_last_name

END FUNCTION full_name
```

Notice that an alternative way of writing the function would be to move the declaration of the type of the function to the body of the function:

```
FUNCTION full_name(first_name,last_name)
   IMPLICIT NONE

   ! Function to join two names to form a full name with a
   ! single space between the first and last names

   ! Result type and dummy argument declarations
   CHARACTER(LEN=*), INTENT(IN) :: first_name,last_name
   CHARACTER(LEN=*) :: full_name
   .
   .
   .
```

Which of the two alternative forms of function declaration is used is largely a matter of personal preference, although the authors prefer the first alternative. In both cases, however, the length of the result variable will be the same as the length that was specified in the declaration of the function name in the calling program unit.

The fourth of the data types that we met in Chapter 3, on the other hand, poses a much more fundamental problem. We can understand this problem if we consider the derived data type **complex_number** that we defined in Example 3.4, and then further consider how we might write a procedure which has one or more arguments of this type.

In the procedure we will need to declare the dummy arguments by means of a statement of the form

```
TYPE(complex_number) :: arg1,arg2,arg3
```

However, as we have repeatedly stressed, the only items within a procedure that are known to any calling program unit are its name (and type if it is a function), and the number and types of any dummy arguments. While we can have variables and constants as actual arguments, we cannot have a type definition as an argument.

So how can the calling program unit know about the definition of the new derived type **complex_number** if that definition occurs in the called procedure, and vice versa if the definition occurs in the calling program unit? It is not sufficient to repeat the type definition, because this will create two different types, one of them only for use within the procedure and one only for use outside it, just as declarations of variables of the same name in two different program units create two different variables. The answer to this difficulty requires a new concept that we shall meet in Section 4.8.

This brings us back again to the very important principle of the **locality of variables**. Each program unit is only aware of any variables declared within

Figure 4.13 Local variables!

the program unit itself, referred to as its **local variables**, together with pseudo-variables known as dummy arguments. There are, however, some occasions when it would be useful for several procedures to be able to access the same variables, or other entities, without the use of arguments, and, as we have just seen, there are some things, such as type definitions, that cannot be passed as arguments. We shall see how to deal with this situation later in this chapter, and will meet a rather older, and less flexible approach, in Chapter 17; with the exception of these techniques, every program unit is unaware of, and cannot access, any of the local entities used in other program units.

This is extremely important because it means that when we are writing a subprogram, or a main program, we do not need to be concerned with a clash of names with those used in another program unit. This is exactly analogous to names within a family.

The Ellis family in Figure 4.13 have called their children David, Sarah and Richard, and refer to them within the family by those names, even though their full names are David Ellis, Sarah Ellis and Richard Ellis. The Jones family, who live a long way away and have never met the Ellis family, have called their children Sarah, Emma and David. Because the two families are in different places and don't even know each other there is never any confusion within their respective families about who David and Sarah are; David and Sarah Ellis are *local* to the Ellis family, while David and Sarah Jones ares not part of the Ellis family but are *local* to the Jones family.

The importance of local variables combined with arguments cannot be overemphasized, as it is the reason why it is possible to write libraries of useful subroutines and functions which can subsequently be used in other people's programs. Someone whom you will never meet can write a procedure, freely using any names for dummy arguments or local variables, secure in the knowledge that there is no possibility of names 'clashing' with names that you have chosen because the names used in the procedure are local to that procedure only.

4.6 Procedures as an aid to program structure

One of the great advantages of subprograms is that they enable us to break the design of a program into several smaller, more manageable sections, and then to write and test each of these sections independently of the rest of the program. This paves the way for an approach known as **modular program development**, which is a key concept of software engineering.

This approach breaks the problem down into its major sub-problems, or **components**, each of which can then be dealt with independently of the others. In a large project these components may be developed by different people. If necessary, a component may itself be sub-divided into further components, just as in any other piece of engineering design. All that is necessary is that the interface between each component and the rest of the program is well defined.

An example of this approach in mechanical engineering is the manufacture of the Airbus A-300. The wings for this aircraft are manufactured in the United Kingdom, while part of the fuselage is manufactured in Italy and the remaining part in France. In order that the front and rear parts of the fuselage join correctly, and that the wings fasten onto the fuselage properly, it is only necessary to provide a detailed specification of exactly how the relevant parts will be joined — the *interface* between these sub-assemblies.

The interface for a component of a Fortran program consists of two parts. The first, the interface proper, is the list of arguments supplied to the component (or rather to the subprogram which is, in effect, the main program unit of the component); this is a concept that we have already discussed in the context of a procedure interface. The second is the specification of the action of the component.

A structure plan gives very great assistance in modular development as it identifies, in a natural way, the major components of the program. Rather than expanding these components within a single structure plan, as we have been doing up to now, we can treat each of these major components as a separate sub-problem whose solution is to be developed independently. Once developed, they can be integrated to form the complete program according to the top-level structure plan. We shall develop this idea further in later chapters, but for the present we shall simply combine the concept of a structure plan with that of a modular program structure.

■ **EXAMPLE 4.3**

1 **Problem**

Write a program which will read a set of ten experimental results and calculate their mean and standard deviation.

2 **Analysis**

We can readily identify the three major components of this problem – the input of the data, the calculation of the mean and standard deviation, and the output of the results. Even if we have no statistical knowledge whatsoever, therefore, we could write a structure plan of the following nature:

1 Read ten real data items ($x1, \ldots, x10$) using the subroutine *input*

2 Calculate the mean and standard deviation using the subroutine *statistics*

3 Print results using the subroutine *results*

Notice that we have specified that the input and output are carried out in subroutines. As well as enabling us to keep the structure of the program as clear as possible, this provides two major benefits.

The first of these is that it means that we can test each of the subroutines separately, thus both simplifying the testing procedure and making it easier to find any errors. For example, a substitute *input* subroutine can be used when testing the main *statistics* subroutine:

```
SUBROUTINE input(x1,x2,x3,x4,x5,x6,x7,x8,x9,x10)
   IMPLICIT NONE
   REAL, INTENT(OUT) :: x1,x2,x3,x4,x5,x6,x7,x8,x9,x10
   x1 = 1.5
   x2 = 3.7
     .
     .
     .
   x10 = -7.1
END SUBROUTINE input
```

The second benefit is that by breaking up a program into discrete sections in this way we can keep the size of each procedure down to manageable proportions. Experience shows that the longer the procedure, the more difficult it is to read and to test, and hence the less likely it is to work as well as possible. As a rule of thumb, we would suggest that if a procedure, including any comments, reaches a length of more than about 50 lines, so that it can no longer be printed on a single sheet of paper or viewed easily on a screen, then you should examine it carefully to see whether the problem being solved by the procedure might not be better split into two, or more, sub-problems, each of which could be the subject of a separate, smaller, procedure.

We can, therefore, now write a second level of subsidiary structure plans, such as:

Subroutine statistics($x1, \ldots, x10, mean, st\_dev$)
   REAL :: $x1, \ldots, x10, mean, st\_dev$

1   Calculate mean and standard deviation

This provides sufficient information for the main program unit to be written, since the interface with the subroutine **statistics** is fully defined. The mathematics of how to calculate the standard deviation can be left to the person who is to write this subroutine, since he or she will know the exact form of the subroutine's interface with the calling program unit.

We will not take this problem any further at this stage, however, as the resulting program will be very limited and the concept of modular development has been sufficiently well demonstrated.

SELF-TEST EXERCISES 4.1

1   Why should programs be broken into a main program and a set of procedures?

2   What is the difference between a subroutine and a function?

3   What is an intrinsic procedure?

4   What is a generic function?

5   What is the difference between a dummy argument which is declared with an **INTENT(INOUT)** attribute, and one which is declared as **INTENT(OUT)**?

6   Write the initial statements and the declarations for any dummy arguments for procedures designed to carry out the following tasks. (Don't worry if you don't know how to write the procedure yet; you can specify its interface with a calling program unit without knowing how to write it.)

(a)   Count the number of times a specified character appears in a character string
(b)   Find the roots of a quadratic equation of the form

$$ax^2 + bx + c = 0$$

(c) Establish whether a whole number is prime. (A number is prime if it is only divisible by itself and by 1.)

(d) Reverse the order of the characters in a character string

(e) Print an error message based on an error code which may be −1 or an integer in the range 1 to 10

(f) Read whatever is typed at the default input unit until a whole number greater than zero is typed, and return that number

4.7 Modules

As we have seen, functions and subroutines are very similar in many ways and represent two different types of procedures. Although we shall meet other ways of writing procedures in Chapter 11, they are normally written as independent program units in the form of *external subprograms*.

Another form of program unit, which is used for a rather different purpose and did not exist in FORTRAN 77, is a **module**.

In a similar fashion to a function or a subroutine, a module starts with an initial statement of the form

```
MODULE name
```

and ends with an end statement which, as might be expected, takes the form

```
END MODULE name
```

or one of the simpler forms

```
END MODULE
END
```

As usual, we recommend that the first form always be used.

The purpose of a module is quite different from a function or a subroutine. Quite simply, a module exists in order to make some or all of the entities declared within it accessible to more than one program unit. A wide range of items may be declared within a module and made accessible to other parts of the program in a way which provides an extremely powerful functionality. Before discussing the full power of modules, however, it is necessary to understand more about some of the other features of Fortran and so the main discussion of modules will be deferred until Chapter 12. One very important use of modules which we can introduce at this stage, however, relates to **global accessibility** of variables, constants and derived type definitions.

As we have already pointed out, the only items in a procedure which are accessible outside the procedure are those which are specified as dummy arguments or as the result variable of a function. Similarly, the only items in a calling program unit which are accessible within a procedure are those which are specified as actual arguments in the subroutine call or function reference. A module allows a defined set of variables and/or constants to be made available to any program units which access them by means of an appropriate USE statement. The USE statement takes the form

USE *name*

where *name* is the name of the module in which the variables, constants and/or derived type definitions are declared.

The concept is most easily explained by means of an example. Let us suppose that several procedures wish to use the values of π and $\pi/2$ in calculations, and that they all wish also to have access to five variables which we shall call global_1, global_2, global_3, global_4 and global_5. A module to declare these items would be as follows:

```
MODULE global_data
   IMPLICIT NONE
   SAVE

   ! Constant declarations
   REAL, PARAMETER :: pi=3.1415926, piby2=pi/2.0

   ! Variable declarations
   REAL :: global_1, global_2, global_3, global_4, global_5

END MODULE global_data
```

Note that the statement immediately following the IMPLICIT NONE statement consists of the single word SAVE. This is recommended in order to avoid a theoretical difficulty which will be described in Chapter 11. For the present, it should always be included in any module which declares any variables.

Any program unit which wishes to access items from the module need only include a statement of the form

```
USE global_data
```

to make all five variables and two constants available. Entities which are made available in this way are said to be made available by USE **association**.

Note that the USE statement comes after the initial statement (PROGRAM, SUBROUTINE or FUNCTION) but *before any other statements*:

```
SUBROUTINE component
   USE global_data
   IMPLICIT NONE

   ! Any additional specification statements
   .
   .
   .
```

```
   ! Executable statements
   .
   .
   .
END SUBROUTINE component
```

As can be seen from this skeleton example, the use of modules can significantly simplify the interface of procedures, although this is only a meaningful thing to do when, as is often the case in large programs, several procedures wish to have access to the same constants and variables and would otherwise have to pass this information between themselves by means of long argument lists.

One point that should be emphasized is that all procedures which use a module that includes a **SAVE** statement are sharing the same copy of any variables, constants, type definitions or other entities accessed from it by **USE** association, as can be seen in the following example, which refers to the module `global_data` defined above:

```
SUBROUTINE sub1
   USE global_data
   IMPLICIT NONE

   global_1 = pi        ! both accessed from module
   PRINT *,global_1     ! prints 3.14159 (approximately!)
   CALL sub2            ! global_1 now has the value 2.5
   PRINT *,global_1     ! prints 2.5
END

SUBROUTINE sub2
   USE global_data
   IMPLICIT NONE
   global_1 = 2.5       ! variable is accessed from module
END
```

Note, incidentally, that one module can **USE** another module in order to gain access to items declared within it, and those items then also become available along with the module's own entities:

```
MODULE first
   IMPLICIT NONE
   SAVE
   INTEGER :: first_int
END MODULE first

MODULE second
   USE first
   IMPLICIT NONE
   SAVE
   INTEGER :: second_int
END MODULE second
```

```
SUBROUTINE module_user
  USE second
  IMPLICIT NONE
  ! This subroutine has access to second_int from the
  ! module second, and first_int from the module first
  .
  .
  .
```

Finally, note that it is not allowed for a module to **USE** itself, either directly or indirectly (via a recursive chain of other modules).

4.8   Modules and derived data types

A particularly important use of modules is in connection with derived data types. It will be remembered that in Section 4.5 it was pointed out that it was not possible to use derived type variables or constants as arguments to a procedure because the procedure would not be aware of the type of actual arguments whose type was defined in the calling program unit, and the calling program unit would not be aware of the type of any dummy arguments whose type was defined in the procedure. Simply defining two derived types with the same name and identical components would not suffice, as this would define two *different* data types, each one local to the program unit in which it was defined. A module, however, enables us to resolve this problem by placing the type definition in a module and then using it in any program units requiring variables or constants of this type, as shown in the following example.

■ EXAMPLE 4.4

1 Problem

Write four functions for use in a complex arithmetic package using the **complex_number** derived type which was created in Example 3.4. The functions should each take two complex arguments and return as their result the result of adding, subtracting, multiplying or dividing the two numbers.

2 Analysis

We calculated three of these in Example 3.4, and we can easily confirm that the result of dividing (x_1, y_1) by (x_2, y_2) is $((x_1x_2 + y_1y_2)/(x_2^2 + y_2^2),$ $(x_2y_1 - x_1y_2)/(x_2^2 + y_2^2))$. All that is necessary, therefore, is to define a module containing the definition of the derived data type and use this in each of the four functions.

3 Solution

```fortran
MODULE complex_data
   IMPLICIT NONE
   SAVE

   ! This module defines a complex data derived data type
   TYPE complex_number
      REAL :: real_part,imag_part
   END TYPE complex_number

END MODULE complex_data

FUNCTION c_add(z1,z2)
   USE complex_data
   IMPLICIT NONE

   ! Declare function type and dummy arguments
   TYPE(complex_number) :: c_add
   TYPE(complex_number), INTENT(IN) :: z1,z2

   ! Calculate function result
   c_add%real_part = z1%real_part + z2%real_part
   c_add%imag_part = z1%imag_part + z2%imag_part
END FUNCTION c_add

FUNCTION c_sub(z1,z2)
   USE complex_data
   IMPLICIT NONE

   ! Declare function type and dummy arguments
   TYPE(complex_number) :: c_sub
   TYPE(complex_number), INTENT(IN) :: z1,z2

   ! Calculate function result
   c_sub%real_part = z1%real_part - z2%real_part
   c_sub%imag_part = z1%imag_part - z2%imag_part
END FUNCTION c_sub

FUNCTION c_mult(z1,z2)
   USE complex_data
   IMPLICIT NONE

   ! Declare function type and dummy arguments
   TYPE(complex_number) :: c_mult
   TYPE(complex_number), INTENT(IN) :: z1,z2

   ! Calculate function result
   c_mult%real_part = z1%real_part*z2%real_part - &
                      z1%imag_part*z2%imag_part
   c_mult%imag_part = z1%real_part*z2%imag_part + &
                      z1%imag_part*z2%real_part
END FUNCTION c_mult
```

```
FUNCTION c_div(z1,z2)
   USE complex_data
   IMPLICIT NONE

   ! Declare function type and dummy arguments
   TYPE(complex_number) :: c_div
   TYPE(complex_number), INTENT(IN) :: z1,z2

   ! Local variable to save calculating denominator twice
   REAL :: denom

   ! Calculate function result
   denom = z2%real_part**2 + z2%imag_part**2
   c_div%real_part = (z1%real_part*z2%real_part + &
                      z1%imag_part*z2%imag_part)/denom
   c_div%imag_part = (z2%real_part*z1%imag_part - &
                      z1%real_part*z2%imag_part)/denom
END FUNCTION c_div
```

Any program or procedure that wishes to use these functions to carry out complex arithmetic will also, of course, need to use the same module to obtain access to the **complex_number** data type, as in the following example, which uses each of the above procedures:

```
PROGRAM complex_example
   USE complex_data
   IMPLICIT NONE

   ! Declare external functions
   TYPE(complex_number), EXTERNAL :: c_add,c_sub,c_mult,c_div

   ! Declare two complex variables
   TYPE(complex_number) :: z1,z2

   ! Read data
   PRINT *,"Please supply two complex numbers as two pairs &
           &of numbers"
   PRINT *,"Each pair represents the real and imaginary parts &
           &of a complex number"
   READ *,z1,z2

   ! Calculate and print sum, difference, product and quotient
   PRINT *,"The sum of the two numbers is ",c_add(z1,z2)
   PRINT *,"The difference between the two numbers is ", &
           c_sub(z1,z2)
   PRINT *,"The product of the two numbers is ",c_mult(z1,z2)
   PRINT *,"The result of dividing the first number by the &
           &second is ",c_div(z1,z2)
END PROGRAM complex_example
```

4.9   Modules and explicit procedure interfaces

We have several times referred to the *interface* of a procedure in a relatively informal manner, and have indicated that it consists of the name of the procedure (and its type if it is a function), together with the number and type of its arguments. We must now, briefly, examine this concept in slightly more detail.

Traditionally, in FORTRAN 77 and earlier versions of FORTRAN, a call to a subroutine or reference to a function was made without the calling program unit knowing anything about the procedure being called at all! After all the program units that constituted the complete program had been compiled a special program would **link** them together and would ensure that if, somewhere in the set of program units being linked together, there was a call or reference to the procedure **MINE** then a procedure called **MINE** was indeed available; if it was not, then an error would be generated. When the call or reference to the procedure **MINE** was obeyed, the actual arguments would be made available, in the correct order, and the procedure **MINE** would use them, in the same order, as its dummy arguments.

This process meant that the calling program unit knew nothing about the procedure, and vice versa. In this situation the called procedure is said to have an **implicit interface**. Although this form of interface does not provide the information necessary for checking that the actual arguments match the dummy arguments, it was a convenient approach, and had the great advantage that procedures could be written without any knowledge about other procedures being utilized in the same program, apart from the programmer's knowledge of the interface specification of any called procedures.

However, as we saw in Section 4.5, if the additional features provided in Fortran 90 for security and other purposes are to operate properly, they need more information about any procedures being used than is available from an implicit interface. Furthermore, as we shall see in later chapters, some of the most powerful features of Fortran 90 can *only* work if they have a full knowledge of any relevant procedure interfaces. This requires that the procedures concerned have an **explicit interface**.

We shall investigate exactly what is meant by an explicit interface in Chapter 11, and will see how we can specify this to a calling program unit. However, there is one way that we can always make the interface of a procedure explicit, namely by placing the procedure in a module. The rules relating to modules specify that

- the interfaces of all the procedures defined within a single module are explicit to each other
- the interfaces of any procedures made available by **USE** association are explicit in the program unit that is using the module

Although, as we shall see in Chapter 12, we can include procedure definitions in the same modules as both type and variable declarations, there are certain complications that it is not appropriate to discuss at this stage. For the present, therefore, we recommend that procedures are contained in one module, or possibly more than one, while other entities are contained in a different module, or modules.

There is one additional statement required in a module that contains a procedure, which is occasioned by the fact that a procedure in a module is a program unit nested within another program unit. This statement consists of the single word

```
CONTAINS
```

which must be placed before the first procedure within a module. Thus, if the subroutine **problem_sub** (see Figure 4.12) which was used earlier to illustrate the use of the **INTENT** attribute were to be placed in a module, the module might be as follows:

```
MODULE my_procedures
   IMPLICIT NONE

CONTAINS
   SUBROUTINE problem_sub(arg1,arg2,arg3)
      IMPLICIT NONE

      ! This subroutine returns the product of its first two
      ! arguments via the third argument

      INTEGER :: arg1,arg2,arg3

      arg1 = arg2*arg3
   END SUBROUTINE problem_sub

END MODULE my_procedures
```

The program that called the subroutine would then **USE** this module:

```
PROGRAM intent_demonstration
   USE my_procedures
   IMPLICIT NONE

   INTEGER, PARAMETER :: a=2
   INTEGER :: b=3,c=4,d

   CALL problem_sub(a,b,c)
   CALL problem_sub(b,c,d)
END PROGRAM intent_demonstration
```

Because the subroutine `problem_sub` is made available through **USE** association its interface is explicit in the calling program, and so checking that the actual arguments and the corresponding dummy arguments agree in type as well as in intent is carried out, thus providing much greater security at compile time. In addition, if the module `my_procedures` contains several procedures, then each of these has an explicit interface to all the other procedures within that module. Thus a group of related procedures can all be encapsulated within a single module, with consequent benefits in manipulation of the group and of their links with each other.

If the procedures contained in one module reference procedures contained in another module then, as we have already seen, the first module may **USE** the second. However, care must be taken that the second module does not also, either directly or indirectly, **USE** the first one, for that is forbidden, as was stated in Section 4.7.

We shall investigate the use of modules in more detail in Chapter 12 and recommend that until then you keep your use of modules as simple as possible. However, we strongly recommend that all procedures are encapsulated in a module henceforth, both to enable the processor to carry out a higher level of argument checking than might otherwise be the case and, possibly even more important, so that some of the valuable features of Fortran that we shall meet in the next few chapters, but which require an explicit interface, can be used without any difficulty.

■ **EXAMPLE 4.5**

1 Problem

In Example 3.3 we created two geometric derived types, **point** and **line**, and wrote a program to determine the line joining two points. Rewrite this example so that the types are stored in a module, and the line is determined by a procedure which is stored in another module. (We shall add further types and procedures to these two modules in later chapters.)

2 Analysis

We have already carried out the analysis for this problem, and it merely remains to create two structure plans for the procedure and a main program with which to test it:

> 1 Read coordinates of two points
> 2 Call subroutine (*line_two_points*) to calculate the line joining the points
> 3 Print the equation of the line

Subroutine *line_two_points(line_1,point_1,point_2)*
   TYPE(*line*) :: *line_1*
   TYPE(*point*) :: *point_1,point_2*

1 Calculate coefficients of the line joining the points

3 **Solution**

```
MODULE geometric_data
   IMPLICIT NONE
   SAVE

   ! Type definitions
   TYPE point
      REAL :: x,y      ! Cartesian coordinates of the point
   END TYPE point

   TYPE line
      REAL :: a,b,c    ! coefficients of defining equation
   END TYPE line

END MODULE geometric_data


MODULE geometric_procedures
   USE geometric_data
   IMPLICIT NONE

CONTAINS
   SUBROUTINE line_two_points(line_1,point_1,point_2)
      IMPLICIT NONE

      ! Dummy arguments
      TYPE(line), INTENT(OUT) :: line_1
      TYPE(point), INTENT(IN) :: point_1,point_2

      ! Calculate coefficients of equation representing the line
      line_1%a = point_2%y - point_1%y
      line_1%b = point_1%x - point_2%x
      line_1%c = point_1%y*point_2%x - point_2%y*point_1%x
   END SUBROUTINE line_two_points

END MODULE geometric_procedures


PROGRAM geometry
   USE geometric_procedures
   IMPLICIT NONE

   ! A program to test the subroutine line_two_points
```

```
! Variable declarations
TYPE(point) :: p1,p2
TYPE(line) :: p1_to_p2

! Read data
PRINT *,"Please type coordinates of first point"
READ *,p1
PRINT *,"Please type coordinates of second point"
READ *,p2

! Call procedure to calculate the equation of the line
CALL line_two_points(p1_to_p2,p1,p2)

! Print result
PRINT *,"The equation of the line joining these two points is"
PRINT *,"ax + by + c = 0"
PRINT *,"where a = ",p1_to_p2%a
PRINT *,"      b = ",p1_to_p2%b
PRINT *,"      c = ",p1_to_p2%c
END PROGRAM Geometry
```

Note that it is not necessary for the subroutine **line_two_points** to USE the module **geometric_data** since the module **geometric_procedures**, in which it is placed, already does so. In a similar fashion, it is not necessary for the program **geometry** to USE both modules, since accessing **geometric_procedures** also makes the entities declared in **geometric_data** available by USE association.

4.10 Modules as an aid to program design

Since Chapter 2 we have been designing all our programs with the aid of a *structure plan* as an aid in planning the logic of our programs. Another important aspect of programming is the design of the program's **data structure**.

Thus far, all the programs that we have written, or indeed that we have been capable of writing, have had very simple data requirements, consisting of little more than a handful of variables. However, in a real-world environment programs are often manipulating hundreds or thousands of separate items of information and the design and control of this data is every bit as important as the design and control of the program itself. Modules are of great assistance in this as they enable a programmer to group the data in such a way that all those procedures that require access to a particular group can do so by simply using the appropriate module.

This will become particularly relevant when we learn how to process sets of similar data in Chapter 7, but can help in the design of programs even now.

Consider, for example, a program that will be required to read data relating to a series of experiments, and then to carry out certain preliminary statistical analyses on the data before using it in the calculation of some of the physical properties of the specimens which were the subject of the experiment. The data provided might be as follows:

   (1)   Date of experiment (day, month, year)

   (2)   Time experiment started (hours, minutes, seconds)

   (3)   Time experiment ended (hours, minutes, seconds)

   (4)   Sample number

   (5)   Material of sample

   (6)   Measurement 1 (start)

   (7)   Measurement 1 (end)

   (8)   Measurement 2 (start)

   (9)   Measurement 2 (end)

 (10)   Measurement 3 (start)

 (11)   Measurement 3 (end)

 (12)   Measurement 4 (start)

 (13)   Measurement 4 (end)

The statistical analysis will calculate three further items

 (14)   Statistical measure 1

 (15)   Statistical measure 2

 (16)   Statistical measure 3

and the four main analysis programs will calculate four physical properties of the sample, each of which will be required in the calculation of the remaining three physical properties and in the printing of the final analysis of the sample.

 (17)   Property 1

 (18)   Property 2

 (19)   Property 3

 (20)   Property 4

We can help to design the data structure for our program and for the individual procedures within it by writing the various entities in three columns. The first of these is a short description of the purpose of the entity, the second is its type, and the third its name. A data design for the module that will be used to implement the above data structure might, therefore, look as follows:

Purpose	Type	Name
A Global data types:		
Date (day,month,year)	[Int,Int,Int]	date
Time (hours,mins,secs)	[Int,Int,Real]	time
B Global data:		
Date of experiment	date	experiment_date
Times at start and end of experiment	time	start_time end_time
Sample number	INTEGER	sample_number
Material type	CHARACTER*20	material_type
Measurements 1–4 at start	REAL	start_measurement_1 ..., etc.
Measurements 1–4 at end	REAL	end_measurement_1 ..., etc.
Stats measurements 1–3	REAL	stats_measurement_1 ..., etc.
Properties 1–4	REAL	property_1, ... etc.

This information could all be *encapsulated* in a module, such as the following:

```
MODULE data_design
   IMPLICIT NONE

   ! Declare derived types
   TYPE date
      INTEGER :: day,month,year
   END TYPE date

   TYPE time
      INTEGER :: hours,mins
      REAL :: seconds
   END TYPE time

   ! Declare global variables
   TYPE(date) :: experiment_date
   TYPE(time) :: start_time,end_time
   INTEGER :: sample_number
   CHARACTER(LEN=20) :: material_type
   REAL :: start_measurement_1,start_measurement_2, &
           start_measurement_3,start_measurement_4, &
           end_measurement_1,end_measurement_2, &
           end_measurement_3,end_measurement_4, &
           stats_measurement_1,stats_measurement_2, &
           stats_measurement_3,property_1,property_2, &
           property_3,property_4

END MODULE data_design
```

The various procedures responsible for reading the data, calculating the various results required, and for outputting those results to the appropriate output device, can then use this module to obtain access to the relevant information. For example, an output procedure might begin as follows:

```
SUBROUTINE output_data
   USE data_design
   IMPLICIT NONE

   PRINT *,"Experiment conducted on ",experiment_date%day, &
           "/",experiment_date%month,"/",experiment_date%year
   PRINT *,"At start time (",start_time%hours,":", &
           start_time%mins,":",start_time%secs,") &
          &measurements were:"
   PRINT *,start_measurement_1
   PRINT *,start_measurement_2
   PRINT *,start_measurement_3
   PRINT *,start_measurement_4
   .
   .
   .
```

In all the programming examples throughout the remainder of this book we shall, when appropriate, present a data design structure as well as a structure plan before starting to write any Fortran code.

SELF-TEST EXERCISES 4.2

1   What is the purpose of a module?

2   What does **USE** association do? How?

3   Why are modules especially important in programs that use derived types?

4   What is the difference between an explicit and an implicit interface for a procedure?

5   Give three situations in which modules are either essential or highly beneficial in Fortran 90 programs.

SUMMARY

- Fortran procedures may be subroutines or functions.
- Intrinsic procedures are a special class of procedures which form part of the Fortran language.
- External procedures are normally implemented as Fortran subprograms.
- A Fortran 90 program consists of one main program unit, and any number of external subprogram program units (function or subroutine), module program units and block data program units.

- A function is given information to operate on by means of one or more arguments, and delivers a single result.

- A subroutine's arguments are used both to receive information to operate on and to return results.

- The INTENT attribute is used to control the direction in which arguments are used to pass information.

- Many intrinsic functions exist in several versions, each of which operates on arguments of different types; such functions are called generic functions.

- The type of the result of a function can be specified either in the initial FUNCTION statement, or in a declaration of a special result variable having the same name as the function.

- Execution of a function is initiated by the appearance of the function name in an expression; execution of a subroutine is initiated by a CALL statement.

- Only the arguments of a procedure are accessible outside the procedure; all other variables and constants declared in the procedure are local to that procedure.

- Modules allow more than one program unit to have access to the objects declared or defined within the module.

- Objects of derived types can only be used as arguments to procedures if their type is defined in a module which is used by the relevant program units.

- Procedures which are contained within a module have an explicit interface to each other and to any program units which use that module; such an interface is desirable for some security aspects, and essential for some of the language features that will be met in future chapters.

- Procedures provide the basic building block for modular development and top-down program design.

- Modules provide the basic encapsulation device for designing a program's data structure.

- Fortran 90 syntax introduced in Chapter 4:

Initial statements	**SUBROUTINE** *name* (*dummy argument list*)
	SUBROUTINE *name*
	type **FUNCTION** *name* (*dummy argument list*)
	type **FUNCTION** *name* ( )
	FUNCTION *name* (*dummy argument list*)
	FUNCTION *name* ( )
	MODULE *name*
Function reference	*function_name* (*actual argument list*)
	function_name ( )
Subroutine call	**CALL** *subroutine_name* (*actual argument list*)
	CALL *subroutine_name*
Module use	**USE** *module_name*

Assumed length character declaration	`CHARACTER(LEN=(*))` :: *character_dummy_arg* `CHARACTER*(*)` :: *character_dummy_arg*
Argument intent attribute	`INTENT(`*intent*`)` where *intent* is `IN`, `OUT` or `INOUT`
External procedure attribute	`EXTERNAL`
`SAVE` statement	`SAVE`
`CONTAINS` statement	`CONTAINS`

PROGRAMMING EXERCISES

Most larger programs are structured in such a way that each of the major functions (input of data, calculation of each type of analysis, printing of results) is handled by a different procedure, or group of procedures, which can be written and tested independently. In the following exercises you should write your solutions in this way, even though it may not be strictly necessary.

Write a structure plan for the program before you start coding.

*4.1   Write a subroutine which, when supplied with the coordinates of two points (x_1, y_1) and (x_2, y_2), calculates the distance of each point from the origin and the distance between the points.

Note that the distance d_1 of point 1 from the origin is given by the formula

$$d_1 = \sqrt{x_1{}^2 + y_1{}^2}$$

while the distance d between the two points is given by

$$d = \sqrt{(x_2 - x_1)^2 + (y_2 - y_1)^2}$$

Test your subroutine in a short program to check that it works correctly with several different sets of data.

4.2   Write a function which, when supplied with the coordinates of two points (x_1, y_1) and (x_2, y_2), calculates the distance between the points.

Test your function to make sure that it works correctly.

Now modify the subroutine that you wrote for Exercise 4.1 so that it uses this function to carry out all the necessary calculations.

4.3   Write a function to give the logarithm of a number to base b. (Use the equation $\log_b x = \log_{10} x / \log_{10} b$.)

*4.4   Write a module that contains four integers. Use this module in a program which contains a main program and three subroutines, one to input three integer values from the keyboard, one to calculate the sum of the three integers, and the third to print the result of adding the three numbers together.

Although a trivial program (to put it mildly!) this approach mirrors that used in larger programs where each of the three activities may be quite complicated, and the use of a module to enable data to be easily shared is extremely useful.

4.5 A credit card company produces monthly statements for its customers. Each statement shows the following information:

(a) The amount outstanding from last month
(b) The interest due on that amount for the month
(c) Any payment received since the last statement
(d) The total spent with the card since the last statement
(e) The total amount now outstanding

The customer can then pay any amount as long as it is at least 5% of the outstanding amount.

Write a program which reads the amount outstanding, details of payments made and total spending, and the current interest rate, and then produces an appropriate statement.

4.6 Write a function which, when supplied with two arguments of type **point**, as already defined on several occasions, returns the distance between the two points as its result. (Note that this is similar to Exercise 4.2, but using derived type arguments.)

Test your function to ensure that it works correctly.

4.7 A builder, possibly the same one as in Exercise 3.10, wishes to calculate the relative costs of building a wall using different sizes of bricks, and different types of mortar. The thickness of the wall will always be one brick's depth. Regardless of the size of brick and the type of mortar, the thickness of the mortar will always be $\frac{1}{2}$ inch. Write a program to help her.

The program should read the size of the bricks and their cost, the cost of the mortar per cubic inch, and the height and length of the wall. It should calculate how many bricks will be required and their cost, how much mortar is required and its cost, and the total cost (excluding labour!).

4.8 The force F due to gravity between two bodies of masses m_1 and m_2 is given by the formula

$$F = \frac{Gm_1m_2}{r^2}$$

where $G = 6.673 \times 10^{-11}$ Nm^{-2}kg^{-2}, r is the distance between the bodies (in metres), and the masses m_1 and m_2 are measured in kilograms.

Write a program that uses a **REAL** function to evaluate the force of gravity between two bodies given their masses and separation. Define G as a parameter (and think about where it should be specified).

4.9 In Einstein's famous equation $E = mc^2$, the energy E is in joules if the mass m is in kilograms and c is the speed of light in metres per second ($= 2.9979 \times 10^8$). Write a function to calculate the energy equivalent of a given mass. Roughly how much energy is equivalent to the mass of a sugar cube (approximately 1 gram)?

4.10   Write a program consisting of a main program and two *subroutines*. The main program should read up to ten positive numbers. It should then use the first subroutine to calculate the arithmetic mean of these numbers (that is, the sum of the numbers divided by *n*, the number of numbers) and the second to calculate their geometric mean (the *n*th root of the product of the *n* numbers). The main program should then print these two means. (Note that the *n*th root of a real value can be obtained by raising it to the power of 1/*n*.)

Now modify the program so that the subroutines do not have any arguments, but obtain their data, and return their results, through variables made available from a module by **USE** association.

4.11   Write a function whose only argument is a time interval in seconds, and whose result is the same time interval expressed in hours, minutes and seconds. (Hint: the result of the function will have to have a derived type.)

4.12   Write a subroutine that calculates the position, velocity and acceleration of a body undergoing simple harmonic motion using the equations given below:

$$\text{position} = a \, \sin(nt + \epsilon)$$
$$\text{velocity} = na \, \cos(nt + \epsilon)$$
$$\text{acceleration} = -an^2 \, \sin(nt + \epsilon)$$

Use as starting values $n = 3.141\,592\,65$, $\epsilon = 0$, $a = 2.5$. Test by specifying your own set of values for t.

4.13   In Example 4.5 we wrote a subroutine which calculated the line joining two points. Using the same derived types, write a further subroutine for the module **geometric_procedures** which calculates the point at the intersection of two lines. Ignore the possibility that the lines might be parallel and, therefore, have no point of intersection; we shall see how to deal with this in the next chapter.

4.14   The escape velocity from the surface of a planet (the velocity that a spacecraft must reach to escape from the gravitational field of the planet and travel off into space) is given by the expression:

$$V_{esc} = \frac{(2GM)^{1/2}}{R}$$

where G is the gravitational constant (6.673×10^{-11} Nm^{-2} kg^{-2}), M is the mass of the planet (in kg) and R is the planet's radius (in metres).

Write a function that accepts the planetary mass and radius as its input and returns the escape velocity. Use your function to compare the escape velocities from the Earth, Jupiter and the Moon using the following data:

Planet	Mass (kg)	Radius (m)
Earth	6.0×10^{24}	6.4×10^{6}
Moon	7.4×10^{22}	1.7×10^{6}
Jupiter	1.9×10^{27}	7.1×10^{7}

4.15 Write a program to convert the ecliptic latitude β and longitude λ of an astronomical object into right ascension α and declination δ using the formulae

$$\alpha = \tan^{-1} \frac{\sin \lambda \, \cos \epsilon - \tan \beta \, \sin \epsilon}{\cos \lambda}$$

$$\delta = \sin^{-1}(\sin \beta \, \cos \epsilon + \cos \beta \, \sin \epsilon \, \sin \lambda)$$

where $\epsilon = 0.4091$. Assume that all quantities are in radians.
(Note: Use the **ATAN2** intrinsic function for the first expression.)

In fact, the right ascension of an astronomical object is generally given in units of time, where 24 hours equals 360 degrees, while the declination is usually given in degrees. Write a subroutine to convert the two quantities from radians into these units, and incorporate it into your solution.

Controlling the flow of your program

Up to now, our programs have started at the beginning and proceeded to the end without interruption. However, in practice, most problems require us to choose between alternative courses of action, depending upon circumstances which are not determined until the program is executed. The ability of a program to specify how these decisions are to be made is one of the most important aspects of programming.

This chapter introduces the concept of comparison between two numbers or two character strings, and explains how such comparisons can be used to determine which one of two, or more, alternative sections of code are obeyed.

An alternative form of choice, which was not available in earlier versions of Fortran, uses a list of possible values of some variable or expression to determine which of the several alternative blocks of code is actually executed.

5.1 Choice and decision-making

All the programs that we have written so far have started execution at the beginning of the main program, and have then proceeded to execute each statement in turn, in the same unvarying sequential order, until the last statement of the main program is executed. Even the use of procedures has not really altered this sequential processing, for the effect has been to transfer control temporarily to another part of the program, obey that sequentially, and then return to carry on at the statement after the procedure reference. What makes computers so powerful — apparently even mimicking some of the powers of the human brain — is their ability to vary the order of execution of statements according to logical criteria which are not determined until after the program has started execution.

In everyday life we frequently encounter a situation which involves several possible alternative courses of action, requiring us to choose one of them based on some decision-making criteria. For example, Figure 5.1 shows a hypothetical discussion about how to get from Vienna to Budapest. Clearly there are several answers, based upon the preferred method of travel and the time available. If we eliminate the details of the answer we see that it has a definite structure, as shown in Figure 5.2.

Each of the various alternative forms of transport (or 'actions') is preceded by a condition or test of the form '*if* some criterion holds *then* ...', apart from the last form (travel by road) which is included as a final alternative if none of the others are suitable and is preceded by the word *otherwise*.

Fortran 90 has a very similar construction, shown in Figure 5.3, which uses the words **IF** and **THEN** exactly as they were used in the English language example, the words **ELSE IF** where the English used *but if*, and the word **ELSE**

Q: How do I get to Budapest from Vienna?

A: It depends how you want to travel.
  If you are in a hurry *then*
      you should fly from Schwechat airport in Vienna to Ferihegy
      airport in Budapest;
  but if you are a romantic or like trains *then*
      you should take the Orient Express from the Sudbanhof to
      Budapest's Keleti palyudvar;
  but if you have plenty of time *then*
      you can travel on one of the boats which ply along the
      Danube;
  otherwise
      you can always go by road.

Figure 5.1 An example of decisions in English.

If criterion *then*
    action
but if criterion *then*
    action
but if criterion *then*
    action
otherwise
    action

Figure 5.2 English language alternatives.

instead of *otherwise*. In addition, so that there is no doubt about the end of the final 'action', the words **END IF** are placed at the very end. The only other difference is that the criterion on which the decision will be based is enclosed in parentheses. This structure is known as a **block IF construct** and the initial **IF ... THEN** is called a **block IF statement**.

    The way a block **IF** works is that each decision criterion is examined in turn. If it is true then the following action or 'block' of Fortran statements is executed. If it is not true then the next criterion (if any) is examined. If none of the criteria are found to be true then the block of statements following the **ELSE** (if there is one) is executed; if there is no **ELSE** statement, as in Figure 5.4, then no action is taken and the computer moves on to the next statement; that is, the one

```
IF (criterion_1) THEN
   action_1
ELSE IF (criterion_2) THEN
   action_2
ELSE IF (criterion_3) THEN
   action_3
ELSE
   action_4
END IF
```

Figure 5.3 Fortran 90 alternatives.

```
IF (criterion) THEN
   action
END IF
```

Figure 5.4 A minimal block IF.

following the **END IF** statement. There must always be an **IF** statement (with its corresponding block of statements) and an **END IF** statement, but the **ELSE IF** statements and the **ELSE** statement may be omitted if they are not required.

Before we can start to use this facility for taking one of several alternative courses of action we must define the criteria on which the decisions will be based. These all consist of a new type of expression — a **logical expression**.

5.2 Logical expressions and LOGICAL variables

In the English language discussion about how to get from Vienna to Budapest the decision depended upon the truth of certain assertions. Thus, '*if* you are in a hurry *then* travel by plane' could be expressed (rather quaintly) as '*if* it is true that you are in a hurry *then* travel by plane', and similarly for the other decision criteria. We see therefore that each decision depends upon whether some assertion is true or false.

The Fortran decision criterion is also an assertion which is either true or false. This is a new concept, not to be confused with numbers or character strings, in which the values *true* and *false* are called **logical values**, and an assertion (or expression) which can take one of these two values is called a **logical expression**. The simplest forms of logical expressions are those expressing the relationship between two numeric values, thus

```
a > b
```

is true if the value of **a** is greater than the value of **b**, and

```
x == y
```

is true if the value of **x** is equal to the value of **y**. Notice that the sign for the equality relation is two consecutive equals signs.

The two expressions shown above, which express a relationship between two values, are a special form of logical expression called a **relational expression**, and the operators are called **relational operators**. Figure 5.5 shows the six relational operators which exist in Fortran 90, and a few moments' thought will show that they define all possible relationships between two arithmetic values. It will also be noticed that each of the six relational operators has two possible forms. The first of these uses the conventional mathematical symbols, or a slight variation on them, while the alternative form consists of two letters enclosed between periods. This is because when Fortran was first defined in 1954 it was not possible to punch signs such as <, > etc. onto cards and therefore all relational operators consisted of two letters enclosed between periods. These forms are still valid, but we recommend that you use the forms based on mathematical symbols in your programs, for clarity.

a < b   and a.LT.b are *true* if a is less than b
a <= b and a.LE.b are *true* if a is less than or equal to b
a > b   and a.GT.b are *true* if a is greater than b
a >= b and a.GE.b are *true* if a is greater than or equal to b
a == b and a.EQ.b are *true* if a is equal to b
a /= b and a.NE.b are *true* if a is not equal to b

Figure 5.5 Relational operators and expressions.

There is a certain amount of redundancy in this range of operators, which leads to the possibility of expressing the same condition in several different ways. An example of this is that the following four relational expressions are identical in their effect and will always give the same results:

```
b**2 >= 4*a*c
b**2-4*a*c >= 0
4*a*c <= b**2
4*a*c-b**2 <= 0
```

The mathematically-oriented reader will recognize these as expressing the condition for a quadratic equation to have real roots.

This variety means that programmers are free to choose their own way of expressing such conditions. For example, two of the authors would always use the first form shown above, as it is the way in which they always think of the condition (that is, $b^2 \geqslant 4ac$), while the third of us prefers the second form.

Notice that in these examples the values being compared are not necessarily expressed as variables or constants but as arithmetic expressions. *All arithmetic operators have a higher priority than any relational operator* and the arithmetic expression, or expressions, are therefore evaluated *before* any comparisons take place.

As we would expect, a relational operator may also be used to evaluate the relation between two character expressions:

string_1 <= *string_2*

However, this is not quite as straightforward as it appears, as we must first establish what we mean when we state that one character string is greater than another. Because this issue has a number of complexities which are unrelated to the primary question of controlling the flow of control in a program, we shall therefore defer further discussion of comparison of character strings until Section 5.5, and will restrict ourselves to numeric comparisons until then.

We can now return to the consideration of relational expressions. We have already established that the result of evaluating such an expression is a logical value, taking one of the two values *true* or *false*, and it will come as no surprise to learn that we can declare **LOGICAL** variables in which to store such values. A logical variable is declared in much the same way as a real or integer variable:

```
LOGICAL :: var_1,var_2,var_3
```

Once we can declare logical variables the next question is how we can write the two possible logical values, *true* and *false* in a Fortran program. We have already mentioned that in earlier versions of Fortran the six relational operators were written as two letters enclosed between periods and, following the same style, the logical literal constants are written as follows:

```
.TRUE.
.FALSE.
```

Moreover, since we can have logical variables and logical expressions it is natural that we should also be allowed to write functions which deliver a logical value:

```
LOGICAL FUNCTION logical_fun(arg1,...)
   .
   .
   .
```

or

```
FUNCTION logical_fun(arg1,...)
   LOGICAL :: logical_fun
   .
   .
```

We now return to examining the nature of logical expressions, but before doing that we shall return to consideration of the discussion about the best means of travelling from Vienna to Budapest, which was shown in Figure 5.1. In this discussion, the second decision took the following form

but if you are a romantic *or* like trains *then*

Here we have not one decision criterion but two criteria, only one of which needs to be satisfied for the appropriate action to be taken:

you should take the Orient Express from the Sudbanhof to Budapest's Keleti palyudvar.

A similar double criterion could have been used to cater for the fact that some people are afraid of flying:

If you are in a hurry *and* you are not afraid of flying *then*
>> you should fly from Schwechat airport in Vienna to Ferihegy airport in Budapest.

In this case the use of the word *and* indicates that *both* the criteria must to satisfied for the specified action to be carried out.

In Fortran we use the same two words to form composite logical expressions, but written as .OR. and .AND. in the now familiar way. They are called **logical operators** and are used to combine two logical expressions or values. Thus we could write

```
(a<b) .OR. (c<d)
```

or

```
(x<=y) .AND. (y<=z)
```

In fact the parentheses shown in these examples are not strictly necessary because the relational operators have a higher priority than logical operators, but to human eyes expressions such as

```
a<b.OR.c<d
```

can sometimes be confusing, although the judicious use of blank spaces can make the meaning clear:

```
a<b .OR. c<d
```

The inclusion of (redundant) parentheses ensures that there is no room for doubt over the true meaning of the expression, and hence of its value:

```
(a<b) .OR. (c<d)
```

The effect of the .OR. and .AND. operators is as one would expect, with .OR. giving a true result if *either* of its operands is true, while .AND. gives a true result only if *both* are true. Figure 5.6 illustrates this.

L1	L2	L1.OR.L2	L1.AND.L2
true	*true*	*true*	*true*
true	*false*	*true*	*false*
false	*true*	*true*	*false*
false	*false*	*false*	*false*

Figure 5.6 The logical operators .OR. and .AND..

L1	L2	L1.EQV.L2	L1.NEQV.L2
true	*true*	*true*	*false*
true	*false*	*false*	*true*
false	*true*	*false*	*true*
false	*false*	*true*	*false*

Figure 5.7 The logical operators .EQV. and .NEQV..

Two other logical operators exist which do not have an exact equivalent in normal English usage, namely .EQV. and .NEQV. The first of these (.EQV.) gives a true result if its operands are *equivalent* (that is, they both have the same logical value), while the other (.NEQV.) is the opposite (*not equivalent*) and gives a true result if they have opposite logical values. Figure 5.7 illustrates this.

Essentially, these operators are used in logical expressions to simplify their structure. Thus the following two expressions are identical in their effect:

```
(a<b .AND. x<y) .OR. (a>=b .AND. x>=y)
a<b .EQV. x<y
```

There is one further logical operator, .NOT. which, unlike all the other relational and logical operators is a unary operator, and has a single operand. The .NOT. operator inverts the value of the following logical expression.

Thus if the logical expression `logical_exp` is *true* then `.NOT.logical_exp` is *false*, and vice versa. As is the case with the relational operators, the effect of the .NOT. operator on an expression can always be obtained in some other way; for example the following expressions are equivalent in their effect:

```
.NOT.(a<b .AND. b<c)
a>=b .OR. b>=c
```

and, of course

```
.NOT.(a<b .EQV. x<y)
a<b .NEQV. x<y
```

In some circumstances, especially when using logical variables, the .NOT. operator can make a logical expression much clearer.

Just as with arithmetic operators, it is important that the relative priorities of the various logical operators are understood. Figure 5.8 shows their priority order, although it should be noted that, as with arithmetic operators, parentheses can be used to change this order. It should also be noted that any arithmetic operators or relational operators (*in that order*) have a higher priority than any logical operators.

Operator	Priority
.NOT.	highest
.AND.	
.OR.	
.EQV. and .NEQV.	lowest

Figure 5.8 Logical operator priorities.

5.3 The block IF construct

We can now return to the basic block **IF** construct which was informally introduced in Section 5.1, and examine its structure in more detail. The initial statement of the construct is a block **IF** statement which consists of the word **IF** followed by a logical expression enclosed in parentheses, followed by the word **THEN**:

IF (*logical_expression*) **THEN**

This is followed by a sequence, or *block*, of statements which will be executed only if the logical expression is true. The block of statements is terminated by an **ELSE IF** statement, an **ELSE** statement or an **END IF** statement.

The **ELSE IF** statement has a very similar syntax to that of an **IF** statement:

ELSE IF (*logical_expression*) **THEN**

It is followed by a block of statements which will be executed if the logical expression is true, and if the logical expression in the initial **IF** statement of the block construct, and those of any preceding **ELSE IF** statements are false. The block of statements is terminated by another **ELSE IF** statement, an **ELSE** statement or an **END IF** statement.

The **ELSE** statement simply consists of the single word **ELSE** and introduces a final block of statements which will be executed only if the logical expressions in all preceding **IF** and **ELSE IF** statements are false.

The construct is always ended by an **END IF** statement.

There are no restrictions upon what types of statements may appear within a block of statements other than that any multi-statement constructs, such as further block **IF** constructs, or the **CASE** and **DO** constructs that we shall meet later, must be wholly contained within a single block. It is obvious that no other situation would make any sense!

A block **IF** construct is, therefore, always introduced by a block **IF** statement and terminated by an **END IF** statement. There may be any number of **ELSE IF** statements, each followed by a block of statements, or there may be none.

```
IF (logical expression) THEN
     block of Fortran statements
ELSE IF (logical expression) THEN
     block of Fortran statements
ELSE IF (logical expression) THEN

     .
     .
     .

ELSE
     block of Fortran statements
END IF
```

Figure 5.9 The block IF structure.

There may be one **ELSE** statement followed by a block of statements, or there may be none; if there is an **ELSE** statement then it, and its succeeding block of statements, must follow all **ELSE IF** blocks. This structure is shown in Figure 5.9.

■ EXAMPLE 5.1

1 Problem

Example 4.1 calculated the number of bags of wheat that were required to sow a triangular field. Modify this program to deal with the situation in which an exact number of full bags is required in a more aesthetically pleasing manner (and one which is easier to follow).

2 Analysis

In Example 4.1 we added 0.9 to the result of dividing the quantity of seed required by 10000 (to calculate the number of multiples of 10 kilos required). This used the truncation mechanism to specify an extra bag (which will only be partially used) if the true quantity is not an exact multiple of 10 kilos. A better way would be to use a block **IF**. Since we have already fully analysed this problem in Chapter 4 we shall not repeat the data design, but will merely show a revised structure plan:

1 Read lengths of sides of field (a, b and c)
2 Calculate the area of the field
3 Read the sowing density
4 Calculate the quantity of seed required

> 5 Calculate number of full bags needed
> 6 If any more seed is needed then
>   **6.1** Add one to number of bags
> 7 Print size of field and number of bags

We can find out if any more is needed by testing if the amount required is greater than the amount in the bags.

3 **Solution**

```fortran
PROGRAM wheat_sowing
   IMPLICIT NONE

   ! A program to calculate the quantity of wheat required to
   ! sow a triangular field

   ! Variable declarations
   REAL :: a,b,c,s,area,density,quantity
   INTEGER :: num_bags

   ! Read the lengths of the sides of the field
   PRINT *,"Type the lengths of the three sides of the field &
         &in metres: "
   READ *,a,b,c

   ! Calculate the area of the field
   s = 0.5*(a+b+c)
   area = SQRT(s*(s-a)*(s-b)*(s-c))

   ! Read sowing density
   PRINT *,"What is the sowing density (gm/sq.m.)? "
   READ *,density

   ! Calculate quantity of wheat in grams and the number of
   ! full 10 kg bags
   quantity = density*area
   num_bags = 0.0001*quantity   ! Any part-full bag is excluded

   ! Check to see if another bag is required
   IF (quantity > 10000*num_bags) THEN
      num_bags = num_bags+1
   END IF

   ! Print results
   PRINT *,"The area of the field is ",area," sq. metres"
   PRINT *,"and ",num_bags," 10 kilo bags will be required"

END PROGRAM wheat_sowing
```

Multiply 25.39 by 17.25 to six significant figures:

$$25.39 \times$$
$$\underline{17.25}$$
$$2539$$
$$17773$$
$$5078$$
$$\underline{12695}$$
$$\overline{4379775}$$

Answer is 437.978

Figure 5.10 Rounding errors in hand calculations.

There are two important points to note here. The first is that the relational expression is comparing a real value (**quantity**) with an integer one (**10000*num_bags**). In this case the expression is evaluated as if comparing the difference between the two operands with zero; thus the expression

```
quantity > 10000*num_bags
```

is evaluated as if it were

```
(quantity-10000*num_bags) > 0.0
```

To do this, **10000*num_bags** is converted to its real equivalent and then the real subtraction is performed.

The second point concerns the accuracy of real arithmetic. Real numbers are stored in the computer as an approximation to a defined degree of accuracy, and therefore when such numbers are used in arithmetic expressions the least significant digits may get lost as a result of round-off. Figure 5.10 illustrates this in the context of hand calculation to six digits of accuracy, where the product of two four-digit numbers requires seven digits to be accurate; the answer is therefore expressed as a six digit number after rounding the sixth digit. The normal rule is that if the first digit to be omitted (the seventh in this case) is in the range 0–4 then it (and any subsequent ones) are simply dropped, but if it is in the range 5–9 (as in this example) then the last significant digit is increased by one (from 7 to 8 in this case) before the remainder are dropped.

A computer operates in exactly the same way and therefore any real arithmetic operation is liable to introduce such a rounding error. Frequently this is of no consequence as the computer is working to a greater accuracy than required for the problem. However there are four cases where it *does* matter a great deal. One of these is where a large amount of numerical calculation is being carried out and in this case a higher level of accuracy (or *precision*) can be specified, as we shall see in Chapter 10. The second case was mentioned in Section 3.3 and relates to the situation when a large integer value is converted to its real equivalent, with a consequent loss of precision. The third case is the related conversion problem in which a real number is to be truncated before being stored as an integer. The final case is more interesting, and concerns the situation in which we wish to compare or subtract two real numbers which are almost exactly the same. We can illustrate the last two situations by reference to the program we have just written.

Let us suppose that the sides of the field are 130 m, 100 m and 130 m, and that the sowing density is 25 g/m^2. A few moments' calculation shows that the area of the field is 6000 m^2, and hence that 150 kg of seed are required. **num_bags** should therefore be 15 and the test should find that these contain exactly enough seed. In practice, though, it probably won't be like that. For example, the calculation of the area could lead to a value such as 5999.999 999 (to 10 significant figures) or to 6000.000 001. The subsequent calculation of the quantity of seed will give further possible rounding errors leading to a (real) value for 0.0001*quantity of perhaps 14.999 999 99 or 15.000 000 01.

Although for all practical purposes these two values are the same as the true value of 15, when they are truncated to calculate **num_bags** they will lead to integer values of 14 and 15 respectively. In the first case **quantity** will clearly be less than **10000*num_bags** and so the situation will be compensated for. In the second case, however, it is possible that **quantity** is fractionally more than 150 000.0 (for instance 150 000.000 1) and that the relational expression will be true, leading to a calculation of 16 bags!

We can deal with this by *never* testing whether two real values are equal (which is essentially what we are doing here in the borderline case) but rather by testing whether their difference is acceptably small. In this case, therefore, we could say that since the numbers being compared are of the order of 100 000 (actually 150 000 in this example) and since any errors in calculation will, hopefully, be much less than 1%, we should alter the test to read

```
IF (quantity > 10000*num_bags+1000) THEN
   num_bags = num_bags + 1
END IF
```

A better way might be to avoid any reference to **num_bags** and to express the test as follows:

```
IF (0.0001*quantity - INT(0.0001*quantity) > 0.1) THEN
   num_bags = num_bags + 1
END IF
```

thereby eliminating multiplying **quantity** by 0.0001, and then multiplying the result by 1000. In this form, the intrinsic function **INT** calculates the integer equivalent of **0.0001*quantity**, which is the value of **num_bags**, and subtracts it from the original, real, value. The result of this will be the amount that was lost through truncation, which in this case represents the amount of seed required in the last, partially filled, bag as a fraction of one bag. We decided in Example 4.1

that if such a bag was less than 10% full then the amount of seed could be ignored. It would probably be advisable, however, to add a comment to explain the test, whichever one is used!

■ **EXAMPLE 5.2**

1 Problem

Write an external function which will return the cube root of its argument.

2 Analysis

In Section 4.3 we wrote a function to meet this requirement which was only valid for positive arguments. We can use a block **IF** construct to deal with the negative and zero argument cases, which were not included in the earlier version.

If the argument is negative then we can use the fact that $\sqrt[3]{(-x)} = -\sqrt[3]{x}$.

The zero argument situation is, however, slightly more complicated, since it is not possible to calculate the logarithm of zero. However, rather than comparing the value of the argument with zero, which is not sensible when working with real numbers, we should rather state that if the absolute value of the argument is less than a specified small number then it is sufficiently close to zero to create possible calculation problems in the **log** function, and we shall therefore treat it as zero and return zero as the result of the function. Our data design and structure plan are therefore as follows:

Data design

Purpose	Type	Name
A Dummy argument: Value whose cube root is required	REAL	x
B Result variable: Cube root of x	REAL	cube_root
C Local constant: A very small number	REAL	epsilon

Structure plan

Real function cube_root(x)

1   If $|x| < epsilon$
    1.1   Return zero
            else if $x < 0$

> **1.2** Return $-\exp(\log(-x)/3)$
> else
> **1.3** Return $\exp(\log(x)/3)$

The only remaining question is what value to use for *epsilon*. Since the cube root of a positive number less than 1.0 is *greater* than the number itself it should not be too large, but equally it should not be so small that problems might occur with the **log** function. We shall, somewhat arbitrarily, use the value 10^{-20}.

3 Solution

```
REAL FUNCTION cube_root(x)
   IMPLICIT NONE

   ! Function to calculate the cube root of a
   ! real number
   ! Dummy argument declaration
   REAL, INTENT(IN) :: x

   ! Local constant
   REAL, PARAMETER :: epsilon=1E-20

   ! Eliminate (nearly) zero case
   IF (ABS(x)<epsilon) THEN
      cube_root = 0.0

   ! Calculate cube root by using logs
   ELSE IF (x<0) THEN
      ! First deal with negative argument
      cube_root = -EXP(LOG(-x)/3.0)
   ELSE
      ! Positive argument
      cube_root = EXP(LOG(x)/3.0)
   END IF

END FUNCTION cube_root
```

One final point that should be made about this function is that calculating the logarithm and then dividing by three is *not* a particularly good way of calculating a cube root. We use it here to demonstrate the use of the block **IF** rather than introducing the lengthy mathematics that a full solution would involve!

■ EXAMPLE 5.3

1 Problem

In Example 4.5 we started to create two modules for use with various geometric entities. When first introducing this topic in Example 3.3 we noted that the calculation of a line joining two points required that the two points be distinct, but were not, at that time, able to check for this situation. Modify the subroutine **line_two_points** that was developed in Example 4.5 so that it returns an error flag to indicate that either (a) the two points were distinct, and the equation of the joining line was therefore calculated, or (b) it was not possible to calculate the line because the points were coincident.

2 Analysis

For this example, a logical error flag would seem to be most appropriate, but for some of the similar procedures which might be required for other geometric calculations there will be more than one reason for error. It is preferable that all the procedures in the module return their error information in the same way, and we shall, therefore, use an integer flag. Following a commonly-used convention, we shall return zero if the equation of the line was calculated satisfactorily, and a non-zero value if there was an error. We shall arbitrarily return −1 if the two points are coincident.

The structure plan can therefore be modified as follows:

Subroutine line_two_points(*line_1,point_1,point_2,status*)
  TYPE(line) :: *line_1*
  TYPE(point) :: *point_1,point_2*
  INTEGER :: *status*

1 If *point_1* and *point_2* are coincident
  1.1 Set *status* to −1
  else
  1.2 Calculate coefficients of the line joining the points
  1.3 Set *status* to 0

3 Solution

We give the complete module so that the context of the subroutine is clear.

```
MODULE geometric_procedures
   USE geometric_data
   IMPLICIT NONE

CONTAINS

   SUBROUTINE line_two_points(line_1,point_1,point_2,status)
      IMPLICIT NONE
```

```
      ! Dummy arguments
      TYPE(line), INTENT(OUT) :: line_1
      TYPE(point), INTENT(IN) :: point_1,point_2
      INTEGER :: status

      ! Check to see whether points are coincident
      IF (point_1%x==point_2%x .AND. point_1%y==point_2%y) THEN
         ! Points are coincident - return error flag
         status = -1

      ELSE
         ! Points are distinct, so calculate the coefficients
         ! of the equation representing the line
         line_1%a = point_2%y - point_1%y
         line_1%b = point_1%x - point_2%x
         line_1%c = point_1%y*point_2%x - point_2%y*point_1%x

         ! Set status to indicate success
         status = 0
      END IF

   END SUBROUTINE line_two_points

 END MODULE geometric_procedures
```

Note that, in order to concentrate on the major issue, we have not included a tolerance factor in the test for coincident points. Since we are comparing real values for 'equality' this should be done in a final version.

5.4   The logical IF statement

Until the advent of FORTRAN 77, the most powerful decision-making statement in Fortran was the **logical IF** statement, which took the form

   IF (*logical expression*) *Fortran statement*

This is exactly equivalent to a block **IF** with a block consisting of a single statement:

   IF (*logical expression*) **THEN**
      Fortran statement
   END IF

Because the second part of the logical **IF** statement is only a single statement, however, there are some restrictions which must be observed. Thus it is not permissible to have a block **IF** statement, a **SELECT CASE** statement (see Section 5.5) or a **DO** statement (see Chapter 6) following the logical expression, nor is it permissible to have another logical **IF** statement there.

Although the logical **IF** statement is the chronological ancestor of the block **IF** construct, because it is limited to making the execution of a single statement conditional upon the value of a logical expression it should be considered as merely a 'shorthand' version of the minimal block **IF** with a single-statement block. Nevertheless, because it is more compact, it can be used in a number of situations without any loss of clarity or efficiency. In particular, as we shall see in Chapter 6, it is an extremely useful form of statement in the control of blocks of statements which are to be repeated a number of times — a very common programming requirement.

5.5 Comparing character strings

In Section 5.2 we mentioned that the six relational operators could be used to compare character expressions and constants (or character *strings* as they are usually referred to), but that the question of determining when one string was greater than another would be left until later. The key to this determination is the **collating sequence** of letters, digits and other characters. Fortran 90 lays down six rules for this covering letters, digits and the space or blank character.

(1)   The 26 upper case letters are collated in the following order:

   A B C D E F G H I J K L M N O P Q R S T U V W X Y Z

(2)   The 26 lower case letters are collated in the following order:

   a b c d e f g h i j k l m n o p q r s t u v w x y z

(3)   The 10 digits are collated in the following order:

   0 1 2 3 4 5 6 7 8 9

(4)   Digits are either all collated before the letter **A**, or all after the letter **Z**

(5)   Digits are either all collated before the letter **a**, or all after the letter **z**

(6)   A space (or blank) is collated before both letters and digits

The other 22 characters in the Fortran character set, and any others which may be available on a particular computer system, do not have any defined position in the collating sequence. In practice they will usually be ordered according to the internal code used by the computer as long as this code satisfies the above rules.

When two character operands are being compared there are three distinct stages in the process:

(1)   If the two operands are not the same length, the shorter one is treated as though it were extended on the right with blanks until it is the same length as the longer one.

(2) The two operands are compared character by character, starting with the leftmost character, until either a difference is found or the end of the operands is reached.

(3) If a difference is found, then the relationship between these two different characters defines the relationship between the two operands, with the character which comes earlier in the collating sequence being deemed to be the lesser of the two. If no difference is found, then the strings are considered to be equal.

The result of this process is that the relational expression always has the value we would instinctively expect it to have. Thus

```
"Adam" > "Eve"
```

is *false* because **A** comes before **E**, and is thus *less than* **E**.

```
"Adam" < "Adamant"
```

is *true* because after **Adam** has been extended the relationship reduces to " " **< "a"** after the first four characters have been found to be the same. Since a blank comes before a letter, this is *true*.

```
"120" < "1201"
```

is *true* because the first difference in the strings leads to an evaluation of " " **< "1"**, which is *true* since a blank also comes before a digit.

Notice, however, that the values of the expressions

```
"ADAM" < "Adam"
"XA" < "X4"
```

and

```
"var_1" > "var-1"
```

are not defined in Fortran. In the first case the standard does not define whether upper case letters come before or after lower case letters or, indeed, whether they are even interleaved, and so the value of **"ADAM" < "Adam"** will depend upon the particular computer system being used. Similarly, in the second case the standard does not define whether digits come before or after letters. Finally, in the third case the special characters are not defined at all in the collating sequence, so that, once again, the value of **"_" > "-"** depends upon the computer system.

These undefined areas are not normally any problem. It is unlikely that most applications would expect to compare character strings (other than for equality) if the order was to be determined by characters other than letters, digits

LGT(s1,s2) is the same as s1 > s2 using ASCII character ordering
LGE(s1,s2) is the same as s1 >= s2 using ASCII character ordering
LLE(s1,s2) is the same as s1 <= s2 using ASCII character ordering
LLT(s1,s2) is the same as s1 < s2 using ASCII character ordering

Figure 5.11 Intrinsic functions for lexical comparison.

or blanks. The concepts of alphabetic or numeric ordering are natural ones, as is the concept of shorter strings coming before longer ones which start with the same characters as the shorter one (that is, *John* comes before *Johnson*, *alpha* before *alphabet*). The only practical area of doubt concerns the question of whether digits come before or after letters.

If, for reasons of portability, it is required to define the ordering of *all* characters, then another way of comparing them is available. This uses one of the four intrinsic functions shown in Figure 5.11. These functions return the value *true* or *false* after a comparison which uses the ordering of characters defined in the American National Standard Code for Information Interchange (ANSI X3.4 1977), which is usually referred to as ASCII. This code, which is widely used as an internal code, is also defined in the International Reference Version (IRV) of the International Standard ISO 646 : 1983; it is included, for reference, in Appendix D of this book.

Thus, for example, whereas the value of

```
"Miles" > "miles"
```

cannot be defined with complete certainty, because the Fortran standard does not state whether upper case letters come before or after lower case letters, the value of

```
LGT("Miles","miles")
```

will always be *true*, because upper case letters *do* come before lower case letters in the **ASCII collating sequence**.

■ EXAMPLE 5.4

1 Problem

Write a function which takes a single character as its argument and returns a single character according to the following rules:

- If the input character is a lower case letter then return its upper case equivalent
- If the input character is an upper case letter then return its lower case equivalent
- If the input character is not a letter then return it unchanged

2 Analysis

The major problem here is establishing the relationship between upper and lower case letters, so that conversions may be easily made. Here we can use the ASCII code (see Appendix D) to good effect due to the existence of the two intrinsic functions **IACHAR** and **ACHAR**. The first of these provides the position of its character argument in the ASCII collating sequence, while the second returns the character at a specified position in that sequence. Thus **IACHAR("A")** is 65, while **ACHAR(97)** is the character **a**. An examination of the ASCII character set (see Figure D.1 in Appendix D) quickly shows that every lower case character is exactly 32 positions after its upper case equivalent. We now have both the information and the means to carry out the conversion and so are ready to design our function.

Although we could simply add or subtract 32 from the ASCII code for the character, as appropriate, it is not then obvious what is happening. We shall therefore define a constant which has the value of this offset, calculated by subtracting the code for an upper case letter from its lower case equivalent. Furthermore, to avoid unecessary complication, we shall assume that the upper case letters are contiguous in the processor's character set (that is, there are no other characters intervening) and that the lower case characters are also contiguous in the processor's character set. If we wished to guarantee this then the tests could be carried out using the ASCII collating sequence by means of the intrinsic functions **LLE** etc., but this would be something of an overkill in this instance!

Data design

	Purpose	*Type*	*Name*
A	Dummy argument: Character to be converted	CHARACTER*1	char
B	Result variable: Converted character	CHARACTER*1	change_case
C	Local constant: Offset between upper and lower case in the ASCII character set	INTEGER	upper_to_lower

Structure plan

Character function change_case(*char*)

1 If A $\leqslant$ *char* $\leqslant$ Z
   1.1 Return character *upper_to_lower* after *char* in ASCII
   else if a $\leqslant$ *char* $\leqslant$ z
   1.2 Return character *upper_to_lower* before *char* in ASCII
   else
   1.3 Return *char* unaltered

☐3 **Solution**

```
CHARACTER FUNCTION change_case(char)
   IMPLICIT NONE

   ! This function changes the case of its argument (if it
   ! is alphabetic)

   ! Dummy argument
   CHARACTER, INTENT(IN) :: char

   ! Local constant
   INTEGER, PARAMETER :: upper_to_lower = IACHAR("a")-IACHAR("A")

   ! Check if argument is lower case alphabetic, upper case
   ! alphabetic, or non-alphabetic
   IF ("A"<=char .AND. char<="Z") THEN
      ! Upper case - convert to lower case
      change_case = ACHAR(IACHAR(char)+upper_to_lower)

   ELSE IF ("a"<=char .AND. char<="z") THEN
      ! Lower case - convert to upper case
      change_case = ACHAR(IACHAR(char)-upper_to_lower)

   ELSE
      ! Not alphabetic
      change_case = char

   END IF

END FUNCTION change_case
```

SELF-TEST EXERCISES 5.1

1   What is the difference between a logical operator and a relational operator?

2   What are the values of the following expressions?

   (a) 1>2
   (b) (1+3).GE.4
   (c) (1+3)<=4
   (d) (0.1+0.3).LE.0.4
   (e) 2>1 .AND. 3<4
   (f) 3>2 .AND. (1+2)<3 .OR. 4<=3
   (g) 3>2 .OR. (1+2)<3 .AND. 4<=3
   (h) 3>2 .AND. (1+2)<3 .EQV. 4<=3

3   What is the purpose of the block **IF** construct?

4   What is the advantage of a block **IF** construct over a logical **IF** statement?

5   What are the rules for collating characters?

6   What are the values of the following expressions?

   (a) "Me"<"You"
   (b) "Me"<"ME"
   (c) "Me"<"Men"
   (d) "Me"<"Me?"
   (e) LLT("Me","Me?")

5.6   The CASE construct

In some situations it is necessary to have an ordering built in to the decision as to which choice to take because there is an overlap between some of the possible decision criteria. For example, if you are a baseball addict, but especially a Cubs fan, then the decision as to what to do on a Saturday afternoon might look like this:

> *If* it is the baseball season *and* the Cubs are at home *then*
>   Go to Wrigley Field
> *Else if* it is the baseball season *and* the Cubs game is on TV *then*
>   Get a six-pack and watch the game on TV
> *Else if* it is the baseball season *then*
>   Go to any nearby baseball game
> *Else*
>   Rent a baseball video and watch it at home.

It is very clear that the order in which the choices are considered is of vital importance!

Frequently, however, the decision criteria are mutually exclusive, and there is no overlap between them. For example, if you are a Liverpool fan, and are only interested in watching football matches in which they are playing (whether at home or away) then your Saturday afternoon decision plan might be rather different:

> *If* it is the football season *and* Liverpool are playing at home *then*
>   Go to Anfield and support the Reds
> *Else if* it is the football season *and* Liverpool are playing away *then*
>   Go to wherever they are playing and support the Reds
> *Else*
>   Get a six-pack and watch some of your old Liverpool videos at home.

Although this has been written in the same way as the previous example, there is clearly no ordering involved in this decision process and the use of *if . . . else* style is rather misleading. An alternative approach would be to write

> *Select the appropriate case from the following alternatives:*
> *Case 1:* It is the football season and Liverpool are playing at home
>   Go to Anfield and support the Reds
> *Case 2:* It is the football season and Liverpool are playing away
>   Go to wherever they are playing and support the Reds
> *Case 3:* Any other situation
>   Get a six-pack and watch some of your old Liverpool videos at home.

As well as the block **IF** construct, which caters for the ordered choice situation, Fortran 90 provides another form of selection, known as the **CASE** construct, to deal with the alternative situation in which the various alternatives are mutually exclusive, and the order in which they are expressed is unimportant. Its overall structure is shown in Figure 5.12.

Both the block **IF** and the **CASE** constructs provide a means of selecting one from a set of blocks of statements and executing that block, or of executing

---

```
SELECT CASE (case expression)
CASE (case selector)
  block of Fortran statements
CASE (case selector)
  block of Fortran statements
    .
    . .
    .
END SELECT
```

Figure 5.12   The CASE structure.

none of them if none of the decision criteria is satisfied. As we have already mentioned, one difference between the two constructs is that in the **CASE** construct the decision criteria must not overlap. The other major difference is that the expression which determines the selection must be a logical expression in a block **IF** construct, but may be an integer expression, a character expression or a logical expression in a **CASE** construct. This means that, in many situations, a more natural form of defining the different cases can be used than is possible with any form of **IF** construct.

The initial statement of a **CASE** construct takes the form

SELECT CASE (*case_expression*)

where, as already indicated, *case_expression* is either an integer expression, a character expression or a logical expression; real expressions are *prohibited* for this purpose. When the **SELECT CASE** statement is encountered the value of *case_expression* is evaluated and the block of statements which follow the appropriate **CASE** statement (if any) is executed.

Each **CASE** statement takes the form

CASE (*case_selector*)

or

CASE DEFAULT

although there may only be one **CASE DEFAULT** statement in a **CASE** construct.

The *case_selector* determines which, if any, of the blocks of statements will be obeyed, while the **CASE DEFAULT** statement, if any, precedes the block of statements to be obeyed if none of the other **CASE** statements produces a match.

The *case_selector* can take one of four forms:

case_value
low_value:
:*high_value*
low_value:*high_value*

or it may be a list of any combination of these. Note, however, that only the first form is permitted for logical values since it would be meaningless to list more than one of the possible two values. The meaning of these four alternatives is almost self-evident, but we shall elaborate them for the avoidance of any doubt:

(1) If the *case_selector* takes the form *case_value* then the following block of code is executed if and only if *case_expression* **==** *case_value*, where *case_expression* is an integer expression or a character expression, and if and only if *case_expression* **.EQV.** *case_value*, where it is a logical expression.

(2) If the *case_selector* takes the form *low_value*: then the following block of code is executed if and only if *low_value* <= *case_expression*.

(3) If the *case_selector* takes the form :*high_value* then the following block of code is executed if and only if *case_expression* <= *high_value*.

(4) If the *case_selector* takes the form *low_value*:*high_value* then the following block of code is executed if and only if *low_value* <= *case_expression* .**AND**. *case_expression* <= *high_value*.

If none of the specified values or value ranges matches the value of the *case_expression* then the block of code following the **CASE DEFAULT** statement, if any, is executed; if there is no **CASE DEFAULT** statement then an exit is made from the **CASE** construct without any code being executed.

Notice that the order in which the various **CASE** statements, and their following blocks of statements, are written does not matter, since the rules governing **CASE** statements require that there is no overlap. However, we recommend that, for clarity, any **CASE DEFAULT** statement be placed either as the first **CASE** statement, or as the last, even though this is not necessary as far as the syntax is concerned. The choice as to which is preferable depends upon whether the **CASE DEFAULT** statement is expected to be the most normal selection, with the specified cases being exceptions, or whether it is a 'catch-all' to deal with those cases which are sufficiently rare not to justify individual treatment.

■ EXAMPLE 5.5

1 Problem

Read a date in the international standard form (yyyy-mm-dd) and print a message to indicate whether on this date in Sydney, Australia, it will be winter, spring, summer or autumn. For the purpose of this exercise we shall assume that winter consists of June and July, that spring is August, September and October, that summer is from November until March, and that the autumn is April and May.

2 Analysis

There are clearly four mutually exclusive cases, depending upon the value of the character string mm, and so the problem is ideally suited for a **CASE** statement. Although it might be reasonable to assume that the date will be a valid one, this is, in general, a dangerous assumption and we should always check that data is valid. In this example a **CASE DEFAULT** statement can easily be used to identify any invalid data. Our data design and structure plan will be as follows:

Data design

Purpose	Type	Name
Date (yyyy-mm-dd)	CHARACTER*10	date
Month (for CASE)	CHARACTER*2	month

Structure plan

1 Read date

2 Extract month from date

3 Select case on *month*

    3.1 *month* is 8, 9 or 10
        Print "spring"

    3.2 *month* is 11, 12, 1, 2 or 3
        Print "summer"

    3.3 *month* is 4 or 5
        Print "autumn"

    3.4 *month* is 6 or 7
        Print "winter"

    3.5 *month* is anything else
        Print an error message

3 Solution

```
PROGRAM seasons
   IMPLICIT NONE

   ! A program to calculate in which season a specified date lies

   ! Variable declarations
   CHARACTER(LEN=10) :: date
   CHARACTER(LEN=2) :: month

   ! Read date
   PRINT *,"Please type a date in the form yyyy-mm-dd"
   READ *,date

   ! Extract month number
   month = date(6:7)

   ! Print season
   SELECT CASE (month)
   CASE ("08":"10")
      PRINT *,date," is in the spring"
   CASE ("11","12","01":"03")
      PRINT *,date," is in the summer"
```

```
      CASE ("04","05")
         PRINT *,date," is in the autumn"
      CASE ("06","07")
         PRINT *,date," is in the winter"
      CASE DEFAULT
         PRINT *,date," is not a valid date"
      END SELECT

END PROGRAM seasons
```

Note that, because the case selector is a character expression, the case values must be expressed as character constants. Furthermore, we have assumed that there are no possible two-character strings which will lie between "08" and "10" other than "09", or between "01" and "03" other than "02". No character coding system known to the authors fails to encode the ten digits 0 to 9 in successive places, but there is no formal requirement to do so. An alternative would be to write the selectors for the spring and summer as

```
CASE ("08","09","10")
```

and

```
CASE ("11","12","01","02","03")
```

respectively.

Another alternative would be to convert the month to integer form, but since this is slightly awkward it would be difficult to justify in such a simple program, and we shall leave it as an exercise for the adventurous reader.

Finally, it is not necessary to use the variable **month** at all. The **SELECT CASE** statement could equally well have been written as

```
SELECT CASE (date(6:7))
```

although it is then marginally less clear what is going on.

■ EXAMPLE 5.6

1 **Problem**

Write a program to read the coefficients of a quadratic equation and print its roots.

2 **Analysis**

This program will use the formula

$$x = \frac{-b \pm \sqrt{(b^2 - 4ac)}}{2a}$$

where

$$ax^2 + bx + c = 0 \quad \text{and} \quad a \neq 0$$

It is immediately apparent that there are three possible cases:

(1) $b^2 > 4ac$
     in which case the equation will have two real roots

(2) $b^2 = 4ac$
     in which case the equation will have one root (or two coincident roots)

(3) $b^2 < 4ac$
     in which case the equation will have no roots (or at least no real roots, and
     we are not concerned with imaginary roots in this example)

At first sight, since there are three mutually exclusive cases, this seems a
natural problem in which to use a **CASE** statement. However, there are two major
difficulties.

The first of these is that the values of the coefficients in this sort of
problem will normally be real, and therefore the expression $b^2 < 4ac$ will also be
real. The *case_expression* in a **CASE** statement must, however, be integer, character
or logical.

The other problem concerns case 2, where the value of the expression is
zero. We have stressed on many occasions that real arithmetic is only an
approximation. In particular we should *never* compare two real numbers for
equality, as two numbers which are mathematically equal will often differ very
slightly if they have been calculated in a different way. We avoid this difficulty by
comparing the difference between two real numbers with a very small number.
Thus we could rewrite the second case as follows:

(2) $|b^2 - 4ac| < epsilon$
     where *epsilon* is a very small number, in which case the equation will have
     one root

If we wish to use a **CASE** statement then we could deal with both of these
problems at the same time by dividing the value of $b^2 - 4ac$ by *epsilon* and then
assigning the result to an integer for use in the **CASE** statement. This will mean that
if $|b^2 - 4ac| < epsilon$ the result of the division will be between -1 and $+1$, and
the integer stored will, as a result of truncation, be zero. If $b^2 - 4ac > epsilon$ then
the result stored will be a positive integer, while if $b^2 - 4ac < epsilon$ the result
stored will be a negative integer. Notice, however, that there is a further problem
in choosing the value of *epsilon* arising from the fact that we shall be dividing
$b^2 - 4ac$ by this very small number; it is always possible that dividing by a very

small number might lead to a result which is larger than the largest number that can be stored on the computer! This indicates that the approach that we have chosen is not a particularly good one and should *not* be used in a real programming situation; it will, however, suffice for this example of how to use **CASE** statements.

Note that this analysis has also ignored two other theoretical difficulties. The first of these is the situation if $a = 0$. In this situation the equation is not a quadratic equation and so for this example, in which the coefficients are being typed at the keyboard, we shall simply assume that a non-zero value will be typed for a; it would not be difficult to test for this case and return an appropriate value for x. It does not, of course, matter if b or c is zero, since the equation will still be a quadratic.

The second problem is that the calculation of b^2 and that of $4ac$ could lead to problems if a, b or c is so large that the resulting calculation leads to a value greater than the maximum capable of being stored on the computer system being used (a condition known as **overflow**). Again, since the coefficients are being typed at the keyboard we shall assume that they are 'reasonable' numbers, and will ignore this problem here. Both of these situations should be considered in a comprehensive solution to this, apparently simple, problem. They are discussed in more detail in Chapter 18.

We can now design our program:

Data design

	Purpose	Type	Name
A	Local constant:		
	A small value	REAL	epsilon
B	Local variables:		
	Coefficients	REAL	a,b,c
	Intermediate value	REAL	d
	CASE selection value	INTEGER	selector

Structure plan

1 Read the three coefficients a, b and c

2 Calculate $d = b^2 - 4ac$

3 Calculate *selector* (int(d/*epsilon*))

4 Select case on *selector*:
  4.1 *selector* > 0
       Calculate and print two roots
  4.2 *selector* = 0
       Calculate and print a single root
  4.3 *selector* < 0
       Print a message to the effect that there are no roots

We may note here that, since all possible cases have been covered, any one of these cases could be treated as the default case. However, for clarity it is preferable, in this example, to specify all three conditions explicitly, with the result that no default case need be specified.

Before writing the actual program we shall note that, despite the fact that the problem appears to be suitable for a **CASE** statement, the awkwardness in calculating a suitable value for use as a case selector might make the use of a block **IF** construct more appropriate. In this case a suitable design would be:

Data design

	Purpose	Type	Name
A	Local constant:		
	A small value	REAL	epsilon
B	Local variables:		
	Coefficients	REAL	a,b,c
	Intermediate values	REAL	d,sqrt_d

Structure plan

1 Read coefficients

2 Calculate $b^2 - 4ac$, and store it in d

3 If $d \geqslant epsilon$ then
  3.1 Calculate and print two roots
  but if $d > -epsilon$ then
  3.2 Calculate and print a single root
  otherwise
  3.3 Print a message to the effect that there are no roots

In this situation, the order in which the tests are carried out *does* matter. First we test whether $b^2 - 4ac$ is greater than or equal to *epsilon*, since this is anticipated to be the most usual case. If it is not then it is zero (for our purpose) or negative. We now test whether it is greater than a very small negative value (*epsilon*). If it is, then, since it is also less than a very small positive value, it can be considered to be zero. If neither of these cases holds then there can be no roots.

Which of these two approaches is used is largely a matter of personal style. However, in most cases it will be quite clear which approach is to be preferred.

We shall write programs in both the ways planned above.

3 **Solution**

(a) Using a **CASE** construct

```
PROGRAM quadratic_by_CASE
   IMPLICIT NONE
```

```fortran
! A program to solve a quadratic equation using a CASE
! statement to distinguish between the three cases

! Constant declaration
REAL, PARAMETER :: epsilon=1E-6

! Variable declarations
REAL :: a,b,c,d,sqrt_d,x1,x2
INTEGER :: selector

! Read coefficients
PRINT *,"Please type the three coefficients a, b and c"
READ *,a,b,c

! Calculate b**2-4*a*c and resulting case selector
d = b**2 - 4.0*a*c
selector = d/epsilon

! Calculate and print roots, if any
SELECT CASE (selector)
CASE (1:)
   ! Two roots
   sqrt_d = SQRT(d)
   x1 = (-b+sqrt_d)/(a+a)
   x2 = (-b-sqrt_d)/(a+a)
   PRINT *,"The equation has two roots: ",x1," and ",x2

CASE (0)
   ! One root
   x1 = -b/(a+a)
   PRINT *,"The equation has one root: ",x1

CASE (:-1)
   ! No roots
   PRINT *,"The equation has no real roots"

END SELECT

END PROGRAM quadratic_by_CASE
```

(b)   Using an **IF** construct

```fortran
PROGRAM quadratic_by_block_IF
   IMPLICIT NONE

   ! A program to solve a quadratic equation using a block IF
   ! statement to distinguish between the three cases

   ! Constant declarations
   REAL, PARAMETER :: epsilon=1E-6

   ! Variable declarations
   REAL :: a,b,c,d,sqrt_d,x1,x2

   ! Read coefficients
   PRINT *,"Please type the three coefficients a, b and c"
   READ *,a,b,c
```

```
! Calculate b**2-4*a*c
d = b**2 - 4.0*a*c

! Calculate and print roots, if any
IF (d>=epsilon) THEN
   ! Two roots
   sqrt_d = SQRT(d)
   x1 = (-b+sqrt_d)/(a+a)
   x2 = (-b-sqrt_d)/(a+a)
   PRINT *,"The equation has two roots: ",x1," and ",x2

ELSE IF (d>-epsilon) THEN
   ! One root
   x1 = -b/(a+a)
   PRINT *,"The equation has one root: ",x1

ELSE
   ! No roots
   PRINT *,"The equation has no real roots"

END IF

END PROGRAM quadratic_by_block_IF
```

5.7   Obsolete forms of control statements

During the period of almost 40 years since the first Fortran system was developed a great deal has been learned about programming style, and its effect upon programming efficiency and the reliability of programs. One of the most obvious effects of this learning process has been the development of new approaches to the ways of controlling the flow of programs. As a result, Fortran 90 contains a number of additional control constructs and statements whose use we do not recommend, but which may, nevertheless, frequently be encountered in older programs. Most of these are now so rare that they will not be described here, although a brief description will be found in Appendix E. One of these older constructs is, however, briefly mentioned here, owing to its widespread use in Fortran 77 programs, although it must be emphasized that its use in new programs is strongly discouraged.

This statement is the computed **GOTO**, which has been replaced by the **CASE** construct, and, to a lesser extent, by the block **IF** construct. It consists of a statement of the form

GOTO (*label_1*, *label_2*, . . .) , *integer_expression*

and caused a transfer of control to one of the statements identified by the labels specified in the parenthesized list. It is described in more detail, for reference, in Appendix E. Its use in new programs is, however, strongly discouraged.

As well as the computed GOTO, Fortran 90 contains two even older, and even less desirable control constructs which are relics from its long past; these are the arithmetic IF and the assigned GOTO. Neither of these should be used in new programs, and both had largely fallen into disuse by the time that Fortran 90 was released. They are briefly described in Appendix E for reference.

SELF-TEST EXERCISES 5.2

1   What is the main difference between a **CASE** construct and a block **IF** construct (apart from their syntax)?

2   What restrictions, if any, are there on the case expression in a **SELECT CASE** statement?

3   What forms may a case selector take? Are there any restrictions on any of these forms?

4   What is meant by overflow on a computer?

5   In a multiple choice situation, when should you use a **CASE** construct, and when should you use a block **IF** construct?

SUMMARY

- The ability of a computer program to choose which one of two or more alternative sequences of statements to obey is a major factor in making computers such powerful tools.

- The block **IF** construct and the **CASE** construct provide the means for a program to select one of several alternative courses of action.

- The logical **IF** statement provides a simpler alternative to the block **IF** construct in a limited number of cases.

- Relational operators are used to derive logical values from a comparison of two numeric expressions or two character expressions.

- Character expressions are compared by the relation operators using the Fortran collating sequence.

- Character expressions may be compared using the ASCII collating sequence by using special intrinsic functions.

- Logical operators are used to combine two logical values, and thus to allow more complex comparisons.

- Logical variables take one of two values: .TRUE. or .FALSE.

- Fortran 90 syntax introduced in Chapter 5:

Variable declaration	**LOGICAL** :: *list of variable names*

Block **IF** construct	**IF** (*logical_expression*) **THEN**
	    block_of_code
	ELSE IF (*logical_expression*) **THEN**
	    block_of_code
	
	    .
	    .
	    .
	
	ELSE
	    block_of_code
	END IF

CASE construct	**SELECT CASE** (*case_expression*)
	CASE (*case_selector*)
	    block_of_code
	
	    .
	    .
	    .
	
	CASE DEFAULT
	    block_of_code
	END SELECT

Logical **IF** statement	**IF** (*logical_expression*) *Fortran_statement*
Relational operators	>, >=, <=, <, ==, /= .GT., .GE., .LE., .LT., .EQ., .NE.
Logical operators	.AND., .OR., .EQV., .NEQV., .NOT.

PROGRAMMING EXERCISES

*5.1   Write a program which will request a number to be typed at the keyboard and will then inform the user whether the number is positive, negative or zero.

Now modify your program so that if it used a block **IF** construct it now uses a **CASE** construct, and vice versa.

5.2   Write a function *that does not use any intrinsic functions* which will determine the larger of two numbers.

5.3   Write a program to print out the truth tables for .OR., .EQV. and .NEQV. in the same form as the following table for .AND.

```
A    B    A.AND.B
T    T       T
T    F       F
F    T       F
F    F       F
```

where the value for the third column is printed as the result of executing a logical expression (and *not* by working out the result and simply printing the table!).

5.4   The logical *NAND* operation is the equivalent of performing the `.AND.` operation on two operands, followed by a `.NOT.` operation on the result. Thus

> *a NAND b* is the same as *not(a and b)*

Write a logical function to perform the *NAND* operation on its two logical arguments.

5.5   Write a program which reads a number between 1 and 6 from the keyboard and prints out the corresponding word: 'one', 'two' etc. If a number outside this range is typed the program should print an appropriate message.
   Now modify your program so that if it used a block `IF` construct it now uses a `CASE` construct, and vice versa.

5.6   Write a program that accepts a positive integer as its input and informs the user of all the following:

(a)   whether the number is odd or even
(b)   whether it is divisible by seven
(c)   whether it is a perfect square (that is, its square root is a whole number).

   Modify your program to find the first even number that is divisible by 7 and is a perfect square.

5.7   Write a program that will determine how much income tax a person pays, given the following basis for taxation:

Income	Tax rate
first £5000	0 %
next £15 000	25 %
everything over £20 000	32 %

5.8   It is often difficult to compare the value of items priced in different currencies. Write a function to convert an amount in any one of the eight currencies shown below to an equivalent amount in one particular currency, which we shall call the *standard currency*. Use this function in a program which reads two amounts in any two of these currencies and calculates which is the lower.
   Use the following table to specify the currencies and their relationships:

1 UK pound	=	1.52 US dollars
	=	2.45 Deutschmarks
	=	8.60 French francs
	=	52.65 Belgian francs
1 US dollar	=	103.95 Japanese yen
	=	1.40 Swiss francs
	=	1.31 Canadian dollars

5.9   The current I drawn by an electrical appliance of power P watts from a supply voltage V volts is given by the formula:

$$I = \frac{P}{V} \text{ amps}$$

An electical supplier stocks three types of cable, suitable for currents of up to 5 amps, 13 amps and 30 amps, respectively. Write a program that asks the user for the power rating and supply voltage of an appliance, and displays the most suitable cable, or a warning if the appliance cannot be safely used with any of the cables in stock.

*5.10   A firm produces digital watches and sells them for £15 each. However it gives a discount for multiple orders as follows:

Number ordered	Discount
2–4	5 %
5–9	10 %
10–29	15 %
30–99	20 %
100–299	25 %
300+	30 %

Write a program to input the number of watches required and to print the gross cost, the discount (if any), and the net cost.

5.11   The brightness of a binary star varies as follows. At time $t = 0$ days its magnitude is 2.5, and it stays at this level until $t = 0.9$ days. Its magnitude is then determined by the formula

$$3.355 - \ln(1.352 + \cos(\pi(t - 0.9)/0.7))$$

until $t = 2.3$ days. Its magnitude is then 2.5 until $t = 4.4$ days, and it is then determined by the formula

$$3.598 - \ln(1.998 + \cos(\pi(t - 4.4)/0.4))$$

until $t = 5.2$ days. It then remains at 2.5 until $t = 6.4$ days, after which the cycle repeats with a period of 6.4 days.
Write a program which will input the value of the time t and print the brightness of the star at that time.

5.12   Exercise 4.13 required the writing of a subroutine to calculate the point of intersection of two lines, but ignored the problem of lines which were parallel and did not, therefore, intersect. In a similar way to that used in Example 5.3, modify your solution for Exercise 4.13 to return an error flag to indicate whether it was possible to calculate the coordinates of the point of intersection.

5.13   Write a function which has two dummy arguments, **first_person** and **second_person**, both of a derived type which contains, among other things, the first and last names of a person, the age of the person, and the sex of the person. The function should return an integer value indicating the relationship between the two people represented by the arguments, according to the following rules:

- If the last names are the same then they are related, otherwise they are unrelated, and the function result should be zero.

- If they are related then a difference in age of over 20 years indicates a parent–child relationship; a difference of less than 20 years, and both ages over 20 implies a marital relationship; a difference of less than 20 years, and at least one aged 20 or less, implies a sibling relationship.

The value of the function should then be as follows:

Husband–wife	1
Father–son	2
Father–daughter	3
Mother–son	4
Mother–daughter	5
Brother–brother	6
Sister–sister	7
Brother–sister	8

If the person represented by the first dummy argument is the older then the result is as shown; if that person is the younger then the value is negated (that is, daughter–father is returned as −3).

Test your function in a program which either reads two sets of personal details from the keyboard or has them as initial values in the main program and uses the function to cause an appropriate message to be printed, along the following lines:

```
Sarah Ellis is the daughter of Miles Ellis
```

5.14 Write a program which reads three real numbers representing three distances. The program should use these as the arguments to a subroutine which will set three further arguments as follows:

triangle   is set *true* if the three distances could represent the sides of a triangle; that is, no number is greater than the sum of the other two numbers

isosceles   is set *true* if **triangle** is *true* and exactly two of the sides are of equal length; that is, an isosceles triangle

equilat   is set *true* if **triangle** is *true* and all three sides are of equal length; that is, an equilateral triangle

The program should then display an appropriate message.

5.15 Write a logical function which has two **CHARACTER** arguments, and which returns the value *true* if the first argument contains the second, and *false* otherwise. Thus, if the function is called **within**, then

```
within("Just testing","test")
```

is *true*, while

```
within("Just testing","Test")
```

is *false*. (Hint: one of the intrinsic functions will help here.)

Test your function with a driver program which inputs pairs of character strings from the keyboard, and uses the result of a function reference to cause one of the following forms of message to be displayed:

(a) `The phrase 'test' is contained within 'Just testing'`

(b) `The phrase 'Test' is not contained within 'Just testing'`

Repeating parts of your program

A very large proportion of mathematical techniques rely on some form of iterative process, while the processing of most types of data requires the same, or similar, actions to be carried out repeatedly for each set of data. One of the most important of all programming concepts, therefore, is the ability to repeat sequences of statements either a predetermined number of times or until some condition is satisfied.

Fortran has a very powerful, yet simple to use, facility for controlling the repetition of blocks of code, and this chapter explains how this facility can be used to control iterative processes as well as more simple repetitive tasks.

The use of repetitive techniques, however, often leads to situations in which it is required to end the repetition earlier than had been anticipated, and Fortran contains a number of statements to assist in these exceptional cases. By their nature, however, such statements interrupt the normal flow of control through the program and must be used with care if they are not to lead to other problems.

6.1   Program repetition and the block DO construct

So far, most of our programs have taken rather longer to write than it would have taken to solve the problem by hand! This is because they have consisted of a series of instructions which are executed in sequence *once only*. In many cases the programs would be much more useful if they could be repeated with different sets of data. For instance, Example 3.1 converted a single Centigrade temperature to Fahrenheit; it would be much more useful if it could convert a series of temperatures or create a table of equivalent temperatures.

Before we see how we can do this in Fortran let us re-examine the structure plan for Example 3.1:

> **1**   Read Centigrade temperature
>
> **2**   Calculate Fahrenheit equivalent
>
> **3**   Print both temperatures

There are three main ways in which we could modify this plan to enable the program to convert more than one temperature. The first of these simply states that the process is to be repeated a predetermined number of times, say 10:

> **1**   Repeat the following 10 times
>   **1.1**   Read Centigrade temperature
>   **1.2**   Calculate Fahrenheit equivalent
>   **1.3**   Print both temperatures

A more flexible approach would be to ask the user how many temperatures are to be converted:

> **1**   Read number of temperatures to be converted (*num*)
>
> **2**   Repeat the following *num* times
>   **2.1**   Read Centigrade temperature
>   **2.2**   Calculate Fahrenheit equivalent
>   **2.3**   Print both temperatures

A variation on this would be to ask after each conversion if any more conversions were required:

> **1**   Repeat the following
>   **1.1**   Read Centigrade temperature

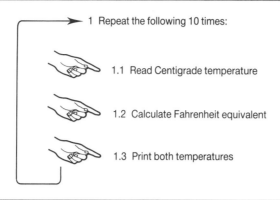

1 Repeat the following 10 times:

1.1 Read Centigrade temperature

1.2 Calculate Fahrenheit equivalent

1.3 Print both temperatures

Figure 6.1 A program loop.

1.2 Calculate Fahrenheit equivalent
1.3 Print both temperatures
1.4 Ask if any more conversions required
1.5 If not then stop repeating this block of code

Another variation would be to produce a table of equivalent temperatures in the following way:

1 Repeat the following for each Centigrade temperature from 0 to 100 in steps of 5
1.1 Calculate Fahrenheit equivalent
1.2 Print both temperatures

Clearly this will produce a table of equivalent temperatures at 5 °C intervals from 0 °C to 100 °C without the need for any data to be read at all.

The repetition of a block of statements a number of times is called a **loop** (see Figure 6.1) and is so important that Fortran contains a special construct with exactly the features that are required. It is called a **DO construct** and takes one of the following forms:

DO *count=initial,final,inc*

.

block of statements

.

END DO

or

(77)   **DO**   *count=initial, final*

      .

     block of statements

      .

END DO

or simply

   DO

      .

     block of statements

      .

   END DO

A loop created by use of a **DO** construct is called a **DO loop**.

6.2   Count-controlled DO loops

The first statement of a **DO** loop is called a **DO statement** and, as we have already seen, takes one of the forms:

   DO   *count=initial, final, inc*
   DO   *count=initial, final*
   DO

The first two alternatives define a **count-controlled DO loop** in which an integer variable, known as the **DO variable**, is used to determine how many times the block of statements which appear between the **DO** statement and the **END DO** statement are to be executed. We shall discuss the third alternative in Section 6.3. There are also two other forms of the **DO** statement which we do not advocate using, but which will be briefly discussed in Section 6.6.

Informally, we can consider the second, slightly simpler, form, in which *inc* is absent, as meaning that the loop is executed for *count* taking the value *initial* the first time that the loop is executed, *initial* + 1 the next time, and so on until it takes the value *final* on the last pass through the loop.

In a similar manner, we can informally consider the first form to mean that the loop is executed for *count* taking the value *initial* the first time that the loop is executed, *initial* + *inc* the next time, and so on, with the value of *count* being incremented by *inc* for each subsequent pass; in this case the final pass through the loop will be the one which would result in the *next* pass having a value of *count* greater than *final*.

DO *statement*	Iteration *count*	DO *variable values*
DO i=1,10	10	1,2,3,4,5,6,7,8,9,10
DO j=20,50,5	7	20,25,30,35,40,45,50
DO p=7,19,4	4	7,11,15,19
DO q=4,5,6	1	4
DO r=6,5,4	0	6
DO x=-20,20,6	7	−20,−14,−8,−2,4,10,16
DO n=25,0,-5	6	25,20,15,10,5,0
DO m=20,-20,-6	7	20,14,8,2,−4,−10,−16

Figure 6.2 Some examples of DO statements and their effect.

The formal definition of this process is that when the DO statement is executed an **iteration count** is first calculated using the formula

$$\textbf{MAX}\,(\,(\textit{final}-\textit{initial}+\textit{inc})\,/\textit{inc},0\,)$$

and the loop executed that many times. On the first pass the value of *count* is *initial*, and on each subsequent pass its value is increased by *inc*. If *inc* is absent then its value is taken as 1. The effect of the **MAX** function is that if *final* < *initial* and *inc* > 0 then the iteration count will be zero, and the statements in the loop will not be executed at all. Notice, however, that *count* will be set to the value *initial* since this assignment takes place before the iteration count is tested.

The DO variable, *count*, must be an integer variable, while *initial*, *final* and *inc* must be integer expressions.

Because of its special role, it is not permitted to alter the value of the DO variable between the initial DO statement and the corresponding END DO statement by any means other than the automatic incrementation which is part of the DO loop processing.

Figure 6.2 shows some examples of the iteration counts for a number of different DO statements, and the values that will be taken by the DO variable on each pass through the corresponding loops, and it can be seen that our informal description is perfectly adequate as long as care is taken over the last value. It must always be remembered, however, that the way that a loop works is *not* by looking at the value of the DO variable on each pass, but by calculating the iteration count once and then decrementing it by one after each pass is completed. One effect of this is that once the loop has been completed (that is, it has been executed the number of times defined by the iteration count) the DO variable will have the value that it would have had on the *next* pass through the loop, if there had been one. Another effect is that if the values of *initial*, *final* and, if it is present, *inc* are such as to result in a zero or negative value for the iteration count then the loop is not obeyed at all, because the value of the iteration count is examined immediately before commencing execution of each pass.

■ EXAMPLE 6.1

1 Problem

Write a program which first reads the number of people sitting an exam. It should then read their marks (or scores) and print the highest and lowest marks, followed by the average mark for the class.

2 Analysis

This is a straightforward problem which will use a **DO** loop to repeatedly read a mark and use it to update the sum of all the marks, the maximum mark so far, and the minimum mark so far.

Data design

Purpose	Type	Name
Number of people (data)	INTEGER	number
Mark (data)	INTEGER	mark
Max and min marks	INTEGER	maximum, minimum
Sum of all marks	INTEGER	sum
Average of all marks	REAL	average
DO variable	INTEGER	i

Structure plan

1   Initialize *sum* to zero, *maximum* to a large negative value, *minimum* to a large positive value

2   Read number of examinees (*number*)

3   Repeat *number* times
   3.1   Read a mark
   3.2   Add it to cumulative sum
   3.3   If it is larger than maximum mark so far set maximum to this mark
   3.4   If it is less than minimum mark so far set minimum to this mark

4   Calculate average

5   Print maximum, minimum and average marks

Since the **DO** variable is only used to control the loop we will follow normal programming (and mathematical) conventions and use the name *i* for this purpose.

One aspect that must be very carefully considered is the initialization of the three variables which will be used to save the accumulated sum of the marks, and the maximum and minimum marks. In this example the cumulative sum must obviously start at zero, but what about the maximum and minimum marks? What we shall do (at steps 3.3 and 3.4) is to compare each mark that is read with the highest (or lowest) read previously and store the higher (or lower) as the new maximum (or minimum). It follows, therefore, that initially the maximum must be set to a lower value than any actual marks can take, and the minimum must be set to a higher value than is possible as a mark. If marks are to lie, for example, in the range 0–100 then any values less than zero or greater than 100 could be used for the initial maximum and minimum, respectively. However, as the intrinsic function **HUGE** is a generic function we can use it to provide the largest possible integer value, which will be more than large enough!

Finally, as there are only three variables to be initialized we could use assignment statements, but as a general rule it is preferable to always carry out such initialization in the declaration statement as this causes the initial values to be stored when the program is first loaded, as well as making it clear that these are *initial* values which will be changed when the program is executed.

3 Solution

```
PROGRAM examination_marks
   IMPLICIT NONE

   ! This program prints statistics about a set of exam results

   ! Variable declarations
   INTEGER :: i,number,mark, &
             sum=0,maximum=-HUGE(1),minimum=HUGE(1)
   REAL :: average

   ! Read number of marks, and then the marks
   PRINT *,"How many marks are there? "
   READ *,number
   PRINT *,"Please type ",number," marks: "

   ! Loop to read and process marks
   DO i=1,number
      READ *,mark
      ! On each pass, update sum, maximum and minimum
      sum = sum+mark
      IF (mark>maximum) maximum=mark
      IF (mark<minimum) minimum=mark
   END DO

   ! Calculate average mark and output results
   average = REAL(sum)/number
   PRINT *,"Highest mark is ",maximum
   PRINT *,"Lowest mark is ",minimum
   PRINT *,"Average mark is ",average

END PROGRAM examination_marks
```

Notice, incidentally, the line after the end of the loop in which the average is calculated. Since both **sum** and **number** are integers the expression **sum/number** would cause integer division to take place, which would not be appropriate when calculating an average. The intrinsic function **REAL** converts an integer to its real equivalent, thus forcing a real division to take place.

It must be emphasized that there are no restrictions on the types of statements that may appear in the block of statements which constitute the **range** of a **DO** loop. In particular, other **DO** loops may be **nested** within a **DO** loop, although the whole of the nested loop must, of course, lie within the outer loop. Example 6.2 shows an example of a nested **DO** loop.

■ EXAMPLE 6.2

1 Problem

Write a program to print a set of multiplication tables from 2 times up to 12 times, where each table should take the form:

> x times 1 is x
> x times 2 is $2x$
> .
> .
> x times 12 is $12x$

2 Analysis

This is an extremely simple program to visualize:

Data design

Purpose	Type	Name
Two values in table	INTEGER	i,j

Structure plan

```
1    Repeat for i from 2 to 12
     1.1    Print heading
     1.2    Repeat for j from 1 to 12
            1.2.1    Print 'i times j is i*j'
```

3 Solution

```fortran
PROGRAM multiplication_tables
   IMPLICIT NONE

   ! A program to print multiplication tables from 2 to 12 times

   ! Variable declarations
   INTEGER :: i,j

   ! Outer loop defines which 'times table'
   DO i=2,12
      PRINT *," "
      PRINT *,i," times table"
      DO j=1,12
         PRINT *,i," times ",j," is ",i*j
      END DO
   END DO
END PROGRAM multiplication_tables
```

Figure 6.3 shows part of the results produced by running this program.

```
                           .
                           .
                           .
              3 times      9 is      27
              3 times     10 is      30
              3 times     11 is      33
              3 times     12 is      36

              4 times table
              4 times      1 is       4
              4 times      2 is       8
              4 times      3 is      12
              4 times      4 is      16
              4 times      5 is      20
              4 times      6 is      24
              4 times      7 is      28
              4 times      8 is      32
              4 times      9 is      36
              4 times     10 is      40
                           .
                           .
                           .
```

Figure 6.3 Part of the results produced by `multiplication_tables`.

■ **EXAMPLE 6.3**

1 Problem

Write a program to print a set of multiplication tables from 2 times up to 12 times, where each table only goes up to 'x times x is x^2'.

2 Analysis

This is a very similar problem to that in Example 6.2, except that the final value of the DO variable in the inner loop will be different each time it is entered to print a new table. This is more like the situations in which counting loops are normally used, in which some or all of the controlling values are variables, rather than constants.

Data design

Purpose	Type	Name
Two values in table	INTEGER	i,j

Structure plan

> **1** Repeat for *i* from 2 to 12
> **1.1** Print heading
> **1.2** Repeat for *j* from 1 to *i*
> **1.2.1** Print '*i* times *j* is *i*j*'

3 Solution

```
PROGRAM multiplication_tables
   IMPLICIT NONE

   ! A program to print multiplication tables from 2 to 12 times

   ! Variable declarations
   INTEGER :: i,j

   ! Outer loop defines which 'times table'
   DO i=2,12
      PRINT *," "
      PRINT *,i," times table"
      DO j=1,i
         PRINT *,i," times ",j," is ",i*j
      END DO
   END DO
END PROGRAM multiplication_tables
```

```
                    .
                    .
                    .
         3 times      1 is     3
         3 times      2 is     6
         3 times      3 is     9

         4 times table
         4 times      1 is     4
         4 times      2 is     8
         4 times      3 is    12
         4 times      4 is    16

         5 times table
         5 times      1 is     5
         5 times      2 is    10
                    .
                    .
                    .
```

Figure 6.4   Part of the results produced by the revised `multiplication_tables`.

Figure 6.4 shows part of the results produced by running this program.

6.3   More flexible loops

The examples that have been discussed above all use the **DO** variable to control the number of times that the loop is executed. However, there are a great many situations in which it is not possible to determine this number in advance, for example in a mathematical calculation which is to be terminated when some value becomes less than a predetermined value. In this situation we can use the third form of the **DO** statement mentioned in Section 6.1, together with a new statement, **EXIT**, which causes a **transfer of control** to the statement immediately following the **END DO** statement. Since this statement will, when executed, cause all the remaining statements in the loop to be omitted, it follows that it is *always* used in association with one of the control statements discussed in Chapter 5.

Thus, for example, the following loop will continue to be executed until the value of **term** becomes less than the value of **epsilon**:

```
DO
   .
   .
   .
IF (term < epsilon) EXIT
   .
   .
   .
END DO
! After obeying the EXIT statement execution continues
! from the next statement
   .
   .
   .
```

However, using this form of the **DO** statement does incur the risk that the condition for obeying the **EXIT** statement may never occur. In that situation the loop will become what is known as an **infinite loop**, and will continue executing until the program is terminated by some external means such as exceeding a time limit or switching off the computer! In order to avoid this possibility, we strongly recommend that this non-counting form of the **DO** statement is only used when the programmer can be absolutely certain that there is no possible situation in which the terminating condition will not occur. Since such a 100% certainty is rare, we recommend that such loops should normally contain a **fail-safe mechanism** in which a **DO** variable is used to limit the number of repetitions to a predefined maximum. Thus, the simple example above should be extended as follows:

```
DO count=1,max_iterations
   .
   .
   .
IF (term < epsilon) EXIT
   .
   .
   .
END DO
! After obeying the EXIT statement, or after obeying
! the loop max_iterations times, execution continues
! from the next statement
   .
   .
   .
```

One additional advantage of this approach is that the number of times that the loop was executed is always available after an exit has been made from the loop. If this exit was made because the maximum number of iterations had been carried out then the rules stated in Section 6.2 tell us that the count will have the value that it would have had on the *next* iteration (**max_iterations+1** in the example above). It is therefore trivially easy to determine whether the loop ended because the terminating condition was met, or whether it had carried out the maximum number of allowable iterations without achieving the terminating condition, which, in some cases, may indicate that there is an error in the logic of the program. Example 6.4 illustrates this situation, and also shows how using a **DO** variable can bring other benefits to loops that do not apparently require one.

■ EXAMPLE 6.4

1 Problem

A set of exam marks, or scores, for a class is provided consisting of three items for each examinee: a number which will be used to identify the student, the mark and a code (F = female, M = male) to indicate the sex of the examinee. The data is terminated by a record containing anything other than F or M for the sex code. It is required to calculate the average mark for the class, and also the average mark for the boys and girls separately.

2 Analysis

The program for this problem needs to produce a sum of all the marks and to count the examinees in order to calculate the class average, and also needs to do the same for the boys and the girls separately. We can use the **DO** variable to count the total number of examinees. Our design is therefore as follows:

Data design

	Purpose	Type	Name
A	Constants:		
	Codes for male/female	CHARACTER	male, female
	Max no. of marks	INTEGER	max_pupils
B	Variables:		
	Student number (data)	INTEGER	student
	Exam mark (data)	INTEGER	mark
	Sex code (data)	CHARACTER	code
	Number of each sex	INTEGER	num_boys, num_girls
	Total marks and by sex	INTEGER	total_marks, marks_boys, marks_girls
	DO variable	INTEGER	num_pupils

Structure plan

> 1   Initialize counts and sums of marks for boys and girls
> 2   Repeat the following for *num_pupils* up to *max_pupils*
>   **2.1**   Read next set of data

> **2.2** Select case on code
>   code is female (= F)
>   **2.2.1** Update sum of girls' marks
>   **2.2.2** Add 1 to count of girls
>   code is male (= M)
>   **2.2.3** Update sum of boys' marks
>   **2.2.4** Add 1 to count of boys
>   code is anything else
>   **2.2.5** Exit from loop
> **3** Calculate sum of all marks
> **4** Calculate and print required averages

Notice that we have defined two constants (*male* and *female*) to represent the relevant codes (M and F). This is not strictly necessary, especially in such a simple program as this, but it makes the program easier to follow and is good programming practice. Notice also that, since the three averages are not required except at the very end for printing, it is not necessary to declare any variables in which to store them. The only remaining difficulty is deciding on the maximum number of times we shall allow the loop to be repeated. Since the problem refers to a school class a maximum of 100 should be more than sufficient.

3 Solution

```
PROGRAM examination_statistics
   IMPLICIT NONE

   ! This program calculates some simple examination statistics

   ! Constant and variable declarations
   CHARACTER, PARAMETER :: male="M",female="F"
   INTEGER, PARAMETER :: max_pupils=100
   INTEGER :: student,mark,num_pupils,num_boys=0,num_girls=0,  &
              total_marks,marks_boys=0,marks_girls=0
   CHARACTER :: code

   ! Read at most max_pupils sets of data
   PRINT *,"Type up to ",max_pupils," exam results."
   PRINT *,"Each result must consist of the student number,   &
           &the mark, and a code"
   PRINT *,"The code is F for a female student and M for a male"
   PRINT *,"Data should be ended by a zero student number and &
           &mark, followed by any code other than M or F"

   DO num_pupils=1,max_pupils
      ! Read next mark and code
      READ *,student,mark,code
```

```
      ! Select appropriate action
      SELECT CASE (code)

      ! Female pupil
      CASE ("F")
         num_girls = num_girls+1
         marks_girls = marks_girls+mark

      ! Male pupil
      CASE ("M")
         num_boys = num_boys+1
         marks_boys = marks_boys+mark

      ! End of data
      CASE DEFAULT
         EXIT
      END SELECT
   END DO


   ! Adjust num_pupils to correct number
   num_pupils = num_pupils-1


   ! Calculate total marks
   total_marks = marks_boys+marks_girls


   ! Calculate and print averages
   IF (num_pupils == 0) THEN
      PRINT *,"There was no data!"
   ELSE
      ! Deal with no terminator case
      IF (num_pupils == max_pupils) THEN
         PRINT *,max_pupils," sets of data read without a &
                 &terminating record"
         PRINT *,"Results are based on these pupils only"
      END IF
      PRINT *,"There are ",num_pupils," pupils. Their average &
              &mark is ",REAL(total_marks)/num_pupils
      IF (num_girls > 0) THEN
         PRINT *,"There are ",num_girls," girls. Their &
                 &average mark is",REAL(marks_girls)/num_girls
      ELSE
         PRINT *,"There are no girls in the class"
      END IF
      IF (num_boys > 0) THEN
         PRINT *,"There are ",num_boys," boys. Their average &
                 &mark is ",REAL(marks_boys)/num_boys
      ELSE
         PRINT *,"There are no boys in the class"
      END IF
   END IF

END PROGRAM examination_statistics
```

Notice that at the exit from the loop we subtracted 1 from `num_pupils`. We should briefly examine why this was done. There are two cases to consider – either the special terminator data is read, or the maximum number of marks are read with no terminator. Let us look at each of these cases separately.

Assume that the class has 35 pupils. On the first pass through the loop `num_pupils` is 1 and the first pupil's mark is read. On the next pass `num_pupils` is 2 and the second pupil's mark is read. On the 35th pass `num_pupils` is 35 and the 35th, and last, pupil's mark is read. On the next pass `num_pupils` is therefore 36 and the terminator data is read. On exit from the loop `num_pupils` is thus one more than the number of pupils.

If no terminator is read, then after `max_pupils` marks have been read the loop will finish. In Section 6.2 we saw that if a `DO` loop completes its specified number of iterations then the `DO` variable will have the value it would have had on the next iteration. In our case this will be `max_pupils+1` – one more than the number of pupils whose marks were read.

In both cases therefore the number of pupils is `num_pupils-1`. Nevertheless, it is appropriate to print a warning message in the latter case to draw attention to the possible omission of some marks if the fail-safe action of the `DO` loop came into effect before data for all the pupils had been processed.

There are two points to note about the calculation and printing of the averages. The first is that a test is made to see if there are any pupils in each category (so as to avoid dividing by zero) and a suitable message printed if there are not. The second concerns the calculation of the average. The program has assumed that the marks are integers, and of course the number of pupils is an integer. An expression such as `total_marks/num_pupils` would therefore lead to an integer division being carried out and the average given in integer form (truncated, not even rounded!). This is not suitable and so steps must be taken to force a real division.

One approach would be for the sums of marks to be kept in real variables. The ensuing expressions would be mixed-mode and would therefore be evaluated using real arithmetic. Alternatively, the sums can be converted to real form once they have been calculated. The easiest way to do this is to use the intrinsic function `REAL` which simply produces as its result the real equivalent of its argument, thus once again leading to a mixed-mode expression. It is not necessary to also make the divisor real as the compiler will take care of this anyway when processing the mixed-mode expression.

The program written for Example 6.4 omitted to deal with one important situation, namely what happens if the data supplied is invalid, for example if a mark is read which is outside an acceptable range (for example, 0–100). A more serious situation would be if the code was incorrectly typed, leading to premature exit from the loop before all the data had been read. Defining a termination code, say X, and treating anything other than M, F or X as an error would deal with this, if we knew what to do once we had detected the error.

The difficulty, therefore, is not how to detect these situations, but what to do when we have done so. Here we can make use of another new statement, **CYCLE**. This is very similar to the **EXIT** statement except that instead of transferring control to the statement *after* the **END DO** statement it transfers control back to the start of the loop in exactly the same way as if it, in fact, transferred control *to* the **END DO** statement. This means, of course, that the iteration count is decreased by one and the **DO** variable, if any, incremented appropriately, before a test is made to determine whether another pass through the loop is required. Although the use of a **CYCLE** statement will, therefore, avoid incorrectly updating the various counts and sums it will lead to the wrong figure for the total number of pupils. This is easily dealt with, however, by using the sum of the number of boys and the number of girls for this purpose.

A possibly more serious problem is that this will reduce the maximum number of iterations of the loop, and hence the maximum number of sets of data that can be read. Since this maximum number is meant to be a fail-safe value, and should never even be closely approached, we shall ignore this problem for the moment.

An additional case can therefore be added to the **CASE** construct in the **DO** loop to deal with an invalid code:

```
! End of data
CASE ("X")
  EXIT
! Invalid code
CASE DEFAULT
  PRINT *,"Invalid code - please re-enter data"
  CYCLE
END SELECT
```

In a similar manner, the two cases which deal with the boys and girls could be modified to deal with invalid marks, using either a nested **CASE** construct or a block **IF** construct:

```
! Female pupil
CASE ("F")
  SELECT CASE (mark)
  CASE (0:100)
    num_girls = num_girls+1
    marks_girls = marks_girls+mark
  CASE DEFAULT
    PRINT *,"Invalid mark - please re-enter data"
    CYCLE
  END SELECT
```

or

```
! Male pupil
CASE ("M")
  IF (mark>=0 .AND. mark<=100) THEN
    num_boys = num_boys+1
    marks_boys = marks_boys+mark
  ELSE
    PRINT *,"Invalid mark - please re-enter data"
    CYCLE
  END IF
```

SELF-TEST EXERCISES 6.1

1   What is a DO loop?

2   What restrictions (if any) are there on the statements which can appear in a DO loop?

3   What is the difference between a count-controlled DO loop and other DO loops? When should the count-controlled form be used?

4   What is a DO variable? What restrictions (if any) are there on the ways in which it is used?

5   What is the iteration count? How is it calculated?

6   How many times will each of the loops controlled by the following DO statements be executed?

   (a)   DO i=-5,5
   (b)   DO j=1,12,2
   (c)   DO k=17,15,-1
   (d)   DO l=17,15
   (e)   DO m=100,350,15
   (f)   DO n=10,10,10

7   What is the value of the DO variable after normal termination of a DO loop?

8   What will be printed by the following programs?

   (a)   PROGRAM loop_test_1
            IMPLICIT NONE
            INTEGER :: i=1,j=2,k=4,l=8,m=0,n=0
            DO i=j,k,l
               k=i
```
```

```
          DO j=1,m,k
             n=j
             DO k=1,n
                DO l=i,k
                   m=k*l
                END DO
             END DO
          END DO
          PRINT *,i,j,k,l,m,n
       END PROGRAM loop_test_1

  (b)  PROGRAM loop_test_2
       IMPLICIT NONE
       INTEGER :: i=1,j=2,k=4,l=8,m=0,n=0
       DO i=j,k,l
          k=-i
          DO j=1,m,k
             n=j
             DO k=1,n
                DO l=i,k
                   m=k*l
                END DO
             END DO
          END DO
       END DO
      PRINT *,i,j,k,l,m,n
      END PROGRAM loop_test_2
```

9   What is an infinite loop? How can it be avoided?

10   What is an **EXIT** statement used for? What is the effect of executing one?

11   What is a **CYCLE** statement used for? What is the effect of executing one?

6.4   Giving names to control constructs

The examples that we have given above of the use of the **EXIT** and **CYCLE** statements should cause no confusion regarding the next statement to be executed. However the situation with nested loops is less clear. For example, to which statement will the **EXIT** statement in Figure 6.5 transfer control?

     The rule for determining this is that the **EXIT** statement transfers control to the statement immediately following the **END DO** statement belonging to the innermost **DO** construct that contains the **EXIT** statement. Thus, in the code fragment shown in Figure 6.5 the **EXIT** statement will transfer control to the first executable statement following the second **END DO**. This is usually what is wanted, but there will be occasions when it is required to exit from *all* of the enclosing

```
          DO
           .
          DO
           .
          DO
              .
              EXIT
              .
              DO
               .
              END DO
              ! This one (1)?
                .
            END DO
            ! or this one (2)?
              .
          END DO
          ! or this one (3)?
            .
      END DO
      ! or this one (4)?
```

Figure 6.5 Exiting from a nested DO loop.

loops, or even from more than the immediately enclosing loop, but not from all of them. A similar rule applies to the **CYCLE** statement.

For this reason, it is possible to give a name to a block **DO** construct, by preceding the **DO** statement by a name, which follows the normal Fortran rules for names and is separated from the **DO** by a colon, and by following the corresponding **END DO** by the same name:

block_name: **DO**

.

.

.

END DO *block_name*

Note that if the initial **DO** statement is named in this way then it is mandatory for the same name to appear on the corresponding **END DO** statement, and vice versa.

The **CYCLE** and **EXIT** statements may also be followed by the name of an enclosing **DO** construct, in which case control is transferred to, or after, respectively, the **END DO** statement having the same name:

```
outer:    DO
              .
              .
              .
inner:        DO
                  .
                  .
                  .
              SELECT CASE (n)
              CASE (1)
                EXIT outer
              CASE (2)
                EXIT inner
              CASE (3)
                CYCLE outer
              CASE (4)
                CYCLE inner
              END SELECT
                  .
                  .
                  .
          END DO inner
              .
              .
              .
          END DO outer
```

Note that, in this example, the references to **inner** in two of the case selections is redundant, since that is where they would transfer control to in any case, if no construct name was specified. However it helps to ensure that there is no doubt in the (human) reader's mind about what is intended.

A similar naming facility also exists for the block **IF** and **CASE** constructs as shown in Figures 6.6 and 6.7, but in these cases the names are purely for clarity in the case of complex structures. Similar rules apply in these cases as for the block **DO** as regards the requirements for matching names on corresponding **IF** and **END IF** statements, and on corresponding **SELECT CASE** and **END SELECT** statements.

```
if_construct_name:    IF (condition) THEN
                          .
                          .
                          .
                      END IF if_construct_name
```

Figure 6.6 A named block IF construct.

```
case_construct_name:   SELECT CASE (case_expression)
                       CASE (case_range_1)
                         .
                         .
                         .

                       END SELECT case_construct_name
```

Figure 6.7   A named **CASE** construct.

There is no requirement for any of the **ELSE IF** or **ELSE** statements in a named block **IF** construct to include a name, but if they do then it must be the name of the block **IF** construct of which they are a part, as shown in Figure 6.8.

Similarly, there is no requirement for any of the **CASE** statements in a **CASE** construct to include a name, but if they do then it must be the name of the **CASE** construct of which they are a part.

```
outer_if_construct:   IF (condition_1) THEN
                        .
                      ELSE IF (condition_2) THEN outer_if_construct
                        .
inner_if_construct:    IF (condition_3) THEN
                        .
                       ELSE IF (condition_4) THEN inner_if_construct
                        .
                       ELSE inner_if_construct
                        .
                       END IF inner_if_construct
                        .
                      ELSE outer_if_construct
                        .
                      END IF outer_if_construct
```

Figure 6.8   Comprehensively named nested block **IF** constructs.

As a general rule we do not recommend the naming of any of these structures except when there is a clear need for a name to be used with an **EXIT** or **CYCLE** statement in a **DO** loop, as the syntax is rather messy. Nevertheless, there will be occasions such as, for example, where an **IF**, **SELECT CASE** or **DO** statement is a long way from the corresponding **END IF**, **END SELECT** or **END DO** statement when the use of named constructs will make the program easier to follow for the human reader.

6.5   Dealing with exceptional situations

All of the control constructs that we have discussed so far have shared one common feature, namely that the construct is entered at only one place (the **IF**, **SELECT CASE** or **DO** statement) and is only left at one place (the corresponding **END IF**, **END SELECT** or **END DO** statement). This is good programming practice, as it enables the programmer to control the logic of the program much more easily than would otherwise be the case. Nevertheless, there are occasionally situations in which this is either inconvenient, or makes programming very difficult, and three additional statements exist to help us in these exceptional situations.

The first of these statements simply terminates execution without the need to find a way of reaching the **END** statement of the main program unit. It consists of the word

STOP

and causes execution of the program to be terminated immediately. Typically this statement will be used when the program has detected some error from which it is not possible to recover.

A closely related statement causes a return from a procedure without the need to find a way of reaching the **END** statement of the procedure. It consists of the word

RETURN

and causes execution of the procedure to be terminated immediately and control transferred back to the program unit which called or referenced the procedure.

The third statement is quite different and causes a transfer of control to any specified statement in the program unit currently being executed. This is, potentially, an extremely dangerous thing to do since it interrupts the normal processing flow in an almost arbitrary way; however, as we shall see, there are some situations in which it is the only way out of an awkward situation. This statement takes either of the forms

GOTO *label*

or

GO TO *label*

where *label* is a **statement label** which identifies the statement to which control is to be transferred. Since a GOTO statement causes an unconditional transfer of control to the specified statement it follows that it should always be used under the control of an IF or CASE construct, as any statements immediately following it will otherwise be inaccessible (unless they are labelled and are also the target of a GOTO statement elsewhere in the program; this leads rapidly to so-called *spaghetti programs*, because of their heavily intertwined logical structure, and is to be deplored).

A statement label consists of from one to five consecutive digits, at least one of which must be non-zero, and which precedes the statement being labelled. The statement label must be separated from the statement it is labelling by at least one space:

```
100 READ *,a

001    STOP

99999 PRINT *,error_number
```

In the old fixed form source a statement label must be written in columns 1–5 of the line, with the statement starting in, or after, column 7.

Each statement label is interpreted as though it were an integer, with the result that the labels 00123, 0123 and 123 are treated as being identical. Every statement label in a program unit must be unique (for obvious reasons!).

Wherever possible, the use of GOTO *statements should be avoided, as experience over many years has shown them to be the single biggest cause of bad programming habits and consequent programming errors.* Like the STOP and RETURN statements, however, they are sometimes needed to recover from an error situation.

6.6 Obsolete forms of loops

It has been pointed out in earlier chapters that Fortran 90 contains a number of statements and constructs which are included for compatibility with earlier versions of Fortran, but which should not be used in new programs. Nowhere is this more apparent than in the areas of program control and looping, where programming ideas and practice have developed markedly over the last 20 years. In particular, there are several alternative forms of the DO loop available, but whose use we do not recommend in new programs.

The first of these constructs is known as the **DO WHILE** construct and takes a similar form to the DO construct already discussed earlier, except that the initial statement takes the form

DO **WHILE** (*logical_expression*)

The interpretation of this form of DO statement is identical to the two consecutive statements

DO
IF (.NOT. *logical_expression*) **EXIT**

and this is, in fact, the way in which the Fortran 90 standard defines it. This construct was not, in fact, part of FORTRAN 77, although it did exist as an extension in several FORTRAN 77 compilers, and its inclusion in Fortran 90 is a reflection of an earlier style of programming, since it does *not* mean that the loop is to be executed *while* (or *as long as*) the logical expression is true, but rather that the next iteration will be initiated as long as the logical expression is true *at the point at which the decision is made about another iteration;* that is, in the DO statement. The use of an **EXIT** statement under the control of an IF statement makes it clear exactly what is happening and is, in any case, far more flexible since it may be placed anywhere in the loop and not only at the beginning.

A second variation on the DO construct allows the inclusion of a statement label on the END DO statement, and a reference to the same label in the corresponding DO statement:

DO *label*, *var=initial,final*
DO *label*, *var=initial,final,inc*
DO *label*, **WHILE** (*logical_expression*)

A third variation, which was the only standard possibility prior to Fortran 90, uses either of the first two forms above as the initial statement of the loop, but instead of an END DO statement the final statement of the loop may be one of a wide range of Fortran statements, with the same label as that referred to in the corresponding DO statement. More information about this form of loop will be found in Appendix E.

SELF-TEST EXERCISES 6.2

1   What is the purpose of naming a block DO construct? What form does the name take?

2   What is the purpose of naming a block IF construct or a **CASE** construct?

3   What does a **RETURN** statement do? When should it be used?

4   What does a **STOP** statement do? When should it be used?

5   What does a **GOTO** statement do? When should it be used?

6   What is a statement label? What restrictions (if any) are there on statement labels?

SUMMARY

- A sequence of statements which are repeated is called a loop.

- The DO construct provides the means for controlling the repetition of statements within a loop.

- In a count-controlled DO loop the number of times the loop is repeated is determined by the value of the iteration count, which is calculated before the first iteration.

- In a count-controlled DO loop the DO variable is incremented on each pass through the loop.

- It is not permitted for the program to alter the value of a DO variable during the execution of the loop, other than through the automatic incrementation process.

- On normal completion of a count-controlled DO loop the DO variable will have the value that it would have had on the next pass through the loop, had there been one.

- Block DO constructs, block IF constructs and CASE constructs may be named.

- Execution of an EXIT statement in a loop causes the next statement to be executed the one immediately after the END DO statement of the innermost loop surrounding the EXIT statement, unless the EXIT statement is named, in which case it will be the statement immediately after the END DO statement having the same name.

- Execution of a CYCLE statement in a loop causes the next statement to be executed to be as though execution had continued with the END DO statement of the innermost loop surrounding the EXIT statement, unless the EXIT statement is named, in which case it will be as though execution had continued with the END DO statement having the same name.

- The STOP statement causes an immediate termination of the execution of the program.

- The RETURN statement causes an immediate termination of the execution of the current procedure.

- A statement label may be used to identify a statement.

- A GOTO statement transfers execution to the statement in the same procedure having a specified label.

- Fortran 90 syntax introduced in Chapter 6:

Block DO construct   DO *do_var=initial, final, inc*

                                      .

                                      .

                                      .

                        END DO

```
                          DO do_var=initial, final
                          .
                          .
                          .
                          END DO
                          DO
                          .
                          .
                          .
                          END DO
```

Loop control statements	**EXIT**
	CYCLE
Named block construct statements	*do_block_name*: **DO** *do_var=initial, final, inc*
	do_block_name: **DO** *do_var=initial, final*
	do_block_name: **DO**
	EXIT *do_block_name*
	CYCLE *do_block_name*
	END DO *do_block_name*
	if_block_name: **IF** (*logical_expression*) **THEN**
	ELSE IF (*logical_expression*) **THEN** *if_block_name*
	ELSE *if_block_name*
	END IF *if_block_name*
	case_block_name: **SELECT CASE** (*case_expression*)
	CASE (*case_selector*) *case_block_name*
	CASE DEFAULT *case_block_name*
	END SELECT *case_block_name*
STOP statement	**STOP**
RETURN statement	**RETURN**
GOTO statement	**GOTO** *label*
	GO TO *label*

PROGRAMMING EXERCISES

6.1   Halley's comet appears approximately every 76 years, and its last appearance was in 1986. Write a program to display the dates of the comet's next 10 appearances.

6.2   Write a program that prints a 'countdown', starting at a count which is input from the keyboard, and which ends by printing 'Blast Off!' when the count reaches zero.

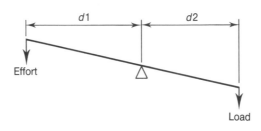

Figure 6.9   Diagram for Exercise 6.6.

6.3   Write a program that produces the sine, cosine and tangent of an angle typed in at the keyboard.

Modify the program so that the user can try more than one angle without having to rerun the program, but can stop the program from executing when desired.

*6.4   Find out how many characters there are in the character set used by your computer; it will probably be 64, 128 or 256. Then write a program to print a list of all the characters in the order of their internal representation (that is, from 0 to 63, 0 to 127, 0 to 255 etc., as appropriate).

6.5   The international standard paper sizes, such as A4, are defined by the formula

$$2^{1/4-n/2} \times 2^{-1/4-n/2} \text{ metres}$$

where n is the number following the letter A. Write a program to print the international paper sizes in both centimetres and inches (1 inch $=$ 2.54 cm) from A0 down to A6.

6.6   A lever is the simplest machine known to mankind, and provides a means of lifting loads that would otherwise be too heavy.

In Figure 6.9, the relationship between the human *Effort* and the actual *Load* is given by the equation

$$Effort \times d_1 = Load \times d_2$$

Write a program that will produce a table of the effort required to raise a load of 2000 kg when the distance of the load from the fulcrum (d_2) is fixed at 2 metres. The program should print out the effort required for levers of lengths differing in steps of 2 metres between two limits (minimum and maximum), which should be input from the keyboard.

Use the results produced by the program to determine the shortest lever that could be used to raise the load if the maximum effort is equivalent to 25 kg.

6.7   Mrs Smith is moving from Cambridge, Massachusetts, to Cambridge, England, and wants to be able to convert her recipes from American measures to British measures using the following conversions:

US	British
1 cup flour	4 oz flour
1 cup butter	8 oz butter
1 cup sugar	6 oz sugar
1 cup confectioner's sugar	4 oz icing sugar
1 cup milk	8 fl oz milk *or* 0.4 pints milk

Write a program which will read lines of the recipe, each containing the quantity, followed by a space, then the units (which may be ignored), followed by another space and then the name of the ingredient. Your program should convert this data into the number of ounces of the ingredient (or the number of pints in the case of milk), and print the revised list of ingredients. Any lines not containing one of the above ingredients should be left unaltered.

6.8 A sheet metal stamping company buys its metal in rectangular sheets of various sizes: 2, 5 or 10 metres long by 2, 4 or 6 metres wide. It has an order for a number of circular discs of a given diameter (less than one metre) and wishes to waste as little metal as possible.

Write a subroutine which takes the number and diameter of discs required and the size of the sheet, and then calculates the number of sheets of this size required and the percentage of the metal wasted.

Use this subroutine in a program which requests the number and diameter of discs required, and then cycles through all the available sheet sizes automatically and prints the relevant information for each sheet size so that the user can decide which sheet size will produce least wastage.

Finally, modify the program so that the program decides which sheet size to use, based on the least amount of metal wasted.

6.9 The yield of a chemical reaction after time t seconds at a temperature of $T\,°C$ is given by $1 - e^{-kt}$, where $k = e^{-q}$ and $q = 2000/(T + 273.16)$.

Write a program which allows the user to enter the temperature, and which then prints out the yield for each minute until it reaches 95%.

6.10 A simple method of determining whether an integer is a prime number is to try dividing it by all integers less than or equal to its square root, and checking to see whether there is any remainder.

Write a function which will determine whether a number is a prime using this method, and will return the value of the first factor found or one if it is a prime.

Test this function by including it in a simple test program that reads a number from the keyboard and either informs the user that it is a prime or displays one of its factors.

Finally, modify your program to print a list of primes less than 32 768.

6.11 The length, L, of a bar of metal at a temperature T is given by the equation

$$L = L_0 + ETL_0$$

where the temperature is measured in degrees Celsius, L_0 is the length of the bar at $0\,°C$, and E is the coefficient of expansion.

Write a program that will produce a set of tables showing the lengths of various bars of metal at various temperatures, assuming that each bar is exactly one metre long at 20 °C. For each type of metal the program should read the coefficient of expansion and the range of temperatures to be covered.

6.12   The Fibonacci Sequence of numbers is one in which each number is the sum of the previous two. It starts

1, 1, 2, 3, 5, 8, ... etc.

Write a program to generate the first 36 members of the sequence.

The ratio of consecutive numbers in the series (1/1, 1/2, 2/3, 3/5, ...) tends to the so-called Golden Ratio:

$$\frac{\sqrt{5} + 1}{2}$$

Modify your program so as to determine how far along the sequence you have to go until the difference between the Golden Ratio and that of consecutive numbers is less than 10^{-6}.

6.13   The value of $\sin x$ (where x is in radians) can be expressed by the infinite series

$$\sin x = x - \frac{x^3}{3!} + \frac{x^5}{5!} - \frac{x^7}{7!} + \frac{x^9}{9!} - \dots$$

where $n! = n \times (n - 1) \times (n - 2) \times \dots \times 2 \times 1$

Write a function that uses the above series to calculate $\sin x$ to an accuracy that is provided as an argument to the function.

(Hint: $\sin(x + 2\pi) = \sin x$ and we may therefore use a value of x which lies between $-\pi$ and $+\pi$ to reduce the size of the terms of the expression. Once this has been done every term after the second is smaller than its predecessor, and so it is easy to know when to stop the calculation.)

Use this function in a program that calculates the sine of an angle input from the keyboard to an accuracy which is also input from the keyboard.

Finally, modify this program so that it produces a table showing the value of $\sin x$ for x taking values from 0° to 90° in steps of 1, where 360° $= 2\pi$ radians. Each line should show the angle (in degrees), the value of $\sin x$ calculated by the program, and the value of $\sin x$ calculated by use of the intrinsic function **SIN**.

*6.14   The pressure inside a can of carbonated drink is given by the expression

$$0.00105 \times T^2 + 0.0042 \times T + 1.352 \text{ atm}$$

where T°C is the temperature of the drink. When the pressure exceeds 3.2 atm the can will explode.

Write a program to print the pressure inside the can for the temperature rising in one degree steps from 15 °C until the can explodes.

6.15   In a simple simulation of a lunar lander, the downward speed V at time $T + 1$ seconds is related to the speed at time T by the expression:

$$V(T + 1) = V(T) + 5 - F$$

where the number 5 allows for the acceleration due to gravity, and F is the number of units of fuel burnt in that second. The height H of the lander above the moon's surface changes according to the equation

$$H(T + 1) = H(T) - V(T)$$

Write a program to implement this simple simulation. The lander starts at a height of 200 units, and the user may choose every second how much fuel to burn (between 0 and 10 units). The user should try to achieve a soft landing (which means having a speed of less than 10 units when H first drops below zero) using the minimum total quantity of fuel.

Your program should print an appropriate message when the lander reaches ground level!

An introduction to arrays

In scientific and engineering computing it is commonly necessary to manipulate ordered sets of values, such as vectors and matrices. There is also a common requirement in many applications to repeat the same sequence of operations on successive sets of data.

In order to handle both of these requirements, Fortran provides extensive facilities for grouping a set of items of the same type as an array which can be operated on either as an object in its own right, or by reference to each of its individual elements.

This chapter explains the principles of Fortran 90's array processing features. These are considerably more powerful than those of any other programming language, and include the construction of array-valued constants, the input and output of arrays, the use of arrays as arguments to procedures, and the returning of an array as the result of a function. For ease of comprehension, the description in this chapter is restricted to arrays having one subscript only; arrays having more than one subscript will be discussed in Chapter 13.

7.1 The array concept

In all that we have said so far, and in all the programs we have written, we have used one name to refer to one location in the computer's memory. However there are a great many situations when we should like to repeat a sequence of operations on a set of related entities, either by repeating the statements in a loop and having the computer use different variables for each iteration, or by simply referring to a complete set and instructing the computer to carry out the same operations on each item in the set.

One way to do this would be to have a group, or **array**, of locations in the memory, all of which are identified by the same name but with an index, or **subscript**, to identify individual locations. Figure 7.1 illustrates this concept, using the same types of boxes as were originally used in Chapter 1 to introduce the concept of named memory locations.

In this example the whole set of n boxes is called A, but within the set we can identify individual boxes by their position within the complete set. Mathematicians are familiar with this concept and refer to an ordered set like this as the *vector* A, and to the individual elements as $A_1, A_2, \ldots A_n$.

In Fortran we call such an ordered set of related variables, which have the same name and type, an **array**, and we refer to the individual items within the array as **array elements**. In Fortran, we cannot use the exact mathematical notation for a subscript to identify these elements (although we do borrow the name); instead we follow the name of the array by an identifying *integer* value enclosed in parentheses:

```
A(1), A(2), ..., A(n)
```

More precisely, an array element is defined by writing the name of the array followed by a subscript, where the subscript consists of an integer

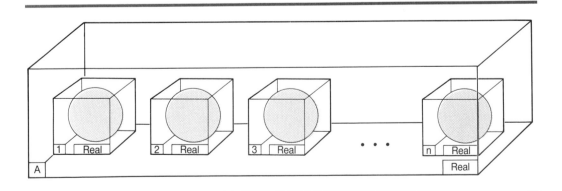

Figure 7.1 An array of memory locations.

expression (known as the **subscript expression**) enclosed in parentheses. Thus, if
x, **y** and **z** are arrays, of any type, and **i**, **j** and **k** are integer variables, then the
following are all valid ways of writing an array element:

```
x(10)
y(i+4)
z(3*i+MAX(i,j,k))
x(INT(y(i)*z(j)+x(k)))
```

Notice that function references are allowed as part of the subscript expression, as
are array elements (including elements of the same array).

7.2 Array declarations

Up to this point all the variables that we have used have been **scalar variables**,
and the declaration of such a variable (or its first use if implicit typing is being used) has
caused the compiler to allocate an appropriate storage unit to contain its value.
When we declare an **array variable**, however, the compiler will need to allocate
several storage units, and the form of the declaration must be modified to provide
information about the size of the array, and hence the number of storage units
that will be required.

There are two ways of doing this, using either a **dimension attribute** or
an **array specification** applied to the variable name.

Let us consider, for example, a situation in which we require three real
arrays, each containing 50 elements. The easiest way to declare these is as
follows:

```
REAL, DIMENSION(50) :: a,b,c
```

This informs the compiler that each of the three variables specified is an array
having 50 elements. The alternative approach is to provide the dimension
information with the variable name:

```
REAL :: a(50),b(50),c(50)
```

In a similar way to that used in declaring the length of character variables,
the two forms may be combined in a single declaration statement, in which case
the value specified in the dimension attribute applies to all variables which do not
have their own array specification:

```
REAL, DIMENSION(50) :: a,b,c,x(20),y(20),z
```

As with character lengths, however, we recommend that you should always write
a separate declaration for arrays of different sizes:

```
REAL, DIMENSION(50) :: a,b,c,z
REAL, DIMENSION(20) :: x,y
```

By default the subscripts will start at 1, but if we wish the subscripts to have a different range of values then we may, instead, provide the **lower bound** and the **upper bound** explicitly, separated by a colon:

```
REAL, DIMENSION(11:60) :: a,b,c
REAL, DIMENSION(-20:-1) :: x
REAL, DIMENSION(-9:10) :: y
REAL, DIMENSION(0:49) :: z
```

Notice that both negative and zero subscript values are allowed, and that the *sizes* of the six arrays declared in this declaration are identical to those declared in the earlier declaration; only their *bounds* are different.

At this point we must mention five technical terms that are of great importance when discussing arrays in Fortran.

- Although all the arrays that have been discussed so far have only had one subscript, Fortran permits up to seven subscripts, each of which relates to one **dimension** of the array. For each dimension there are two bounds which define the range of values that are permitted for the corresponding subscript, the lower bound and the upper bound.

- The number of permissible subscripts for a particular array is called its **rank**.

- The **extent** of a dimension is the number of elements in that dimension, and is equal to the difference between the upper and lower bounds for that dimension plus one.

- The **size** of the array is the total number of elements which make up the array; this is, of course, the same as the extent for a rank-one array.

- Finally, the **shape** of an array is determined by its rank and the extent of each dimension; it is possible to store the shape of any array in a rank-one array where the value of each element represents the extent of the corresponding dimension.

In this chapter we shall only consider rank-one arrays, since this is sufficient for many purposes and will enable us to appreciate many of the particular features of Fortran's array processing facilities without undue complexity. Chapter 13 will then build on this knowledge and experience to discuss the full range of array features.

An array declared in the way shown in the above examples is called an **explicit-shape array** because its bounds are declared explicitly. As we shall see later in this chapter and in Chapter 13, there are other forms of array which do not need explicit declaration of the bounds. For the present, we shall also assume

```
PROGRAM array_or_function
   IMPLICIT NONE
   REAL,DIMENSION(10) :: first    ! first is an array
   REAL :: second                 ! second is not an array
   INTEGER :: i
   REAL :: first_i,second_i
   .
   .
   .
   first_i = first(i)
   second_i = second(i)
   .
   .
   .
END PROGRAM array_or_function
```

Figure 7.2 Array and function references.

that the bounds are constant, although Section 7.7 will discuss situations in which this restriction may be lifted.

Although the primary reason for declaring an array is to enable the compiler to allocate sufficient storage space, there is also another reason which arises from the fact that an array reference and a function reference look the same. A Fortran compiler, just like a human reader, can only tell which is intended by looking at the specification statements and seeing whether a dimension attribute has been specified. This can be illustrated by considering the program extract shown in Figure 7.2.

It can clearly be seen that the two executable statements have exactly the same form in every way, and that the only way of determining what is intended is by noting that the declaration for **first** includes a dimension attribute, while that for **second** does not. The first executable statement therefore assigns the value of the array element **first(i)** to the variable **first_i**. Since there is no dimension attribute specified for **second** the second executable statement is assumed to refer to a real external function **second**, and the compiler will insert the appropriate instructions to transfer control to the function **second** with the actual argument being specified by **i**; the value returned by the function will then be assigned to the variable **second_i**. It is not unknown, therefore, for missing array declarations to result in misleading error messages about missing functions!

7.3 Array constants and initial values

Before we examine how to use arrays we must establish how an array constant is defined. Since an array consists of a number of array elements it is necessary to provide values for each of these elements by means of an **array constructor**. In its simplest form an array constructor consists of a list of values enclosed between special delimiters, the first of which consists of the two characters (/ and the second of the two characters /) :

```
(/ value_1,value_2, ... /)
```

If **arr** is an integer array of size 10, its elements could therefore be set to the values 1, 2, ..., 10 by the following statement:

```
arr = (/ 1,2,3,4,5,6,7,8,9,10 /)
```

This is perfectly satisfactory for a small array, but what if the array had been 500 elements in size? To deal with this situation, as well as for the general, and very common, situation in which an array constant is required which has some regular pattern, we can use an **implied** DO. This is a special syntax used with arrays in a number of situations which uses the DO loop counting control mechanism to step through a set of values and/or array elements. It takes the general form

```
(value_list,implied_do_control)
```

where the *implied_do_control* takes exactly the same structure as the DO variable control specification in a DO statement. Thus the assignment statement shown above for the array **arr** could also be written in the more compact, and less error-prone, form

```
arr = (/ (i,i=1,10) /)
```

An implied DO element does not have to appear on its own, and may be freely mixed with single constants, or other implied DO elements, in the overall list of values which make up an array constructor. For example, the following array constructor defines the sequence of 50 values which are all zero except for the first, which take the values −1, and the last, which takes the value 1:

```
(/ -1,(0,i=2,49),1 /)
```

Note that the values of i in this example are only used for counting and that using the values from 2 to 49 is simply to emphasize to the human reader which elements will have zero values. We could equally well have written

```
(/ -1,(0,i=1,48),1 /)
```

or even, somewhat confusingly,

```
(/ -1,(0,i=37,84),1 /)
```

Although the above examples only have a single item in the list of values controlled by the implied DO, there may be as many as required, including other (nested) implied DO elements if necessary. Thus the following array constructor defines a sequence of 100 values which are all zero apart from every tenth value, which takes the value of its position in the list:

```
(/ ((0,i=1,9),10*j,j=1,10) /)
```

The list of values in an array constructor must contain exactly the same number of values as the size of the array to which it is being assigned in either an assignment statement or in an initial value assignment in the array declaration statement:

```
INTEGER, DIMENSION(50)  :: an_array = (/ (0, i=1,50) /)
INTEGER, DIMENSION(100) :: another_array = &
         (/ ((0,i=1,9),10*j,j=1,10) /)
```

The first of these two initial value declarations can, in fact, be further simplified, as we shall see in Section 7.5 when we examine the way in which arrays are used in expressions and assignment statements.

7.4   Input and output with arrays

Before we can start to use arrays in our programs, however, we must be able to input data to arrays and output results from arrays. There are three possibilities here, depending upon whether we wish to refer to individual array elements, to groups of array elements, or to complete arrays.

- Array elements are treated in just the same way as scalar variables, and so need no further discussion.
- An array name may appear in an input or output list, in which case it refers to the whole array.
- Part of an array may be identified in an input or output list by use of an implied DO in a similar manner to the way that this feature is used in an array constructor. In this case, the item in the input or output list takes the form

    (*object_list*,*implied_do_control*)

Thus, for example, the following statement would output the odd-numbered elements of the array **p** whose subscripts lie in the range 1 to 99, followed by the third and fourth elements of the array **q** and the whole of the array **r**:

```
PRINT *,(p(i),i=1,99,2),q(3),q(4),r
```

One point to note is that it is permitted for one or more of the controlling values for an implied DO in an input statement to be themselves input by the same statement:

```
READ *,first,last,(arr(i),i=first,last)
```

This form of input statement must, however, be used with care, for it opens the door to a frequent cause of errors. Consider, for example, what would happen if the value read for **first** was less than the lower bound of the array **arr**, or if the value read for **last** was more than the upper bound. The READ statement would read these values and then, under the control of the implied DO list, would read sufficient data to occupy the array elements **arr(first)** to **arr(last)**. Unfortunately, checking that the subscript value is within the defined bounds is a time-consuming task and many compilers will only insert the code for such checking into the compiled program upon request, for example during testing. If such checking is absent or inactive the program will store the input values in consecutive storage units starting at what it believes to be **arr(first)**, even if this involves using other memory locations which are not part of the array **arr**!

The fact that these memory locations have been overwritten may not be immediately apparent, and the subsequent incorrect results and/or program

```
PROGRAM array_input
   IMPLICIT NONE
   INTEGER,PARAMETER :: lower=-50,upper=50
   INTEGER :: first,last,i
   REAL,DIMENSION(lower:upper) :: arr
   .
   .
   .
   READ *,first,last
   IF (first>=lower .AND. last<=upper) THEN
      READ *,(arr(i),i=first,last)
   ELSE
      PRINT *,'Invalid array subscript specification!'
   .
   .
   .
   END IF
   .
   .
   .
END PROGRAM array_input
```

Figure 7.3 A safe way of reading data with an implied DO.

failure can be very difficult to identify. In order to guard against this possibility it is often preferable first to read the controlling information and check that it is acceptable before reading the full set of data. Figure 7.3 shows one way in which this might be done for the case shown above.

7.5 Using arrays and array elements in expressions and assignments

An array element can be used anywhere that a scalar variable can be used. In exactly the same way as a scalar variable, it identifies a unique location in the memory to which a value can be assigned or input, and whose value may be used in an expression or output list, etc. The great advantage is that by altering the value of the array element's subscript it can be made to refer to a different location.

The use of array variables within a loop therefore greatly increases the power and flexibility of a program. This can be seen in Figure 7.4, where a short

```
PROGRAM survey_analysis
   IMPLICIT NONE
   TYPE person
      CHARACTER(LEN=12) :: first_name, middle_initial*1, &
                           last_name
      INTEGER :: age
      CHARACTER :: sex     ! M/F
      CHARACTER(LEN=11) :: social_security
      REAL :: height, weight
   END TYPE person
   INTEGER, PARAMETER :: max_people=100
   INTEGER :: i
   TYPE(person),DIMENSION(max_people) :: individual
   .
   .
   .
   DO i=1,max_people
      READ *,individual(i)
      IF (individual(i)%age) < 0) EXIT   ! age<0 ends data
   END DO
   .
   .
   .
END PROGRAM survey_analysis
```

Figure 7.4 Inputting data to an array.

loop enables up to 100 sets of survey data to be input *and stored* for subsequent analysis in a way which is not otherwise possible.

In FORTRAN 77, and most other programming languages, this is the only way that arrays can be used in most types of operations. However Fortran 90 enables an array to be treated as a single *object* in its own right, in much the same way as a scalar object. We have already used this fact when we assigned an array constant to an array variable in the previous section with a statement of the form

array_name = (/ *list of values* /)

and we should now establish the rules for working with whole arrays.

- Two arrays are **conformable** if they have the same shape
- A scalar, including a constant, is conformable with any array
- All intrinsic operations are defined between two conformable objects

When two conformable arrays are the operands in an intrinsic operation then the operation is carried out on an element-by-element basis. Thus the following code fragment will result in the arrays **a** and **b** having identical values:

```
    .
    .
    .
REAL, DIMENSION(20) :: a,b,c,d
    .
    .
    .
a = c*d                 ! Fortran 90 array processing

DO i=1,20               ! FORTRAN 77 style
  b(i) = c(i)*d(i)      ! array manipulation
END DO
    .
    .
    .
```

It is immediately obvious that the Fortran 90 style is much easier to read than the earlier FORTRAN 77 style, as well as avoiding the need for the extraneous DO loop variable, i.

An important point to notice is that the rule is that the *shapes* of two arrays must be the same for them to be conformable. This means that the arrays must have the same rank (that is, the same number of dimensions) and the same extent in each dimension. It does *not* mean that the range of the subscripts need be the same. The importance of this can be seen from Figure 7.5, which shows exactly the same program fragment as that above, except that the bounds of the four arrays are all different, even though their extents are the same. Here the advantage of the Fortran 90 array processing capability becomes really apparent!

```
      .
      .
      .
REAL :: a(1:20),b(0:19),c(10:29),d(-9,10)
      .
      .
      .
a = c*d                      ! Fortran 90 style
DO i=1,20                    ! FORTRAN 77 style
   b(i-1) = c(i+9)*d(i-10)
END DO
      .
      .
      .
```

Figure 7.5 Fortran 90 array processing.

The rule that a scalar is conformable with any array means that we can write statements such as

    array_1 = 10*array_2

which will cause every element of the array **array_1**, whatever its shape, to be assigned a value 10 times the corresponding element of the array **array_2**, as long as its shape is the same as that of **array_1**. Furthermore, it means that the statement

    arr = 0

will set every element of the array **arr** to zero, regardless of its rank and size. In particular, this means that all the elements of an array may be initialized to zero in exactly the same way as for scalar variables:

    REAL :: a=0.0, b=0.0
    REAL, DIMENSION(50) :: c=0.0, d=0.0

7.6 Using intrinsic procedures with arrays

The Fortran intrinsic procedure library, as we have already seen, contains a considerable number of functions and subroutines which are of great importance in many programming situations. A particularly valuable aspect of the Fortran 90 array processing facilities is that of **elemental intrinsic procedures**, whereby arrays may be used as arguments to many of the intrinsic procedures in just the same way that scalars are. If an elemental function has an array as an argument then the result of the function reference will be an array with the same shape as the argument. Thus the statement

```
array_1 = SIN(array_2)
```

assigns the sine of each element of the array **array_2** to each corresponding element of the array **array_1**. Where an intrinsic function has more than one argument then they must all be conformable, as we would expect. Thus the statement

```
arr_max = MAX(100.0,a,b,c,d,e)
```

will assign to the elements of **arr_max** the maximum value of the corresponding elements of the arrays **a**, **b**, **c**, **d** and **e**, or 100.0 if that is greater, as long as the five arrays are all conformable; the scalar value 100.0 is, of course, conformable with any array.

All of the intrinsic functions which it might be reasonable to expect to work with either array-valued or scalar arguments are elemental, so that, in particular, the wide range of mathematical functions may be applied equally to array or scalar arguments.

There are also two elemental intrinsic subroutines which can take either scalar or array arguments, **MVBITS** and **RANDOM_NUMBER**. The list of all intrinsic procedures in Appendix A indicates, among other things, which ones are elemental.

SELF-TEST EXERCISES 7.1

1   What is an array? What is an array element?

2   What is the difference between an array variable and a scalar variable?

3   How is an array specification written? What is the difference between a dimension attribute and an array specification?

4   What (if any) are the constraints on a subscript expression?

5   What are the rank, extent, size and shape of an array?

6   Write declarations for suitable arrays in which to store the following sets of data:

   (a)   The information collected in an (anonymous) survey of people attending a meeting of Gamblers Anonymous. Each person is asked how much they earn each week, how many times they go gambling each week, how much they lose on average each week gambling, what is their largest single win, what is their largest single loss, and how many weeks they have been a gambling addict.

(b) The data collected in an experiment in which a sample piece of metal (or other material) is fixed in a device which then allows it to be repeatedly hit by a mass of variable weight (but fixed for each experiment) dropped from a specified height until the sample fractures. The mass, height and number of blows are recorded.

(c) The heights above a base plane at various points on the surface of a three-dimensional model.

(d) The temperature at 6 a.m., noon, 6 p.m. and midnight on each day of a year, and the number of days on which the noon temperature was below $-10\,°C$, was exactly $10\,°C$, $-9\,°C$, $-8\,°C$, ... $+30\,°C$, and was over $30\,°C$.

7   What is an array constructor?

8   What is an implied DO? How is one used with an array constructor?

9   What are the differences (if any) between input and output to and from arrays and input and output to and from scalars?

10   What differences are allowed between an implied DO used in an array constructor, and an implied DO used in a READ statement?

11   What is meant by the statement that two arrays are conformable?

12   What is the particular importance of conformable objects?

13   How can arrays be used in expressions?

14   What is an elemental procedure?

7.7   Arrays and procedures

So far, all the array declarations that we have used have had constant bounds. However, the requirement for constant bounds would cause a great many difficulties when working with procedures, as can readily be seen by examining the situation that arises if we wish to use an array as an argument to a procedure, for how can we declare the dummy argument array in the procedure when we do not know any details about the size or shape of the actual arguments that may be used in references to the procedure?

As we saw in Chapter 4, one of the most important aspects of the argument-passing mechanism is that the procedure does not need to know the details of the calling program unit, and that program unit, in turn, does not need to know anything about the procedure except the information about its arguments which form part of the procedure's interface. It would make no sense at all for the bounds of a dummy argument array to be fixed, and for all arrays passed as actual arguments to be required to have the same bounds!

One solution to this is the **assumed-shape array**.

An assumed-shape array is a dummy argument array whose shape, as its name implies, is not known but which *assumes* the same shape as that of any actual argument that becomes associated with it. The shape of an array, as we have already seen, is defined by its rank and the extent of each of its dimensions, but since we are only concerned with rank-one arrays at present we need only consider the extent.

The array specification for an assumed shape array can take one of two forms:

(*lower_bound*:)

or, simply

(:)

The second form is equivalent to the first with a lower bound equal to 1. In both cases the upper bound will only be established on entry to the procedure, and will be whatever value is necessary to ensure that the extent of the dummy array is the same as that of the actual array argument. An example will make this clear.

Let us consider a subroutine which starts with the following statements:

```
SUBROUTINE array_example(dummy_array_1,dummy_array_2)
   IMPLICIT NONE
   REAL, DIMENSION(:) :: dummy_array_1,dummy_array_2
   .
   .
   .
```

If this subroutine is called from a program unit which contains the declarations

```
REAL,DIMENSION(10:30) :: a,b
```

by the statement

```
CALL array_example(a,b)
```

then the two dummy argument arrays will both have lower bounds of 1 and upper bounds of 21. If it is subsequently called from another program unit (or even from the same one) which contains the declarations

```
REAL :: p(-5:5),q(100)
```

by the statement

```
CALL array_example(p,q)
```

then on this occasion both dummy argument arrays will have a lower bound of 1, while the upper bound of **dummy_array_1** will be 11 and the upper bound of **dummy_array_2** will be 100.

One very important point must be made here. In Section 4.9 we stated that there are some situations in which the calling program unit *must* have full details about the interface of the called procedure, in other words the procedure must have an *explicit interface* available at the point of the call. A call or reference to a procedure which has an assumed-shape dummy argument is one of those situations. We have already recommended that, at least for the time being, all procedures should be placed in a module to avoid this problem, and until we meet an alternative solution in Section 11.2 it is *essential* that any procedures having assumed-shape dummy arguments are treated in this way.

For many purposes this may be all that is needed, but there will also be occasions when it will be necessary for the procedure to know the size and/or the bounds of its dummy argument arrays. To resolve this problem there are three intrinsic procedures available to provide the necessary information. These are designed to work with arrays of any rank, and we may specify them in a slightly simplified form as long as we are only dealing with rank-one arrays; a complete specification will be given in Chapter 13. For a rank-one array argument **arr** the three procedures are used as follows:

- **SIZE**(*arr*)   returns the size of the rank-one array *arr*
- **LBOUND**(*arr*,1)   returns the lower bound of the rank-one array *arr*
- **UBOUND**(*arr*,1)   returns the upper bound of the rank-one array *arr*

The second argument for **LBOUND** and **UBOUND** specifies that the value returned is to be the lower or upper bound for the first dimension (the only one for a rank-one array) and must be present, even though its value is always 1 for a rank-one array.

■ **EXAMPLE 7.1**

1 **Problem**

Write a subroutine which will sort a set of names into alphabetical order.

2 **Analysis**

The need to sort data into numerical or alphabetical order is a very common one in many computer programs, and is a need which is easily satisfied with the tools

Initial order		⑦	①	8	4	6	3	5	2
After first exchange		1	⑦	8	4	6	3	5	②
After second exchange		1	2	⑧	4	6	③	5	7
After third exchange		1	2	3	④	6	8	5	7
After fourth exchange		1	2	3	4	⑥	8	⑤	7
After fifth exchange		1	2	3	4	5	⑧	⑥	7
After sixth exchange		1	2	3	4	5	6	⑧	⑦
After seventh exchange		1	2	3	4	5	6	7	8

Figure 7.6 Sorting by straight selection.

we now have at our disposal. Sorting is a subject into which much research has been carried out over many years; however, for our purposes a simple general-purpose sorting method will suffice. If small amounts of data are to be sorted it is perfectly adequate; but if large amounts are to be sorted one of many specialist sorting methods, such as Quicksort or Pigeon Sort, should be used.

We shall investigate the method of **straight selection** because it is reasonably efficient and easy to understand. Essentially the method involves searching through all the items to be sorted and finding the one which is to go at the head of the sorted list. This is then *exchanged* with the item currently at the head of the list. The process is then repeated, starting immediately after the item just sorted into its correct place, and so on. Each time, one more item is moved to its correct place. Figure 7.6 shows the progress of such a sort, in which eight numbers are sorted so that the lowest is on the left and the highest is on the right. The two numbers to be exchanged at each stage are circled, although it should be noted that the fourth exchange does not actually take place because the number at the head is already in the correct place.

This is quite a simple method to code in Fortran, but before planning the logic we must first consider how the data to be sorted will be provided, and how the sorted list of names will be returned. The major question to be decided is whether the original data is to be sorted, or whether a copy is to be made and sorted so that the data is also available in its original order. A third possibility, which we shall briefly discuss later, is to leave the original data unchanged but to provide a sorted **index array** which can be used to access the data in alphabetical order. For this example, however, we shall simply re-order the original data.

We can now prepare our data design and structure plan:

Data design

Purpose	Type	Name
A Argument		
Array of names to be sorted	CHARACTER*(*)	name(:)
B Local variables		
Number of items to be sorted	INTEGER	number
First name on this pass	CHARACTER*n [n = LEN(name)]	first
Subscript of first name	INTEGER	index
Temp for swapping names	CHARACTER*n	temp
DO variables	INTEGER	i, j

Structure plan

Subroutine alpha_sort(*name*)

1 Repeat for *i* from 1 to *number* − 1
    1.1 Save *i* and *name(i)* as current 'earliest' name
    1.2 Repeat for *j* from *i* + 1 to *number*
        1.2.1 If *name(j)* is 'earlier' than current 'earliest' store it and its index
    1.3 If step 1.2 found an 'earlier' name swap with *name(i)*

3 **Solution**

```
SUBROUTINE alpha_sort(name)
   IMPLICIT NONE

   ! A subroutine to sort the contents of the array name into
   ! alphabetic order
   ! THIS SUBROUTINE MUST HAVE AN EXPLICIT INTERFACE WHERE CALLED

   ! Dummy argument
   CHARACTER(LEN=*),DIMENSION(:),INTENT(INOUT) :: name

   ! Local variables
   CHARACTER(LEN=LEN(name)) :: first,temp
   INTEGER :: number,index,i,j

   ! Set number to the number of names to be sorted
   number = SIZE(name)

   ! Loop to sort number-1 names into order
   DO i=1,number-1

      ! Initialize earliest so far to be the first in this pass
      first = name(i)
      index = i
```

```
      ! Search remaining (unsorted items) for earliest one
      DO j=i+1,number
         IF (name(j) < first) THEN    ! An earlier one has been
            first = name(j)           ! found, so save it
            index = j                 ! and its position
         END IF
      END DO

      IF (index /= i) THEN            ! An earlier name was found
         temp = name(i)               ! so exchange it with the
         name(i) = name(index)        ! 'head' of the list
         name(index) = temp
      END IF
   END DO


END SUBROUTINE alpha_sort
```

Notice, in particular, that this subroutine can be written without any knowledge of either the length of the character strings being sorted, because the array **name** is declared with assumed length, or the number of items being sorted, because it is an assumed-shape array.

The length *is* needed for the declaration of the two temporary character variables **first**, which is used to store the current earliest name on each iteration, and **temp**, which is used for temporary storage when two names are being exchanged. It is obtained by use of the intrinsic function **LEN** applied to the dummy array **name**.

The number of items to be sorted is required in order to control how many times the two loops are to be obeyed, and is obtained by use of the intrinsic function **SIZE**. It should be noted, however, that this will return the number of *elements* in the actual argument associated with the dummy argument array **name**; if the actual argument array is not full with data to be sorted then the value returned will not, in fact, be the number of items to be sorted. An easy way round this problem would be to provide the number of items to be sorted as a second argument. However a more elegant way is to use an **array section** in the calling program unit to pass only that part of the array which is to be sorted. We shall discuss the use of array sections in Chapter 13.

Finally, note that the array argument **name** is declared to have **INTENT(INOUT)** since the array must be defined with a set of values before entry to the subroutine (as otherwise there would be nothing to sort!), but it is also used to return the sorted array. If it was required to keep the original order as well as having a sorted array then a slightly modified version of the subroutine might have two array arguments, one with **INTENT(IN)** and the other with **INTENT(OUT)**.

One problem with an assumed-shape array, however, is that only the shape of the dummy argument array is known, and hence the extent in each dimension, but not the bounds of the actual argument array. Frequently this does not matter, but if the bounds are required then we may use an *explicit-shape array*, but with the bounds supplied though other arguments, or by some other means.

In the simplest case this might take the form:

```
SUBROUTINE explicit(a,b,lower,upper)
   IMPLICIT NONE
   INTEGER,INTENT(IN) :: lower,upper
   REAL,DIMENSION(lower:upper),INTENT(IN) :: a,b
   .
   .
   .
```

However, it is not necessary for the relevant values to be provided by means of a dummy argument if they can be provided in some other way, for example in a module:

```
SUBROUTINE explicit_2(a,b)
   USE database      ! This module includes the lower
                     ! and upper bounds of a large group
                     ! of arrays, including a and b
                     ! These are called lower and upper
   IMPLICIT NONE
   REAL,DIMENSION(lower:upper),INTENT(IN) :: a,b
   .
   .
   .
```

There are a number of other ways in which the bounds might be made available, such as by host association (see Chapter 11), or in a **COMMON** block (see Chapter 17). Whatever the means by which they are made available, or values from which they may be calculated are made available, the bounds are determined using the values that the relevant variables had *on entry to the procedure*, and any subsequent change in their value has no effect on the array bounds.

In Example 7.1 we created two temporary variables in which to save information during (part of) the execution of the procedure, but whose values were not required outside the procedure. Where there is a requirement for scalar variables of this type there is no problem, but if a local array is required for the duration of the execution of the procedure, how do we know what size to declare it? It cannot be declared as an assumed-shape array, since these must be dummy argument arrays. However, there is a special form of explicit-shape array, known as an **automatic array**, which is provided for this precise purpose.

An automatic array is an explicit-shape array which is *not* a dummy argument array, and whose bounds, or the information necessary to calculate the bounds, are made available through dummy arguments, by use association from a module, or by any other means which can provide the necessary information at the time of entry to the procedure. An automatic array is declared, therefore, in a very similar manner to an explicit-shape array which has non-constant bounds, except that the automatic array is not a dummy argument.

It is important to emphasize that there are only three situations in which an explicit-shape array may have non-constant bounds:

- if the array is a dummy argument of a procedure
- if the array is an automatic array in a procedure
- if the array is the result of a function

We have met the first two of these cases in this section; the third will be discussed in the next section.

There is one further type of dummy argument array which is known as an **assumed-size array**, and which was the only form of non-constant array in earlier versions of Fortran apart from an explicit-shape dummy array argument with variable bounds. For a rank-one array the declaration of an assumed-size array takes the form:

```
INTEGER,DIMENSION(*) :: as_size_arr_1
```

or

```
INTEGER :: as_size_arr_2(*)
```

For rank-one arrays, whose shapes are, in effect, the same as their sizes, there is little significant difference between an assumed-shape array and an assumed-size array. However, when we investigate the use of more sophisticated arrays in Chapter 13 it will be apparent that the assumed-size array is far less useful than the assumed-shape array.

We strongly recommend that you do not use assumed-size arrays in any new programs.

7.8   Array-valued functions

We have now met most of the ways in which arrays can be passed to procedures as arguments, and in which a subroutine can return information by means of an array. However, it would often be convenient for a function to return its result in the form of an array of values, rather than as a single scalar value. Such a function is called an **array-valued** function.

There is one important difference between the initial statement of an array-valued function and the initial statements of the functions that we have been writing up to now, namely that the type of an array-valued function is not specified in the initial **FUNCTION** statement, but in a type declaration in the body of the function, which must also specify the appropriate dimension attribute:

```
FUNCTION name(...)
   IMPLICIT NONE
   REAL, DIMENSION(dim) :: name
     .
     .
     .
```

The type declaration for *name* is, of course, actually a type declaration for the result variable and this may be an explicit-shape array, including an automatic array, without any difficulty. Thus, for example, the following function will return an array which is the same size as its dummy argument *arr*:

```
FUNCTION name(arr,...)
   IMPLICIT NONE
   REAL, DIMENSION(:) :: arr
   REAL, DIMENSION(SIZE(arr)) :: name
     .
     .
     .
```

It is, of course, the responsibility of the program unit which references this function to ensure that its result is assigned to a large enough array. Although it is not a requirement, the result variable of an array-valued function will usually be an automatic array, linked to the size of one or more of its dummy arguments.

Note, however, that the result of an array-valued function cannot be an assumed-shape array because, as was stated in Section 7.7, such arrays must be dummy arguments. Nevertheless, it is possible to achieve the same effect in another way.

Let us first consider a trivial subroutine which simply adds two arrays together, returning the result through a third dummy argument array:

```
SUBROUTINE trivial_sub(a,b,c)
   IMPLICIT NONE
   REAL,DIMENSION(:),INTENT(OUT) :: a
   REAL,DIMENSION(:),INTENT(IN) :: b,c
   a = b+c
END SUBROUTINE trivial_sub
```

In this situation all three dummy argument arrays are assumed-shape arrays and the result will be returned through the dummy argument **c**, whose shape (the extent in this rank-one case) is determined by the corresponding actual argument.

It would seem more natural to write this procedure as a function, but although we can still have two assumed-shape dummy arguments, what about the result array variable? The answer in this case is that, since it must be conformable with the two dummy arguments in order for the assignment to take place, we can use their shape in the declaration of the result variable:

```
FUNCTION trivial_fun(x,y)
  IMPLICIT NONE
  REAL,DIMENSION(:),INTENT(IN) :: x,y
  REAL,DIMENSION(SIZE(x)) :: trivial_fun
  trivial_fun = x+y
END FUNCTION trivial_fun
```

Note that since all three arrays **x**, **y** and the result array variable **trivial_fun** must be conformable they must all have the same size and it does not matter which of the two dummy arguments is referred to in the array specification for **trivial_fun**. Of course, if this function was being written for other than demonstration purposes it would be advisable to check that the two arrays were conformable by means of a statement such as

```
IF (SIZE(x) /= SIZE(y)) THEN
  ! Take appropriate error action
  .
  .
  .
```

In most cases where an array-valued function, of varying size or shape, is required there will be at least one dummy argument which can be used to provide the information necessary for the declaration of result array variable.

Although the concept of an array-valued function is a very straightforward one, it was not available in earlier versions of Fortran because they did not allow any whole-array operations, and without the ability to assign a whole array an array-valued function could not have been used!

■ EXAMPLE 7.2

1 Problem

Write a function which takes two real arrays as its arguments and returns an array in which each element is the maximum of the two corresponding elements in the input arrays.

2 Analysis

This is a very simple exercise which only requires a very simple data design and structure plan. The only complication would be if the two input arrays were of different sizes; however, we shall ignore this and assume that they have identical bounds:

Data design

	Purpose	Type	Name
A	Dummy arguments Input arrays	REAL(:)	array_1, array_2
B	Local variables Result variable	REAL(:)	max_array

Structure plan

> **1** Repeat for each element of input *array_1*
>   **1.1** *max_array*(*i*) = maximum of *array_1*(*i*) and *array_2*(*i*)

3 Solution

```
FUNCTION max_array(array_1,array_2)
   IMPLICIT NONE

   ! This function returns the maximum of two arrays on an
   ! element by element basis

   ! Dummy arguments
   REAL, DIMENSION(:) :: array_1,array_2

   ! Result variable
   REAL, DIMENSION(SIZE(array_1)) :: max_array

   ! Use the elemental intrinsic MAX to compare elements
   max_array = MAX(array_1,array_2)

END FUNCTION max_array
```

Note that the use of the intrinsic function **MAX** in an elemental fashion avoids the need to write a loop of the form

```
DO i=1,SIZE(array_1)
   max_array(i) = MAX(array_1(i),array_2(i))
END DO
```

7.9 Arrays as components of derived types

When we introduced the derived type concept in Chapter 3 we simply stated that the definitions of the various components took a similar form to the declaration of variables of the same type. As we might expect, therefore, we may include array-valued components in a derived type definition:

```
TYPE golfer
   CHARACTER(LEN=15) :: first_name,last_name
   INTEGER :: handicap,last_rounds(10)
END TYPE golfer
```

In this type definition the fourth component, **last_rounds**, is an array having bounds of 1 and 10, and will, presumably, be used to record the golfer's most recent scores.

It is important to fully understand the placing of the subscript expression in a reference to an element of an array component of an array object. If the details of the members of a golf club are to be held in an array declared as

```
TYPE(golfer),DIMENSION(250) :: member
```

then the last name of an individual golfer will be referred to as

```
member(i)%last_name
```

and the third of the golfer's last ten rounds will be referred to as

```
member(i)%last_rounds(3)
```

An array component of a derived type definition must be an explicit-shape array having constant bounds. It may also be a **deferred-shape array**, but further discussion of this last type of array will be left until Chapter 13.

One important restriction is that, in a reference to an object of a derived type having one, or more, array components, at most one array must have a rank greater than zero. In other words, all array components, except possibly one, must be subscripted. It is therefore permitted to write

```
member%last_rounds(i) = 72
```

in order to set the *i*th round for every member to 72, and it is permitted to write

```
member(j)%last_rounds = 72
```

in order to set every round for the *j*th member to 72. However, the statement

```
member%last_rounds =72      ! ILLEGAL
```

is not allowed, because both **member** and **last_rounds** are rank-one arrays.

■ EXAMPLE 7.3

1 Problem

Write a function which will take as its arguments an array of type **golfer** (as defined above) and an array of golf scores for the same set of golfers. For each golfer, the function should move the golf scores in elements 1–9 of the **last_rounds** component to elements 2–10, and insert the new score in the first element. The function should then create an internal sorted list of the aggregate scores for the last five rounds, taking into account their handicaps, and should return as its result an array containing the names of the leading six members of the club over the last five rounds, and their average scores over those rounds, after taking into account their handicaps; this array is to be of type **competitor**, where this is defined in the same module, **golf_details**, as the type **golfer** and has two components – an index to the main list of members and the average score:

```
TYPE competitor
   INTEGER :: index,score
END TYPE competitor
```

Note (for non-golfers): In golf, each player has an official *handicap*, which is the number of strokes by which, in theory, the golfer is expected to exceed the *par*, or standard number of strokes, for a round of 18 holes. The net score is, therefore, obtained by subtracting the handicap from the actual number of strokes taken to complete the round. If everyone played exactly to their handicaps then all the net scores would be the same, but it isn't usually like that! In this example, in order to calculate the net scores for the last five rounds it will be necessary, therefore, to add the actual scores for the last five rounds together and then subtract five times the player's handicap. The leading player is, of course, the one with the lowest net total.

2 Analysis

This problem requires some simple manipulation of the elements of the array, followed by a sort of the arrays into ascending order of subtotals. As these are quite separate processes, however, it is preferable to carry each out in a separate procedure. An initial structure plan for the function might be as follows:

> 1 Call subroutine *update* to update the golfers' scores and return the aggregates for the last five rounds, allowing for handicaps
>
> 2 Call subroutine *sort* to sort golfers into order, based on their five-round aggregates
>
> 3 Store indexes to the six leading names and their scores in result array

A refinement would be to use an index array to the aggregate scores as an actual argument to the sorting subroutine, both to simplify the sorting and to provide exactly the form of result that will be required for the final result array.

The data design for this function is straightforward, and will use two automatic arrays for the aggregate totals and the index array:

Data design

Purpose	Type	Name
A Result:		
Array of six leading players	COMPETITOR	leaders(6)
B Arguments:		
Array of players and scores	GOLFER	members(:)
Array of recent scores	INTEGER	scores(:)
C Local variables		
Array of total scores	INTEGER	total(n)
		[n = SIZE(scores)]
Index array	INTEGER	index(n)
Number of players	INTEGER	number
DO variable	INTEGER	i

Structure plan

> Function leaders(*members,scores*)
>
> 1 Call *update* to update members' records and calculate aggregates
>
> 2 Create an index array to *members*
>
> 3 Call *sort* to sort index array into ascending order of totals
>
> 4 Return indexes and average scores for top six

The two subsidiary subroutines are both so straightforward that we shall not give further details, but will proceed to the solution.

3 **Solution**

```
FUNCTION leaders(members,scores)
   USE golf_details
   IMPLICIT NONE
```

```fortran
! A function to determine the leading golfers in a golf club

! Result and argument declarations
TYPE(competitor),DIMENSION(6) :: leaders
TYPE(golfer),DIMENSION(:),INTENT(IN) :: members
INTEGER,DIMENSION(:),INTENT(IN) :: scores

! Local variables
INTEGER,DIMENSION(SIZE(members)) :: total,member_index
INTEGER :: i, number
number = SIZE(members)

! Update golfers records and create array of aggregate
! scores for the last five rounds, allowing for handicaps
CALL update(members,scores,number,total)

! Set up initial index array
member_index = (/ (i,i=1,number) /)

! Sort index array to members and totals into ascending
! order of totals
CALL sort(total,member_index,number)

! Indexes sorted, so return first six
DO i=1,6
   leaders(i)%index = member_index(i)
   ! Round average scores
   leaders(i)%score = REAL(total(member_index(i)))/5.0 + 0.5
END DO

END FUNCTION leaders

SUBROUTINE update(members,scores,n,total)
   USE golf_details
   IMPLICIT NONE

   ! This subroutine updates the records of a set of golfers,
   ! and then creates an array of aggregate scores for their
   ! last five rounds, allowing for their individual handicaps

   ! Dummy arguments
   TYPE(golfer), DIMENSION(n), INTENT(IN) :: members
   INTEGER, DIMENSION(n), INTENT(IN) :: scores
   INTEGER, INTENT(IN) :: n
   INTEGER, DIMENSION(n), INTENT(OUT) :: total

   ! Local variable
   INTEGER :: i

   ! Move most recent 9 scores into last_rounds 2-10
   DO i=9,1,-1
     members%last_rounds(i+1) = members%last_rounds(i)
   END DO
```

```
      ! Insert latest scores into last_rounds(1)
      members%last_rounds(1) = scores


      ! Calculate aggregate scores allowing for handicap
      total = members%last_rounds(1) + &
              members%last_rounds(2) + &
              members%last_rounds(3) + &
              members%last_rounds(4) + &
              members%last_rounds(5) - 5*members%handicap


END SUBROUTINE update


SUBROUTINE sort(total,index,n)
   USE golf_details
   IMPLICIT NONE


   ! This subroutine sorts an index array to the array total


   ! Dummy arguments
   INTEGER, DIMENSION(n), INTENT(IN) :: total
   INTEGER, DIMENSION(n), INTENT(INOUT) :: index
   INTEGER, INTENT(IN) :: n


   ! Local variables
   INTEGER :: i,j,temp,first,i_first


   ! Sort index array into ascending order of aggregate scores
   DO i=1,n-1

      ! Initialize lowest so far to be first in this iteration
      first = total(index(i))
      i_first = i

      ! Search remaining unsorted items for lowest one
      DO j=i+1,n
         IF (total(index(j)) < first) THEN   ! A lower total has
            first = total(index(i))          ! been found, so
            i_first = j                      ! save it and index
         END IF
      END DO

      ! Exchange indexes if necessary
      IF (i_first /= i) THEN
         temp = index(i)
         index(i) = index(i_first)
         index(i_first) = temp
      END IF
   END DO


END SUBROUTINE sort
```

Note that the function declares two automatic arrays and then uses these as actual arguments to the two subsidiary procedures. In those procedures the corresponding dummy arguments are both declared as explicit-shape arrays, with the extent being passed as an argument from the calling procedure.

Note also that near the end of the subroutine **update** there is a rather lengthy summation of the members' last five rounds, while near the end of the function **leaders** a loop is used to calculate and store the averages for the leading six players. Both of these could be greatly simplified by use of the array sections that will be described in Chapter 13.

SELF-TEST EXERCISES 7.2

1   What is an assumed-shape array? When can one be used?

2   What are the advantages of an assumed-shape array over an explicit-shape array? What are the disadvantages?

3   What is an automatic array?

4   What are the three situations in which an explict-shape array may have non-constant bounds?

5   How is the type of an array-valued function declared? What restrictions (if any) are there on the form of the array that it may return as its value?

6   What are the restrictions (if any) on the inclusion of an array-valued component in a derived type definition?

SUMMARY

- An array is an ordered set of related variables which are referred to by a single name.

- The individual items in an array are called array elements.

- Array elements are identified by following the name of the array by an integer subscript expression, enclosed in parentheses.

- An array may have up to seven subscripts, each of which relates to one dimension of the array.

- Each dimension of an array has a lower and an upper bound which, together, define the range of allowable subscript values for that dimension.

- The number of permissible subscripts for an array is called its rank.

- The extent of a dimension is the number of elements in that dimension.

- The size of an array is the total number of elements in the array.

- The shape of an array is determined by its rank and the extent of each dimension.

- The declaration of an array must specify its rank and the bounds for each dimension.

- An explicit-shape array is an array whose bounds are specified explicitly.

- An assumed-shape array is a dummy array argument whose bounds are not specified in the declaration of the array, but which assumes the same shape as the corresponding actual array argument.

- An automatic array is an array in a procedure, which is not a dummy argument, which has non-constant bounds, and which obtains the information required to calculate its bounds from outside the procedure at the time of entering the procedure.

- An array-valued constant is specified by a structure constructor, which may include one or more implied DO elements.

- Input and output of arrays may be specified element-by-element, by whole arrays, or by use of an implied DO.

- Two arrays are conformable if they have the same shape; a scalar is conformable with any array.

- All intrinsic operators are defined for conformable arrays in addition to scalars.

- Intrinsic operations on arrays take place element-by-element.

- Many intrinsic procedures are elemental and may be used with array arguments to deliver array-valued results.

- An array valued function must have the bounds of the array-valued result variable declared in a type declaration statement within the body of the function subprogram.

- Derived type definitions may have arrays as components, provided that they are explicit-shape arrays having constant bounds.

- Fortran 90 syntax introduced in Chapter 7:

Array declaration

```
type, DIMENSION (extent) :: list of names
type, DIMENSION (extent) :: name_1, name_2 (extent) , . . .
type, DIMENSION (lower_bnd : upper_bnd) :: list of names
type, DIMENSION (lower_bnd :) :: list of names
type, DIMENSION (:) :: list of names
```

Array element	*array_name*(*integer_expression*)
Array constructor	(/ *list of values* /)
	(/ (*value_list*,*int_var*=*initial*,*final*,*inc*) /)
Array input/output	**READ** *,*array_element*,*array_name*
	PRINT *, (*array_element_list*,*int_var*=*initial*,*final*,*inc*)
	.
	.
	.
Whole array operations	**a = b*c**
	etc., where **a**, **b** and **c** are conformable arrays

PROGRAMMING EXERCISES

7.1 Write a program which will read up to 20 integer numbers and print them out in the reverse order to that in which they were typed.

7.2 The normal probability function ϕ is defined as:

$$\phi(x) = \frac{1}{\sqrt{2\pi}}\,e^{-x^2/2}$$

Write a program to evaluate $\phi(x)$ for values of x from -3.0 to $+3.0$ in steps of 0.2, and store these in an array. Display the results in a table, with five values to a line.

7.3 In a psychology experiment volunteers are asked to carry out ten simple tests, and a record is kept of which tests they pass and which they fail. This record consists of a one for a pass, and a zero for a fail.

Write a program which inputs the test results of a set of volunteers and prints the percentage of the volunteers who passed each test.

(Hint: Use an array of size ten in which to accumulate the passes.)

*7.4 Write a subroutine that has an explicit-shape array with variable bounds as one of its arguments, providing a set of angles (in radians) at which it is required to evaluate the sine of the angle. The subroutine should print a table of all the angles and their sines.

Write a simple program to enable you to test your subroutine. Use an array constructor to establish the set of angles to be used.

Modify your program so that the subroutine uses an assumed-shape array for the angles instead of an explicit-shape array.

7.5 In a television quiz game, each of six competitors takes part in five rounds and is awarded a score of between 0 and 10 for each round. The winner of each round gains a bonus of five points.

Write a program which reads the names and scores in each round for each competitor. The program should then calculate any bonuses due for winning a round before calculating the final score for each competitor. Finally, the program should print the names and scores (round by round and total) for the winner and runner-up.

7.6   Write a program that reads and stores two distinct sets of integer numbers and then finds and prints their union and their intersection. (The union is the collection of those items that are in at least one of the sets; the intersection is the collection of those items that are in both sets.)

Use an array in which to store a set, with unused elements being set to a special value which is not allowed to appear in the set, and write one subroutine to determine the union, and another to determine the intersection.

When you are satisfied that the two subroutines work correctly, alter your program so that the union and intersection are calculated by array-valued functions.

7.7   In an examination a student is awarded a distinction if he or she has obtained more than 30% above the average obtained by the whole class. To ensure fair marking, the students are identified only by a unique number in the range 1000 to 1999.

Write a program which will input the marks obtained by the members of the class, and which will then print out the average mark, and the identifying numbers of any students obtaining distinction, together with their marks.

7.8   In Philipsville all goods sold in shops, other than food, attract a 5% City sales tax. In addition, all goods other than printed materials (books, newspapers etc.) attract a State tax of 3% intended to subsidize the State Printing House.

Write a program which takes as its input the details about a number of purchases, each consisting of the price and a sales code (1 = food, 2 = books, 3 = newspapers, 4 = other printed material, 9 = other items), and prints a bill in the following order:

(1)   The number of food purchases, their basic cost, the State tax, and the total cost

(2)   The number of book and other printed material purchases, their basic cost, the City tax, and the total cost

(3)   The number of other purchases, their basic cost, the City and State taxes, and the total cost

(4)   The total cost of the goods, the total City tax, and the total State tax

7.9   Modify the program that you wrote for Exercise 7.6 so that a set is represented by a derived type consisting of two components: an array to contain the members of the set, and an integer count of the number of elements in the set. This avoids the problem of determining which elements of the array are not being used.

7.10   The number of entries in a cycle race is so large that it is decided to divide them into two separate races, based upon their times in an initial time trial.

Write a program which reads the total number of riders and then, for each rider, the rider's name, race number and time in the trial. All those whose time is less than the mean time of all the riders will be in race A, with the remainder being in race B. The program should print a list, showing each rider's name and number and the race (A or B) to which the rider has been allocated.

7.11   The bubble sort is a very simple (and very inefficient) means of sorting an array. It works as follows.

Compare the first and second elements of the array; if they are in the wrong order then exchange them, otherwise do nothing. Repeat this process for the second and third elements, then for the third and fourth elements, etc. At the conclusion of this process the last value in the sorted sequence will have 'bubbled' along to the last element of the array, and will therefore be in the correct place. Now repeat the process, which will result in the next-to-last value being moved to the next-to-last element. Repeat the process until all the values have been moved to their correct places.

(Clearly, improvements can be made by, for example, examining all n elements of the array in the first pass, the first $n - 1$ elements in the second pass etc., but you should not feel any obligation to refine your program in this way — the simplest approach will be sufficient for now.)

Write a subroutine to sort the contents of a **CHARACTER** array using a bubble sort, and test it in a program that reads a set of words from the keyboard.

*7.12   Write two procedures to convert an 8-digit binary number to its decimal equivalent, and vice versa. Note that you can store the binary number in an eight-element integer array, in which each array element contains either a 1 or 0.

Use these procedures in a program which requests two positive binary numbers in the range 00000000 to 11111111 and calculates their sum by converting them both to integers, adding the integers, and converting the result back to a binary representation. (Hint: you will need to read and write the binary numbers as character strings.)

7.13   An 8-bit binary number can also be stored in an eight-element **LOGICAL** array, where a *true* value indicates a 1, and a *false* value indicates a 0. Write a program to add two 8-bit binary numbers by using **LOGICAL** arrays to represent the numbers.

7.14   The dot product of two three-dimensional vectors a and b is defined as

$$a \cdot b = (a_1 \times b_1) + (a_2 \times b_2) + (a_3 \times b_3)$$

where a is the vector (a_1, a_2, a_3) and b is the vector (b_1, b_2, b_3).

The vector product, c, of the same vectors a and b is defined as the vector

$$c = a \times b$$

where $c_1 = a_2 \times b_3 - a_3 \times b_2$, $c_2 = a_3 \times b_1 - a_1 \times b_3$, and $c_3 = a_1 \times b_2 - a_2 \times b_1$

Write and test two functions to calculate the dot product and the vector product of two such vectors.

Now use these functions in a third function to evaluate the scalar triple product of three vectors a, b and c, which is defined as

$$[abc] = a \cdot (b \times c)$$

Write a program to test this function and also to determine the relationship between $[abc]$, $[bca]$ and $[cab]$.

7.15 An (unordered) set S of the integers between 1 and 100 can be represented as a **LOGICAL** array A of dimension 100, where n is an element of S if $A(n)$ is *true*. Write and test subroutines to give the union and intersection of sets represented in this way.

Unfortunately, using a **LOGICAL** array with a very large number of elements may take up more space than is available. Devise a way of using an **INTEGER** array to represent a **LOGICAL** array in such a way that more than one **LOGICAL** value can be stored in one **INTEGER** value. (Hint: remember that integers are stored as binary numbers consisting of a fixed number of bits, each of which can take the value 0 or 1.)

Write a subroutine to insert a **LOGICAL** value into such a simulated logical array, and a **LOGICAL** function to obtain the value of any given element, and use them to modify your earlier program so as to allow for sets of integers between 1 and 4000.

More control over input and output

The input and output facilities of any programming language are extremely important, because it is through these features of the language that communication between the user and the program are carried out. However, this frequently leads to a conflict between ease of use and complexity and Fortran 90, therefore, provides facilities for input and output at two quite different levels.

The list-directed input and output statements that we have been using up to now provide the capability for straightforward input from the keyboard and output to the printer. These statements, however, allow the user very little control over the source or the layout of the input data, or over the destination or layout of the printed results.

This chapter introduces the more general input/output features of Fortran 90, by means of which the programmer may specify exactly how the data will be presented and interpreted, from which of the available input units it is to be read, exactly how the results are to be displayed, and to which of the available output units the results are to be sent. Because of the interaction with the world outside the computer, input and output has the potential for more execution-time errors than most other parts of a program, and Fortran's approach to the detection of such errors is also briefly discussed.

8.1 The interface between the user and the computer

We have now learned how to instruct the computer to manipulate both numeric and character information, to repeat sequences of instructions and to take alternative courses of action depending upon decisions which are only made during the execution of the program. We have seen how we may use procedures to simplify our program structure while simultaneously adding greatly to the flexibility of the options before us, and we have even been able to create new data types to meet our own particular needs. Compared with the sophistication of which we are now capable in these areas, our control over the layout and interpretation of input data and the presentation of results has so far been woefully primitive. The problem arises because it is in this area that the world of the computer (where everything is stored as an electric, magnetic or optical signal in one of only two states) comes face-to-face with the world of the human computer user (where there are an almost infinite number of ways of storing or presenting information). It is the interface between these two worlds that we must now examine.

123456789

Figure 8.1 A line of input data.

A graphic example of this problem can be seen in the line of data shown in Figure 8.1, which has the digits 1 to 9 typed in the first nine positions. There are an enormous number of possible interpretations of this, apparently simple, line.

- It could be the number 123456789
- Or it could be the nine numbers 1, 2, 3, 4, 5, 6, 7, 8 and 9
- Or it could be the three numbers 123, 456, 789
- Or it could even be the number 12345.6789
- Or it could be the four numbers 1.23, 0.45, 67 and 8900
- Or it could be one of hundreds of other valid interpretations of these nine digits

Although these are all real possibilities, we have had little difficulty in dealing with input from the keyboard since the rules that were laid down in Section 3.4 accord with the natural way of presenting data, in most cases, and lead to a quite unambiguous interpretation of what has been typed.

The situation with output, however, has been more problematical since there have been many occasions when we should have liked to have had more control over the way in which the results are laid out on the screen. For example, if we wished to print the character string **The answers are** followed by the values of two variables (which are approximately **12.34** and **-7.89**) we have a potentially vast choice of ways in which to arrange our results. They could all be on one line like this:

```
The answers are 12.34 -7.89
```

or they could be on three lines:

```
The answers are

12.34    -7.89
```

or

```
The answers are
       12.34
       -7.89
```

or a number of other variations. They could also be printed immediately below the last item, or separated from it by one or more blank lines, or at the top of a new page, or in the middle of one. The number might be printed with two decimal places, or with five, or in any other way that we might wish. The possibilities are enormous.

As if this was not enough, there is also the question of where the data comes from and where the results are to be sent. The data will often be typed directly at a keyboard, but in larger systems, or for large amounts of data, it will probably be first input to a file in the file store by some quite different means and then read from there. In a similar fashion, results may be displayed on a screen, printed on a printer, or sent to a file. Furthermore, the peripheral device being used for the input or the output may be a local one which is more or less directly attached to the computer, or it may be at some remote site, possibly many miles away.

All of these questions need to be resolved every time any data is input to, or results are output from, a program.

Up to this point all our input and output has been carried out using list-directed **READ** and **PRINT** statements, and we have not, apparently, considered any of these difficulties at all! In fact, however, the Fortran processor has been taking care of everything on our behalf, and it is now time for us to learn how to specify those aspects over which we wish to exercise control — while leaving the processor to look after the rest.

If we consider the **READ** statement first, we find that the source of the data is dealt with by a neat piece of sleight-of-hand. When first introducing the list-directed input and output statements in Chapter 3 we said that the data would be read from the default input unit, which is defined by the particular computer system being used; typically, for personal computers and workstations, it will be the keyboard. In a similar way, the **PRINT** statement sends its results to the default output unit, which is also processor-dependent, but which will usually be the computer's display or printer.

The interpretation of the data by a list-directed **READ** statement has been dealt with primarily by treating a space or a comma (or a /) as a separator between items of data, and using the 'obvious' interpretation of the data items between the separators.

We should now define more formally how this process actually operates.

The data is considered to be a sequence of alternating values and **value separators**, with the occurrence of a value separator indicating the termination of the previous value. The value separators are of four types:

- a comma, optionally preceded and/or followed by one or more blanks
- a slash (/), optionally preceded and/or followed by one or more blanks
- one or more consecutive blanks
- the end of the record (that is, of the line), optionally preceded by one or more blanks

If there are no values between two consecutive value separators, for example there are two consecutive commas, then the effect is to read a **null value**. The effect of this is to leave the value of the corresponding variable in the input list *unchanged*. This often surprises people!

If a slash value separator is encountered then no more data items are read, and processing of the input statement is ended. If there are any remaining items in the input list then the result is as though null values had been input to them; in other words, their values remain unchanged.

For numeric data, that is all that is to be said, but for character data there is the further rule concerning the requirement for delimiting apostrophes or quotation marks. Because of the above rules concerning terminators, character strings being input by a list-directed **READ** statement must be delimited by matching apostrophes or quotation marks unless *all* of the following conditions are met:

- the character data does not contain any blanks, any commas or any slashes (that is, it does not contain any of the value separators discussed earlier)
- the character data is all contained within a single record or line
- the first non-blank character is not a quotation mark or an apostrophe, since this would be taken as a delimiting character
- the leading characters are not numeric followed by an asterisk, since this would be confused with the multiple data item form ($n*c$)

If all of these conditions are met, which essentially means that the character data being input is a single 'word' then it is treated in exactly the same way as numeric data and, in particular, is terminated by any of the value separators which will terminate a numeric data item (blank, comma, slash or end of record); it may also be repeated by means of a multiple data item of the form $n*c$.

For a great many purposes, therefore, list-directed input is perfectly satisfactory. However, the layout of the results by a list-directed **PRINT** statement has been less satisfactory, since each **PRINT** statement causes output to start at the beginning of the next line and prints the various items in a 'reasonable' format. Although the style in which each type of data is output is defined in general terms by the Fortran standard, the detail is left to the processor to determine; in particular, the field width and the number of decimal places displayed for real values is entirely processor-dependent. The effect is that the results will always be printed in a readable fashion, but the programmer has virtually no control over their layout.

These two list-directed input/output statements are thus restricted in their ability to define both the format of the information and, especially, its source or destination. The remainder of this chapter will examine how we can provide the flexibility needed in many cases for both input and output.

8.2 Formats and edit descriptors

An input statement must contain three distinct types of information – where the data is to be found, where it is to be stored in the computer's memory, and how it is to be interpreted. Similarly an output statement must define where the results are currently stored, where they are to be sent, and in what form they are to be displayed. These processes are illustrated in diagrammatic form in Figure 8.2, and

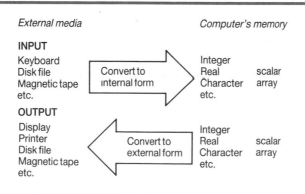

Figure 8.2 Input and output editing.

it can be seen that both processes are, in one sense, the same in that they both take information from one place, transform (or edit) it into a different format, and put the edited version in another place.

We have already discussed in some detail how the relevant locations in the computer's memory are identified and, although some minor extensions to the methods already discussed will be presented in later chapters, there is nothing more to add in this regard for the present.

Furthermore, the input/output statements that we have been using so far do not allow us to specify the nature of the external medium, but always use the default input or output unit. We shall see how to change this situation in Section 8.6.

The key element in both the input and output processes, however, is the **editing** of information in one form for presentation in another form, and it is this aspect of input and output which we shall now examine in some detail.

The input and output statements that we have been using thus far have taken the forms

```
READ *,input_list
PRINT *,output_list
```

but this has, in fact, been a considerable simplification. Each of these statements actually has three forms:

```
READ ch_var,input_list
READ label,input_list
READ *,input_list
```

and

```
PRINT ch_var,output_list
PRINT label,output_list
PRINT *,output_list
```

where *ch_var* is a character constant, character variable, character array, character array element or other character expression, and *label* is a statement label.

In all three variations the item following the keyword (**READ** or **PRINT**) is a **format specifier** which provides a link to the information necessary for the required editing to be carried out as part of the input or output process. This information is called a **format** and consists of a list of **edit descriptors** enclosed in parentheses:

```
(ed_des1,ed_des2, ...)
```

The first variation, where the format specifier is a character expression, is called an **embedded format** because the format itself appears as part of the **READ** or **PRINT** statement:

READ ' (*edit_descriptor_list*) ' , *input_list*

or

READ " (*edit_descriptor_list*) " , *input_list*

Because, as we shall see, an output format will often contain a character constant it is usually more convenient to use apostrophes to delimit character constants which represent formats than to use quotation marks. We shall always use the first of the two forms shown above, therefore, although it must be emphasized that either is permissible.

In the second variation of the **READ** and **PRINT** statements, however, the statement label is the label of a new type of statement called a **FORMAT statement** which contains the appropriate format. In the third variation, the asterisk indicates that the format to be used is a list-directed format which will be created by the processor to meet the perceived needs of the particular input or output list – hence its name.

The first two variations are, therefore, identical in their effect; the difference lies solely in the manner in which the format is actually provided. In the next section we shall present the details of the various edit descriptors, and the ways in which they are used, in the context of an embedded format, since this is usually the more convenient approach in most Fortran programs. Section 8.4 will then show how the same concept is implemented using **FORMAT** statements.

8.3 Input editing using embedded formats

We shall start by considering the various edit descriptors that are used for input in conjunction with a **READ** statement, since these are the easiest to understand. They fall into two categories – those concerned with the editing of actual data, and those concerned with altering the order in which the characters in the input record are edited. Figure 8.3 shows most of the available edit descriptors, and it will be seen that the first five fall into the first category; we shall investigate these first.

The first, and simplest, edit descriptor is used for inputting whole numbers which are to be stored in an *integer* variable, and takes the form

Iw

This indicates that the next w characters are to be read and interpreted as an integer. Thus if we wished to read the line shown in Figure 8.1 (which had the digits 1 to 9 typed in positions 1 to 9) as a single integer to be stored in the integer variable **n** we could write

Descriptor	Meaning
Iw	Read the next w characters as an integer
Fw.d	Read the next w characters as a real number with d digits
Ew.d	after the decimal place if no decimal point is present
Aw	Read the next w characters as characters
A	Read sufficient characters to fill the input list item, stored as characters
Lw	Read the next w characters as the representation of a logical value
nX	Ignore the next n characters
Tc	Next character to be read is at position c
TLn	Next character to be read is n characters before (TL) or
TRn	after (TR) the current position

Figure 8.3   Edit descriptors for input.

```
READ '(I9)',n
```

If we wished to read the same line as three separate integers (123, 456, 789) then we could write

```
READ '(I3,I3,I3)', n1,n2,n3
```

where **n1**, **n2** and **n3** are integer variables. This format interacts with the rest of the **READ** statement in the following way:

- First the **READ** statement recognizes that it requires an integer to store in **n1**; the format indicates that the first item to be read is an integer occupying the first three character positions (**I3**). The characters '123' are therefore read and converted to the internal form of the integer 123 before being stored in **n1**.

- The **READ** statement then requires another integer and the format indicates that this is to come from the *next* three character positions (**I3**). The characters '456' are therefore read and converted to the internal form of the integer 456 before being stored in **n2**.

- Finally, the process is repeated a third time, causing the characters '789' to be read, converted, and stored in **n3** as the integer 789.

- The **READ** statement is now satisfied, since data has been read for all of the variables in its input list, and so input of this line of data is complete.

Notice that there is an implied concept of an *index* which is always indicating which is the next character of the input record to be read. Normally this index is moved through the record as characters are read; however the **X**, **T**, **TL** and **TR** edit descriptors allow the index to be moved without any characters being read.

The **X** edit descriptor takes the form n**X** and causes the index to be moved forward across n characters. The next character to be read will be n positions to the right of the current position and the effect is to ignore the next n characters. Thus, using the same data line as before, the statement

```
READ '(4X,I5)', num
```

will ignore the first four columns and then read the next five as an integer; the value 56789 will therefore be stored in **num**. Similarly, the statement

```
READ '(I2,3X,I3)', i,j
```

will cause the value 12 to be stored in **i** and 678 in **j**. Notice that in this case the 9 typed in character position 9 is ignored because the format only specifies the first eight positions.

The next three edit descriptors are, essentially, three variations on a single theme:

```
Tc
TRn
TLn
```

The first of these causes a tab to character position c; in other words the next character to be read will be from position c. Thus the statement

```
READ '(T4,I2,T8,I2,T2,I4)', x,y,z
```

will, when used with the same line of data, first move the index to position 4 and read the number 45 into **x**, then move it to position 8 before reading 89 into **y**, and then move it to position 2 before reading the number 2345 into **z**. The **T** edit descriptor thus provides a means of not only skipping over unwanted characters, but also of going back in the record and reading it (or parts of it) again.

The **T** edit descriptor moves to a character position which is defined *absolutely* by its position in the record, or line of data. The **TL** and **TR** edit descriptors, on the other hand, specify a *relative* tab — that is a move to a character position which is defined relative to the current position. The letters **TR** followed by a number n indicate that the next character is to be n positions to the right of the current position; it is thus identical in its effect to n**X**. The letters **TL** followed by a number n specify a tab to the left, and cause the next character to be n positions to the left of (or before) the current position. If **TL**n would cause the next position to be before the first character of the record then the pointer is positioned at the start of the record (at the beginning of the line of input data).

The next data edit descriptor is the **F** edit descriptor, which is used for reading real values, and takes a slightly more complicated form than any of the other edit descriptors that we have met so far:

$Fw.d$

This edit descriptor can be used in two rather different ways, depending upon the layout of the data.

If the data is typed with a decimal point in the appropriate position then the edit descriptor causes the next w characters to be read and converted into a real number. The value of d is irrelevant (although it must be included in the format).

On the other hand, if the w columns which are to be read as a real number do not contain any decimal point then the value of d indicates where one may be assumed to have been omitted, by specifying that the number has d decimal places. Thus (assuming our usual input record, as shown in Figure 8.1) the statement

```
READ '(F9.4)', real_num
```

will cause the first nine characters to be read as a real number with four decimal places. The variable **real_num** will therefore have the number 12345.6789 stored in it. In a similar way

```
READ '(F3.1,F2.2,F3.0,TL6,F4.2)', r1,r2,r3,r4
```

will cause the value 12.3 to be stored in **r1**, 0.45 in **r2**, 678.0 in **r3**, and 34.56 in **r4**.

Let us now consider what will happen if the same statement is used to read the line shown in Figure 8.4. The first edit descriptor requires three columns to be read, and since these (.23) contain a decimal point the second part of the edit descriptor is ignored and the value 0.23 stored in **r1**. In a similar way the **F2.2** descriptor causes the characters '.5' to be read, and **r2** is therefore given the value 0.5. The **F3.0** edit descriptor also has its second part overridden by the decimal point in 6.8 and so this is the value stored in **r3**. Finally, **TL6,F4.0** causes the characters '3.56' to be read, and so this value is stored in **r4**. Figure 8.5 summarizes the result of reading these two lines of data.

.23.56.8

Figure 8.4 Another line of data.

```
       READ '(F3.1,F2.2,F3.0,TL6,F4.2)', r1,r2,r3,r4
Data:          123456789   .23.56.8
A contains     12.3        0.23
B contains      0.45       0.5
C contains    678.0        6.8
D contains     34.56       3.56
```

Figure 8.5 The effect of the F edit descriptor during input.

As a general rule, data which is to be stored as real values will be presented to the computer with the decimal points in their correct places. However sometimes, and especially when the data has been collected independently from the programmer, it is presented as whole numbers which need to be processed by the computer as real numbers.

There is also an **E** edit descriptor, which takes a very similar form to the **F** edit descriptor:

$$Ew.d$$

and, on input, is interpreted in an identical way. On output, however, as we shall see, it is different from an **F** edit descriptor.

The third major data edit descriptor is the **A** edit descriptor, which is used to control the editing of character data. It takes one of the forms

$$Aw$$
$$A$$

During input, the edit descriptor **A**w refers to the next w characters (just as **I**w and **F**$w.d$ refer to w characters). However, a character variable has a defined length and any string which is to be stored in it must be made to have the same length. If we assume that length of the input list item is *len* then the following rules apply:

- If w is less than *len* then extra blank characters will be added at the end so as to extend the length of the input character string to *len*. This is similar to the situation with assignment.

- If w is greater than *len*, however, the rightmost *len* characters of the input character string will be stored in the input list item. This is the *opposite* of what happens with assignment! The reason for this apparent incongruity will become apparent when we consider the outputting of characters in Section 8.5.

An **A** edit descriptor without any field width *w* is treated as though the field width was identical to the length of the corresponding input list item. Thus, if the three variables **ch1**, **ch2** and **ch3** are declared by a statement of the form

```
CHARACTER :: ch1*10, ch2*6, ch3*15
```

then the following two statements will have an identical effect:

```
READ '(A10,A6,A15)', ch1,ch2,ch3
READ '(A,A,A)', ch1,ch2,ch3
```

Since the form without a field width requires the **READ** statement to provide exactly the same number of characters as the length of the variable into which they are to be stored, the question of blank padding or truncation never occurs.

The remaining data edit descriptor is used with logical data, and takes the form

L*w*

This edit descriptor processes the next *w* characters to derive either a *true* value, a *false* value, or an error. There are exactly two ways of representing *true* and *false* in the data, namely as a string of characters in one of the following forms, optionally preceded by one or more spaces:

T*ccc...c*   or   .T*ccc...c*

and

F*ccc...c*   or   .F*ccc...c*

where *c* represents any character.

Data items interpreted as true	*Data items interpreted as false*
T	F
TRUE	FALSE
.T	.F
.T.	.F.
.TRUE	.FALSE
.TRUE.	.FALSE.
Truthful	Fanciful
terrible	futile
true	false
.t	.f

Figure 8.6 Logical data for input with an L8 edit descriptor.

The lower case letters **t** and **f** are treated as being equivalent to the upper case letters **T** and **F** in a logical input field. Figure 8.6 shows some examples of data which would be interpreted by the edit descriptor **L8** as either *true* or *false*. If the first non-blank character, other than a period, is not **T** or **F**, or their lower case equivalents, then an error will occur.

■ **EXAMPLE 8.1**

1 **Problem**

A survey, consisting of a maximum of 1000 respondents, has recorded the name, age, sex, marital status, height and weight of a number of people. The information has been recorded as follows:

First name	in columns 1–15
Last name	in columns 21–40
Sex	coded in column 43
	F = female
	M = male
Marital status	coded in column 45
	0 = single
	1 = married
	2 = widowed
	3 = divorced
	4 = cohabiting
	9 = unknown
Age (yrs)	in columns 47, 48
Height (cm)	in columns 51–53
Weight (kg)	in columns 56–62 in the form *kkk.ggg*

The data is terminated by a line which has **END OF DATA** typed in columns 1 to 11.

Write and test a procedure to read this data and store it in a form suitable for subsequent analysis. Such analysis will require the heights to be stored in metres.

A module, **Global_Data**, is available which contains, among other things, the type definition for a type **person** with components defined as follows

```
CHARACTER(LEN=15) :: first_name
CHARACTER(LEN=20) :: last_name
CHARACTER :: sex    ! M or F
INTEGER :: marital_status, age
REAL :: height, weight
```

2 Analysis

When developing a large program it is always a good idea first to write and thoroughly test an input procedure. When developing the rest of the program we can then be confident that the data is being correctly input, and can concentrate on the other parts of the program.

The procedure will use a **DO** loop to carry out the input, and the only areas to require any particular attention will be the detection of the terminating condition and the conversion of the height in centimetres into metres. This last matter can be dealt with during input by use of an edit descriptor of **F3.2**, which will cause the data to be interpreted as though it had a decimal point in the required place. The data will be stored in an array of type **person** which will be supplied as an argument to the procedure. The maximum number of respondents is not relevant as far as the procedure is concerned since this can be provided as another argument or, better, derived by the procedure from the shape of the actual argument array.

Data design

Purpose	Type	Name
A Arguments:		
Array of personal data	PERSON	people
Number of people in survey	INTEGER	number_people
B Local variables:		
Maximum number of data sets	INTEGER	max_people
DO variable	INTEGER	i

Structure plan

Subroutine input(*people,number_people*)
   using *Global_data*

1 Set *max_people* to the size of the dummy argument *people*
2 Repeat up to *max_people* times
   2.1 Read next record
   2.2 If terminator found then exit
3 Return number of data sets read

Although the problem, as specified, did not ask for the number of sets of data that were read, this is clearly information that will probably be required during any subsequent processing, and so it seems sensible to provide it.

3 Solution

```fortran
SUBROUTINE input(people,number_people)
   USE Global_Data
   IMPLICIT NONE

   ! An input subroutine for a survey

   ! Dummy arguments
   TYPE(person),DIMENSION(:) :: people
   INTEGER :: number_people

   ! Local variables
   INTEGER :: i,max_people

   ! Store maximum number of allowable data sets
   max_people = SIZE(people)

   ! Display data format
   PRINT *,"Type data as follows: "
   PRINT *,"Cols.  1-15  First name"
   PRINT *,"Cols. 21-40  Last name"
   PRINT *,"Col.    43   Sex (F=female, M=male)"
   PRINT *,"Col.    45   Marital status (0=single, 1=married,"
   PRINT *,"             2=widowed, 3=divorced, 4=cohabiting,"
   PRINT *,"             9=unknown)"
   PRINT *,"Cols. 47,48  Age (in years)"
   PRINT *,"Cols. 51-53  Height (in cm)"
   PRINT *,"Cols. 56-62  Weight (in kg in the form kkk.ggg)"
   PRINT *," "
   PRINT *,"Data should be terminated by the words &
           &'END OF DATA' typed in cols. 1-11"
   PRINT *," "

   ! Loop to read data
   DO i=1,max_people
      READ '(A15,5X,A20,2X,I1,1X,I1,1X,I2,2X,F3.2,2X,F7.3)', &
           people(i)

      ! Check if this is the terminator record
      IF (people(i)%first_name(1:11) == "END OF DATA") EXIT

   END DO

   ! Check to see if a terminator was found
   IF (i>max_people) THEN
      PRINT *,"Maximum number of records (",max_people,") read"
      PRINT *,"with no terminator - input halted"
      ! Save number of data records read
      number_people = max_people
   ELSE
      number_people = i-1
   END IF

END SUBROUTINE input
```

8.4 FORMAT statements

We have now seen how the format, which defines the layout of the data and how it is to be interpreted, works together with the **READ** statement, which specifies where the data is to come from and where the converted data is to be stored. The inclusion of the format as part of the **READ** statement is normally the most natural way to link these two aspects of the input process, but there are occasions when this can lead to confusing statements or to unnecessary duplication. For example, if the nature of a program is such that there are several **READ** statements, all requiring the identical format, then it is both wasteful and potentially a source of errors to repeat the format in each of the **READ** statements. In these circumstances we can define the format in a special, non-executable, **FORMAT** statement which takes the form

label **FORMAT** (*edit_descriptor_list*)

A **FORMAT** statement must *always* be preceded by a label because that is the only means by which it can be referenced in a **READ** statement, which will take the second of the three forms introduced in Section 8.2:

READ *label*, *output_list*

The labelled **FORMAT** statement may appear anywhere in the program unit after the initial statement and any **USE** statements, and before the **END** statement. As we shall see in Chapter 11, it must also come before any internal procedures. We recommend that any **FORMAT** statements in a program unit should be kept together for ease of reference, either near the start of the program unit, for example immediately after the declarations and other specification statements and before the start of the executable statements, or after all the executable statements in the program unit.

Figure 8.7 shows part of a program in which personal data in the same format as that used in Example 8.1 is read into one of three arrays, depending on the value of an integer variable, and it can be seen that the use of a single **FORMAT** statement helps to keep the structure of the program clearly visible.

8.5 Output editing

As we might expect, the edit descriptors used for output are essentially the same as those used for input, although there are some additional ones that are only available for output and the interpretation of the others is slightly different. Figure 8.8 shows the main edit descriptors that are available for output, and we shall briefly examine each in turn.

The **I** edit descriptor (**I**w) causes an integer to be output in such a way as to utilize the next w character positions. These w positions will consist of (if

```
SUBROUTINE format_statement_demo(group_1,group_2,group_3)
  USE Global_Data
  IMPLICIT NONE

  ! An input subroutine for a survey

  ! Dummy arguments
  TYPE(person),DIMENSION(:) :: group_1,group_2,group_3

  ! Local variables
  INTEGER :: i1,i2,i3,code
  .
  .
  .
  ! Input format
100 FORMAT (A15,5X,A20,2X,I1,1X,I1,1X,I2,2X,F3.2,2X,F7.3)
  .
  .
  .
  SELECT CASE (code)
  CASE (:-1)            ! code<0 - group_1
    READ 100,group_1(i1)
    .
    .
    .
  CASE (0)             ! code=0 - group_2
    READ 100,group_2(i2)
    .
    .
    .
  CASE (1:)            ! code>0 - group_3
    READ 100,group_3(i3)
    .
    .
    .
  END SELECT
  .
  .
  .
END SUBROUTINE input
```

Figure 8.7 An example of the use of **FORMAT** statements.

necessary) one or more spaces, followed by a minus sign if the number is negative, followed by the value of the number. Thus the statements

```
tom = 23
dick = 715
harry = -12
PRINT '(I5,I5,I5)',tom,dick,harry
```

will produce the following line of output (where the symbol ♦ represents a space)

♦♦♦23♦♦715♦♦-12

Descriptor	Meaning
Iw	Output an integer in the next w character positions
F$w.d$	Output a real number in the next w character positions with d decimal places
E$w.d$	Output a real number in the next w character positions using an exponent format with d decimal places in the mantissa and four characters for the exponent
Aw	Output a character string in the next w character positions
A	Output a character string, starting at the next character position, with no leading or trailing blanks
Lw	Output $w - 1$ blanks, followed by T or F to represent a logical value
nX	Ignore the next n character positions
Tc	Output the next item starting at character position c
TLn TRn	Output the next item starting n character positions before (TL) or after (TR) the current position
"$c_1c_2 \dots c_n$" '$c_1c_2 \dots c_n$'	Output the string of characters $c_1c_2 \dots c_n$ starting at the next character position

Figure 8.8 Edit descriptors for output.

If the output is to go to the computer's *printer* then the results which actually appear will be very slightly different, as the first character on the line (a space in this example) will not be printed; the reason for this is discussed in Section 8.7. If it is sent to a display screen, or most other peripheral devices, the layout will normally be exactly as defined, although in some cases it may be the same as if it had been sent to the printer.

The F edit descriptor operates in a similar way, and F$w.d$ indicates that a real number is to be output occupying w characters, of which the last d are to follow the decimal point. Note that the real value to be output is *rounded* (not truncated) to d places of decimals before it is sent to the relevant output device. Rounding is carried out in the usual arithmetic way. Thus the statements

```
x = 3.14159
y = -275.3024
z = 12.9999
PRINT '(F10.3,F10.3,F10.3)',x,y,z
```

will produce the following line of output:

```
♦♦♦♦♦3.142♦♦-275.302♦♦♦♦♦13.000
```

```
361.764
3.61764+2
361764-3
0.0361764E4
3617.64D-1
3.61764E +2
361.764+0
```

Figure 8.9 Some of the ways in which the real data item 361.764 may be written.

Notice that, because the edit descriptors each specify only three places of decimals, the value of **x** is printed as 3.142 (rounded up), the value of **y** as −275.302 (rounded down), and the value of **z** as 13.000 (rounded up).

The **E** edit descriptor is also used for outputting real numbers, but using a form of notation which represents the number as a mantissa and an exponent. Before discussing it, however, we must briefly review the representation of the format of real numbers.

We have already seen, in Section 3.3, that a real constant may be written followed by an exponent (for instance, **1.5E-6**) and a similar format is allowed for numbers being input by a **READ** statement. In this case the exponent may take one of three forms:

- a signed integer constant
- **E** followed by an optionally signed constant
- **D** followed by an optionally signed constant

In the latter two cases the letter (**D** or **E**) may be followed by one or more spaces.

Thus a real data value may be written in a great many different ways; for example, some of the ways in which the number 361.764 may occur in data are shown in Figure 8.9.

As was mentioned in Section 8.3, such data may be input using either the $Fw.d$ or $Ew.d$ edit descriptors. However, on output the two edit descriptors operate in quite different ways.

We have already seen that $Fw.d$ will output a real number rounded to d decimal places with an external field of width w. The **E** edit descriptor, however, produces a representation of a real number consisting of a decimal fraction, m, in the range $0.1 \leqslant m < 1.0$, with d digits of precision, followed by a four character exponent; the whole number will occupy a field width of w characters. It is therefore much more flexible, and will cater more easily than the **F** edit descriptor with very large or very small numbers. The number 0.000 036 176 4, for instance, will be output as shown below with various edit descriptors:

```
F10.4      ◆◆◆◆0.0000
F12.6      ◆◆◆◆0.000036
F14.8      ◆◆◆◆0.00003618
E10.4      0.3618E-04
E12.6      0.361764E-04
E14.8      0.36176400E-04
```

If the exponent is greater than 99, or less than −99, then the exponent will be output as a plus or minus sign, followed by a three digit exponent. Some Fortran 90 processors may choose to use this form of representation for all values of the exponent.

It is important to realize that, for *all* numeric edit descriptors, if the number does not require the full field width w it will be preceded by one or more spaces. By allowing more room than is necessary, several numbers may be spaced across the page and the printing of tables becomes relatively easy, as can be seen in Figure 8.10. In this case the format being used specifies that the three items to be printed $(x, \sqrt{x}, \sqrt[3]{x})$ are all to use an edit descriptor of **F15.4**. The three numbers are therefore spread evenly across the page, with the next three directly below them, and so on.

As we might expect, the **A** edit descriptor works in a similar fashion for output as for input. **A**w will, therefore, cause characters to be output to the next w character positions of the output record, and, as was the case for input, we need

```
PROGRAM tabular_output
   IMPLICIT NONE
   REAL,PARAMETER :: third=1.0/3.0
   REAL :: x
   INTEGER :: i
   DO i=1,10
      x=i
      PRINT '(F15.4,F15.4,F15.4)', x,SQRT(x),x**third
   END DO
END PROGRAM tabular_output
```

The output from this program will be

```
       1.0000         1.0000         1.0000
       2.0000         1.4142         1.2599
       3.0000         1.7321         1.4422
       4.0000         ·2.0000        1.5874
       5.0000         2.2361         1.7100
       6.0000         2.4495         1.8171
       7.0000         2.6458         1.9129
       8.0000         2.8284         2.0000
       9.0000         3.0000         2.0801
      10.0000         3.1623         2.1544
```

Figure 8.10 An example of tabular printing.

to establish exactly what happens if the length of the output list item is not exactly w. The rules that apply here are similar to those that we had for input, where *len* is the length of the character variable or constant being output:

- If w is greater than *len* then the character string will be right-justified within the output field, and will be preceded by one or more blanks. This is similar to what happens with the **I**, **F** and **E** edit descriptors.
- If w is less than *len* then the leftmost w characters will be output.

It will be remembered that, during the discussion of the use of the **A** format for input in Section 3.3, the apparent incongruity between the truncation on the left during input and truncation on the right during assignment was raised. We can now see that this was necessary to ensure compatibility between input and output. If a character string is output to a field larger than its length then it will have spaces added at the beginning, as with all other types of data. If that same external representation were to be subsequently read back into the computer, using the same format, then it is necessary that the extra blanks at the beginning be removed, and not the important characters at the end! The apparent incompatibility with assignment is, therefore, much less important than the major incompatibility between input and output that would occur if a character string were to be input with truncation at the right.

Note, however, that for *list-directed input* assignment rules apply, and a character string which is too long for the variable it is to be input to will be truncated on the right.

Just as was the case with input, we may omit the field width with an **A** edit descriptor, in which case the character string being output will occupy exactly the space it requires, with neither leading nor trailing blanks. This form of the **A** edit descriptor is, therefore, particularly useful on output, since it can enable the same basic format to be used with character variables of different lengths.

Finally, there is the **L** edit descriptor for use in outputting a representation of logical values. This is perfectly straightforward, and the descriptor **L**w will cause $w - 1$ blanks to be output, followed by the letter **T** or the letter **F** to indicate *true* or *false*.

There is one further point that should be made at this stage. In the example shown in Figure 8.10, as in several other programs in this section, the same edit descriptor has been repeated several times. A number, called a **repeat count**, may be placed *before* the **I**, **F**, **E**, **A** or **L** edit descriptors to indicate how many times they are to be repeated. Thus the format

```
(I5,I5,I5,F6.2,F6.2,F6.2,F6.2)
```

could be written more succinctly, and more clearly, as

```
(3I5,4F6.2)
```

A repeat count may be used in formats for both input and output to cause repetition of an edit descriptor which is used in conjunction with an input or output list item; it cannot be used to repeat the other edit descriptors, such as **X**, **TL**, etc.

For output there is also a common requirement to display a fixed text string to identify, or otherwise clarify, the meaning of the results being output. We have used this feature extensively in list-directed output statements of the form

```
PRINT *,"The result is ",result
```

A format may also include a **character constant edit descriptor**, which takes the form of a character constant, and is output at the next character position. Thus, the above example could also be written as

```
PRINT '("The result is ",I5)', result
```

It is because of the frequent requirement for character constant edit descriptors in most output formats that we have been adopting the convention that apostrophes will be used to delimit embedded formats. We could, of course, have equally well written

```
PRINT "('The result is ',I5)", result
```

and if you prefer to normally use apostrophes to delimit character constants then you should use this form for embedded formats. The important thing is to be consistent.

The remaining edit descriptors that we shall discuss here are all concerned with layout. The **X** edit descriptor (*n***X**) operates in a similar manner to that which was described for input, and is used to ignore, or skip over, the next *n* character positions. If no output has yet been sent to these positions the effect is to insert *n* spaces; if some output has already been sent to these position, however, the **X** edit descriptor merely moves the index recording where the next character is to be output. The effect of *n***X** is best appreciated by assuming that an output record always consists of spaces before the start of a **PRINT** statement, and that *n***X** always moves the index *n* character positions to the right.

The **T**, **TL** and **TC** edit descriptors also operate in essentially the same way as for input, if we assume that the output record consists initially of spaces, and enable items to be positioned in an exact place in the record (or line).

SELF-TEST EXERCISES 8.1

1   What is a value separator during list-directed input?

2   What are the possible value separators during list-directed input?

3   Under what circumstances may character data be read by a list-directed **READ** statement without being enclosed between apostrophes or quotation marks?

4   What is an embedded format? What is a **FORMAT** statement?

5   When is it preferable to use an embedded format, and when is it preferable to use a **FORMAT** statement?

6   What is an edit descriptor?

7   If the user responds to the following program by typing the nine digits 1 to 9 without any intervening characters, what *exactly* will be printed?

```
PROGRAM test1
   IMPLICIT NONE
   INTEGER :: a,b
   REAL :: c,d
   READ 101,a,b,c,d
   PRINT 200,a,b,a-b,c,d,c-d
   101 FORMAT(T6,I4,TL6,I4,TL6,F4.1,TL6,F4.2)
   200 FORMAT(5X,I4," minus",I5," is",I5,TR4,F6.2, &
              " minus",F6.2," is",F8.3)
END PROGRAM test1
```

8   If the user responds to the following program by typing the nine digits 1 to 9 without any intervening characters, what *exactly* will be printed?

```
PROGRAM test2
   IMPLICIT NONE
   CHARACTER(LEN=6) :: a,b,c
   READ '(A8,T1,A4,T1,A)',a,b,c
   PRINT '(5X,A8,5X,A4,5X,A)',a,b,c
   PRINT '(5X,A,5X,A,5X,A)',a,b,c
END PROGRAM test2
```

8.6   READ, WRITE and PRINT statements

Now that we have discussed all the major edit descriptors that can be used to assist in the interpretation of data and the presentation of results, it is time to return to the question that we deferred in Section 8.2, namely the source of data and the destination of results.

The three variants of the **READ** statement that we have used up to now have taken their input from the default input unit. In order to vary this source of data, and also to allow the possibility of monitoring the success or otherwise of the reading process, we must use a more general form of **READ** statement:

READ (*cilist*) *input_list*

where *cilist* is a **control information list** consisting of one or more items, known as **specifiers**, separated by commas. There are a number of specifiers that can be used in conjunction with the **READ** statement, but we shall only discuss three of them here; further specifiers will be introduced as they are needed in Chapters 9 and 15. All specifiers take the same basic form:

keyword = *value*

although the keyword may be omitted in two cases, in certain circumstances. Such specifiers as are used in a particular case may appear in any order as long as the full form (with keyword) is used.

There must always be a **unit specifier** in the control information list, which takes the form

UNIT = *unit*

where *unit* is the input device (or **unit** in Fortran parlance) from which input is to be taken. *unit* may also be the name of an **internal file**, as we shall see in Chapter 15. It either takes the form of an integer expression whose value is zero or positive, or it may be an asterisk to indicate that the default input unit is to be used. The way in which the unit number is related to a particular peripheral device is, to a large extent, dependent upon the computer system being used. Normally, some units will be **preconnected** and will be automatically available to all programs. The default input unit and the default output unit will always be preconnected in this way, but each Fortran 90 implementation may well have different unit numbers associated with them. Any other peripheral devices or files which the program requires must be given a unit number and connected to the program by an **OPEN** statement (see Section 9.3).

The default input unit will usually be preconnected as unit 1 or unit 5. (This is purely for historical reasons, since IBM, and several other manufacturers, used unit 5 for the card reader and unit 6 for the printer in their early Fortran systems, while others used units 1 and 2 for these devices. A great many programs written in earlier versions thus expect their input from unit 1 or 5 and send their results to unit 2 or 6, depending upon the type of computer being used. For compatibility, a Fortran 90 system is likely to preserve the convention previously in use at a particular site.) We shall assume that it is unit 5, but it must be emphasized that *this is only an assumption*; a particular implementation may use any positive number, or zero, for the default input unit.

With this assumption we may write

```
UNIT = 5
```

or

```
UNIT = *
```

to identify the default input unit. If, and only if, the unit specifier is the *first* item in the control information list we may omit the **UNIT** keyword and the **=** sign, and simply write

```
5
```

or

```
*
```

For clarity, however, we recommend that the **UNIT** keyword should always be included.

Normally the input will need to be converted from some *external* form, such as the characters sent by a keyboard, to an *internal* form suitable for storing in the computer's memory. To carry out this conversion we have already seen that we need a format, and this is identified by a **format specifier** which takes one of the forms

```
FMT = ch_var
FMT = label
FMT = *
```

in an analogous fashion to the format specifications discussed earlier in this chapter. If the format specifier is the second item in the control information list *and* the first item is a unit specifier without any keyword then the **FMT** keyword and **=** sign may also be omitted from the format specifier. Thus the following are all acceptable alternatives for the same statement:

```
READ (UNIT=5,FMT='(3F6.2)') x,y,z
READ (FMT='(3F6.2)',UNIT=5) x,y,z
READ (5,FMT=100) x,y,z
READ (5,100) x,y,z
READ (5,'(3F6.2)') x,y,z
100 FORMAT (3F6.2)
```

As with the **UNIT** keyword, however, we strongly recommend that the **FMT** keyword should always be included.

We can also see that the statement

```
READ (*,*) a,b,c
```

is identical in its effect to the earlier list-directed input statement

```
READ *,a,b,c
```

The remaining specifier that we shall discuss here is concerned with monitoring the outcome of the reading process, and takes the form

```
IOSTAT = io_status
```

where *io_status* is an integer variable. At the conclusion of the execution of the **READ** statement *io_status* will be set to a value which the program can use to determine whether any errors occurred during the input process. There are four possibilities:

- The variable is set to zero to indicate that no errors occurred.
- The variable is set to a processor-dependent positive value to indicate that an error has occurred.
- The variable is set to a processor-dependent negative value to indicate that a condition known as an end-of-file condition has occurred; we shall discuss this condition, and the situations in which it can occur, in Chapter 9.
- The variable is set to a processor-dependent negative value to indicate that a condition known as an end-of-record condition has occurred; we shall discuss this condition, and the situations in which it can occur, in Chapter 15.

For the present, therefore, we may simply use **IOSTAT** to determine whether or not the reading of data was carried out successfully by testing the value of the variable in an **IF** or **CASE** construct:

```
READ (UNIT=*,FMT='(5F6.3)',IOSTAT=ioerror) p,q,r,s,t
IF (ioerror /= 0) THEN     ! ioerror is non-zero
   .                       ! Print error/warning message
   .                       ! and take remedial action
   .                       ! before exit from procedure
   RETURN
END IF
! Continue with normal processing
   .
   .
   .
```

Output is essentially the reverse of input so far as the transfer of information is concerned, and as one would expect, the facilities available are essentially the same. The most obvious difference is that for input the word **READ** is used in all cases, but for output we have two words. We have used the **PRINT** statement for list-directed output for user-formatted output to the default output unit. To take advantage of the full range of facilities, however, we must use a different word, **WRITE**, in a form of statement which is almost identical to that used for input:

WRITE (*cilist*) *output_list*

Exactly the same specifiers are available as was the case for the **READ** statement, although it is impossible to encounter an end-of-file condition or an end-of-record condition during output. The only other difference is the obvious one that an asterisk as a unit identifier refers to the default *output* unit.

As was the case for input, the choice of a unit number for the default output unit is dependent upon the particular implementation. It will usually be 6 (when 5 is used for input) or 2 (when 1 is used for input). In this book *we shall assume that the default output unit is 6* and that, therefore, the following statements are equivalent:

```
WRITE (UNIT=6,FMT=150) d,e,f
WRITE (UNIT=*,FMT=150) d,e,f
```

8.7 Printer control characters

We have seen how a format can be used to define the layout of data or of results. However, when the results are being output on a printer there is one further level of control possible, namely a (limited) control of the vertical spacing of the printed output.

When a line of output is to be sent to the output device designated as the *printer*, the Fortran output system will remove the first character of the line and interpret it as a **printer control character** which determines how much the paper is to be moved up before any remaining characters of the line are printed. This apparently bizarre behaviour reflects the way in which some of the very early printers, back in the 1950s, actually worked and has remained in Fortran ever since.

There are four characters which have a particular significance in this regard, as shown in Figure 8.11. If the first character is not one of these four then the effect on the printer is undefined; in practice, however, any other character will usually have the same effect as does a space, that is, printing will take place on the *next* line.

Character	Vertical spacing before printing
♦ (space)	one line
0 (zero)	two lines
1 (one)	first line of next page
+ (plus)	no paper advance (overprint)

Figure 8.11   Printer control characters.

Because the first character is removed and not printed it is important that we insert an extra (control) character at the start of each record that is to be output to the printer; Figure 8.12 shows what can happen if we do not do so.

Because the edit descriptor in format 200 (**F5.2**) only allowed room for two digits before the decimal point, and format 201 only allowed room for one, the output records actually produced are as follows:

```
♦3.00
♦4.00
12.00
0.750
```

The first character, however, will be removed for printer control. In the first two lines this merely means that the leading space, shown as ♦, is removed, causing the correct number to be printed on the next line. The third line, however, starts with a one. This is removed and the remainder of the record (**2.00**) is printed at the top of the *next page*, as specified by the (apparent) control character (**1**). In a similar way, the leading zero of the last line causes double spacing (that is, a blank line before printing).

There are several ways in which a control character can be inserted at the start of a line, especially if it is a space (as is usually the case). It is preferable to include the control character explicitly, rather than simply incorporating it into the first format specifier, so that it stands out as not being part of the format proper, and will not get removed inadvertently when modifying the program at a later date. It is also easier to modify the program to remove the printer control character at a subsequent date, if required, if it is physically separate from the next edit descriptor. The two formats shown in Figure 8.12 could therefore be rewritten as

```
200 FORMAT (1X,F5.2)
201 FORMAT (1X,F5.3)
```

It is important to realise that this only applies to the *printer*, or to other units which the compiler designates as *printing units*, including, in some cases, the computer's display screen; other output devices, including, possibly, others which

```
        PROGRAM poor_printer_control
          IMPLICIT NONE
          REAL :: x,y
          x = 3.0
          y = 4.0
          WRITE (UNIT=*,FMT=200) x
          WRITE (UNIT=*,FMT=200) y
          WRITE (UNIT=*,FMT=200) x*y
          WRITE (UNIT=*,FMT=201) x/y
          200 FORMAT (F5.2)
          201 FORMAT (F5.3)
        END PROGRAM poor_printer_control
```

The output from this program will be

```
3.00
4.00
- - - - - - - - - - - - - - - - - - - - - - - - (new page)
2.00

.750
```

Figure 8.12 An example of printer control errors.

produce some form of printed output, do not need a control character and will print the complete record. Note also that the **PRINT** statement automatically inserts a (space) control character at the start of each line if the default output unit is the printer.

8.8 More powerful formats

This chapter has described the means whereby a program may define formats for both input and output of considerable complexity. However, a number of other features are available to facilitate still more control of input and output. Probably the most important of these concern multi-records formats, and the repetition of formats.

Let us consider a program that wishes to read 12 real numbers into an array **arr**, of size 12, typed four to a line. With our present knowledge we could write

```
READ 100,(arr(i),i=1,4)
READ 100,(arr(i),i=5,8)
READ 100,(arr(i),i=9,12)
100 FORMAT (4F12.3)
```

However, consider what would happen if we wrote

```
READ 100,arr
```

which is the same as writing

```
READ 100,(arr(i),i=1,12)
```

After the READ statement has used the format to input four real numbers (which are placed in the first four elements of **arr**) it finds that the input list is not yet exhausted, and that another real number is required. The format *is* completed, however, and it follows that this input record contains no more useful information. There is only one sensible thing to do at this stage – namely to read a new record and interpret its contents using the same format. This is exactly what happens.

Whenever a format is fully used up and there are still items in the input (or output) list awaiting processing the format will be repeated. The rules governing the point from which it will be repeated are straightforward:

- If there are no nested parentheses then the format is repeated from the beginning.
- If the format contains any nested parentheses then it is repeated from immediately after the left parenthesis corresponding to the rightmost nested parenthesis.
- If the left parenthesis defined above is preceded by a repeat count then the format is repeated including the repeat count.

The following examples should make this clear; an arrow (↑) is shown below the point from which repetition (if any) will take place:

```
(I6,10X,I5,3F10.2)
↑
(I6,10X,I5,(3F10.2))
           ↑
(I6,(10X,I5),3F10.2)
    ↑
(F6.2,(2F4.1,2X,I4,4(I7,F7.2)))
      ↑
(F6.2,2(2F4.1,2X,I4),4(I7,F7.2))
                     ↑
(F6.2,(2(2F4.2,2X,I4),4(I7,F7.2)))
      ↑
((F6.2,2(2F4.2,2X,I4),4(I7,F7.2)))
 ↑
```

The repetition of a format can be extremely useful; however, in many cases it is also desirable to be able to define a format which processes two or more

```
- - - - - - - - - - - - - - - - - - - - - - (new page)
        Multi-record example

The sum of 12.25 and 23.50 is   35.75
Their product is   287.875
```

Figure 8.13 An example of a multi-line output format.

separate lines, or (more accurately) **records**. This is achieved by the / edit descriptor, which can, but need not be, separated from any preceding or succeeding descriptor by a comma, and which indicates the end of the current record.

On input, a / causes the rest of the current record to be ignored and the next input item to be the first item of the *next* record. On output, a / terminates the current record and starts a new one. Thus the statement

```
READ '(3F8.2/3I6)',a,b,c,p,q,r
```

will read three real numbers from the first record and three integers from the second.

Similarly, the statements

```
WRITE (UNIT=6,FMT=201) a,b,a+b,a*b
201 FORMAT("1",T10,"Multi-record example"/            &
           "0","The sum of",F6.2," and",F6.2," is",F7.2/ &
           1X,"Their product is",F10.3)
```

will cause output as shown in Figure 8.13 to be printed starting at the top of a new page.

Multiple consecutive / descriptors cause input records to be skipped or null (blank) records to be output. Thus the statement

```
READ '(3F8.2//3I6)',a,b,c,p,q,r
```

will cause three real numbers to be read from the *first* record and three integers from the *third*. The second record will be skipped and not read.

Multiple / descriptors are particularly useful on output, as we can see in the following variation of the program extract used earlier, which will produce the output shown in Figure 8.14:

```
WRITE (UNIT=6,FMT=202) a,b,a+b,a*b
202 FORMAT("1"////T10,"Another multi-record example"/// &
           1X,"The sum of",F6.2," and",F6.2," is",F7.2// &
           1X,"Their product is",F10.3////)
```

- *(new page)*

    Another multi-record example

The sum of 12.25 and 23.50 is 35.75

Their product is   287.875

Figure 8.14 Another example of multi-line output formatting.

Finally, it should be pointed out that the combination of a / edit descriptor and a repeated format can provide a very powerful degree of flexibility; thus the following format

```
(I6/(I4,3F12.2))
```

specifies that the first record consists of a single integer, and that the following ones all consist of an integer followed by three real numbers, since the format will be repeated as many times as necessary from the left parenthesis before the **I4** descriptor.

■ EXAMPLE 8.2

1 Problem

A piece of experimental apparatus is monitoring the radioactive decay of a specimen. At approximately regular intervals it records the time since the start of the experiment (in hundredths of a second), the number of α-particles emitted during the interval, the number of β-particles emitted and the amount of γ-radiation in the same period. These are output as an eight-digit number (for the time) and three six-digit numbers. There are five spaces between each number.

Write a program to read this data and to print a table containing the following information: a sequence number for each interval, the length of the interval, the three readings obtained and the average emission of α-particles, β-particles and γ-rays (per second) during the interval. After 1000 time intervals print the time interval which had the highest rate of emission of γ-radiation.

2 Analysis

This is a straightforward problem, which is primarily concerned with the use of formats to read the data and lay out the results. We shall use constants (*in* and *out*) in which to store the unit numbers, thus making it much easier to change these if it should subsequently be desired to do so.

Data design

Purpose	Type	Name
A Constants:		
I/O unit numbers	INTEGER	in, out
Maximum number of readings	INTEGER	max_readings
B Variables:		
Time since start (data)	REAL	time
Experimental readings (data)	INTEGER	alpha, beta, gamma
DO variable (and sequence no.)	INTEGER	i
Time of last reading and interval	REAL	last_time, period
Average emissions	REAL	av_alpha, av_beta, av_gamma
Maximum average gamma	REAL	max_av_gamma
Interval with max ave. gamma	INTEGER	max_interval

Structure plan

> **1**   Initialize maximum gamma radiation and interval
>
> **2**   Print column headings
>
> **3**   Repeat *max_readings* times
> > **3.1**   Read next set of data
> > **3.2**   Calculate length of interval and average emissions
> > **3.3**   Print details
> > **3.4**   If γ-radiation > max γ-radiation then
> > > **3.4.1**   Save maximum γ-radiation and interval number
>
> **4**   Print details of maximum γ-radiation

This is fairly straightforward except for step 2. We shall be printing a table with eight columns and it is sensible to identify these by headings. We can do this by means of a **WRITE** statement which has no output list, but which uses a format consisting solely of character constant edit descriptors together with any necessary positioning descriptors.

We also need to consider the formats for both input and output. As is often the case, the format of the data is already defined and our format definition must therefore reflect it. In this case it is quite simple:

```
(F8.2,5X,I6,5X,I6,5X,I6)
```

The time is provided in hundredths of a second so the easiest approach is to read it as a real number in seconds with an implied decimal point before the last two digits. The other items are all integers. Notice that we have a repeated sequence (**5X,I6**) in the format shown above. We can shorten this format in one of two ways, either by enclosing this sequence in parentheses and preceding it by a repeat count, or by including the leading spaces as part of the numeric field — although this could be dangerous as there is no guarantee that there is not some other data in the input records that we are ignoring (i.e. not reading):

```
(F8.2,3(5X,I6))
```

or

```
(F8.2,3I11)
```

Notice that, although we stated earlier that only data edit descriptors were repeatable, the **X** edit descriptor in the first alternative has also been repeated. This is allowed when it is part of a repeated sequence which contains at least one repeatable edit descriptor.

Output is always rather different from input in one important respect, namely that we usually have complete control over its format. In this case we wish to produce a table of eight items — a sequence number, a time interval (to one hundredth of a second), three integer values and three averages. Although, at first sight, a suitable format might be

```
(I6,F8.2,3I8,3F8.2)
```

more detailed examination of the layout, and of the expected size of the results, leads to the conclusion that a more aesthetically pleasing layout might be obtained with the format

```
(I6,F8.2,2I6,I7,2F9.2,F10.2)
```

Notice that all the edit descriptors in this format have a field width wider than is necessary in order to space the columns across the page, and also to leave room for column titles.

3 Solution

```
PROGRAM Radioactive_decay
  IMPLICIT NONE

  ! This program processes experimental data relating
  ! to radioactive decay

  ! Constant declarations
  ! max_readings is maximum number of sets of data
  ! in and out are the unit numbers for reading and writing
  INTEGER,PARAMETER :: max_readings=1000,in=5,out=6
```

```
! Variable declarations
INTEGER :: alpha,beta,gamma,i,max_interval=0
REAL :: time,last_time=0.0,period, &
        av_alpha,av_beta,av_gamma,max_av_gamma=0.0

! Print headings
WRITE (UNIT=out,FMT=201)

! Process max_readings sets of data in a loop
DO i=1,max_readings
    READ (UNIT=in,FMT=101) time,alpha,beta,gamma

    ! Calculate interval since last readings
    period = time-last_time
    last_time = time

    ! Calculate average rates of emission
    av_alpha = alpha/period
    av_beta = beta/period
    av_gamma = gamma/period

    ! Print statistics for this interval
    WRITE (UNIT=out,FMT=202) i,period,alpha,beta,gamma,   &
                             av_alpha,av_beta,av_gamma

    ! Check for maximum gamma radiation in this period
    IF (av_gamma > max_av_gamma) THEN
        max_av_gamma = av_gamma
        max_interval = i
    END IF
END DO

! Print details of interval with maximum gamma radiation
WRITE (UNIT=out,FMT=203) max_av_gamma,max_interval.

! Format statements
101 FORMAT (F8.2,3(5X,I6))
201 FORMAT ("1","Interval",T11,"Time",T17,"Alpha", &
    T24,"Beta",T30,"Gamma",T37,"Average",T46,"Average", &
    T55,"Average"/ &
    T38,"Alpha",T47,"Beta",T56,"Gamma")
202 FORMAT (I6,F8.2,2I6,I7,2F9.2,F10.2)
203 FORMAT ("0",T3,"Maximum average gamma radiation was", &
    F7.2," in interval",I5)

END PROGRAM Radioactive_decay
```

An example of part of the results produced by this program can be seen in Figure 8.15.

This example is typical of the class of problems for which the **E** edit descriptor will often be better than the **F** edit descriptor, since the size and range of the results may be unknown when it is written and may vary quite widely

Interval	Time	Alpha	Beta	Gamma	Average Alpha	Average Beta	Average Gamma
.	.	.	.	.	.	.	.
.	.	.	.	.	.	.	.
.	.	.	.	.	.	.	.
990	2.56	175	23	401	68.36	8.98	156.64
991	2.59	168	22	395	64.86	8.49	152.51
992	2.48	181	27	412	72.98	10.89	166.13
993	2.51	177	25	410	70.52	9.96	163.35
994	2.48	166	29	391	66.94	11.69	157.66
995	2.54	181	25	397	71.26	9.84	156.30
996	2.51	169	28	407	67.33	11.16	162.15
997	2.58	159	23	388	61.63	8.91	150.39
998	2.51	177	26	401	70.52	10.36	159.76
999	2.47	173	24	398	70.04	9.72	161.13
1000	2.52	183	28	403	72.62	11.11	159.92

Maximum average gamma radiation was 174.28 in interval 741

Figure 8.15 Results produced by the `Radioactive_decay` program.

between different experiments. Thus, while the average values for alpha particles shown in Figure 8.15 are all printed to four significant digits, the averages for beta particles vary between three and four and the average gamma radiation always has five significant digits. And yet all data was collected at the same time with, presumably, the same intrinsic level of accuracy. Using an **E** edit descriptor

Int.	Time	A	B	G	Average Alpha	Average Beta	Average Gamma
990	2.56	175	23	401	0.68359E+02	0.89844E+01	0.15664E+03
.	.	.	.	.	.	.	.
.	.	.	.	.	.	.	.
.	.	.	.	.	.	.	.
990	2.56	175	23	401	0.68359E+02	0.89844E+01	0.15664E+03
991	2.59	168	22	395	0.64865E+02	0.84942E+01	0.15251E+03
992	2.48	181	27	412	0.72984E+02	0.10887E+02	0.16613E+03
993	2.51	177	25	410	0.70518E+02	0.99602E+01	0.16335E+03
994	2.48	166	29	391	0.66935E+02	0.11694E+02	0.15766E+03
995	2.54	181	25	397	0.71260E+02	0.98425E+01	0.15630E+03
996	2.51	169	28	407	0.67331E+02	0.11155E+02	0.16215E+03
997	2.58	159	23	388	0.61628E+02	0.89147E+01	0.15039E+03
998	2.51	177	26	401	0.70518E+02	0.10359E+02	0.15976E+03
999	2.47	173	24	398	0.70040E+02	0.97166E+01	0.16113E+03
1000	2.52	183	28	403	0.72619E+02	0.11111E+02	0.15992E+03

Maximum average gamma radiation was 0.17428E+03 in interval 741

Figure 8.16 Results produced by the modified `Radioactive_decay` program.

for these three values will enable them all to be shown to the same level of accuracy.

Do not, however, fall into the trap of believing that just because the results are printed to d digits of precision that they are necessarily accurate to that degree! We shall have more to say about this in Chapter 10.

Figure 8.16 shows the result of running a slightly modified version of the same program with the same data as before. The only change is to the three format statements 201, 202 and 203 to allow all averages to be printed to five digits of precision.

SELF-TEST EXERCISES 8.2

1   Find out which are the default input and output units for the computer that you are using, and also if any other units are preconnected.

2   What is the major difference between a **WRITE** statement and a **PRINT** statement?

3   What is the purpose of an **IOSTAT** specifier?

4   What is a printer control character? What values of the printer control character have specified effects?

5   When is a format, or part of one, repeated?

6   If necessary, where will each of the following formats be repeated from?

    (a)   `(3I8,2F8.2)`
    (b)   `(3I8,2(3X,F5.2))`
    (c)   `(3(3X,I5),2F8.2)`
    (d)   `(3(3X,I5),2(3X,F5.2))`
    (e)   `(3I8/2F8.2)`
    (f)   `(3I8/2(3X,F5.2))`

7   Write formats and associated input or output statements to read or print the dimensions of a box as follows:

    (a)   Read the dimensions in metric form, where each side is less than ten metres and the data is typed in the form

        `m.cc by m.cc by m.cc`

    (b)   Print the dimensions and the volume of the box in the form

        `a * b * c (=v cubic metres)`

    (c) Read the dimensions in feet and inches, where each side is less than 30 feet and the data is typed in the form

        `ff'ii" by ff'ii" by ff'ii"`

    (d) Print the dimensions and the volume of the box in the form

        `a * b * c (=v cubic feet)`

SUMMARY

- During list-directed input data values are separated by value separators, each of which may be a comma, a slash, a blank, or the end of record, preceded and/or followed by any number of consecutive blanks.

- If there is no value between two consecutive value separators then a null value is read, leaving the corresponding input list item unchanged.

- Character data read by a list-directed **READ** statement must be delimited by apostrophes or quotation marks unless it is contained on a single line, does not contain any blanks, commas or slashes, does not begin with an apostrophe or quotation mark, and does not begin with a sequence of digits followed by an asterisk.

- A format specifier is used to provided user-specified data editing on input and output, and may be embedded in the input/output statement or contained in a separate **FORMAT** statement.

- **I** edit descriptors are used to edit integer data.

- **F** or **E** edit descriptors are used to edit real data.

- **A** edit descriptors are used to edit character data.

- **L** edit descriptors are used to edit logical data.

- **X**, **T**, **TL** and **TR** edit descriptors are used to control where data is read from in an input record and where it is placed in an output record.

- **/** edit descriptors are used to identify the end of a record.

- Formats, or parts of formats, are repeated as many times as required until the input or output list has been exhausted.

- **READ** and **WRITE** statements with control information lists are used to provide greater flexibility than is possible with the simple **READ** and **PRINT** statements which always use the default input and output units.

- The control information list in a **READ** or **WRITE** statement consists of a list of specifiers which provide additional information for use during input or output.

- A **UNIT** specifier is used to specify the input or output unit to be used for a **READ** or **WRITE** statement.

- An `FMT` specifier is used to specify the format to be used with a `READ` or `WRITE` statement.

- An `IOSTAT` specifier is used to determine whether a `READ` or `WRITE` statement was executed without any error, and to provide information about the type of error if one occurred.

- The first character of each output record being sent to the unit designated by the processor as a printer is removed before printing takes place and used to control vertical printer movement; it is called the printer control character.

- Fortran 90 syntax introduced in Chapter 8:

Input/output statements	`READ` (*cilist*) *input_list*
	`WRITE` (*cilist*) *output_list*
Format specifier	(*list of edit descriptors*)
`FORMAT` statement	*label* `FORMAT` (*list of edit descriptors*)
Edit descriptors	I*w*, F*w.d*, E*w.d*, A*w*, `A`, L*w*
	*n*X, T*c*, TL*n*, TR*n*, /
Control information	`UNIT` = *unit*
list specifiers	`UNIT` = ⋆
	`FMT` = *label*
	`FMT` = '*format_specifier*'
	`FMT` = ⋆
	`IOSTAT` = *int_var*

PROGRAMMING EXERCISES

8.1   Find out which are the standard input and output units for the computer that you are using. Also find out if any other units are preconnected. If *In* represents the default input unit, and *Out* represents the default output unit, find out what happens if you refer to unit ⋆ and either *In* or *Out* in the same program.

When you have established the answers to these questions run the following programs to see if they behave as you expect.

```
PROGRAM unit_test_1
   IMPLICIT NONE
   ! Note that "input_unit" and "output_unit" should be
   ! replaced in the following declaration by the correct
   ! unit numbers for the computer you are using
   INTEGER, PARAMETER :: in=input_unit, out=output_unit

   INTEGER :: num1,num2

   WRITE (UNIT=*,FMT=*) "Please type a 4 digit integer "
   READ (UNIT=*,FMT=*) num1
   WRITE (UNIT=out,FMT=*) "Please type a 3 digit integer "
   READ (UNIT=in,FMT=*) num2
   WRITE (UNIT=out,FMT=*) "The numbers you typed were &
                          &as follows"
   PRINT '(" ",I4," and",I4)',num1,num2
END PROGRAM unit_test_1
```

```
PROGRAM unit_test_2
   IMPLICIT NONE

   ! Note that "input_unit" and "output_unit" should be
   ! replaced in the following declaration by the correct
   ! unit numbers for the computer you are using
   INTEGER, PARAMETER :: in=input_unit, out=output_unit

   INTEGER :: num1,num2

   WRITE (UNIT=out,FMT=*) 'Please type a 4 digit integer '
   READ (UNIT=in,FMT=*) num1
   WRITE (UNIT=*,FMT=*) 'Please type a 3 digit integer '
   READ (UNIT=*,FMT=*) num2
   PRINT *, 'The numbers you typed were as follows'
   WRITE (UNIT=out,FMT='(" ",I4," and",I4)') num1,num2
END PROGRAM unit_test_2
```

8.2   The actual implementation of printer control characters, especially **+** (to produce output on the same line as the previous record) and **1** (to start a new page) can vary — especially when the output device is a display screen. Run the following program to establish what happens on your computer system.

```
PROGRAM ptest
   IMPLICIT NONE
   ! This program tests the effect of printer control
   ! characters on the display and on the printer

   ! In the following declaration statement display_unit
   ! should be replaced by the unit number of the display
   ! on your computer, and printer_unit by the unit number
   ! of the printer (if one is available)
   INTEGER, PARAMETER :: display=display_unit,            &
                         printer=printer_unit

   INTEGER :: n

   WRITE (UNIT=display,FMT=100)
   WRITE (UNIT=printer,FMT=100)
100 FORMAT                                                &
     ("1","This line should be at the top of a new page"/ &
      " ","This should be on the next line"/              &
      "0","This line should be after a blank line"/       &
      " ","This line should be"/                          &
      "+","                       on the next line"/      &
      "0",23X,"after a blank line"/                       &
      "+","And this one should be")

   ! Wait until you have checked the output to the display
   WRITE (UNIT=display,FMT=*)                             &
        "Check the display and then type an integer"
   READ *,n

   ! Repeat the output - to see what happens to the display
   WRITE (display,FMT=100)
   WRITE (printer,FMT=100)
END PROGRAM ptest
```

8.3   Write a program to display a 'multiplication square'. The numbers 1–12 should run across the top of the table and down the side, with the entries holding the relevant product. Thus the first few lines would be:

```
       1  2  3  4  5  6  7  8  9  10 11 12
    X
1      1  2  3  4  5  6  7  8  9  10 11 12
2      2  4  6  8  10 12 14 16 18 20 22 24
3      3  6  9  12  ...
```

etc.

8.4   Write a program which will input a date in the form *dd mmm yyyy*, where *dd* and *yyyy* are numeric, and *mmm* is a 3-letter representation of the month, and convert it to the number of days since 1 January 1900.

8.5   Write a program that finds the positive difference between two 3-digit integer numbers and produces the result of the calculation in the form:

The positive difference between *n1* **and** *n2* **is** *n3*

Use formatted **READ** and **PRINT** statements in your program.

*8.6   Store twelve 5-digit numbers in an array. Purely by changing the output format, print the numbers as

- **(a)**   a single column of numbers
- **(b)**   four rows of three numbers
- **(c)**   a single line of numbers

Now modify the program so that the format is unchanged, but that altering the way in which a *single* **READ** statement is used can produce the same three formats for the results.

8.7   A railway timetable has to be produced in the following form

Station no.	Arrival	Departure
1	-	1.20
2	2.05	2.15
3	2.35	2.45
4	3.20	3.30
5	3.40	-

Write a program that prints out the timetable on the screen as given above.

8.8   Find a printed four-figure logarithm table. Write a program to print such a table.

8.9   Write a program to print a bank statement. The user should be asked for the opening balance and the amount of each of a number of transactions, which may be debits or credits. Once all transactions have been entered, the program should calculate the final balance and generate a printout of the form:

```
Opening balance:      123.45
Transactions:
Debit      Credit     Total
11.23                 112.22
50.00                  62.22
           25.00       87.22
Closing balance:       87.22
```

Is the **REAL** data type suitable for such financial calculations?

8.10 The expression

$$\sin \theta \sin \phi - \frac{(\cos(\theta - \phi) - \cos(\theta + \phi))}{2}$$

should be zero for all values of θ and ϕ. Write a program which will produce a square table showing the calculated values of the function for values of θ and ϕ between 0 and 3 radians in steps of 0.25.

8.11 Angles are often expressed in degrees, minutes and seconds, where there are 360 degrees in a full circle, 60 minutes in a degree, and 60 seconds in a minute.

Define a derived type suitable for this form of representation. Then write a program that reads an angle as three integer values, representing the degrees, minutes and seconds, and which then computes its value as a decimal number of degrees, and also its value in radians (where there are 2π radians in a full circle, and π may be taken as 3.141 592 36). The program should display the angle in all three forms, using four decimal places for the value in decimal degrees, and an appropriate number of decimal places for the value in radians.

8.12 A chemist makes five measurements of the rates of three different reactions. The data collected is shown below:

Reaction A	Reaction B	Reaction C
20.6	16.9	90.6
31.2	20.2	100.2
10.9	30.7	98.7
15.4	30.2	117.2
12.1	30.0	88.6

Write a program that calculates the mean rate and standard deviation for each reaction. The standard deviation is given by the formula

$$\sigma = \sqrt{\frac{1}{N} \sum (x_i - \mu)^2}$$

where N is the number of measurements, μ is the mean and x_i is the ith measurement for each reaction. Use formatted output to produce a table consisting of three columns for the experimental data followed by the mean and standard deviation for each reaction.

*8.13 Following an earthquake it is required to print out the seismic measurements recorded at a number of different centres around the world. Write a program which reads several sets of data from the keyboard, each consisting of the longitude and latitude of the recording instrument (as two pairs of integer numbers) and the strength measured on the Richter scale (as a real number). Each set of figures should be stored in a derived type array, each element of which holds the position and strength of the measurement.

Latitudes to the west of the Greenwich meridian are recorded as negative values (thus 23°48′ W is recorded as −23,48), and those to the east as positive values. Similarly, longitudes north of the equator are recorded as positive, and those to the south as negative.

Your program should read all the data, and then print the measurements as a table in the following form:

```
Seismic measuremnts recorded after Laheytown earthquake
    Recording Station           Richter
    Longitude      Latitude     Strength
    nn°nn' N      nnn°nn' W      nn.nn
    nn°nn' S      nnn°nn' E      nn.nn
        .             .             .
        .             .             .
        .             .             .
```

8.14   Even on a computer without graphics facilities, simple plots can be produced by, for instance, printing an asterisk in the appropriate column of the screen to represent a point. Use this technique to make a plot of the function $y = \cos x$ for x taking values from 0 to 4π radians. Can you make the x-axis run across the page instead of down?

8.15   Write and test a subroutine which prints a real number x, using a field width of 8, according to the following rules:

(a)   If $x = \text{INT}(x)$ then the number should be displayed as an integer
(b)   Otherwise, if it is possible, x should be printed in fixed point format to at least 3 significant figures
(c)   Otherwise x should be printed in floating point format to as many decimal places as will fit in the space available

Using files to preserve data

One of the most important aspects of computing is the ability for a program to save the data that it has been using for subsequent use either by itself or by another program. This involves the output of the data to a file, usually on some form of magnetic or optical medium, for input at some later time. Files may be written and read sequentially or, on some types of media, the information in a file may be written and read in a random order. In either case the file may be stored permanently within the computer system, for example on a magnetic or magneto-optical disk which is an integral part of the computer, or it may be stored on some medium, such as a disk or tape, which may be removed from the computer either for safe-keeping or for physical transport to another computer.

This chapter shows how the READ and WRITE statements discussed in Chapter 8 can be used to read data from a file and write data to a file, in a sequential manner, and introduces several additional statements which are required when dealing with files. More sophisticated uses of files, including random access to information stored in a file, is discussed later, in Chapter 15.

9.1 Files and records

The input and output facilities that we have met so far allow us to input data and to output results in a wide variety of different ways; however there has been one major omission which we shall now address. All the programs that we have written have been based on the assumption that when the program is run it reads some data from the keyboard (or other default input unit), processes it, produces some results which are displayed on the screen or sent to a printer, and finishes. Once the program has finished nothing remains within the computer system.

This ignores two very important aspects of the normal computing process.

The first is that if there are more than a few lines of data it is usually far more appropriate to type the data into a **file**, possibly using the same editor as is used to type and edit the program, and for the program to then read the data directly from the file. This has the advantage that the data need only be typed once; on all subsequent runs of the program (for example, during testing) there is no need to retype the data. Even if it is not intended to process the data more than once this mode of operation is preferable for larger amounts of data, since it allows for error corrections and/or changes to be made to the data *before* it is read by the program.

For similar reasons, where there are more than a few lines of results to be displayed it is often more convenient to send them to a file which can subsequently be displayed in sections or sent to a printer, or both, as appropriate.

The second aspect that we must consider occurs when the results produced by one program, or some of the results, are required as data for another program, or even another run of the same program. Examples of this type of application range from data processing activities such as payroll calculation or financial accounting, where past records are essential, to analysis of scientific experiments over a period of time, control of airline reservations, scheduling of production, or any other activity which requires knowledge of some past events of the same or similar type.

The **file store** of the computer system is used for this purpose. This consists of special input/output units usually, though not always, based on either magnetic disks or magnetic tapes, or a combination of the two. Information may be transferred to and from these units by using **READ** and **WRITE** statements in a similar manner to that used for data and results transferred via the default input and output units. However, before we examine this in more detail, we must first define two important concepts, namely those of a **record** and of a **file**.

We have already referred to records informally when discussing input and output, and have understood it to refer to a sequence of characters such as a line of typing or a printed line of results. However, a record does not necessarily correspond in this way to some physical entity, but refers to some defined sequence of characters *or of values*. There are three types of records in Fortran 90, formatted, unformatted and endfile records, and we shall discuss these in some detail in the next section.

A sequence of records forms a file, of which there are two types – external and internal. We shall investigate external files in more detail before we start to examine the records of which they are comprised; internal files will be discussed in Chapter 15.

An **external file** is an identifiable sequence of records which is stored on some external medium. Thus a sheet of printed results is a file. Although this is the formal definition of a file, in general usage a file is normally understood to refer to a file which is part of the computer system's file store. As we have already indicated, there are two main types of storage medium used for this purpose, magnetic tape and magnetic or optical disk, and before discussing files any further it is important to recognize one very important difference between these two types of storage medium, and the effect that this has on the use of files in Fortran programs.

A magnetic tape, which is the older storage medium, is a **sequential** storage medium, in that each record written will normally be written directly after the previous record, so that the normal way of reading magnetic tape records is in the same order as that in which they were written. Magnetic tapes on large computer systems are typically over 2000 ft long (or almost 0.75 km) and may contain as many as 50 million characters or their equivalent, although standard audio cassettes are also used on some small computers, and it would be extremely time-consuming to search for individual records in a random order. On the other hand, magnetic tapes are easy to store and the tape decks that are used to read and write information are relatively economical to manufacture.

A magnetic or optical disk, however, does not record information in a single spiral, like a record, but stores it in the form of a large number of concentric circular **tracks**. This means that information can be retrieved from any part of the surface of the disk in a fraction of a second since, at worst, the read head only needs to travel a few inches to position itself on the required part of the disk. Such a storage unit can therefore be used for **random access** of information as well as sequential access. Moreover, because the technology used in the manufacture of disk drives permits data to be stored very much more densely than is possible on a magnetic tape, a $3\frac{1}{2}$ inch diameter exchangeable **diskette** (or **floppy disk**) on a personal computer can hold almost 3 million characters, while the disks attached to larger computers may store as much as several billion characters.

Because the information anywhere on a magnetic disk (or other similar device) can be accessed so rapidly, and because a disk can hold so much information, a single disk will usually store a large number of separate files of information. Most computers will have some disks permanently (or semi-permanently) mounted, while others will only be loaded when required. On a personal computer, for example, there will normally be a permanently mounted **fixed disk** (or **hard disk**) capable of storing between 100 million and 500 million characters, while diskettes of 1–3 million characters will be loaded as and when required to provide more transitory data storage, or to provide a second copy for backup or for transfer of information to another computer.

In the case of computers which are used simultaneously by more than one user, the files on a single disk will often belong to a number of different users of the computer, and it is the job of the computer's operating system to keep a catalogue of all the files so that the correct files can be made available to a program when required. Because of the problems associated with sequential access, on the other hand, a magnetic tape often consists of a single file, but the computer's operating system will often catalogue this so that a record is kept of which file is stored on which physical magnetic tape. Thus the operating system will, usually, be able to request that the appropriate tape be loaded whenever a program wishes to use a file which is stored on that tape.

For most purposes we may ignore the differences between the various types of file store units and simply consider their mode of access – sequential or direct. In this chapter, moreover, we shall only consider sequential access files; the use of direct access files will be discussed in Chapter 15. However, before we start to use any type of file we must investigate in more detail the three types of record which may make up a file.

9.2   Formatted, unformatted and endfile records

The first type of record is called a **formatted record**, and consists of a sequence of characters selected from those which can be represented by the processor being used – that is the 58 characters in the Fortran character set plus any other characters which may be available. A formatted record is written by the same type of formatted output statement that we introduced in Chapter 8:

```
WRITE 200, var_1,var_2,var_3
```

or by an output statement which uses list-directed formatting:

```
WRITE *, var_1,var_2,var_3
```

Each such output statement creates a new record, or several new records if the format used defines multiple records.

A formatted record may also be created by some means other than a Fortran program; for example it may be typed at a keyboard.

A formatted record is read by a formatted input statement, including one which uses list-directed formatting.

A formatted record is formatted so that it can be represented in a form that human beings (or a different type of computer) can understand. The work involved in converting values from their internal (binary) representation into character form, or vice versa, imposes a considerable overhead, and if the information is being written to a file so that the same program, or another one on the same computer, can subsequently read it back there is clearly no need to convert it to character form. Furthermore, where real numbers are concerned, the process of converting them to character form and then converting back to internal form will almost invariably introduce round-off errors due to the difference in precision of the internal and external (character) representations. Fortran 90 therefore contains a second type of record, called an **unformatted record**, which consists of a sequence of values (in a processor-dependent form) and is, essentially, a copy of some part, or parts, of the memory of the computer. An unformatted record can only be produced by an unformatted output statement, which is the same as a formatted **WRITE** statement but without any format specifier:

```
WRITE (UNIT=9) var_1,var_2,var_3
WRITE (UNIT=3,IOSTAT=ios) x,y,z
```

As we might expect, an unformatted record can only be read by an unformatted input statement:

```
READ (UNIT=9) var_4,var_5,var_6
READ (UNIT=3,IOSTAT=io_status) a,b,c
```

One important difference between the input/output of formatted and unformatted records is that whereas a formatted input or output statement may read or write more than one record by use of a suitable format, for example

```
WRITE (UNIT=3,FMT='(2I8/(4F12.4))') int_1,int_2,arr
```

an unformatted input or output statement will always read or write exactly *one* record. The number of items in the input list of an unformatted **READ** statement must therefore be the same as the number in the output list of the unformatted **WRITE** statement that wrote it, or fewer (in which case the last few items in the record are ignored).

As well as formatted and unformatted records there is a third type of record which is particularly important for files which are to be accessed sequentially; this is the **endfile record**, which is a special type of record which can only occur as the last record of a file and is written by a special statement

```
ENDFILE unit
```

or

```
ENDFILE (auxlist)
```

In the first case *unit* is the output unit to which an endfile record is to be written, while in the second case *auxlist* consists of a **UNIT** specifier and, optionally, an

IOSTAT specifier, where these specifiers are the same as those already introduced in Section 8.6 for use with a WRITE statement. As is the case with the READ and WRITE statements, the UNIT= may be omitted if the unit specifier is the first specifier in the list, but, as for those statements, we strongly recommend that, for clarity, the full form is used.

An ENDFILE statement writes a special endfile record to the specified file and leaves the file positioned after that record. Any information which physically exists after an endfile record becomes inaccessible thereafter, and may be considered to have been deleted. It is not subsequently possible to write to, or read from, that file without first repositioning it by using either a REWIND or a BACKSPACE statement (see Section 9.4).

An endfile record has no defined length, but if it is read by an input statement it will cause an **end-of-file condition** which can be detected by an IOSTAT specifier in a READ statement. *If it is not specifically detected in this way an error will occur and the program will fail.*

It is good practice to place an endfile record at the end of all sequential files in order that a program which subsequently reads the file can easily detect the end of the information in the file without the need for any other special records or counts. It also acts as a safeguard against an error which might cause the program not to detect the end of the information in the file.

9.3   Connecting external files to your program

There is one further important difference between input and output using files and the forms of input and output that we have been concerned with up to now, and that concerns the identification of the input or output unit which is to be used. Before any input or output unit can be used by a program to read or write data it has to be **connected** to the program, although certain peripheral units (such as the default input unit and the default output unit) will always be **preconnected**. We need to examine how we can connect a particular file to our program and what implications this has.

Every computer system normally has a very large number of files which, in some sense or other, *belong* to that computer. Some, such as a printer listing, do not belong to it for very long, while others, such as files in its permanent file store, may belong to it for a considerable period of time. These files have been created by the various users of the computer, or by those who are responsible for its operation, or even by the computer's own operating system, and have various levels of accessibility. For example, a file containing a library of widely used subroutines, or a Fortran 90 compiler, will probably be available to all users of the computer; a file created by a user to contain private research data, on the other hand, will almost certainly only be accessible by the user, or by the user and a small group of colleagues working on the same project. At any given time,

```
UNIT = unit_number
FILE = file_name
STATUS = file_status
FORM = format_mode
ACTION = allowed_actions
POSITION = file_position
IOSTAT = ios
```

Figure 9.1 Some of the specifiers available for use with OPEN.

therefore, a particular program will only be allowed to access a certain number of the files held by the computer; only these files are said to **exist** for that program.

Before a file can exist it must be created, and in Fortran's terminology **creating** a file means causing a file to exist that did not previously exist. Notice that this action does not necessarily have any effect on the total number of files known to the whole computer system – the act of creating a file simply means that the file exists for the program that creates it. For example, a program may wish to access a file belonging to another user; the act of creating the file in this case merely means granting access to it, whereupon it will exist for this program. In a similar way, **closing** a file means terminating the existence of a file; once again it does not *necessarily* mean that the file is removed from the computer system. One effect of this is that a file may exist and yet not contain any records, for example when it has just been created but not yet written to.

For any information to be transferred between a file and a program the file must be **connected** to a unit; in other words, a logical connection, or relationship, must be established between the file and the unit number that will be used in any **READ** or **WRITE** statements which are to use that file. In some cases a physical connection must also be established, such as, for example, loading a particular diskette into a personal computer. This connection is initiated by means of an **OPEN** statement, which takes the form

    OPEN (*open_specifier_list*)

where *open_specifier_list* is a list of specifiers, as shown in Figure 9.1, although we shall meet some further permissible specifiers in Chapter 15.

The **UNIT** specifier must be present, and takes the same form as in the **READ**, **WRITE** and **ENDFILE** statements. All the remaining specifiers are optional and enable us to specify various requirements regarding the file that is to be opened and to monitor the opening process itself.

If we are concerned with files in the file store they will normally have a name by which they are known to the computer system. This name is specified by using the **FILE** specifier, which takes the form

    FILE = *file_name*

where *file_name* is a character expression which, after the removal of any trailing blanks, takes the form of a filename for the particular computer system. Thus, if the name of the required file is `MILES-ELLIS`, we could connect the file of that name to a program by means of a statement such as

```
OPEN (UNIT=9,FILE="MILES-ELLIS")
```

which will connect unit 9 to the specified file; thereafter any input or output using unit 9 will read from or write to that file.

Alternatively, we could read the name of the required file from the keyboard by a program fragment such as the following:

```
PRINT *,"Please give the name of the input file"
READ '(A)', in_file
OPEN (UNIT=9,FILE=in_file,IOSTAT=open_status)
```

We sometimes wish to define certain restrictions on our use of the file; for example we may wish to ensure that we do not overwrite an existing file by accident. We can use the `STATUS` specifier for this purpose by writing

STATUS = *file_status*

where *file_status* is a character expression which, after removing any trailing blanks, is one of `OLD`, `NEW`, `REPLACE`, `SCRATCH` or `UNKNOWN`. Note that *file_status* is a character expression and therefore we actually write

```
STATUS="OLD"
STATUS="NEW"
```

etc.

If *file_status* is `OLD` then the file *must already exist*, whereas if it is `NEW` then it *must not already exist*. If `NEW` is specified then the `OPEN` statement will attempt to create the file, and if successful will change its status to `OLD`, after which any subsequent attempt to open the file as `NEW` will fail.

If *file_status* is `REPLACE`, and the file already exists, then it is deleted and an attempt made to create a new file with the same name; if this is successful the status is changed to `OLD`. If the file does not already exist then the action taken will be the same as if `NEW` had been specified.

If *file_status* is `SCRATCH` then a special un-named file is created for use by the program; when the program ceases execution (or when the file is `CLOSE`d, see Section 15.1) the file will be deleted and will cease to exist. Such a file can therefore be used as a temporary file for the duration of execution only. It is not permitted, for obvious reasons, to specify that the status of a named file (one with a `FILE` specifier) is `SCRATCH`.

Finally, if *file_status* is **UNKNOWN**, or if no **STATUS** specifier is included, the status of the file is dependent upon the particular implementation. In most cases if the file exists it will be treated as **OLD**, whereas if it does not exist it will be treated as **NEW**. Some implementations, however, have different interpretations of **UNKNOWN** status, and so no assumptions should be made without checking on the exact situation for the Fortran system being used. We strongly recommend, therefore, that you should always be specific in order to avoid potential problems if the program is subsequently moved to a different system.

Because of the different ways in which they are written and read, the records in a file must either all be formatted or all be unformatted, and the specifier

FORM = *format_mode*

is used to specify which is required. The character expression *format_mode* must take one of the two values **FORMATTED** or **UNFORMATTED**, after the removal of any trailing blanks; if it is omitted then the file is assumed to be formatted if it is connected for sequential access, but unformatted if it is connected for direct access (see Section 15.4). Thus the statement

```
OPEN (UNIT=9,FILE="DATAFILE")
```

will connect the file **DATAFILE** to unit 9 as a formatted sequential access file. On the other hand

```
OPEN (UNIT=7,STATUS="SCRATCH",FORM="UNFORMATTED")
```

will create a temporary scratch file and connect it to unit 7 as an unformatted sequential access file.

As well as specifying the initial status of the file, we may also wish to specify what type of input/output actions are allowed with the file. The **ACTION** specifier may be used for this purpose, and takes the form

ACTION = *allowed_actions*

where *allowed_actions* is a character expression which, after the removal of any trailing blanks, must take one of the three values **READ**, **WRITE** or **READWRITE**.

If *allowed_actions* is **READ** then the file is to be treated as a *read-only* file, and only **READ** statements, together with the two file positioning statements **BACKSPACE** and **REWIND** (see Section 9.4), are allowed on this file; **WRITE** and **ENDFILE** statements are not allowed, thus preventing a program from accidentally overwriting information in the file.

If *allowed_actions* is **WRITE** then the file is to be treated as an output file, and only **WRITE** and **ENDFILE** statements, together with the two file positioning statements **BACKSPACE** and **REWIND**, are allowed on this file; **READ** statements are not allowed.

If *allowed_actions* is **READWRITE** then all input/output statements are allowed for this file.

If no **ACTION** specifier is included in an **OPEN** statement then the effect is determined by the particular implementation. It will normally allow any input/output actions (that is, it will behave as though **ACTION = "READWRITE"** had been specified), but it is possible that some implementations might choose a different set of allowable actions for a file depending upon its initial status.

Sometimes it is convenient, when opening a sequential file, to specify that it is to be positioned at some point other than at the beginning, the most obvious case being when a file is being used to store data in a cumulative fashion. The **POSITION** specifier allows the programmer to instruct the **OPEN** statement to cause the file to be positioned in this way, and takes the form

POSITION = *file_position*

where *file_position* is a character expression which, after the removal of any trailing blanks, must take one of the three values **REWIND**, **APPEND** or **ASIS**.

If the file did not previously exist then this specifier is ignored and the new file will always be positioned at its initial point. After all, there is nowhere else to position a new file!

If the file does already exist and *file_position* is **REWIND** then the file is positioned at its initial point and a subsequent **READ** or **WRITE** statement will either read the first record in the file, or write a new first record, as appropriate.

If the file already exists and *file_position* is **APPEND** then the file is positioned immediately before the endfile record, if there is one, or immediately after the last record of the file (at its terminal point) if there is no endfile record. A subsequent **WRITE** statement will therefore write the next record immediately after the end of the existing information in the file; a **READ** statement would, of course, lead to either an error or an end-of-file condition since the file has no records remaining to be read other than an endfile record, if one exists.

The third possibility, that the file already exists and *file_position* is **ASIS**, exists to allow for the possibility that a program attempts to open a file that is already open and connected to the same unit. In this situation the inclusion of the specifier **POSITION = "ASIS"** in the **OPEN** statement ensures that the position of the file is not altered by the execution of the **OPEN** statement. If the file exists but is not already connected then the position of the file after execution of the **OPEN** statement is unspecified.

Rather surprisingly, if no **POSITION** specifier is included in an **OPEN** statement the effect is as though **ASIS** had been specified; that is, the initial position is not defined if the file already exists but is not connected. In practice, however, it is probable that the Fortran 90 implementation will position an existing file at its initial point, ready to read the first record, unless explicitly instructed otherwise by means of a **POSITION = "APPEND"** specifier.

The final specifier that will be discussed here, **IOSTAT**, is concerned with recognizing when an error occurs during the connection process, for example if the named file does not exist or is of the wrong type, and operates in the same way as has already been discussed in connection with the **READ**, **WRITE** and **ENDFILE** statements. In the event of an error during the opening of a file the execution of the program will be terminated unless it is detected by the program:

```
OPEN(UNIT=13,FILE="Problem_file",IOSTAT=ios)
IF (ios /= 0) THEN
   PRINT *,"Error during opening of 'Problem_file'"
      .
      .
      .
END IF
! Continue processing
   .
   .
   .
```

As we have already mentioned, in certain circumstances it is permitted to obey an **OPEN** statement which refers to a unit which is already connected to a file. These situations will be discussed in more detail in Chapter 15 when we examine the remaining, more sophisticated, aspects of Fortran file-handling. However, we should mention at this point that if a unit is already connected to a file when an **OPEN** statement referring to the same unit but a *different* file is obeyed, then the currently connected file is **disconnected** and the specified, new, file is connected in its place. *It is never permitted to attempt to connect a unit to a file if that file is already connected to a different unit.*

■ **EXAMPLE 9.1**

[1] **Problem**

In Example 8.2 we wrote a program which read up to 1000 sets of experimental data. This is clearly a situation in which it would be absurd to read the data directly from the keyboard; it would be far more sensible to store the data in a file and then to read the data from that file. In this way the data can be created at any convenient time, not necessarily all at once, and checked for accuracy, before being processed by the computer at a later time.

Rewrite the solution to Example 8.2 so that the data is read from a file whose name is provided by the user when running the program.

[2] **Analysis**

We have already carried out the main analysis for this problem, and the main change is that an additional **CHARACTER** variable will be required for the name of the file containing the data, and an `INTEGER` variable to record the success, or otherwise, of the attempt to open the required file, together with a small amount of additional 'housekeeping' to open the file at the start of the program.

③ Solution

```fortran
PROGRAM Radioactive_decay
   IMPLICIT NONE
   ! This program processes experimental data relating to
   ! radioactive decay which is stored in a file whose name
   ! is supplied at execution time

   ! Constant declarations
   ! max_readings is maximum number of sets of data
   ! in and out are the unit numbers for reading and writing
   INTEGER,PARAMETER :: max_readings=1000,in=3,out=6

   ! Variable declarations
   INTEGER :: alpha,beta,gamma,i,ios,max_interval=0
   REAL :: time,last_time=0.0,period, &
           av_alpha,av_beta,av_gamma,max_av_gamma=0.0
   CHARACTER(LEN=20) :: data_file_name
   ! Obtain name of data file
   DO
      PRINT *,"Please give name of data file"
      READ '(A)',data_file_name

      ! Open data file on unit number "in"
      OPEN (UNIT=in,FILE=data_file_name,STATUS="OLD",IOSTAT=ios)

      ! Repeat request if file not opened satisfactorily
      IF (ios==0) EXIT
      PRINT *,"Unable to open file - please try again"
   END DO

   ! Print headings
   WRITE (UNIT=out,FMT=201)

   ! Process max_readings sets of data in a loop
   DO i=1,max_readings
      READ (UNIT=in,FMT=101) time,alpha,beta,gamma
      ! Calculate interval since last readings
      period = time-last_time
      last_time = time

      ! Calculate average rates of emission
      av_alpha = alpha/period
      av_beta = beta/period
      av_gamma = gamma/period

      ! Print statistics for this interval
      WRITE (UNIT=out,FMT=202) i,period,alpha,beta,gamma,  &
                               av_alpha,av_beta,av_gamma
```

```
      ! Check for maximum gamma radiation in this period
      IF (av_gamma > max_av_gamma) THEN
         max_av_gamma = av_gamma
         max_interval = i
      END IF
   END DO

   ! Print details of interval with maximum gamma radiation
   WRITE (UNIT=out,FMT=203) max_av_gamma,max_interval

   ! Format statements
   101 FORMAT (F8.2,3(5X,I6))
   201 FORMAT ("1","Interval",T11,"Time",T17,"Alpha", &
       T24,"Beta",T30,"Gamma",T37,"Average",T46,"Average", &
       T55,"Average"/ &
       T38,"Alpha",T47,"Beta",T56,"Gamma")
   202 FORMAT (I6,F8.2,2I6,I7,2F9.2,F10.2)
   203 FORMAT ("0",T3,"Maximum average gamma radiation was", &
       F7.2," in interval",I5)

END PROGRAM Radioactive_decay
```

Note, incidentally, that it was not necessary to open unit **out** since this was assumed to be the default output unit. However, if the output was being saved to a file on a non-default output unit for subsequent use, then it would need to have been explicitly opened.

9.4 File-positioning statements

There are often situations in which it is required to alter the position in a file without reading or writing any records, and Fortran provides two additional file-positioning statements for this purpose. The first of these

BACKSPACE *unit_number*

or

BACKSPACE (*auxlist*)

causes the file to be positioned just before the *preceding* record (that is, it enables the program to read the immediately previously read record again). If the second form is used then, as with the **ENDFILE** statement, *auxlist* consists of a **UNIT** specifier and, optionally, an **IOSTAT** specifier.

The other file-positioning statement is

REWIND *unit_number*

or

REWIND (*auxlist*)

which causes the file to be positioned just before the *first* record so that a subsequent input statement will start reading or writing the file from the beginning.

These two statements are particularly important when we are dealing with endfile records because, as was mentioned in Section 9.3, if a program has either read or written an endfile record it cannot read or write any more records until either a **BACKSPACE** or a **REWIND** statement has positioned the file before the endfile record.

One further important point about the positioning of a file particularly concerns the writing of information to a file in a sequential manner. The rule in Fortran is that *writing a record to a sequential file destroys all information in the file after that record*. This is, in part, a reminder of the days when all sequential files were on magnetic tape and the physical characteristics of a magnetic tape unit had exactly this effect.

Thus it is not possible to use **BACKSPACE** and/or **REWIND** in order to position a file so that only one particular record can be overwritten by a new one, but only so that the rest of the file can be overwritten, or so that a particular record or records can be read. If it is required to overwrite individual records selectively within a file then the file must be opened for direct access (see Section 15.4).

A common use of **BACKSPACE** in conjunction with **ENDFILE** is to add information at the end of a previously written file, as in the following example:

```
.
.
.
! Read up to end-of-file
DO
    READ (UNIT=8,IOSTAT=ios) dummy
    IF (ios<0) EXIT    ! Negative ios means end-of-file
END DO
! Backspace to before end-of-file record
BACKSPACE 8
! Now add new information
WRITE (UNIT=8) ...
.
.
.
! Terminate file with an end-of-file ready for next time
ENDFILE 8
.
.
.
```

In FORTRAN 77 and earlier versions of FORTRAN this was the only way of achieving this objective. However the use of the **POSITION** specifier in the **OPEN** statement provides a much easier alternative in most such situations:

```
    .
    .
    .
! Open file at the end
OPEN (UNIT=8,FILE=datafile,POSITION="APPEND",IOSTAT=ios)
IF (ios /= 0) ...      ! Error during opening
! File is now positioned for adding new information
WRITE (UNIT=8) ...
    .
    .
    .
! Terminate file with an end-of-file ready for next time
ENDFILE 8
    .
    .
    .
```

■ **EXAMPLE 9.2**

---

1 **Problem**

A survey has been carried out to obtain statistics concerning the occupation of people in a certain area. The results of the survey are available in a file for input to the computer in the following format:

Columns 1–20 Name

Column 23 Sex = F if female
              = M if male

Column 25 Job status = 1 if in full-time education
              = 2 if in full-time employment
              = 3 if in part-time employment
              = 4 if temporarily unemployed
              = 5 if not working or seeking a job

This is followed by one or more items depending upon the job status of the respondent:

Job status = 1   columns 28, 29   Age

        = 2   columns 28–31   Monthly salary

        = 3   columns 28–31   Monthly salary
                   columns 34–37   Other monthly income

        = 4   columns 28, 29   Age
                   columns 32–34   No. of months unemployed

        = 5   columns 28, 29   Age
                   column 31   Code
                                     = 1 if looking after children
                                     = 2 if looking after other relatives
                                     = 3 for any other reason

Since the data is stored in a file there is no need for any special terminating record, as the end of the file can be easily recognized.

Write an input procedure to read the data for processing by another part of the program.

2 Analysis

The major problem here is the variable format of the data, depending on the code which is used to describe the job status (in column 25). In Chapter 15 we shall meet two approaches which can be used to deal with this problem, but we can deal with it here in a cruder, and more time-consuming, way by backspacing and reading the record again using the correct format.

Although it was not specified in the problem, it will clearly be desirable to define a derived type to represent the data for one person, and to place this definition, together with the various codes, in a module which can be used by both the input procedure and the other parts of the program which will deal with the analysis of the data and the printing of results.

The form of this derived type will clearly allow for all possible variations in the data, even though several of these will not be relevant for any one person. We must therefore set any unused fields to a special value to indicate that they are unused. Since the relevant fields are all numeric, and none of them will be negative, we can set the unused fields to a negative value, which will easily be distinguished from the real data.

The other question which was not specified concerns the opening of the input file. It would be possible for the main program to identify the appropriate file and then open this on a particular unit, communicating this unit number to the input procedure, or the input procedure could deal with this itself. If the file were to be used elsewhere in the program then the former option would probably be preferable, but if the file is only to be accessed to read the data then it would seem better to keep all access to it within the one procedure. We shall adopt this option. Nevertheless, to avoid possible unit number clashes, the unit number to be used will be provided as an argument to the procedure.

Finally, there is always the possibility that an input procedure may detect an error when reading the data and it is important that the calling program unit is aware of this. There are three obvious errors that might occur in a procedure such as this:

(1) There is an error during the opening of the file. This will obviously mean that no data has been read! However, it may be possible for the procedure to advise the user of the difficulty if, as here, the filename is being requested interactively, in which case it might be preferable to allow, say, three attempts to open the file before failing.

(2) There is an error during the reading of the data.

(3) The maximum number of records is read without a terminator.

We shall return the value -1 in the first case, -2 in the second case, and -3 in the last. In the last two cases the actual number of valid records read will also, of course, be returned in the same way as for an error-free case. If there were no errors then the value zero will be returned.

We can now define our data structure and write a structure plan.

Data design

MODULE survey_details

	Purpose	Type	Name
A	Constants:		
	Sex codes	CHARACTER*1	female, male
	Job codes	INTEGER	ft_ed, ft_job, pt_job, no_job, at_home
	At home codes	INTEGER	ch_minder, rel_minder, other
	Code for unused data entries	INTEGER	unused
B	Data type		
	Individual survey response	[CHARACTER*20, CHARACTER*1, INT,INT,INT, INT,REAL,REAL]	survey_info

Subroutine input (using survey_details)

	Purpose	Type	Name
A	Arguments:		
	Unit number for data	INTEGER	unit
	Maximum no of data sets	INTEGER	max_datasets
	Survey data	survey_info	survey_data(:)
	Number of data sets read	INTEGER	num_datasets
	Error code	INTEGER	error_code

B Local variables:

File name for data	CHARACTER*30	data_file
DO variable	INTEGER	i
IOSTAT return code	INTEGER	ios
Name (current record)	CHARACTER*20	name
Sex	CHARACTER*1	sex
Job status	INTEGER	status
Age	INTEGER	age
No. months unemployed	INTEGER	months
At home code	INTEGER	code
Monthly salary	REAL	salary
Other monthly income	REAL	income

Structure plan

> 1 Request name of data file and open it on *unit*
>
> 2 Repeat up to *max_datasets* times
>   2.1 Read next record as though job status is 5
>   2.2 If end of file then exit from loop
>   2.3 If error then set *error_code* to −2 and exit from loop
>   2.4 Select case on job status
>   status is 1 or 5
>   2.4.1 Set unused items to unused
>   status is 2, 3 or 4
>   2.4.2 Backspace and read record again
>   2.4.3 Set unused items to unused
>   2.5 Copy local record to array
>
> 3 If end of file read set *error_code* to −3
>
> 4 Return number of data sets read

Note that a set of local variables are being used for initial input to simplify the programming, and that when the full record has been read in the correct format the final data is then copied to the next element of the main data array.

3 Solution

```
MODULE survey_details
   IMPLICIT NONE

   ! This module contains a type definition and constants
   ! for use with the input and processing of survey data

   ! Type definition for survey response
   TYPE survey_info
      CHARACTER(LEN=20) :: name
      CHARACTER :: sex
      INTEGER :: job_status,age,months_jobless,at_home_code
      REAL :: salary,other_income
   END TYPE survey_info
```

```fortran
   ! Various codes
   CHARACTER, PARAMETER :: female="F", male="M"  ! Sex
   INTEGER, PARAMETER ::                      &
           ft_ed=1,ft_job=2,pt_job=3,         &! Job status
           no_job=4,at_home=5,                &! ----------
           ch_minder=1,rel_minder=2,other=3,  &! At home code
           unused=-1                           ! Unused code


END MODULE survey_details



SUBROUTINE input(unit,max_datasets,survey_data,num_datasets, &
                 error_code)
   USE survey_details
   IMPLICIT NONE

   ! This subroutine reads up to max_datasets records prepared
   ! as follows, returning the number read in num_datasets

   ! Columns 1-20 Name
   !          23 Sex (M or F)
   !          25 Job status (1-5)
   !       28,29 Age - for status 1, 4 or 5
   !       28-31 Monthly salary - for status 2 and 3
   !       32-34 Other monthly income - for status 3
   !       32-34 Months unemployed - for status 4
   !          31 Special code (1-3) - for status 5

   ! Arguments
   INTEGER, INTENT(IN) :: unit,max_datasets
   INTEGER, INTENT(OUT) :: num_datasets,error_code
   TYPE(survey_info), DIMENSION(:), INTENT(OUT) :: survey_data

   ! Local variables
   CHARACTER(LEN=30) :: data_file
   CHARACTER(LEN=20) :: name
   CHARACTER :: sex
   INTEGER :: i,ios,status,age,months,code
   REAL :: salary,income

   ! Ask for name of data file
   ! A maximum of three attempts will be allowed to open the file
   DO i=1,3
      PRINT *,"Type name of data file"
      READ '(A)',data_file
      ! Open file at beginning
      OPEN (UNIT=unit,FILE=data_file,POSITION="REWIND",    &
            IOSTAT=ios)
      IF (ios==0) EXIT
      ! Error when opening file - try again
      PRINT *,"Unable to open file - please try again"
   END DO
```

```
! If open was unsuccessful after 3 attempts return error=-1
IF (ios /= 0) THEN
   error_code = -1
   RETURN

   ! Successful file opening
   error_code = 0
END IF

! Loop to read data
DO i=1,max_datasets
   ! Read (part of) next set of data
   READ (UNIT=unit,FMT='(A20,2X,A1,1X,I1,2X,I2,1X,I1)',   &
         IOSTAT=ios)name,sex,status,age,code

   ! Check for errors and end of file
   SELECT CASE (ios)
   CASE (:-1)               ! End of file - no more data
      EXIT

   CASE (1:)               ! Error during reading
      error_code = -2
      EXIT
   END SELECT

   ! Process data read and backspace for more if necessary
   SELECT CASE (status)
   CASE (ft_ed,at_home)
      ! All data for this person already read
      ! Set unused items to unused code
      months = unused
      salary = unused
      income = unused
      IF (status == ft_ed) code = unused

   CASE (ft_job,pt_job)
      ! Backspace and read financial details
      BACKSPACE unit
      READ (UNIT=unit,FMT='(T28,F4.0,2X,F4.0)')salary,income
      ! Set unused items to unused code
      age = unused
      months = unused
      code = unused
      IF (status == ft_job) income = unused

   CASE (no_job)
      ! Backspace and read unemployment details
      BACKSPACE unit
      READ (UNIT=unit,FMT='(T32,I3)')months
      ! Set unused items to unused code
      salary = unused
      income = unused
      code = unused
   END SELECT
```

```
          ! Record is now fully input, so copy to main data array
          survey_data(i) = survey_info (name,sex,status,age, &
                                        months,code,salary,income)

      END DO

      ! All data input - check if end of file was read
      IF (i > max_datasets) error_code = -3

      ! Save number of records read and return
      num_datasets = i-1
   END SUBROUTINE input
```

Notice that the checks made that the reading of data from the data file has been error-free have only been carried out the first time that a record is read. This will deal with the problem of detecting the end of file, but there is always a theoretical possibility of some hardware problem causing an error during reading, and this should be checked for in all cases in a 'production' program.

Note also the use of the **RETURN** statement when the procedure is unable to open the data file. This statement was introduced in Section 6.5 and provides a means to return directly to the calling program unit without executing the **END** statement. This is a good example of when it is particularly useful.

SELF-TEST EXERCISES 9.1

1   What is the difference between a formatted record and an unformatted record? When should each type be used?

2   What is the difference between a formatted **READ** or **WRITE** statement and an unformatted **READ** or **WRITE** statement?

3   What is an endfile record? How is one created?

4   Why must a file be connected to a program before it is used? How is this done?

5   Write appropriate **OPEN** statements to enable a program to use the following files in the manner specified:

   (a)   A file called **Payroll_Data** which has been prepared by a data preparation operator and is to be read by the program from unit 7

   (b)   A file called **Intermediate_results-1** which was produced by another program which carried out the initial analysis of raw data, and which is to be read from unit 11

   (c)   A file called **Intermediate-results-2** which is to be produced by this program for further analysis by another program, and which is to be written on unit 8

(d) A file called **Results** which will be read from and written to on unit 10, and contains experimental results to which additional results will be added as a result of the program's execution

(e) A file which will be written to and read from on unit 9, and which will be used for storing very large arrays, and other information, during the execution of the program

(f) A file which will be written to on unit 10, and which will contain the tabulated results produced as a result of the execution of the program

SUMMARY

- Information that is to be preserved after the execution of a program is ended is stored in a file.

- A file consists of a sequence of records.

- The records in a file may be accessed in a sequential manner, or in a random access manner.

- Writing to a sequential file destroys all records after the one written.

- A file may consist of formatted records and, optionally, one endfile record, or it may consist of unformatted records and, optionally, one endfile record.

- A formatted record is written by a formatted **WRITE** statement, or by some means external to Fortran, and consists of a sequence of characters; it is read by a formatted **READ** statement.

- An unformatted record is written by an unformatted **WRITE** statement, and consists of a sequence of values in a processor-dependent form; it is read by an unformatted **READ** statement.

- An endfile record is written by an **ENDFILE** statement.

- Reading an endfile record causes an end-of-file condition, which will lead to failure of the program unless detected, for example by use of an **IOSTAT** specifier in a **READ** statement.

- A file must be connected to a program by an **OPEN** statement before it is first used.

- An **OPEN** statement may include specifiers to specify the type of file, the type of access allowed to the file, and the position at which reading or writing will start in the file.

- **BACKSPACE** and **REWIND** statements may be used to position the file prior to a **READ** or **WRITE** statement.

- Fortran 90 syntax introduced in Chapter 9:

  File connection statement **OPEN** (*open_specifier_list*)

Unformatted input/ output statements	**READ** (*control_information_list*) *input_list* **WRITE** (*control_information_list*) *input_list* where the *control_information_list* does not include a format specifier
ENDFILE statement	**ENDFILE** *unit* **ENDFILE** (*auxlist*)
File positioning statements	**BACKSPACE** *unit* **BACKSPACE** (*auxlist*) **REWIND** *unit* **REWIND** (*auxlist*)
Control information list specifiers	**FILE** = *file_name* **STATUS** = *file_status* where *file_status* is one of **"OLD"**, **"NEW"**, **"REPLACE"**, **"SCRATCH"** or **"UNKNOWN"** **FORM** = *format_mode* where *format_mode* is either **"FORMATTED"** or **"UNFORMATTED"** **ACTION** = *allowed_actions* where *allowed_actions* is one of **"READ"**, **"WRITE"** or **"READWRITE"** **POSITION** = *file_position* where *file_position* is one of **"REWIND"**, **"APPEND"** or **"ASIS"**

PROGRAMMING EXERCISES

Most of the exercises in this chapter involve the writing of a program to read data from a file. Data can be put in a file either by another program or by typing it into the file using your computer's editor — normally the same one that you use when typing your program.

9.1   Establish how to type data into a file on your computer, and any conventions and/or requirements imposed on you with regard to the names that you may give to your files.

   To ensure that you have the details correct, use your editor to create a file containing three lines (or records) each containing four numbers (in any form you wish). Then write a program which reads these 12 numbers into a 12 element array, prints the 12 numbers in any format that you choose, and writes them to a second file as four rows of three. Finally, list the contents of this second file by whatever means is most appropriate on your computer — other than by use of a Fortran program.

*9.2   A file contains a list of 10 integers, stored one per line. Write a program to read this list and write it to another file with the order of the numbers reversed.

9.3   Type the following data into a file:

```
21♦♦♦32.642♦♦♦♦0.103E6
48   41.001   0.792E7
62   12.608   0.465E5
```

where ♦ indicates a space.

Write a program to read this data from the file using an appropriate format statement, and display it on the screen in exactly the same format.

9.4   Exercise 5.8 involved writing a program to compare prices in different currencies. Modify this program (or write a new one) so that the table of currency exchange rates is read from a file. The table should consist of a series of records in the following format:

curr1 rate curr2

where curr1 and curr2 are codes of up to five characters which identify the two currencies concerned, and rate is the number of units of curr2 which are equal to one unit of curr1. The first record in the file should consist of a single integer, which indicates how many exchange rate records follow. A suitable table, based on the rates used in Exercise 5.8, might be as follows:

```
7
UK£     1.52   US$
UK£     2.45   DMark
UK£     8.60   FFr
UK£    52.65   BFr
US$   103.95   yen
US$     1.40   SwFr
US$     1.31   Can$
```

9.5   Modify your solution to Exercise 9.2 so that it can cope with a file with a variable number of integers, up to a maximum of, say, 100. (Hint: you will need to use an **IOSTAT** specifier in your **READ** statement to detect the end of the file.)

Can you think of a way of writing the program so it can deal with an arbitrary, and possibly very large, number of integers (that is, so large that they cannot all be held in an array)?

9.6   Type two or three paragraphs from this book into a file. Then write a program to locate the longest word in the file and display it on the screen, together with a count of the number of letters in the word.

9.7   Write a program that allows a user to type a series of real numbers into a file. Your program should enable the user to check that the data written to the file has been correctly entered (by use of the **BACKSPACE** command).

9.8   Write a program to read in the following data from a file:

```
122.25   120.00
135.26   140.00
141.00   100.00
 56.21    50.00
 17.20    17.00
```

The figures in the two columns represent actual and estimated costs of office equipment for a university department. Calculate the error of each estimate as a percentage of the estimate, and write a new file consisting of three columns, the first two being those in the original file and the third column containing the percentage error in the estimate.

Now modify your program so that the output data overwrites the original data in the input file without closing and reopening the file.

9.9   Type the following data into a file:

12.36	0.004	1.3536E12	2320.326
13.24	0.008	2.4293E15	5111.116
15.01	0.103	9.9879E11	3062.329
11.83	0.051	6.3195E13	8375.145
14.00	0.001	8.0369E14	1283.782

(Note that this file will be used again for Exercise 15.5.)

By constructing an appropriate formatted input statement, read each line of data from the file into four variables, and determine the number of numbers, n, there are in the file and the absolute value of the largest number, m (that is, the largest number ignoring its sign). Do *not* presume in your program that you know how many lines of data are in the file.

Now read the data again, but this time store each number in an array as its input value divided by the largest value, m. This process is known as *normalizing* the data. Print the values of the normalized array four to a line.

*9.10   A file contains a list of names and telephone numbers in the format shown below:

```
Arthur Jones (365) 271-8912
John Smith (011-44-235) 135246
Simon Addison (699) 987-6543
Rachel Jones (444) 361-8990
Jean-Paul Maronne (011-33-1) 34567890
Hideo Takata (011-81-3) 3456-1212
```

etc.

Write a program to search the file for a particular name (surname, forename or both) and display the line or lines with the phone number.

9.11   Using the same file as in Exercise 9.10, write a program to read the contents of the file and sort it into alphabetical order as the names would appear in a telephone directory (sorted first by surname, with identical surnames appearing in alphabetical order of first name).

Now write a new program (or modify this one) which can be used to update the master file by adding a new name and telephone number at the correct place in the file.

9.12   A file contains the text of a business letter – up to 100 lines with no more than 80 characters on a given line. Write a program to count the number of occurrences of the word 'very' in the letter.

Your program should cope with:

(a) 'Every care has been taken...'
(b) 'Very sincerely yours,'
(c) 'We are VERY concerned...'

9.13 Modify the program you wrote for Exercise 8.13 so that the seismic data is read from a file in which the data from each seismic recording centre is stored as follows:

ccc♦♦$\pm ll,mm$♦♦$\pm LL,MM$♦♦$rr.rr$

where *ccc* is the centre's identifying number, *ll,mm* are the degrees and minutes of latitude of the centre (with negative degrees representing west of Greenwich and positive representing east of Greenwich), *LL,MM* are the degrees and minutes of longitude of the centre (with negative degrees representing north of the equator and positive representing south of the equator), *rr.rr* is the strength of the shock on the Richter scale, and ♦ represents a space.

9.14 A bank wishes to write a simple program to produce statements from a file containing details of the transactions that have taken place during a given period. Each record of the file is laid out as follows:

aaaaaaaa♦♦♦dd♦mm♦yy♦♦♦*cccccc*♦♦♦*nnnnnnn.nn*

where	*aaaaaaaa*	is the 8-digit account number
	dd♦*mm*♦♦*yy*	is the date of the transaction
	cccccc	is the 6-digit cheque number for a debit, and is blank for a credit
	nnnnnnn.nn	is the (positive) amount of the credit or debit

A second file contains details of the balances on the various accounts at the beginning of the period, with each record taking the form

aaaaaaaa♦♦♦$\pm$*nnnnnnn.nn*

where *aaaaaaaa* is the 8-digit account number

nnnnnnn.nn is the balance at the end of the last statement period (positive or negative)

The program should read an account number from the keyboard, find the existing balance (if any), and print a statement showing all the transactions which have taken place on that account in the form

Statement for Account *aaaaaaaa*

			Previous balance	$\pm$*nnnnnnn.nn*
dd/mm/yy	*cccccc*	**Debit**	−*nnnnnnn.nn*	$\pm$*nnnnnnn.nn*
dd/mm/yy	*cccccc*	**Debit**	−*nnnnnnn.nn*	$\pm$*nnnnnnn.nn*
dd/mm/yy		**Credit**	*nnnnnnn.nn*	$\pm$*nnnnnnn.nn*
.	.	.	.	.
.		.		.
.	.	.	.	
dd/mm/yy				$\pm$*nnnnnnn.nn*
		Current balance		$\pm$*nnnnnnn.nn*

The program should also produce an updated file containing the current balances of all account holders. (Note: don't forget about any accounts where there has been neither a credit nor a debit during the period.)

9.15   The heliocentric coordinates L, R, ψ of a planet can be calculated from its elements M_0, tp, e, i, Ω, a, ω as follows.

Take D to be the number of days since 1 January 1990. Then M can be calculated using the formula

$$M = 2\pi(D/tp - \text{INT}(D/tp)) + M_0$$

We can now solve Kepler's equation

$$E - e\sin E = M$$

for E by first setting E to the value of M, and then successively setting E to

$$E - \frac{E - e\sin E - M}{1 - e\cos E}$$

until the change between successive estimates is less than 10^{-6}.
Then

$$\nu = 2\tan^{-1}\left(\left(\frac{1+e}{1-e}\right)^{1/2}\tan\frac{E}{2}\right)$$

$$L_1 = \nu + \omega$$

$$R_1 = \frac{a(1 - e^2)}{1 + e\cos\nu}$$

$$\psi = \sin^{-1}(\sin(L_1)\sin i)$$

$$L = \tan^{-1}(\tan(L_1)\cos i)$$

$$R = R_1\cos\psi$$

Given the following elements for the Earth and Jupiter:

Planet	M_0	tp	e	i	Ω	a	ω
Earth	6.2435	365.2564	0.01672	0	0	1.0000	1.7906
Jupiter	3.9028	4332.287	0.04808	0.02277	1.7535	5.2026	4.8027

write a program which reads a date and calculates the heliocentric coordinates of the Earth and Jupiter, and also calculates the ecliptic coordinates of Jupiter from the formulae

$$\alpha = \tan^{-1}\left(\frac{R_E\sin(L_J - L_E)}{R_J - R_E\cos(L_J - L_E)}\right) + L_J$$

$$\beta = \tan^{-1}\left(\frac{R_J\tan\psi\sin(\lambda - L_J)}{R_E\sin(L_J - L_E)}\right)$$

Finally, your program should convert these coordinates to right ascension α and declination δ using the formulae

$$\alpha = \tan^{-1} \frac{\sin \lambda \cos \epsilon - \tan \beta \sin \epsilon}{\cos \lambda}$$

$$\delta = \sin^{-1}(\sin \beta \cos \epsilon + \cos \beta \sin \epsilon \sin \lambda)$$

(where $\epsilon = 0.4091$), as was carried out in Exercise 4.15.

When you have tested this program, modify it so that it reads a date from the keyboard and writes the predicted weekly positions of Jupiter for the following twelve months to a file (which can subsequently be inspected and/or listed).

INTERMISSION –
Designing, coding and debugging programs

The first part of this book has presented the fundamental capabilities of the Fortran 90 programming language. With the features that have been discussed it is possible to write a program to solve almost any problem that you wish. However, as in almost all human activities, providing more powerful capabilities means that more complicated tasks can be more easily and efficiently accomplished. Fortran 90 is no exception to this general principle, and the second part of this book is devoted to describing the advanced features of Fortran 90 that make programming tasks easier to accomplish.

More powerful features can, however, lead to confusion if they are not used properly. Before presenting them, therefore, we shall return once more to a brief discussion of programming techniques in general.

After completing the first part of this book, you should have developed a clear programming style and a thorough understanding of the principles of good programming design. In particular, we have frequently emphasized the importance of developing a program by the method of incrementally refining the design. From bitter experience, the authors are all aware of the temptation to truncate the design stage prematurely and plunge into writing code – and of the disastrous results that succumbing to this temptation usually brings. By repeatedly reminding our readers that effort expended in the design stage invariably saves more effort at later stages, we hope to save the readers of this book from many frustrating experiences.

Unfortunately, in a book such as this, you can only be exposed to small programs, and you are presented with solutions where you have not seen the effort that went into creating them. You will not see any programs in this book where, in terms of the order in which they are referenced, procedures are nested ten or more deep; and yet such programs are commonplace in the real world of programming.

Real-world problems take from weeks to years to develop and may, in extreme cases, involve hundreds of programmers. In such situations, a disciplined style of programming is essential, and it is important to develop good habits when working with the relatively small problems presented in this book.

It is impossible to be specific, because programming projects are so enormously varied; however, when creating a program, it is reasonable to expend about one-third of the total effort on the design phase. The writing of the code is usually a relatively small part, perhaps less than one-fifth, of the total effort. What consumes the remainder of the time — often more than half of the total effort — is making the code function correctly, or **debugging** the code.

We advocate that you should always adopt an incremental approach to both writing and debugging a program. In other words, you should always break your code into small procedures, each one of which has a logically coherent, single, purpose. *Do not write procedures that do too many unrelated tasks.* The motivation is to keep different parts of a program from interacting with each other in subtle and obscure ways. Breaking a program into procedures means that such interactions can occur in a controlled way, only via procedure calling sequences. A good rule of thumb here is to keep procedures to no more than 50 lines of code. In that way, they can be printed on a single sheet of paper and more readily understood.

To debug a program incrementally, each procedure should be thoroughly tested *by itself*. This means that input to the procedure is generated by another part of the program, or by hand, and the output examined for correctness. The set of inputs used to test a procedure should exercise all branches of the code it contains.

It is often very tempting not to test every procedure but, instead, to start trying to make a complete program function. This almost always results in errors being looked for in the wrong place — which is probably the most time-consuming and frustrating part of debugging a program.

Do not build your house without foundations. The incremental debugging approach means that the lowest-level procedures are tested first, then the procedures that use those procedures, and so on until the whole program is verified. The process of developing a set of test problems can often take half of the debugging effort.

Finally, you should keep all the test problems and the results produced during testing. In the course of time almost all non-trivial programs will be modified, and when that day comes it will both save time, and provide an added degree of confidence, if the modified program can be shown to perform correctly on the same sets of test data as the original version. This does not mean, however, that you should not develop additional tests for any new features added to the program. Thus over the life of a program the test suite will gradually grow with each new modification.

During the second part of this book, many of the exercises at the ends of chapters will involve writing rather more complex programs than has been the case up to now. It will, therefore, be even more important than before that you should develop good testing habits as well as good programming habits.

PART II

Towards Real Programming

An introduction to numerical methods in Fortran 90 programs

10.1 Numerical calculations, precision and rounding errors
10.2 Parameterized REAL variables
10.3 Conditioning and stability
10.4 Data fitting by least squares approximation

10.5 Iterative solution of non-linear equations
10.6 Obtaining increased precision with DOUBLE PRECISION variables

The main area of application for Fortran programs is, and always has been, the solution of scientific and technological problems – a process which usually involves the solution of mathematical problems by numerical, as opposed to analytical, means.

This chapter introduces some of the major limitations that are imposed on numerical problem solving by the physical characteristics of computers, as well as by the nature of the problems being solved, and the means that are provided in Fortran 90 to ensure that the effects of these constraints are both predictable and controllable. Two of the most common numerical problems, the fitting of a straight line through a set of experimental or empirical data and the solution of non-linear equations, are then discussed, and examples given of how these problems may be solved in Fortran.

For those particularly interested in this aspect of programming, Chapter 18 will return to the subject in rather more detail, with examples of several other commonly required numerical methods.

10.1 Numerical calculations, precision and rounding errors

The Fortran language was originally designed to help in the solution of numerical problems, and this is still, by far, the largest class of problems for which Fortran programs are used. However, it is extremely important that the writer *and the user* of such programs should be aware of the intrinsic limitations of a computer in this area, and of the steps that may be taken to improve matters.

We have already met and used the two main types of numbers used in Fortran programs (**REAL** and **INTEGER**), but it is appropriate at this stage to briefly review their characteristics.

INTEGER numbers are stored exactly, without any fractional part, and all calculations performed upon them, other than division, lead to a result which is mathematically accurate. There could, however, be a problem if, for example, the sum of two integers exceeded the largest integer that a computer could hold. In the case of division, any fractional part in the (mathematical) result is discarded. Typically, **INTEGER** numbers can be in the range -10^9 to $+10^9$. **INTEGER** numbers are normally used for counting and similar operations.

REAL numbers, on the other hand, are stored as an *approximation* to the mathematical value using a **floating-point** representation which allows a wide range of values to be stored with the same degree of precision. Typically, a **REAL** number will be stored in a computer to about six or seven decimal digits of precision, with an exponent range of around -10^{38} to $+10^{38}$. Some computers, typically those in the supercomputer class, exceed these ranges considerably. Numerical calculations normally use **REAL** numbers and, unless otherwise stated, the following discussion of numerical methods will assume that all numbers are **REAL** numbers.

Having established that **REAL** numbers used in numerical calculations are approximations, held to a specified degree of precision, we must analyse what effect this may have on the results of such calculations. We discussed this briefly in Chapter 5, when we referred to the manner in which we deal with precision when carrying out manual calculations, but we must now examine the problem in slightly more depth.

In order to illustrate this more easily, we shall assume the existence of a computer which stores its numbers in a **normalized decimal floating-point form**, i.e. in a decimal equivalent of the way in which (binary) floating-point numbers are stored in a typical computer. We shall further assume that these numbers are stored with four digits of precision. Finally, we shall assume that the exponent must lie in the range -9 to $+9$. Thus, a non-zero normalized decimal number will be of the form $0.d_1d_2d_3d_4 \times 10^p$, where d_1 lies in the range 1–9, and d_2, d_3 and d_4 all lie in the range 0–9. The number $0.d_1d_2d_3d_4$ is called the mantissa, while p is called the exponent; we shall assume for this purpose that the exponent, p, must lie in the range -9 to $+9$. Figure 10.1 shows some examples of the way numbers will be stored in this computer.

External value	Internal representation
37.5	0.3750×10^2
123.456	0.1235×10^3
123456789.12345	0.1234×10^9
9876543210.1234	cannot be represented – exponent is 10
0.0000012345678	0.1234×10^{-5}
0.9999999999999	0.1×10^1
0.0000000000375	cannot be represented – exponent is -10

Figure 10.1 Number storage on the decimal floating-point computer.

Notice that two of the numbers shown in Figure 10.1 cannot be represented on our decimal computer. The first of these, 9 876 543 210.123 45, would require an exponent of 10, which is more than the computer will allow. Any attempt to store a number whose exponent is too large, as here, will create a condition known as **overflow**, and will normally cause an error at this stage of the processing. Obviously, once a calculation has overflowed then any subsequent calculations using this result will also be incorrect.

A similar situation arose with the final number shown in Figure 10.1, 0.000 000 000 037 5, which would have required an exponent of -10, which is less than the computer will allow. This situation, which is known as **underflow**, is less serious than overflow since the effect is that a number is too close to zero to be distinguished from zero. Many computers will not report this form of error, and will store the number as zero; in some numerical calculations, however, it is important to know when underflow has occurred and so some computer systems do report its occurrence as a non-fatal error. In particular, an unreported underflow can result in an attempt to divide by zero if the divisor is very small, or in the wrong result of a test for a number being zero.

We can now look at how our decimal computer will carry out simple arithmetic calculations. Before progressing further, however, we note that most computers carry out arithmetic in a special set of **registers** which allow more digits of precision than does the main memory; we shall, therefore, assume that our computer has arithmetic registers capable of storing numbers to eight decimal digits of precision – that is, twice the memory's precision. When the result of an arithmetic calculation is stored in memory we will assume that it will be rounded to the computer precision – in our case, four decimal digits.

Consider first the sum of the two fractions 11/9 and 1/3. The first number, 11/9, will be stored as 0.1222×10^1 on our computer, while the second, 1/3, will be stored as 0.3333×10^0. However, before these two numbers can be added together they must be converted so that they both have the same exponent, where the digits following the space in the following description represent the extra digits available in the arithmetic registers:

$$0.1222 \times 10^1 + 0.0333\ 3 \times 10^1 \rightarrow 0.1555\ 3 \times 10^1 \quad \text{(in registers)}$$
$$\rightarrow 0.1555 \times 10^1 \quad \text{(in memory)}$$

Observe that the process is to take the number with the lowest exponent, then raise its exponent until it matches the exponent of the other number while correspondingly shifting the mantissa to the right (thus denormalizing it).

The correct internal representation of $(11/9 + 1/3)$, i.e. $14/9$, is 0.1556×10^1 and it is worth noting that even this simple calculation, performed in floating-point arithmetic, has therefore introduced an error in the fourth significant figure due to round-off during the calculation.

Consider now the result of a slightly longer calculation in which the five numbers 4, 0.0004, 0.0004, 0.0004 and 0.0004 are added together. Since arithmetic on computers always involves only two operands at each stage, the steps are as follows:

(1) $0.4000 \times 10^1 + 0.0000\ 4 \times 10^1 \rightarrow 0.4000\ 4 \times 10^1$ (in registers)
$\rightarrow 0.4000 \times 10^1$ (in memory)

(2) $0.4000 \times 10^1 + 0.0000\ 4 \times 10^1 \rightarrow 0.4000\ 4 \times 10^1$ (in registers)
$\rightarrow 0.4000 \times 10^1$ (in memory)

etc.

The result will be 0.4000×10^1, that is, 4.0, when we can easily see that it should be 4.002 when rounded to four significant digits! The denormalization has forced some of the numbers to be effectively zero as far as addition is concerned.

Now consider what would have happened if the addition had been carried out in the reverse order:

(1) $0.4000 \times 10^{-3} + 0.4000 \times 10^{-3} \rightarrow 0.8000 \times 10^{-3}$ (in registers)
$\rightarrow 0.8000 \times 10^{-3}$ (in memory)

(2) $0.8000 \times 10^{-3} + 0.4000 \times 10^{-3} \rightarrow 1.2000 \times 10^{-3}$ (in registers)
$\rightarrow 0.1200\ 0 \times 10^{-2}$ (in registers)
$\rightarrow 0.1200 \times 10^{-2}$ (in memory)

(3) $0.1200 \times 10^{-2} + 0.0400\ 0 \times 10^{-2} \rightarrow 0.1600 \times 10^{-2}$ (in registers)
$\rightarrow 0.1600 \times 10^{-2}$ (in memory)

(4) $0.0001\ 6 \times 10^1 + 0.4000 \times 10^1 \rightarrow 0.4001\ 6 \times 10^1$ (in registers)
$\rightarrow 0.4002 \times 10^1$ (in memory)

Thus, in this case the result will be 4.002, which is the correct answer to four significant digits.

This example shows that, whenever possible, it is preferable to add positive numbers in order of increasing value in order to minimize errors due to round-off. Similarly, it is preferable to add negative numbers in order of decreasing value in order to minimize errors due to round-off.

A much more serious example of round-off problems comes when we subtract two numbers. Consider, for example, the effect of subtracting 12/41 from 5/17. 5/17 is represented as 0.2941×10^0, and 12/41 as 0.2927×10^0, in our decimal computer and so the subtraction proceeds as follows:

$$0.2941 \times 10^0 - 0.2927 \times 10^0 \rightarrow 0.0014 \times 10^0 \qquad \text{(in registers)}$$
$$\rightarrow 0.1400 \times 10^{-2} \qquad \text{(in memory)}$$

However, $5/17 - 12/41$ is equal to $1/697$, or 0.1435×10^{-2}. The error in the calculation is, therefore, over 2.4%, which is hardly the accuracy we might expect from a computer — even our hypothetical one.

This example illustrates that great care must always be exercised when subtracting numbers which may be almost identical (or summing a series of numbers that may be both positive and negative), as the loss of precision resulting from floating-point calculations can seriously affect the accuracy of the overall calculation.

The reader is cautioned that even though we used a hypothetical computer with only four significant digits, real machines with six or more significant digits encounter the same round-off problems. We have shown that there can be round-off problems after only four or five additions. Modern computers are capable of speeds in excess of a billion floating-point operations a second. Moreover, some problems can run for days even on such fast machines. The issue of determining the validity of the answers obtained by performing as many as the 10^{14} floating point operations such problems may involve is an important one.

It is not intended to continue this discussion here, since the question of arithmetic precision is quite complicated, especially when we turn to multiplication and division. It is enough at this stage to draw attention to the problem. There are several excellent books on this topic if the problems are particularly important for a particular class of work, some of which are listed in the bibliography at the end of this book.

To mitigate the effects of round-off, attention must be paid to the numerical algorithms to be employed and to the precision with which the arithmetic operations are to be performed. The first topic is discussed in more detail in books on numerical analysis. In this book we only discuss these topics in an introductory matter. With regard to the second topic, the Fortran language provides different types of numeric variable for those parts of a calculation where loss of precision may be serious. For many problems, although not all, increasing the accuracy of the floating-point calculations is sufficient to obtain satisfactory answers. This is described in the next section.

10.2 Parameterized REAL variables

As we have seen, a real value is an *approximation* which represents a numeric value to a specified precision using a **floating point** representation. The accuracy of this approximation is determined by the form of the floating point number which is allocated a fixed number of **bits** for the **mantissa** (thus defining the *precision*), and a fixed number for the **exponent** (thus defining the *range* of the numbers). The precision and exponent range are potentially different for every computer. This is a serious hindrance to portability. A program that executes acceptably on one machine may fail on another because of less accuracy or a smaller exponent range.

To permit more precise control over the precision and exponent range of floating point numbers, **REAL** variables are, in fact, **parameterized**. That is, they have a parameter associated with them that specifies *minimum precision and exponent range* requirements. This is called the **kind type parameter**. When this parameter is not specified explicitly, the type of the floating-point number is said to be **default real**. The kind type parameter value assigned to a default real is processor-dependent.

So far, in this book, all **REAL** variables have been of type default real. The rest of this section will explain what the kind type parameter means, and how to specify the kind type parameter explicitly.

The following statements illustrate the concept:

```
REAL :: a,b
REAL :: c,d
REAL,DIMENSION(10) :: x,y
REAL :: p(20),q(40),r(60)

REAL(KIND=4) :: e,f
REAL(KIND=1) :: g,h
REAL(KIND=4),DIMENSION(10) :: u,v
REAL(KIND=2) :: s(8),t(5)
```

The scalar variables **a**, **b**, **c** and **d** are of type default real, as are the arrays **x**, **y**, **p**, **q** and **r**. The second set of variables have been given explicit values for their kind type parameters. Thus, the scalar variables **e** and **f** are of kind type 4, as are the arrays **u** and **v**. The scalars **g** and **h** are of kind type 1 and the arrays **s** and **t** are of kind type 2.

For any variable or constant that is an intrinsic type, the value of its kind type can be found by using the intrinsic function **KIND**. Thus

```
REAL(KIND=3) :: x
REAL :: y
INTEGER :: i,j

i = KIND(x)
j = KIND(y)
```

will set **i** to 3 and **j** to have the value for the kind type of a default real number. Note that the kind of **y** is processor-dependent, while that of **x** is not.

In the above statements the **KIND=** is optional. Thus the second set of type declarations could be given as

```
REAL(4) :: e,f
REAL(1) :: g,h
REAL(4),DIMENSION :: u,v
REAL(2) :: s(8),t(5)
```

However, we believe that including the **KIND=** is a clearer, less cryptic, way of expressing the intent of the code.

The reader will note that, so far, no specific precision or exponent ranges have been attached to a particular value for a kind type. In fact, each Fortran processor is free to attach any precision and exponent range values to a particular kind type value it wishes. Thus, at first sight, it appears that no portability has been gained, since a variable of kind type 2, for example, may have 14 significant digits of precision and an exponent range of 100 on one machine while it has 6 digits of precision and an exponent range of 30 on another.

However, using the kind type in association with the intrinsic function **SELECTED_REAL_KIND** will provide complete portability. This intrinsic function has two optional arguments **P** and **R**. (The subject of optional arguments is discussed in detail in Section 11.3; for the present, references to this and similar functions should be written exactly as shown.)

P is a scalar integer argument specifying the minimal number of decimal digits required and **R** is a scalar integer argument specifying the minimal decimal exponent range required. The result of the function is the kind type that meets, or minimally exceeds, the requirements specified by **P** and **R**. If more than one kind type parameter meets the requirements, the value returned is the one with the smallest decimal precision. If there are several such values the smallest one is returned. If the precision is not available the result is -1, if the range is not available it is -2, and if neither is available it is -3.

The following statements illustrate the concept:

```
REAL(KIND=SELECTED_REAL_KIND(P=8,R=30)) :: m
REAL(KIND=SELECTED_REAL_KIND(P=6,R=30)) :: n
```

Most computers have provision to store floating-point numbers using one of two precisions, usually referred to as **single-precision** and **double-precision**, with corresponding hardware registers to perform arithmetic operations on them. On a computer that has six significant digits and an exponent range of 40 for its single-precision numbers, **m** will be stored as a double-precision number, and arithmetic operations on it will be performed using double-precision hardware registers. The variable **n**, on the other hand, will be stored on the same computer as a single-precision number, and arithmetic operations on it will be performed using single-precision registers.

On a computer that has 15 significant digits and an exponent range of 300 for its single-precision numbers, however, both **m** and **n** will be stored as single-precision numbers, and arithmetic operations on them will use single-precision registers.

The important point to notice here is that, regardless of the computer on which the above code is compiled and executed, it will not have to be changed in any way to meet the specified precision and range requirements. The values returned by the **SELECTED_REAL_KIND** function may change, but that is of no consequence to the program as far as portability is concerned. In fact, because of the lack of portability of the kind type parameter values, we recommend that they *only* be used via the **SELECTED_REAL_KIND** function. The easiest way to do this is to define a constant for use in subsequent variable declarations:

```
INTEGER, PARAMETER :: real_8_30 = SELECTED_REAL_KIND(P=8,R=30)
   .
   .
   .
REAL(KIND=real_8_30) :: x,y,z
```

Figure 10.2 shows the results of calculating the value of the expression

$$\sqrt{\left(\frac{1}{2} \times \frac{3}{4} \times \frac{5}{6} \times \ldots \times \frac{2n-1}{2n}\right)^2} \times \frac{2}{1} \times \frac{4}{3} \times \frac{6}{5} \times \ldots \times \frac{2n}{2n-1}$$

for different values of n.

n	*Six digits of precision*		*Fourteen digits of precision*	
	Result	*Time (s)*	*Result*	*Time (s)*
10000	1.000 01	0.07	0.999 999 999 999 98	0.10
20000	0.999 995	0.13	0.999 999 999 999 98	0.19
30000	0.999 993	0.21	0.999 999 999 999 99	0.29
40000	0.999 988	0.27	0.999 999 999 999 98	0.38
50000	0.999 989	0.34	0.999 999 999 999 98	0.48
100000	0.999 941	0.69	0.999 999 999 999 98	0.98
500000	1.000 84	3.43	0.999 999 999 999 94	4.75
1000000	1.007 32	7.31	0.999 999 999 999 97	9.51
1500000	0.998 708	10.60	0.999 999 999 999 87	14.23
2000000	0.985 693	13.66	0.999 999 999 999 78	18.93
2500000	0.999 439	17.06	0.999 999 999 999 80	23.72

Figure 10.2 A comparison of the effect of different precisions.

The program was executed on a 32-bit workstation with the precision required set first at six digits, then at 14 digits. Mathematically, the result of the calculation should be 1, but round-off and truncation effects cause this not to happen exactly. Such effects increase as n increases. Note that the precision 14 answers are better than the precision 6 answers. This additional precision was, however, obtained at the cost of increasing the execution time by 40%.

Real constants also, of course, have a kind type parameter and, as with variables, if none is specified then the constant is of type default real. The kind type parameter is explicitly specified by following the constant's value by an underscore and the kind parameter:

`-103.4_7`	Real of kind type 7
`3.14_high`	Real of kind type high
`4.0E7_2`	Real of kind type 2
`2.7`	Default real (processor-dependent kind type)

Unfortunately, the kind mechanism can also lead to problems if used without due care, and we must sound some notes of caution.

- In choosing values for the precision, you cannot, unfortunately, do so in total abstraction, freely choosing any precision you might wish. For example, many computers have a precision of between six and seven decimal digits for their single-precision floating-point numbers. Thus, if you choose a precision of 6 for your floating point variables on such a computer, each real variable will be stored in one single-precision unit of memory and the arithmetic will be performed using single-precision registers. If you choose a precision of 7, on the other hand, then the computer will use one double-precision unit of memory in which to store each number and arithmetic will be performed using double-precision registers. Thus, by choosing a precision of 7, you may have inadvertently doubled the size of your program and made it run slower than necessary.

- Another effect of the underlying hardware may make you think a process has converged when in fact it has not. Again, taking a computer with between six and seven decimal digits of precision, suppose you ran a program with precision set at 4, then ran it again with precision set at 5, and then finally with precision set at 6. Suppose you notice that your answers are not changing. You *may not*, as a consequence, conclude that your computations have been proved correct. What is in fact happening is that your calculations are all being performed at the *same* actual precision, somewhere between six and seven decimal digits. If you re-read the definition of the **SELECTED_REAL_KIND** function, you will notice that it returns a kind type value that meets or *minimally exceeds* your requirements; it does not have to match them exactly. Thus, in effect, you are executing identical programs, even though you are specifying increasing precision.

● A third class of difficulties can be experienced as a result of the computer providing significantly more precision than requested. Suppose that you specify a precision of 6 for your calculations, for example, and your program executes successfully on a computer where the underlying single-precision hardware has 14 digits of accuracy. This means that your calculations are being executed with considerably more precision than you specified. If this program is subsequently moved to a computer where the underlying single-precision hardware has six digits of accuracy, the program may now fail. This is because, on the second machine, you are now executing with exactly the precision you specified. Thus, when you move your program from a high-precision machine to a lower-precision machine, you should test your program carefully to see if the precision you initially specified should be increased.

Let us sound a final note of caution. The mechanism for specifying higher precision or exponent range should not be used blindly to attempt to get out of numerical difficulties.

You may, for example, be using an unstable algorithm or your problem may be ill-conditioned. In such cases you should consider reworking the algorithm or understanding why your problem is ill-conditioned; we shall discuss this topic in Section 10.3.

Furthermore, you cannot specify arbitrarily high precision to get you out of difficulties, as a processor is free to limit the amount of precision it provides. Note that the **SELECTED_REAL_KIND** function will return a negative number when asked for a precision or exponent range that the processor does not support.

Finally, we note that choosing the exponent range is frequently less critical than choosing the precision correctly, and it is permissible to not specify a value for **R** in a reference to **SELECTED_REAL_KIND**, in which case the range provided will be the default range for the precision specified:

```
INTEGER, PARAMETER :: real_8 = SELECTED_REAL_KIND(P=8)
```

10.3 Conditioning and stability

The previous two sections have shown how important it is for the programmer to be aware of the effect of round-off errors in computer calculations, and have indicated some of the approaches that can be used to contain the problem. However, it is also important that the programmer is aware of the likelihood of a particular calculation being seriously affected by such problems. Two factors that are important in assessing this are the **stability** of a numerical process, and the **conditioning** of a problem.

A **well-conditioned** problem is one which is relatively insensitive to changes in the values of its parameters, so that small changes in these parameters only produce small changes in the output. An **ill-conditioned problem**, on the other hand, is one which is highly sensitive to changes in its parameters, and where small changes in these parameters produce large changes in the output.

If a problem is ill-conditioned even the best algorithm that can be applied to it will lead to results that are suspect. In such cases the definition of the problem should be examined to see if it can be redefined so that the results can be obtained from different data which is better conditioned. If it is impossible to improve the problem definition then the answer should be labelled as being sensitive to the values of its input data. It might be appropriate to solve such a problem for sets of slightly different input data to analyse the sensitivity of the answer to the data. The reason for the concern in such situations is that physical data can only be obtained to a certain problem-dependent accuracy. If the data are ill-conditioned the reliability of any answer obtained is correspondingly suspect.

An example of an ill-conditioned problem is the quadratic equation

$$(x - 1)^2 = 10^{-6}$$

whose roots are 0.999 and 1.001. If the problem is changed slightly to be

$$(x - 1)^2 = 10^{-2}$$

the roots are now 0.9 and 1.1. Thus a change of 0.009 99 in the constant term of the equation has changed each root by 0.099; a ten times greater change.

This phenomenon does not only occur when the roots are almost equal. Just how unstable the roots of a polynomial can generally be was well illustrated by Wilkinson (1963), who gave a case of a 20th degree polynomial, where the roots were 1, 2, 3, ..., 20, in which changing the coefficient of x^{19} very slightly caused massive changes in about half of the roots.

Another example of an ill-conditioned problem is the pair of simultaneous equations

$$x + y = 10$$
$$1.002x + y = 0$$

whose solution is clearly

$$x = -5000$$
$$y = 5010$$

However, if some round-off, for example on the four decimal digit machine referred to in Section 10.1, had led to the second equation being expressed as

$$1.001x + y = 0$$

then the solution would have been

$$x = -10000$$
$$y = 10010$$

which is a very great change from the original solution, while if the round-off error had led the coefficient of x in the second equation to be 1.000 (to four significant digits) then the problem would have been insoluble!

Clearly, in this case the reason for this extremely ill-conditioned behaviour is that the two equations represent two lines which are almost parallel, and therefore a very small change in the gradient of one will cause a very large movement of their point of intersection. Thus, a computer program which generated these equations and then solved them would stand a high probability of being so inaccurate as to be completely useless.

On the other hand, the two equations

$$x + y = 10$$
$$1.002x - y = 0$$

which have the solution

$$x = 4.995$$
$$y = 5.005$$

are well-conditioned, and a change of the coefficient of x in the second equation to 1.001 or 1.000 would lead to solutions of

$$x = 4.998$$
$$y = 5.002$$

or

$$x = 5.0$$
$$y = 5.0$$

respectively. This is because, in this case, the two lines are almost perpendicular to each other.

There are techniques which will detect whether, for example, a system of simultaneous linear equations is ill-conditioned, but a discussion of these is beyond the scope of this book. An excellent description of these and other related problems can be found in the book by Atkinson *et al.* (1989).

Related to the conditioning of a numerical process is its stability. A numerical process (algorithm) is said to be **stable** if the answer it gives is the mathematically exact answer to a problem that is only slightly different from the problem given. It is said to be **unstable** if the answer it provides is to a problem substantially different from the one given.

The two principal causes of unstable algorithms are **round-off error**, which we have already discussed, and **truncation error**. Truncation error is the name given to the error caused by terminating a calculation before it is mathematically correct. For example, if a function is being evaluated by a power series, on a computer, it will be necessary to sum only a finite number of terms. In this case the truncation error is the sum of the infinite number of dropped terms. Providing this sum is sufficiently small, and round-off errors are also small, the algorithm will be stable. Other examples of truncation error are estimating the derivative of a function by evaluating it at two close-together points, and estimating the value of a definite integral by evaluating the function at a finite set of well-chosen points.

An example of an unstable algorithm is the following method for calculation of e^{-5}. Suppose we use the power series expansion

$$e^{-x} = 1 - \frac{x}{1!} + \frac{x^2}{2!} - \frac{x^3}{3!} + \dots$$

with $x = 5$. This series converges for all values of x. Moreover, if the series is truncated after the nth term, it can be shown that the error, E_n, satisfies the relationship

$$|E_n| \leqslant \frac{|x|^n e^{-t}}{n!}$$

for some t such that $0 < t < x$. Thus, if $x = 5$, and we take the first 25 terms of the series, we are guaranteed that the mathematical error (the truncation error) will be no more than 2×10^{-8}.

The following program to implement this algorithm was executed on a computer with between six and seven decimal digits of precision:

```fortran
PROGRAM exponential_unstable
   IMPLICIT NONE
   REAL :: x=5.0, ans=0.0, term=1.0
   INTEGER :: i

   PRINT '(T5,"i",T14,"TERMi",T29,"SUMi")'
   DO i = 1,25
      ans = ans+term
      PRINT '(I5,2X,2E15.6)',i,term,ans
      term = term*(-x)/REAL(i)
   END DO

END PROGRAM exponential_unstable
```

i	TERMi	SUMi
1	0.100000E+01	0.100000E+01
2	-0.500000E+01	-0.400000E+01
3	0.125000E+02	0.850000E+01
4	-0.208333E+02	-0.123333E+02
5	0.260417E+02	0.137083E+02
6	-0.260417E+02	-0.123333E+02
7	0.217014E+02	0.936806E+01
8	-0.155010E+02	-0.613294E+01
9	0.968812E+01	0.355518E+01
10	-0.538229E+01	-0.182711E+01
11	0.269114E+01	0.864040E+00
12	-0.122325E+01	-0.359208E+00
13	0.509687E+00	0.150479E+00
14	-0.196033E+00	-0.455547E-01
15	0.700119E-01	0.244571E-01
16	-0.233373E-01	0.111986E-02
17	0.729290E-02	0.841276E-02
18	-0.214497E-02	0.626779E-02
19	0.595825E-03	0.686361E-02
20	-0.156796E-03	0.670682E-02
21	0.391990E-04	0.674602E-02
22	-0.933311E-05	0.673668E-02
23	0.212116E-05	0.673880E-02
24	-0.461122E-06	0.673834E-02
25	0.960671E-07	0.673844E-02

Figure 10.3 Results produced by using an unstable algorithm to calculate e^{-5}.

Figure 10.3 shows the results of running this program, and it can be seen that the answer obtained is $0.673\,844 \times 10^{-2}$. Since the correct answer, to six digits of precision, is $0.673\,795 \times 10^{-2}$, something has gone wrong!

The truncation error was controlled mathematically to be acceptable, and, therefore, the problem must be due to round-off error. Note that each successive term of the calculation is alternating in sign, and that, after the sixth term, they are getting smaller in absolute value. This algorithm has, therefore, been designed with bad round-off characteristics.

To produce a stable algorithm, we can rearrange the calculation as follows. Observe that

$$e^{-x} = (e^x)^{-1} = \left(1 + \frac{x}{1!} + \frac{x^2}{2!} + \frac{x^3}{3!} + \ldots \right)^{-1}$$

The error, E_n, after truncating n terms of the series satisfies the relationship

$$|E_n| \leqslant \frac{|x|^n e^t}{n!}$$

for some t such that $0 < t < x$. Thus, if $x = 5$, and we take the first 25 terms of the series, the truncation error is less than 2.9×10^{-6}. Notice that now the terms do not alternate in sign. The error in using the reciprocal of the truncated series as an approximation to e^{-x} is

$$\frac{E_n}{e^x(e^x - E_n)}$$

Therefore, for $x = 5$ the error is less than 1.3×10^{-10}. Proving this is left as an exercise for the interested reader.

A program to implement this algorithm is:

```
PROGRAM exponential_stable
  IMPLICIT NONE

  REAL :: x=5.0, r_ans=0.0, term=1.0
  INTEGER :: i

  PRINT '(T5,"i",T14,"TERMi",T29,"SUMi")'
  DO i = 1,25
    r_ans = r_ans+term
    PRINT '(I5,2X,2E15.7)',i,term,1.0/r_ans
    term = term*x/FLOAT(i)
  END DO

END PROGRAM exponential_stable
```

Figure 10.4 shows the results of running this program, and this time the result obtained, $0.673\,795 \times 10^{-2}$, is accurate to six digits of precision. You will observe that the sum does not change after the 21st addition; this is because, with the modified algorithm, taking the first 23 terms of the series guarantees that the truncation error is less than 3.1×10^{-9}.

Before leaving this example we must express a final note of caution. This method is almost certainly not the way that the **EXP** intrinsic function is implemented by your compiler, which will probably use the techniques of range reduction and a rational approximation. Our purpose in presenting this example is to show that unstable algorithms can usually be replaced by something better. Furthermore, while we have eliminated the problems caused by subtracting numbers, we have not rearranged the calculations to accumulate the sum by adding the various components in order of ascending magnitude. This omission is simply to improve the clarity of the example, and we leave this improvement as an exercise for the interested reader.

i	TERMi	SUMi
1	0.1000000E+01	0.1000000E+01
2	0.5000000E+01	0.1666667E+00
3	0.1250000E+02	0.5405406E-01
4	0.2083333E+02	0.2542373E-01
5	0.2604167E+02	0.1529637E-01
6	0.2604167E+02	0.1093892E-01
7	0.2170139E+02	0.8840321E-02
8	0.1550099E+02	0.7774897E-02
9	0.9688121E+01	0.7230282E-02
10	0.5382289E+01	0.6959451E-02
11	0.2691145E+01	0.6831505E-02
12	0.1223248E+01	0.6774890E-02
13	0.5096865E+00	0.6751576E-02
14	0.1960333E+00	0.6742652E-02
15	0.7001188E-01	0.6739471E-02
16	0.2333729E-01	0.6738411E-02
17	0.7292904E-02	0.6738080E-02
18	0.2144972E-02	0.6737982E-02
19	0.5958255E-03	0.6737955E-02
20	0.1567962E-03	0.6737948E-02
21	0.3919905E-04	0.6737946E-02
22	0.9333106E-05	0.6737946E-02
23	0.2121161E-05	0.6737946E-02
24	0.4611219E-06	0.6737946E-02
25	0.9606706E-07	0.6737946E-02

Figure 10.4 Results produced by using a stable algorithm to calculate e^{-5}.

SELF-TEST EXERCISES 10.1

1   Define overflow and underflow. Which usually causes the most problems in numerical calculations?

2   In each of the following cases two possible orders of calculation are shown which are mathematically equivalent. Which is the best to use on a computer, and why?

	Order 1	Order 2
(a)	$a \times a - b \times b$	$(a + b) \times (a - b)$
(b)	$(a - b)/c$	$a/c - b/c$
(c)	$(a + b)/c$	$a/c + b/c$
(d)	$a + b + c + d + e$	$e + d + c + b + a$
	(where $0 < a < b < c < d < e$ in both cases)	
(e)	$a/b - c/d$	$((a \times d) - (b \times c))/(b \times d)$

3   How are **REAL** variables parameterized?

4   What does it mean to be of type default real?

5 To achieve numeric portability, how should you use the **KIND=** capability of **REAL** variables?

6 Which of the following two programs will give the more accurate results, assuming that you use a machine that has about six digits of precision for single-precision operations? Explain your answer.

```
PROGRAM test_10a
  IMPLICIT NONE
  REAL(KIND=SELECTED_REAL_KIND(P=3)) :: x,y,z
  READ '(2F10.4)',x,y
  z = x-y
  PRINT '(5X,"The difference between",F14.8," and",F14.8,&
         " is",F14.8)',x,y,z
END PROGRAM test_10a

PROGRAM test_10b
  IMPLICIT NONE
  REAL(KIND=SELECTED_REAL_KIND(P=12)) :: x,y,z
  READ '(2F10.4)',x,y
  z = x-y
  PRINT '(5X,"The difference between",F14.8," and",F14.8,&
         " is", F14.8)', x, y, z
END PROGRAM test_10b
```

7 What are the two types of effects that determine the accuracy of a calculation?

8 What are the two effects that contribute to the stability of an algorithm?

9 Define a well-conditioned problem and an ill-conditioned one.

10 Define a well-conditioned numerical process and an ill-conditioned one. What is the effect of round-off errors on the stability of a numerical process?

10.4 Data fitting by least squares approximation

A frequent situation in experimental sciences is that data has been collected which, it is believed, will satisfy a linear relationship of the form

$$y = ax + b$$

However, due to experimental error, the relationship between the data collected at different times will rarely be identical, and can typically be represented graphically as shown in Figure 10.5. Fitting a straight line through the data in such a way as to obtain the fit which most closely reflects the true relationship is, therefore, a widespread need. One well-established method is known as the **method of least squares**.

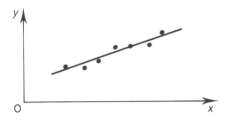

Figure 10.5 Experimental data which exhibits a linear relationship.

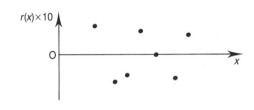

Figure 10.6 Residuals for the data from Figure 10.5.

This method can be applied to any polynomial, or even to more general functions, but for the present we shall only consider the linear case. If we assume that the equation

$$y = ax + b$$

is a possible best fit then we can test its accuracy by calculating the predicted values of y for the actual data values of x and comparing them with the corresponding data values. The difference between a calculated value y' and an experimental value y is called the **residual**, and the method of least squares attempts to minimize the sum of the squares of the residuals for all the data points. Figure 10.6 shows the residuals for the data in Figure 10.5 in graphical form, and it can easily be seen that using the square of the residuals eliminates the problem caused by some predicted values being too large and others being too small.

Simple differential calculus leads to the conclusion that the equation that minimizes the square of the residuals is when the two coefficients a and b are defined as follows:

$$a = \frac{\sum x_i \sum y_i - n \sum x_i y_i}{\left(\sum x_i\right)^2 - n \sum x_i^2}$$

$$b = \frac{\sum y_i - a \sum x_i}{n}$$

It is worth noting that it is quite common for one item (or sometimes more) of a set of experimental data to be less accurate than the rest. Clearly this can lead to an erroneous result, and it is therefore sometimes appropriate to ignore one item of a data set and then to attempt to fit a straight line through the remaining items.

The value of the sum of the squares of the residuals, often referred to as simply the **residual sum**, can be a good guide as to how closely the equation fits the data. If it is a perfect fit then all data points will lie on the line and the residual sum will be zero. If it is required to compare the **goodness of fit** of two or more equations, then the one with the lowest residual sum can be taken to be the best fit. It would clearly be possible to use this technique, for example, to first use all data points, and then to repeat the fitting process leaving each data point out of the calculation in turn. Points which contribute excessively to the residual sum would then be candidates for being ignored, on the grounds that they contain too much experimental error.

■ EXAMPLE 10.1

1 Problem

Figure 10.7 shows the results obtained from an experiment to calculate the Young's modulus of the material used to make a piece of wire. Write a program to calculate the value of Young's modulus for this material and the natural (unstretched) length of the wire.

Weight	Length
10	39.967
12	39.971
15	39.979
17	39.986
20	39.993
22	40.000
25	40.007
28	40.016
30	40.022

The diameter of the wire (in inches) is 0.025

Figure 10.7 Experimental data from Young's modulus experiment.

2 **Analysis**

In this experiment the extensions produced in the wire by suspending various weights from it were measured very accurately. Young's modulus is defined by the equation

$$E = \frac{\text{stress}}{\text{strain}}$$

which can be expressed as

$$E = \frac{f/A}{e/L} \qquad \text{or} \qquad E = \frac{fL}{Ae}$$

where f is the applied force (the weight), A is the cross-sectional area of the wire (measured at several points and averaged), e is the extension, and L is the unstressed length of the wire.

In this case, in order to eliminate the effect of any curl or kinking in the wire no measurements were taken in a completely unstressed condition, but the length of the wire was measured instead under an initial load and then under various heavier loads, as indicated in Figure 10.7.

From the above definition of Young's modulus we can derive the equation

$$e = kf$$

where

$$k = \frac{L}{AE}$$

However, we do not have the value of e, but rather the value of l, where

$$e = l - L$$

We therefore need to fit the equation

$$l = kf + L$$

to the experimental data. We shall then be able to calculate the value of E.

We are now in a position to design our program, and, in accordance with good practice, will place all the constants required for problem in a module so that they can be easily accessed from any procedure in the program. As both the main program and the subroutine which will carry out the least squares fitting follow the method already discussed we shall omit the detailed data design and structure plan and proceed directly to the program.

3 Solution

```
MODULE constants
   IMPLICIT NONE

   ! This module contains the physical and other constants
   ! for use with the program youngs_modulus

   ! Define a real kind type q with at least 6 decimal
   ! digits and an exponent range from 10**30 to 10**(-30)
   INTEGER,PARAMETER :: q = SELECTED_REAL_KIND(P=6,R=30)

   ! Define pi
   REAL(KIND=q),PARAMETER :: pi = 3.1415926536_q

   ! Define the mass to weight conversion factor
   REAL(KIND=q),PARAMETER :: g = 386.0_q

   ! Define the size of the largest problem set that can be
   ! processed
   INTEGER,PARAMETER :: max_dat=100

END MODULE constants


PROGRAM youngs_modulus
   USE constants
   IMPLICIT NONE

   ! This program calculates Young's modulus for a piece of wire
   ! using experimental data, and also calculates the unstretched
   ! length of the wire

   ! Input variables
   REAL(KIND=q), DIMENSION(max_dat) :: wt,len
   REAL(KIND=q) :: diam
   INTEGER :: n_sets

   ! Other variables
   REAL(KIND=q) :: k,l,e
   INTEGER :: i

   ! Read data
   PRINT *,"How many sets of data?"
   READ *,n_sets

   ! End execution if too much or too little data
   SELECT CASE (n_sets)
   CASE (max_dat+1: )
      PRINT *,"Too much data!"
      PRINT *,"Maximum permitted is ",max_dat," data sets"
      STOP
   CASE ( :1)
      PRINT *,"Not enough data!"
      PRINT *,"There must be at least 2 data sets"
      STOP
   END SELECT
```

```
          PRINT *,"Type data in pairs: weight (in lbs), &
                  &length (in inches)"
          DO i = 1,n_sets
             PRINT '("Data set ", I4, ": ")',i
             READ *,wt(i),len(i)
          END DO

          PRINT *,"What is the diameter of the wire (in ins.)?"
          READ *,diam

          ! Convert mass to weight
          wt = g*wt

          ! Calculate least squares fit
          CALL least_squares_line(n_sets,wt,len,k,l)

          ! Calculate Young's modulus
          e = (4.0_q*l)/(pi*diam*diam*k)

          ! Print results
          PRINT '(//,5X,"The unstressed length of the wire is",&
                  F7.3,"ins.")',l

          PRINT '(5X,"Its Young's modulus is ",E10.4, &
                  " lbs/in/sec/sec"//)',e

      END PROGRAM youngs_modulus


      SUBROUTINE least_squares_line(n,x,y,a,b)
          USE constants
          IMPLICIT NONE

          ! This subroutine calculates the least squares fit line ax+b
          ! to the x-y data pairs

          ! Dummy arguments
          INTEGER,INTENT (IN) :: n
          REAL(KIND=q),DIMENSION(n),INTENT (IN) :: x,y
          REAL(KIND=q),INTENT (OUT) :: a,b

          ! Local variables
          REAL(KIND=q) :: sum_x,sum_y,sum_xy,sum_x_sq

          ! Calculate sums
          sum_x = SUM(x)
          sum_y = SUM(y)
          sum_xy = DOT_PRODUCT(x,y)
          sum_x_sq = DOT_PRODUCT(x,x)

          ! Calculate coefficients of least squares fit line
          a = (sum_x*sum_y - n*sum_xy)/(sum_x*sum_x - n*sum_x_sq)
          b = (sum_y - a*sum_x)/n

      END SUBROUTINE least_squares_line
```

```
How many sets of data?
9
Type data in pairs: weight (in lbs), length (in ins.)
Data set    1:
10 39.967
Data set    2:
12 39.971
Data set    3:
15 39.979
Data set    4:
17 39.986
Data set    5:
20 39.993
Data set    6:
22 40.0
Data set    7:
25 40.007
Data set    8:
28 40.016
Data set    9:
30 40.022
What is the diameter of the wire (in ins.)?
0.025
        The unstressed length of the wire is   39.938ins.
        Its Young's modulus is 0.1131E+11 lbs/in/sec/sec
```

Figure 10.8   Results produced by the program `youngs_modulus`.

Figure 10.8 shows the result of running this program with the data shown in Figure 10.7.

10.5 Iterative solution of non-linear equations

Although a straight line fit is often appropriate, many real-life situations will not result in a straight line fit but, rather, in some non-linear relationship of the form

$$y = f(x)$$

If $f(x)$ is a quadratic function then we can solve the equation

$$ax^2 + bx + c = 0$$

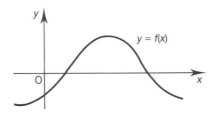

Figure 10.9 $y = f(x)$ and the roots of the equation $f(x) = 0$.

as we showed in Example 5.6, although it should be noted that a deeper analysis of this well-known, but often imperfectly understood, problem will be found in Section 18.2. In general, the equation will be more complex than a simple quadratic and analytic solutions are not possible. In this section, therefore, we shall start to investigate methods to solve the equation numerically; we shall return to this topic in more detail in Sections 18.3 and 18.4.

Numerical methods are usually based on calculating an approximation to the true value of a root (or **zero**) of the equation

$$f(x) = 0$$

and then successively refining this approximation until further refining would achieve no useful purpose.

Figure 10.9 shows the graphical representation of a continuous function $y = f(x)$ and it is clear that the roots of the equation

$$f(x) = 0$$

are the values of x at which the curve intersects the y-axis. This leads us to a simple, yet powerful, approach to calculating these roots, based on the observation that if $f(x_i) < 0$ and $f(x_j) > 0$ then there must be at least one root in the interval $x_i < x < x_j$. Notice, incidentally, that there may be more than one root in the interval; in this discussion, however, we are only interested in finding one of them.

The **bisection method** uses this fact by then evaluating the value of $f(x)$ at the point mid-way between x_i and x_j and then repeating the process until the value of x is sufficiently close to the true value of the root. As in all **iterative methods** the problem is in deciding when it is time to stop, or what the **convergence criteria** for the problem are.

Essentially, there are three possible criteria that we might use to terminate an iterative search for a root of the equation, all of which depend upon some value becoming less than some small number ϵ. Suppose that the iterative method

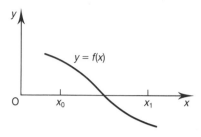

Figure 10.10 Finding an initial interval which contains a root of $f(x) = 0$.

successively generates the values x_0, x_1, x_2, ... Then the convergence criteria are:

(1) The magnitude of the function $|f(x_i)|$ should be less than ϵ.

(2) The error $|x_i - x_r|$, where x_r is the true value of the root, should be less than ϵ;

(3) The difference between successive approximations $|x_i - x_{i-1}|$ should be less than ϵ.

Different methods will use different criteria to terminate the iteration.

In the case of the bisection method it is clear that at each step the interval which surrounds the true value of the root is halved. For example, if the two initial values $f(x_0)$ and $f(x_1)$ have opposite signs then the root must lie between them, as shown in Figure 10.10, and the value of $f(x_2)$ is calculated, where

$$x_2 = \frac{x_0 + x_1}{2}$$

If the sign of $f(x_2)$ is the same as that of $f(x_0)$ then the root must lie in the interval $x_2 < x < x_1$, while if it is opposite then the root must lie in the interval $x_0 < x < x_2$. In either case the new interval is half the size of the first one (which is, of course, the reason for the name of this method).

After n iterations the interval containing the root will therefore be of size t, where

$$t = \frac{x_1 - x_0}{2^n}$$

The true root must, therefore, differ from any point within this interval by no more than t and, in particular, must differ from the mid-point of this interval by no more than $t/2$. Rather surprisingly, therefore, even though we do not know the value of the true root we can use criterion 2 to stop the iteration when we are within a predetermined tolerance of the true value.

The observant reader will have noticed one problem with the procedure outlined above, namely the assumption that we have two initial values x_0 and x_1 between which the root lies. How do we find these two initial values? And how do we ensure that there is only one root between x_0 and x_1? For the moment we shall ignore this problem and assume that we have already determined, possibly by graphical means, an initial rough approximation to the root, which allows us to choose suitable values for x_0 and x_1; we shall return to this topic in Chapter 18.

■ EXAMPLE 10.2

1 Problem

Write a program to find the root of the equation $f(x) = 0$ which lies in a specified interval. The program should use an external function to define the equation, and the user should input the details of the interval in which the root lies and the accuracy required.

2 Analysis

We have already discussed the mathematics underlying this method, and so can proceed directly to the design of our program.

An initial structure plan might be as follows:

> 1 Read range (*left* and *right*), *tolerance* and *maximum_iterations*
> 2 Call subroutine *bisect* to find a root in the interval (*left*, *right*)
> 3 If root found then
>   **3.1** Print root
>   otherwise
>   **3.2** Print error message

> Subroutine *bisect*
> Real dummy arguments: *xl_start*, *xr_start*, *tolerance*, *zero*, *delta*
> Integer dummy arguments: *max_iterations*, *num_bisecs*, *error*
>
> [Note that *zero* is the root, *delta* is the uncertainty in the root (it will not exceed *tolerance*), *num_bisecs* is the number of interval bisections taken and *error* is a status indicator]
>
> 1 If *xl_start* and *xr_start* do not bracket a root then
>   **1.1** Set error = −1 and return

> **2** Set $x\_left = xl\_start$, $x\_right = xr\_start$
>
> **3** Repeat *max_iterations* times
>
>   **3.1** Calculate mid-point (x_mid) of interval
>
>   **3.2** If $(x\_mid - x\_left) \leq tolerance$ then exit with $zero = x\_mid$ $delta = x\_mid - x\_left$, and $error = 0$ to indicate success
>
>   **3.3** Otherwise, determine which half interval the root lies in and set x_left and x_right appropriately
>
> **4** No root found so set $error = -2$ to indicate failure to converge quickly enough

The only slightly tricky step is step 3.3 in which we determine which of the two half intervals the root lies in. We can expand this step as follows:

> **3.3.1** If $f(x\_left) \times f(x\_mid)$ is less than 0 then
>
>   **3.3.1.1** $f(x\_left)$ and $f(x\_mid)$ have opposite signs so set x_right to x_mid
>
>   otherwise
>
>   **3.3.1.2** $f(x\_left)$ and $f(x\_mid)$ have the same sign so set x_left to x_mid

Step 1 will test for the initial condition in a similar way.

It will be noted that we appear to have overlooked the situation in which $f(x\_mid)$ is equal to zero, that is, x_mid is the true root. *This is not actually the case, however, for we must be careful not to mix up different convergence criteria.*

We already know that since real numbers are approximations we should never compare two real numbers for equality during this type of process, but should rather compare their difference with a very small number. However, the value of a function with a steep gradient near to a root may be quite large near to the root, while a function with a small gradient may have quite small values even at points distant from the root. It is to avoid these problems that the bisection method uses the second convergence criterion, in which the size of the bracketing interval is successively halved until *it* becomes less than a specified tolerance.

It will be noticed that once a function value is calculated it is used again, if possible, when the interval is bisected. That is, if the root is in the left half interval, x_left does not change and so $f(x\_left)$ need not be recalculated. The same is true for $f(x\_right)$ if the root is in the right half interval. This is valuable because most functions encountered in engineering and scientific applications will be expensive to evaluate. The prime measure of a root-finding algorithm's efficiency is how many function evaluations it requires.

We shall not continue with a full data design and structure plan, but will proceed to the solution.

3 Solution

```fortran
MODULE constants
   IMPLICIT NONE

   ! Define a kind type q to have at least 6 decimal
   ! digits and an exponent range from 10**30 to 10**(-30)
   INTEGER,PARAMETER :: q = SELECTED_REAL_KIND(P=6,R=30)
END MODULE constants

PROGRAM zero_find
   USE constants
   IMPLICIT NONE

   ! This program finds a root of the equation f(x)=0 in a
   ! specified interval to within a specified tolerance of the
   ! true root, by using the bisection method

   ! Input variables
      REAL(KIND=q),EXTERNAL :: f
      REAL(KIND=q) :: left,right,tolerance
      INTEGER :: maximum_iterations

   ! Other variables
   REAL(KIND=q) :: zero,delta
   INTEGER :: number_of_bisections,err

   ! Get range and tolerance information
   PRINT *,"Give the bounding interval (two values)"
   READ *,left,right

   PRINT *,"Give the tolerance"
   READ *,tolerance

   PRINT *,"Give the maximum number of iterations allowed"
   READ *,maximum_iterations

   ! Calculate root by the bisection method
   CALL bisect(f,left,right,tolerance,maximum_iterations, &
                zero,delta,number_of_bisections,err)

   ! Determine type of result
   SELECT CASE (err)
   CASE (0)
      PRINT *,"The zero is ",zero,"+- ",delta
      PRINT *,"obtained after ",number_of_bisections, &
                " bisections"

   CASE (-1)
      PRINT *,"The input is bad"

   CASE (-2)
      PRINT *,"The maximum number of iterations has been &
              &exceeded"
      PRINT *,"The x value being considered was ",zero
   END SELECT

END PROGRAM zero_find
```

```fortran
SUBROUTINE bisect(f,xl_start,xr_start,tolerance,max_iterations,&
                  zero,delta,num_bisecs,error)
   USE constants
   IMPLICIT NONE

   ! This subroutine attempts to find a root in the interval
   ! xl_start to xr_start using the bisection method

   ! Dummy arguments
   REAL(KIND=q),INTENT(IN) :: xl_start,xr_start,tolerance
   INTEGER,INTENT(IN) :: max_iterations
   REAL(KIND=q),INTENT(OUT) :: zero,delta
   INTEGER,INTENT(OUT) :: num_bisecs,error

   ! Function used to define equation whose roots are required
   REAL(KIND=q),EXTERNAL :: f

   ! Local variables
   REAL(KIND=q) :: x_left,x_mid,x_right,v_left,v_mid,v_right

   ! Initialize the zero-bounding interval and the function
   ! values at the end points
   IF (xl_start < xr_start) THEN
      x_left = xl_start
      x_right = xr_start
   ELSE
      x_left = xr_start
      x_right = xl_start
   END IF

   v_left = f(x_left)
   v_right = f(x_right)

   ! Validity check
   IF (v_left*v_right >= 0.0 .OR. tolerance <= 0.0 .OR. &
       max_iterations < 1) THEN
      error = -1
      RETURN
   END IF

   DO num_bisecs = 0,max_iterations
      delta = 0.5*(x_right-x_left)
      x_mid = x_left+delta
      IF (delta < tolerance) THEN
         ! Convergence criteria satisfied
         error = 0
         zero = x_mid
         RETURN
      END IF

      v_mid = f(x_mid)
```

```
! ****************************************************
! Remove the following print statement when the
! program has been thoroughly tested
PRINT '("Iteration",I3,4X,3F12.6,"   (",F10.6,")")', &
       & num_bisecs,x_left,x_mid,x_right,v_mid
! ****************************************************

      IF (v_left*v_mid < 0.0) THEN
         ! A root lies in the left half of the interval
         ! Contract the bounding interval to the left half
         x_right = x_mid
         v_right = v_mid
      ELSE
         ! A root lies in the right half of the interval
         ! Contract the bounding interval to the right half
         x_left = x_mid
         v_left = v_mid
      END IF
   END DO

   ! The maximum number of iterations has been exceeded
   error = -2
   zero = x_mid

END SUBROUTINE bisect
```

Note that the declaration of the function **f** specifies the **EXTERNAL** attribute, as introduced in Section 4.3, in order to inform the compiler that it is the name of an external function. The disadvantage of this approach is that the function must be called **f**. In the next chapter we shall learn how to specify a procedure as an argument to a procedure, which would eliminate this difficulty.

Note also that we have included an extra **PRINT** statement in **bisect** to print the value of the various values being calculated at each iteration. Once the program has been tested this statement would normally be removed.

Figure 10.11 shows the result of running this program using the following function subprogram to define the equation to be solved:

```
FUNCTION f(x)
   USE constants
   IMPLICIT NONE

   ! Function type
   REAL(KIND=q) :: f

   ! Dummy argument
   REAL(KIND=q),INTENT(IN) :: x

   f = x + exp(x)

END FUNCTION f
```

```
Give the bounding interval (two values)
-10, 0
Give the tolerance
1E-5
Give the maximum number of iterations allowed
100

Iteration  0 -10.000000   -5.000000    0.000000   ( -4.993262)
Iteration  1  -5.000000   -2.500000    0.000000   ( -2.417915)
Iteration  2  -2.500000   -1.250000    0.000000   ( -0.963495)
Iteration  3  -1.250000   -0.625000    0.000000   ( -0.089739)
Iteration  4  -0.625000   -0.312500    0.000000   (  0.419116)
Iteration  5  -0.625000   -0.468750   -0.312500   (  0.157034)
Iteration  6  -0.625000   -0.546875   -0.468750   (  0.031881)
Iteration  7  -0.625000   -0.585938   -0.546875   ( -0.029354)
Iteration  8  -0.585938   -0.566406   -0.546875   (  0.001155)
Iteration  9  -0.585938   -0.576172   -0.566406   ( -0.014126)
Iteration 10  -0.576172   -0.571289   -0.566406   ( -0.006492)
Iteration 11  -0.571289   -0.568848   -0.566406   ( -0.002670)
Iteration 12  -0.568848   -0.567627   -0.566406   ( -0.000758)
Iteration 13  -0.567627   -0.567017   -0.566406   (  0.000199)
Iteration 14  -0.567627   -0.567322   -0.567017   ( -0.000280)
Iteration 15  -0.567322   -0.567169   -0.567017   ( -0.000041)
Iteration 16  -0.567169   -0.567093   -0.567017   (  0.000079)
Iteration 17  -0.567169   -0.567131   -0.567093   (  0.000019)
Iteration 18  -0.567169   -0.567150   -0.567131   ( -0.000011)
The zero is    -0.5671406 +-     9.5367432E-06
obtained after  19  bisections
```

Figure 10.11   The solution of $x + e^x = 0$ using **bisect**.

For simplicity, we have determined if two values have opposite signs by multiplying them together and testing whether their product is negative. This can lead to underflow or overflow problems. The reader should consider alternate approaches.

We shall present an alternative solution to this problem in Chapter 11 when we discuss the recursive use of procedures in Fortran 90.

SELF-TEST EXERCISES 10.2

1   What are the three main types of convergence criteria for an iterative process?

2   In the method of data fitting by least squares approximation, what is the meaning of the residual and the residual sum?

3 How is the residual sum used as a measure of goodness of fit in a least squares approximation?

4 Name two potential problems with the bisection method for finding the roots of a non-linear equation.

10.6 Obtaining increased precision with DOUBLE PRECISION variables

As was shown in Section 10.2, the precision of a variable can be specified precisely and portably by using parameterized **REAL** variables. However, before the release of Fortran 90, real variables were not parameterized, and all **REAL** variables were the equivalent of default reals in Fortran 90. If more precision was required than a **REAL** variable provided, a second type of variable called DOUBLE PRECISION was available for storing real numbers with both higher precision and, usually, a wider exponent range than was provided for **REAL** entities.

When developing new programs you should use parameterized **REAL** entities in preference to DOUBLE PRECISION, because they provide portable control over precision and range. However, you may be required to maintain or convert a program written in FORTRAN 77 involving DOUBLE PRECISION variables, and this section therefore explains their principal features, even though we advocate not using them.

A **DOUBLE PRECISION** variable uses two consecutive numeric storage units (although it does not necessarily hold numbers to exactly twice as many significant digits of precision as a default real). Double precision variables must be declared in a type specification statement which takes the form

DOUBLE PRECISION *name1*, *name2*, . . .

The input and output of double precision values is performed by **F** or **E** edit descriptors in exactly the same way as for real values.

Double precision constants are written in the exponent and mantissa form, but with a **D** to separate the two parts instead of an **E** as with real constants (see Section 3.3), thus

1D-7 is double precision 0.000 000 1
14713D-3 is double precision 14.713
9.413D5 is double precision 941 300.0

When using double precision values in a mixed-mode arithmetic expression a similar process occurs to that with which we are already familiar. The expression is evaluated in stages using the normal priority rules: if one operand is double precision and the other is real or integer, the latter is converted to double precision before the operation is carried out, to give a double precision result. Note, however, that it is not permitted to combine double precision and complex entities (see Section 14.7) in a single mixed-mode expression.

SUMMARY

- REAL numbers are stored in a computer as floating-point approximations to their true mathematical values.

- All REAL calculations are subject to round-off errors, and the programmer must take care to perform complicated calculations in such a way as to minimize these effects.

- Overflow will occur if a calculation would result in an exponent for a real number being larger than the maximum possible exponent allowed. Overflow results in an error condition.

- Underflow will occur if a calculation would result in an exponent for a real number being smaller than the minimum possible exponent allowed. The result of underflow is that the result of the calculation is treated as zero; it is not treated as an error by many processors.

- REAL variables may be parameterized in order to provide more than one representation of real numbers, with differing degrees of precision or exponent range.

- A processor which supports more than one representation of real numbers will specify a different kind type parameter for each representation.

- A REAL variable or constant whose kind type parameter is not specified is of default real type.

- The SELECTED_REAL_KIND intrinsic function may be used to determine the kind type parameter of the real number representation on the current processor which meets, at least, a specified degree of precision and exponent range.

- The use of parameterized REAL variables and constants, in conjunction with the SELECTED_REAL_KIND intrinsic function, provides a portable means of specifying the precision and exponent range for numerical algorithms.

- An ill-conditioned problem is one whose results are highly sensitive to changes in its input parameters; a well-conditioned problem is relatively insensitive to such changes.

- A stable numerical algorithm is one which provides a mathematically exact answer to a problem that is only very slightly different from that specified; an unstable process provides an answer to a substantially different problem.

- It is often possible to restate a numerical problem in order to provide a stable algorithm for its solution instead of an unstable one.

- The method of least squares approximation is a simple and effective method of fitting a straight line through a set of data points.

- The residual sum of a least squares approximation can be a good guide as to how closely the line fits the data, and can be used to improve the approximation by omitting data points which contain too much experimental error

- Iterative methods are normally used to solve non-linear equations.

- The bisection method is a simple iterative method for finding a root of a non-linear equation in a specified interval.

- The DOUBLE PRECISION type is an older, and non-portable, method of obtaining greater precision than is provided by REAL numbers.

- Fortran 90 syntax introduced in Chapter 10:

| Variable declarations | REAL(KIND=*kind_type*) ... :: *list of variable names* |
| Literal constant definition | *numeric_literal_kind_type* |

PROGRAMMING EXERCISES

10.1   Write a program that calculates π using default REAL variables. Print out the answers to as many decimal places as your machine will allow and compare the result with a tabulated value. Repeat this exercise using parameterized REALs having KIND types giving 6, 10, 14 and 18 decimal digits of precision. What does this tell you?

10.2   Tabulate the values of $1 - \cos x$ to four decimal places for x between 0 and 10^{-4} in steps of 10^{-5}, using a REAL variable, parameterized to have a precision of 6, for x. Repeat this with a precision for x of 14.
  Now repeat all of the above using the fact that

$$1 - \cos x = 2\sin^2(x/2)$$

Are you getting better answers? If so, why?

*10.3   Write a program to evaluate the factorial of 200. (Hint: use logs.)
  Compare your result with Stirling's approximation for large n:

$$\log_e(n!) = (n + 0.5)\log_e n - n + \frac{\log_e(2\pi)}{2}$$

(Note that these are all logs to base e.)

10.4   The polynomial

$$63x^3 - 183x^2 + 97x + 55$$

has three real roots between -10 and $+10$. Write a program to find them, using the bisection method.
  (Hint: You must first find intervals in which the roots lie; this can be achieved by tabulating the value of the polynomial for various values of x.)

*10.5 Use the program you wrote for Exercise 10.4 to find those roots of the following equations which lie in the range $-10 \leqslant x \leqslant 10$.

(a) $10x^3 - x^2 - 69x + 72$
(b) $20x^3 - 52x^2 + 17x + 24$
(c) $5x^3 - x^2 - 80x + 16$
(d) $10x^4 + 13x^3 - 163x^2 - 208x + 48$
(e) $x^4 + 2x^3 - 23x^2 - 24x + 144$
(f) $9x^4 - 42x^3 - 1040x^2 + 5082x - 5929$

10.6 The Taylor series is a method of calculating an approximation to a particular function. For example, the Taylor series for the function $\sin(x)$ is

$$\sin(x) = x - \frac{x^3}{3!} + \frac{x^5}{5!} - \frac{x^7}{7!} + \frac{x^9}{9!} - \ldots$$

where x is an angle in radians and $n!$ is the factorial function of n, that is, $n \times (n-1) \times (n-2) \times \ldots \times 2 \times 1$.

Write a program to evaluate the first five terms of the above series, and compare the accuracy achieved with the intrinsic function sin. The algorithm provided by your compiler for the sin function is almost certainly more sophisticated than that given here. Now modify your program so that it uses a variable number of terms in the series, and keeps adding terms until they become sufficiently small. Note that an efficient program should calculate each term in the series from the previous one. Compare the accuracy obtainable with **REAL** variables with the precision set to 6 and then set to 14. (Note that if you are using a machine whose single-precision hardware has more than 14 digits of precision you should set the precision to 14 and then 28 for this exercise.)

10.7 The following set of experimental data is to be fitted to a curve of the form $y = e^{ax}$:

x	0.0	0.1	0.2	0.3	0.4	0.5	0.6	0.7	0.8	0.9	1.0
y	1.07	1.40	1.56	2.30	2.92	3.52	4.57	6.00	7.33	9.69	12.04

This can be done as follows. The sum of the squares of the residuals is given by

$$\sum_{i=0}^{10} \left(y_i - \exp(a x_i) \right)^2$$

and this must be minimized with respect to a. Simple differentiation with respect to a, therefore, tells us that the following equation needs to be solved for a:

$$\sum_{i=0}^{10} x_i \left(y_i - \exp(a x_i) \right) \exp(a x_i) = 0$$

Write a program to solve this using the bisection method, and hence find the estimated value of a.

10.8 In engineering or scientific problems it is often required to calculate the derivative of a function; frequently, however, such a derivative is expensive or impossible to compute analytically. One method of calculating the first derivative $f'(x)$ of a function $f(x)$ uses the so-called Newton quotient:

$$f'(x) = \frac{f(x+h) - f(x)}{h}$$

where h is small. Write a program to compute the Newton quotient for the function

$$f(x) = x^2 - 3x + 2$$

at the point $x = 2$ (where we can readily calculate that the exact answer is 1). Your program should print a table showing the value of h and the calculated value of $f'(x)$, for values of h starting at 1 and decreasing by a factor of 10 on each repetition. You will find that when h becomes too small the calculation loses all semblance of accuracy due to rounding errors.

Modify your program to use a new set of values for h in the region which showed the greatest accuracy. What is the best value for h for this function when $x = 2$?

10.9 Exercise 10.8 showed how rounding errors affected the calculation of the first derivative of a function by means of the Newton quotient. Repeat the exercise, but carry out all the calculations using **REAL** numbers in which the precision is set to 14. (Once again, if you are using a machine whose single-precision hardware has more than 14 digits of precision you should set the precision to 14 and then 28 for this exercise.)

Now repeat the same process, using both default reals and the higher precision reals used above, for the following functions at the points specified:

(a) $x^2 - 3x + 2$ at $x = 1.5$ (exact value is 0)
(b) $x^3 - 6x^2 + 12x - 5$ at $x = 1$ (exact value is 3)
(c) $x^3 - 6x^2 + 12x - 5$ at $x = 2$ (exact value is 0)
(d) $x^3 - 6x^2 + 12x - 5$ at $x = 3$ (exact value is 12)

What does this tell you about choosing the value for h?

10.10 This exercise analyses an unstable algorithm. Write a program to calculate the integrals $I_0, I_1, \ldots, I_{10}$, where

$$I_n = \int_0^1 x^n e^{-x}\, dx \qquad \text{for } n = 0, 1, 2, \ldots, 10$$

by the recursion formula

$$I_0 = 1 - e^{-1}$$
$$I_n = -e^{-1} + nI_{n-1} \qquad \text{for } n \geqslant 1$$

where e is the basis of the natural logarithms. Those who are mathematically inclined can easily verify that this recursion formula is correct by integration by parts.

Use six significant decimal digits of accuracy. Mathematically, the results should all be positive (and should decrease as the subscript increases). Your answers, unless you are using considerably more than the specified accuracy, will show that something is clearly going wrong. What is the problem?

Hint: think about what happens to the small round-off error made in calculating I_0. How does it get magnified in calculating I_1, I_2, I_3, etc.?

A stable algorithm for this problem can be created in a very interesting way. Rewrite the recursion formula as

$$I_{20} = 0$$

$$I_n = \frac{e^{-1} + I_{n+1}}{n+1}$$

Write a program based on this algorithm. You will note that the values of $I_0, I_1, \ldots, I_{10}$ are all positive and that the values decrease as the subscript increases. In fact, the answers obtained are all correct to six figures of precision. How can this algorithm work when we have arbitrarily set I_{20} to 0 and then worked backwards?

Hint: think about the error made in I_{19} by setting $I_{20} = 0$. Then the resulting error in $I_{18}, \ldots$.

So, starting with an initial value that was good to six significant digits we obtained wrong answers to the problem. However, starting with a very poor initial value, we were able to obtain six figure accuracy. This demonstrates some of the power and elegance of numerical analysis.

More flexible procedures

11

Procedures were first introduced in Chapter 4 as one of the fundamental building blocks in Fortran programming. This chapter re-examines some of the concepts introduced in that and subsequent chapters and, in particular, provides a more formal basis for the relationship between actual and dummy arguments, as well as introducing the concept of optional arguments.

Another important topic introduced in this chapter is concerned with the relationship between the variables and other entities defined in different parts of a program, where they are accessible, and the ways in which they may be accessed in other parts of the program.

Several extensions to the simple procedures used up to now are also introduced which allow for recursion, for the writing of generic procedures which operate on different types of arguments in a similar manner to generic intrinsic procedures, and for the nesting of procedures within a main program or subprogram.

11.1 A brief review of procedures

We have made extensive use of procedures throughout this book since first introducing them in Chapter 4, but there are a number of other important features relating to procedures and their use that we have not yet met. Before discussing these, however, it is appropriate to review briefly what we have learned about procedures so far and, in particular, to re-examine the relationship between actual arguments and dummy arguments.

The primary purpose of a procedure is to enable a program to be broken up into small segments, each of which carries out a single task. Not only does this mean that it is easier to develop *and test* a program than would be the case if it were written as a single program unit, but it provides many advantages in efficiency and reusability. In particular, a well-designed procedure can deal with many related problems through variations in its arguments.

We have seen that a procedure can interact with the program unit from which it is **invoked** (that is, called, in the case of a subroutine, or referenced, in the case of a function) in two ways. The first of these is through its arguments and, in the case of a function, the result variable; we shall examine this process in more detail in this chapter. The second form of interaction is through **USE** association of data which is stored in a module; we shall examine ways in which greater control can be exercised over this process in Chapter 12.

All of the procedures that we have met so far have been either intrinsic or external. Intrinsic procedures are part of the Fortran 90 language and are supplied automatically by the Fortran processor; many of the intrinsic functions in Fortran 90 are generic functions which, in effect, exist in several versions suitable for different types of arguments. External procedures are written in Fortran in the form of a function subprogram or a subroutine subprogram. We shall meet a third type of procedure in Section 11.8.

Unless some action is taken by the programmer, an external procedure has what is called an *implicit* interface in any program units from which it is invoked, with the result that the invoking program unit has no information about the number and type of the arguments. For some purposes it is desirable, or even essential, that such a procedure has an *explicit* interface. For many purposes an explicit interface can be most easily provided simply by placing the procedure in a module, since procedures which are contained within a module have explicit interfaces inside that module, and also in any program unit that uses that module. This approach also has the advantage of packaging groups of related procedures in a single program unit, and we recommended in Chapter 4 that all procedures should be encapsulated in modules in this way to avoid unforeseen problems. Note, incidentally, that all intrinsic procedures automatically have explicit interfaces in any program unit that invokes them.

However, it is not always appropriate to place all procedures in a module, and the next section shows how an explicit interface for a procedure can be provided wherever one is required without recourse to modules.

11.2 Procedure interfaces and interface blocks

Although we have emphasized the difference between an *implicit interface* for a procedure, as was the case for all procedures in FORTRAN 77 and earlier versions of Fortran, and an *explicit interface*, as required for some of the new features in Fortran 90, in order that the compiler has all the necessary information available, we have not yet fully defined exactly what is meant by a procedure's interface. The formal definition is actually quite complicated, but for most purposes we can adopt a more informal definition:

> The interface of a procedure determines the forms of reference through which it may be invoked, and consists of the name of the procedure and whether it is a subroutine or a function, the name and characteristics of each of its dummy arguments, and, in the case of a function, the characteristics of the result variable.

We shall not define exactly what is meant by the *characteristics* of a dummy argument or result variable, as it is sufficient to state that they comprise all the information which must appear in the declarations of a procedure's dummy arguments or a function's result variable.

We have already advised that, when writing programs or developing libraries, there are many advantages to be gained from placing groups of related procedures in a module, one of which is that the interfaces of any procedures contained within the module will be explicit in any program unit that uses the module. However, this is not always possible or appropriate, and in these cases the use of an **interface block** in the calling program unit will ensure that all possible consistency checks can be carried out and that, when required, the procedure's interface is explicit.

An interface block for a procedure is specified by duplicating the heading information of that procedure, and takes the following form:

```
INTERFACE
     interface_body_1
     interface_body_2
     .
     .
     .
END INTERFACE
```

Each *interface_body* consists of the initial **SUBROUTINE** or **FUNCTION** statement of the corresponding external procedure, the specification statements relating to its dummy arguments and, where relevant, its result variable, and the final **END** statement. Thus, an interface block for the subroutine written in Example 7.1 to sort a set of names into alphabetical order might be as follows:

```
INTERFACE
   SUBROUTINE alpha_sort(name)
      IMPLICIT NONE
      CHARACTER(LEN=*), DIMENSION(:), INTENT(INOUT) :: name
   END SUBROUTINE alpha_sort
END INTERFACE
```

Note that an interface block must not specify the interface of a procedure in a module that is available by USE association, as the interface of such a procedure is already explicit and it is not permitted to have two explicit interfaces for a procedure available at the same time.

One other important point that must be made is that, although the specifications of the dummy arguments in the interface block must be consistent with those in the actual procedure, it is not necessary for their names to be the same and it would be allowable for the interface block above to use, for example, **string_array** instead of **name**. However, we do not recommend this, as there is no obvious advantage in changing the names and the possibility of introducing errors is increased. It is suggested that, as already implied above, the best way to create an interface block is to copy the relevant lines of code directly from the procedure itself into the interface block in order to ensure that they are identical.

11.3 Actual and dummy arguments

The initial **SUBROUTINE** or **FUNCTION** statement normally contains a list of dummy arguments, enclosed in parentheses. A **CALL** to that subroutine, or a reference to that function, contains a list of actual arguments which must agree, exactly, with the dummy arguments with respect to the number of arguments and their types. During the execution of a **CALL** statement or a function reference appropriate steps will be taken to link the values of the dummy arguments with those of the actual arguments. The method used is not important, but two common approaches are

(1) to pass the locations of the actual arguments in the memory to the procedure in such a way as to enable the dummy arguments to refer to the same memory locations as did the actual arguments, and

(2) to copy the values of the actual arguments to variables in the procedure representing the dummy arguments when the procedure is entered, and then to copy the value of the dummy arguments back to the actual arguments when the procedure has finished.

Both approaches may be used by a compiler, depending upon the type of an argument, but the approach used will not affect the behaviour of the program. However, it is possible for the programmer to constrain the way in which dummy arguments are used within a procedure by means of the **INTENT** attribute, as was described in detail in Section 4.5.

Up to this point, dummy arguments have been either scalar variables or arrays. It is, however, also possible to pass the name of a procedure as an argument to a procedure, in which case a new form of declaration is required for the corresponding dummy argument.

In the case of a function dummy argument the declaration of the type of the function dummy argument should include an **EXTERNAL** attribute:

REAL, EXTERNAL :: *dummy_function_name*

This specifies that the dummy argument is the name of a function and not the name of a data object, as would otherwise be the case. The corresponding actual argument must also be declared in the calling program unit with either an **EXTERNAL** attribute or, if it is the name of an intrinsic function, an **INTRINSIC** attribute:

INTEGER, EXTERNAL :: *my_function*
REAL, INTRINSIC :: SIN

Note that in the case of intrinsic functions that are passed as actual arguments only the *specific* names of functions may appear in a declaration statement specifying the **INTRINSIC** attribute; this is because the type of the function must be specified in both the calling program unit and in the called procedure. Some specific names are not allowed in such declarations, but these are ones which it is difficult to imagine ever wanting to use in this way, such as the lexical comparison functions (**LLT** etc.) and type conversion functions (**REAL** etc.); a full list of those intrinsic function names which cannot be used in this way will be found in Appendix A.

In the case of a subroutine dummy argument, since a subroutine name does not have a type a different approach must be used, and the dummy argument must be declared in a special **EXTERNAL** statement:

EXTERNAL *dummy_subroutine_name*

or

EXTERNAL *list of dummy_subroutine names*

In the calling program unit, the corresponding actual arguments must appear in an **EXTERNAL** statement:

EXTERNAL *my_subroutine*

or

EXTERNAL *list of subroutine names*

It is not permitted to pass any of the intrinsic subroutine names as actual arguments (and it is very difficult to imagine why anyone should ever want to!). Notice also that the **EXTERNAL** statement does not contain a double colon.

■ **EXAMPLE 11.1**

1 Problem

The intrinsic functions for trigonometrical functions (**SIN**, **COS**, **ASIN** etc.) operate in radians. Write a general purpose function which will calculate the sine (or cosine or tangent) of an angle whose value is given in degrees, minutes and seconds of arc. (For non-mathematicians, 2π radians $= 360$ degrees, where $\pi = 3.141\,592\,653\,6$, and 1 degree $= 60$ minutes, 1 minute $= 60$ seconds.)

2 Analysis

The function will operate by being passed the name of the intrinsic function to be used and converting the angle to radians before using the appropriate intrinsic function to calculate the required trigonometrical result. We shall assume that the value of π is available from a general module **Universal_Constants** which contains all the generally required physical and universal constants relevant to our work. If such a module is not available, then one could be written for this problem as follows:

```
MODULE Universal_Constants
   IMPLICIT NONE

   REAL, PARAMETER :: pi=3.1415926536

END MODULE Universal_Constants
```

We can now proceed with the data design and structure plan, both of which are quite straightforward.

Data design

Purpose	Type	Name
A Dummy arguments		
Degrees part of angle	INTEGER	degrees
Minutes part	INTEGER	minutes
Seconds part	INTEGER	seconds
B Global constant in module *Universal_Constants*		
π	REAL	pi
C Local variable		
Angle in radians	REAL	angle

Structure plan

1 Convert angle in degrees etc. to radians
2 Calculate *trig_fun(angle)*
3 Return

3 **Solution**

```
REAL FUNCTION trig_fun_degrees(trig_fun,degrees,minutes,seconds)
   USE Universal_Constants
   IMPLICIT NONE
   ! This function is a general trigonometry procedure for
   ! angles in degrees, minutes and seconds.

   ! Dummy arguments
   REAL, EXTERNAL :: trig_fun
   INTEGER, INTENT(IN) :: degrees,minutes,seconds

   ! Local variable
   REAL :: angle

   ! Convert angle to radians
   angle = (degrees + minutes/60.0 + seconds/3600.0)*pi/180.0

   ! Use supplied intrinsic to calculate required function
   trig_fun_degrees = trig_fun(angle)

END FUNCTION trig_fun_degrees
```

An appropriate test program for this function is as follows:

```
PROGRAM test_for_trig_fun_degrees
   IMPLICIT NONE

   ! This program is a test program for trig_fun_degrees

   ! Declarations
   REAL, INTRINSIC :: SIN,COS,TAN
   REAL, EXTERNAL :: tri_fun_degrees
   INTEGER :: degrees,mins,secs
   CHARACTER :: answer

   ! Loop to ask for an angle
   DO
      PRINT *,"Please give an angle in degrees, minutes&
            & and seconds"
      PRINT *,"without any fractional parts"
      PRINT *,"Degrees: "
```

```
READ *,degrees
PRINT *,"Minutes (0-59): "
READ *,mins
PRINT *,"Seconds (0-59): "
READ *,secs

! Calculate and display its sin, cosine and tangent
PRINT *,"Its sine is ", &
        trig_fun_degrees(SIN,degrees,mins,secs)
PRINT *,"Its cosine is ", &
        trig_fun_degrees(COS,degrees,mins,secs)
PRINT *,"Its tangent is ", &
        trig_fun_degrees(TAN,degrees,mins,secs)

! Ask if another test is required
PRINT *,"Another one? (Y/N) "
READ *,answer
IF (answer/="Y" .AND. answer/="y") EXIT

! If answer was Y or y then repeat the loop
END DO

END PROGRAM test_for_trig_fun_degrees
```

It will be seen that the three intrinsic functions **SIN**, **COS** and **TAN** are declared with the **INTRINSIC** attribute. If this were not done, then the three references to the function **trig_fun_degrees** would be interpreted by the compiler as though the first actual argument in each case was an implicitly defined variable, and since **IMPLICIT NONE** has been specified, this would cause an error.

Note that if **IMPLICIT NONE** had *not* been specified, then this error would not have been discovered until the program was executed, unless the function being tested was placed in a module, or otherwise provided with an explicit interface, in which case there would have been an apparent mis-match between the types of the corresponding arguments which would have been discovered during compilation.

We can now summarize the rules which relate to the association of actual arguments with their corresponding dummy arguments when a procedure is invoked:

- If the dummy argument is a scalar variable then the actual argument must be a scalar object of the same type, such as a scalar variable, an array element, a character substring, a constant or an expression.

- If the dummy argument is an array then the actual argument must be an array of the same type.

- If the dummy argument is a procedure, then the actual argument must either be the name of an external procedure or the specific name of an intrinsic function.

However, there is still one important aspect of procedure arguments to discuss.

Up to this point, we have always stated that the actual argument list and the dummy argument list must match exactly, and that the first dummy argument will correspond to the first actual argument, and so on. This was the situation in FORTRAN 77 and earlier versions of Fortran, but in Fortran 90 it is permissible to specify actual arguments for only some of the dummy arguments, or to present them in a different order, *as long as the interface of the procedure being called in this way is explicit in the calling program unit*. This is the second situation in which an explicit interface is required (the first was the use of assumed-shape array dummy arguments), and it may be provided either by placing the procedure in a module and then accessing the module by **USE** association, as was recommended in Section 4.9, or by including an interface block for the procedure in the calling program unit, as discussed in Section 11.2.

These enhanced facilities are provided by **keyword arguments** in which one or more of the actual arguments take the form

keyword = *actual_argument*

and *keyword* is the name of the dummy argument which is to be associated with the actual argument specified.

This is most easily explained by means of an example. We shall assume that a subroutine exists with the following initial statements:

```
SUBROUTINE keywords(first,second,third,fourth)
   IMPLICIT NONE
   INTEGER, INTENT(INOUT) :: first,second,third,fourth
   .
   .
   .
```

If we wish to call this subroutine with the corresponding actual integer arguments **one**, **two**, **three** and **four** then any of the following forms of the **CALL** statement would have the identical effect:

```
CALL keywords(one,two,three,four)          ! Positional

CALL keywords(first=one,second=two,        &! Keyword in
      third=three,fourth=four)              ! same order
```

```
CALL keywords(third=three,first=one,      &! Keyword in
    fourth=four,second=two)                 ! different order

CALL keywords(one,fourth=four,            &! Mixed positional
    third=three,second=two)                 ! and keyword
```

Note, especially, the last example. It is permitted to mix positional arguments and keyword arguments, but once a keyword argument has appeared then *all* remaining actual arguments must also be keyword arguments.

In itself, the ability to provide the actual arguments in a different order, at the cost of rather more writing, does not seem to be any great advantage. However, when combined with the ability to define **optional arguments** it can become extremely useful.

An optional argument is specified by the inclusion of the OPTIONAL attribute in the declaration of the dummy argument:

```
REAL,INTENT(IN),OPTIONAL :: dummy_argument_name
```

Obviously, it will normally be necessary for the procedure to know if an actual argument corresponding to an optional dummy argument has been specified or not, and a logical intrinsic function, **PRESENT**, is available for this purpose. This function takes the name of an optional dummy argument as its argument and returns the value *true* if there is a corresponding actual argument, and *false* if there is no corresponding actual argument. Note that a procedure having any optional arguments must have an explicit interface in the calling program unit.

Thus if the subroutine **keywords** was modified so that its last three arguments were all optional:

```
SUBROUTINE keywords(first,second,third,fourth)
    IMPLICIT NONE
    INTEGER, INTENT(INOUT) :: first
    INTEGER, INTENT(INOUT), OPTIONAL :: second,third,fourth
    .
    .
    .
```

then it could be called with statements such as

```
CALL keywords(one,two)
```

```
CALL keywords(one,third=three)
```

```
CALL keywords(one,two,fourth=four)
```

and the procedure **keywords** would be able to detect which of the three optional arguments had been supplied and take appropriate action. Note that without using keyword arguments it is only possible to omit arguments from the end of the list of arguments; by using keyword arguments it is possible to omit any argument.

■ EXAMPLE 11.2

1 Problem

Write a function which calculates the mean of the elements of an array, which is supplied as an argument. The function should use two optional arguments to provide the possibility of ignoring values above or below specified values.

2 Analysis

This is a very simple problem, apart from the use of the optional arguments to eliminate some of the elements of the array from the calculation. One important point to note, however, is that if both optional arguments are omitted then the calculation can be carried out using whole array operations, whereas if either, or both, of the optional arguments is provided then a loop will be required so that each element can be checked against the limit(s) provided.

Data design

Purpose	Type	Name
A Dummy arguments		
Data array	REAL(:)	array
Minimum value	REAL, OPTIONAL	min_value
Maximum value	REAL, OPTIONAL	max_value
B Local variables		
Indication of upper limit	LOGICAL	maximum_check
Indication of lower limit	LOGICAL	minimum_check
Do loop variable	INTEGER	i
No. of elements used	INTEGER	count
Sum of elements used	REAL	sum_elems

Structure plan

1 Set *maximum_check* and *minimum_check* to indicate if limits required
2 Select case on presence of optional arguments:
   2.1 Both absent
       Calculate mean of whole array
   2.2 Otherwise
       2.2.1 Set *sum_elems* and *count* to zero

> **2.2.2** Repeat for each element in *array*
> **2.2.2.1** If element is in allowed range add it to *sum_elems* and add 1 to *count*
> **2.2.3** Calculate mean

3 Solution

```
REAL FUNCTION mean(array,min_value,max_value)
   IMPLICIT NONE

   ! This function calculates the mean of the elements of array,
   ! ignoring any elements outside the range specified by the two
   ! optional arguments

   ! Dummy arguments
   REAL,DIMENSION(:),INTENT(IN) :: array
   REAL,INTENT(IN),OPTIONAL :: min_value,max_value

   ! Local variables
   LOGICAL :: minimum_check,maximum_check
   INTEGER :: i,count=0
   REAL :: sum_elems=0.0

   ! Establish whether any limits are supplied
   minimum_check = PRESENT(min_value)
   maximum_check = PRESENT(max_value)

   ! Take different actions depending on whether any limits
   ! are set
   SELECT CASE (minimum_check .OR. maximum_check)
   CASE (.FALSE.)
      ! No limits - use whole array processing
      sum_elems = SUM(array)
      count = SIZE(array)

   CASE (.TRUE.)
      ! One or both limits specified - examine each element
      DO i=LBOUND(array,1),UBOUND(array,1)
         ! Ignore element if below minimum value - if specified
         IF (minimum_check .AND. array(i)<min_value) CYCLE
         ! Ignore element if above maximum value - if specified
         IF (maximum_check .AND. array(i)>max_value) CYCLE

         ! Include this element in the calculation
         sum_elems = sum_elems + array(i)
         count = count + 1
      END DO

   END SELECT
```

```
    ! Calculate mean
    IF (count>0) THEN
        mean = sum_elems/count
    ELSE
        PRINT *,"No items in specified range - zero returned"
        mean = 0.0
    END IF

END FUNCTION mean
```

Notice that the function checks to see if the value of **count** is zero, which would be the case if all the elements of **array** were either greater than **max_value** or less than **min_value**. As written, if **count** is zero the function prints a message and then returns zero as the mean; a better solution would, perhaps, have been to write the procedure as a subroutine and use another argument to return *true* if a mean was calculated and *false* if there were no values to take the mean of.

Finally, it should be noted that the **INTENT**, **INTRINSIC** and **OPTIONAL** attributes can also be specified by means of statements, in much the same way as was possible for the **EXTERNAL** attribute:

INTENT (*intent_specifier*) *list of dummy arguments*
INTRINSIC *list of specific names*
OPTIONAL *list of optional dummy arguments*

It is strongly recommended that the attribute forms be used, rather than the statement form, as all the attributes of an entity will then be present in one statement, with consequent improvements in clarity. The only exception is the case in which it is required to have an optional dummy subroutine argument, when the statement form is the only possibility.

11.4 Saving the values of local objects on exit from a procedure

We must now examine in more detail the role of local variables and arrays in a procedure and, in particular, what happens to these local objects when an exit is made from the procedure.

We have stated on many occasions that the local entities within a procedure are not accessible from outside that procedure (unless, of course, they are used as actual arguments in a call to another, subsidiary, procedure). It follows, therefore, that once an exit has been made from the procedure then none of the local entities within that procedure can be accessed in any way from anywhere else in the program; in effect, they cease to exist. But what happens if a further call is made to the procedure? Are its local variables still in the state in which they were left when an exit was last made? Or are they, in effect, a new set of local entities which will 'exist' only for this *instance*, or use, of the procedure? (An instance of a procedure is the formal term for its being executed as a result of a **CALL** or function reference, as appropriate.)

The simple answer is that if a local object is given an initial value in its declaration then its value, whatever that may be by then, is preserved on exit from the procedure; otherwise it is not. Formally, an object which is given an initial value as part of its declaration has the **save attribute**.

An obvious example of a procedure which uses a saved object is one which prints a heading at the top of the next page of output, including the page number:

```
SUBROUTINE new_page
   IMPLICIT NONE

   ! This subroutine prints a heading and the page number
   ! at the top of the next page

   ! Local variable
   INTEGER :: page=0

   ! Update page number and print heading
   page = page + 1
   PRINT '("1",20X,"Example Page Heading",15X,I3//)',page

END SUBROUTINE new_page
```

In this example, the page number is initialized to zero at the time of the first entry to the subroutine, but on each entry thereafter it has the same value that it had on exit the previous time. Since its value is increased by one each time the subroutine is entered, this has the desired effect.

An important point to note, arising from this, is that if a local variable which is given an initial value has its value changed during the execution of the procedure then the next time the procedure is entered the variable is *not* re-initialized, and will retain the value that it had at the time of the last exit from the procedure.

Clearly, however, there will be many cases in which local variables are not given an initial value, but *are* required to retain their values from one instance of the procedure to the next. In such cases it is possible to specify that such a variable is to have the save attribute by including the attribute **SAVE** in its declaration:

REAL, SAVE :: *list of real variables*

Note, however, that it is not possible to give the save attribute to a dummy argument or to an automatic array (that is, an array whose bounds are only determined on entry to the procedure).

As with most other attributes, there is also a statement form:

SAVE *list of variables to be saved*

although, as usual, we recommend that you should always use the attribute form in preference to the statement form.

There is, however, a special form of the **SAVE** statement which is often useful, in which the list of variables to be saved is omitted:

SAVE

This form of the **SAVE** statement saves *all* local objects in the procedure that could be saved, and is thus a convenient way of ensuring that on each entry to the procedure everything is just as it was at the time of the last exit. In practice, however, this situation does not often occur, and it is preferable for reasons of clarity and efficiency to save only those objects which are specifically required to preserve their values from one instance to the next.

Finally, we should point out that, in our experience, the automatic saving of all objects which are given an initial value in their declarations covers almost all of the situations in which it is required to save local objects, and the need for explicit use of the **SAVE** attribute or statement is relatively rare.

One point that must be made here, however, relates to the definition status of variables that are declared in a module. In Chapter 4 we stated that all modules which contain any variable declarations should also include a **SAVE** statement, and we can now understand that this is to ensure that these variables do not become undefined.

When an exit is made from a procedure that is accessing variables from a module by **USE** association these variables will become undefined, just like local variables, unless either they have the **SAVE** attribute or the module is also being referenced by at least one other program unit at that time. If the module is being **USE**d by the main program unit, or by another procedure that, directly or indirectly, calls the procedure from which an exit is being made, then all variables in the module will, therefore, remain defined. To avoid the possibility of such module variables ever becoming undefined, therefore, you should either include a **SAVE** statement in the module, as recommended in Chapter 4, or include a **USE** statement for the module in the main program unit. Of course, if all the variables already have the **SAVE** attribute, for example because they are initialized, then this is not necessary.

11.5 Recursive procedures

In Chapter 4 we stated that it was not normally permitted for a function or subroutine to reference itself, either directly or indirectly. This was an absolute prohibition in FORTRAN 77, but there are a number of classes of problem which lend themselves very naturally to a recursive solution, and Fortran 90 has therefore added the possibility of specifying that a function or subroutine may call itself recursively.

We shall examine the situation with subroutines first, since the concept is easier to understand in this case, and will then extend it to functions.

If we wish to allow a subroutine to be called recursively, either directly or indirectly, we simply add the word **RECURSIVE** before the initial statement:

```
RECURSIVE SUBROUTINE my_recursive_subroutine(...)
```

We can illustrate how this may be used by considering the classic recursive algorithm, namely the calculation of factorials.

■ EXAMPLE 11.3

1 Problem

Write a subroutine to calculate $n!$

2 Analysis

The factorial of n is written by mathematicians as $n!$ and is defined as follows:

$$n! = n \times (n-1) \times (n-2) \times \ldots \times 2 \times 1 \qquad \text{for } n \geqslant 0, \text{and } 0! = 1$$

Another, recursive, way of expressing this is:

$$\text{for } n > 0 \qquad n! = n \times (n-1)!$$
$$\text{for } n = 0 \qquad n! = 1$$

We note that n must be not less than zero, and we should therefore take appropriate steps in our subroutine to deal with the situation in which it is called with an illegal value for n. One approach, and the one that we shall adopt, is to return zero in this case, since this is an impossible value for a factorial and can easily be detected, therefore, by the calling program.

We can now easily develop a design for a subroutine to implement this algorithm.

Data design

Purpose	Type	Name
Dummy arguments:		
The number (n) whose factorial is required	INTEGER	n
$n!$	REAL	factorial_n

Structure plan

1 Select case on *n*
  1.1 *n* = 0
      1.1.1 *factorial_n* = 1
  1.2 *n* > 0
      1.2.1 Call *factorial* to calculate (*n* − 1)!
      1.2.2 *factorial_n* = *n* × (*n* − 1)!
  1.3 *n* < 0
      1.3.1 Error − return *factorial_n* = 0

3 Solution

```
RECURSIVE SUBROUTINE factorial(n,factorial_n)
    IMPLICIT NONE

    ! Dummy arguments
    INTEGER, INTENT(IN) :: n
    REAL, INTENT(OUT) :: factorial_n

    ! Determine whether further recursion is required
    SELECT CASE(n)
    CASE (0)
       ! Recursion has reached the end
       factorial_n = 1.0

    CASE (1:)
       ! Recursive call(s) required to obtain (n-1)!
       CALL factorial(n-1,factorial_n)

       ! Now calculate n! = n*(n-1)!
       factorial_n = n*factorial_n

    CASE DEFAULT
       ! n is negative - return zero as an error indicator
       factorial_n = 0.0

    END SELECT

END SUBROUTINE factorial
```

It is clear that when this subroutine is called with a value of **n** which is greater than 0 then the subroutine is called again to calculate **(n-1)**!. Once **(n-1)**! has been calculated, after further recursive calls if necessary, then **n!** is easily calculated by multiplying the value returned for **(n-1)**! by **n**.

If the subroutine is called with **n** being equal to 0, as will eventually be the case, then the recursion will end, and a value of 1 will be returned. Note that all recursive algorithms need some condition to end the recursion!

A great many mathematical algorithms lend themselves to a recursive approach, and Example 11.4 is concerned with a more important use of recursion than the simple example of the calculation of factorials. In Chapter 10 we discussed the numerical technique known as the bisection method, which uses repeated subdivision of an interval to find a root of the equation $f(x) = 0$. A program implementing this method was developed in Example 10.2 using an iterative technique; however, the repeated subdivision lends itself so naturally to a recursive approach that Example 11.4 develops an alternative solution to the same problem, using a recursive method.

■ EXAMPLE 11.4

1 Problem

In Example 10.2 we used an iterative implementation of the bisection method to find the roots of the equation $f(x) = 0$. Rewrite this program to use a recursive approach.

2 Analysis

We shall not repeat the discussion of the mathematics of this solution, since that was given in some detail in the discussion of Example 10.2. We simply note that in this program, the recursive subroutine **divide_interval** calls itself whenever an interval bisection is needed. One other change is that this solution uses the (default) real variables that have been used throughout this book, apart from Chapter 10; we shall examine other kinds of real variables in Chapter 14. Finally, since only the subroutine **bisect** in the solution for Example 10.2 has been changed, the main program is not included here.

3 Solution

```
SUBROUTINE bisect(f,xl_start,xr_start,tol,max_iter,  &
                  zero,delta,n_bisecs,error)
   IMPLICIT NONE

   ! Dummy arguments
   REAL,INTENT(IN) :: xl_start,xr_start,tol
   INTEGER,INTENT(IN) :: max_iter
   REAL,INTENT(OUT) :: zero,delta
   INTEGER,INTENT(OUT) :: n_bisecs,error

   ! Local variables
   REAL :: xl,xr
   INTEGER :: iter_count

   ! External function
   REAL,EXTERNAL :: f
```

```
   ! Initialize the zero-bounding interval
   IF (xl_start < xr_start) THEN
      xl = xl_start
      xr = xr_start
   ELSE
      xl = xr_start
      xr = xl_start
   END IF

   ! Check if a solution is possible
   IF (f(xl)*f(xr)>=0.0 .OR. tol<=0.0 .OR. max_iter<1) THEN
      ! No solution possible
      error = -1
   ELSE
      ! Solution is possible, call divide_interval to find it
      iter_count = max iter
      CALL divide_interval(f,xl,xr,tol,iter_count,zero,delta, &
                           error)
      n_bisecs = max_iter - iter_count
   END IF

END SUBROUTINE bisect

RECURSIVE SUBROUTINE divide_interval(f,xl,xr,tol,iter_count,  &
                                     zero,delta,error)
   IMPLICIT NONE

   ! Dummy arguments
   REAL,INTENT(IN) :: tol

   REAL,INTENT(INOUT) :: xl,xr
   INTEGER,INTENT(INOUT) :: iter_count

   REAL,INTENT(OUT) :: zero,delta
   INTEGER,INTENT(OUT) :: error

   ! Local variables
   REAL :: xm

   ! External function
   REAL,EXTERNAL :: f

   ! Remove the following PRINT statements when the
   ! program has been thoroughly tested
   PRINT *, " "
   PRINT *, " Iteration countdown",iter_count
   PRINT *, xl,xr

   delta = 0.5*(xr-xl)
   ! Check to see if within the specified tolerance of the root
   IF (delta < tol) THEN
      ! Yes - return result
      error = 0
      zero = xl + delta
   ELSE
      ! No root yet - check if maximum iterations reached
      iter_count = iter_count - 1
```

```
          IF (iter_count < 0) THEN
            ! Maximum iterations with no solution - return error
            error = -2
            zero = xl + delta
          ELSE
            ! More iterations permitted
            xm = xl + delta
            IF (f(xl)*f(xm) < 0.0) THEN
                CALL divide_interval(f,xl,xm,tol,iter_count,zero, &
                                      delta,error)
            ELSE
                CALL divide_interval(f,xm,xr,tol,iter_count,zero, &
                                      delta,error)
            END IF
          END IF
       END IF

   END SUBROUTINE divide_interval
```

Figure 11.1 shows the results produced by running the program written for Example 10.2, with the above two subroutines in place of the original subroutine

```
Give the bounding interval (two values)
-10, 0
Give the tolerance
1E-5
Give the maximum number of iterations allowed
100

iteration countdown 100
 -10.0000000    0.0000000E+00

iteration countdown 99
  -5.0000000    0.0000000E+00

iteration countdown 98
  -2.5000000    0.0000000E+00

iteration countdown 97
  -1.2500000    0.0000000E+00

iteration countdown 96
  -0.6250000    0.0000000E+00
.
.
.
iteration countdown 82
  -0.5671692   -0.5671310

iteration countdown 81
  -0.5671501   -0.5671310

The zero is   -0.5671406 +-   9.5367432E-06
Obtained after  19  bisections
```

Figure 11.1 The solution of $x + e^x = 0$ using a recursive program.

bisect. Not surprisingly, an identical root is found after the same number of iterations.

The situation with recursive functions is slightly more complicated than with recursive subroutines because the function name is already used within the body of the function as the result variable, and if it was also used as a recursive reference to itself there could be ambiguities in some situations. In order to resolve this problem, it is possible to specify that some name other than the name of the function is used for the result variable. The initial statement of a recursive function therefore takes the following form:

> **RECURSIVE FUNCTION** *function_name*(...) **RESULT**(*result_name*)

Note that this form of initial statement does not have a type specification. The type of the function will be specified in a type declaration statement for the result variable. Any reference to *function_name* in the body of the function will be treated as a recursive reference to itself.

We can illustrate this by rewriting the solution to Example 11.3 as a function:

```
RECURSIVE FUNCTION factorial(n) RESULT(factorial_n)
   IMPLICIT NONE

   ! Result variable
   REAL :: factorial_n

   ! Dummy argument
   INTEGER, INTENT(IN) :: n

   ! Determine whether further recursion is required
   SELECT CASE(n)
   CASE (0)
      ! Recursion has reached the end
      factorial_n = 1.0

   CASE (1:)
      ! Recursive call(s) required
      factorial_n = n*factorial(n-1)

   CASE DEFAULT
      ! n is negative - return zero as an error indicator
      factorial_n = 0.0

   END SELECT

END FUNCTION factorial
```

SELF-TEST EXERCISES 11.1

1   What is meant by *invoking* a procedure?

2   What is a procedure interface? What is the difference between an explicit interface and an implicit interface? Why is an explicit interface sometimes necessary?

3   What is the purpose of an interface block?

4   Write an interface block for each of the following procedures:

   (a) A subroutine, called **demo**, which has four real arguments, used for information transfer in both directions, followed by an optional integer argument which is only used to supply information to the subroutine.

   (b) A function, **mean**, which takes an integer array as its only argument, and returns the arithmetic mean (or average) of all the elements of the array.

   (c) An input subroutine, **input**, which reads data relating to a mesh of points into an array of type **point**, as defined in the module **geometric_data**, returning the points and the number of points through its arguments.

5   When must an object be declared with the **EXTERNAL** attribute?

6   When must an object be declared with the **INTRINSIC** attribute?

7   What is the difference between a keyword argument and a positional argument?

8   What are the rules which govern the association of dummy arguments and their corresponding actual arguments?

9   How is an optional argument specified? How does a procedure establish whether an optional dummy argument has a corresponding actual argument?

10   Which of the local variables in a procedure retain their values between calls to the procedure?

11   What is the **SAVE** attribute?

12   What is the difference between a recursive procedure and a non-recursive procedure? How is each type of procedure specified?

11.6 Writing generic procedures

The form of an interface block discussed in Section 11.2 allows a program unit to include an explicit interface for those procedures it invokes which do not already have an explicit interface by some other means, such as, for example, being made accessible by **USE** association. A far more powerful use for an interface block, however, is to enable you to define your own generic procedures.

We have used generic procedures throughout most of this book, for example when writing **ABS(x)**, where **x** can be real, integer or complex (see Section 14.7), but these have all been intrinsic procedures. It is often useful, however, to be able to define your own generic procedures so that a single procedure name may be used at appropriate places in a program, with the precise action taken being determined by the type of its arguments.

Obviously, since the type and other characteristics of the dummy arguments of a procedure are fixed, it is not possible to write a single procedure to work with alternative types of actual arguments; however a modified form of interface block can be used to specify that two or more distinct procedures can be referred to by the same name – the actual procedure to be used on each occasion being determined by the compiler after examination of the actual arguments.

This is achieved by following the word **INTERFACE** at the start of the interface block with the **generic name** to be used for *all* of the procedures defined in that block:

```
INTERFACE generic_name
    specific_interface_body_1
    specific_interface_body_2
    .
    .
    .

END INTERFACE
```

It is obviously vital that all the procedures specified in interface bodies in such a **generic interface block** can be unambiguously differentiated, and the following rules apply for this purpose:

- All the procedures specified in a generic interface block must be subroutines, or they must all be functions.

- Any two procedures in a generic interface block must be distinguishable by reference to their non-optional dummy arguments, at least one of which must be different when considered both as positional and as keyword arguments.

The distinction between two procedures can therefore be made because one has a dummy argument for which the other has no equivalent dummy argument, or for which the equivalent dummy argument is of a different type or rank. The compiler can then ensure that the correct procedure is used on each occasion that the generic name is referenced.

There is an important further extension to our definition of an interface block, however, which relates to procedures in modules. We said in Section 11.2 that an interface block may not be used to specify an explicit interface for procedures which are available through **USE** association. However, when using an interface block to give a generic name to two or more procedures it is clearly possible that either or both of these procedures may be encapsulated in a module. It is therefore permitted to specify the names of any such **module procedures** in an interface block, but not their interfaces. This is achieved by including, after the specification of any external procedure interfaces, one or more statements of the form

MODULE PROCEDURE *list of module procedure names*

where each name in the list is either the name of a procedure that is available through **USE** association, or, if the interface block is itself in a module, is the name of a procedure in the same module as the interface block.

Note that, as might be anticipated, if a reference is made to a procedure by its generic name, then the procedure interface must be explicit in the calling program unit.

■ EXAMPLE 11.5

1 Problem

In earlier examples we have developed a number of procedures for use in a geometric package. It is now required to provide a generic subroutine which will provide as its result a line which either (a) passes through two specified points, (b) passes through a point perpendicular to a specified line, or (c) passes through a point and is tangent to a specified circle. In the last case, an additional argument specifies which of the two alternatives is to be chosen.

2 Analysis

We developed a subroutine for the first of these cases in Example 5.3 and the others would be relatively straightforward – the last is the subject of Exercise 11.2. It is clear, however, that although the first two arguments for each are a line and a point, the types of the third argument are point, line and circle, respectively, and so the rules for disambiguating are satisfied. All that remains is to write a generic interface block. There are three cases to consider:

(a) An interface block to include in the module **geometric_procedures** so that the generic name may be accessed by **USE** association as well as the specific names.

(b) An interface block to include in a program unit that is accessing only the specific names in the module **geometric_procedures** by **USE** association, but which wishes to refer to them by a generic name.

(c) An interface block for the situation in which the three procedures are not accessed by USE association, but are only available as external procedures.

The final matter to be considered is the generic name to be used to refer to the three definitions. An obvious name might seem to be **line**, but this is not allowed because the name of one of the derived types is **line**. We shall therefore use **gen_line** for the generic name.

3 **Solution**

(a) In the module **geometric_procedures**:

```
INTERFACE gen_line
   MODULE PROCEDURE line_two_points
   MODULE PROCEDURE line_point_perpto_line
   MODULE PROCEDURE line_point_tanto_circle
END INTERFACE
```

(b) In a procedure that uses the module **geometric_procedures**:

```
INTERFACE gen_line
   MODULE PROCEDURE line_two_points
   MODULE PROCEDURE line_point_perpto_line
   MODULE PROCEDURE line_point_tanto_circle
END INTERFACE
```

This is, of course, identical to the interface block for case (a). However, the inclusion of the interface block in the module in case (a) makes the generic name **gen_line** available to any program unit that uses the module, whereas case (b) only specifies the generic name for use in the procedure which contains the generic interface block.

(c) In a procedure which refers to the three specific procedures as external procedures, but which uses the module **geometric_data** to obtain the relevant geometric derived types:

```
INTERFACE gen_line

   SUBROUTINE line_two_points(line_1,point_1,point_2)
      IMPLICIT NONE
      TYPE(line),INTENT(OUT) :: line_1
      TYPE(point),INTENT(IN) :: point_1,point_2
   END SUBROUTINE line_two_points

   SUBROUTINE line_point_perpto_line(line_1,point_1,line_2)
      IMPLICIT NONE
      TYPE(line),INTENT(OUT) :: line_1
      TYPE(point),INTENT(IN) :: point_1
      TYPE(line),INTENT(IN) :: line_2
   END SUBROUTINE line_point_perpto_line
```

```
        SUBROUTINE line_point_tanto_circle(line_1,point_1,    &
                                           circle_1,modifier)
          IMPLICIT NONE
          TYPE(line),INTENT(OUT) :: line_1
          TYPE(point),INTENT(IN) :: point_1
          TYPE(line),INTENT(IN) :: circle_1
          CHARACTER(LEN=6) :: modifier
        END SUBROUTINE line_point_tanto_circle
      END INTERFACE
```

In this case, because the three procedures are not module procedures their full interfaces must be specified; this also, of course, has the effect of making their interfaces explicit within the procedure that contains the interface block.

11.7 Scope and scoping units

When we introduced procedures in Chapter 4 we stated that the local variables in a procedure were not accessible outside that procedure unless they were passed as actual arguments to another procedure. In the same chapter we introduced modules as a means of providing global entities (for example, variables and type definitions) which were accessible to several program units by **USE** association.

We must now consider the relationship between the entities declared or defined in different parts of a program in rather more detail, as it has several important consequences which we have been able to ignore up to now. In particular, we shall introduce the concept of the **scope** of an entity, where an entity is most frequently a named object (for instance a variable, a procedure, a derived type etc.), but may also be some other object such as an input/output unit number or a statement label.

Procedures written in Fortran are implemented as subprograms, and in Chapter 4 we established that external subprograms, modules and the main program are three types of program unit in Fortran 90. However, a program unit may also be considered to consist of a set of non-overlapping **scoping units**, where a scoping unit is one of the following:

- a derived type definition
- a procedure interface body, *excluding* any derived type definitions and procedure interface bodies contained within it
- a program unit or subprogram, *excluding* any derived type definitions, procedure interface bodies and subprograms contained within it

```
        SUBROUTINE scoping_unit_example              ! Line 1
           IMPLICIT NONE                             ! Line 2

   !   Type definition
           TYPE date                                 ! Line 5
              INTEGER :: day
              CHARACTER(LEN=3) :: month
              INTEGER :: year
           END TYPE date                             ! Line 9

   !   Procedure interface body
           INTERFACE                                 ! Line 12
              SUBROUTINE get_date(day,month,year)    ! Line 13
                 IMPLICIT NONE
                 INTEGER,INTENT(IN) :: day,year
                 CHARACTER(LEN=*),INTENT(IN) :: month
              END SUBROUTINE get_date                ! Line 17
           END INTERFACE                             ! Line 18

   !   Local variables
           INTEGER :: day,year                       ! Line 21
           CHARACTER(LEN=10) :: month
           TYPE(date) :: today
                  .
                  .
                  .
        END SUBROUTINE scoping_unit_example          ! Line 99
```

Figure 11.2 An example of nested scoping units.

If one scoping unit surrounds another scoping unit then it is called the
host scoping unit or, more informally, simply the **host** of the inner, or nested,
scoping unit. Thus, for example, Figure 11.2 shows a subroutine subprogram unit
in which the host scoping unit consists of lines 1–4, lines 10–12 and lines 18–99,
while lines 5–9 and lines 13–17 form two independent nested scoping units. Note
that it is the interface *body*, not the whole interface block, that forms the nested
scoping unit.

With a few minor exceptions, which will be discussed later in this section,
the names of all entities within a scoping unit must be different; entities in
different scoping units may have the same name. Thus, in the example shown in
Figure 11.2 the three names **day**, **month** and **year** appear in three sets of
declarations:

- The first set, in lines 6–8, refers to components of the derived type **date**
  and appears within the scoping unit of the derived type definition.

- The second set, in lines 13, 15 and 16, refers to dummy arguments of the
  subroutine **get_date** and appears within the scoping unit of the interface
  procedure body.

- The third set, in lines 21 and 22, refers to local variables declared in the subroutine `scoping_unit_example` and appears within the scoping unit of the external subprogram, which is also host to the other two scoping units.

This brings us back to the consideration of the scope of an entity, and a more formal definition of the concepts of global and local entities:

- Any entity whose scope is that of the whole program is called a **global entity**. Program units, external procedures and `COMMON` blocks (see Chapter 17) are global entities and must all have distinct names.

- Any entity whose scope is that of a scoping unit is called a **local entity**. Within a scoping unit all local entities must have distinct names except that the names of any type components and the names of the arguments of any procedures having an explicit interface may also be used as the names of another entity in the same scoping unit.

It is also possible for an entity to only have the scope of a single statement, or even part of a statement, in which case it is called a **statement entity**. The only case that we have met so far of a statement entity is the `DO` variable in an implied `DO` in an array constructor (see Section 7.3), in which case it has the scope of the implied `DO` list only. In effect, this means that such an implied `DO` variable is different from any variable in the same program unit having the same name, and its appearance in an array constructor will not affect the value of a variable having the same name.

The formal rules concerning the scopes of entities in a program are quite complicated and are summarized in Appendix B for reference. For most purposes, however, the situation is quite straightforward as long as sensible use is made of names; a programmer who is determined to see how many entities in a program unit can have the same name may, possibly, find one or two surprises!

One final point that should be made here concerns the accessibility in one scoping unit of entities in the scope of another scoping unit. We have already met one example of this in connection with modules, namely the concept of `USE` association, by means of which entities such as derived type definitions, named constants or variables within the module can be treated as though they had been declared within the program unit that is using the module. As we shall see in the next section, and also in Chapter 12, it is also possible for entities in a host scoping unit to be used within nested scoping units by a process known as **host association**.

11.8 Internal procedures

Since our first introduction to procedures in Chapter 4, we have either written them as external procedures or as module procedures – the latter being, for all practical purposes, the same as external procedures, but encapsulated in a module for convenience. However, there are many cases where a procedure will only be invoked by one particular program unit, and in this case it is permissible to include that procedure as an integral part of the program unit that will invoke it as an **internal procedure**.

An internal procedure is a form of subprogram, and must follow all the executable statements of its host program unit, and be separated from them by a `CONTAINS` statement. Thus if the subroutine **inner** is only used by the subroutine **outer** it may be written as an internal procedure of **outer** in the following way:

```
SUBROUTINE outer(a,b,c)
   IMPLICIT NONE
   Specification statements
   .
   .
   .
   Executable statements
   .
   .
   .
CONTAINS
   SUBROUTINE inner(x,y,z)
   .
   .
   .
   END SUBROUTINE inner
END SUBROUTINE outer
```

Note that the `CONTAINS` statement and the internal procedure are not part of the executable part of the procedure **outer**. Thus, if the statement immediately preceding the `CONTAINS` statement is executed, and the next statement is not a transfer of control (for example, a `RETURN`, a `STOP` or a `GOTO`) then execution will proceed with the `END SUBROUTINE outer` statement in the normal way, just as though the `CONTAINS` statement and the following internal procedure were not there.

An internal procedure is the same as an external procedure with three exceptions:

- The name of an internal procedure is not global – the procedure may only be invoked by the host program unit.
- The name of an internal procedure may not be passed as an actual argument to a procedure whose corresponding dummy argument is a dummy procedure.
- An internal procedure has access to entities of its host by host association.

The first two of these are quite straightforward, and are what one might expect. The third, however, brings us to the important new concept of host association, which was briefly referred to in the previous section, and which we must now discuss in some detail.

We can explain the concept most easily by considering the example already used to demonstrate how an internal procedure is contained within a host program unit, but with more detail included:

```
SUBROUTINE outer(a,b,c)
   IMPLICIT NONE
   REAL,INTENT(INOUT) :: a,b,c  ! Dummy arguments
   REAL :: aa,bb,cc             ! Local variables
   ! Executable statements follow
   .
   .
   .
CONTAINS
   SUBROUTINE inner(x,y,z)
      ! Note that IMPLICIT NONE is not allowed here
      ! as the IMPLICIT NONE in the host is still in effect
      REAL,INTENT(INOUT) :: x,y,z   ! Dummy arguments
      REAL :: a,bb,xx,yy,zz          ! Local variables

      xx = x+y                      ! Assigns to xx in inner
      aa = y+z                      ! Assigns to aa in outer
      bb = z+x                      ! Assigns to bb in inner
      .
      .
      .
   END SUBROUTINE inner
END SUBROUTINE outer
```

In this example, the subroutine **inner** is a scoping unit in its own right, and has full access to the eight variables declared within that scoping unit – the three dummy arguments **x**, **y** and **z**, and the five local variables **a**, **bb**, **xx**, **yy** and **zz**. It also has access by host association to all the entities of its host *except for any which have the same name as a local entity of the internal procedure*. The Fortran standard contains a long and somewhat complicated list of local entities which block host association, which is summarized in Appendix B, but for most purposes this simple rule will suffice.

Thus, in the example above, the internal subroutine **inner** also has full access to four of the six variables declared in the scope of the host subprogram **outer** – the two dummy arguments **b** and **c**, and the two local variables **aa** and **cc**; the dummy argument **a** and the local variable **bb** are, however, not accessible in the scope of the internal procedure because of the declaration of variables of the same names in that procedure.

An internal procedure, as one might intuitively expect, is therefore more closely linked to its host than is the case with an external procedure and a program unit that invokes it; in particular, its interface is explicit in the host. A further consequence of this closeness is that it is frequently not necessary to use many, or even any, arguments to pass information between an internal procedure and its host, since host association may be used instead.

■ EXAMPLE 11.6

1 **Problem**

Write a program, as a single main program unit, which reads a set of scientific data consisting of the name and density of a number of materials, and then sorts the data either alphabetically or into either increasing or decreasing density. The data is terminated by a dummy item having a zero density. You may assume that there will be no more than 100 materials.

2 **Analysis**

An initial structure plan for this problem might be as follows:

1 Read data
2 Ask which type of sort is required
3 Select one of the following cases
   3.1 Sort into alphabetic order
   or
   3.2 Sort into order of increasing density
   or
   3.3 Sort into order of decreasing density
4 Print sorted list of materials and densities

We developed a subroutine to sort a character array into alphabetic order in Example 7.1, and it will not be difficult to develop a slightly modified version to carry out a numeric sort. It is also clear that sorting into increasing or decreasing order should be a matter which can be determined by an argument to the sort procedure. For clarity, we shall also carry out the input in a further internal subroutine, and can, therefore, revise our structure plan to reflect this:

1 Read data using *input*
2 Ask which type of sort is required
3 Select case on *sort_type*
   3.1 *sort_type* is 'alphabetic'
      Sort into alphabetic order using *alpha_sort*
   3.2 *sort_type* is 'increasing density' or 'decreasing density'
      Sort into order of density using *numeric_sort*
4 Print sorted list of materials and densities

Since the data array and the number of data items will be declared within the scope of the main program they can be accessed by host association by all the subroutines and do not need to be passed as arguments. The same is true of the information regarding the order of numeric sorting, but in this case it may be clearer to the human reader if an argument is used to provide this information. However, since the more usual order is probably that of increasing density we shall write the subroutine with an optional argument whose absence will indicate that the arrays are to be sorted in order of increasing density. Our final data design and structure plan for the main program is therefore as follows.

Data design

Purpose	Type	Name
Array of material names	CHARACTER*20(:)	material
Array of material densities	REAL(:)	density
Number of data items	INTEGER	number
Implied DO variable	INTEGER	i
Type of sort required	CHARACTER*1	sort_type
A = alphabetic		
I = increasing density		
D = decreasing density		

Structure plan

> **1** Read data using *input*
>
> **2** Ask which type of sort is required
>
> **3** Select case on *sort_type*
> > **3.1** *sort_type* is A (alphabetic)
> > Sort into alphabetic order using *alpha_sort*
> > **3.2** *sort_type* is D (decreasing density)
> > Sort into order of density using *numeric_sort(up = .FALSE.)*
> > **3.3** *sort_type* is I (increasing density)
> > Sort into order of density using *numeric_sort*
>
> **4** Print sorted list of materials and densities

Since the input procedure is similar to several that have been written for other examples, and the two sort procedures are very closely based on the subroutine developed for Example 7.1, we shall not carry out a full data design and structure plan here, but will proceed directly to the programming phase.

3 **Solution**

```
PROGRAM material_sort
  IMPLICIT NONE

  ! This program reads a set of material names and densities
```

```
! and lists them in either alphabetical order or in order
! of their densities, either increasing or decreasing

! Declarations
INTEGER, PARAMETER :: max_length=20,max_number=100
CHARACTER(LEN=max_length),DIMENSION(max_number+1) :: material
REAL,DIMENSION(max_number+1) :: density
INTEGER :: number,i
CHARACTER :: sort_type

! Read data
CALL input

! Ask what type of sort is required
DO
   PRINT *,"How do you wish this data to be sorted?"
   PRINT *,"Type A for alphabetic order"
   PRINT *,"Type D for order of decreasing density"
   PRINT *,"Type I for order of increasing density"
   READ *,sort_type
   SELECT CASE (sort_type)
   CASE ("A","D","I")
      ! Valid reply - prepare to sort data
      EXIT
   CASE DEFAULT
      ! Invalid reply - try again
      PRINT *,"You must type A, D or I. Please try again"
   END SELECT
END DO

! Use appropriate sort procedure to sort data
SELECT CASE (sort_type)
CASE ("A")
   CALL alpha_sort
CASE ("D")
   CALL numeric_sort(up=.FALSE.)
CASE ("I")
   CALL numeric_sort
END SELECT

! List sorted data
PRINT '("The materials and their densities are:"//   &
       (A15,F10.4/))', (material(i),density(i),i=1,number)

CONTAINS

SUBROUTINE input
   ! This subroutine reads the data into the arrays material
   ! and density, and stores the number of data items in
   ! number

   ! Local variable
   INTEGER :: count

   PRINT *,"Please type up to ",max_number," sets of data"
   PRINT *,"Each set must consist of the name of the material"
   PRINT *,"followed by its density"
```

```
      PRINT *,"The final set must be followed by a line"
      PRINT *,"consisting of the word END followed by a zero"

      ! Loop to read data
      DO count=1,max_number+1
         READ *,material(count),density(count)
         IF (density==0.0) EXIT
      END DO

      IF (count>max_number) THEN
         ! count>max_number, print warning
         PRINT *,"More than ",max_number,  &
                 " data sets have been entered"
         PRINT *,"Only the first ",max_number," will be used"
         number = max_number
      ELSE
         ! Set number to number of data sets read
         number = count-1
      END IF
   END SUBROUTINE input

   SUBROUTINE alpha_sort
      ! This subroutine sorts the contents of the character array
      ! material into alphabetic order and also sorts the array
      ! density into the same order

      ! Local variables
      CHARACTER(LEN=max_length) :: first,temp_name
      INTEGER :: index,temp_num,i,j

      ! Loop to sort number-1 material names into order
      DO i=1,number-1

         ! Initialize earliest so far to be the first in
         ! this pass
         first = material(i)
         index = i

         ! Search remaining (unsorted items) for earliest one
         DO j=i+1,number
            IF (material(j) < first) THEN
               first = material(j)
               index = j
            END IF
         END DO

         ! Swap both material names and densities if necessary
         IF (index /= i) THEN
            temp_name = material(i)
            material(i) = material(index)
            material(index) = temp_name
            temp_num = density(i)
            density(i) = density(index)
            density(index) = temp_num
         END IF
      END DO
   END SUBROUTINE alpha_sort
```

```
SUBROUTINE numeric_sort(up)
  ! This subroutine sorts the contents of the real array
  ! density into numeric order and also sorts the character
  ! array material into the same order. If the optional
  ! argument up has the value .FALSE. then density is sorted
  ! into decreasing order; otherwise it is sorted into
  ! increasing order.

  ! Dummy argument
  LOGICAL,OPTIONAL :: up

  ! Local variables
  CHARACTER(LEN=max_length) :: temp_name
  INTEGER :: index,first,temp_num,i,j

  ! Set up to .TRUE. if not present as an actual argument
  IF (.NOT.PRESENT(up)) up=.TRUE.

  ! Loop to sort number-1 densities into order
  DO i=1,number-1

    ! Initialize earliest so far to be the first in
    ! this pass
    first = density(i)
    index = i

    ! Search remaining (unsorted items) for earliest one
    DO j=i+1,number
      SELECT CASE (up)
      CASE DEFAULT

        ! Sorting in increasing order
        IF (density(j) < first) THEN
          first = density(j)
          index = j
        END IF
      CASE (.FALSE.)
        ! Sorting in decreasing order
        IF (density(j) > first) THEN
          first = density(j)
          index = j
        END IF
      END SELECT
    END DO

    ! Swap both densities and material names if necessary
    IF (index /= i) THEN
      temp_num = density(i)
      density(i) = density(index)
      density(index) = temp_num
      temp_name = material(i)
      material(i) = material(index)
      material(index) = temp_name
    END IF
```

```
        END DO
    END SUBROUTINE numeric_sort
END PROGRAM material_sort
```

In addition to internal procedures Fortran 90 also includes a much simpler facility called a statement function, which was the only form of internal procedure in FORTRAN 77. This has been totally superseded by the internal subprogram discussed in this section, but is described briefly, for reference, in Appendix E.

SELF-TEST EXERCISES 11.2

1   What is the purpose of a generic interface block? How is it distinguished from a non-generic interface block?

2   What is the purpose of a **MODULE PROCEDURE** statement? Where does it appear?

3   What rules govern the specific procedures that are used in the definition of a generic procedure?

4   How many scoping units are there in the following program extract?

```
SUBROUTINE scoping_test
    IMPLICIT NONE
    INTERFACE
        SUBROUTINE sub_1
            TYPE my_type
               .
               .
               .
            END TYPE my_type
           .
           .
           .
        END SUBROUTINE sub_1

        SUBROUTINE sub_2
           .
           .
           .
        END SUBROUTINE sub_2
    END INTERFACE
    TYPE my_type
       .
       .
       .
    END TYPE my_type
       .
       .
       .
```

```
    CONTAINS
        SUBROUTINE sub_3
            TYPE my_type
                .
                .
                .
            END TYPE my_type
        .
        .
        .
        END SUBROUTINE sub_3
    END SUBROUTINE scope_test
```

5   What is the difference between host association and **USE** association?

6   What are the differences between an internal subprogram and an external subprogram?

7   When are entities in a host scoping unit not accessible within a nested scoping unit?

SUMMARY

- A dummy argument may be a scalar variable, an array or a procedure.

- If a dummy argument is a scalar variable then the corresponding actual argument must be a scalar object of the same type (such as a scalar variable, an array element, a character substring, a constant or an expression); if it is an array then the actual argument must be an array of the same type; if it is a procedure, then the actual argument must either be an external procedure or the specific name of an intrinsic function.

- If a dummy argument is a function then its declaration must include the **EXTERNAL** attribute; if it is a subroutine it must be declared in an **EXTERNAL** statement.

- If an actual argument is an external function then its declaration must include the **EXTERNAL** attribute; if it is the specific name of an intrinsic function then the declaration of its specific name must include the **INTRINSIC** attribute; if it is a subroutine it must be declared in an **EXTERNAL** statement.

- Actual arguments may be related to dummy arguments either by position or by keyword.

- Dummy arguments declared with the **OPTIONAL** attribute may be omitted from the list of actual arguments; the intrinsic function **PRESENT** determines whether an optional dummy argument has a corresponding actual argument.

- Local variables of a procedure are not preserved between invocations unless they have the save attribute or are initialized as part of their declaration; automatic arrays and dummy arguments cannot be saved.

- Procedures may be invoked recursively if the initial statement of the procedure specifies `RECURSIVE SUBROUTINE` or `RECURSIVE FUNCTION`, as appropriate.

- The initial statement of a recursive function should include a `RESULT` specification but no type; the type of the function is specified in a conventional type declaration statement for the result variable.

- An interface block without a name is used to provide an explicit interface for one or more procedures.

- An interface block with a name is used to give a generic name to two or more specific procedures, which must either be all functions or all subroutines.

- Any two specific procedures in a generic interface block must be distinguishable solely by reference to their non-optional dummy arguments.

- The `MODULE PROCEDURE` statement is used in a generic interface block to specify procedures which are accessible through `USE` association.

- A main program unit or a subprogram unit may contain any number of internal procedures, which may only be invoked from within the host program unit; internal procedures follow all the executable statements of the host, and are separated from them by a `CONTAINS` statement.

- The name of an internal procedure may not be used as an actual argument.

- An internal procedure has access to entities of its host by host association unless an entity of the same name is declared in the internal procedure.

- Fortran 90 syntax introduced in Chapter 11:

Initial statements	`RECURSIVE SUBROUTINE` *name* (...) `RECURSIVE FUNCTION` *name* (...) `RESULT` (*res_var*)
Keyword procedure invocation	`CALL` *name* (*dummy_arg_name=actual_arg* , ...) *function_name* (*dummy_arg_name=actual_arg* , ...)
Optional dummy argument attribute	`OPTIONAL`
Intrinsic procedure attribute	`INTRINSIC`
External procedure statement	`EXTERNAL` *subroutine_name*
Save attribute	`SAVE`
Save statement	`SAVE` *list of entities to be saved* `SAVE`

Non-generic interface block	`INTERFACE`
	    interface_body_1
	    interface_body_2
	    .
	    .
	    .
	`END INTERFACE`

Generic interface block	**INTERFACE** *generic_name*
	interface_body_1
	interface_body_2
	.
	.
	.
	MODULE PROCEDURE *list of module procedure names*
	.
	.
	.
	END INTERFACE

PROGRAMMING EXERCISES

*11.1   Write a function which returns the next character from a string which is input from the keyboard. The function should store the string in a suitable location and save it between calls. Each time the function is entered it should check if there are any characters left in the string, and request a new string from the keyboard if there are not. If there are characters left, or if a new string has just been read, the function should return the next one, and set a pointer to indicate the next character.

Test this function by using it to recreate a string input from the keyboard and display it.

(This type of function is often essential in programs such as compilers, and other language processors, which must analyse the input character by character to determine its syntax and meaning. In Chapter 15 we shall discuss input and output in more detail and will meet the concept of non-advancing input, which provides an alternative way of carrying out this exercise.)

11.2   Example 11.5 referred to a subroutine which will define a line which passes through a point and is tangent to a circle, using the types defined in the module **geometric_data**. Note that there are three possibilities:

- the point is inside the circle, in which case there is no solution;
- the point is on the circle, in which case there is a single solution;
- the point is outside the circle, in which case there are two solutions, and some means must be devised of determining which one is required. The method used in many CAD/CAM languages is to imagine that the circle is viewed from the point, and to specify the required line as being the one on the right, or on the left.

Write a suitable subroutine and test it with some of the other procedures already written for these modules.

11.3   Write a function to return a tax based solely on income. The tax is calculated from two tables, one containing upper income limits for each income range and the other the corresponding tax rate. If u is the integer table of income limits and r is the integer table of tax rates (specifying percentages), the tax is calculated by searching u and then applying the corresponding tax rate from r to the whole income. If anyone reports a negative income, do not give them a tax refund, simply charge them no tax. If anyone reports an income greater than the greatest value in u, apply the maximum tax rate in r. Both u and r should have strictly increasing values.

Write a program to test your function, where u and r are initialized (your opportunity to experiment with social engineering!) and test it with several different incomes.

11.4   Change the tax definition used in Exercise 11.3 so the tax rate r_i is applied only to the fraction of the income that lies in u_{i-1} to u_i (up to the maximum relevant rate). The total tax is found by summing the taxes for each income segment. Test this program with several different incomes.

11.5   Write a program which can be used to encrypt or decrypt a message in the following manner. A keyword of up to 10 letters is read, and used to encrypt the message by allocating each letter in the keyword its numeric position in the alphabet, and then replacing each letter of the message by the letter n later in the alphabet, where n is the value of the next letter of the keyword. The keyword is repeated as often as necessary, and the alphabet is considered to be circular (that is, A follows Z). Numbers are spelled out, digit by digit, and spaces are replaced by the next letter in the keyword. All letters are encrypted to lower case.

The coded message is written in groups of the same length as the keyword, which forms the first group, with extra random letters being added to the end of the last group if necessary. Thus, if the keyword is *Fortran* (6, 15, 18, 20, 18, 1, 14) the message *This exercise is fun* will be encrypted as follows:

$$
\begin{aligned}
T &\rightarrow T + 6 &= z \\
h &\rightarrow h + 15 &= w \\
i &\rightarrow i + 18 &= a \\
s &\rightarrow s + 20 &= m \\
\blacklozenge &\rightarrow 18 &= r \\
e &\rightarrow e + 1 &= f \\
x &\rightarrow x + 14 &= l \\
e &\rightarrow e + 6 &= k \\
r &\rightarrow r + 15 &= g \\
\text{etc.}
\end{aligned}
$$

leading to the encrypted message

fortran zwamrfl kguckfn ohrzmob

Note that the same letter does not normally encrypt to the same encrypted letter, thus eliminating the well-known method of code-breaking based on frequency counts.

The decryption part of the program will, of course, use the same procedure in reverse.

(Hint: first write and test the encryption part of the program; this can then be used to test the decryption part.)

11.6   The fact that factoring large integers into prime components is an extremely expensive process forms the basis for many modern encryption algorithms. In 1986 the record was the factoring of an 81 digit number using eight microcomputers, each of which ran for 150 hours. In 1988, a 100 digit number was factorized. Because of such successes, 200 digit numbers are being proposed as the basis for codes used by the United States government. If you wish to work in this area, modern methods for factoring large numbers (the quadratic sieve) are described by Cipra (1988), Gerver (1983) and Richards (1982); Richards also discusses public key codes.

Surprisingly, finding the highest common factor of two integers is a computationally easy problem, solved by the ancient Greeks. The following is Euclid's algorithm for finding the highest common factor of two positive integers a and b:

(1)   Let q and r be the quotient and remainder when a is divided by b. It is easy to prove that the highest common factor of a and b is the highest common factor of b and r.

(2)   If r is zero, then the highest common factor is b. If r is not zero, replace a and b by b and r, respectively, and repeat step 1.

After, at most, $\min(a,\ b) + 1$ iterations, the highest common factor will be found.

Write a program to implement Euclid's algorithm. Use the algorithm to find the highest common factor of 26 379 714 and 876 147 and then the highest common factor of 24 019 and 48 611.

11.7   The potential energy of a diatomic molecule can be expressed as a function of the distance between two atoms, r, using the expression

$$V = D\left(1 - e^{-\alpha(r-r_e)}\right)^2$$

where D, α and r_e are parameters, for instance $D = 10\,000$, $\alpha = 0.1$, $r_e = 1.0$. Use an internal function to evaluate V in a program that calculates V for r taking the values 0.5, 1.0, 1.5, 2.0, 2.5, 3.0, 3.5, 4.0, 4.5 and 5.0. Produce the results in the form of a table consisting of two columns.

11.8   Write a subroutine which sorts an array **a** with **n** elements using the following algorithm for the Quicksort method.

(1)   Start with `i=1, j=n`

(2)   Decrease `j` until `a(i)>a(j)`, then swap `a(i)` and `a(j)`

(3)   Increase `i` until `a(i)>a(j)`, then swap `a(i)` and `a(j)`

(4)   Repeat the last two actions until `i` and `j` are equal, and call this value of `i` (and `j`) **pivot**

a(pivot) is now in the correct place, and the array has been divided into two sections around **pivot**, each of which can be sorted separately.

If both sections have more than one element then save the start and end positions of the smaller section on a stack, and return to sort the larger section. If only one section has more than one element then return to sort that section. If neither section has more than one element then remove the start and end of a section off the stack and return to sort it. If there is nothing left on the stack then the array is fully sorted.

A stack is a means of storing items in which items can only be removed in the reverse order to that in which they were added to the stack ('last in, first out'), and is a very useful concept in many algorithms. It can be implemented in Fortran as an array and an integer pointer to the top of the stack. In this case an array of dimension $2\log_2 n$ will be large enough.

Use your subroutine in a program which reads a list of words from a file and sorts them into alphabetic order.

11.9 Example 7.1 introduced the straight selection sort, Exercise 7.11 introduced the bubble sort and Exercise 11.8 explained Quicksort, but all of the subroutines written to implement these sorts can only sort items of a specific type. Thus a procedure for sorting integers cannot be used to sort characters. However, it can readily be seen that in all methods there are only two situations when the array is referred to: (a) when elements i and j of the array are to be compared, and (b) when elements i and j of the array are to be exchanged.

Write a sorting subroutine using whichever method you prefer which uses optional arguments to allow it to sort an array which is either integer, real or character type. Also include an additional argument to indicate whether the sort array is to be in ascending or descending order. Test the subroutine in a program which calls it three times: first to sort a set of integers into ascending order, second to sort a set of words into alphabetic order, and third to sort a set of real values into descending order.

*11.10 qfpuzkx dutdfjx knuupcm xxqhzef rzptofx nxeoekd fxpzxpp toizzpj vbuizam ztjuftt vfijzef rzpdndr vgtuoqx lyyigkr ykpfeju fxtufzp qkdxoog empvnox uksjdtl xfuvcsx srexkkg kfynzfq vjpjnww qlemzef vfvdrdr qhbjcvx jkcdczj ftpohpp vgvoecx knuupcc moepska fjuyzmj fiauidx lyuyzem qkdxooc quhudpa fjuutsc qtustkm ekpntzn qjkodqh

zhjaq injzf dnrab inebp jujfp djjju gynou agwhu nlpav uqpqn jguiz igoqe wgnfz ogdxo vyeko kaatd ftmsd ciedw cbysm cengt ufhbf vzqqt ozwii bzjru gsjwg sbcwj hopxj qkepj gsnbs wlncg alhrt axizy zxbtn pxpdn

(Hint: See Exercise 11.5.)

Creating your own environment with modules

12

Up to this point modules have been used to provide global access to variables and derived types, and also to provide an explicit interface for external procedures. Modules are, however, far more powerful than this, and provide an extensive capability for creating an environment suited for the particular application area for which a program is being written.

One of the most important tools in this regard is the ability to control which of the entities in a module can be accessed by a program unit which uses the module – a concept known as data hiding. Another is the ability to create new operators and to extend the meaning of intrinsic operators and assignment. Taken together, these provide powerful data abstraction facilities.

As well as explaining how these individual features of Fortran 90 work, this chapter explores how the resulting data abstraction capability can be used to extend the language to provide some of those facilities missing from the language which would be particularly useful in a specific application domain.

12.1 The structure of a module

When we introduced modules in Chapter 4 we identified two uses for them – to enable data entities and derived type definitions to be accessed by more than one procedure, and to provide an easy way of making the explicit interface of procedures available to any program units which invoke them. In both cases the relevant entities are made available through **USE** association.

The only reason that we did not suggest combining specifications and procedures in the same module in Chapter 4 was that host association, as discussed in the context of internal procedures in Chapter 11, applies to module program units as well as to main program and subprogram program units, and our experience indicates that to introduce the concept of host association at that stage would have led to unnecessary confusion.

A procedure that is defined within a module is called a **module procedure**, and Figure 12.1, therefore, shows the complete structure of a module program unit, with the obvious proviso that if there are no module procedures then the **CONTAINS** statement is omitted.

The fact that host association applies to modules means that when developing a group of related procedures their common data entities and derived type definitions can be placed in the same module as the procedures, and will automatically be available to all the procedures, with any name clashes being resolved as described in Section 11.8. Example 12.1 shows how some of the geometric types and procedures that have been developed in earlier chapters might be combined into a single module.

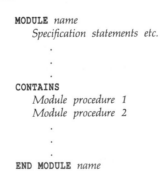

```
MODULE name
     Specification statements etc.
          .
          .
          .
CONTAINS
     Module procedure 1
     Module procedure 2
          .
          .
END MODULE name
```

Figure 12.1 The structure of a module program unit.

■ EXAMPLE 12.1

1 Problem

In Example 11.5 we defined a generic interface block which enabled a generic subroutine called **gen_line** to be used to define a line which either (a) passes through two specified points, (b) passes through a point perpendicular to a specified line, or (c) passes through a point and is tangent to a specified circle. It is now required to write a single module to provide such a capability, as well as providing the necessary derived types for use by any program unit which uses the module.

2 Analysis

We have already done all the necessary work in other examples and exercises, and we shall simply combine what was done before, with appropriate modifications. To save unnecessary repetition of what has already been done elsewhere we shall only give the first of the subroutines in full.

3 Solution

```
MODULE geometry
   IMPLICIT NONE

   ! Type definitions
   TYPE circle
      CHARACTER(LEN=12) :: name
      REAL :: x,y,r    ! coordinates of centre, and radius
   END TYPE circle

   TYPE line
      CHARACTER(LEN=12) :: name
      REAL :: a,b,c    ! coefficients of defining equation
   END TYPE line

   TYPE point
      CHARACTER(LEN=12) :: name
      REAL :: x,y       ! Cartesian coordinates of the point
   END TYPE point

   ! Generic procedure definition
   INTERFACE gen_line
      MODULE PROCEDURE line_two_points
      MODULE PROCEDURE line_point_perpto_line
      MODULE PROCEDURE line_point_tanto_circle
   END INTERFACE

CONTAINS
```

```
SUBROUTINE line_two_points(line_1,point_1,point_2)
   ! Dummy arguments
   TYPE(line),INTENT(OUT) :: line_1
   TYPE(point),INTENT(IN) :: point_1,point_2


   ! Local variable
   REAL :: small=10.0*TINY(1.0)


   ! Calculate coefficients of equation of line
   line_1%a = point_2%y - point_1%y
   line_1%b = point_1%x - point_2%x
   line_1%c = point_1%y*point_2%x - point_2%y*point_1%x


   ! Check for coincident points
   IF (ABS(line_1%a)<small .AND. ABS(line_1%b)<small) THEN
      ! Points are coincident - return all coefficients zero
      line_1 = line(0.0,0.0,0.0)
   END IF
END SUBROUTINE line_two_points


SUBROUTINE line_point_perpto_line(line_1,point_1,line_2)
   ! Dummy arguments
   TYPE(line),INTENT(OUT) :: line_1
   TYPE(point),INTENT(IN) :: point_1
   TYPE(line),INTENT(IN) :: line_2
   .
   .
   .
END SUBROUTINE line_point_perpto_line


SUBROUTINE line_point_tanto_circle(line_1,point_1,    &
                                   circle_1,modifier)
   ! Dummy arguments
   TYPE(line),INTENT(OUT) :: line_1
   TYPE(point),INTENT(IN) :: point_1
   TYPE(line),INTENT(IN) :: circle_1
   CHARACTER(LEN=6) :: modifier
   .
   .
   .
END SUBROUTINE line_point_tanto_circle

END MODULE geometry
```

Note that the test for coincident points is, in effect, testing that both the x and y coordinates of the two points are the same. Any program unit that uses this module will have access through USE association to the derived types circle, line and point, the procedures line_two_points, line_point_perpto_line and line_point_tanto_circle, and the generic procedure gen_line.

All future examples involving the geometric types and procedures will assume that only a single module is involved, and that all the derived types and procedures developed earlier have been rewritten in a similar style to that shown here.

12.2 Gaining more control over USE association

One of the potential problems with obtaining access to the entities in a module by USE association is that the names of one or more of these entities might clash with other names in the same scoping unit, such as local names or the names of entities made accessible by USE association from another module. In order to deal with this situation an extended form of the USE statement allows entities in the module to be referred to by a different name in the scoping unit containing that USE statement:

USE *module_name*, *rename list*

where each item in the *rename list* takes the form

local_name => *name_in_module*

Thus, for example, if it was required to use the module developed in Example 12.1 but with the generic subroutine called **define_line** instead of **gen_line** then the USE statement would be as follows:

```
USE geometry, define_line => gen_line
```

In a similar manner, if it were felt that it would be more convenient to call the generic defining subroutine(s) by the name of the geometric entity that was being defined (line, point, etc.) then the names of the derived types would also have to be changed, for example:

```
USE geometry, circle_def => circle, line_def => line,  &
              point_def => point, line => gen_line
```

Figure 12.2 shows how a program which uses the module in this way would declare various circles, lines and points and then define three lines using each of the three methods defined in Example 12.1.

As well as wanting to rename some of the entities accessed from a module by USE association, it may sometimes be required to restrict their number. We shall see in the next section how the author of a module may restrict the

```
PROGRAM rename_example
    USE geometry, circle_def => circle, line_def => line, &
                  point_def => point, line => gen_line
    IMPLICIT NONE

    TYPE(point_def) :: pt1,pt2
    TYPE(line_def) :: ln1,ln2,ln3
    TYPE(circle_def) :: cir1
    .
    .
    .
    CALL line(ln1,pt1,pt2)
    CALL line(ln2,pt1,ln1)
    CALL line(ln3,pt2,cir1,'xlarge')
    .
    .
    .
END PROGRAM rename_example
```

Figure 12.2 An example of renaming module entities.

entities that are available for **USE** association, but the program unit that is using a module may limit the entities made available from the module by another extension of the **USE** statement:

> USE *module_name*, **ONLY**: *only list*

where each item in the *only list* is either the name of an entity in the module, or a renaming of such an entity, as already described.

Thus, for example, if in both the two cases shown it was required that the names of the three subroutines **line_two_points**, **line_point_perpto_line** and **line_point_tanto_circle** should not be available then the **USE** statements would be as follows:

```
USE geometry, ONLY: circle, line, point,              &
                define_line => gen_line
```

and

```
USE geometry, ONLY: circle_def => circle,             &
                line_def => line, point_def => point, &
                line => gen_line
```

There is one point that should be noted about this form of the **USE** statement, which concerns the situation when there are two or more **USE** statements in the same scoping unit which refer to the same module. There are four possibilities here:

(1)   None of the **USE** statements involves renaming or has an **ONLY** qualifier. In this case the effect is the same as if there had only been a single **USE** statement.

(2)   One or more of the **USE** statements involves renaming, but none has an **ONLY** qualifier. In this case the effect is the same as if there had only been a single **USE** statement which contained all the *rename* lists concatenated into a single list.

(3)   All of the **USE** statements have **ONLY** qualifiers. In this case the effect is the same as if there had only been a single **USE** statement which contained all the **ONLY** qualifiers concatenated into a single list.

(4)   Some, but not all, of the **USE** statements have **ONLY** qualifiers. In this case the effect is the same as if there had only been a single **USE** statement which contained all the *rename* lists concatenated into a single *rename* list, but *without* any **ONLY** qualifier.

In practice, this will rarely be an issue since it would not be sensible to write more than one **USE** statement referring to the same module. Such situations might occur, for example, if an internal procedure accesses a module by **USE** association which is already being accessed by **USE** association in the host program unit, and it is important to understand what will happen. We strongly recommend that you should always remove any duplicate **USE** statements from your programs.

12.3 Restricting access to entities within a module

Although the example in the previous sections relates to geometric entities, the grouping together of related entities into a more complex structure is common everywhere in engineering and mathematics. For example, a complex number consists of two real numbers grouped in such a way that they can then be manipulated as a single entity. This encapsulation is convenient when it is not necessary to think of the real and imaginary parts separately. Similarly, a set of m by n numbers are often combined into a single mathematical structure, an m by n matrix, which then can be manipulated as a single entity. Much of the power of mathematics comes from this combination of simpler entities to form new, more complex, mathematical entities that can then be manipulated as single units at a higher level.

In previous chapters, it has been pointed out that it is good programming practice to group related variables together in a derived type and to encapsulate that derived type definition in a module in order that the type may then be easily used throughout a program. Furthermore, as we saw in the previous section, procedures that provide fundamental manipulation capabilities for entities of that type can, and should, also be put into the same module. This makes program development easier and maintenance simpler, because all the code relating to the creation and fundamental manipulation of a particular data type is encapsulated in one place and not distributed throughout a program.

Thus, it was natural to create a derived type for complex numbers whose components were two real numbers, as we did in Chapters 3 and 4, although, as we shall see in Chapter 14, Fortran does contain an intrinsic **COMPLEX** type, so this was not actually necessary. As we shall see in Example 14.1, electrical and electronic engineers frequently use the amplitude and phase of an alternating electrical signal in calculating the performance of circuits; for many purposes, therefore, it might be more convenient to use a complex data type which used polar coordinates rather than Cartesian coordinates to represent complex values. Figure 12.3 shows the relationship between the two types, and it is clear that it would be a trivial task to create a derived type encapsulating this structure.

However, this example illustrates a potential danger, for if a module was written to contain the derived type definition for a polar **complex_number**, together with procedures to carry out addition, subtraction, multiplication and division with entities of this type, it would still be legal to write a statement such as

```
z = complex_number(1.0,2.0)
```

where the writer (presumably!) assumed that the resulting complex number would have the value $1 + 2j$. This is because both the conventional and the polar representations of a complex number consist of two real numbers.

It is often appropriate, therefore, to go beyond using derived types and modules in the ways already described, in order to provide even greater program reliability.

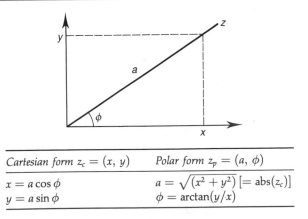

Cartesian form $z_c = (x, y)$	Polar form $z_p = (a, \phi)$
$x = a \cos \phi$	$a = \sqrt{(x^2 + y^2)} \, [= \text{abs}(z_c)]$
$y = a \sin \phi$	$\phi = \arctan(y/x)$

Figure 12.3 Complex numbers in both polar and Cartesian form.

The basic idea is that the component parts of a derived type should *not* be freely available throughout a program, but should only be available, in a controlled manner, through procedures provided in the module containing the derived type definition. This provides greater program safety and control within the program, because if an error in the construction or use of the components of a derived type entity occurs then the problem must be located inside the module. This concept is expressed by saying that the components of a derived type are either **private** (only available without restriction in the defining module) or **public** (freely available without restriction throughout a program).

The components of a derived type are made private by preceding the first component declaration in the derived type definition by the word **PRIVATE** on a line by itself:

```
TYPE complex_number
   PRIVATE
   REAL :: a,phi
END TYPE complex_number
```

Note that a **PRIVATE** statement can only appear in a type definition that is in a module.

Note also that the privacy only applies *outside* the module in which the type definition appears. Within the module, including all its module procedures, the components are fully accessible.

Finally, note that if the components of a derived type are private then not only is it not permitted to use the % notation with that derived type outside the module, but it is also not permitted to write a structure constructor to define a constant of that type outside the module; moreover, entities of that type cannot appear in an input or output statement, since this requires a knowledge of the components of the type. Objects of that type can, therefore, only be manipulated as a whole outside the module, unless they use procedures which have been written for detailed manipulation of components of entities of that type, and which are themselves made available through **USE** association from the module, thus providing the security that we require.

■ **EXAMPLE 12.2**

[1] Problem

Vectors and matrices are two of the most powerful data concepts for many engineering and mathematical applications. Write a module which provides a data type called **vector** and a procedure to multiply two vectors together to obtain their scalar product (or dot product). Note that it will also be necessary to provide procedures to create a vector (from a rank-one array) and to provide access to the individual elements of a vector.

2 Analysis

We shall first need to determine how we shall define a vector. We shall limit ourselves to vectors having real values, and it is clear that the primary means of storing the elements of the vector will therefore be a real array. However, vectors may be of varying sizes, and so, although we shall store the elements in an array of fixed size, we will also store the number of elements used (the *length* of the vector) as another component of the type. A suitable type definition will, therefore, be

```
TYPE vector
   PRIVATE
   INTEGER :: length
   REAL, DIMENSION(max_length) :: elements
END TYPE vector
```

where `max_length` is a named constant which specifies the maximum length of vector permitted. This constant will be declared in the module so that, if it is required to alter the maximum size of vectors, it will only be necessary to make one change to the module, and none to any program that uses the module.

The function to create a vector from an array is quite straightforward, but will need to include a check to ensure that the maximum length of a vector is not exceeded.

Data design

	Purpose	Type	Name
A	Dummy arguments		
	Array containing elements	REAL(:)	array
	Number of elements	INTEGER	n
B	Result variable	vector	create_vector

Structure plan

> **1** If n > max_length
>   **1.1** Print error message, set length of vector to zero, and exit
> **2** Set length of vector to *n*
> **3** Copy first *n* elements of *array* to vector

The means whereby individual elements of a vector are extracted is not specified. We shall simply copy the vector to an array, thereby returning all the elements in a form in which the program can use them. However, it will first be necessary to establish the length of the array in order to ensure that the array is large enough. The two functions to achieve this are extremely simple.

Integer function vector_size

Data design

	Purpose	Type	Name
A	Dummy argument Vector whose size is required	vector	v
B	Result variable	INTEGER	vector_size

Structure plan

> **1** Set function result to length of the dummy argument vector

Real array-valued function vector_array

Data design

	Purpose	Type	Name
A	Dummy argument Vector to be converted to an array	vector	v
B	Result variable	REAL(*l*) where *l* is the length of the vector v	vector_array

Structure plan

> **1** Set function result(1:*l*) to elements 1:*l* of the dummy argument vector

We can now proceed to consideration of the scalar product function.

Data design

	Purpose	Type	Name
A	Dummy argument Vectors to be multiplied	Vector	v1, v2
B	Local variable Scalar product of vectors	REAL	dot_product
	Loop counter	INTEGER	i

Structure plan

> **1** If lengths of two vectors are different
> **1.1** Print error message, set result to zero and exit
>
> **2** Initialize *dot_product* to zero
>
> **3** Repeat for *i* from 1 to *vector%length*
> **3.1** Add product of corresponding vector elements to *dot_product*
>
> **4** Exit with *dot_product* as function value

3 **Solution**

```
MODULE vectors
   IMPLICIT NONE

   ! Maximum length for vectors
   INTEGER, PARAMETER :: max_length = 10

   ! Derived type definition
   TYPE vector
      PRIVATE
      INTEGER :: length
      REAL, DIMENSION(max_length) :: elements
   END TYPE vector

CONTAINS

   TYPE(vector) FUNCTION create_vector(array,n)
   ! This function creates a vector from the first n
   ! elements of an array

      ! Dummy arguments
      INTEGER, INTENT(IN) :: n
      REAL, DIMENSION(n), INTENT(IN) :: array

      ! Validity check
      IF (n > max_length) THEN
         ! Too long - print warning and set length to zero
         PRINT '(" Error: Vector of length",I5," requested"/ &
                 " Maximum permitted is ",I3)',n,max_length
         create_vector%length = 0
      ELSE
         ! OK - copy first n elements of array to vector
         create_vector%length = n
         create_vector%elements(1:n) = array(1:n)
      END IF
   END FUNCTION create_vector

   INTEGER FUNCTION vector_size(v)
   ! This function returns the size of a vector
```

```
   ! Dummy argument
   TYPE(vector), INTENT(IN) :: v

   vector_size = v%length
END FUNCTION vector_size


FUNCTION vector_array(v)
! This function returns the elements of a vector as an array

   ! Dummy argument and function result
   TYPE(vector), INTENT(IN) :: v
   REAL, DIMENSION(v%length) :: vector_array(v%length)

   vector_array(1:v%length) = v%elements(1:v%length)
END FUNCTION vector_array

REAL FUNCTION scalar_product(v1,v2)
! This function returns the scalar product of two vectors

   ! Dummy arguments
   TYPE(vector), INTENT(IN) :: v1,v2

   ! Local variables
   REAL :: dot_product = 0.0
   INTEGER :: i

   ! Validity check
   IF (v1%length /= v2%length) THEN
      ! Vectors have different lengths
      PRINT '(" Error:  Vectors are of different lengths", &
             I4," and",I4 / " Zero result returned")',    &
             v1%length,v2%length
      scalar_product = 0.0
   ELSE
      ! OK - calculate dot product
      DO i=1,v1%length
         dot_product = dot_product +   &
                       v1%elements(i)*v2%elements(i)
      END DO
      scalar_product = dot_product
   END IF
END FUNCTION scalar_product


END MODULE vectors
```

Notice that, because the type definition for **vector** is in the same module as the procedures, it is possible to declare the type of the function **create_vector** in its initial statement in a way which is not possible when the type is obtained through **USE** association.

Figure 12.4 shows a program suitable for testing this module, and Figure 12.5 shows the result of executing this test program.

```
PROGRAM test_vectors
  USE vectors
  IMPLICIT NONE

  INTEGER :: dot,i
  REAL, DIMENSION(3) :: a
  REAL, DIMENSION(20) :: b
  TYPE(vector) :: v,w

  ! Set up to arrays and convert to vectors
  a = (/1.0, 2.0, 3.0/)
  b = (/2.0, 3.0, 4.0, 5.0, (0.0, i=1,16)/)
  v = create_vector(a,3)
  w = create_vector(b,3)

  ! Print details of vectors
  PRINT '(" Length of v is",I3 /    &
          " Its elements are (", 3(F5.1,","), ")")',  &
          vector_size(v),vector_array(v)
  PRINT '(" Length of w is",I3 /    &
          " Its elements are (", 3(F5.1,","), ")")',  &
          vector_size(w),vector_array(w)

  ! Calculate and print their scalar product
  PRINT '(" Their scalar product is ",F6.1)',    &
          scalar_product(v,w)

  ! Test error messages
  w = create_vector(b,20)
  w = create_vector(b,5)
  dot = scalar_product(v,w)

END PROGRAM test_vectors
```

Figure 12.4 A test program for the module **vectors**.

```
Length of v is  3
Its elements are (  1.0,  2.0,  3.0)
Length of w is  3
Its elements are (  2.0,  3.0,  4.0)
Their scalar product is   20.0
Error:  Vector of length   20 requested
Maximum permitted is  10
Error:  Vectors are of different lengths   3 and   5
Zero result returned
```

Figure 12.5 The result of testing the module **vectors**.

Of course, the module **vectors** is far from complete. There are many more fundamental capabilities for creating and manipulating vectors that should be added to it, and we shall return briefly to consideration of some of these in the next section. Furthermore, the definition of the type **vector** is wasteful of space, since all entities of type **vector** are of the same size, regardless of the length of the individual vectors; we shall introduce a technique for dealing with this problem in Chapter 16.

This principle of **data hiding** or, more generally, of only allowing access to a restricted set of the entities in a module is extremely important for secure programming, and does not only apply to the components of a derived type. For example, a module which is being used to provide a common database which will be used by a number of procedures in a program might, nevertheless, not wish to allow unlimited access to everything in that database. In a similar manner, a module which contains a collection of procedures to manipulate data in a particular application area might only wish to allow access to the 'top level' of these procedures, and not to those which are used for internal housekeeping, or other purposes which are not the concern of the program unit which is using the module.

As was the case with derived type components, the accessibility of any entity in a module can be either *private* or *public*, and the writer of the module has complete control over such accessibility for every entity. In the case of data objects or type definitions this is achieved by including a **PRIVATE** or **PUBLIC** attribute in the declaration:

```
REAL, PRIVATE :: internal_value
TYPE, PRIVATE :: internal_type
   REAL :: x,y
END TYPE internal_type
```

Note that making a derived type definition private means that no variables of that type can be declared outside the module. This contrasts with the earlier example in which the *components* of a derived type definition were made private, but the derived type itself was not.

Note also that a double colon must be included in the initial **TYPE** definition statement when a **PRIVATE** or **PUBLIC** attribute is specified. It may be included even if there is no accessibility attribute specified:

```
TYPE :: another_type
   .
   .
   .
END TYPE another_type
```

but we do not believe that this is necessary, as there are no other attributes that can be applied to a type definition and, as we shall see, even this one is not often required.

As is the case with many other attributes, the accessibility may also be specified by a statement:

> **PRIVATE** :: *list of private entities*
> **PUBLIC** :: *list of public entities*

These two statements may also appear without any list, in which case they specify the default accessibility for the module, which is otherwise *public*, of course. It is therefore possible to specify that *all* entities in a module are private, unless they are specifically given a public attribute. We recommend that modules should normally be written this way, and that for the convenience of the reader of the program those entities which are to be public should not be given that attribute in their declarations, but rather that a single list of the public entities should be placed near the beginning of the module:

```
MODULE example
   IMPLICIT NONE
   PRIVATE
   PUBLIC :: list of public entities
   .
   .
   .
```

Thus, for example, if the module written in Example 12.1 had the following two statements inserted at the beginning:

```
PRIVATE
PUBLIC :: circle, line, point, gen_line
```

then only these four entities would be available to any program unit using this module, and the three specific procedure names `line_two_points`, `line_point_perpto_line` and `line_point_tanto_circle` would be hidden from them.

This approach is standard practice among programmers writing modules for a wide audience, and we strongly recommend that all your modules should be written this way.

SELF-TEST EXERCISES 12.1

1 How can a program unit restrict the entities in a module that it has access to through **USE** association?

2   What happens if a subroutine has a local variable of the same name as a public entity in a module that it is using? How can the subroutine have access to both the local variable and the module entity?

3   What is the point of making the components of a derived type private?

4   Can the components of any derived type be made private?

5   What are the consequences of making the components of a derived type private?

6   Under what circumstances can the components of an entity of a derived type with private components be accessed?

7   What is the difference between making the components of a derived type private and making the definition of a derived type private?

8   What is meant by data hiding?

9   What is the recommended way of controlling the accessibility of entities in a module? Why?

12.4 Defining your own operators

We have now seen how a module can be written which will provide the programmer who uses it with new data types and procedures that use the data types both for detailed manipulation of the components of those types and for commonly required operations on objects of these types. This goes a long way towards enabling the programmer to create a special environment for use in a particular application area, but there is still one major gap in this environment – namely the provision of *operators* for use with objects of these types.

For example, in Example 12.2 we wrote a function `scalar_product` which produced the scalar product of two objects of type **vector**. This allows the programmer to write a statement such as

```
v1 dot_v2 = scalar_product(v1,v2)
```

where **v1** and **v2** are vectors and **v1_dot_v2** is an integer. However, it would be more natural to write

```
v1_dot_v2 = v1 .dot. v2
```

or even

```
v1_dot_v2 = v1 * v2
```

Fortran 90 allows us to do both of these by either defining our own operators or extending the meaning of intrinsic operators. The mechanism used is similar to that used to define generic procedures:

```
INTERFACE OPERATOR(operator_symbol)
    interface body
END INTERFACE
```

where *operator_symbol* may be one of the intrinsic operators or may consist of a sequence of up to 31 letters enclosed between periods. If *operator_symbol* is an intrinsic operator then the interface block extends the meaning of the intrinsic operator; otherwise it creates a new operator.

The interface body in the defining interface block must be a function having either one or two arguments; if it has one argument than the operator will be a unary operator, while if it has two then the operator will be a binary operator. In either case, the dummy arguments must be non-optional, and must be specified as having **INTENT(IN)**. Note, however, that since the function being referred to will normally be defined in the same module the interface body will normally be replaced by a **MODULE PROCEDURE** statement referring to the function's name.

Such a **defined operation** will be treated as a reference to the function with the operand(s) as the actual argument(s); in the case of a defined binary operation the first, or left-hand, operand will be the first actual argument and the second, or right-hand, operand will be the second actual argument. Note that the function must have an explicit interface in any program unit that invokes it.

Returning to the example of the function for calculating the scalar product of two vectors, the inclusion of the following interface block in the module would, therefore, allow the operator .dot. to be used in the way shown above:

```
INTERFACE OPERATOR(.dot.)
    MODULE PROCEDURE scalar_product
END INTERFACE
```

If we wish to extend the meaning of one of the intrinsic operators then there are three additional points to bear in mind:

● It is not permitted to *change* the meaning of an intrinsic operator, only to extend it. It must be possible, therefore, to distinguish the extended meaning of the operator from its already defined intrinsic meaning(s) solely by reference to the types of its operands, in much the same way as the alternative procedures in a generic interface block are distinguished.

● The number of function arguments must be consistent with the intrinsic uses of the operator.

- Extending the meaning of any of the six relational operators (<, <=, >, >=, == and /=) makes the same extension to the alternative way of writing these six operators (.LT., .LE., .GT., .GE., .EQ. and .NE.).

We can, therefore, extend the meaning of the intrinsic multiplication operator, *, to calculate the scalar product of two vectors by means of the following interface block:

```
INTERFACE OPERATOR(*)
   MODULE PROCEDURE scalar_product
END INTERFACE
```

so that the user can simply write statements such as

```
v1_dot_v2 = v1*v2
```

where **v1** and **v2** are of type **vector**.

Although in many cases it will only be required to define or extend an operator to deal with one combination of operands, there will also be situations in which it would be convenient to use the same operator in several situations, with different combinations of operands. In this case, we may define a generic defined operator in exactly the same way as we defined a generic procedure:

```
INTERFACE OPERATOR (operator_symbol)
   interface body_1
   interface body_2
   .
   .
   .
END INTERFACE
```

■ EXAMPLE 12.3

1 Problem

Make the necessary additions to the module written in Example 12.2 so that statements of the form **n*v** or **v*n**, where **n** is either integer or real and **v** is a vector, result in a new vector, each of whose elements is **n** times the corresponding element of **v**.

2 Analysis

There are four combinations here, and there will need to be four functions to implement them. They are all so simple that we shall omit the structure plan and proceed directly to coding them.

3 Solution

The following four module procedures must be added to the module **vectors**:

```
TYPE(vector) FUNCTION int_times_vector(n,v)
! This function multiplies every element of the vector v
! by the integer n

   ! Dummy arguments
   INTEGER, INTENT(IN) :: n
   TYPE(vector), INTENT(IN) :: v

   ! Local variable
   INTEGER :: i

   int_times_vector%length = v%length
   DO i=1,v%length
      int_times_vector%elements(i) = n * v%elements(i)
   END DO
END FUNCTION int_times_vector

TYPE(vector) FUNCTION vector_times_int(v,n)
! This function multiplies every element of the vector v
! by the integer n

   ! Dummy arguments
   INTEGER, INTENT(IN) :: n
   TYPE(vector), INTENT(IN) :: v

   ! Local variable
   INTEGER :: i

   vector_times_int%length = v%length
   DO i=1,v%length
      vector_times_int%elements(i) = n * v%elements(i)
   END DO
END FUNCTION vector_times_int

TYPE(vector) FUNCTION real_times_vector(p,v)
! This function multiplies every element of the vector v
! by the real number p

   ! Dummy arguments
   REAL, INTENT(IN) :: p
   TYPE(vector), INTENT(IN) :: v

   ! Local variable
   INTEGER :: i

   real_times_vector%length = v%length
   DO i=1,v%length
      real_times_vector%elements(i) = p * v%elements(i)
   END DO
END FUNCTION real_times_vector
```

```
TYPE(vector) FUNCTION vector_times_real(v,p)
! This function multiplies every element of the vector v
! by the real number p

    ! Dummy arguments
    REAL, INTENT(IN) :: p
    TYPE(vector), INTENT(IN) :: v

    ! Local variable
    INTEGER :: i

    vector_times_real%length = v%length
    DO i=1,v%length
        vector_times_real%elements(i) = p * v%elements(i)
    END DO
END FUNCTION vector_times_real
```

In addition, the following interface block must be added to the body of the module:

```
INTERFACE OPERATOR(*)
    MODULE PROCEDURE int_times_vector
    MODULE PROCEDURE vector_times_int
    MODULE PROCEDURE real_times_vector
    MODULE PROCEDURE vector_times_real
END INTERFACE
```

This is also an example of a situation in which it would be sensible to hide the names of the four procedures and to allow only a program unit which uses the module to have direct access to the extended operator, thus avoiding the possibility of a potential name clash should the programmer wish to use these names for some other purpose. In order to do this the operator name must appear in a **PUBLIC** statement in the same form as it appears in the **INTERFACE** statement:

```
PUBLIC :: OPERATOR(*)
```

This almost completes the set of programming tools necessary for fully utilizing the capabilities inherent in the combination of derived types and modules, but there is one remaining requirement which the reader may not immediately think of, namely assignment.

Although we tend to think of the assignment operator, =, as simply copying the result of the expression on its right to the variable, or other entity, whose name appears on its left, a moment's thought shows us that there is more to assignment than this, for we have already met many cases in which some change is made to the value on the right-hand side of the assignment before it is stored in the location in memory identified by the name on the left-hand side. For example, a real value may be converted to an integer, including truncation, or a character string may be extended with spaces. Assignment is, however, fully defined for all intrinsic data types, but what about derived types?

If an object of a derived type is assigned to an entity of the same type then, by default, every component of the derived type value on the right is copied to the corresponding component of the entity on the left. Since this is normally what is required there is no problem here. But what about assignments where the types are different? In these cases, and possibly even when they are the same, we can define the meaning of assignment in much the same way as we have just learned to define operators:

```
INTERFACE ASSIGNMENT (=)
    interface body
END INTERFACE
```

or

```
INTERFACE ASSIGNMENT (=)
    interface body_1
    interface body_2
       .
       .
       .
END INTERFACE
```

Note that the assignment symbol must be included in the **INTERFACE** statement, even though it cannot be changed from **=**; this is because the syntax would otherwise be the specification of a generic procedure called **ASSIGNMENT**!

The interface bodies in the defining interface block must all be subroutines having exactly two non-optional dummy arguments; the first dummy argument must be specified as having **INTENT(OUT)** or **INTENT(INOUT)**, while the second must be specified as **INTENT(IN)**.

Such a **defined assignment** will be treated as a reference to the subroutine with the left-hand side as the first actual argument and the right-hand, enclosed in parentheses, as the second actual argument. Note that this subroutine must have an explicit interface in any program unit that invokes it.

Thus, for example, the two functions **create_vector** and **vector_array**, which were written in Example 12.2 to create a vector from a rank-one array and to copy the elements of a vector to a rank-one array, respectively, could easily be rewritten as subroutines and used to define assignment between rank-one arrays and vectors by means of the following interface block:

```
INTERFACE ASSIGNMENT (=)
    MODULE PROCEDURE create_vector
    MODULE PROCEDURE vector_array
END INTERFACE
```

Note that there will need to be one change in the specification of the subroutine **create_vector** compared with the equivalent function in Example 12.2. In the original form, the number of elements of the array that was to be used in creating the vector were also passed as an argument. Because this (third) argument is not permitted here it will be necessary to use an assumed-shape dummy array, with the consequence that the length of the vector will be set to the size of the array, regardless of how many elements are really required. We shall see how to get round this problem in Chapter 14.

With these defined assignments added to the module **vectors** it will be possible to write statements such as

```
v1 = a1
```

and

```
a2 = v2
```

where **v1** and **v2** are of type **vector**, and **a1** and **a2** are real arrays, instead of the much clumsier

```
v1 = create_vector(a1,n)
```

and

```
a2 = vector_array(v2)
```

As was suggested for defined operators, it is usually preferable to hide the name of the subroutine which is used to provide the defined assignment, and in a similar way to that used with operators, the assignment symbol must have the **PUBLIC** attribute and the defining subroutine must be **PRIVATE**:

```
PRIVATE
PUBLIC :: ASSIGNMENT(=)
```

12.5 Data abstraction and language extension

The ability to define new data types and to encapsulate them in a module, together with any relevant operators, including defined assignment, and procedures, coupled with the ability to make any of these operators and procedures generic, and the use of the **PRIVATE** and **PUBLIC** attributes to hide the internal details from the user of the module, are collectively known as **data abstraction**, and is a key functionality in modern programming practice. In particular, it means that Fortran 90 modules can provide many of the features required for **object-oriented** programming, although not all of them, and for **language extension**.

Although we have demonstrated language extension in our development of a module for handling various types of geometric objects, and also with the module **vectors** earlier in this chapter, we can best illustrate how language extension works by considering two examples taken from international standards which use modules to extend the Fortran 90 language.

The first of these is included as an example in the Fortran 90 standard itself (ISO/IEC 1539 : 1991), and consists of a module, **INTEGER_SETS**, to provide all the necessary features for programs to use sets, where the elements of each set are integers. The module provides a new type **SET**, together with a number of operators which are detailed in Figure 12.6, and three functions in addition to the five which define the five operators. These functions perform the following additional tasks:

- return the cardinality of a set, that is, the number of elements in the set;
- transfer the elements of a rank-one array to a set, removing any duplicate values;
- transfer the elements of a set to a rank-one array in ascending order.

Although it was not done that way in the example referred to in the standard, it would obviously be possible, arguably even preferable, for the latter two functions to be written as subroutines and then used to define assignment between an integer array and a set, and vice versa.

The second example is the subject of an auxiliary standard to the primary Fortran 90 standard (ISO/IEC 1539-2) and defines the necessary extensions to the Fortran 90 language to provide a **varying string** data type, in addition to the fixed-length character strings available using the intrinsic **CHARACTER** type. This auxiliary standard (which was still undergoing final international processing at the time of writing this book) defines a new data type **VARYING_STRING** and specifies extended meanings for all the intrinsic operators that can be used with characters, defines assignment between objects of type **VARYING_STRING**, between **VARYING_STRING** and **CHARACTER**, and between **CHARACTER** and **VARYING_STRING**, and extends the meaning of all the intrinsic procedures which relate to characters by adding additional cases to their generic meanings. In addition, it specifies a number of generic procedures which must be provided for such purposes as type conversion, input/output and substring manipulation.

Although this auxiliary standard only specifies the meaning of these various operators and procedures, in a very similar manner to the way in which the Fortran 90 language itself is defined in its defining standard, it also includes, in an Annex, a complete Fortran 90 module which could be used to implement all the capabilities specified in this auxiliary standard. This module includes no fewer than 96 module procedures, which are used to define or extend 25 generic

Operator	Example	Meaning
.IN.	x.IN.a	*true* if the integer **x** is a member of the set **a**
<=	a<=b	*true* if the set **a** is a subset of the set **b**; that is, every element of **a** is also a member of **b**
+	a+b	the union of the sets **a** and **b**; that is, the set containing all the elements which are a member of either **a** or **b**, or both
-	a-b	the difference of the sets **a** and **b**; that is, the set containing those elements of **a** or **b** which are not also a member of the other set
*	a*b	the intersection of the sets **a** and **b**; that is, the set containing only those elements which are a member of both **a** and **b**

Figure 12.6 The operators defined in the module INTEGER_SETS.

procedures, to extend the six intrinsic relational operators and the concatenation operator, and to extend the assignment operator. In this module the default accessibility is set to **PRIVATE**, as are the components of the derived type **VARYING_STRING**, and a single **PUBLIC** statement lists the 34 entities (the derived type, 25 generic procedures, 7 operators and the assignment operator) which are accessible outside the module.

This example, in particular, illustrates the power of the features discussed in this chapter to allow a programmer to extend the language to make it more appropriate for a particular application area. The time spent in developing such a language extension will be more than repaid by the easier and more reliable programs that can then be developed in this application domain.

■ EXAMPLE 12.4

1 Problem

A rational number is a number consisting of two parts, an integer numerator and a non-zero integer denominator, whose decimal value is the result of dividing the numerator by the denominator; in other words it is a fraction. It is required to write a module to create a type for rational numbers and to provide the necessary facilities for rational numbers to be used in arithmetic expressions in the same ways as integer and real numbers. Write that part of the module that contains the specifications for all public entities, together with the procedure, or procedures, necessary to add an integer to a rational number and store the result in a rational number variable.

2 Analysis

The specification of a derived type to implement rational numbers is very straightforward:

```
TYPE rational
   PRIVATE
   INTEGER :: num,denom
END TYPE rational
```

We now need to think carefully about the various arithmetic operations that we shall need to provide for, and we shall consider addition first. There are a total of nine possibilities, as shown in Figure 12.7, and an interface block to extend the + operator accordingly might be as follows:

```
INTERFACE OPERATOR(+)
   MODULE PROCEDURE real_real_plus_rat
   MODULE PROCEDURE real_rat_plus_real
   MODULE PROCEDURE rat_real_plus_rat
   MODULE PROCEDURE rat_rat_plus_real
   MODULE PROCEDURE int_int_plus_rat
   MODULE PROCEDURE int_rat_plus_int
   MODULE PROCEDURE rat_int_plus_rat
   MODULE PROCEDURE rat_rat_plus_int
   MODULE PROCEDURE rat_rat_plus_rat
END INTERFACE
```

There are also possible extensions to the unary meaning of the + operator, but we shall ignore these for this example.

Similar interface blocks will be required to extend the subtraction, multiplication, division and exponentiation operators.

Type of result	Type of left operand	Type of right operand
REAL	REAL	rational
REAL	rational	REAL
rational	REAL	rational
rational	rational	REAL
INTEGER	INTEGER	rational
INTEGER	rational	INTEGER
rational	INTEGER	rational
rational	rational	INTEGER
rational	rational	rational

Figure 12.7 Extended cases for operators for rational arithmetic.

Left-hand side	Right-hand side
REAL	rational
rational	REAL
INTEGER	rational
rational	INTEGER
rational	rational

Figure 12.8 Extended assignments for rational arithmetic.

Furthermore, it will be necessary to provide extensions to the assignment operator to cover the five cases shown in Figure 12.8; the fifth case, of rational assigned to rational, could be left to the default assignment of component to component, but it might be desirable to simplify the form of the number on assignment so that, for example, the rational number (37,74) is converted to (1,2) as part of the assignment process.

We should also consider providing a generic conversion function to convert a real or integer number into a rational one, and extended generic specifications for the intrinsic **REAL** and **INTEGER** conversion functions to convert rational numbers to real or integer values, as appropriate.

Finally, we must write the necessary procedures to add an integer to a rational number with a rational result. In this case we know that we shall not require any simplification of the result, assuming that the rational number involved in the expression is already in its simplest form, and so we need only write functions to deal with two cases (integer plus rational, and rational plus integer), although as these will be the same for all practical purposes we shall only develop a structure plan for the first, **rat_rat_plus_int**.

Data design

	Purpose	Type	Name
A	Dummy arguments		
	Integer value to be added	INTEGER	int_num
	Rational value to be added	TYPE(rational)	rat_num
B	Result variable		
	Sum of two arguments	TYPE(rational)	rat_int_rat

Structure plan

> 1 Numerator of result is *rat_num%num* + *int_num*rat_num%denom*
> 2 Denominator of result is *rat_num%denom*

3 Solution

```
MODULE rational_numbers
  IMPLICIT NONE
  PRIVATE
  PUBLIC :: rational, OPERATOR(+),OPERATOR(-),OPERATOR(*),  &
            OPERATOR(/),OPERATOR(**),ASSIGNMENT(=),         &
            rational_convert,REAL,INTEGER

! This module implements rational numbers as an additional
! numeric type

  ! Type definition
  TYPE rational
    PRIVATE
    INTEGER :: num,denom
  END TYPE rational

  ! Extended intrinsic operator specifications
  INTERFACE OPERATOR(+)
    MODULE PROCEDURE real_real_plus_rat
    MODULE PROCEDURE real_rat_plus_real
    MODULE PROCEDURE rat_real_plus_rat
    MODULE PROCEDURE rat_rat_plus_real
    MODULE PROCEDURE int_int_plus_rat
    MODULE PROCEDURE int_rat_plus_int
    MODULE PROCEDURE rat_int_plus_rat
    MODULE PROCEDURE rat_rat_plus_int
    MODULE PROCEDURE rat_rat_plus_rat
  END INTERFACE

  INTERFACE OPERATOR(-)
    MODULE PROCEDURE real_real_minus_rat
    MODULE PROCEDURE real_rat_minus_real
    MODULE PROCEDURE rat_real_minus_rat
    MODULE PROCEDURE rat_rat_minus_real
    MODULE PROCEDURE int_int_minus_rat
    MODULE PROCEDURE int_rat_minus_int
    MODULE PROCEDURE rat_int_minus_rat
    MODULE PROCEDURE rat_rat_minus_int
    MODULE PROCEDURE rat_rat_minus_rat
  END INTERFACE

  ! and three similar interface blocks for *, / and **
  .
  .
  .

  ! Extended assignment
  INTERFACE ASSIGNMENT(=)
    MODULE PROCEDURE real_equals_rat
    MODULE PROCEDURE rat_equals_real
    MODULE PROCEDURE int_equals_rat
    MODULE PROCEDURE rat_equals_int
```

```
                MODULE PROCEDURE rat_equals_rat
        END INTERFACE


        ! Generic type conversion functions
        INTERFACE rational_convert
                MODULE PROCEDURE real_to_rat
                MODULE PROCEDURE int_to_rat
        END INTERFACE

        INTERFACE REAL
                MODULE PROCEDURE rat_to_real
        END INTERFACE

        INTERFACE INTEGER
                MODULE PROCEDURE rat_to_int
        END INTERFACE

CONTAINS

        TYPE(rational) FUNCTION rat_rat_plus_int(rat_num,int_num)
        ! Adds an integer to a rational number to give a rational
        ! result

            ! Dummy arguments
            TYPE(rational), INTENT(IN) :: rat_num
            INTEGER, INTENT(IN) :: int_num

            ! Calculate result
            rat_rat_plus_int%num = rat_num%num + int_num*rat_num%denom
            rat_rat_plus_int%denom = rat_num%denom
        END FUNCTION rat_rat_plus_int

        TYPE(rational) FUNCTION rat_int_plus_rat(int_num,rat_num)
        ! Adds a rational number to an integer to give a rational
        ! result

            ! Dummy arguments
            INTEGER, INTENT(IN) :: int_num
            TYPE(rational), INTENT(IN) :: rat_num

            ! Calculate result
            rat_int_plus_rat%num = int_num*rat_num%denom + rat_num%num
            rat_int_plus_rat%denom = rat_num%denom
        END FUNCTION rat_int_plus_rat
            .
            .
            .

END MODULE rational_numbers
```

Notice, incidentally, that the second of the two functions detailed above could have been written in a slightly shorter way by using the defined operator +, as specified by the first procedure:

```
TYPE(rational) FUNCTION rat_int_plus_rat(int_num,rat_num)
! Adds a rational number to an integer to give a rational
! result

    ! Dummy arguments
    INTEGER, INTENT(IN) :: int_num
    TYPE(rational), INTENT(IN) :: rat_num

    ! Calculate result with defined operator for reverse order
    rat_int_plus_rat = rat_num + int_num
END FUNCTION rat_int_plus_rat
```

In this instance a saving of one line of code is achieved at the cost of an extra procedure call, and so could hardly be justified. However, if each procedure had been substantially longer then such a simplification might be justified. Similarly, it might be worth using the extended meaning of one intrinsic operator in the procedure(s) to define another extended operator.

SELF-TEST EXERCISES 11.2

1   What is meant by a defined operation? How is it defined?

2   What are the constraints on extending the meaning of an intrinsic operator?

3   How many things are wrong with the following interface block?

```
INTERFACE OPERATOR(<)
   INTEGER FUNCTION tom(dick,harry)
      INTEGER :: dick,harry
   END FUNCTION tom

   REAL FUNCTION reduce(array)
      REAL, DIMENSION(:), INTENT(IN) :: array
   END FUNCTION reduce
END INTERFACE
```

4   What is meant by defined assignment? How is it defined?

5   What is meant by data abstraction? What are the benefits of data abstraction?

SUMMARY

- A module will normally contain both specification statements and module procedures.

- Module procedures have access to entities specified in the body of the module by host association.

- A USE statement may specify local names for entities accessible from the module by renaming the module entities.

- A USE statement may restrict the entities accessible from the module by use of an ONLY qualifier.

- The components of a derived type that is defined in a module may be made private by the inclusion of a PRIVATE statement before any component declarations, in which case the components are inaccessible from outside the module other than by use of module procedures from that module.

- All entities in a module may be either public or private; by default everything is public.

- Derived type definitions and data objects declared within a module may be given a public or private attribute as part of their declaration.

- A PRIVATE or PUBLIC statement in a module sets the accessibility attribute of the entities listed to private or public, as appropriate.

- A PRIVATE or PUBLIC statement in a module without an entity list sets the default accessibility for the module to private or public, as appropriate.

- Data hiding provides greater security for programmers.

- An interface block may be used to define a new operator, or to extend the meaning of an intrinsic operator.

- An interface block may be used to extend the meaning of assignment for non-intrinsic data types.

- Data hiding and the ability to define and extend operators and assignment provide the facilities for data abstraction.

- Data abstraction is used for language extension and object-oriented programming.

- Fortran 90 syntax introduced in Chapter 12:

Accessibility attributes	**PRIVATE**
	PUBLIC
Accessibility statements	**PRIVATE** :: *entity1,entity2,...*
	PRIVATE
	PUBLIC :: *entity1,entity2,...*
	PUBLIC
Module entity renaming	**USE** *name*, *local_name* => *module_public_name,...*
Module entity restriction	**USE** *name*, **ONLY**: *list of module public names*

Defined operator
interface block

```
INTERFACE OPERATOR (operator_symbol)
    function_interface_body_1
    function_interface_body_2
        .
        .
        .
    MODULE PROCEDURE list of module function names
        .
        .
        .
END INTERFACE
```

Defined assignment
interface block

```
INTERFACE ASSIGNMENT (=)
    subroutine_interface_body_1
    subroutine_interface_body_2
        .
        .
        .
    MODULE PROCEDURE list of module subroutine names
        .
        .
        .
END INTERFACE
```

PROGRAMMING EXERCISES

12.1   Create two definitions for a derived type called **point** which represents a point in two-dimensional space; the first should use Cartesian coordinates (x, y) and the second polar coordinates (r, θ). Place each definition in a different module. Now write a program which uses *both* modules and declares two variables of each type. The program should ask the user for the polar coordinates of two points, and should calculate the equation of the line joining them, in the form

$$ax + by + c = 0$$

Finally, the program should print the coordinates of the two points in both polar and Cartesian coordinates, followed by the equation of the line joining them.

12.2   Define a derived type to represent a person, which includes the name(s), sex and date of birth of the person. Now define another derived type which represents a family of people of the first type, including the relationship between its various members (father, mother etc.). Allow for a minimum of three generations in a family.

   Now write a program which will initialize a family consisting of four grandparents, their children and their grandchildren and responds to questions from the user of the form 'Who is the mother of Lucy Jones?' or 'How many children does Frances Smith have?'.

Note that the questions need not be phrased in English as shown. It is perfectly acceptable, even desirable, to offer the user a choice of types of questions, and then an appropriate list of names about whom the question can be asked, for example:

```
Who do you want to ask about from the following list?
1. Lucy Jones
2. Frances Smith
   .
   .
   .
Type number of person: response from user

What do you want to know from the following list?
1. Mother
2. Father
3. Maternal grandmother
   .
   .
   .
```

etc.

12.3 Modify the program that you wrote for Exercise 12.2 (if necessary) so that the components of the two derived types are not accessible from outside the module, and add appropriate procedures to the module to provide the names of the people in a specified family, the relationship between two specified people, and any other information that you feel necessary.

Test the program with the same questions as before.

Finally, modify the program so that it reads the family data from a file instead of having this information specified in initialization statements.

*12.4 In Example 4.4 we developed a module containing a derived type **complex_number** and four procedures to implement addition, subtraction, multiplication and division with complex numbers. Write a module based on that one which allows a program to use the intrinsic operators +, -, * and / to carry out these operations on complex numbers instead of using the procedures.

12.5 Exerises 11.5 and 11.10 required you to write programs which would encrypt or decrypt a message. Using either of the techniques described in these exercises, write a module which has only two public entities, namely operators .**encrypt**. and .**decrypt**.. Each of these operators should have two character operands, and should deliver as their result the encrypted or decrypted version of their second operand, using the first operand as the key. Thus, using the technique described in Exercise 11.5,

```
"Fortran" .encrypt. "This exercise is fun"
```

will deliver the result "**zwamrfl kguckfn ohrzmob**", while

```
"Fortran" .decrypt. "zwamrfl kguckfn ohrzmob"
```

will deliver the result "**this exercise is funp**" (where the extra letter at the end is because of the addition by the encrypting operator of an extra letter to complete the last block).

*12.6   Write the necessary code to add to the module **geometry** so that the statement

        point_1 = .centre.circle_1

in a program that uses the module will cause the variable **point_1** of type **point** to be defined with the coordinates of the centre of the circle **circle_1**, which is itself of type **circle**, and the statement

        point_2 = line_1 .intersects. line_2

will cause the variable **point_2**, also of type **point**, to be defined with the coordinates of the point of intersection of the two lines **line_1** and **line_2**, both of type **line**. Remember to take appropriate action if the lines are parallel.

12.7   Create a derived type for rational numbers and make its components private. Place this definition in a module, together with a procedure that will create a rational number given two integers (which may be positive or negative). This procedure should reduce the rational number by finding the highest common factor of the numerator and denominator and dividing it into them (see Exercise 11.6 for one method of doing this).

Write two more procedures for the module that, given a rational number, will return the numerator and the denominator, respectively.

Test your module by creating rational numbers 5/3, 60/84. Then print out the numerator and denominator of each of the resulting rational numbers.

12.8   Extend the module written for Exercise 12.4 so that any combination of real, integer and **complex_number** entities (variables or constants) may be the operands for the four operators **+**, **-**, ***** and **/**. Your module should also extend the assignment operator so that assignment of real or integer values to **complex_number** variables works correctly.

Test the module within a program that uses all possible combinations of operand types.

12.9   Some programming languages contain a data type known as an *enumeration type*, in which a finite set of discrete values are specified, and variables or constants of that type may only take one of these values. For example a character enumeration type called **seasons** might only allow the values **"spring"**, **"summer"**, **"autumn"** and **"winter"**, and an integer enumeration type called **month** might only allow the integers between 1 and 12, inclusive.

Write a module which defines two enumeration types, **int_enum** and **char_enum**, for integers and characters respectively, and appropriate operators etc., to allow variables of these types to be used in expressions and in **CASE** statements. Test your module with a suitable test program.

Note that you will need to determine what to do if the program attempts to assign an illegal value to a variable of one of these types. One possibility might be to print an error message and/or to terminate the program. Another possibility might be to treat such an action in a similar way to overflow during an arithmetic operation, and to store a logical variable as part of the type which specifies whether the last attempt to change the variables value was successful. This could be tested by the module procedures which access an enumerated variable, or by a special validity-check procedure, and appropriate action taken if a variable is found to have been corrupted.

12.10 Create a derived type, with private components, for a company's personnel records. It should have fields for a first name, last name, department, birthday and salary. Create a file with five to ten such records. Write a simple program to do this.

Put an initialized character field into the module containing the definition of records. The value will be used as a secret password. Put a procedure into the module that will search the file of records for those that match a specified name and print out the names and departments of those that match. Put a second procedure into the module that, when also given the correct password, will also print out birthday and salary information.

Test this module by using it in a program that allows the user to search the personnel database and provides the names and departments of those satisfying the matching criteria, together with the birthday and salary information if the user has previously supplied the correct secret password.

It appears to the authors that if the user does not have access to the source code for the module, and does not know the password, then it is impossible to access birth date and salary information using only Fortran 90, even given the data file. Can you see a way to get at the confidential information using only Fortran 90? (Perhaps we don't have sufficiently criminal minds!)

Array processing and matrix manipulation

13

In Chapter 7 we discussed the basic principles of Fortran's array facilities in the context of rank-one arrays. In mathematical terms, such arrays are suitable for representing vectors, but in order to represent matrices, or more complex rectangular structures, more than one subscript is required. The same general principles apply to rank-n arrays as were described earlier in the context of rank-one arrays, although the order of the array elements is occasionally important.

As well as extending the basic array concepts to rank-n arrays, however, Fortran contains several other powerful array features which are the subject of the major part of this chapter. These include dynamic arrays, whose shape is not determined until execution time, and sub-arrays, which are created from either a regular or an irregular set of elements of another array. Finally, the facilities for whole array processing are re-examined in the light of these new, more flexible, types of arrays, and additional concepts are introduced to add still further to the power of Fortran's array processing capability.

13.1 Matrices and two-dimensional arrays

Arrays were first introduced in Chapter 7, and we have already seen how useful they can be in many situations. However, the arrays that we have been using up to now have been restricted to a single subscript, and have been referred to as rank-one or single-dimensional arrays. Although these arrays were perfectly adequate for working with objects such as vectors, they are not appropriate for matrices or objects that are naturally represented by arrays of more than one dimension. Fortran allows us to define arrays with up to seven subscripts, but before dealing with the full generality provided by Fortran for multi-dimensional arrays, we will, because of their connection with matrices and also for illustrative purposes, briefly discuss two-dimensional arrays in particular.

Mathematically, a matrix is a two-dimensional rectangular array of elements. For example, a 3×4 matrix $\mathbf{A}$ consists of the elements

$$\begin{bmatrix} A_{1,1} & A_{1,2} & A_{1,3} & A_{1,4} \\ A_{2,1} & A_{2,2} & A_{2,3} & A_{2,4} \\ A_{3,1} & A_{3,2} & A_{3,3} & A_{3,4} \end{bmatrix}$$

Fortran extends the concept of a one-dimensional array, introduced in Chapter 7, in a natural manner, by means of the **DIMENSION** attribute. Thus, to define a two-dimensional array **a** that could hold the elements of the matrix $\mathbf{A}$ we would write

```
REAL, DIMENSION(3,4) :: a
```

Note that, in the dimension attribute, the number of rows is specified first and the number of columns second. *This order is important.*

As a second example, if we wanted to create three 10×4, two-dimensional arrays, **b**, **c** and **d**, of logical elements, we would write

```
LOGICAL, DIMENSION(10,4) :: b, c, d
```

The elements of a two-dimensional array are scalars (that is, they are single entities of the data type involved) and are referenced by a logical extension of the notation used for one-dimensional arrays. For example, **a(2,3)** is the element of **a** in the second row and third column. Once again, we emphasize that the row position is specified first, followed by the column position. Thus, **a(3,2)** is a different element from **a(2,3)**, just as $A_{2,3}$ is different from $A_{3,2}$.

The elements of an array, being scalars, can be used anywhere it is legitimate to use a scalar. They can occur in arithmetic expressions, be passed as actual arguments, occur in I/O statements, etc. For example,

Name	Result
MATMUL	Matrix product of two matrices, or a matrix and a vector
DOT_PRODUCT	Scalar (dot) product of two vectors
TRANSPOSE	Transpose of a matrix
MAXVAL	Maximum value of all the elements of an array, or of all the elements along a specified dimension of an array
MINVAL	Minimum value of all the elements of an array, or of all the elements along a specified dimension of an array
PRODUCT	Product of all the elements of an array, or of all the elements along a specified dimension of an array
SUM	Sum of all the elements of an array, or of all the elements along a specified dimension of an array

Figure 13.1 Intrinsic functions for use with vectors and matrices.

```
a(3,4) = 2.0*a(3,4) + 1.0   ! Doubles a(3,4) and adds 1 to it.

DO i = 1,4                   ! Replace row 1 of a by row 3 of a.
   a(1,i) = a(3,i)           ! Row 3 is unaltered.
END DO

DO I = 1,3                   ! Replace column 2 of a by column
   a(i,2) = a(i,1)           ! 1 of a. Column 1 is unaltered.
END DO
```

Fortran provides three intrinsic functions specifically designed for vector and matrix operations, where it is assumed that matrices are stored in two-dimensional arrays and vectors are stored in one-dimensional arrays. Figure 13.1 lists these and their purpose, but it should be noted that Fortran 90 contains a large number of other intrinsic functions which operate on arrays of any dimension. These are described in Section 13.4, but it is relevant to mention here that MAXVAL, MINVAL, PRODUCT and SUM are also useful for work with vectors and matrices and are, therefore, included in Figure 13.1.

The use of some of these intrinsic functions is illustrated by the program shown in Figure 13.2 which establishes a 2 × 3 matrix and its 3 × 2 transpose, and then performs a matrix multiplication to create a 2 × 2 result. A similar multiplication is carried out between the 3 × 2 matrix and a three-element vector to give a two-element vector result.

Note, incidentally, that, although the vector **vector_c** has been given an initial value by means of an array constructor, the matrix **matrix_a** has been given its value by means of a series of assignment statements. This is because array constructors are always of rank-one. We shall see in Section 13.3 how to overcome this problem.

```
PROGRAM vectors_and_matrices
  IMPLICIT NONE
  INTEGER, DIMENSION(2,3) :: matrix_a
  INTEGER, DIMENSION(3,2) :: matrix_b
  INTEGER, DIMENSION(2,2) :: matrix_ab
  INTEGER, DIMENSION(2) :: vector_c = (/ 1,2 /)
  INTEGER, DIMENSION(3) :: vector_bc

  ! Initialize matrix_a
  matrix_a(1,1) = 1         ! matrix_a is the matrix:
  matrix_a(1,2) = 2
  matrix_a(1,3) = 3         !    [ 1  2  3 ]
  matrix_a(2,1) = 2         !    [ 2  3  4 ]
  matrix_a(2,2) = 3
  matrix_a(2,3) = 4

  ! Set matrix_b as the transpose of matrix_a
  matrix_b = TRANSPOSE(matrix_a)
  ! matrix_b is now the matrix:   [ 1  2 ]
  !                               [ 2  3 ]
  !                               [ 3  4 ]

  ! Calculate matrix products
  matrix_ab = MATMUL(matrix_a,matrix_b)
  ! matrix_ab is now the matrix:  [ 14  20 ]
  !                               [ 20  29 ]

  vector_bc = MATMUL(matrix_b,vector_c)
  ! vector_bc is now the vector:  [ 5  8  11 ]

END PROGRAM vectors_and_matrices
```

Figure 13.2 An example of matrix and vector multiplication.

13.2 Basic array concepts for arrays having more than one dimension

In Fortran, an array is formally defined as a compound entity that contains an ordered set of scalar entities, each one of the same type, arranged in a rectangular pattern. An array may have from one to seven dimensions. As we mentioned in Chapter 7, the **rank** of an array is defined as the number of its dimensions. (Incidentally, for those knowledgeable about linear algebra, the rank of a Fortran array has no connection at all with the notion of the rank of a matrix!) Although in the previous section we followed the widespread, informal, custom of referring to a rank-two array as a two-dimensional array, we shall, in general, use the more correct terminology from now on; thus a vector is a rank-one array, and a matrix is a rank-two array.

The rank of an array is specified by using the dimension attribute in a type declaration statement. Thus the three declarations

```
REAL, DIMENSION(8) :: a
INTEGER, DIMENSION(3,10,2) :: b
TYPE(point), DIMENSION(4,2,100,8) :: c
```

specify an eight-element rank-one real array **a**, a $3 \times 10 \times 2$ rank-three integer array **b**, and a $4 \times 2 \times 100 \times 8$ rank-four array **c** of the derived type **point**.

Notice that this form of the dimension attribute is very similar to that used for rank-one arrays, except that the **extent** of each dimension is specified, separated by commas. The rank of the array is the number of items in this list. Once specified, the rank of an array cannot be changed.

For arrays with fixed extents, it is generally good programming practice not to use integers for the extents of arrays but, instead, to use named constants. Thus, for example, we might declare the array **c**, above, as follows:

```
INTEGER, PARAMETER :: s1 = 4, s2 = 2, s3 = 100, s4 = s1*s2
   .
   .
   .
TYPE(point), DIMENSION(s1, s2, s3, s4) :: c
```

Consistently using the parameter attribute in this way permits the easy change of array sizes in a complex program where several arrays and their extents may have correlated sizes. This might be required if a program has to be modified to solve larger problems.

On the other hand, if you have arrays dimensioned at three because you are working with three-dimensional vectors, it will not be appropriate to use the parameter attribute in the above way – you are unlikely to decide to change the dimensionality of your space from 3 to 5!

In most of the examples in this book we shall use literal constants for the extents of arrays, for clarity, but when writing real programs you should always consider whether it is more sensible to use a named constant here, just as the same consideration should be applied to *any* use of literal constants in a program.

When we first introduced the various terms used with arrays in Chapter 7, we stated that the **size** of an array is the total number of elements it contains; it is thus equal to the product of the extents of all its dimensions. In the second example above, the array **b** has extent 3 for its first dimension, extent 10 for its second dimension, and extent 2 for its third dimension; its size is therefore $3 \times 10 \times 2$, or 60. Similarly, the array **c** has extent 4 for its first dimension, extent 2 for its second dimension, extent 100 for its third dimension, and extent 8 for its fourth dimension; its size is therefore $4 \times 2 \times 100 \times 8$, or 6400. The size of the first array, **a** is, of course, the same as its extent, since it is a rank-one array.

One point that we must mention here is that, formally, an array may have any non-negative extent, *including zero*, for any of its dimensions. Although the idea of having an extent of zero in one, or more, dimensions may seem a little strange it is very convenient in certain types of problem. However, it has a further implication since the size of an array is equal to the product of the extents, and, consequently, if an array has a zero extent for one of its dimensions, its size will be zero, regardless of the extent of any other dimensions.

We also stated, in Chapter 7, that the **shape** of an array is determined by its rank and the extent of each dimension. The shape of any array is therefore representable as a rank-one array whose elements are the extents. For example, if a rank-three array has extents 10, 20 and 30, respectively, for its first, second and third dimensions, its shape is representable as the rank-one array whose elements are, in order, 10, 20 and 30. This concept of the shape of an array will be important when we come to some of the more advanced uses of arrays later in this chapter.

In Chapter 7 we introduced many of the fundamental features of arrays in the context of rank-one arrays, and all of these features can now be extended to rank-n arrays in a natural fashion. Thus, for example, the array declarations for rank-n arrays may specify lower and upper bounds for one or more of their dimensions, if required:

```
REAL, DIMENSION(11:18) :: a
INTEGER, DIMENSION(5:7, -10:-1, 2) :: b
TYPE(Point), DIMENSION(5:8, 0:1, 100, -3:4) :: c
```

Notice that we have not changed the extents of any of the dimensions of the three arrays **a**, **b** and **c** from the forms in which they were declared earlier, but only the way that the elements of the arrays are to be referenced. This is an important point that should be clearly understood.

Notice also that, when we specify the lower and upper **index bounds** for a dimension, the extent for that dimension is one plus the difference between the upper and lower index bounds. There is, however, one exception to this, namely that if the lower index bound is greater than the upper index bound then the extent of that dimension is defined to be zero.

It is important to stress that the index bounds of an array are not directly part of its shape. Of course the index bounds determine the array extents, which are part of its shape, but, for example, a rank-one array with index bounds 1 and 10 has the same shape as another rank-one array with index bounds 20 and 29.

Before discussing the ways in which the uses of rank-n arrays relate to the similar uses of rank-one arrays with which we are already familiar, we must briefly discuss the order of the elements in an array.

The elements of an array form a sequence known as the **array element order**. It can be visualized as all the elements of an array, of whatever rank, being arranged in a sequence in such a way that the first index of the element specification is varying most rapidly, the next index of the element specification is varying the second most rapidly, and continuing in this manner until the last index of the element specification is varying the least rapidly.

To illustrate the concept, let us consider the array **arr** which is declared as follows:

```
REAL, DIMENSION(4,3) :: arr
```

arr is, therefore, a rank-two array of shape (4,3) with default lower index bounds of 1, and the array element order of **arr** is the sequence

```
arr(1,1), arr(2,1), arr(3,1), arr(4,1), arr(1,2), arr(2,2),
arr(3,2), arr(4,2), arr(1,3), arr(2,3), arr(3,3), arr(4,3)
```

Notice that this is the same as the order obtained by traversing the first column of **arr**, followed by traversing the second column, and finally the third column, and it is for this reason that it is sometimes said that Fortran stores arrays by columns:

The same rule applies regardless of the number of dimensions, although it becomes increasingly difficult to visualize a model, and so it is generally best not to attempt to do so for arrays of rank greater than two!

In general, in Fortran 90, it is not necessary to be concerned with the array element order; however in FORTRAN 77 it was extremely important, since none of the whole array operations of Fortran 90 were available, and it is important that the ordering rules are understood so that any FORTRAN 77 code which is to be maintained or modified will be properly understood. Apart from two situations which we shall discuss in the next two sections, we shall deal with arrays in future without any concern for the order in which the elements are arranged.

13.3 Array constructors for rank-*n* arrays

In Section 7.3 we introduced the concept of an array constructor, as a means of specifying a literal array-valued constant. This takes the form

(/ *value_list* /)

where each item in *value_list* is either a single value or a list in parentheses controlled by an implied **DO**, for example:

```
(/ -1, (0,i=1,48), 1 /)
```

An array constructor, however, always creates a rank-one array of values, and if it is required to use this in a context in which an array of some other rank is required, such as assigning it to such an array, then further steps need to be taken to transform it into an array of the correct shape. This is achieved by using the intrinsic function **RESHAPE**.

This function constructs an array of a specified shape from the elements of a given array. For the current purpose we will use it in the simplest way, in which there are only two arguments. The first argument is the source array (in this application, an array constructor), and the second argument is a rank-one array specifying the required shape. For example

```
RESHAPE( (/ 1.0, 2.0, 3.0, 4.0, 5.0, 6.0 /), (/ 2, 3 /)
```

takes the rank-one real array whose elements are 1.0, 2.0, 3.0, 4.0, 5.0, 6.0 and produces, as a result, the 2 × 3 real array whose elements are

$$\begin{bmatrix} 1.0 & 3.0 & 5.0 \\ 2.0 & 4.0 & 6.0 \end{bmatrix}$$

Notice that the elements of the source array are used *in array element order*; this is one of the few places in Fortran 90 where knowing the array element order is necessary.

The **RESHAPE** function may also be used in a declaration statement to provide an initial value or to define a named constant, and Figure 13.3 shows how the example program used in Figure 13.2 can be improved by declaring the value of the matrix **matrix_a** using an array constructor and the **RESHAPE** function.

Finally, as might be expected, implied **DO** elements may be nested, so that an integer array **a** could be declared and given the value

$$\begin{bmatrix} 11 & 12 \\ 21 & 22 \end{bmatrix}$$

by the following declaration statement:

```
INTEGER :: i,j
REAL, DIMENSION(2,2) :: a = &
    RESHAPE((/ ((10*i+j, i = 1,2), j = 1,2) /), (/ 2,2 /))
```

```
PROGRAM vectors_and_matrices
  IMPLICIT NONE
  INTEGER, DIMENSION(2,3) :: matrix_a = &
         RESHAPE((/1,2,2,3,3,4/), (/ 2,3 /))
  INTEGER, DIMENSION(3,2) :: matrix_b
  INTEGER, DIMENSION(2,2) :: matrix_ab
  INTEGER, DIMENSION(2) :: vector_c = (/ 1,2 /)
  INTEGER, DIMENSION(3) :: vector_bc

  ! Set matrix_b as the transpose of matrix_a
  matrix_b = TRANSPOSE(matrix_a)
  ! matrix_b is now the matrix:   [ 1   2 ]
  !                               [ 2   3 ]
  !                               [ 3   4 ]

  ! Calculate matrix products
  matrix_ab = MATMUL(matrix_a,matrix_b)
  ! matrix_ab is now the matrix:  [ 14   20 ]
  !                               [ 20   29 ]

  vector_bc = MATMUL(matrix_b,vector_c)
  ! vector_bc is now the vector:  [ 5   8   11 ]

END PROGRAM vectors_and_matrices
```

Figure 13.3 An improved example of matrix and vector multiplication.

13.4 Input and output with arrays

In Section 7.4 we stated that, in the context of rank-one arrays, input and output of arrays, or of parts of arrays, could be handled in three ways:

- as a list of individual array elements;
- as a list of array elements under the control of an implied DO;
- as the complete array, by including the unsubscripted array name in the input or output list.

The first two of these cases need no further elaboration, but the third case needs some care, as the array elements will be transferred *in array element order*. This is the second place in Fortran 90 in which knowledge of the array element order is required.

In general we would advise you always to use an implied DO when reading or writing whole arrays as it makes it absolutely clear in which order the data is to be presented or the results are to be printed. In many situations, moreover, the obvious way of providing data is not the same as the array element order. For example, consider the situation in which an array **x** is being used to store a 50×8 array of data values.

Since the data may be considered as 50 rows of 8 columns, we would normally wish to input or output the array row by row. However a statement such as

```
PRINT '(8F8.2)', x
```

will print out the data in the following way:

```
x(1,1)   x(2,1)   x(3,1)   x(4,1)   x(5,1)   x(6,1)   x(7,1)   x(8,1)
x(9,1)   x(10,1)  x(11,1)  x(12,1)  x(13,1)  x(14,1)  x(15,1)  x(16,1)
  .        .        .        .        .        .        .        .
  .        .        .        .        .        .        .        .
  .        .        .        .        .        .        .        .
x(49,1)  x(50,1)  x(1,2)   x(2,2)   x(3,2)   x(4,2)   x(5,2)   x(6,2)
x(7,2)   x(8,2)   x(9,2)   x(10,2)  x(11,2)  x(12,2)  x(13,2)  x(14,2)
  .        .        .        .        .        .        .        .
  .        .        .        .        .        .        .        .
  .        .        .        .        .        .        .        .
```

which is not at all what was wanted!

On the other hand, the statement

```
PRINT '(8F8.2)', ((x(i,j),j=1,8),i=1,50)
```

will cause the results to be printed in the correct arrangement:

```
x(1,1)   x(1,2)   x(1,3)   x(1,4)   x(1,5)   x(1,6)   x(1,7)   x(1,8)
x(2,1)   x(2,2)   x(2,3)   x(2,4)   x(2,5)   x(2,6)   x(2,7)   x(2,8)
  .        .        .        .        .        .        .        .
  .        .        .        .        .        .        .        .
  .        .        .        .        .        .        .        .
```

13.5 The five classes of arrays

When discussing rank-one arrays in Chapter 7 we met four different classes of arrays, namely explicit-shape arrays, assumed-shape arrays, automatic arrays (which are actually a sub-class of explicit-shape arrays) and assumed-size arrays. In this section we shall review these four classes and draw attention to the (minor) differences in their use when their rank is greater than one. There is also a fifth class, deferred-shape arrays, which we have not yet met; this will be discussed in detail in Section 13.6.

Explicit-shape arrays are arrays whose index bounds for each dimension are specified when the array is declared in a type-declaration statement. In this context, specified does not necessarily mean fixed. It means that the index bounds can be calculated from information available when the arrays are declared.

The dimension attribute for an explicit-shape array takes the form

DIMENSION (*list of explicit-shape specifiers*)

The rank of the array is the number of *explicit-shape specifiers* given. Each *explicit-shape specifier* specifies the lower and upper index bounds for one dimension of the array and takes the form

lower_bound : *upper_bound*

or

upper_bound

where *lower_bound* and *upper_bound* are **specification expressions**. A specification expression may be considered for all practical applications as being a scalar integer expression; there are some restrictions on the form of this expression but they are unimportant in practice, and will not be given here. If the *lower_bound* is omitted it is taken to be 1.

An example of an explicit-shape array whose bounds are fixed is:

```
TYPE(person), DIMENSION(101:110,20) :: company
```

The variable **company** is a rank-two array of the derived type **person**, where, for example, the first dimension might represent the department within the company, and the second dimension might represent the people in the department; thus **company(i,j)** would be the **j**th person in the **i**th department. The lower and upper index bounds of the array are 101 and 110 for the first dimension, and 1 (default) and 20 for the second dimension. The extents are 10 and 20 for the first and second dimensions, respectively, and the size of the array is 200 (10×20). The shape of the array is specifiable as a rank-one array whose elements have the values 10 and 20.

Explicit-shape arrays with constant index bounds can be specified in type declaration statements in either main programs or procedures.

In a procedure, a dummy argument may be an explicit-shape array whose bounds are integer expressions, the values of which can be determined at the time of entry to the procedure. Such bounds usually involve other dummy arguments, but the relevant information may also be provided by other means, such as host or **USE** association. An example of a procedure with explicit-shape dummy arguments is

```
SUBROUTINE explicit(a,b,m,n)
   IMPLICIT NONE
   INTEGER, INTENT(IN) :: m,n
   REAL, DIMENSION(m,n*n+1), INTENT(INOUT) :: a
   REAL, DIMENSION(-n:n,m,INT(m/n)), INTENT(OUT) :: b
```

.
.
.

```
END SUBROUTINE explicit
```

In this example **a** is a rank-two array and **b** is a rank-three array. Note that **a** has default lower index bounds of 1 for each dimension, whereas **b** has an explicit lower index bound of $-n$ for the first dimension and default lower index bounds of 1 for the second and third dimensions. It is not necessary for the bounds of the actual and dummy arguments to be the same even though the extents should match, so that, for example a call to this subroutine of the form

```
REAL, DIMENSION(15,50) :: p
REAL, DIMENSION(15,15,2) :: q
  .
  .
  .
CALL explicit(p,q,15,7)
```

will establish the dummy argument **a** with subscripts from 1 to 15 in the first dimension and 1 to 50 in the second, which exactly matches the index bounds for the corresponding actual argument **p**, while the dummy argument **b** will have subscripts from -7 to $+7$ in the first dimension, 1 to 15 in the second, and 1 to 2 in the third, which match the extents of the corresponding actual argument **q**, but not their index bounds in the case of the first dimension.

One of the difficulties with explicit-shape dummy arguments, unless they have fixed shape, is the need to provide the information from which the bounds can be calculated, usually by means of additional dummy arguments. *Assumed-shape arrays* eliminate this need, as the information about extents is carried implicitly when an actual array is associated with an assumed-shape dummy argument. Notice that it is information about the *extents* of the actual argument that is implicitly available, not information about *index bounds*. The index bounds used inside a procedure are always local to that procedure, constrained only by the need to be consistent with the corresponding extents of the actual arguments.

Assumed-shape arrays may only be dummy arguments of a procedure that has an explicit interface; they cannot occur in a main program. They take their shape from association with actual arguments when a procedure is referenced, hence the name assumed-shape. The actual argument must be of the same type and have the same rank as the dummy argument.

The dimension attribute for an assumed-shape array takes the form

DIMENSION(*list of assumed-shape specifiers*)

The rank of the array is the number of *assumed-shape specifiers* given. Each *assumed-shape specifier* specifies the lower index bound for one dimension of the array and takes the form *lower bound* :

or

:

If the *lower bound* is omitted, it is taken to be 1. For example, the following program extract has two assumed-shape dummy array arguments, **a** and **b**:

```
REAL FUNCTION assumed_shape(a,b)
   IMPLICIT NONE
   INTEGER, DIMENSION(:,:) :: a
   REAL, DIMENSION(5:,:,:) :: b
   .
   .
   .
```

The first dummy array argument, **a**, is of rank 2, with the lower index bounds for both subscripts being 1; the second dummy array argument, **b**, is of rank 3, with the lower index bound for the first subscript being 5, and the lower index bounds for the other subscripts being 1.

When discussing assumed-shape arrays in Chapter 7 we briefly mentioned the three intrinsic functions **SIZE**, **LBOUND** and **UBOUND** in the context of rank-one arrays, and it is now appropriate to re-examine how these functions operate with rank-*n* arrays.

The function **SIZE** has two arguments, the second of which is optional. The first argument is the name of the array, and the second argument, **DIM**, is an integer which, if present, must lie in the range $1 \leqslant DIM \leqslant rank$, where *rank* is the rank of the array. If **DIM** is not present, **SIZE** returns the size of the whole array. If **DIM** is present, **SIZE** returns the extent of the array for the specified dimension.

The function **LBOUND** also has two arguments, of which the second is optional. These arguments follow the same pattern as those for **SIZE**, with the first argument being the name of the array, and the second argument specifying the dimension. If the second argument, **DIM** is present, then **LBOUND** returns the lower index bound of the specified dimension in the form of an integer. If **DIM** is not present, however, the result of the function reference is a rank-one array containing *all* the lower index bounds.

This explains why, in Chapter 7, we stated that these procedures should be used with two arguments, the second being 1, when asking for the bounds of a rank-one array. If, for example, a reference was made to **LBOUND(rank_1)**, where **rank_1** is a rank-one array, then the result of the function reference will be a rank-one array, consisting of a single element, and not a scalar value as might have been expected.

The third function, **UBOUND**, is similar to **LBOUND**, but returns the upper bound(s) of its first argument.

A procedure that uses assumed-shape dummy arguments usually has a small increase in internal complexity, compared with using explicit-shape arrays, because of the added need to determine the array bounds within the procedure. However, the decrease in complexity of the procedure interface more than compensates for this; incorrect calling sequences are a major source of programming errors.

■ **EXAMPLE 13.1**

1 Problem

Write a program to determine whether a polygon is convex.

2 Analysis

This type of problem frequently occurs in writing software for computer-aided design (usually abbreviated as CAD) and computer-aided manufacture (usually abbreviated as CAM). Such problems also occur in writing programs for virtual reality applications.

A polygon is an n-sided figure whose boundary consists of straight line segments joining adjacent vertices. Triangles and quadrilaterals, for example, are special cases of polygons (Figure 13.4).

An area is said to be convex if, for any two points in the area, the straight line segment joining them is completely contained in the area. Thus, in Figure 13.5 area A is convex, while area B is not. It is easy to prove that a triangle is always convex, whereas a quadrilateral may not be.

The problem of determining convexity will be solved by using a derived-type **point**, consisting of two real numbers, in which to store the coordinates of the vertices. This is similar to the derived type used on several occasions as part of

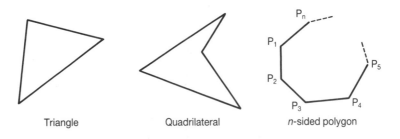

Triangle   Quadrilateral n-sided polygon

Figure 13.4 3-sided, 4-sided and n-sided polygons.

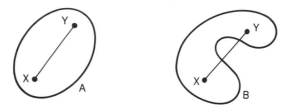

Figure 13.5   Convexity of two-dimensional areas.

the module **geometry**, but we shall not need the rest of that module for this example. An array of points will then be used to store the definitions of polygons.

The mathematical analysis is based on the observation that a polygon is convex if and only if the rotation angles (restricted to be in the range $-180 < \theta \leqslant 180$) between adjacent sides are either always positive (that is, each side is always rotated in an anticlockwise (counterclockwise) direction from its predecessor side) or always negative (that is, each side is always rotated in a clockwise direction from its predecessor side). Thus, in the five-sided polygon shown in Figure 13.6 it can be seen visually that the five rotation angles are always in the clockwise direction. Therefore, the five-sided polygon $P_1P_2P_3P_4P_5$ is convex.

By contrast, in the six-sided polygon shown in Figure 13.7 it can be seen visually that the rotation angle between sides P_3P_4 and P_4P_5 is clockwise, whereas all the other angles are anticlockwise. Hence the six-sided polygon $P_1P_2P_3P_4P_5P_6$ is not convex.

It is easily proved by vector analysis that, for convexity, we require, for every three adjacent vertices P_i, P_{i+1}, P_{i+3}, with coordinates (x_i, y_i),

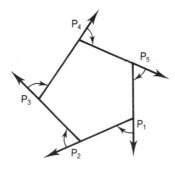

Figure 13.6   A five-sided polygon.

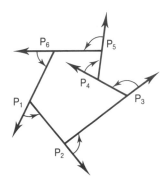

Figure 13.7 A six-sided polygon.

(x_{i+1}, y_{i+1}) and (x_{i+2}, y_{i+2}), respectively, that $(x_{i+1} - x_i)(y_{i+2} - y_{i+1})$ − $(y_{i+1} - y_i)(x_{i+2} - x_{i+1})$ always have the same sign around the polygon. This algorithm will work whether the vertices are given in clockwise or anticlockwise order. (For those interested in the mathematics, the proof is based on taking the cross product of two adjacent edges. The polygon is convex if the sine of the angle between the edges is always of the same sign − ignoring degenerate cases when three adjacent vertices are collinear.)

An initial structure plan for the main subroutine is easily developed.

> **1** Obtain number of sides of the polygon
> **2** Set convex flag *true*
> **3** Calculate the direction of rotation at the first vertex
> **4** Repeat for each remaining vertex
>   **4.1** If direction of rotation has changed
>   **4.1.1** Set convex flag *false*
>   **4.1.2** Exit from loop

The only difficulty here is the calculation of the direction of rotation at each vertex, and so we shall place this in a function which will return a positive value if the direction is positive (anticlockwise) and a negative value if it is negative (clockwise). We can then easily detect if the direction of rotation has changed by multiplying two successive orientations together and testing to see whether the result is negative. In practice, a few moments' thought shows that we need only use the orientation at the *first* vertex and the current one.

We can now proceed with our data design and structure plan for each procedure; however, we shall not go into the detail of the mathematics involved in calculating the direction of rotation at a vertex.

Subroutine convex_polygon

Data design

	Purpose	Type	Name
A	Arguments		
	Array of points	point	polygon
	Convexity of the polygon	LOGICAL	convex
B	Local variables		
	Orientation at first vertex	REAL	anti
	Number of vertices	INTEGER	n_vertices
	DO loop variable	INTEGER	i

Structure plan

1 Obtain number of sides of the polygon from SIZE(*polygon*)

2 Set *convex* to *true*

3 Calculate the direction of rotation at the first vertex (*anti*) using the function *orientation*

4 Repeat for each remaining vertex
    4.1 If *anti*orientation*(this vertex) < 0
        4.1.1 Set *convex* to *false*
        4.1.2 Exit from loop

Real function orientation

Data design

	Purpose	Type	Name
A	Arguments		
	Array of points	point	p
	Number of vertex	INTEGER	vertex
B	Local variable		
	Number of vertices	INTEGER	n

Structure plan

1 Obtain number of vertices from SIZE(*p*)

2 Calculate direction of rotation and return as the value of the function

Note that, by using assumed-shape arrays for the two dummy argument arrays of points which represent the polygon, our procedures will work for any size of polygon.

3 Solution

```
MODULE convexity
   IMPLICIT NONE

   ! Derived type definition
   TYPE point
      REAL :: x,y
   END TYPE point

CONTAINS

SUBROUTINE convex_polygon(polygon,convex)
   IMPLICIT NONE

   ! This subroutine determines whether a polygon is convex

   ! Dummy arguments
   TYPE(point), DIMENSION(:), INTENT(IN) :: polygon
   LOGICAL, INTENT(OUT) :: convex

   ! Local variables
   REAL :: anti = 0.0
   INTEGER :: i,n_vertices

   ! Set initial value for convex and obtain number of vertices
   convex = .TRUE.
   n_vertices = SIZE(polygon,1)     ! n_vertices is the number
                                    ! of vertices

   ! Get direction of rotation at first vertex
   IF (orientation(polygon,1) > 0.0) THEN
      anti = 1.0
   ELSE
      anti = -1.0
   END IF

   ! Check direction of rotation at remaining vertices
   DO i = 2,n_vertices
      IF (anti*orientation(polygon,i) < 0.0) THEN
         ! Return immediately a different orientation occurs
         convex = .FALSE.
         EXIT
      END IF
   END DO
END SUBROUTINE convex_polygon

REAL FUNCTION orientation (p,vertex)
   IMPLICIT NONE

   ! This function returns the direction of angular
   ! rotation at a specified vertex of a polygon
   ! positive if counterclockwise, negative if clockwise
```

```
! Dummy arguments
TYPE(point), DIMENSION(:), INTENT(IN) :: p
INTEGER, INTENT(IN) :: vertex


! Local variable
INTEGER :: n

n = SIZE(p,1)          ! n is the number of vertices

! Calculate orientation at this vertex
IF (vertex == n-1) THEN
   orientation = (p(n)%x-p(n-1)%x)*(p(1)%y-p(n)%y)      &
                 - (p(n)%y-p(n-1)%y)*(p(1)%x-p(n)%x)
ELSE IF (vertex == n) THEN
   orientation = (p(1)%x - p(n)%x)*(p(2)%y - p(1)%y)    &
                 - (p(1)%y - p(n)%y)*(p(2)%x - p(1)%x)
ELSE
   orientation = (p(vertex+1)%x - p(vertex)%x)          &
                 *(p(vertex+2)%y - p(vertex+1)%y)       &
                 - (p(vertex+1)%y - p(vertex)%y)        &
                 *(p(vertex+2)%x - p(vertex+1)%x)
END IF
END FUNCTION orientation


END MODULE convexity
```

The first three points are used to determine the sign of $(x_2 - x_1)(y_3 - y_2)$ $- (y_2 - y_1)(x_3 - x_1)$. We then require that the sign of the corresponding quantity for every three adjacent points have the same sign. This is done in the subroutine **convex_polygon**.

There is one complication with indexing. When we get to P_{n-1} we must use the points P_{n-1}, P_n, P_1 (not P_{n-1}, P_n, P_{n+1}, because P_{n+1} does not exist, and we want to continue with the first point P_1), and when we get to P_n we must use the points P_n, P_1, P_2. This is taken care of in the function **orientation**.

We can then easily write a program to test these procedures by asking for, say, six points and then calling **convex_polygon** to determine the convexity of the resulting polygon:

```
PROGRAM polygon_test
   USE convexity
   IMPLICIT NONE

   ! This program uses the module convexity to establish
   ! whether a set of points make a convex polygon

   INTEGER, PARAMETER :: number_of_points = 6
   TYPE(point), DIMENSION(number_of_points) :: polygon
   INTEGER :: i
   LOGICAL :: convex
```

First program run	*Second program run*
Give vertex number 1	Give vertex number 1
0,0	1,1
Give vertex number 2	Give vertex number 2
1,0	3,1
Give vertex number 3	Give vertex number 3
2,1	2,2
Give vertex number 4	Give vertex number 4
2,2	3,3
Give vertex number 5	Give vertex number 5
1,3	1,3
Give vertex number 6	Give vertex number 6
-1,1	0,2
Polygon is convex	Polygon is not convex

Figure 13.8 Results produced by the program `polygon_test`.

```
! Ask for six points
DO i = 1,number_of_points
    PRINT '(1X,"Give vertex number ",I2)', i
    READ *, polygon(i)%x, polygon(i)%y
END DO

! Establish the polygon's convexity
CALL convex_polygon(polygon,convex)
IF (convex) THEN
    PRINT *, "Polygon is convex"
ELSE
    PRINT *, "Polygon is not convex"
END IF
END PROGRAM polygon_test
```

Figure 13.8 shows the result produced by running this program for two polygons, the first with vertices (0,0), (1,0), (2,1), (2,2), (1,3), (-1,1) and the second with vertices (1,1), (3,1), (2,2), (3,3), (1,3), (0,2).

Figure 13.9 shows the result of changing the value of **number_of_points** in the main program to 5 and running the program again with a different set of points.

The third class of arrays which were introduced for rank-one arrays in Chapter 7 are **automatic arrays**. An automatic array is a special type of explicit-shape array which can only be declared in a procedure, which is not a dummy argument, and which has at least one index bound that is not constant. The space

```
Give vertex number 1
1,1
Give vertex number 2
3,1
Give vertex number 3
3,3
Give vertex number 4
1,3
Give vertex number 5
0,2
Polygon is convex
```

Figure 13.9 Results produced by the modified program `polygon_test`.

for the elements of an automatic array is created dynamically when the procedure is entered and is removed upon exit from the procedure. In between entry and exit, an automatic array may be used in the same manner as any other array — including passing it or its elements as actual arguments to other procedures. This contrasts with the space for explicit-shape or assumed-shape arrays which, somewhere in the program, must be defined as having some fixed size, and which are passed to procedures as actual arguments.

We can see the difference in the following example:

```
SUBROUTINE abc(x,y,n)
   IMPLICIT NONE

   ! Dummy arguments
   INTEGER,INTENT(IN) :: n
   REAL,DIMENSION(n),INTENT(INOUT) :: x    ! Explicit-shape
   REAL,DIMENSION(:),INTENT(INOUT) :: y    ! Assumed-shape

   ! Local variables
   REAL,DIMENSION(SIZE(y,1)) :: e          ! Automatic
   REAL,DIMENSION(n,n) :: f                ! Automatic
   REAL,DIMENSION(10) :: g                 ! Explicit-shape
   .
   .
   .
END SUBROUTINE abc
```

In subroutine **abc**, the arrays **e** and **f** are not dummy arguments, but their index bounds are not constant. The upper index bound of **e**, a rank-one array, is dependent on the shape of the dummy argument **y**. Both the upper index bounds of the rank-two array **f** depend on the extent of the dummy argument **x**, which is supplied as a dummy argument. Hence, both **e** and **f** are automatic arrays. The array **g** is not a dummy argument, but its index bounds are constant; it is, therefore, not an automatic array.

Automatic arrays are convenient when array space (of variable shape) is needed on a temporary basis inside a procedure, and such arrays are, therefore, often called **work arrays**. The use of automatic arrays for such temporary purposes can enormously simplify calling sequences by eliminating the need for arrays of complicated shape to be passed as arguments. Automatic arrays did not exist in FORTRAN 77, with the result that many programs and general-purpose mathematical, or other, subprogram libraries were frequently very much more complex (in terms of array shape requirements for work space) than would otherwise have been the case.

In Chapter 7 we also mentioned a fourth type of array, known as an **assumed-size array**. An assumed-size array, like an assumed-shape array, may only appear as a dummy argument to a procedure. In the declaration of an assumed-size array, all the extents *except that of the last dimension* must be specified explicitly; the extent of the last dimension takes one of the forms *lower_bound:* * or *.

The most common usage for assumed-size arrays is to have the extents of the actual and dummy arguments explicitly agree for all but the last dimension. The dummy argument will then get the extent for its last dimension from the last dimension of the actual argument, and the dummy and actual arguments will have the same shape. A more complicated case occurs when the dummy and actual arguments do not have the same shape. In this case the extent of the last dimension of the assumed-size dummy argument is such as to make the sizes of the actual and dummy arguments agree, and a full understanding of the array element order is required to ensure that the elements of the dummy argument correspond to the required elements of the actual argument.

We strongly recommend that assumed-size arrays are never used in writing new Fortran 90 programs; however more information about their use will be found, for reference, in Appendix E, together with other obsolescent and deprecated features.

SELF-TEST EXERCISES 13.1

1 What are the index bounds, extents and size of an array?

2 What is the shape of an array? How can it be denoted?

3 What is the array element order for the array **wow**, which is declared as follows?

```
REAL, DIMENSION(2,3,4) :: wow
```

4 Write a **READ** statement to read 24 values into the real array **wow** declared in Exercise 3, if the data is provided in the order **wow(1,1,1)**, **wow(1,1,2)**, **wow(1,1,3)**, **wow(1,1,4)**, **wow(1,2,1)**, **wow(1,2,2)**, **wow(1,2,3)**, **wow(1,2,4)**, etc.

5 How is the **RESHAPE** intrinsic function used in connection with array constructors?

6 What are explicit-shape arrays? Can they occur in main programs and procedures?

7 What are assumed-shape arrays? Can they occur in main programs and procedures? Are there any restrictions on the use of assumed-shape arrays?

8 How may the index bounds of a dummy procedure argument be determined?

9 What are automatic arrays and when should they be used?

13.6 Allocatable arrays

In the previous section we stressed the importance of being able to create temporary arrays whose size could only be determined during the execution of the program. Automatic arrays provide a partial solution to this problem, but a more complete solution is provided by **allocatable arrays**. These provide more flexibility than automatic arrays, because the allocation and deallocation of space for their elements is completely under user control. This is not the case for automatic arrays, since their space is always allocated on entry to a procedure and is always deallocated on exit.

Using allocatable arrays is slightly more complicated than using any other class of arrays, and consists, essentially, of three steps:

- Firstly, the allocatable array is specified in a type declaration statement.

- Secondly, space is dynamically allocated for its elements in a separate **allocation statement**, after which the array may be used in the normal way.

- Finally, after the array has been used and is no longer required, the space for the elements is deallocated by a **deallocation statement**.

Once space has been allocated for them, allocatable arrays may be used in the same way as any other arrays. Their elements may be defined or referenced, and they may be passed as actual arguments to other procedures although, as might be expected, they may not be used as dummy arguments in a procedure.

An allocatable array is declared in a type declaration statement which includes an **ALLOCATABLE** attribute. However, since its size is not known when it is declared, it must initially have its shape specifiers set to be undefined by omitting all index bound information for every dimension, and representing the shape of the array in the dimension attribute by a single colon for each dimension:

```
REAL, ALLOCATABLE, DIMENSION(:,:,:) :: allocatable_array
```

The rank of the array is, of course, the same as the number of colons, so that the above statement declares a rank-three array.

It will be noted that the type declaration statement for an allocatable array is similar to the type declaration statement for an assumed-shape array. However, an assumed-shape array *must* be a dummy argument to a procedure, and *must not* have an **ALLOCATABLE** attribute, whereas the opposite is true for allocatable arrays. The two types of declaration statements are, therefore, readily distinguished from each other.

Note that the **ALLOCATABLE** attribute may also be specified by means of a separate **ALLOCATABLE** statement, in a similar way to that which we have already seen with most other attributes:

ALLOCATABLE :: *list of deferred_array_specifications*

where each *deferred_array_specification* takes the same form as in the earlier example:

ALLOCATABLE :: arr_1(:), arr_2(:,:), arr_3(:,:,:)

We recommend, however, that you should always use an **ALLOCATABLE** attribute in the type declaration statement in preference to a separate **ALLOCATABLE** statement, for reasons of both clarity and security; it is always best if *all* the information about a single entity is contained in a single statement, wherever possible.

Allocatable arrays are called **deferred-shape** arrays because, when they are initially declared in a type declaration statement, the extent along each dimension is not specified, but is *deferred* until later. We shall meet another form of deferred shape array in Chapter 16. Like assumed-shape arrays and automatic arrays, deferred-shape arrays were not available in FORTRAN 77.

Unlike all other forms of array that we have met, the declaration of an allocatable array does not, in itself, allocate any space for the array, and it is therefore not usually possible to use the array until further action has been taken. An allocatable array is said to have an **allocation status**, and until space is allocated for its elements, this allocation status is said to be *not currently allocated*, or simply *unallocated*.

An unallocated array has its status changed to *currently allocated*, or simply *allocated*, by means of an **ALLOCATE** statement which dynamically allocates space for an allocatable array. It takes the form

ALLOCATE (*list of array_specifications*, **STAT=***status_variable*)

or

ALLOCATE (*list of array_specifications*)

Each *array_specification* must consist of the name of an allocatable array, followed by the index bounds for each dimension, enclosed in parentheses:

ALLOCATE (arr_1(20), arr_2(10:30,-10:10), arr_3(20,30:50,5))

The **STAT=***status_variable* element of the **ALLOCATE** statement enables the processor to report on the success, or otherwise, of the allocation process in a

```
.
.
.
INTEGER :: error
REAL, ALLOCATABLE, DIMENSION(:,:) :: p
INTEGER, ALLOCATABLE, DIMENSION(:,:,:) :: q
TYPE(vector), ALLOCATABLE, DIMENSION(:) :: r
.
.
.
ALLOCATE(p(5,1000), q(10,m,n+7), r(-10:10), STAT=error)
IF (error /= 0) THEN
   ! Space for p, q, and r could not be allocated
   PRINT *,"Program could not allocate space for p, q, and r"
   STOP
END IF
! Space for p, q, and r successfully allocated
.
.
.
```

Figure 13.10 An example of allocation of allocatable arrays, with error checking.

similar way to that in which an **IOSTAT** specifier reports on the success of an input/output statement. If the allocation is successful then the integer variable *status_variable* will be set to zero; if there is an error during the allocation, for example if there is insufficient memory for the array or if it is currently allocated, then *status_variable* will be assigned a processor-dependent positive value.

Note that if an error condition arises during the execution of an **ALLOCATE** statement and there is no **STAT** element in the statement then the program will fail. We recommend, therefore, that you should always include a **STAT** element, as illustrated in Figure 13.10.

A currently allocated allocatable array is deallocated by the related **DEALLOCATE** statement, which has the effect of changing its status to *not currently allocated* and making the memory space that it was using available for other purposes. This statement takes the form

DEALLOCATE(*list of currently_allocated_arrays*, **STAT**=*status_variable*)

or

DEALLOCATE(*list of currently_allocated_arrays*)

where the meaning and use of the **STAT** element is identical to that for the

ALLOCATE statement. Once an array has been deallocated then the values stored in its elements are no longer available.

It may appear unnecessary to check the deallocation of an array for errors, since it will, presumably, have already been allocated. However, suppose that the program was subsequently modified by inserting some extra statements between the allocation and deallocation of the array. The inserted code might, after performing its calculations, erroneously deallocate the array. It is to guard against such difficult-to-find programming errors that the success or failure of allocation and deallocation statements should always be checked.

The use of **ALLOCATE** and **DEALLOCATE** statements enables an allocatable array to have its size repeatedly changed, as is shown in the following example:

```
REAL, ALLOCATABLE, DIMENSION(:) :: varying_array
INTEGER :: i,n,alloc_error,dealloc_error
   .
   .
   .
READ *, n                            ! Read maximum size needed
DO i=1,n
   ALLOCATE(varying_array(-i:i), STAT=alloc_error)
   IF(alloc_error /= 0) THEN
      PRINT *,"Insufficient space to allocate array &
              &when i = ",i
      STOP
   END IF
   ! Calculate using varying_array
      .
      .
      .
   DEALLOCATE(varying_array, STAT=dealloc_error)
   IF(dealloc_error /= 0) THEN
      PRINT *,"Unexpected deallocation error"
      STOP
   END IF
END DO
   .
   .
   .
```

This code fragment first allocates **varying_array** to be a rank-one array, with index bounds of -1 and $+1$. It performs calculations using the array with this size and shape, and then deallocates it. Next it allocates **varying_array** again, but this time with index bounds of -2 and $+2$, performs calculations using the array with this new size, and then again deallocates it. This cycle is repeated **n** times.

If **varying_array** were not deallocated at the end of every iteration, an error would occur in the second iteration of the loop when the second attempt to allocate **a** is made.

Note that execution of a **DEALLOCATE** statement is not the only way in which an allocated array can lose its allocated status. Exit from a procedure causes the allocation status of any currently allocated allocatable arrays without the save attribute to become **undefined**. Such undefined arrays cannot subsequently be referenced, defined, allocated or deallocated!

As well as causing potential problems, it is bad programming practice to permit the status of an allocatable array to become undefined. An allocatable array which is no longer required should, therefore, always be deallocated before an exit is made from the procedure in which it was allocated. If it will be required again, and its current values need to be preserved, then it should be declared with the **SAVE** attribute:

```
CHARACTER(LEN=50), ALLOCATABLE, DIMENSION(:), SAVE :: name
```

If this is done, then the allocatable array will remain allocated when an exit is made from the procedure and the elements of the array will maintain their values. If it is not currently allocated on exit from the procedure then it remains in that state.

This ability for an allocatable array to be saved between references to a procedure is a major advantage over automatic arrays, which always cease to exist on exit from the procedure in which they are declared.

The greater control provided by allocatable arrays can also be used to write programs with more capacity than is possible with automatic arrays, as can be seen from the following example:

```
SUBROUTINE space(n)
  IMPLICIT NONE
  INTEGER, INTENT(IN) :: n
  REAL, ALLOCATABLE, DIMENSION(:,:) :: a,b

  ALLOCATE(a(2*n,6*n))       ! Allocate space for a
  ! Calculate using a
  .
  .
  .
  DEALLOCATE(a)              ! Free space used by a
  ALLOCATE(b(3*n,4*n))      ! Allocate space for b
  ! Calculate using b
  .
  .
  .
  DEALLOCATE(b)              ! Free space used by b
END SUBROUTINE space
```

The subroutine **space**, therefore, uses $12n^2$ elements for **a** during execution of the first part, and then releases this space, and then uses $12n^2$ elements for **b** during execution of the second part. Thus, the maximum space required for the two arrays is that required for $12n^2$ real numbers.

Now suppose the subroutine **space** was rewritten to use automatic arrays instead of allocatable arrays:

```
SUBROUTINE space(n)
   IMPLICIT NONE
   INTEGER, INTENT(IN) :: n
   REAL, DIMENSION(2*n,6*n) :: a
   REAL, DIMENSION(3*n,4*n) :: b
   ! Calculate using a
   .
   .
   .

   ! Calculate using b
   .
   .
   .
END SUBROUTINE space
```

In this case, when the subroutine **space** begins execution $12n^2$ elements are allocated for **a** and $12n^2$ elements are allocated for **b**. A total of $24n^2$ elements are therefore created, and are not released until exit from the subroutine.

Consequently, the version of **space** using automatic arrays requires twice as many real numbers as does the version using allocatable arrays. If **n** is large, this extra space requirement could be the difference between success and failure of a program, since a computer only has finite resources available!

The decision as to whether to use automatic arrays or allocatable arrays will depend upon individual circumstances. If very large arrays are required, or if they need to be saved between procedure calls, then allocatable arrays should be used; on the other hand, if only small arrays are involved, and there is no need to save array values between procedure references, the greater simplicity of automatic arrays may tip the balance in their favour.

There are three main restrictions on allocatable arrays:

- Allocatable arrays cannot be dummy arguments of a procedure.
- The result of a function cannot be an allocatable array.
- Allocatable arrays cannot be used in a derived type definition.

Because of the first of these restrictions, allocatable arrays that are defined in a main program or procedure must be allocated and deallocated in the main program or procedure in which they were initially defined. However, if the type declaration for an allocatable array is placed in a module then the array can be allocated and deallocated by any main program or procedures using the module. We shall see an example of this in Example 13.2.

If it is necessary to have a derived type with a variable-size array as a component, pointers must be used; see Chapter 16.

One other point that should be made is that, although an unallocated allocatable array cannot be used in most of the ways in which arrays are normally used, it can be used as an actual argument in a reference to some of the intrinsic inquiry functions, namely **ALLOCATED** (which returns the allocation status of an allocatable array), the intrinsic inquiry functions that give information about a type (for example, **DIGITS**), and the intrinsic inquiry functions that give information about type parameters (**KIND** and **LEN**). More information about these functions will be found in Appendix A, but it is worth pointing out that the **ALLOCATED** function can be used to guard against trying to deallocate an unallocated array, or to allocate an array which has already been allocated:

```
        .
        .
        .
REAL, ALLOCATABLE, DIMENSION(:) :: work_array
        ı
        .
        .
IF ALLOCATED(work_array) DEALLOCATE(work_array)
ALLOCATE(work_array(n:m),STAT=alloc_stat)
        .
        .
        .
```

The **ALLOCATED** function can, of course, only be used on arrays with the allocatable attribute.

■ EXAMPLE 13.2

[1] Problem

Write a program which will determine the minimum and maximum numbers in a file of real numbers, where they occur, and how many of the numbers are less than the mean of all the numbers in the file.

[2] Analysis

This is a fairly straightforward problem, apart from the fact that there will need to be an array in which to store the values read from the file, and yet the size of the array clearly cannot be known until execution time. It is thus an ideal situation for an allocatable array.

An initial structure plan might be:

1	Allocate a suitable work array
2	Carry out analysis of file

Further thought leads to a refined plan:

> 1 Request maximum size of work array required
> 2 Allocate a suitable work array
> 3 Carry out analysis of file
>   **3.1** Get name of file
>   **3.2** Find maximum and minimum values, and their positions in the file (or array)
>   **3.3** Calculate mean, and count the number of values less than the mean

Steps 1 and 2 can be readily placed in one procedure, while steps 3.2 and 3.3 lend themselves to being placed in separate procedures. If the work array is declared in a module, **work_space**, then the final program structure can easily be developed. Because the data requirements are so simple, as is most of the logic, we shall not give a full data design, nor shall we give detailed structure plans for each procedure, but will simply show the overall structure:

> 1 Call *allocate_space* to do the following:
>   **1.1** Request maximum size of file
>   **1.2** Allocate a suitable work array
> 2 Call *calculate* to do the following:
>   **2.1** Get name of file and open it
>   **2.2** Read all the numbers in the file into the work array
>   **2.3** Call *minmax* to find minimum and maximum values, and their positions
>   **2.4** Call *num_less_than_mean* to find the number less than the mean

3 Solution

```
MODULE work_space
   IMPLICIT NONE
   SAVE
   INTEGER :: work_size
   REAL, ALLOCATABLE, DIMENSION(:) :: work
END MODULE work_space

PROGRAM flexible
   IMPLICIT NONE

   ! Allocate space for the array work
   CALL allocate_space

   ! Carry out calculations using the array work
   CALL calculate

END PROGRAM flexible
```

```fortran
SUBROUTINE allocate_space
   USE work_space
   IMPLICIT NONE

   ! This subroutine allocates the array work at a size
   ! determined by the user during execution

   ! Local variable
   INTEGER :: error

   ! Ask for required size for array
   PRINT *,"Please give maximum size of file"
   READ *,work_size

   ! Allocate array
   ALLOCATE(work(work_size+1), STAT=error)
   IF (error /= 0) THEN

   ! Error during allocation - terminate processing
      PRINT *,"Space requested not possible"
      STOP
   END IF

   ! Work array successfully allocated
END SUBROUTINE allocate_space

SUBROUTINE calculate
   USE work_space
   IMPLICIT NONE

   ! Local variables
   INTEGER :: i,n,min_p,max_p,open_error,io_stat
   REAL :: min, max
   CHARACTER(LEN=20) :: file_name

   ! Get name of data file
   PRINT *,"Please give name of data file"
   READ '(A)',file_name

   ! Open data file
   OPEN(UNIT=7, FILE=file_name, STATUS ="OLD", &
        ACTION="READ", IOSTAT=open_error)
   IF (open_error /= 0) THEN
      PRINT *,"Error during file opening"
      STOP
   END IF

   ! Read data until end of file
   DO i=1,work_size
      READ (UNIT=7, FMT=*, IOSTAT=io_stat) work(i)
      ! Check for end of file
      IF (io_stat < 0) EXIT
   END DO
```

```
          ! Save number of numbers read
          n = i-1

          ! Find maximum and minimum values
          CALL minmax(n,min,max,min_p,max_p)

          ! Print details of minimum and maximum numbers
          PRINT '(1X,"Minimum value is",F15.4,              &
                    " and occurs at position ",I10/         &
                 1X,"Maximum value is",F15.4,               &
                    " and occurs at position ",I10)',       &
                 min, min_p, max, max_p

          ! Calculate number that are less than the mean
          CALL num_less_than_mean(n)

          ! Deallocate work array
          DEALLOCATE(work)

       END SUBROUTINE calculate

       SUBROUTINE minmax(n,minimum,maximum,min_pos,max_pos)
          USE work_space
          IMPLICIT NONE
          ! This subroutine calculates the largest and smallest
          ! element values in work(1) to work(n)

          ! Dummy arguments
          INTEGER, INTENT(IN) :: n
          REAL, INTENT(OUT) :: minimum, maximum
          INTEGER, INTENT(OUT) :: min_pos, max_pos

          ! Local variable
          INTEGER :: i

          ! Establish initial values
          minimum = work(1)
          maximum = work(1)
          min_pos = 1
          max_pos = 1

          ! Loop to find maximum and minimum values
          DO i = 2,n
             IF (work(i) < minimum) THEN
                minimum = work(i)
                min_pos = i
             ELSE IF (work(i) > maximum) THEN
                maximum = work(i)
                max_pos = i
             END IF
          END DO

       END SUBROUTINE minmax
```

```
SUBROUTINE num_less_than_mean(n)
   USE work_space
   IMPLICIT NONE


   ! This subroutine calculates and prints the number of
   ! elements of work(1) to work(n) that are less than
   ! the mean of all the numbers


   ! Dummy argument
   INTEGER, INTENT(IN) :: n


   ! Local variables
   INTEGER :: i,less=0
   REAL :: sum=0.0,mean


   ! Calculate mean
   DO i=1,n
      sum = sum+work(i)
   END DO
   mean = sum/n


   ! Count number less than mean
   DO i = 1,n
      IF (work(i) < mean) less = less+1
   END DO


   ! Print number below mean
   PRINT '(1X,"There are ",I10," numbers less than the &
          &mean of all numbers in the file")', less


END SUBROUTINE num_less_than_mean
```

Notice that the module **work_space** contains only type declaration statements. One is for an allocatable array **work**, used to hold the array of real numbers, and the other is for **work-size**, an integer that is the size of **work** when it has been allocated. Notice, also, that the module **work_space** is used by all the procedures, but that it is not used by the main program because it does not need to reference any of the entities in the module. The inclusion of a **SAVE** statement in the module is, therefore, essential in order to ensure that neither of these entities becomes undefined on exit from one of the procedures, as discussed in Section 11.4.

As is usually the case in our example programs, we have not taken all the error-checking steps that are desirable, in the cause of clarity and of shortening the length of the program. Figure 13.11, however, shows an alternative version of the subroutine **allocate_space** which checks that the allocation process has been successful, and allows the user to try twice more if it is not successful.

```
SUBROUTINE allocate_space
   USE work_space
   IMPLICIT NONE

   ! This subroutine allocates the array work at a size
   ! determined by the user during execution

   ! Local variables
   INTEGER :: i,error

   ! Ask for required size for array
   DO i=1,3
      PRINT *,"Please give maximum size of file"
      READ *,work_size

      ! Allocate array
      ALLOCATE(work(work_size), STAT=error)
      IF (error == 0) EXIT

      ! Error during allocation - try again (max of 2 times)
      PRINT *,"Space requested not possible - try again"
   END DO

   ! Check to see if array was (finally) allocated
   IF (.NOT. ALLOCATED(work)) THEN
   ! No allocation - even after three tries
      PRINT *,"Three attempts to allocate without success!"
      STOP
   END IF

   ! Work array successfully allocated
END SUBROUTINE allocate_space
```

Figure 13.11 An alternative version of the subroutine `allocate_space`.

Exactly how far to go in this type of checking will depend upon the environment in which the program is to be used, and, for example, if it will be used only by the programmer or will be part of a widely distributed piece of general-purpose software.

13.7 Whole array operations

In Chapter 7, in the context of rank-one arrays, we introduced the Fortran 90 concept of whole array processing, whereby two conformable arrays (that is, two arrays which have the same shape) could appear as operands in an expression or an assignment, and the operation or assignment would be carried out on an element-by-element basis. Thus, if two arrays are declared as follows:

```
REAL, DIMENSION(10) :: p,q
REAL, DIMENSION(10:19) :: r
```

then the statement

```
p = q+r
```

has exactly the same effect as the DO loop

```
DO i=1,10
   p(i) = q(i)+r(i-9)
END DO
```

As we might expect, the same rule applies to arrays of any rank so that if, for example, three rank-four arrays are declared as follows:

```
REAL, DIMENSION(10,10,21,21) :: x
REAL, DIMENSION(0:9,0:9,-10:10,-10:10) :: y
REAL, DIMENSION(11:20,-9:0,0:20,-20:0) :: z
```

then the statement

```
x = y+z
```

has exactly the same effect as the following nest of DO loops:

```
DO i=1,10
   DO j=1,10
      DO k=1,21
         DO l=1,21
            x(i,j,k,l) = y(i-1,j-1,k-11,l-11) +   &
                         z(i+10,j-10,k-1,l-21)
         END DO
      END DO
   END DO
END DO
```

This example makes it very clear that using whole-array expressions is simpler, and hence less error-prone, than using DO loops! For machines with multiple processing units, they can also make it easier for the compiler to parallelize the code. They should be used, wherever possible, to simplify code.

We should now remind ourselves of the rules for working with whole arrays which were stated in Chapter 7:

- Two arrays are conformable if they have the same shape.
- A scalar, including a constant, is conformable with any array.
- All intrinsic operations are defined between conformable objects.

So far, we have discussed whole-array assignment and expressions in the context of numeric arrays, but the capability to write whole-array expressions is also available for character arrays and logical arrays. Thus, the following code fragment will concatenate each element of **string_1** with each corresponding element of **string_2**, storing the resulting strings in the corresponding elements of **long_string**:

```
CHARACTER(LEN=7), DIMENSION(3,4) :: string_1,string_2
CHARACTER(LEN=14), DIMENSION(3,4) :: long_string
     .
     .
     .
long_string = string_1//string_2
     .
     .
     .
```

The fact that scalars are conformable with any array means that the following code fragment has the effect of placing quotation marks around the strings in every element of the array **unquoted** and storing the resulting strings in the array **quoted**:

```
CHARACTER(LEN=20), DIMENSION(4,50) :: unquoted
CHARACTER(LEN=22), DIMENSION(4,50) :: quoted
     .
     .
     .
quoted = '"'//unquoted//'"'
     .
     .
     .
```

Logical operators also follow the same rules, with the result that the conditional expression in the statement

```
IF (ALL(a > 1.0)) ...
```

where a is a real array, will evaluate as *true* if, and only if, every element of a is greater than 1. Note that the intrinsic function **ALL** has been used to convert the array-valued expression (a > 1.0) to a scalar value (see Appendix A.8). Similarly, if a and b are conformable arrays, the conditional expression in the statement

```
IF (ANY(a == b)) ...
```

```
FUNCTION outer(x, y)
   IMPLICIT NONE
   REAL, DIMENSION(:), INTENT(IN) :: x, y
   REAL, DIMENSION(SIZE(x,1),SIZE(y,1)) :: outer
   INTEGER :: i,j
   DO i = 1,SIZE(x,1)
      DO j = 1,SIZE(y,1)
         outer(i, j) = x(i)*y(j)
      END DO
   END DO
END FUNCTION outer
```

Figure 13.12   An array-valued function to calculate the outer product of two vectors.

will evaluate as *true* if any element of **a** is equal to the corresponding element of **b**.

The final aspect of whole array processing that we introduced in Chapter 7 is the concept of an array-valued function. As with all the other concepts that we met originally in the context of rank-one arrays, there is no significant difference in applying the concept to arrays of any rank.

There are only three rules to remember when writing and using an array-valued function:

- An array-valued function must have an explicit interface.

- The type of the function, and an appropriate dimension attribute, must appear within the body of the function, not as part of the **FUNCTION** statement.

- The array that is the function result must be an explicit-shape array, although it may have variable extents in any of its dimensions.

An example of an array-valued function which calculates the outer product of two vectors is given in Figure 13.12.

The mathematical definition of the outer product of two vectors x and y is the matrix whose (i, j)th element is $x_i y_j$. In this function we assume that the two vectors are provided as rank-one arrays; the result of the function will be a rank-two array. Note how the extents of the (vector) arrays **x** and **y** are obtained by means of the intrinsic function **SIZE**, and then used to define the shape of the function result, **outer**, and also to control the two **DO** loops.

Many of Fortran's intrinsic procedures may be used in an **elemental** manner in whole-array expressions; in other words, they will accept arrays as actual arguments, and will return as their result an array of the same shape as the actual argument in which the procedure has been applied to every element of the array. Thus if **a** is a rank-three real array with shape (l, m, n), **SIN(a)** is a rank-three real array of shape (l, m, n) in which the (i, j, k)th element is **sin(a(i,j,k))**, for

Vector or matrix multiply functions

`DOT_PRODUCT(VECTOR_A,VECTOR_B)`	Dot product of two rank-one arrays
`MATMUL(MATRIX_A,MATRIX_B)`	Matrix multiplication

Array reduction functions

`ALL(MASK[,DIM])`	True if all values are true
`ANY(MASK[,DIM])`	True if any value is true
`COUNT(MASK[,DIM])`	Number of true elements in an array
`MAXVAL(ARRAY[,DIM][,MASK])`	Maximum value in an array
`MINVAL(ARRAY[,DIM][,MASK])`	Minimum value in an array
`PRODUCT(ARRAY[,DIM][,MASK])`	Product of array elements
`SUM(ARRAY[,DIM][,MASK])`	Sum of array elements

Array inquiry functions

`ALLOCATED(ARRAY)`	Array allocation status
`LBOUND(ARRAY[,DIM])`	Lower dimension bounds of an array
`SHAPE(SOURCE)`	Shape of an array or scalar
`SIZE(ARRAY[,DIM])`	Total number of elements in an array
`UBOUND(ARRAY[,DIM])`	Upper dimension bounds of an array

Array construction functions

`MERGE(TSOURCE,PSOURCE,MASK)`	Merge under mask
`PACK(ARRAY,MASK[,VECTOR])`	Pack an array into an array of rank one under a mask
`SPREAD(SOURCE,DIM,NCOPIES)`	Replicate an array by adding a dimension
`UNPACK(VECTOR,MASK,FIELD)`	Unpack an array of rank one into an array under a mask

Array reshape function

`RESHAPE(SOURCE,SHAPE[,PAD]` & `         [,ORDER])`	Reshape an array

Array manipulation functions

`CSHIFT(ARRAY,SHIFT[,DIM])`	Circular shift
`EOSHIFT(ARRAY,SHIFT` & `       [,BOUNDARY][,DIM])`	End-off shift
`TRANSPOSE(MATRIX)`	Transpose of an array of rank two

Array location functions

`MAXLOC(ARRAY[,MASK])`	Location of a maximum value in an array
`MINLOC(ARRAY[,MASK])`	Location of a minimum value in an array

Note that in the above table `[,XYZ]` indicates that the argument `XYZ` is optional

Figure 13.13 Intrinsic procedures designed for use in array processing.

$i = 1, \ldots, l, j = 1, \ldots, m$ and $k = 1, \ldots, n$. The term elemental is used to describe this behaviour because the intrinsic function is applied element-by-element to its array arguments. If an intrinsic function is used elementally, then all its array arguments must be of the same shape; if not, the situation would be meaningless.

As a slightly more complicated example, if **a** and **b** are rank-one integer arrays of size n, then **MAX(0,a,b)** is a rank-one array whose ith element is **MAX(0,a(i),b(i))**, for $i = 1, \ldots, n$. Note that the scalar **0** is conformable with **a** and **b**.

Fortran 90 also provides many intrinsic procedures specifically designed for array operations, in addition to the intrinsic procedures that can be used elementally; a list of these can be seen in Figure 13.13, while a more detailed description of each of them will be found in Appendix A.

The use of these array intrinsics is strongly recommended when writing code that manipulates arrays for three main reasons:

- The resulting code will almost always be cleaner and more compact than code written without them.
- The intrinsic procedures are usually provided in assembly language, by the compiler writers, and are consequently very efficient.
- It will require less effort.

In addition to the extension of scalar operations to arrays, and the intrinsics provided to simplify the manipulation of arrays, Fortran 90 also contains two further powerful array handling features which complete the facilities required for powerful and flexible array processing, and these will be described in the final two sections of this chapter.

13.8 Masked array assignment

The first of these new features allows a finer degree of control over the assignment of one array to another, by use of a **mask** which determines whether the assignment of a particular element should take place or, alternatively, which of two alternate values should be assigned to each element. This concept is called **masked array assignment**, and comes in two forms.

The first, simpler, form is known as a **WHERE** statement, and takes the general form

WHERE (*mask_expression*) *array_assignment_statement*

where *mask_expression* is a logical expression of the same shape as the array variable being defined in the *array_assignment_statement*. The effect is that the assignment statement is only executed for those elements where the elements in the corresponding positions of the *mask_expression* are true. Note, however, that the assignment statement must not be a defined assignment, as described in Section 12.4.

For example, if **arr** is a real array, then the effect of the statement

```
WHERE (arr<0.0) arr = -arr
```

is to change the sign of all the elements of **arr** having negative values, and to leave those having positive values unchanged. This is because the expression **a<0.0** is an array logical expression, of the same shape as **arr**, in which an element is *true* if the corresponding element of **arr** is less than 0, and is *false* otherwise. Consequently, the assignment statement **arr = -arr** is only performed for those elements whose value is less than zero.

The **WHERE** statement is sufficient for many situations, but there are often cases in which it is desirable either to control more than one assignment statement by the masked assignment, or in which it is required to carry out one of two alternative assignments, depending on the value of the corresponding element of the mask array. In these cases we can use the **WHERE** construct, which takes the form

```
WHERE (mask_expression)
    array_assignment_statements
ELSEWHERE
    array_assignment_statements
END WHERE
```

or

```
WHERE (mask_expression)
    array_assignment_statements
END WHERE
```

The effect of the **WHERE** construct is that the set of array assignment statements immediately following the **WHERE** are only executed for those elements where the elements in the corresponding positions in the mask expression are *true*. Conversely, the set of array assignment statements immediately following the **ELSEWHERE** are only executed for those elements where the elements in the corresponding positions in the mask expression are *false*. Note that all the arrays being assigned values must be conformable with each other, and with the mask array.

The following example illustrates how a **WHERE** construct can be used to replace every non-zero element of the array **array** by its reciprocal, and every zero element by 1.0:

```
WHERE (array /= 0.0)
    array = 1.0/array
ELSEWHERE
    array = 1.0
END WHERE
```

One very important point to emphasize is that, despite its syntactic similarity with the block **IF** construct, the **WHERE** construct is *not* a sequential construct. The mask is always an array which is conformable with the array, or arrays, which appear on the left-hand side of the assignment statement, or statements, in the construct, and the effect is as if all the array elements were assigned simultaneously, with the mask either preventing some of the assignments taking place, or causing different ones to take place.

13.9 Sub-arrays and array sections

Although we have seen how to use whole arrays in expressions, and we can use individual array elements in the same way that any other scalar can be used, it is frequently useful, especially in scientific programming, to be able to define a sub-array, consisting of a selection of elements of an array, and to then manipulate this sub-array in the same way that a whole array can be manipulated.

In Fortran 90, **array sections** can be extracted from a parent array in a rectangular grid (that is, with regular spacing) using **subscript triplet** notation, or in a completely general manner using **vector subscript** notation. In either case the resulting array section is itself an array, and can be used in the same way as an array – for example, in whole array expressions or passed as an argument to a procedure.

We have already defined an array element as

$$array\_name(i_1, \ldots, i_k)$$

where *array_name* is the name of a variable with the dimension attribute (that is, an array), k is the rank of *array_name*, and the i_j are subscripts.

If any or all of the i_j are replaced by what are called subscript triplets or vector subscripts, then, instead of defining an array element, we have defined an array section. The rank of the array section so defined is the number of subscript triplets and vector subscripts it contains. This definition fits well with the convention that an array element has rank zero, since its definition contains no subscript triplets or vector subscripts.

We will describe subscript triplets first, because they are conceptually simpler than vector subscripts.

A subscript triplet takes the following form:

$$subscript\_1 : subscript\_2 : stride$$

or one of the simpler forms

$$subscript\_1 : subscript\_2$$
$$subscript\_1 :$$

> *subscript_1* : : *stride*
> : *subscript_2*
> : *subscript_2* : *stride*
> : : *stride*
> :

where *subscript_1*, *subscript_2* and *stride* are all scalar integer expressions. A subscript triplet is interpreted as defining an ordered set of subscripts that start at *subscript_1*, that end on or before *subscript_2*, and have a separation of *stride* between consecutive subscripts. The value of *stride* must not be zero.

If *subscript_1* is omitted, it defaults to the lower index bound for the dimension; if *subscript_2* is omitted, it defaults to the upper index bound for the dimension; and if *stride* is omitted, it defaults to the value 1. Note that the first colon must always be included, even if the first subscript is not specified.

Thus if the array **arr** is declared as

```
REAL, DIMENSION(10) :: arr
```

then 2:8:3 is a subscript triplet that defines a set of integers that starts at 2 and proceeds in increments of 3 until 8 is reached. So the set of subscripts is 2, 5, 8, and **arr(2:8:3)** is an *array* whose elements are **arr(2)**, **arr(5)** and **arr(8)**, in that order.

If the stride is negative, then the subscript order is reversed with the result that **arr(8:2:-3)** is an array whose elements are **arr(8)**, **arr(5)** and **arr(2)**, in that order.

Some other sub-arrays of **arr** are as follows:

arr(1:10)   is a rank-one real array containing all the elements of **arr**; it is, in fact, identical to **arr**.

arr(3:5)   is a rank-one real array containing the elements **arr(3)**, **arr(4)** and **arr(5)**.

arr(:9)   is a rank-one real array containing the elements **arr(1)**, **arr(2)**, ..., **arr(9)**.

arr(::4)   is a rank-one real array containing the elements **arr(1)**, **arr(5)** and **arr(9)**.

arr(:)   is a rank-one real array containing all the elements of **arr**; it is the same as **arr**.

A simple example of how array sections can simplify code can be seen if we refer to the subroutine **num_less_than_mean** that was developed as part of Example 13.2. This subroutine had to calculate the sum of the first n elements of the array **work** in order to calculate the mean of those values, and did so by means of a **DO** loop:

```
DO i=1,n
   sum = sum+work(i)
END DO
mean = sum/n
```

The use of an array section and the intrinsic procedure **SUM** would enable us to write simply

```
mean = SUM(work(1:n))/n
```

This defines an array section consisting of the first **n** elements of **work**, which is therefore an array, and then uses **SUM** to calculate the sum of all the elements of that array, before dividing by **n**. This version is both easier to read and, since it uses the intrinsic function instead of a **DO** loop, almost certainly more efficient — which might be important if **n** is very large.

Of course, arrays of rank greater than 1 can have sections defined, so that if the array **array_2** is declared as

```
INTEGER, DIMENSION(2:9,-2,1) :: arr_2
```

then **arr_2(4:5,-1:0)** is a rank-two integer array containing the elements

$$\begin{bmatrix} arr2(4,-1) & arr2(4,0) \\ arr2(5,-1) & arr2(5,0) \end{bmatrix}$$

So far, the ranks of the array sections have been the same as those of their parent arrays; however this is not necessary. For example, if **arr_3** is declared as

```
REAL, DIMENSION(3,4) :: arr_3
```

then

arr_3(2,:)	is a rank-one real array (because there is only one subscript triplet) whose elements are **arr_3(2,1)**, **arr_3(2,2)**, **arr_3(2,3)** and **arr_3(2,4)**. In other words, it is the second row of **arr_3**.
arr_3(:,3)	is a rank-one real array whose elements are **arr_3(1,3)**, **arr_3(2,3)** and **arr_3(3,3)**. It is, therefore, the third column of **arr_3**.
arr-3(2,3:4)	is a rank-one array whose elements are **arr_3(2,3)** and **arr_3(2,4)**.

A good example of the use of array sections defined by subscript triplets will be found in Chapter 18, in the procedure for solving a system of linear equations by Gaussian elimination (Section 18.5).

We shall now turn from subscript triplets to vector subscripts. These are used when a non-regular pattern of indices is needed and, hence, a subscript triplet would not work.

A vector subscript is an integer array expression of rank 1, each of whose elements has the value of a subscript in the array section being defined. Thus, if the rank-one array **v** has a size of 4, and its elements have the values 3, 7, 4 and 5, then the array section **arr(v)** is a rank-one array of size 4, whose elements are, in order, **arr(3)**, **arr(7)**, **arr(4)** and **arr(5)**. The array **v** is the vector subscript.

Note that, in the preceding example, the size of **arr(v)** was equal to the size of **v**, and the size of **arr** was irrelevant in determining the size of the array section **arr(v)**. Hence, a vector subscript can be used to construct a vector from an array that is longer than that array; for example, if the arrays **p** and **u** are declared as follows:

```
LOGICAL, DIMENSION(3) :: p
INTEGER, DIMENSION(5) :: u = (/3,2,2,3,1/)
```

then **p(u)** is a rank-one logical array of size 5, whose elements are, in order, **p(3)**, **p(2)**, **p(2)**, **p(3)** and **p(1)**. Notice that some of the elements of **p** are repeated.

This is an example of a **many–one array section**. That is, it is an array section with a vector subscript having at least two elements with the same value. A many–one array section must not appear on the left-hand side of an assignment statement, nor may it be an input item in a **READ** statement. In both cases, such uses would be ambiguous and are, therefore, forbidden.

Finally, we note that subscripts, subscript triplets and vector subscripts can be used together to define an array section. Thus, if the arrays **string** and **vec** are declared as follows:

```
CHARACTER(LEN=10), DIMENSION(3,4,9) :: string
INTEGER, DIMENSION(5) :: vec = (/7,1,3,1,4/)
```

then **string(vec,3,5:9:4)** is a rank-two character array whose elements are

$$
\begin{bmatrix}
\text{string}(7,3,5) & \text{string}(7,3,9) \\
\text{string}(1,3,5) & \text{string}(1,3,9) \\
\text{string}(3,3,5) & \text{string}(3,3,9) \\
\text{string}(1,3,5) & \text{string}(1,3,9) \\
\text{string}(4,3,5) & \text{string}(4,3,9)
\end{bmatrix}
$$

SELF-TEST EXERCISES 13.2

1   How would you specify two rank-two allocatable arrays called A and B?

2   How would you allocate space so that the array A of the previous exercise has dimension 3 × 4 and B has shape (m, n), where m and n are integer variables?

3　Under what circumstances can an allocatable array, or one of its elements, be passed as an argument to a procedure or be used in an arithmetic expression?

4　What is the allocation status of an array? What are the possible states? How do they occur?

5　How can the allocation status of an allocatable array be prevented from becoming undefined?

6　How can the allocation status of an array be determined while a program is executing?

7　What are the differences between automatic arrays and allocatable arrays? What are the criteria for choosing which to use?

8　How are operators applied in a whole-array expression?

9　How can some intrinsic Fortran functions be used in a whole-array expression?

10　What are the advantages of using whole-array expressions?

11　What is the purpose of a masked array assignment?

12　What is an array section? How is it used?

13　What is the difference between a subscript triplet and a vector subscript? When should each be used?

SUMMARY

- An array may have up to seven dimensions; its rank is the number of dimensions it has.

- The extent of a dimension is the number of permissible index values for that dimension.

- The size of an array is the number of elements it contains and is equal to the product of its extents.

- The shape of an array is determined by the number of its dimensions and the extent along each dimension. It is representable as a rank-one array.

- The elements of an array are stored in a sequence known as the array element order, in which the first subscript varies most rapidly, then the second, and so on.

- Array constructors define array-valued constants in the form of rank-one arrays. The **RESHAPE** intrinsic function can be used to change this into any specified shape for assignment to an array whose rank is greater than one.

- An allocatable array is an array whose rank is declared initially, but none of its extents, and which is subsequently allocated with bounds specified dynamically during execution.

- The space required for an allocatable array may be released at any time during execution by deallocating the array.

- Allocatable arrays cannot be dummy arguments, function results or components of a derived type.

- The whole array processing capability is complemented by a number of intrinsic functions designed for manipulating arrays.

- Masked array assignment is a generalization of whole array assignment. It is used to control the assignment at the individual element level by employing a conformable logical array expression.

- An array section is a sub-array defined by specifying a subset of the elements of another array.

- Array sections are defined by the use of subscript triplets and vector subscripts.

- Fortran 90 syntax introduced in Chapter 13:

Array declaration	*type*, **DIMENSION**(*dim_spec*,...) :: *list of names*
	where each *dim_spec* (up to a maximum of 7) takes one of the forms:
	   extent
	   lower_bound:*upper_bound*
	   lower_bound:
	   :*upper_bound*
	   :

Allocatable attribute	**ALLOCATABLE**
Allocate and deallocate statements	**ALLOCATE** (*list of array_specifications*, **STAT**=*stat_var*) **ALLOCATE** (*list of array_specifications*) **DEALLOCATE** (*list of allocated arrays*, **STAT**=*stat_var*) **DEALLOCATE** (*list of allocated arrays*)

Masked array assignment	**WHERE** (*conformable_log_expr*) *array_name* = *expression*
	WHERE (*conformable_log_expr*)
	  array assignment statements
	END WHERE
	
	WHERE (*conformable_log_expr*)
	  array assignment statements
	ELSEWHERE
	  array assignment statements
	END WHERE

Array section $array\_name$ ($subscript\_triplet$)
                                 $array\_name$ ($vector\_subscript$)
                                 where $subscript\_triplet$ is one of
                                  $subscript1$: $subscript2$: $stride$
                                  $subscript1$: $subscript2$
                                  $subscript1$:
                                  $subscript1$: : $stride$
                                  : $subscript2$
                                  : $subscript2$: $stride$
                                  : : $stride$
                                  :

                                 and $vector\_subscript$ is an integer array expression of
                                 rank-one

PROGRAMMING EXERCISES

*13.1 Write a program that has an explicit-shape rank-two integer array of shape (4,5) with default index bounds. Fill the array so that the (i, j)th element has the value $10 \times i + j$. Print out all the array element values in a rectangular pattern that reflects the array structure.

 Now modify your program so that the printed pattern is rotated through 90°; that is, if the original version treated the first subscript as the row number and the second subscript as the column, then this version should treat the first subscript as the column number and the second as the row number.

13.2 A bus leaves the terminus on the hour and every half-hour between 7.30 a.m. and midnight on Saturdays and Sundays. On all other days it runs on the hour and every 20 minutes between 7.00 a.m. and 6.00 p.m., and on the hour and half-hour between 6.00 p.m. and 11.00 p.m.

 Write a program that generates the timetable for the whole week, using a 24-hour clock, and stores it in a rank-two array in which each column contains the times of buses on one day of the week. The program should then print the complete timetable using a single **WRITE** or **PRINT** statement.

 When you have tested your program, modify it so that for each day of the week it reads up to three triplets which specify the start time of a particular frequency, the end time and the frequency; in the above example the data for Tuesday would therefore be 0700, 1800, 20, 1800, 2300, 30. Test your program with several different patterns. Remember to ensure that buses at the change between frequency pattens (for instance at 6.00 p.m. in the above example) are not scheduled twice!

13.3 The infinity-norm of a vector is defined as the largest of the absolute values of the elements of the vector. Write a function that returns the infinity norm of a vector whose elements are stored in a rank-one assumed-shape real array which is the only argument to the function. The function should use elemental references to the intrinsic functions to do as much of the work as possible. Test your function on several vectors that have mixtures of positive and negative elements.

The two-norm of a matrix whose elements are a_{ij}, $i = 1, \ldots, m$, $j = 1, \ldots, n$ is defined to be

$$\sqrt{\sum_{i=1}^{m} \sum_{j=1}^{n} a_{ij}^2}$$

Modify the function just written so that it calculates the two-norm of a matrix, and test it with several matrices of different sizes.

13.4 The intersection of two sets is the set of all elements that occur in both sets. Write a subroutine that has two rank-one integer assumed-shape dummy arguments as input and one rank-one integer explicit-shape dummy argument as output. The output array should contain the intersection of the two input arrays. The fourth argument should be the size of the explicit-shape array. The fifth argument of the subroutine should be the number of elements in the intersection.

Test your subroutine with different size sets. For each array, the elements inside the array should be distinct from each other. Be careful that the array used for output is of sufficient size to hold the answer. The subprogram should perform a validity check to test for too small an output array.

Now modify your subroutine so that the output array is also an assumed-shape array, and test it. Which approach is preferable, and why?

13.5 Write a function that has two assumed-shape rank-one real dummy arguments. Internally, form a rank-two real array whose (i, j)th element is the product of the ith element of the first array and the jth element of the second array. The function should scan the product array systematically, to find a 2×2 sub-array that has the largest value for the sum of its elements. Return this sum. Test your function with several sets of inputs.

13.6 The ancient Greeks developed a method of finding all prime numbers up to a specified maximum which is called the Sieve of Eratosthenes. The method is, given the maximum integer n:

(1) Create an integer array **a** of size n.
(2) Fill **a** with integers such that `a(i)=i`, `i=1, ..., n`.
(3) Set `p=2`.
(4) Go through the array **a**, setting all integers exactly divisible by **p** to 0.
(5) Advance **p**, until either a non-zero **a(p)** is found, in which case go to step 4, or $p = n$, in which case go to step 6.
(6) All the numbers in the array that are non-zero must be prime (nothing divided them exactly). Print them out.

Implement this algorithm using an allocatable array for **a**. The integer n is to be read as input. Try your program for different sizes of n starting at 100. Be careful that you do not set n too large and thereby use an inordinate amount of computer time!

*13.7 Write a function that takes a rank-one integer array as input and whose result is the input array with its elements reversed. Use a vector subscript to accomplish this.

Use this function to reverse the elements of the ith row of a rank-two integer array.

13.8   Write a function that takes a rank-one real array as input, and an integer that lies between 1 and the size of the input array, and whose result is the input array with elements shifted to the left the number of places specified by the integer input. Those element values from the beginning of the array that are replaced by new values should be appended at the other end of the array. This is commonly called a left circular shift. There is an intrinsic function to do this, but the point of this exercise is to write your own.

13.9   Write a subroutine that has a rank-two square integer array as input and as output. The array will contain positive integer values between 0 and 10. The subroutine should modify the input array so that, when an element has a value 10 it is set to 0, when it has a value between 6 and 8 it is increased by 1, when it has a value between 1 and 5 it is decreased by 1, and when it has a value of 0 it is left unchanged.

Test the subroutine by running an array through it repetitively.

13.10   A conservation group is investigating the relative populations of various woodland animals, such as badgers, foxes and squirrels, in a wooded area on the basis of identifying their 'homes'.

The area under observation has been divided into small 'regions', each 100 m^2, forming an n km $\times$ m km rectangular area. These regions are identified by a coordinate system in which they are numbered from 0 to $10n - 1$ west–east, and from 0 to $10m - 1$ south–north; thus region (12,7) is the region whose south-west corner is 1200 m east of the 'origin' and 700 m north of it (where the 'origin' of the coordinate system is the south-west corner of the larger area being surveyed).

Within each region the number of fox holes, badger setts, squirrel dreys etc., has been recorded in the form of the coordinates of the region, followed by several counts of the form

   nn `animals`

where **animals** is **Badgers**, **Foxes** or whatever animal's home has been identified.

Thus a particular record, for region (12,17) might read

   `12 17 2 Foxes 1 Badger 5 Squirrels`

Write a program to read this data (from a file) and to produce the following initial analyses:

   (a)   The total population of each type of animal, assuming one animal per hole, sett, drey or other type of home;
   (b)   The region or regions with the highest population of each type of animal;
   (c)   The region or regions with the lowest population of each type of animal.

The program should read the dimensions of the area being surveyed (n and m) at the beginning, but it will not be possible to determine the number of different types of animals until all the data has been input.

Test your program with several different sets of data.

Parameterized and other data types

14

14.1 Non-default data types
14.2 Specifying kinds of variables
14.3 Specifying kinds of constants
14.4 Using non-default kinds to improve portability

14.5 Using non-default kinds to improve flexibility
14.6 Mixed kind expressions
14.7 COMPLEX variables

Almost all computers have more than one physical representation for real numbers, providing different degrees of precision and exponent range, and many also provide more than one representation of integers, providing different ranges of integer values. This chapter shows how Fortran 90 allows the programmer to specify, in a portable fashion, the degree of precision and/or the range of values required, so that the compiler can ensure that the most suitable of the hardware representations is used.

In a similar fashion, many computers support more than one character set, in order that the computer can operate with the characters used in the language of the user. This chapter also describes how Fortran 90 uses the same concept as is used for numbers to allow the programmer to specify which character set is to be used for a particular character entity.

As well as the INTEGER, REAL, CHARACTER and LOGICAL data types discussed in earlier chapters, Fortran includes an intrinsic COMPLEX type, whose use is also described in this chapter.

14.1 Non-default data types

We first introduced the intrinsic INTEGER, REAL and CHARACTER data types in Chapter 3, LOGICAL in Chapter 6, and DOUBLE PRECISION in Chapter 10. However, apart from the discussion of parameterized real data in Chapter 10, we have not yet presented the full potential of any of these data types. For example, the range of values that may be stored in an integer will vary according to how many bits are used to represent it in a computer's memory, while both the range and the precision of real values can vary enormously depending on how they are actually represented by the computer being used. This presents considerable numerical difficulties when attempting to write portable programs.

In order to overcome these problems, Fortran 90 allows all the intrinsic types other than DOUBLE PRECISION to have more than one form, known as different **kinds**, and provides the means for a program to define which kinds of variables and constants it wishes to use. Each implementation of Fortran 90 will provide at least one kind of each intrinsic data type, known as the **default kind**, and may provide as many other kinds as it wishes. The non-default kinds are identified by means of **kind type parameters**.

For the numeric data types, the kind type parameters allow the specification of the numeric ranges and, for REAL and COMPLEX (see Section 14.7), the precisions available. By selecting a kind with a defined range and precision the precision problems resulting from moving programs from one computer to another are greatly reduced.

The kind type parameter for the character data type is rather different as it identifies which character set is being used – for example, a natural language character set such as Cyrillic or Kanji, or a character set containing special graphics symbols such as those required for printing music.

The kind type parameter for the logical data type, however, is something of an anomaly – possibly because it was included in the language as much for consistency with the other intrinsic data types as for any good technical reason. Even though a logical entity may have a kind type parameter, the Fortran standard attaches no specific meaning to it! A processor is free to use it in whatever way it wishes for processor-dependent purposes.

Before discussing how kind type parameters are specified we should briefly examine under what circumstances kind type parameters should be explicitly specified.

Essentially, the numeric data types should have their kind type parameters explicitly specified when the program is expected to be run on more than one type of machine (which is the usual situation) and the degree of precision used in calculations is important, or when the default precision or range provided by the machine being used is inadequate for the type of calculations being undertaken.

For character entities, the default character set will be adequate for most purposes. However, if programs are being written for other than an English-speaking environment, or if special symbols which are not part of the default character set are required, then it will be necessary to specify explicitly the kind type parameter of character entities.

On the other hand, since non-default logicals are inherently non-portable we recommend that only default logicals should normally be used.

The next section will explain how to specify **kind type parameters** for **variables** and **constants** of different types, without going into details of what the values mean. The subsequent sections will then show how to obtain specific effects by varying the values of the kind type parameters for each of the main intrinsic Fortran data types.

14.2 Specifying kinds of variables

The kind type parameter associated with a variable is specified by the **kind selector** in the declaration of the variable. If no kind selector is specified then the type is said to be of **default type**. Up to this point (other than during a similar discussion in Chapter 10), all the variables and constants that we have used have been of default type. Thus, in Figure 14.1, the variables **x** and **y** are of type default real, **z** is a rank-one default real array of size **n**, **i** is a default integer named constant whose value is 25, **a** is a rank-two default character array of size 10 × 20, each of whose elements is five characters long, and **danger** is of type default logical.

Each data type has its explicit parametrization specified in an identical manner in a modified version of the type declaration statement that we have been using up to now:

    TYPE(KIND=_kind_num_**)** , ... :: _var_1_, ...

where **TYPE** is one of **INTEGER**, **REAL**, **COMPLEX**, **CHARACTER** or **LOGICAL**. It _cannot_ be **DOUBLE PRECISION**. If the parenthesized **KIND=** phrase is omitted then the type is a default type.

_kind_num_ is either a positive integer constant or a constant integer expression which will evaluate to a positive value. In fact, it is a special type of constant expression, known as an **initialization expression**, which must be

```
REAL :: x, y
REAL, DIMENSION(n) :: z
INTEGER, PARAMETER :: i = 25
CHARACTER(LEN = 5), DIMENSION(10, 20) :: a
LOGICAL :: danger
```

Figure 14.1 Default kind type declarations.

capable of being evaluated when the program is compiled – it *cannot* be varied during execution.

We may omit the **KIND=** part of the specification:

TYPE (*kind_num*) , ... :: ...

but we recommend that the first form should always be used to avoid any confusion, especially when dealing with character declarations.

In the case of character declarations, there is a complication because the length of the character variable also has to be specified. The type declaration statement, when kind type parameter values are given explicitly, can take any of the following forms:

CHARACTER(LEN=*len*, **KIND=***kind_num*) , ... :: ...
CHARACTER(*len*, **KIND=***kind_num*) , ... :: ...
CHARACTER(*len*, *kind_num*) , ... :: ...
CHARACTER(KIND=*kind_num*, **LEN=***len*) , ... :: ...
CHARACTER(KIND=*kind_num*) , ... :: ...

Both keywords are optional, and if the first item does not have a keyword it is taken to refer to the *length*, as in the second and third examples shown above. In the last example the length specification defaults to 1, but note that while

REAL(*number*) , ... :: ...

declares a real variable of kind *number*, the similar statement

CHARACTER(*number*) , ... :: ...

declares a character variable of default kind and of length *number*, as we saw in Chapter 3. We strongly recommend, therefore, that both keywords should always be used to avoid confusion and potential errors.

Figure 14.2 shows how the same variables and arrays as in Figure 14.1 would be declared with each data type having an explicit value for its kind selector.

It must be emphasized that only intrinsic data types have kind selectors, and that it is impossible, therefore, to associate a kind selector with a derived

```
REAL(KIND = 2) :: x, y
REAL(KIND = 1), DIMENSION(n) :: z
INTEGER(KIND = 10), PARAMETER :: i = 25
CHARACTER(KIND = 0, LEN = 5), DIMENSION(10, 20) :: a
LOGICAL(KIND = 3) :: danger
```

Figure 14.2 Explicit kind type declarations.

type, although kind selectors can, of course, be used with the *components* of a derived type. Thus

```
TYPE my_point
    REAL(KIND = 3) :: x, y, z
END TYPE my_point
```

defines a derived type each of whose components is real of kind type 3.

14.3 Specifying kinds of constants

Since variables can be of different kinds, it follows that the same must also apply to constants. Unfortunately, however, the situation here is not quite as straightforward as is the case with variable declarations. In order to specify the kind of a constant, the kind type parameter follows the constant, separated from it by an underscore, except in the case of characters, where the kind type parameter precedes the constant, separated from it by an underscore. The kind type parameter is either a literal integer constant or a named constant, and takes the value of the required kind type. If the kind type parameter is omitted then the constant is, of course, of the appropriate default type.

The following are examples of integer literal constants:

`-124`	Default integer
`628_3`	Integer of kind 3
`-628_small`	Integer of kind **small**
`628_large`	Integer of kind **large**

where **small** and **large** are scalar integer named constants whose values are non-negative. They could, for example, have been defined by a statement of the form

```
INTEGER, PARAMETER :: small = 5, large = 1
```

Real literal constants take a similar form:

`-1.0`	Default real
`12.34`	Default real
`401.2E-5`	Default real
`155.0_1`	Real of kind 1
`-704.2E-3_3`	Real of kind 3
`-704.2E-3_low`	Real of kind **low**
`-704.2E-3_high`	Real of kind **high**

where **low** and **high** are scalar integer named constants whose values are non-negative.

For characters, the kind type parameter *precedes* the character literal, separated by an underscore. (The reason for this is so that the processor can know what kind of characters it is dealing with before it gets to them.) The following are examples of character literal constants:

"ABC_XYZ" is a default character literal, using the default character set which must include the Fortran Character Set

12_"жз и" is a kind 12 character literal, where kind type 12 identifies a character set on the processor which includes Cyrillic characters

cyrillic_"жз и" is a kind **cyrillic** character literal, where **cyrillic** is a named constant whose value has been set to the kind type of a character set on the processor which includes Cyrillic characters

greek_"αβγ" is a kind **greek** character literal, where **greek** is a named constant whose value has been set to the kind type of a character set on the processor which includes Greek characters

Note that the kind type identifies a *processor-defined character set*, or **repertoire**. There is no standard interpretation of the kind values and, for example, if a processor supports the 'universal' coded character set defined in ISO/IEC 10646 it would probably result in **greek** and **cyrillic** having the same values on that processor, whereas on most processors, which do not support the universal coded character set, they will each have different values.

For logical constants, the kind parameter follows the literal:

.TRUE. Default logical

.FALSE._5 Logical of kind 5

14.4 Using non-default kinds to improve portability

Before discussing how non-default kinds can be used to provide greater control and portability of programs than is possible with default data types there is an important point that must be dealt with. The Fortran standard does *not* require that the values of the kind type parameters have the same meaning on all processors.

At first sight, this would seem to eliminate the possibility of writing portable programs, even though this has been stated to be one of the advantages of using non-default data types. Fortran 90, however, provides a number of intrinsic functions that completely eliminate this difficulty for numeric data types. For **CHARACTER** data types, as we shall see, modules can be used to largely eliminate portability difficulties.

For *integers*, the value of the kind type parameter specifies what range of integers is required. To provide a convenient way of *portably* specifying the range requirements, the intrinsic function **SELECTED_INT_KIND** can be used to specify the range required, and cause the Fortran processor to provide a suitable kind type. Thus a reference to

SELECTED_INT_KIND (r)

returns a value of the kind type parameter for an integer data type that can represent, *at least*, all integer values n in the range $-10^r < n < 10^r$. If it is not possible to represent all the integer values in this range then the function will return a result of -1.

In some cases there may be more than one available kind type which will satisfy the requirement, in which case the one with the smallest exponent range will be returned. If there are several of these then the smallest of these kind type values is returned.

The following example uses this function to define a constant which is, in turn, used in the declaration of a number of variables.

```
PROGRAM degree
    IMPLICIT NONE
    INTEGER, PARAMETER :: range = SELECTED_INT_KIND(20)
    INTEGER(KIND = range) :: x, y, z
    x = 360_range
    y = 180_range
    z = 90_range
    .
    .
    .
END PROGRAM degree
```

This extract defines three integer variables **x**, **y** and **z** that can contain values in the range $-10^{20} < n < 10^{20}$. They are initially set to the values 360, 180 and 90, respectively.

Notice that the named constant **range** is used to set the precision requirements for all integer constants and variables in the program. If the program is moved to a different computer system it will still use variables and constants of a kind which will allow at least the specified range because, even though the relevant kind types returned by the function **SELECTED_INT_KIND** are processor-dependent, it is known that they will be such as to meet the specified range requirement.

Note, however, that the program is not totally portable, because it is possible that the processor cannot support the requested integer range. In this case, the value -1 will be returned by **SELECTED_INT_KIND**, and the subsequent attempt to declare a variable or constant of this kind will lead to an error. For most programs, though, this should be an extremely rare occurrence.

In the above program fragment we have specified the kind of the constants by writing them in the form **360_range**. This is not normally necessary, however, when dealing with integers, since the default integer will almost certainly have a sufficiently large range for any literal constants. We can therefore write statements such as

```
x = 360
```

which are easier to read, and let the compiler take care of the necessary conversions. When we come to consider the situation with non-default reals, however, we shall have to be more careful.

It is important to note that the kind type parameter value returned by the intrinsic function **SELECTED_INT_KIND** may be for an integer data type that *exceeds* the requirements specified. Therefore, in subsequent calculations, it would not necessarily be an error to set **x**, **y** or **z** to 10^{25}. Whether or not this produced an error, or any type of warning at all, would be completely dependent on the processor on which the program is run – it is not required by the Fortran standard.

There is one final point to be made before we leave our discussion of non-default integers. In general, we shall require all the integers in the program, or certainly a substantial proportion of them, to be of the same kind. It will therefore be more satisfactory to place the definition of the kind type in a module so that it can easily be made available to all procedures that require it and, moreover, so that a global change to the range required in the program can be made by simply changing the kind type number in just one statement. Figure 14.3 shows how this program extract would look if written in this way.

```
MODULE constants
   IMPLICIT NONE
   INTEGER, PARAMETER :: range = SELECTED_INT_KIND(20)
END MODULE constants

PROGRAM degree
   USE constants
   IMPLICIT NONE
   INTEGER(KIND = range) :: x, y, z

   x = 360_range
   y = 180_range
   z = 90_range
   .
   .
   .
END PROGRAM degree
```

Figure 14.3 Using a module to specify the kind types of variables and constants.

In all future examples we will normally adopt this approach of using modules for entities that permeate entire programs.

For *real numbers*, the value of the kind type parameter specifies the precision as well as the exponent range that is required. Furthermore, in a similar manner to the case with integers, we can use the intrinsic function `SELECTED_REAL_KIND` to assist with portability. Thus the statement

```
INTEGER, PARAMETER :: real_kind = SELECTED_REAL_KIND(p,r)
```

sets the constant **real_kind** to a kind type parameter for a real data type that has at least p decimal digits of accuracy and a decimal exponent range of at least r. If no such kind type parameter is available on a particular processor for the range requested, the function will return a value of -1. If the precision requested is unsupported, the function will return a value of -2. If neither the precision nor range requested are available, the function will return a value of -3. If any of these values are used as the kind type in a declaration statement they will, of course, cause a compilation error. If more than one kind type parameter value meets the criteria, the one with the smallest decimal precision is returned. If there are several such kind values, then the smallest of the values is returned.

The exponent range argument r is optional. This reflects the fact that, for most calculations and processors, selection of the precision is usually (but not always) a more critical issue than selection of the exponent range. If the range argument is omitted, the processor will choose the value of r.

Figure 14.4 shows a program fragment which uses real numbers having six decimal digits of accuracy and an exponent range of 30.

```
MODULE constants
   IMPLICIT NONE
   INTEGER, PARAMETER :: real_kind=SELECTED_REAL_KIND(6,30)
END MODULE constants

PROGRAM satellite
   USE constants
   IMPLICIT NONE
   REAL(KIND = real_kind) :: r, theta, phi

   r = 321.172_real_kind
   theta = 1.47239_real_kind
   phi = 0.172341E-1_real_kind
   .
   .
   .
END PROGRAM satellite
```

Figure 14.4 Specifying the precision and range of real variables and constants.

Just as was the case with integers, it is important to note that the kind type parameter value returned by the intrinsic function **SELECTED_REAL_KIND** may specify a kind type that *exceeds* the specified precision and exponent range requirements. For example, on a computer which had two real kind types 1 and 2, which had precisions and ranges of $(5, 30)$ and $(10, 60)$, respectively, kind type 2 would be selected for the program shown in Figure 14.4, with the result that all calculations would use variables and constants which held values to 10 digits of precision. If the program was subsequently run on a computer which also had two kind types 1 and 2, but with precisions and ranges of $(6, 40)$ and $(12, 70)$, respectively, then kind type 1 would be selected, and all calculations would use only six digits of precision. The result might be different from that obtained on the first computer, therefore, but *it would not be different to six digits of precision*, since both computer systems were working to at least that level of precision.

Parameterization of real numbers involves more subtle issues (of a numerical nature) than for any other Fortran data type, and has already been discussed in some detail in Section 10.2, for those interested in such matters.

14.5 Using non-default kinds to improve flexibility

Unlike the numeric types, where it is possible to use the intrinsic functions **SELECTED_INT_KIND** and **SELECTED_REAL_KIND** to guarantee portability of range and precision, non-default character and logical types are inherently non-portable, since different processors will, almost certainly, not provide equivalent types or kind numbers. The primary use for non-default character and logical types is, therefore, to provide greater flexibility in certain important aspects.

For *characters*, the value of the kind type parameter specifies what **character repertoire** is required, or what set of characters is to be available. The whole question of **coded character sets** (the actual binary codes used to represent characters) and character repertoires (the set of available characters regardless of their internal coding) is quite complicated and beyond the scope of this book. It is the goal of the International Organization for Standardization, and of most major computer manufacturers, that in the not-too-distant future a single coding system will be used on all computers which will deal with all possible characters, even those contained in very large character repertoires such as are required for Chinese, Japanese and certain other East Asian languages. Despite the work being done in this area, however, it seems probable that most computer systems will not accept more than a relatively small subset of the known characters for many years to come, and that some means will be required to specify those that are required in a particular application. In Fortran 90, as we have already seen, that specification is provided as the kind type parameter.

The kind type parameter for characters is, however, just as processor-dependent as are those for the numeric types. Moreover, no intrinsic functions are provided to assist in developing portable code. We therefore recommend that *all* character repertoire specifications be put into a module where they may be readily adjusted, in one place only, if the program is moved to a different processor.

Let us suppose, for example, that a program is being written which requires access to both Cyrillic and Kanji characters. If the processor that we are using provides both the Cyrillic and Kanji character repertoires with kind parameter values 3 and 5, respectively, then a suitable module would be as follows:

```
MODULE constants
   IMPLICIT NONE
   INTEGER, PARAMETER :: cyrillic = 3
   INTEGER, PARAMETER :: kanji = 5
END MODULE constants
```

We could then use both character repertoires, as well as the default repertoire, in a program which would, in itself, be portable as long as the necessary changes were made to the module if it were to be moved to another processor:

```
PROGRAM translate
   USE constants
   IMPLICIT NONE

   CHARACTER(LEN = 80, KIND = cyrillic) :: russian_text
   CHARACTER(LEN = 240, KIND = kanji) :: japanese_text
   CHARACTER(LEN = 80) :: english_text
   .
   .
   .
   russian_text = cyrillic_"Без неё ничто невозможно"
   japanese_text = kanji_"彼女なしでは何もできない"
   english_text = "Without her, nothing is possible"
   .
   .
END PROGRAM translate
```

Of course, if this program is moved to a computer system which does not support either of these two character repertoires then there will be problems! However, as long as the characters are supported, the program will run correctly, even though the relevant kind parameters may have quite different values.

For *logical* data, the Fortran standard assigns no specific meaning to the kind type parameter. The reason for this is that non-default logical data types were included in Fortran 90 mainly because the other intrinsic data types could be parameterized, and so why not logicals?

Because there is no requirement for a Fortran 90 processor to provide any logical data types other than the default kind, and because there is no guarantee, even if they do, that the non-default logical types have any particular relationship to each other, the concept is inherently non-portable and not to be recommended.

14.6 Mixed kind expressions

In Chapter 3 we explained how (default) real and (default) integer values could be used in the same expression, and elaborated the rules relating to the evaluation of such expressions. We also presented the rules governing the assignment of values of one type to a variable of another type.

Clearly, we must now extend these rules to cover the case of expressions involving explicitly parameterized variables and constants. Of course, if all the operands in an expression are of the same type and have the same value for their kind type parameter values, then matters are quite straightforward and, as we would expect, the expression will have a value for its kind type parameter that is the same as that of its operands. It is only when expressions involve operands of different types or different kind type parameter values that the situation may become slightly more complicated.

A number of intrinsic functions are provided to give precise control of kind type parameter values in expressions. The first of these, the intrinsic inquiry function **KIND**, will return the kind type parameter value of any integer, real, complex, character or logical entity. Thus the statement

```
k1 = KIND(0.0)
```

sets **k1** to the value of the kind type parameter for default reals, the statement

```
k2 = KIND("ABC")
```

sets **k2** to the value of the kind type parameter for default characters, while the statements

```
INTEGER(KIND=3), DIMENSION(3) :: a
k3 = KIND(a)
```

set **k3** to 3.

At first sight this function does not appear to be particularly useful other than for establishing the kind type parameter values of the default intrinsic data types, since it is necessary to know the kind type of a variable before it can be declared, and of a constant before it can be written. However, as we shall see, it does have a role to play in writing portable programs.

A rather more useful feature in this regard, however, is the inclusion of an extra, optional, argument in the type conversion functions **INT**, **REAL** and **CMPLX**. We have already met the first two of these functions in their simple form, but we shall now briefly re-examine them in their new, more powerful, role.

The intrinsic function **INT(A,KIND)** converts the argument **A** to an integer. **A** can be integer, real or complex and can be scalar or array-valued. The value of the result is the integer part of **A** if it is of type integer or real. If **A** is complex, the value is the integer part of the *real* component of **A**. If the argument **KIND** is present then the result of the conversion will be an integer of kind `KIND`; if it is not present, as has been the case when we have used it before, then the result will be of type default integer. In all cases, if the value of the number being converted lies outside the range of integers which can be represented in the specified kind of integer then the result is undefined — although it will usually result in an error.

Thus the expression

```
j = j + INT(x,KIND(j))
```

will convert the value of the variable **x** to an integer of the same kind as the (integer) variable **j**, before adding it to **j** and storing the result in **j**.

In a similar way, the intrinsic function `REAL(A,KIND)` converts the argument **A** to real. **A** can be integer, real or complex and be scalar or array-valued. The value of the result is a floating point approximation to **A** if it is of type integer or real. As was the case with `INT`, the result will be real of kind `KIND` if the argument `KIND` is present, and will be default real otherwise.

Note, however, that the statement

```
j = INT(REAL(i,KIND(x)),KIND(i))
```

does not necessarily result in **j** taking the same value as **i**, even if they are both of the same integer kind. For example, if the three variables in the above statement were declared by means of the following statements:

```
INTEGER, PARAMETER :: k = SELECTED_INT_KIND(10)
INTEGER, PARAMETER :: p = SELECTED_REAL_KIND(6)

INTEGER(KIND=k) :: i,j
REAL(KIND=p) :: x
```

then the integer variable **i** potentially has 10 decimal digits of accuracy. When it is converted to a real with a requirement for six decimal digits of accuracy, therefore, it must be assumed that some loss of precision may result. When it is subsequently converted back to an integer of the same kind as the original value it is too late to retrieve the lost precision!

For logical entities, there is an intrinsic function `LOGICAL(L,KIND)` that converts between different kinds of logicals. The argument **L** must be of type logical. The result has the same value as **L** and will be of logical kind `KIND` if the argument `KIND` is present, and will be default logical otherwise.

Characters are, of course, different from other data types in that different kinds are quite distinct and conversion from one character set to another would be quite meaningless. There is, therefore, no intrinsic function to convert between character entities having differing kind type parameter values.

Function name and arguments	Purpose
`AINT(A,KIND)`	Truncation
`ANINT(A,KIND)`	Nearest whole number
`CHAR(I,KIND)`	Character in given position in collating sequence
`CMPLX(X,Y,KIND)`	Convert to complex
`INT(A,KIND)`	Convert to integer
`LOGICAL(L,KIND)`	Convert between kinds of logical
`NINT(A,KIND)`	Nearest integer
`REAL(A,KIND)`	Convert to real

Figure 14.5 Intrinsic functions which have an optional KIND argument.

There are a number of other intrinsic functions which have an optional argument which defines the kind of the result in the same way as in those described above; a full list can be seen in Figure 14.5. A specification of these, and of all Fortran's intrinsic procedures, can be found in Appendix A.

We now come to the kind type parameter values of expressions, and here we would strongly recommend that the intrinsic functions discussed above are always used to ensure that all the elements of an expression are converted to the same kind before any other operations are carried out.

For characters there is only one operator, namely the concatenation operator (//), and both operands must be of the same kind. As we would expect, assignment is only allowed when the kind of the expression is the same as the kind of the variable to which the value of the expression is being assigned.

For logical entities the various logical operators are only fully defined for operands of the same kind; if they are of different kinds then the kind of the result is processor-dependent. It is unlikely that this will cause any difficulties, since interpretation of one kind of *true* as another kind is unlikely to be beyond the capability of any Fortran processor! Whatever the kind of the value of a logical expression, if it is assigned to a logical variable then it will be converted to the kind of that variable.

The rules for determining the kind type parameter value of a numeric expression, however, appear to be quite complicated, although they are quite logical once you sit down and think about them! Figure 14.6 shows how the kind of a simple binary operation is determined, and the kind type parameter value of a more complex expression can then be determined by systematic application of these rules.

It is clear, therefore, that if the kind type parameter values of the operands in an expression are not identical, then the rules for their evaluation are quite complicated, and code written in this way will be difficult to understand, maintain and convert to a new computer. Whenever possible, therefore, expressions involving operands with differing kind type parameter values should be avoided.

		Operand x_2		
		INTEGER	**REAL**	**COMPLEX**
Operand x_1	**INTEGER**	Kind type parameter value of x_1 if the kind type parameter values of the two operands are equal. Otherwise it is the kind type parameter value of whichever operand has the greatest[a] decimal exponent range.	Kind type parameter value of the real operand.	Kind type parameter value of the complex operand.
	REAL	Kind type parameter value of the real operand.	Kind type parameter value of x_1 if the kind type parameter values of both operands are equal. Otherwise, it is the kind type parameter value of whichever operand has the greatest* decimal precision.	
	COMPLEX	Kind type parameter value of the complex operand.		

* If they are equal, the kind type parameter value is processor-dependent.

Figure 14.6   Kind type parameter value of x_1 **op** x_2.

SELF-TEST EXERCISES 14.1

1   What is a kind type parameter? Why are kind type parameters important?

2   How are explicit kind type parameters specified for variables?

3   How are explicit kind type parameters specified for constants?

4   What are the default **REAL** and default **CHARACTER** data types?

5   What implicit functions are used to specify values for the kind type parameters of **INTEGER** and **REAL** entities? How are they used?

6   What happens if an impossible **INTEGER** range or **REAL** precision is requested?

7   Why is it undesirable to write an expression like

   `x + 1234567_2`

   where **x** is a default **REAL**?

8   Why should logical entities always be default logicals?

14.7 COMPLEX variables

There is one more type of numeric variable which, although it is not used as much as real or integer variables, does occur from time to time in general applications, and is very important in certain application areas, such as electrical engineering. This type is called **complex** and consists of two parts – a **real part** and an **imaginary part**. In Chapter 4 we defined a derived type for this purpose which enabled us to illustrate several aspects of derived types. In a similar way, the intrinsic **COMPLEX** type stores a complex number in two consecutive numeric storage units as two separate real numbers – the first representing the real part and the second representing the imaginary part.

A complex variable is declared in a type specification statement of the form

```
COMPLEX :: name1,name2,...
```

As with all other intrinsic types, other than DOUBLE PRECISION, a complex variable may have a kind type parameter:

```
COMPLEX(KIND=3), DIMENSION(4) :: v,w
```

Note, however, that since complex numbers are compound entities, consisting of an ordered pair of **REAL** numbers, the value of the kind selector, whether explicitly or implicitly specified, applies to both of the two real components. Thus, in the above example, the two rank-one complex arrays, **v** and **w**, each consist of eight real components of kind type 3 – a real and an imaginary component of each element of each array.

Because its components are real values, the value of the kind type parameter for a complex entity specifies the decimal precision and exponent range required for the two component real numbers. Thus, we can use the intrinsic function **SELECTED_REAL_KIND** to specify precision and exponent range requirements for complex numbers in a portable manner. Figure 14.7 illustrates the use of non-default complex numbers in a program fragment which declares an array of complex numbers, each of whose elements has real and imaginary parts having at least 12 digits of precision and an exponent range of at least 70.

A complex constant is written as a pair of numeric constants, either real or integer, separated by a comma and enclosed in parentheses:

```
(1.5,7.3)
(1.59E4,-12E-1)
(2.5,6)
(19,2.5E-2)
```

The situation regarding kind type parameters with complex literal constants is, however, slightly more complicated than for other data types

```
MODULE constants
   IMPLICIT NONE
   INTEGER, PARAMETER :: complex_kind = &
                          SELECTED_REAL_KIND(12, 70)
END MODULE constants

PROGRAM accurate
   USE constants
   IMPLICIT NONE
   COMPLEX(KIND = complex_kind), DIMENSION(4) :: z

   z(1) = (3.72471778E-45_complex_kind, &
           723.115798E-56_complex_kind)
   .
   .
   .

END PROGRAM accurate
```

Figure 14.7 Specifying the precision and range of complex variables and constants.

because of the fact that a complex constant is specified as an ordered pair of numbers that may be real or integer constants, and every possible combination of component data types must be considered. If integers are used, they are converted to their real equivalents.

If both component constants are of the default real type, then the complex constant has the same kind as default real. Thus $(1.23,4.28)$ is a default complex constant whose kind type is the same as default real.

If both component constants are integer, with any kind type parameter, they are converted to default reals and the complex constant is of type default complex. Thus

$(1\_2,3)$
$(1,3)$
$(1\_2,3\_4)$

are all default complex constants.

If only one of the component constants is an integer constant, it is converted to a real with the kind type of the real component, and the complex constant also has that kind type. Thus

$(1,2.0)$ is a default complex constant

$(1,2.0\_3)$ has a kind type parameter of 3

If both component numbers are real, the kind type parameter of the complex constant is the value of the kind type parameter of the component that has the greater decimal precision. If both precisions are the same, the processor can select the kind type parameter of either component as the kind type parameter of the complex constant. Thus

> (1.2_3,3.4_3)   has a kind type parameter of 3.
>
> (1.2_3,1E6_4)   has a kind type parameter of 3 if the processor provides more decimal precision for real constants of kind 3 than for real constants of kind 4;
>
> has a kind type parameter of 4 if the processor provides more decimal precision for real constants of kind 4 than for real constants of kind 3;
>
> and has a kind type parameter either 3 or 4 (the processor's choice) if the processor provides the same decimal precision for real constants with kind parameter 3 and 4.

To avoid these complications we recommend always using a pair of real constants of the same kind type to form a complex constant.

Finally, in a similar manner to the intrinsic functions **REAL** and **INTEGER**, the intrinsic type conversion function **CMPLX(X,Y,KIND)** combines the arguments **X** and **Y** (if present) to be the real and imaginary parts of a complex type. The arguments **X** and **Y** can be integer, real or complex, and may be scalar or array-valued. The argument **Y** is optional; if it is omitted it is taken to have the value 0 unless **X** is complex, in which case only **X** is used to form the result value and **Y** *must* be omitted. If **X** is not complex, then the real and imaginary parts of the result are **X** and **Y**, respectively. The value of the kind type parameter of the result is **KIND**, if it is present; otherwise it will be that of default real.

We can now move to examining how complex numbers are used, and first we note that, in mathematical terms, the complex number (x, y) is written $x + iy$, where $i^2 = -1$. Electrical engineers usually use the letter j rather than i, and we shall use j in the following discussion. This definition of a complex number leads to the rules for complex arithmetic which we met in Chapter 4 when defining our own complex derived type; for convenience they are shown again in Figure 14.8.

Both real and integer numbers may be combined with complex numbers in a mixed-mode expression, and the evaluation of such a mixed-mode expression is achieved by first converting the real or integer number to a complex number with a zero imaginary part. Thus, if **z1** is the complex number **(x1,y1)**, and **r** is a real number then

    r*z1

is converted to

    (r,0)*(x1,y1)

If

$$z_1 = (x_1, y_1)$$
$$z_2 = (x_2, y_2)$$

then

$$z_1 + z_2 = (x_1 + x_2, y_1 + y_2)$$
$$z_1 - z_2 = (x_1 - x_2, y_1 - y_2)$$
$$z_1 z_2 = (x_1 x_2 - y_1 y_2, x_1 y_2 + x_2 y_1)$$
$$z_1 / z_2 = \left(\frac{x_1 x_2 + y_1 y_2}{x_2{}^2 + y_2{}^2}, \frac{x_2 y_1 - x_1 y_2}{x_2{}^2 + y_2{}^2} \right)$$

Figure 14.8 Complex arithmetic.

which will be evaluated as

`(r*x1,r*y1)`

Similarly, if **n** is an integer, then

`n+z1`

is evaluated as

`(REAL(n)+x1,y1)`

Several intrinsic functions are available for use with complex numbers. For example

`AIMAG(z)`   obtains the imaginary part of **z**

and

`CONJG(z)`   obtains the complex conjugate `(x,-y)`

All of the generic intrinsic functions, such as **SIN**, **LOG**, etc. can also be used with complex arguments. Full details of all intrinsic functions which can be used with complex numbers can be found in Appendix A.

```
PROGRAM complex_arithmetic
   IMPLICIT NONE

   COMPLEX :: a,b,c

   ! Read two complex numbers
   READ '(2F10.3)',a,b
   c = a*b

   ! Print data items and their product
   PRINT 200,a,b,c
   200 FORMAT(" a = (",F10.3,",",F10.3,")"/    &
              " b = (",F10.3,",",F10.3,")"/    &
              "a*b = (",F10.3,",",F10.3,")")

END PROGRAM complex_arithmetic
```

Output:

```
  a = (    12.500,     8.400)
  b = (     6.500,     9.600)
a*b = (     0.610,   174.600)
```

Figure 14.9 An example of complex arithmetic.

Finally, we should mention that the input and output of complex numbers is achieved by reading or writing two real numbers, corresponding to the real and imaginary parts, using any appropriate edit descriptor. Figure 14.9 shows an example of both complex input and complex output.

■ EXAMPLE 14.1

1 Problem

When an alternating voltage is applied to an electrical circuit both its phase and its amplitude will be affected by the characteristics of the circuit. In order to simplify calculations relating to such situations, electrical engineers calculate a *transfer function* for the circuit. If the value of the transfer function at a frequency w is $H(w)$, then the amplitude of the output voltage is simply the amplitude of the input voltage multiplied by the magnitude of $H(w)$, while the phase of the output voltage is the phase of the transfer function added to the phase of the input voltage. (The magnitude of the transfer function is its absolute value, while its phase is the arctangent of the imaginary part divided by the real part.)

A very common type of circuit in electronic equipment is a *filter circuit*, such as that shown in Figure 14.10, which consists of a capacitor and an inductor in series, with a resistor in parallel. By varying the sizes of the three components

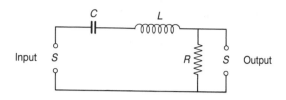

Figure 14.10 A simple electronic filter.

it is possible to produce a *high-pass filter* that passes high frequencies with little attenuation but substantially reduces the amplitude of low-frequency signals, a *low-pass filter* that does the reverse, or a *band-pass filter* that reduces both high- and low-frequency signals, allowing only frequencies within an intermediate band to pass without attenuation.

Write a program to produce a table showing the phase and amplitude of the output signal from the circuit shown in Figure 14.10 at different input frequencies, and for different values of the components.

2 Analysis

We can use Kirchhoff's laws to derive the transfer function for this system, which is

$$H(f) = \frac{R}{1/2\pi j f\, C + 2\pi j f L + R}$$

or

$$H(f) = \frac{2\pi j f\, RC}{1 - (2\pi f)^2 LC + 2\pi j f\, RC}$$

where f is the frequency of the signal in hertz (cycles s^{-1}).

The data design and structure plan for the program is then straightforward.

Data design

Purpose	Type	Name
A Module constants		
π	REAL	pi
2π	REAL	two_pi

B Local variables

Initial and final frequencies	INTEGER	f1, f2
Frequency interval	INTEGER	f_inc
Loop variable (frequency)	INTEGER	f
Capacitance	REAL	c
Inductance	REAL	l
Resistance	REAL	r
Transfer function	COMPLEX	h
Output phase	REAL	phase
Output amplitude	REAL	amplitude
Yes/no reply	CHARACTER*1	answer

Structure plan

> 1 Repeat as long as necessary
> 1.1 Read data values for next case – using *input*
> 1.2 Repeat for *f* from *f1* to *f2* in steps of *f_inc*
> 1.2.1 Calculate transfer function
> 1.2.2 Calculate amplitude and phase shift
> 1.2.3 Print frequency, amplitude and phase shift
> 1.3 Ask if another case required
> 1.3.1 If not 'yes' then exit from loop

Since the input procedure simply asks for the relevant information it hardly needs a structure plan.

3 Solution

```
MODULE constants
   IMPLICIT NONE
   REAL,PARAMETER (pi = 3.1415926536, twopi = 2.0*pi)
END MODULE constants

PROGRAM filter
   USE constants
   IMPLICIT NONE

   ! This program calculates the transfer function for a simple
   ! electronic filter, consisting of a capacitor and an
   ! inductor in series, with a resistor in parallel, and then
   ! prints the voltage amplification and phase shift that it
   ! produces on input signals in a specified range of
   ! frequencies.

   ! Declarations
   INTEGER :: f1,f2,f_inc,f
   REAL :: r,c,l,amplitude,phase
   COMPLEX :: h
   CHARACTER :: answer
```

```
      DO
          ! Get data for next case
          CALL input

          ! Print title for this circuit, and column headers
          PRINT '("1","Frequency response between ",I5," Hz. &
                  &and ",I5," Hz." / &
                " ","for a filter with a series capacitance &
                  &of ",F7.3, " microfarads", / &
                " ","and a series inductance of ",F7.3, &
                  " millihenries"/ &
                " ","in parallel with a resistance of ", &
                  F7.3," kilo-ohms is:", // &
                " ","Frequency",T15," Voltage",T30, &
                  "Phase"/ &
                " "," (Hz.)",T15,"amplification",T30, &
                  "shift"//)', f1,f2,c,l,r

          ! Convert capacitance to farads, inductance to henries,
          ! and resistance to ohms
          c=c*1.0E-6
          l=l*1.0E-3
          r=r*1.0E3

          ! Loop for required frequencies
          DO f=f1,f2,f_inc
             ! Calculate transfer function
             h=CMPLX(r,0.0)/CMPLX(r,twopi*f*l-1.0/(twopi*f*c))

             ! Amplification factor is absolute value of H
             amplitude=ABS(h)

             ! Phase shift is arctangent of imaginary part
             ! divided by real part
             phase=ATAN2(AIMAG(h),REAL(h))
             ! Convert to degrees
             phase=180.0*phase/pi

             ! Print results for this frequency
             PRINT '(" ",I6,T15,F9.3,T30,F5.1)',f,amplitude,phase
          END DO

          ! Ask if another case required
          PRINT *,"Another case? (Y/N)"
          READ *,answer
          IF (answer /= "Y" .AND. answer /= "y") EXIT
      END DO

CONTAINS

   SUBROUTINE input

      ! This is the input routine for the main program
```

```
        PRINT *,"What is the value of the capacitance &
                &(microfarads)?"
        READ *,c
        PRINT *,"What is the value of the inductance &
                &(millihenries)?"
        READ *,l
        PRINT *,"What is the value of the resistance &
                &(kilo-ohms)?"
        READ *,r
        ! Read frequency data
        DO
            PRINT *,"Give initial and final frequencies, and &
                    &increment (Hz)"
            READ *,f1,f2,f_inc
            ! Check for validity
            IF (f1<=f2 .AND. f_inc>0.0) THEN
                EXIT
            ELSE
                PRINT *,"Data is inconsistent. Please try again"
            END IF
        END DO
    END SUBROUTINE input

END PROGRAM filter
```

Note that when calculating the transfer function h we used the first form shown in the earlier discussion, namely

$$H(f) = \frac{R}{1/2\pi j f C + 2\pi j f L + R}$$

which was coded in Fortran as

```
h=CMPLX(r,0.0)/CMPLX(r,twopi*f*l-1.0/(twopi*f*c))
```

where the expression $1/2\pi j f C$ was converted to $-j/2\pi f C$ by multiplying top and bottom by j, remembering that $j^2 = -1$. We could, alternatively, have used the second form of the relationship

$$H(f) = \frac{2\pi j f R C}{1 - (2\pi f)^2 L + 2\pi j f R C}$$

which was derived as a result of multiplying both top and bottom of the first form by $2\pi j f C$. In that case the Fortran expression would have been

```
h=CMPLX(0.0,twopi*f*r*c)/ &
  CMPLX(1.0-twopi*twopi*f*f*l*c,twopi*f*r*c)
```

Frequency response between 1000 Hz. and 20000 Hz.
for a filter with a series capacitance of 0.022 microfarads
and a series inductance of 72.000 millihenries
in parallel with a resistance of 4.700 kilo-ohms is:

Frequency (Hz.)	Voltage amplification	Phase shift
1000	0.570	55.3
2000	0.866	30.0
3000	0.976	12.6
4000	1.000	0.0
5000	0.985	-9.8
6000	0.952	-17.8
7000	0.911	-24.4
8000	0.866	-30.0
9000	0.821	-34.8
10000	0.778	-39.0
11000	0.736	-42.6
12000	0.698	-45.8
13000	0.662	-48.6
14000	0.628	-51.1
15000	0.598	-53.3
16000	0.569	-55.3
17000	0.543	-57.1
18000	0.519	-58.7
19000	0.497	-60.2
20000	0.476	-61.6

Figure 14.11 An extract from the results obtained from **FILTER**.

Note also that the input subroutine has been written as an internal procedure, thus avoiding the need to pass all the input variables as arguments. Since input routines are, by definition, normally only called from one place, they are usually better written as internal procedures in this way.

Figure 14.11 shows the result of running this program for a particular circuit. It can clearly be seen that at 4000 Hz there is no attenuation at all, and that there is only a relatively slight attenuation between 2 kHz and 8 kHz. This circuit is therefore a band-pass filter which substantially attenuates frequencies below 1 kHz and above 15 kHz; it is thus suitable for use in audio equipment, since this is the frequency band which is of most relevance in this type of application. (In practice, since the circuit only contains passive elements, it is unlikely that such a primitive filter would actually be used in high fidelity equipment, but we are not concerned here with the finer points of electronic circuit design!)

SELF TEST EXERCISES 14.2

1   If a **REAL** constant or variable is defined by explicitly stating range or precision requirements, why does it not always meet these requirements exactly?

2   How is a complex number represented by the **COMPLEX** type?

3   What is the relationship between the kind type of a complex variable and the kind types of its components?

4   What will be printed by the following program?

```
PROGRAM test14_2_4
   IMPLICIT NONE
   COMPLEX :: p=(1,2),q=(3,4)
   REAL :: x=5.0

   PRINT *,p,q,x
   PRINT *,p+q,p-q,p+x
   PRINT *,p*q,x*q,p/q
   PRINT *,p/x,x/p,CONJG(x/p)
END PROGRAM test14_2_4
```

5   Why is it undesirable to write a complex number in the following form?

    (1.0,x_4)

SUMMARY

- All intrinsic data types have a parameter called the kind type parameter.

- If the kind type parameter is omitted, the type is said to be of default kind.

- The values of the kind type parameter are system-dependent.

- For the numeric data types, the kind type parameter specifies range and precision requirements.

- For the **CHARACTER** data type, the kind type parameter specifies the character set required. The default character set will always include the Fortran character set.

- The intrinsic functions **SELECTED_INT_KIND** and **SELECTED_REAL_KIND** enable precision and range requirements to be specified in a portable fashion.

- If all the components of an expression have the same kind type parameter values, the result of the expression also has this kind type parameter value.

- The rules for determining the kind type parameter of an expression in which the components have different kind type parameter values are complicated, and such expressions should be avoided.

- **COMPLEX** entities use two consecutive numeric storage units to represent the real and imaginary parts by two real numbers.

- The kind type parameter of a **COMPLEX** variable is the same as the kind type parameter of the two real numbers which represent its two component parts.

- To avoid complications, a **COMPLEX** literal constant should always have two components with the same kind types.

- Fortran 90 syntax introduced in Chapter 14:

Variable declarations	**COMPLEX** ... :: *list of variable names*
	REAL(KIND=*kind_type***)** ... :: *list of variable names*
	INTEGER(KIND=*kind_type***)** ... :: *list of variable names*
	COMPLEX(KIND=*kind_type***)** ... :: *list of variable names*
	LOGICAL(KIND=*kind_type***)** ... :: *list of variable names*
	CHARACTER(LEN=*length***,KIND=***kind_type***)** ... :: **&** *list of variable names*
	CHARACTER(KIND=*kind_type***,LEN=***length***)** ... :: **&** *list of variable names*
Literal constant definitions	(*real_part,imaginary_part*)
	numeric_literal_kind_type
	logical_literal_kind_type
	kind_type_character_literal

PROGRAMMING EXERCISES

14.1   Find out how many kinds of integers your Fortran 90 processor supports. Then write a program which calculates factorials of integers from 1 upwards until the program fails due to integer overflow when the calculation of the next factorial would result in a larger value than the maximum integer value of the kind being used. Repeat this program using each of the available kinds of integers. (Note that Section 11.5 contains two recursive procedures for calculating factorials, one a subroutine and one a function.)

Now modify your program so that it first requests a maximum range for integers and then uses integers of a kind which will allow integers to represent numbers of this size. The program should then request a maximum value of *n* for which it will calculate *n*! before starting to produce a list as before.

Use the results of the first program to select several pairs of ranges and maximum factorials, and check that the program now runs without failing.

14.2   Repeat Exercise 14.1 using real variables instead of integers. What does this tell you?

*14.3   Write a program which calculates $1/n!$ for real values of *n* increasing in steps of 1.0, starting from 1.0 and continuing until the calculated result is not distinguishable from zero. Run this program using default **real** kind, and then run it again using each available **real** kind in turn.

What does this exercise tell you?

14.4   If your processor supports more than one kind of character variable write a program which prints out a table of decimal values and their character representations for each kind of character. For example, if one kind is ASCII (or ISO 646) then part of the table for that kind might read as follows (see Appendix D):

	0	1	2	3	4	5	6	7	8	9
.	.	.	.	.	.	.	.	.	.	.
.	.	.	.	.	.	.	.	.	.	.
.	.	.	.	.	.	.	.	.	.	.
60	<	=	>	?	@	A	B	C	D	E
70	F	G	H	I	J	K	L	M	N	O
80	P	Q	R	S	T	U	V	W	X	Y
90	Z	[	\	]	^	_	'	a	b	c
.	.	.	.	.	.	.	.	.	.	.
.	.	.	.	.	.	.	.	.	.	.
.	.	.	.	.	.	.	.	.	.	.

14.5   If your processor supports more than one different kind of character, experiment by writing a program that can read a file of data consisting of a sequence of words. Sort this data into increasing order and print the sorted data. Your program should be designed so that it can be readily changed to use different kinds of characters. Modify your program for a different kind of character and execute it again. You will have to create one data file for each kind of character.

14.6   In Section 14.4 we discussed the importance of the mapping between kind type parameters for real variables and the precision used in the hardware of the computer you are using; understanding this relationship will prevent inappropriate precision requests. Write a program to print out a table of the number of decimal digits specified and the actual decimal precision given by your machine. The decimal precision should range from 1 to 30.

*14.7   Write a program which reads the values of two complex numbers w and z from the keyboard as two pairs of real numbers, and calculates the following values:

$$w + z$$
$$\bar{z}$$
$$\bar{w}$$
$$z^2$$
$$z\bar{z}$$

where $\bar{z}$ is the complex conjugate of z. (If $z = x + jy$, then $\bar{z} = x - jy$)
Test your program with several sets of data, including the following:

(a) $w = 2 + 1j$, $z = 4 + 3j$
(b) $w = 8 + 3j$, $z = 5 + 2j$

14.8   The polar form of the complex number z ($= x + jy$) is written as (r, θ), where $r = |z|$ (the absolute value of z, which is equal to $\sqrt{x^2 + y^2}$ and $\theta = \tan^{-1}(y/x)$.
Write a subroutine to convert a complex number to its polar form.

If $z = 1 + j$ and $w = 1 + 3j$, write a program which uses your subroutine to print the values of the following expressions in polar form, with θ given in degrees:

z

w

$z \times w$

z/w

$z + w$

$z - w$

$2 \times z$

z^2

$\sqrt{z}$

14.9   The roots of the quadratic equation

$$az^2 + bz + c = 0$$

are given by the formula

$$z = \frac{-b \pm \sqrt{b^2 - 4ac}}{2a}$$

Allowing for the fact that the expression $b^2 - 4ac$ may be negative (by using **COMPLEX** variables), write a program that calculates the roots of such an equation, and use it to find the roots of the following equations:

$z^2 - 1 = 0$
$z^2 + 1 = 0$
$z^2 - 3z + 4 = 0$
$z^2 - 3z - 4 = 0$

14.10   Write a program that calculates the roots of $ax^2 + bx + c = 0$, where a, b, c are complex numbers. Try your program in the case where $a = 1$, $b = -6.000\,01 - 7.999\,99j$, $c = -6.999\,93 + 24.000\,01j$. Run it with the precision first set to 6 and then to 14 decimal digits. The exact answers are $3 + 4j$ and $3.000\,01 + 3.999\,99j$.

   Unless you have used a sophisticated algorithm, or have a 64-bit machine, you will probably not get very accurate answers when the precision is 6.

Additional input/output and file handling facilities

15

Input and output of information is both the most important part of any computing process, because it is the computer's only means of communicating with the outside world, and one of the most awkward, because the mechanical aspects of the interaction involve many compromises and inelegant activities.

In earlier chapters we have met the most useful features of Fortran's input and output facilities, but there is a great deal more which, although less widely used, is of very great importance in particular classes of work. This chapter first discusses the many remaining edit descriptors and input/output specifiers which complete the forms of input and output that have already been introduced, before moving on to introduce four additional categories of input and output – two of which (non-advancing and NAMELIST input/output) did not exist in FORTRAN 77.

15.1 More control over external files

In Chapter 9 we introduced the concept of external files, and described how the **OPEN** statement was used to *connect* a file with a unit number, which could then be used in **READ** and **WRITE** statements to cause input or output to take place using that file. Although the specifiers described in Chapter 9 for use with the **OPEN** statement are sufficient for most purposes, there are several additional specifiers, as shown in Figure 15.1, which can be used to exercise a finer degree of control when required. The first three of these are only applicable to files opened for formatted input or output and affect the way that certain aspects of the formatting are processed.

The first specifier is only applicable to formatted input, and allows blank characters in a numeric field to be treated as zeros instead of as blanks. It takes the form

BLANK = *blank_mode*

where *blank_mode* is a character expression which, after the removal of any trailing blanks, is either **NULL** or **ZERO**. If it is **NULL**, or if there is no **BLANK** specifier present in the **OPEN** statement, then any blank characters in a numeric field are ignored; if it is **ZERO** then any blank characters in a numeric field are treated as zeros.

Thus, if a program contains the following statements

```
OPEN (UNIT=9,FILE=input_file,BLANK="ZERO",IOSTAT=open_stat)
READ (UNIT=9,FMT='(2I6)',IOSTAT=read_stat) int1,int2
```

and the record that is read is as follows, where ♦ represents a blank character

♦♦12♦♦♦♦34♦♦

then, after the record has been read, int1 will have the value 1200 and int2 will have the value 3400, since the trailing blanks in each field would have been treated as zeros. (Whether the leading blanks are treated as zeros or blanks does not, of course, make any difference.)

On the other hand, if the **OPEN** statement had taken the form

```
OPEN (UNIT=9,FILE=input_file,BLANK="NULL",IOSTAT=open_stat)
```

or

```
OPEN (UNIT=9,FILE=input_file,IOSTAT=open_stat)
```

then int1 would have taken the value 12 and int2 would have taken the value 24.

BLANK = *blank_mode*
PAD = *padding_mode*
DELIM = *delimitor_character*
RECL = *record_length*
ACCESS = *access_type*

Figure 15.1 Some more specifiers for use with OPEN.

Note, incidentally, that a numeric field that is all blanks will always be interpreted as zero, regardless of the setting of the BLANK specifier.

The BLANK specifier establishes the interpretation of blanks in numeric fields for all input statements on that file; as we shall see in the next section, it is also possible to specify the interpretation of blanks on a record-by-record basis by use of a BN or BZ edit descriptor.

The PAD specifier is also concerned with formatted input only and specifies whether the processor is to supply any necessary trailing blanks for a record that does not contain as many characters as specified by the format. It takes the form

PAD = *padding_mode*

where *padding_mode* is a character expression which, after the removal of any trailing blanks, is either YES or NO. If it is YES, or if the PAD specifier is omitted, then the processor will supply as many additional blank characters as are required to match the length of the record specified in the format. If it is NO then the length of the record must be at least as long as that specified by the format.

Thus, if a program contains the following statements:

```
OPEN (UNIT=9,FILE=input_file,PAD="YES",IOSTAT=open_stat)
READ (UNIT=9,FMT='(2I6)',IOSTAT=read_stat) int1,int2
```

and the record that is read is as follows

12♦♦♦♦34

then, after the record has been read, int1 will have the value 12 and int2 will have the value 34, since the record will first have been padded with four additional trailing blanks, and then the blanks in each field will have been ignored.

If the OPEN statement omitted any PAD specifier, then the effect would have been the same. However, if the OPEN statement were changed to read

```
OPEN (UNIT=9,FILE=input_file,PAD="NO",IOSTAT=open_stat)
```

then the READ statement would have given rise to an error, because the length of the input record was only eight characters, but the format specified twelve.

When reading from the keyboard, or from a file which had been created from the keyboard, the **PAD** specifier would not normally ever be used, therefore, as records created in this way will not normally contain additional blanks after the last meaningful character. On the other hand, if the file has been written by another program, and the exact length of the records is known, the use of **PAD="NO"** provides an additional check that data has been read correctly.

Note that the character used for a padding character is not defined for non-default character sets.

The third specifier is only for use with formatted output, and takes the form

DELIM = *delimiter_character*

where *delimiter_character* is a character expression which, after the removal of any trailing blanks, is one of **APOSTROPHE**, **QUOTE** or **NONE**, and is used to specify what character, if any, should be used to delimit character values which are output using list-directed formatting or namelist formatting (see Section 15.7).

If it is **NONE**, or if the **DELIM** specifier is omitted, then the character value is output without any delimiting characters. If it is **APOSTROPHE** then the character value is delimited by apostrophes, and any apostrophes contained within the string are doubled. If it is **QUOTE** then the character value is delimited by quotation marks, and any quotation marks contained within the string are doubled. Thus, if a program contains the following lines:

```
OPEN (UNIT=8,FILE=output_file,DELIM="NONE",IOSTAT=open_stat)
WRITE (UNIT=8,FMT=*,IOSTAT=write_stat) "David's Score"
```

the following will be printed

```
David's Score
```

which is the same as would be printed if no **DELIM** specifier were included in the **OPEN** statement. If the **DELIM** specifier is changed to **DELIM="QUOTE"** then the output will be

```
"David's Score"
```

while if it is changed to **DELIM="APOSTROPHE"** then the output will be

```
'David''s Score'
```

If the output is destined for the printer then no **DELIM** specifier will normally be required. However, if the output is being sent to a file which will subsequently be read by another program, or even by the same one, using list-directed or namelist formatting, then it may be essential to delimit any character strings in this way.

The next specifier, **RECL**, behaves slightly differently depending upon whether the file is connected for sequential or direct access. We shall discuss direct access files in Section 15.4 and, therefore, will only consider its use in a sequential statement for the present. It takes the form

RECL = *record_length*

where *record_length* is an integer expression which defines the *maximum* length that the records in the file may have. If the file is a formatted file the length is expressed in characters; if it is an unformatted file then the length is expressed in processor-defined units. In general, this specifier is not required for sequential files, and its main use in this regard is to limit the size of records in a file which will be transferred to another processor which restricts the size of records in files.

The remaining specifier that may be used with the **OPEN** statement is the **ACCESS** specifier; this will be discussed in Section 15.4.

Up to this point we have assumed that once a file has been opened it will remain open for the remainder of the execution of the program. This is frequently what is required, but there are occasions when it is required to disconnect a file from the program before the end of execution, or when it is required to specify that some specific action is to take place when such disconnection does take place. A file which has been connected to a program by means of an **OPEN** statement can, therefore, be disconnected by means of a **CLOSE** statement, which takes the form

CLOSE (*close_specifier_list*)

where the possible specifiers are as shown in Figure 15.2.

The **UNIT** and **IOSTAT** specifiers take the usual form, while the **STATUS** specifier may be used to determine what is to happen to the file when it has been disconnected from the program. It takes the form

STATUS = *file_status*

where *file_status* is a character expression which, after the removal of any trailing blanks, is either **KEEP** or **DELETE**. If it is **KEEP** then the file will continue to exist after it has been disconnected from the program; if it is **DELETE** then the file will cease to exist after it has been disconnected. Note that, as was emphasized in

---

```
UNIT = unit_number
STATUS = file_status
IOSTAT = ios
```

Figure 15.2 Specifiers for use with **CLOSE**.

Section 9.3, this does not *necessarily* mean that it is physically deleted, merely that it is no longer accessible to the program; for example, if the file is a magnetic tape it may simply be removed from the index of tapes available.

If a file has been opened with status **SCRATCH** then it will automatically be deleted when it is disconnected from the program, and it is not allowed to specify a close status of **KEEP**!

Finally, we mention two further specifiers which can be used with the various input and output statements that use a list of specifiers. The first of these can be used with the **OPEN, READ, WRITE, ENDFILE, BACKSPACE, REWIND, CLOSE** and **INQUIRE** (see Section 15.6) statements, and takes the form

    ERR = *label*

It causes a transfer of control to the statement labelled *label* if an error occurs. Its use is not recommended because the use of the **IOSTAT** specifier gives greater control, since it can provide a processor-specified integer to indicate the cause of the error, and, more importantly, enables the program to be written in a better style than is possible with the uncontrolled transfers of control to labelled statements elsewhere in the program.

The second specifier is similar, but can be used only with a **READ** statement. It takes the form

    END = *label*

and causes a transfer of control to the statement labelled *label* if an endfile record is encountered during the reading of the file. Its use is not recommended for the same reasons as given for not using the **ERR** specifier.

The **ERR** and **END** specifiers will frequently be encountered in older programs, but we do not recommend their use in any new programs.

15.2 Additional edit descriptors for formatted input and output

In Chapter 8 we introduced the principles of formats and edit descriptors, and described those edit descriptors which are most generally used for formatted input and output. However, there are a number of further edit descriptors (Figure 15.3) which can be extremely useful in certain situations, and we shall briefly describe these before moving on to some new features of Fortran's input and output capabilities.

The first group of these are extensions to the edit descriptors that we have already met for numeric editing, together with one new numeric edit descriptor.

Iw.m is an extended form of the **I** edit descriptor which only affects the output of integers; if used for input it is treated as though it were Iw. On output it specifies the minimum number of digits which are to be printed including, if necessary, one or more leading zeros. The value of m must not be greater than w, while if it is zero and the value of the integer is also zero only blanks are output. Figure 15.4 gives an example of its use.

As well as the **F** and **E** edit descriptors there are a number of other ways of inputting and outputting real numbers which provide slight variations on those methods.

Descriptor	Meaning
I*w*.*m*	Output integer with at least *m* digits
E*w*.*d* E*e* EN*w*.*d* EN*w*.*d* E*e* ES*w*.*d* ES*w*.*d* E*e* D*w*.*d*	Input or output real or double-precision values (see text for details)
B*w*	Input or output a binary number
B*w*.*m*	Output a binary number with at least *m* binary digits
O*w*	Input or output an octal number
O*w*.*m*	Output an octal number with at least *m* octal digits
Z*w*	Input or output a hexadecimal number
Z*w*.*m*	Output a hexadecimal number with at least *m* hexadecimal digits
G*w*.*d* G*w*.*d* E*e*	Generalized editing (see text for details)
:	Terminate format if there are no more list items
SP	Print + signs before positive numbers
SS	Do not print + signs before positive numbers
S	Processor decides whether to print + signs before positive numbers
BN	Ignore blanks in numeric input fields
BZ	Treat blanks in numeric input fields as zeros

Figure 15.3 More edit descriptors for input and output.

```
PROGRAM extended_integer_editing
   IMPLICIT NONE
   INTEGER i
   DO i=-10,10,5
      PRINT '(I5,I5.2,I5.0)',i,i,i
   END DO
END PROGRAM extended_integer_editing
```

Output

```
-10  -10  -10
 -5  -05   -5
  0   00
  5   05    5
 10   10   10
```

Figure 15.4 An example of I*w*.*m* editing.

For *input*, all of the following edit descriptors have the identical effect:

F*w*.*d*
E*w*.*d*
EN*w*.*d*
ES*w*.*d*
D*w*.*d*
E*w*.*d*E*e*
EN*w*.*d*E*e*
ES*w*.*d*E*e*

where *e* may have any value (and is ignored).

For output, however, there are significant differences. As we have already seen, F*w*.*d* will output a real number rounded to *d* decimal places with an external field of width *w*; E*w*.*d*, on the other hand, will output such a number in an external field of width *w* using an exponential format consisting of a decimal fraction of *d* digits in the range 0.1 to 0.9999..., followed by a four-character exponent.

The **EN** and **ES** edit descriptors are variants of the **E** edit descriptors which conform with normal practice in the engineering and scientific fields, respectively.

EN*w*.*d* produces an output field of a similar form to that produced by E*w*.*d*, but with the constraint that the exponent is divisible by three and that the absolute value of the mantissa lies in the range 1 to 999, except when the value being output is zero.

ES*w*.*d* also produces an output field of a similar form to that produced by E*w*.*d*, but in this case with the constraint that the absolute value of the mantissa lies in the range 1 to 9, except when the value being output is zero.

Figure 15.5 shows the effect of these three variants of the **E** edit descriptor.

```
PROGRAM e_en_and_es_editing
  IMPLICIT NONE
  REAL, DIMENSION(4) :: x=(/1.234,-0.5,0.00678,98765.4/)
  PRINT '(E14.3/EN14.3/ES14.3)',x,x,x
END PROGRAM e_en_and_es_editing
```

Output

```
    0.123E+01    -0.500E+00    0.678E-02     0.988E+05
    1.234E+00  -500.000E-03    6.780E-03    98.765E+03
    1.234E+00    -5.000E-01    6.780E-03     9.877E+04
```

Figure 15.5 The differences between **E**, **EN** and **ES** edit descriptors for output.

If $Ew.d$, $ENw.d$ or $ESw.d$ is followed by Ee then the exponent will consist of e digits. Thus, the number 0.000 023 143 6 will be output as shown below with various edit descriptors:

```
E12.5      0.23144E-04
E12.5E3    0.23144E-004
E12.5E1    0.23144E-4
```

The D edit descriptor ($Dw.d$) is identical to the $Ew.d$ descriptor for input, and for output is identical except that the letter E in the formatted output may be replaced by a letter D, but does not have to be. It exists mainly for compatibility with earlier versions of Fortran, and cannot be used with an Ee suffix. Its use is not recommended in new programs.

The next group of edit descriptors are used for the input or output of integers in the form of binary, octal or hexadecimal numbers. They operate in exactly the same way as the corresponding Iw and $Iw.m$ edit descriptors, except that

- For Bw and $Bw.m$ a number being input must only use the digits 0 and 1 and will be interpreted as a binary number, while on output the integer value being output will be output in its binary representation.

- For Ow and $Ow.m$ a number being input must only use the digits 0–7 and will be interpreted as an octal number (a number to base 8), while on output the integer value being output will be output in its octal representation.

- For Zw and $Zw.m$ a number being input may use the digits 0–9, together with the letters A–F, to represent a hexadecimal number (a number to base 16), while on output the integer value being output will be output in its hexadecimal representation.

Fortran also provides a **generalized edit descriptor** which can be used to input or output values of any intrinsic type.

When used with an integer, logical or character input/output list item both $Gw.d$ and $Gw.dEe$ behave as though the corresponding edit descriptor was Iw, Lw or Aw, respectively, with the values of d and e, if present, being ignored.

When used with real or complex input/output items, however, the situation is slightly more complicated. On input it is the same as $Fw.d$, but on output it uses either the $Fw.d$, $Ew.d$ or $Ew.dEe$ formats depending upon the magnitude of the number being output.

If the magnitude (absolute value) of the number to be output lies between 0.1 and 10^d (that is, the exponent in E format would lie between 0 and d inclusive) then F formatting is used; otherwise E formatting takes place. If F formatting is used the field width is reduced by four for $Gw.d$ and by $e + 2$ for $Gw.dEe$, and the number is followed by four spaces or $e + 2$ spaces, respectively; the number of

```
PROGRAM e_f_and_g_editing
   IMPLICIT NONE
   REAL :: x=123456.0
   INTEGER :: i
   DO i=1,7
      PRINT '(F12.5,3X,E12.5,3X,G12.5)',x,x,x,-x,-x,-x
      x = x/100.0
   END DO
END PROGRAM e_f_and_g_editing
```

Output

```
  123456.00000      0.12346E+06      0.12346E+06
 ************      -0.12346E+06     -0.12346E+06
    1234.56000      0.12346E+04      1234.56
   -1234.56000     -0.12346E+04     -1234.56
      12.34560      0.12346E+02      12.3456
     -12.34560     -0.12346E+02     -12.3456
       0.12346      0.12346E+00      0.12345
      -0.12346     -0.12346E+00     -0.12346
       0.00123      0.12346E-02      0.12346E-02
      -0.00123     -0.12346E-02     -0.12346E-02
       0.00001      0.12346E-04      0.12346E-04
      -0.00001     -0.12346E-04     -0.12346E-04
       0.00000      0.12346E-06      0.12346E-06
      -0.00000     -0.12346E-06     -0.12346E-06
```

Figure 15.6   A comparison of F, E and G editing.

decimal digits in the mantissa (*d*) is then modified according to a formula which ensures that the maximum degree of accuracy, consistent with the revised field width, is maintained. In all cases the number is printed with *d* significant digits. Figure 15.6 shows a comparison of F, E and G editing, and the advantage of the G format when a wide range of numbers is possible is readily apparent. Notice in particular that −123 456.0 has proved to be too large for the F format (and is therefore output as an equivalent number of asterisks), while 0.000 012 345 6 has lost most semblance of accuracy in the F format and 0.000 000 123 456 has been printed as zero.

The effect of the numeric edit descriptors on the input and output of real values can be altered by use of a scale factor. This is applied by means of a P edit descriptor (*k*P), which causes a scale factor of *k* to be applied to all numeric edit descriptors following it in a format. Its effect can be somewhat confusing and its use is not, therefore, recommended. It is briefly discussed in Appendix E, together with other obsolete or little-used features of Fortran 90.

The remaining additional edit descriptors are of three types. The first of these is the : edit descriptor, which is used to terminate a format if there are no more list items. This is not usually necessary, as the format will terminate in any case at the next edit descriptor which requires a list item. In an output format,

```
PROGRAM colon_editing
   IMPLICIT NONE
   REAL :: a=3.5,b=7.2
   PRINT 201,a,b,a+b
   PRINT 202,a,b,a+b
   201 FORMAT ("1","With no colon:"/               &
               "The sum of ",F5.2," and ",F5.2," is ", &
               F6.2/" Their product is ",F8.2)
   202 FORMAT ("0","With a colon:"/                &
               "The sum of ",F5.2," and ",F5.2," is ", &
               F6.2:/" Their product is ",F8.2)
END PROGRAM colon_editing
```

Output

```
With no colon:
The sum of  3.50 and  7.20 is  10.70
Their product is

With a colon:
The sum of  3.50 and  7.20 is  10.70
```

Figure 15.7   An example of the effect of using a : edit descriptor for output.

however, this could cause some unnecessary printing to occur. Figure 15.7 shows the effect of the : edit descriptor on output.

The second type controls the display of plus signs during the output of numbers by any of the numeric edit descriptors. The **SP** edit descriptor affects any numbers output by any following edit descriptors in this format, and causes a $+$ sign to be placed before positive numbers (just as a $-$ sign is placed before negative ones). An **SS** edit descriptor has the opposite effect, and prevents a $+$ sign being placed before positive numbers. Finally, an **S** edit descriptor restores the normal (default) situation which, for most systems, will be to omit $+$ signs.

The final two edit descriptors, **BN** and **BZ** are used to control the interpretation of blanks in numeric input fields. This is normally best achieved by use of the **BLANK** specifier in an **OPEN** statement, but these two edit descriptors are described, for reference, in Appendix E, together with other obsolete and little-used features of Fortran 90.

15.3 Non-advancing input and output

One of the fundamental principles of input and output in FORTRAN 77 was that every **READ**, **WRITE** or **PRINT** statement begins a new record. This is the default behaviour in Fortran 90 as well, but there are situations when it would be convenient to be able to read part of a record, and read the rest later, or to write part of a record, and write some more later.

Fortran 90 provides for this requirement by means of **non-advancing input and output**.

Non-advancing input/output can only take place on a formatted file that is connected to an input or output unit for sequential access, and which is using an explicit format (that is, it is not using list-directed or namelist formatting). With non-advancing input/output it is possible to:

- read or write a record by a sequence of statements, each statement accessing a portion of the record instead of one statement processing the complete record;
- be informed of the length (number of characters read) of a formatted sequential input record; and
- be notified when an end-of-record has been encountered during the processing of a **READ** statement.

Non-advancing input or output is specified by the inclusion of an **ADVANCE** specifier in a **READ** or **WRITE** statement. This takes the form

ADVANCE = *advance_mode*

where *advance_mode* is a character expression which, after the removal of any trailing blanks, is either **YES** or **NO**.

If it is **YES**, or if the **ADVANCE** specifier is omitted, then input or output, as appropriate, is carried out in the normal, advancing, mode, in which the file is positioned after the end of the last record read or written at the completion of the statement.

However, if it is **NO** then the input or output is carried out in non-advancing mode.

In the case of a non-advancing **READ** statement there are three possibilities:

- If the **READ** statement did not attempt to read beyond the end of the record, and there were no errors and no end-of-file condition set, then the file position is unchanged, and the next **READ** statement will start to read the same record, starting immediately after the last character read.
- If the **READ** statement did attempt to read beyond the end of the record then an end-of record condition will be set, and can be tested for by use of the **IOSTAT** specifier. The file will be positioned immediately after the end of the record just read.

  Note that an end-of-record condition is not an error, and so if it is not detected by means of an **IOSTAT** or **EOR** specifier then the program will continue without any indication that some of the data items read may have been null. However, it is worth noting that if the **PAD** specifier has been set to **NO** then an error will occur in this situation, since the number of characters read must exactly match or exceed that required by the format.

- If there was an error, or if an end-of-file condition was set, then the file will be positioned immediately after the end of the record just read.

It is frequently useful, when carrying out non-advancing input, to be able to determine how many characters have been read. This is achieved by use of the **SIZE** specifier, which takes the form

SIZE = *character_count*

where *character_count* is an integer variable. At the conclusion of the non-advancing **READ** statement the variable *character_count* becomes defined with the number of characters read, excluding any inserted as padding characters.

Thus, the statement

```
READ (UNIT=input,FMT=123,ADVANCE="NO",SIZE=count,  &
      IOSTAT=read_status) var1,var2,var3
```

will carry out non-advancing input from the file connected to unit **input** using the format defined by the statement labelled 123, and will store the number of characters read in the integer variable **count**. The integer variable **read_status** will be set to an appropriate value to indicate the success, or otherwise, of the reading operation.

Note that there is also another specifier for taking action when an end-of-record condition is set, which takes the form

EOR = *label*

and causes a transfer of control to the statement labelled *label* if an end-of-record is set up during the reading of the file. Its use is not recommended for the same reasons as given for not using the **END** and **ERR** specifiers in Section 15.1.

Non-advancing output is more straightforward than non-advancing input, and there are only two possibilities:

- If there were no errors then the file position is unchanged, and the next **WRITE** statement will write to the same record, starting immediately after the last character written.
- If there was an error then the file will be positioned immediately after the end of the record just written.

■ **EXAMPLE 15.1**

1 **Problem**

In Example 9.2 a set of data was read from a file, in which each record had the following format:

Columns 1–20   Name
Column   23   Sex = F if female
                        = M if male
Column   25   Job status = 1 if in full-time education
                                    = 2 if in full-time employment
                                    = 3 if in part-time employment
                                    = 4 if temporarily unemployed
                                    = 5 if not working or seeking a job

This was followed by one or more items depending upon the job status of the respondent:

Job status = 1   columns 28, 29   Age
              = 2   columns 28–31   Monthly salary
              = 3   columns 28–31   Monthly salary
                     columns 34–37   Other monthly income
              = 4   columns 28, 29   Age
                     columns 32–34   No. of months unemployed
              = 5   columns 28, 29   Age
                     column 31   Code
                                           = 1 if looking after children
                                           = 2 if looking after other relatives
                                           = 3 for any other reason

In Example 9.2 an input subprogram was written which would read up to a specified number of records and store the relevant details in suitable arrays for subsequent use by other subprograms. The problem of not knowing the format of the whole record until the first part had been read was dealt with by the crude method of only reading the first part of each record, and then backspacing the file and re-reading the rest in the correct format.

Rewrite the input procedure written in Example 9.2 to use non-advancing input, so that each record is only read once.

2 Analysis

The only change that needs to be made to the previous version is in the actual reading of the records. In this case the first three items will first be read using non-advancing input, and then the remaining one or two items, depending upon the code read as the third item. The data design will therefore be exactly as in the previous example, except that we shall place the processor-dependent codes for end-of-file and end-of-record in a module; the structure plan will, however, be altered slightly:

Structure plan

1 Request name of data file and open it on *unit*

2 Repeat up to *max_datasets* times
    2.1 Read first three items of next record
    2.2 If end of file then exit from loop
    2.3 If error then set *error_code* to −2 and exit from loop
    2.4 Select case on job status
       status is 1
       2.4.1 Read age
       2.4.2 Set salary, other income, months unemployed and code
               to unused
       status is 2
       2.4.3 Read salary
       2.4.4 Set age, other income, months unemployed and code to
               unused
       status is 3
       2.4.5 Read salary and other income
       2.4.6 Set age, months unemployed and code to unused
       status is 4
       2.4.7 Read age and months unemployed
       2.4.8 Set salary, other income and code to unused
       status is 5
       2.4.9 Read age and code
       2.4.10 Set salary, other income and months unemployed to
               unused
    2.5 Copy local record to array

3 If no end of file read set *error_code* to −3

4 Return number of data sets read

3 Solution

```
MODULE error_codes
   IMPLICIT NONE

   ! This module contains processor-dependent error codes

   INTEGER, PARAMETER :: end_of_record = -2, end_file = -1

END MODULE error_codes

MODULE survey_details
   IMPLICIT NONE

   ! This module contains a type definition and constants
   ! for use with the input and processing of survey data
```

```
! Type definition for survey response
TYPE survey_info
   CHARACTER(LEN=20) :: name
   CHARACTER :: sex
   INTEGER :: job_status,age,months_jobless,at_home_code
   REAL :: salary,other_income
END TYPE survey_info

! Various codes
CHARACTER, PARAMETER :: female="F", male="M"   ! Sex
INTEGER, PARAMETER ::                       &
        ft_ed=1,ft_job=2,pt_job=3,          &! Job status
        no_job=4,at_home=5,                 &! ----------
        ch_minder=1,rel_minder=2,other=3,   &! At home code
        unused=-1                            ! Unused code

END MODULE survey_details

SUBROUTINE input(unit,max_datasets,survey_data,num_datasets, &
               error_code)
   USE error_codes
   USE survey_details
   IMPLICIT NONE

   ! This subroutine reads up to max_datasets records prepared
   ! as follows, returning the number read in num_datasets

   ! Columns 1-20   Name
   !           23   Sex (M or F)
   !           25   Job status (1-5)
   !        28,29   Age - for status 1, 4 or 5
   !        28-31   Monthly salary - for status 2 and 3
   !        32-34   Other monthly income - for status 3
   !        32-34   Months unemployed - for status 4
   !           31   Special code (1-3) - for status 5

   ! Arguments
   INTEGER, INTENT(IN) :: unit,max_datasets
   INTEGER, INTENT(OUT) :: num_datasets,error_code
   TYPE(survey_info), DIMENSION(:), INTENT(OUT) :: survey_data

   ! Local variables
   CHARACTER(LEN=30) :: data_file
   CHARACTER(LEN=20) :: name
   CHARACTER :: sex
   INTEGER :: i,ios,status,age,months,code
   REAL :: salary,income

   ! Ask for name of data file
   ! A maximum of three attempts will be allowed to open the file
   DO i=1,3
      PRINT *,"Type name of data file"
      READ '(A)',data_file
      ! Open file at beginning
      OPEN (UNIT=unit,FILE=data_file,POSITION="REWIND",      &
            IOSTAT=ios)
```

```
      IF (ios==0) EXIT
      ! Error when opening file - try again
      PRINT *,"Unable to open file - please try again"
END DO

! If open was unsuccessful after 3 attempts return error=-1
IF (ios/=0) THEN
   error_code = -1
   RETURN
END IF

! Successful file opening
error_code = 0

! Loop to read data
DO i=1,max_datasets
   ! Read first part of the next set of data
   READ (UNIT=unit,FMT='(A20,2X,A1,1X,I1)',ADVANCE="NO",  &
         IOSTAT=ios)name,sex,status
   ! Check for errors and end of file
   SELECT CASE (ios)
   CASE (end_file)            ! End of file - no more data
      EXIT

   CASE (1:)                  ! Error during reading
      error_code = -2
      EXIT
   END SELECT

   ! Read more data according to status code
   SELECT CASE (status)

   CASE (ft_ed)
      ! Read age and set other items to unused code
      READ (UNIT=unit,FMT='(2X,I2)')age
      months = unused
      salary = unused
      income = unused
      code = unused

   CASE (ft_job)
      ! Read salary details and set other items to unused
      READ (UNIT=unit,FMT='(2X,F4.0)')salary
      age = unused
      income = unused
      months = unused
      code = unused

   CASE (pt_job)
      ! Read income details and set other items to unused
      READ (UNIT=unit,FMT='(2X,F4.0,2X,F4.0)')salary,income
      age = unused
      months = unused
      code = unused
```

```
       CASE (no_job)
         ! Read age and months unemployed
         ! and set other items to unused
         READ (UNIT=unit,FMT='(2X,I2,2X,I3)')age,months
         salary = unused
         income = unused
         code = unused

       CASE (at_home)
          ! Read age and code, and set other items to unused
          READ (UNIT=unit,FMT='(2X,I2,1X,I1)')age,code
          salary = unused
          income = unused
          months = unused

     END SELECT

       ! Record is now fully input, so copy to main data array
       survey_data(i) = survey_info (name,sex,status,age, &
                                     months,code,salary,income)

   END DO

   ! All data input - check if end of file was read
   IF (i > max_datasets) error_code = -3

   ! Save number of records read and return
   num_datasets = i-1

 END SUBROUTINE input
```

Note that non-advancing input is not specified when reading the record for the second time, as this will always be the last time that a record is read, and it is important that the file is positioned after the end of the record so that the next record will be read properly.

Notice also that, as in the previous version, the checks made that the reading of data from the data file has been error-free have only been carried out the first time that a record is read. This will deal with the problem of detecting the end-of-file which indicates that there is no more data, but there is always a theoretical possibility of some hardware problem causing an error during reading, and this should be checked for in all cases in a 'production' program.

SELF-TEST EXERCISES 15.1

1   When should you use a **BLANK** specifier, and when should you use a **BN** or **BZ** edit descriptor?

2 How can a file which has been connected to a peripheral unit by an **OPEN** statement be disconnected before the end of the program? Give two reasons why this action might be required.

3 What will be printed by the following program?

```
PROGRAM test_15_1_3
   IMPLICIT NONE
   INTEGER, DIMENSION(0:6) :: powers_of_two
   INTEGER :: i, j
   powers_of_two = (/ 2**i,i=0,6 /)
   DO i=0,6
       PRINT '(I10,I10.6,B10.6,O10.6,Z10.6,G10.6)',   &
               (powers_of_two(i), j=1,6)
   END DO
END PROGRAM test_15_1_3
```

4 What will be printed by the following program?

```
PROGRAM test_15_1_4
   IMPLICIT NONE
   REAL :: x=8E7
   INTEGER :: i
   DO i=1,5
       PRINT '(F12.3,E12.3,EN12.3,ES12.3,G12.3)', x,x,x,x,x
       x = x/5000.0
   END DO
END PROGRAM test_15_1_4
```

5 What is the difference between advancing and non-advancing input? When should you use each type?

6 What is the difference between advancing and non-advancing output? When should you use each type?

15.4 Direct access files

In Chapter 9 we defined an external file as a sequence of records, either formatted or unformatted, which exists outside the program on some external medium. We also indicated that such a file could be stored either in a sequential manner, in which records are written and read in sequence, or in a random manner, in which records are written and read in any specified order.

We learned, in Chapter 9, how to read and write sequential files and, in most cases, this is perfectly satisfactory. However, there are a considerable number of situations in which it is more convenient to write and/or read records in a non-sequential fashion, for example when interrogating a database. Fortran, therefore, allows a file to be written and read in a **direct access** manner as well as in a sequential manner.

To do this, however, the file must first be connected to the program for direct access, rather than the (default) sequential access mode that we have used up to now. This is achieved by use of the **ACCESS** specifier in the **OPEN** statement for the file; this takes the form

ACCESS = *access_type*

where *access_type* is a character expression which, after the removal of any trailing blanks, is either **SEQUENTIAL** or **DIRECT**. If it is **SEQUENTIAL**, or if the **ACCESS** specifier is omitted, then the file is connected for sequential access. If it is **DIRECT** then the file is connected for direct access.

If an **OPEN** statement contains an **ACCESS="DIRECT"** specifier then there must also be a **RECL** specifier, which, as we saw in Section 15.1, takes the form

RECL = *record_length*

When used with a direct access file this specifies that *all* the records in the file will have the same length, *record_length*, which is measured in characters if the file is formatted and in processor-defined units if it is an unformatted file. Since direct access files cannot normally be transferred to another type of computer there is normally no reason for converting the values being written to the file into their character representation, with the result that direct access files are, almost invariably, also unformatted files.

In order to write to, or read from, a direct access file it is necessary to define which record is to be written or read by use of a **REC** specifier in the **READ** or **WRITE** statement. This takes the form

REC = *record_number*

where *record_number* is an integer expression *with a positive value*, which specifies the **record number** of the record to be read or written. Thus the statement

WRITE (UNIT=7,REC=20) a,b,c,d

will write the values of **a**, **b**, **c** and **d** as an unformatted record to record 20 of the direct-access file connected to unit 7, and

READ (UNIT=7,REC=next_rec) w,x,y,z

will read the record from the same file whose record number is the value of the integer variable **next_rec**.

Note also that if a format used to write (or read) a formatted direct access file specifies more than one record, then each successive record will be given a number one greater than the previous one. Thus the statement

WRITE (UNIT=8,FMT=' (10F12.2)' ,REC=75) (array(i),i=1,100)

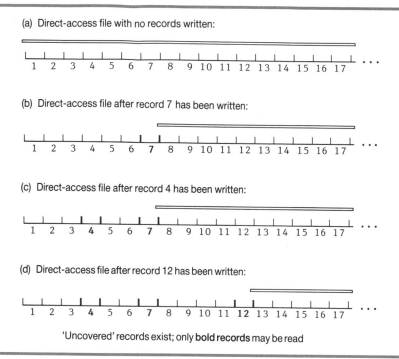

(a) Direct-access file with no records written:

(b) Direct-access file after record 7 has been written:

(c) Direct-access file after record 4 has been written:

(d) Direct-access file after record 12 has been written:

'Uncovered' records exist; only **bold records** may be read

Figure 15.8 A representation of a direct access file.

will cause ten records to be written, since the format specifies that each record contains ten real numbers; these records will be numbered from 75 to 84, inclusive.

If an input or output statement includes a **REC** specifier then it is a direct-access input or output statement; if it does not include a **REC** specifier then it is a sequential input or output statement. *Note, however, that direct-access input or output may not use list-directed formatting or namelist formatting (see Section 15.7), nor may it use non-advancing input or output.*

It is important to understand that, although the records in a file are numbered consecutively, starting at record 1, they may be written in any order. Once a record has been written it may never be deleted, but it may be overwritten. The effect of this can be visualized by imagining a file to consist of a very large number of potential, fixed-size, records available in the file, all of which are 'hidden' by a movable cover in a newly created file, as shown in Figure 15.8. Once record n has been written then it becomes available by sliding the cover, thus also making visible all those records that 'precede it' (that is, records 1 to $n - 1$) – although such a record cannot be read until some value has been written to it.

It may appear, at first sight, that the rule that requires every record in a direct access file to have the same length, namely that defined by the **RECL** specifier in the **OPEN** statement, may be somewhat restrictive. This is not the case, however, since the record will always be extended to the specified length if it would otherwise be too short; the specified record length can, therefore be considered as a maximum record length, and as long as there is no attempt to exceed this maximum there will be no problem.

Note that if an unformatted record would be too short then it will be extended with undefined values in order to make it the correct length. If a formatted record would be too short then it will be extended with trailing blanks.

■ EXAMPLE 15.2

1 Problem

The superintendent of a college chemistry department wishes to keep a record of all the chemicals in the department's store on a computer, so that each day the record of all material moved from the store to the laboratories can be used to update the quantities held in the store, and identify which items need to be re-ordered from the suppliers. In other words, the department wishes to develop a simple stock control system.

Define the structure of the master file used to store details of stocks held, and write a program which can be used to update this file with the daily stock movements. Ignore the problems associated with adding new chemicals to the master file and of deleting unused chemicals and assume that only the quantities will change.

2 Analysis

The major difficulty with any problem of this nature is that the updating information (the store's documents recording the issue of chemicals, in this case) will be in an arbitrary order, whereas the information in the master file which is to be updated will be stored in a predefined order – which will, by definition, be different from the 'random' order of the data. There are three, well-established, approaches to overcoming this incompatibility:

(1) (a)   The master data is stored in a sequential file and read into memory at the start of processing.

   (b)   All updating of the master file is then carried out in memory.

   (c)   At the completion of processing, the updated information is written to a new sequential file, ready for next time.

(2) (a)   The master data is stored in a sequential file.

   (b)   Before starting to update the master file, all the updating details are sorted into the same order as the records in the master file.

   (c)   The master file is then updated sequentially.

(3) (a) The data is stored in a direct access file.

(b) The master file is updated in the order of the input data.

Each of these approaches has its advantages and disadvantages. For example, if the master file is small then the much faster updating possible through carrying out the whole process in memory is the dominant factor; however, this approach will not work for large master files because of its memory requirements.

The second approach was the only approach in the days before the widespread availability of disk-drives, with their inherent random-access capability. For many years, almost all business and commercial data-processing programs spent a significant amount of their time sorting files into the correct order for the next operation, with the result that significant efforts were devoted to developing faster and more effective sorting algorithms for different types of sorting needs.

However, with the advent of large and economical random-access storage, in the form of magnetic and magneto-optical disks, the third approach is the preferred one, other than for small master files, when the first method may still be preferred. We shall, therefore, use a direct-access file to store the details of the stocks held of the various chemicals.

Each record in the file will contain the following fields:

Name of chemical (in its symbolic form, for example, H2SO4 for sulphuric acid, H_2SO_4)

Current stock level

Units (grams, litres, etc.)

Reorder level

Unit order quantity

Maximum stock

The program will update the current stock levels and then, when all input data has been processed, will compare the current stocks of every chemical with the reorder level and issue a request to order additional supplies of those below that level. These orders will be for multiples of the unit order quantity to bring the total stock to a level as close as possible *below* the maximum stock. A refinement would be to include the name and address of the supplier in the file and to print the orders, but that is not necessary for this example.

The only remaining problem is identifying which record in the master file contains the information relating to a particular chemical. Since records in a direct-access file are identified by their record number, running upwards from 1, it is clearly necessary to relate the name of the chemical to a record number. We shall adopt a simple, albeit inefficient, method of storing all the chemical symbols in an array and using the index of the name in the array as the record number. We shall, however, return to this in a subsequent refinement to the program. In order to simplify such a subsequent refinement, and in order to allow any extension to the program to identify easily which record relates to a particular chemical, we shall package this **look-up table** and a function which will use it to return the record number for a specified chemical in a module. We shall also keep the name of the master file and the unit to which it will be connected in this module, together with the length of each record in the file.

We can now proceed to the final design of the program.

Module file_control

Data design

Purpose	Type	Name
A Module entities		
Size of look-up table	INTEGER, PARAMETER	max_names
Length of names	INTEGER, PARAMETER	max_len
Look-up table of names	CHARACTER*max_len	chemical
Name of master file	CHARACTER*20	master_file_name
Master file unit	INTEGER, PARAMETER	master_file
Record length	INTEGER, PARAMETER	rec_len
B Procedure variables		
Dummy argument	CHARACTER*max_len	item
Procedure name	INTEGER	record_number
Loop variable	INTEGER	i

Structure plan

> **1** Repeat for *i* from 1 to *max_names*
>   **1.1** If *item* = *chemical(i)* exit from loop
> **2** If a match was made
>   **2.1** Return value of *i*
>   otherwise
>   **2.1** Return zero

Program stock_control

Data design

Purpose	Type	Name
Name of chemical	CHARACTER*max_len	name
Current stock level	REAL	current_stock
Units	CHARACTER*8	units
Reorder level	REAL	re_order
Unit order quantity	REAL	unit_order
Maximum stock	REAL	max_stock
Amount issued	REAL	amount
Loop variable	INTEGER	i
IOSTAT variable	INTEGER	ios
Record number	INTEGER	record

Structure plan

> **1** Repeat the following
>   **1.1** Read next update record (*name, amount*)
>   **1.2** Find *record_number* for this chemical
>   **1.3** If *record_number* > 0 then
>   **1.3.1** Read record *record_number*
>   **1.3.2** Update current stock level
>   **1.3.3** Write updated record back to master file
>   otherwise
>   **1.3.4** Exit from loop
> **2** Repeat for each record in the file
>   **2.1** Read the record
>   **2.2** If current stock level < reorder level then
>   **2.2.1** Calculate number of order units required
>   **2.2.2** Print order details

3 **Solution**

```
MODULE file_control
  IMPLICIT NONE
  PRIVATE
  PUBLIC :: max_names,max_len,record_number,rec_len,  &
            master_file_name,master_file


  ! This module contains the data and procedure required to
  ! find the record_number for a specified chemical

  INTEGER, PARAMETER :: max_names=200,max_len=20
  CHARACTER(LEN=max_len), DIMENSION(max_names) :: chemical=
    (/"HCl","H2SO4","CuSO3",         &! Full list of
                                     &! chemicals in the
                                     &! same order as in
     "FeSO3","NaCl"/)                &! the master file
  CHARACTER(LEN=20) :: master_file_name="Chemical_supplies"
  INTEGER, PARAMETER :: master_file=7


  ! Note that the calculation of the record length is processor
  ! dependent; the following assumes one unit per character
  ! and four units per real value
  INTEGER, PARAMETER :: char_store=1,real_store=4
  INTEGER, PARAMETER :: rec_len = char_store*(max_len+8) + &
                                  real_store*4


CONTAINS
```

```
INTEGER FUNCTION record_number(item)
   ! This function returns the index of item in the look-up
   ! table chemical (in the module)

   ! Dummy argument
   CHARACTER(LEN=max_len), INTENT(IN) :: item

   ! Local variable
   INTEGER :: i

   ! Search for item name in look-up table
   DO i=1,max_names
      IF (item==chemical(i)) EXIT
   END DO

   ! Check to see if a match was found
   IF (i>max_names) THEN
      ! No match made - return zero
      record_number = 0
   ELSE
      record_number = i
   END IF
END FUNCTION record_number
END MODULE file_control


PROGRAM stock_control
   USE file_control
   IMPLICIT NONE

   ! This program updates a stock control file of chemicals
   ! and produces a list of order requests

   ! Fields in the master file records
   CHARACTER(LEN=max_len) :: name
   REAL :: current_stock,re_order,unit_order,max_stock
   CHARACTER(LEN=8) :: units

   ! Other variables
   REAL :: amount,quantity
   INTEGER :: i,ios,record,num_units

   ! Open master file
   OPEN (UNIT=master_file, FILE=master_file_name,        &
         ACCESS="DIRECT, RECL=rec_len, IOSTAT=ios)
   IF (ios/=0) THEN
      ! Error during opening master file
      PRINT *,"Error during opening of master file"
      PRINT *,"Please check file and try again"
      STOP
   END IF
```

```
! Update master file
PRINT *,"Type stock issues as chemical followed by quantity"
PRINT *,"issued (negative) or received (positive)"
PRINT *,"To end data type the word UPDATE"
DO
    READ *,name,amount
    ! Get record number for this chemical
    record = record_number(name)


    ! Check if this was a valid name
    IF (record>0) THEN
       ! Update master file
       READ (UNIT=master_file,REC=record,IOSTAT=ios) name,  &
            current_stock,units,re_order,unit_stock,max_stock
       IF (ios/=0) THEN
          ! Error during reading - ignore this data
          PRINT *,"Error during reading this chemical's &
                  &record in the master file."
          PRINT *,"The record is unchanged"


       ELSE
          ! Update current stock and rewrite record
          current_stock = current_stock+amount
          WRITE (UNIT=master_file,REC=record,IOSTAT=ios)  &
                name,current_stock,units,re_order,           &
                unit_stock,max_stock
          IF (ios/=0) THEN
             ! Error during writing
             PRINT *,"Error during updating this chemical's &
                     &record in the master file."
             PRINT *,"The record may now be incorrect!"
          END IF
       END IF


    ELSE
       ! Invalid chemical name - check if end of data
       IF (name=="UPDATE") THEN
          EXIT
       ELSE
          ! Unknown chemical - print error message
          PRINT *,name," is not in the master file."
          PRINT *,"This line of data has been ignored!"
       END IF
    END IF
END DO


! All updating now carried out - search for chemicals
! in need of reordering
PRINT '(" ","The following items need reordering:"/  &
        "0","Chemical",T30,"Quantity"//)'
```

```
DO i=1,max_names
    READ (UNIT=master_file,REC=record,IOSTAT=ios) name,  &
        current_stock,units,re_order,unit_stock,max_stock
    IF (ios/=0) THEN
        ! Error during reading - ignore this data
        PRINT *,"Error during checking this chemical's &
            &record in the master file."
        PRINT *,"No check for reordering made!"

    ELSE
        ! Check if stocks are below reorder level
        IF (current_stock<re_order) THEN
            ! More stock required - calculate order quantity
            quantity = max_stock-current_stock
            num_units = INT(quantity/unit_order)
            quantity = num_units*unit_order
            PRINT '(" ",A,",",T30,F8.0,1X,A," (in units of ",  &
                I8,1X,A,")")',name,quantity,units,           &
                unit_order,units
        END IF
    END IF
END DO


END PROGRAM stock_control
```

Note that the program has checked, at each stage, that the master file has been read or written without error. *This is extremely important when updating a master file in this way.* However, there is always a danger that an execution error might leave the file in a damaged state, and so it is normally not recommended to update such a file directly in the way that we have done here. One approach is to make a **back-up** copy before updating commences, so that if an error should occur the original version of the file can still be used. An alternative is to have a cycle of, typically, three files and to update from one to the next in the cycle; this approach, which is conventionally referred to as the **grandfather–father–son** method, ensures that the previous *two* versions of the file are always available in case an error is detected during, or after, processing. We shall return to this topic in Section 15.6.

The other point that should be mentioned concerns the method of identifying the record number of the master file record associated with a specified chemical. Obviously a sequential search is not very efficient, particularly if there are a large number of records, and so we shall briefly examine an alternative approach.

This establishes the record number corresponding to a particular chemical by using a different form of table, which must be kept in a file because of the method used for inserting new names. It uses what is known as a **hashing technique** to create a special form of table, known as a **hash table**, in which the names are not stored sequentially but, instead, are used to derive an integer in a given range (the same as the extent of the table) which identifies the place in the table at which the name will be stored. If that place is already in use then a new index is calculated, possibly by as simple an algorithm as adding one, and tried.

The advantage of this approach is that it is only necessary to search a small number of elements of the table to find a name instead of carrying out a sequential search through the whole table until a match is found. A further advantage is that the identical method can be used for inserting new entries, since if an empty cell in the table is encountered before a match is made then that is the correct place to insert the new name; deletion is more difficult as it requires a reorganization of the whole table, but deletion of items from the simpler look-up tables will also require the restructuring of the master file if the 'empty' spaces are to be used for other purposes.

We shall not provide a complete solution to the problem using a hash table, but will merely present an alternative version of the function `record_number` which assumes that some other procedure has read the hash table from a file into the array `chemical`, which is now organized as a hash table and not as a simple look-up table:

```
INTEGER FUNCTION record_number(item)
    ! This function returns the index of item in the hash
    ! table chemical (in the module)

    ! Dummy argument
    CHARACTER(LEN=max_len), INTENT(IN) :: item

    ! Local variables
    INTEGER :: i,start

    ! Calculate start point for table search
    start = MOD(ICHAR(item(1:1))*ICHAR(item(2:2)),max_names)+1

    ! Search from here to end of table
    DO i=start,max_names
        IF (chemical(i)==item) THEN
            ! Match made - return index
            record_number = i
            RETURN

        ELSE IF (chemical(i)==0) THEN
            ! Empty cell means item is not in table - return 0
            record_number = 0
            RETURN
        END IF
    END DO
```

```
        ! No match yet made, and all cells full
        ! Search remainder of table
        DO i=1,start-1
           IF (chemical(i)==item) THEN
              ! Match made - return index
              record_number = i
              RETURN

           ELSE IF (chemical(i)==0) THEN
              ! Empty cell means item is not in table - return 0
              record_number = 0
              RETURN
           END IF
        END DO

        ! Complete table has been searched without either finding
        ! a match or finding an empty cell
        ! Return -1 to indicate that table is full
        record_number = -1

     END FUNCTION record_number
```

Note that the initial point to start searching the table has been determined by multiplying the numeric value of the first two characters in the chemical's name together and then taking the remainder after dividing by the size of the hash table; finally, one is added to obtain a value which lies between 1 and **max_names**. The method used to calculate the initial value, **start**, is not particularly important as long as it gives a fairly wide spread of values for any group of names, and it can be determined quickly.

The final point to make about this version is that if the table is full then a negative value has been returned. This can be treated in the same way as zero in this program, but would be of importance in a further procedure which used this function to establish where to insert a new name. If the function returned the value zero, then the name could be inserted at that point, but if it returned a negative value then it would indicate that it was not possible to add any more entries to the table.

15.5 Internal files

An **internal file** is not really a file at all but behaves like one, and can be used to great advantage in particular situations. It is actually a means whereby the power and flexibility of Fortran's formatting process can be used to convert information from one format to another without the use of any external media. Such a file may be a **CHARACTER** scalar variable, a **CHARACTER** array element, a **CHARACTER** substring, or a **CHARACTER** array.

In the first three cases the internal file consists of a single record, while if it is an array it consists of a sequence of records, each of which corresponds to one element of the array. In the latter case the whole file must be input or output by means of a single statement, since a **READ** or **WRITE** statement on an internal file *always* starts at the beginning of the file.

An internal file can only be read by a sequential formatted **READ** statement that does not use namelist formatting. It can only be written by a sequential formatted **WRITE** statement that does not use namelist formatting, or it can be created by any other appropriate means – for example by an assignment statement or by input from some other source.

An internal file is identified by using the name of the character entity in an input or output statement in place of the unit identifier. Thus we may write

```
CHARACTER(LEN=30) :: line
WRITE (UNIT=line,FMT='(3F10.4)') x,y,z
READ (UNIT=line,FMT='(3(F6.0,4X)') x,y,z
```

which would first create a character string in the variable **line** consisting of the representations of the values of **x**, **y** and **z** with four decimal places, and would then read these back into the same variables in such a way as to ignore the digits following the decimal point. The effect would, therefore, be to truncate the values of the three variables by eliminating any fractional parts. (Note that the same effect could be achieved by use of the intrinsic function **INT**.)

The following example illustrates another use of an internal file, namely to allow a record of an external file to be read more than once without the need to backspace the external file.

■ EXAMPLE 15.3

1 Problem

Example 15.1 used non-advancing input to read data in which the format of the second part of each record varied, depending upon the value of a code in the earlier part of the record. An alternative approach would be to use an internal file.

2 Analysis

The program will be very similar to that written for Example 15.1 except that after the first three items in each record have been read, the rest of the record will be read into a **CHARACTER** variable, and then the relevant parts read from that variable, acting as an internal file.

Data design

This will be as before, except for the addition of a **CHARACTER** variable, *input_record*, of length 10 (which is sufficient for the longest case).

Structure plan

> **1** Request name of data file and open it on *unit*
>
> **2** Repeat up to *max_datasets* times
>> **2.1** Read first three items of next record, and the rest of the record into *input_record*
>> **2.2** If end of file then exit from loop
>> **2.3** If error then set *error_code* to −2 and exit from loop
>> **2.4** Select case on job status
>>> status is 1
>>>> **2.4.1** Read age from *input_record*
>>>> **2.4.2** Set salary, other income, months unemployed and code to unused
>>>
>>> status is 2
>>>> **2.4.3** Read salary from *input_record*
>>>> **2.4.4** Set age, other income, months unemployed and code to unused
>>>
>>> status is 3
>>>> **2.4.5** Read salary and other income from *input_record*
>>>> **2.4.6** Set age, months unemployed and code to unused
>>>
>>> status is 4
>>>> **2.4.7** Read age and months unemployed from *input_record*
>>>> **2.4.8** Set salary, other income and code to unused
>>>
>>> status is 5
>>>> **2.4.9** Read age and code from *input_record*
>>>> **2.4.10** Set salary, other income and months unemployed to unused
>>
>> **2.5** Copy local record to array
>
> **3** If no end of file read set *error_code* to −3
>
> **4** Return number of data sets read

3 Solution

The two modules are as in Example 15.1.

```
SUBROUTINE input(unit,max_datasets,survey_data,num_datasets, &
                 error_code)
    USE error_codes
    USE survey_details
    IMPLICIT NONE
```

```
! This subroutine reads up to max_datasets records prepared
! as follows, returning the number read in num_datasets


! Columns 1-20  Name
!          23   Sex (M or F)
!          25   Job status (1-5)
!       28,29   Age - for status 1, 4 or 5
!       28-31   Monthly salary - for status 2 and 3
!       32-34   Other monthly income - for status 3
!       32-34   Months unemployed - for status 4
!          31   Special code (1-3) - for status 5


! Arguments
INTEGER, INTENT(IN) :: unit,max_datasets
INTEGER, INTENT(OUT) :: num_datasets,error_code
TYPE(survey_info), DIMENSION(:), INTENT(OUT) :: survey_data


! Local variables
CHARACTER(LEN=30) :: data_file
CHARACTER(LEN=10) :: input_record
CHARACTER(LEN=20) :: name
CHARACTER :: sex
INTEGER :: i,ios,status,age,months,code
REAL :: salary,income


! Ask for name of data file
! A maximum of three attempts will be allowed to open the file
DO i=1,3
   PRINT *,"Type name of data file"
   READ '(A)',data_file
   ! Open file at beginning
   OPEN (UNIT=unit,FILE=data_file,POSITION="REWIND",      &
         IOSTAT=ios)
   IF (ios==0) EXIT
   ! Error when opening file - try again
   PRINT *,"Unable to open file - please try again"
END DO


! If open was unsuccessful after 3 attempts return error=-1
IF (ios/=0) THEN
   error_code = -1
   RETURN
END IF


! Loop to read data
DO i=1,max_datasets
   ! Read next data record
   READ (UNIT=unit,FMT='(A20,2X,A1,1X,I1,2X,A10)',      &
         IOSTAT=ios), name,sex,status,input_record
```

```fortran
! Check for errors and end of file
SELECT CASE (ios)
CASE (end_file)            ! End of file - no more data
   EXIT

CASE (1:)                  ! Error during reading
   error_code = -2
   EXIT
END SELECT

! Read remaining data from internal file according to
! status code
SELECT CASE (status)
CASE (ft_ed)
   ! Read age and set other items to unused code
   READ (UNIT=input_record,FMT='(I2)'), age
   months = unused
   salary = unused
   income = unused
   code = unused

CASE (ft_job)
   ! Read salary details and set other items to unused
   READ (UNIT=input_record,FMT='(F4.0)'), salary
   age = unused
   income = unused
   months = unused
   code = unused

CASE (pt_job)
   ! Read income details and set other items to unused
   READ (UNIT=input_record,FMT='(F4.0,2X,F4.0)'),  &
        salary,income
   age = unused
   months = unused
   code = unused

CASE (no_job)
   ! Read age and months unemployed
   ! and set other items to unused
   READ (UNIT=input_record,FMT='(I2,2X,I3)'), age,months
   salary = unused
   income = unused
   code = unused

CASE (at_home)
   ! Read age and code, and set other items to unused
   READ (UNIT=input_record,FMT='(I2,1X,I1)'), age,code
   salary = unused
   income = unused
   months = unused
END SELECT
```

```
      ! Record is now fully input, so copy to main data array
      survey_data(i) = survey_info (name,sex,status,age, &
                                    months,code,salary,income)
  END DO

      ! All data input - check if end of file was read
      IF (i > max_datasets) error_code = -3

      ! Save number of records read and return
      num_datasets = i-1

END SUBROUTINE input
```

Note that it would also have been possible for the **READ** statement which actually reads the data from the input file to have read the whole record into **input_record**, and then read everything, including the three common items, from the internal file. This would have had the advantage that the whole input record was always available, at the cost of slightly more complicated formats.

15.6 The INQUIRE statement

For most purposes the statements already described will enable a program to carry out any file operations it requires. There are, however, occasions, especially when writing a general purpose subroutine, when it would be useful to find out, or check up on, the various details which are applicable to files (for example, whether they are formatted, connected for direct access etc.). This can be achieved by using the **INQUIRE** statement, which takes the form

   INQUIRE (*list of specifiers*)

where the specifiers which may appear in the list are shown in Figures 15.9–15.12.

With one exception, which we shall meet later, an **INQUIRE** statement is either an inquire-by-unit or an inquire-by-file. An inquire-by-unit statement must include a **UNIT** specifier in the same form as in an **OPEN** statement, but must not include a **FILE** specifier; an inquire-by-file statement must include a **FILE** specifier in the same form as in an **OPEN** statement, but must not include a **UNIT** specifier. In both cases, the statement may include an **IOSTAT** or **ERR** specifier, in the usual way.

The specifiers, and their purpose, fall into five groups.

The first group, shown in Figure 15.9, is used in an inquire-by-unit and enables the program to establish whether a specified unit exists, whether a file is connected to a specified unit, and if so, what its name is.

Specifier	Target values and meaning
EXIST=*file_existence*	.**TRUE**. or .**FALSE**. Existence of the named unit
OPENED=*open_status*	.**TRUE**. or .**FALSE**. Whether a file is connected to this unit
NAMED=*name_status*	.**TRUE**. or .**FALSE**. Whether the file connected to this unit has a name
NAME=*file_name*	The name of the file connected to this unit, or undefined

Figure 15.9   Unit status specifiers for use with the **INQUIRE** statement.

Thus, the statement

```
INQUIRE (UNIT=unit_number, OPENED=connected,   &
         NAMED=named_file, NAME=file_name)
```

will set the logical variable **connected** *true* if there is a file connected to unit number **unit_number** and will set the logical variable **named_file** *true* if the file connected to unit **unit_number** has a name (that is, it is not a scratch file). If the file has a name then the character variable **file_name** will be assigned the name of the file; otherwise it will become undefined.

The second group, shown in Figure 15.10, is used in an inquire-by-file to provide similar information.

The third group of specifiers is shown in Figure 15.11, and may be used in either an inquire-by-unit or an inquire-by-file to determine the record length of a file, or the next record in a direct-access file, respectively. In the latter case, the

Specifier	Target values and meaning
EXIST=*file_existence*	.**TRUE**. or .**FALSE**. Existence of the named file
OPENED=*open_status*	.**TRUE**. or .**FALSE**. Whether this file is connected to an input/output unit
NUMBER=*unit_number*	The unit number of the unit connected to this file, or undefined
NAME=*file_name*	The name of this file in a processor-defined form

Figure 15.10   File status specifiers for use with the **INQUIRE** statement.

Specifier	Target values and meaning
RECL=*record_length*	The record length of a file connected for direct access, or the maximum record length for a file connected for sequential access, or undefined
NEXTREC=*record_number*	The number of the next record of a file connected for direct access, or undefined

Figure 15.11   Record-related specifiers for use with the INQUIRE statement.

value returned is $n + 1$ if the last record read or written was record number n, and 1 if the file is connected but no records have yet been read or written.

The fourth and largest group of specifiers is shown in Figure 15.12, and enables the program to determine the values of the various attributes which could have been set in an OPEN statement for a file.

These specifiers all require a character target and most of them assign it the value that was used for the corresponding specifier in the OPEN statement, or the default value if appropriate, or undefined if the file is not yet connected or it is not possible to determine the correct value. Some of these specifiers, however, ask whether a particular action is allowable and set the target to the characters YES or NO (or UNKNOWN), as appropriate. Thus, if the file **Toms_file** has been opened for direct access, the statement

```
INQUIRE (UNIT="Toms_file",ACCESS=access_type)
```

will set the character variable **access_type** to the value DIRECT. The statement

```
INQUIRE (UNIT="Toms_file",SEQUENTIAL=seq,DIRECT=dir)
```

will set the character variable **dir** to the value YES. It is not possible, however, to state what value will be assigned to the character variable **seq**, since if sequential access is also allowed on the file it may be YES, if sequential access is never allowed on the file it may be NO, but if the processor cannot determine which of these possibilities is true then the value UNKNOWN will be assigned to **seq**.

Note that any character values which are assigned as a result of executing an INQUIRE statement will always be in upper case, except in the case of the NAME specifier, which will be in whatever form the actual filename is specified.

Note also that if an error condition occurs during execution of an INQUIRE statement then all inquiry specifier variables become undefined, other than the IOSTAT variable, if one is specified.

Finally, it should be noted that the value assigned to the target variable of the POSITION specifier assumes that the file has not been repositioned since it was

Specifier	Target values and meaning
ACCESS=*access_type*	**SEQUENTIAL, DIRECT** or **UNDEFINED**
SEQUENTIAL=*yes_or_no*	**YES, NO** or **UNKNOWN**
DIRECT=*yes_or_no*	**YES, NO** or **UNKNOWN**
	The type of access for which the file is connected
FORM=*format_type*	**FORMATTED, UNFORMATTED** or **UNDEFINED**
FORMATTED=*yes_or_no*	**YES, NO** or **UNKNOWN**
UNFORMATTED=*yes_or_no*	**YES, NO** or **UNKNOWN**
	The type of formatting for which the file is connected
ACTION=*io_type*	**READ, WRITE, READWRITE** or **UNDEFINED**
READ=*yes_or_no*	**YES, NO** or **UNKNOWN**
WRITE=*yes_or_no*	**YES, NO** or **UNKNOWN**
READWRITE=*yes_or_no*	**YES, NO** or **UNKNOWN**
	The type of input/ouput for which the file is connected
BLANK=*blank_action*	**NULL, ZERO** or **UNDEFINED**
	The type of blank interpretation in effect for the file
POSITION=*file_position*	**REWIND, APPEND, ASIS** or **UNDEFINED**
	The initial file position specifed when the file was connected
DELIM=*delimiter*	**APOSTROPHE, QUOTE, NONE** or **UNDEFINED**
	The character delimiter specified for list-directed and namelist character output when the file was connected
PAD=*padding_type*	**NO** or **YES**
	Whether padding of input fields is specified for the file

Figure 15.12 Attribute specifiers for use with the **INQUIRE** statement.

opened. If it has been repositioned then the target will be assigned a processor-dependent value.

The final group, which consists of the single specifier, **IOLENGTH**, is used in the third type of **INQUIRE** statement, known as an inquire-by-output-list. This takes a different form from the other types of **INQUIRE** statement:

   INQUIRE (IOLENGTH=length**)** *output_list*

where *length* is an integer variable and *output_list* is a list of entities in the same form as an output list for a **WRITE** statement. The effect of this statement is to assign the target variable *length* with the length of the record that would result from using the specified output list in an unformatted **WRITE** statement.

It will be remembered that this is measured in processor-defined units, and that, moreover, it is required when opening a file for direct access. Thus, for example, in Example 15.2, the module **file_control** included the following lines:

```
INTEGER, PARAMETER :: char_store=1,real_store=4
INTEGER, PARAMETER :: rec_len = char_store*(max_len+8) + &
                                real_store*4
```

A better approach, using the **INQUIRE** statement, would be to replace these lines in the module by the following declaration:

```
INTEGER :: rec_len
```

and to add the following statement before the **OPEN** statement in the main program:

```
INQUIRE (IOLENGTH=rec_len) name,current_stock,units,  &
                          re_order,unit_stock,max_stock
```

which will set **rec_len** to the correct value for the records which constitute the master file.

Another way in which the **INQUIRE** statement can be useful is in connection with establishing, and maintaining a Grandfather–Father–Son cycle of tapes in a program which updates a master file. Example 15.2, for example, could be modified so that a cycle of three tapes was used, say **Master_1**, **Master_2** and **Master_3** in the following manner:

nth run   Update from **Master_1** to **Master_2**; delete **Master_3** at end of run;

$(n + 1$th run)   Update from **Master_2** to **Master_3**; delete **Master_1** at end of run;

$(n + 2$th run)   Update from **Master_3** to **Master_1**; delete **Master_2** at end of run;

etc. It is a relatively trivial task to write a procedure which will use **INQUIRE** to determine which two of the three possible files exist, and then to open the one that does not exist as the new master tape (for writing), the one that was created on the last run for reading only, and the third tape so that it can be closed *and deleted* at the successful conclusion of the program's execution. The program will then automatically look after this aspect of its data security.

15.7 NAMELIST input and output

In all of the output operations that we have met so far the values that are to be output are determined by the list of variables and other objects in the **WRITE** or **PRINT** statement, while in all of the input operations the variables to which values are to be input are determined by the list of variables in the **READ** statement.

Sometimes, however, it is convenient to specify a group of variables which will always be output together, or to which new values will always be input together. In this case we may use a new feature within Fortran's comprehensive input/output facilities, namely **NAMELIST input/output**, which uses list-directed formatting to output a set of values determined by a predefined list of variables or to input values to some or all of the variables in such a list.

Before any **NAMELIST** input or output can take place a **NAMELIST** group name must be defined by means of a statement of the form

NAMELIST /*namelist_group_name*/*list of names*

where *namelist_group_name* is the name that will be used to identify the set of variables whose names constitute the following list. Note that a name in a **NAMELIST** group must not be an array dummy argument with a non-constant bound, a variable with non-constant character length, an automatic object, a pointer (see Chapter 16), a variable that has an ultimate component that is a pointer, or an allocatable array.

A name in a **NAMELIST** group may have an optional qualification, such as a derived-type component name or an integer constant for subscript(s), stride, and substring expression. If the name of an array or a derived-type variable appears in a *namelist_group_name*, then all the elements or components of the array or derived-type variable name are eligible for input, and all the elements or components are output.

Two **NAMELIST** statements may be combined in either of the following ways

NAMELIST /*nl_group_name1*/*list of names*,/*nl_group_name2*/*list of names* ...

or

NAMELIST /*nl_group_name1*/*list of names*/*nl_group_name2*/*list of names* ...

although we recommend that you do not use these forms of the statement.

If two **NAMELIST** statements have the same **NAMELIST** group name then they are considered as though the second list was a continuation of the first. Thus, the statements

```
NAMELIST /group_1/x,y,z(3:5)
NAMELIST /group_1/a,b,c
```

have exactly the same effect as the single statement

```
NAMELIST /group_1/x,y,z(3:5),a,b,c
```

Note that the **NAMELIST** statement is a specification statement and must, therefore, appear before any executable statements in the program unit in which it is defined.

A **NAMELIST** input or output statement takes the form of a formatted input or output statement except that

- the format specifier is replaced by a **NAMELIST** specifier, which takes the form NML=*namelist_group_name*;
- there must be no input or output list.

Thus, the statement

```
WRITE (UNIT=*,NML=group_1,IOSTAT=ios)
```

will output the values of *all* the variables specified as being part of the **NAMELIST** group **group_1**, in the order in which they were specified. Note that **NAMELIST** output cannot be used with a **PRINT** statement.

The output produced will take the following form:

(1)   An ampersand character (**&**), optionally preceded by any number of blanks, and *immediately* followed by the **NAMELIST** group name which appears in the **WRITE** statement. The name will always be in upper case.

(2)   A **name-value subsequence** for each variable in the **NAMELIST** group. Each name-value subsequence consists of the name of the variable being output, an equals sign, and the value of the variable in the format that would be used for list-directed output; in the case of an array, the equals sign will be followed by a list of values, corresponding to all the elements of the array. If two or more consecutive values are the same the processor is allowed to output them in the form *r*∗*c*, where *c* is the value and *r* is the number of repetitions. Additional blank characters may be inserted before or after the name-value subsequence, and on either side of the equals sign, and each name-value subsequence may optionally be followed by a comma, surrounded by any number of blank characters.

(3)   A terminating slash (/) character.

The processor will begin new output records as necessary, but only character and complex values may be split between two records.

Figure 15.13 shows an example of how the output from a **NAMELIST** output statement might appear.

Note, however, that character values are output, as with list-directed output, without any delimiting characters. This is normally what is required for other forms of output, but since **NAMELIST** output is frequently intended for subsequent input by means of a **NAMELIST** input statement (see below) it may not be what is required in this case. If it is required to output character values

```
PROGRAM namelist_output
   IMPLICIT NONE
   INTEGER :: a=987, b=-123
   INTEGER, DIMENSION(3:5) :: c=(/3,4,5/)
   REAL :: x=6.54, y=0.00009876
   COMPLEX :: q=(4.5,6.7)
   CHARACTER(LEN=22) :: s="The cat sat on the mat"
   NAMELIST /xyz/a,b,c,x,y,q,s

   WRITE (UNIT=*,NML=xyz)
END PROGRAM namelist_output
```

Output

```
&XYZ
A=      987,   B=    -123,   C=       3       4       5,
X=    6.543,   Y=    0.9876E-04,   Q=(    4.500,   6.700),
S= The cat sat on the mat/
```

Figure 15.13 An example of NAMELIST output.

enclosed in delimiters then the output file must be opened with the **DELIM** specifier set to either **APOSTROPHE** or **QUOTE**. (Note that it is permissible to open a pre-connected file, such as the default output unit, in order to change some of the default attributes.)

If a **NAMELIST** specifier appears in a **READ** statement, the format for the data is exactly the same as the format in which **NAMELIST** output is produced. It is not necessary, however, to supply values for all the variables in the **NAMELIST** group, and users need only input values for those variables that they wish to change. Note, however, that if a name is assigned values more than once within the input record, the last occurrence of the name specifies the value or values that will be used.

In the case of an array or derived-type variable name, the number of values following the equals sign must not exceed the number of items represented by the name (for instance the number of elements in the array), but may be less. If it is less, then the remaining list items are not changed.

Thus, if the program contained the following **READ** statement, for the **NAMELIST** group defined earlier,

```
READ (UNIT=*,NML=group_1,IOSTAT=ios)
```

and the data took the form

```
&group_1
a=3.2 b=6.1
z=9.6,3.1/
```

then the variables **a** and **b** would have their values changed to 3.2 and 6.1, respectively, while elements three and four of the array **z** would be set to 9.6 and 6.1. The values of **x**, **y** and **c**, and of **z(5)** would remain unchanged.

Note that the same rules apply to the representation of numeric, logical and character values, and for the separation of such values, as apply to list-directed input.

It will be noted that the format used for input is identical to that used by the processor for output, apart, possibly, from character values that have been output without delimiters, although the *namelist_group_name* and the names of the variables may be in either upper or lower case on input, but will always be in upper case on output. Results produced by a **NAMELIST** output statement to a file can, therefore, be input directly by a **NAMELIST** input statement as long as they do not contain non-delimited character values with embedded blanks.

The statement is particularly useful, therefore, if it is required to write a set of variable data to a file for subsequent input by the same or another program.

SELF-TEST EXERCISES 15.2

1 What is the difference in the meaning of the **RECL** specifier in an **OPEN** statement for a sequential file and its meaning in an **OPEN** statement for a direct-access file?

2 Can a file which has been written with direct-access **WRITE** statements subsequently be read as a sequential file?

3 Can a file which has been written with sequential **WRITE** statements subsequently be read as a direct-access file?

4 What restrictions are there on the form of input and output on direct-access files?

5 What is a hash table? How is it used, and what are its advantages over a conventional look-up table? What is its major disadvantage?

6 What will be printed by the following program?

```
PROGRAM test_15_2_6
   IMPLICIT NONE
   CHARACTER(LEN=5), DIMENSION(10) :: line1,line2
   INTEGER :: i
   line1 = (/"One","Two","Three","Four","Five","Six",  &
            "Seven","Eight","Nine","Ten"/)
   DO i=1,10
      READ (UNIT=line1,FMT='(A5)') line2(i)
   END DO
   WRITE (UNIT=*,FMT='(10A6)') line2
   READ (UNIT=line1,FMT='(A5)') line2
   WRITE (UNIT=*,FMT='(10A6)') line2
END PROGRAM test_15_2_6
```

7 How would you find out the length of the record produced on your computer by the **WRITE** statement in the following program extract? What is it?

```
.
.
.
INTEGER :: next
REAL :: p,q
REAL, DIMENSION(7) :: x
REAL(KIND=SELECTED_REAL_KIND(12,30)) :: y,z
.
.
.
WRITE(UNIT=8,REC=next)p,q,x,y,z
.
.
.
```

SUMMARY

- Default treatment of blanks in numeric fields may be overridden by a specifier in the OPEN statement, or by edit descriptors on a record-by-record basis.

- Other input/output defaults, such as padding character strings on input, may be overridden by use of specifiers when the file is opened.

- Various other edit descriptors may be used to provide additional control over input and output editing.

- Non-advancing input and output does not start a new record each time an input/output statement is executed.

- Non-advancing input and output may only occur on a sequential file that uses explicit formatting.

- Files may be sequential, direct-access or internal.

- The records in a direct-access file can be written or read in any order.

- An internal file is a character variable or array, and enables the edit descriptors used in formatting to be used to convert an item in memory into another format.

- A hash table is a convenient method of storing a random set of identifying names for subsequent retrieval.

- The INQUIRE statement enables a program to establish details about files at execution time; it can also be used to establish the length of an input/output list.

- Fortran 90 syntax introduced in Chapter 15:

File disconnection statement	CLOSE (*close_specifier_list*)
NAMELIST statement	NAMELIST /*namelist_group_name*/ *list of names*

INQUIRE statement	INQUIRE (*inquire_specifier_list*)
	INQUIRE (IOLENGTH=*integer_variable*) *output_list*
Edit descriptors	Iw.m, Ew.dEe, ENw.d, ENw.dEe, ESw.d, ESw.dEe, Dw.d,
	Bw, Bw.m, Ow, Ow.m, Zw, Zw.m, Gw.d, Gw.dEe,
	:, SP, SS, S, BN, BZ
Input/output specifiers	BLANK = *blank_mode*
	PAD = *padding_mode*
	DELIM = *delimiter_character*
	RECL = *record_length*
	STATUS = *file_status*
	ADVANCE = *advance_mode*
	SIZE = *character_count*
	END = *label*
	EOR = *label*
	ERR = *label*
	ACCESS = *access_type*
	REC = *record_number*
	NML = *namelist_group_name*
INQUIRE specifiers	See Figures 15.9, 15.10, 15.11 and 15.12

PROGRAMMING EXERCISES

15.1 Write a program to calculate the values of y, where $y = e^x \sin x$, for x varying from 0 to 20 in steps of 0.5. The sets of values for x and y should be written to an unformatted file, and should also be printed using list-directed formatting.

Now write a second program which reads the results produced by the first program and prints them in the form of a table containing the values of x and y. The program should print this table several times using different formats for both x and y as follows:

(a) Both in F format
(b) x in F format and y in E format
(c) Both in E format
(d) x in F format and y in ES format
(e) x in F format and y in EN format
(f) Both in G format
(g) x in F format and y in G format

15.2 Write a program which carries out the following input and output actions:

(a) Prints an opening (welcome) message
(b) Prints a request for two integers to be typed
(c) Reads one integer from the keyboard
(d) Reads the second integer from the keyboard
(e) Prints the two numbers
(f) Prints the sum of the two numbers
(g) Prints a farewell message

The program should use list-directed input and output statements.

Note that each printed message will begin on a new line and that the two integers must also be typed on separate lines; if two numbers are typed on the same line in response to the request for two integers then the second will not be read, but the computer will wait for the second number to be typed on a new line.

Now modify the program so that it uses formatted **READ** and **WRITE** statements, specifying the default input and output units. Other than a probably slightly different field width when printing the numbers and their sum, the format of the input and output should be identical.

Now modify the program again by changing the first **READ** statement (step c, above) to use non-advancing input and run the program again. Was the result what you expected?

Now change each of the **READ** and **WRITE** statements in turn to use non-advancing input or output until all statements are non-advancing. Were the effects what you had expected?

Finally, *without changing anything apart from the specification of advancing or non-advancing input/output*, modify the program so that the initial welcome is on the first line, followed by the request for two integers and the input of both integers on the next line, followed by the listing of the two numbers, their sum, and the farewell message on a third line.

You should now understand how advancing and non-advancing input and output work!

15.3 A simple integer calculator can be simulated by reading a numerical expression from the keyboard involving the operators +, -, * and / and ending with =, and then displaying the result. There are three obvious ways of dealing with the problem of reading the line of data and analysing it:

(a) Read an integer using non-advancing input. Then read characters until a non-space character is read – this must be an operator or an equals sign. If it is an operator then read the next integer and calculate a partial result before looking for the next operator as before; if it is an equals sign then the result can be printed.

(b) Read the complete line into a character variable or array and then use this as an internal file in a similar manner to that described above.

(c) Read the complete line into a character variable or array and then examine each character in turn in order to either create an integer value or identify it as an operator; this is, essentially, what a compiler does when reading a source program, although the number of possibilities in a Fortran 90 program are considerably greater than is the case for the very simple syntax of this exercise.

Write a program to simulate a calculator using each of these three methods. Which did you find the best method? Why?

*15.4 Write a program that asks the user for the name of a file and then writes the alphabet, as 26 elements of a character array, to the file. The program should check to see if the file already exists, and if it does it should inform the user and request a new name (which should also be checked in the same way).

Test the program by running it twice with exactly the same filename supplied as input.

*15.5 The following data was stored in a file for Exercise 9.9. If this file is no longer available then type it in again.

12.36	0.004	1.3536E12	2320.326
13.24	0.008	2.4293E15	5111.116
15.01	0.103	9.9879E11	3062.329
11.83	0.051	6.3195E13	8375.145
14.00	0.001	8.0369E14	1283.782

Write a program that reads each record of the file as one long character string. The program should then use an internal file to extract the four numbers from each line and store them in one row of a matrix as real numbers. Finally, the program should calculate the mean of each column of the matrix.

15.6 A census has been carried out on the population of Smalltown, during which the following data was collected:

Name	Age	Address	Economic status
Sandy T Shaw	26	10, High Street	A
Alan M Jones	56	2, Largeville Road	B
Chris D Jones	54	2, Largeville Road	B
Simon B Taylor	32	7, High Street	D
Paul K Smith	72	5, Largeville Road	C
Tristan T Bloggs	44	8, High Street	E

Enter this information into a file. Write and test a program that reads the file and provides the user of the program with the following options:

(a) Obtain the address of a named person;

(b) Obtain the age of a named person;

(c) Obtain the names of people with a given economic status.

Now modify the program to allow you to add new census data to the file.

15.7 Use the file described in Exercise 15.6 as a direct-access file. Write a program that reorders the records in the data file according to age, with the youngest first, and write the reordered data back to the same file.

15.8 When a large database is being processed it is often neither possible nor appropriate to read all the data from a file into the computer's memory. In these cases the data should be stored in a direct-access file in such a way that the required record can easily be identified and read whenever it is required. The solution for Example 15.2 illustrated how a hash table could be used to quickly identify the correct record.

However, that example did not provide the means for inserting and/or deleting entries in the hash table.

Either modify the program written in Example 15.2 or write a separate program which will do this. The program should

(a) *for insertion* read the name of the chemical, and then find the first vacant position in the hash table (using the hashing method used in the example program). If there is a vacant position, and the chemical name is not already in the table (human errors can occur!), then the appropriate entry should be made in the table, and the relevant stock control details should be read and written to the master file;

(b) *for deletion* read the name of the chemical and find its entry in the hash table. The corresponding record in the master file can easily be deleted, but deleting the entry from the hash table is not necessarily straightforward. Remember that simply deleting it might mean that another entry which originally selected this position, and then used another because it was already in use, would then fail to be found by the hashing routine. There are several possibilities – see if you can find a satisfactory one.

15.9 Data obtained from separate runs of the same experiment are usually stored in different files. The data shown below represent the results of four experiments that each measure the length (x) of a support girder five times:

Experiment 1	Experiment 2	Experiment 3	Experiment 4
15.523	15.518	15.538	15.529
15.534	15.536	15.526	15.541
15.519	15.544	15.545	15.530
15.525	15.527	15.550	15.539
15.532	15.549	15.519	15.532

Type each column of data into a separate file.

Now write a program that uses a subroutine to open all four files on different unit numbers. When the user supplies a name of a file to be opened, the subroutine should check that the file is not already open. All the data should then be read by the main program, and the mean length (x) calculated, together with the standard deviation from the mean length (σ) for each experiment using the formulae

$$\bar{x} = \sum_{i=1}^{N} \frac{1}{N} x_i$$

$$\sigma = \sqrt{\frac{1}{N} \sum_{i=1}^{N} (x_1 - \bar{x})^2}$$

15.10 A hospital's intensive care unit records various measurements from patient monitoring equipment every five minutes. It is required to write a program to analyse the changes in these measurements over a period of 24 hours. As the first step, you should write a program to read this data and produce some simple statistics, and then test it with data for a period of one hour (12 sets of data).

The first set of data will contain the time as a six digit number (*hhmmss*), the patient's temperature, pulse rate, respiration rate, blood pressure (two numbers) and blood sugar level. Thereafter, only those figures that are different from the last time will be included. The program should read all the data using namelist input, and for each type of reading print the mean value, and the maximum and minimum values during the observed period.

(A typical set of test data might, therefore, begin as follows:

```
&itu_data
time=090000   temp=99.7   pulse=85   resp=65
bp1=138   bp2=75   sugar=5.1/
&itu_data
time=090459   temp=99.8   resp=67/
&itu_data
time=091002   pulse=81   resp=64   bp1=136/
.
.
.
```

You should create a suitable set of test data to cover all possibilities with regard to frequency of data changes.)

Pointers and dynamic data structures

16

It is often convenient to have a pointer to a variable, which can be used to access the variable indirectly. Fortran 90 provides this capability by giving a pointer attribute to a variable, which allows it to point at variables of a specified type.

The use of pointers provides several benefits, of which the two most important are the ability to provide a more flexible alternative to allocatable arrays, and the tools with which to create and manipulate linked lists. This latter form of dynamic data structure opens the door to powerful recursive algorithms as well as providing the means to tailor the storage requirements exactly to the needs of the problem and the data.

This chapter shows how to use Fortran pointers, and illustrates their potential by several examples which are both powerful and yet elegant.

16.1 Fundamental pointer concepts

All of the variables that we have met so far in Fortran, whether scalar or array, have shared one common feature, namely that they contain some form of data. However, there is one further class of variable which does not contain any data; instead it *points* to a scalar or array variable where the data is actually stored (see Figure 16.1). Because their function is to point at where data is stored, rather than to contain data themselves, variables in this class are called **pointers**.

Pointers are commonly used in situations where data entities are being created and destroyed dynamically (that is, while a program is executing) and it is not known beforehand how many such events are going to occur, or in what order. Simulating the flight control system at an airport is such a case, or handling a list of requests for cash withdrawals on a national network of cash machines. It is not feasible to use dynamically allocated arrays efficiently in such situations, because, when such an array became full, it would be necessary to allocate another, larger, array and then to copy all the data from the first array to the second. This would involve significant computer time and enough memory to contain both arrays simultaneously.

Pointers are also used to manipulate connections between data objects efficiently. Consider, for example, the situation in which it is required to sort a large set of data into order, where each item is of a derived type containing many fields. As we have already seen, sorting an array can involve a considerable number of data movements, and if this is done by moving the objects themselves into the required order there will be a considerable overhead. If, however, there is an array of pointers to the data objects then, instead of interchanging large-sized data objects, it is only necessary to interchange the pointers that are pointing to them. Since pointers are generally small objects, occupying typically only one memory location this is much more efficient.

Finally, it should be noted that arrays force a rectangular structure on data. This is acceptable if the data is of that nature. However, much data does not fit well into a rectangular pattern, such as sparse matrices, the structure of neural nets, a road or railroad system, and almost all biological systems. Pointers provide a natural way to emulate the structure of such entities.

A variable in Fortran is declared to be a pointer by specifying that it has the **POINTER** attribute in a type declaration statement. For example, the statement

```
REAL, POINTER :: p
```

specifies that the variable **p** is a pointer that can point to objects of type real. It does *not* specify a real entity that **p** is pointing to, only that it *can* point to one. An extremely important feature of this statement is that **p** can *only* be set to point to entities of type real. Any attempt to make it point to data of some other type (intrinsic or derived) will cause a compilation error.

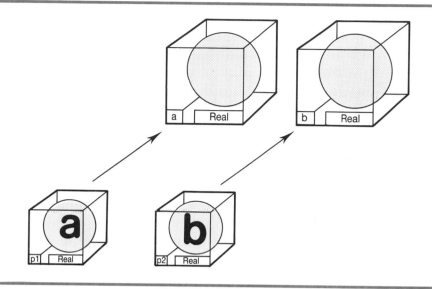

Figure 16.1 Pointers!

Pointers can, of course, be defined that can point to derived-type objects as well as to intrinsic-type objects. For example

```
TYPE(employee), POINTER :: q
```

defines **q** to be a pointer variable that can point to objects of the derived type **employee**.

The general pattern for a pointer type declaration statement is

type specifier, *attribute list*, **POINTER** :: *list of pointer variables*

The *type specifier* specifies what type of object can be pointed to, the *attribute list* gives the other attributes (if any) of the data type, and the *list of pointer variables* is a list of all the pointers being defined.

An important aspect of pointers is that every pointer has an **association status** which indicates whether or not it is currently pointing at anything. A pointer's association status, when it is initially specified in a type declaration statement, is said to be **undefined**.

Before discussing pointer type declaration statements in more detail, it is appropriate to examine how to make a pointer variable point to an object and, in particular, to introduce a concept that makes Fortran's pointers different from those of most other languages.

One potential problem with pointers is that, for reasons that we do not need to elaborate here, they can very easily have a severely detrimental effect upon the execution efficiency of programs. Since execution efficiency has always been of great importance for the class of problems that Fortran is primarily used for, certain steps have been taken to ensure that Fortran compilers can produce as efficient code as possible even though a program uses pointers. This is achieved by restricting the variables to which a pointer may point by requiring that all objects to which a pointer may point have an additional attribute, called the **TARGET attribute**, which, as its name implies, specifies that the object may be pointed to — in other words, that it may be the target of a pointer. Thus, in the following statements

```
REAL :: a
REAL, TARGET :: b
REAL, POINTER :: p
INTEGER, POINTER :: q
```

the variable **p** can point to the variable **b** because the types match and **b** has the target attribute; it cannot point to **a** (even though **a** is a real variable), because **a** does not have the target attribute. The variable **q** cannot point to **b** because, although **b** possesses the target attribute, it is of the wrong type, since **q** can only point to an integer entity.

Note that, as with other attributes, the **POINTER** and **TARGET** attributes can also be specified by means of statements:

```
POINTER :: list of names of pointer objects
TARGET :: list of names of target objects
```

As has been emphasized before, in other contexts, we strongly recommend that the attribute forms are always used, rather than the statement forms, in order that all the attributes of an entity are present in one statement, with consequent improvements in clarity.

A pointer can be associated with a target by a **pointer assignment statement**. This is an executable statement which takes the form

```
pointer => target
```

where *pointer* is a variable with the pointer attribute and *target* is a variable which has either the target attribute or the pointer attribute, and which has the same type, type parameters, and rank as the *pointer* variable. Note that the pointer assignment operator is a composite symbol consisting of an equals sign followed by a greater than sign, without any intervening spaces.

When a pointer points to a target, its association status is said to be **associated**.

Figure 16.2 illustrates some pointer assignment statements and their effect. In this example, the pointer association status of **p**, **q** and **r** is initially undefined. The status of **p** changes to associated after the third statement is executed, that of **q** after the fourth statement, and that of **r** after the fifth. Notice that it is legitimate for two or more pointers to be associated with the same target.

```
   .
   .
   .
INTEGER, POINTER :: p, q, r
INTEGER, TARGET :: a, b
p => a                          ! p points to a
q => a                          ! q also points to a
r => b                          ! r points to b
p => b                          ! Now q points to a
   .                            ! and p and r point to b
   .
   .
```

Figure 16.2 Examples of pointer assignment.

In Figure 16.2 the targets all had the target attribute. However, it is also permitted for pointer assignment to take place between two pointers, as illustrated in Figure 16.3. In this example, the pointer association status of u, **v** and **w** is initially undefined. The pointer **u** then becomes associated with **x** and its association status becomes defined. The next statement

```
v => u
```

does not, however, set **v** to point to the pointer **u**. Instead, the effect is to make **v** point to *the same target* that **u** is pointing to. Thus **v** now points to **x**, since the pointer **u** points to **x**, and the association status of **v** becomes associated. In Fortran you cannot point to a pointer; however, if you do need pointers to pointers, they can be created indirectly through the use of derived types.

If the *target* is a pointer whose association status is undefined, then the status of *pointer* becomes undefined, as can be seen in the final statement in Figure 16.3, which sets the association status of **u** to that of **w**; that is, undefined.

```
   .
   .
   .
REAL, POINTER :: u, v, w
REAL, TARGET :: x
u => x                          ! u points to x
v => u                          ! v points to x
u => w                          ! u now has an undefined
   .                            ! association status
   .
   .
```

Figure 16.3 Examples of pointer assignment where the target is a pointer.

Sometimes it is required to break a pointer's association with a target without setting it to point to another target with a pointer assignment statement, and the **NULLIFY** statement exists for this purpose. This takes the form

    NULLIFY (*list of pointers*)

and breaks the association between the specified pointers and their targets, setting the pointer association status of each pointer to *disassociated*:

```
   .
   .
   .
REAL, TARGET :: a, b
REAL, POINTER :: p, q
p => a                         ! p points to a
q => a                         ! q also points to a
NULLIFY(p)                     ! p is disassociated
   .                           ! q still points to a
   .
   .
p => b                         ! p now points to b
   .
   .
   .
NULLIFY(p,q)                   ! p and q are disassociated
   .
   .
   .
```

There are several things to observe in this example. In the fifth line, the disassociation of **p** did not affect **q** even though they were both pointing at the same object. After being disassociated, **p** can be associated again later in the program, either with the same or with a different object. Finally, the last line illustrates that a **NULLIFY** statement can disassociate several pointers simultaneously.

Because of the importance, in many applications using pointers, of knowing the current pointer association status of pointers, Fortran 90 includes an intrinsic function, **ASSOCIATED**, that will return the association status of a pointer. This can be used in two ways — with one argument or with two.

In the first case, the function reference **ASSOCIATED(p)**, where **p** is a variable with the pointer attribute, has the logical value *true* if the pointer is currently associated with a target and *false* if it is not.

If a reference to this function contains a second argument, then that argument must have the target attribute, and the result of the function reference will be *true* if and only if the pointer is associated with the specified target.

There is one important restriction concerning the use of this function, namely that the (first) argument must not have an undefined pointer association status. A pointer only has this status from the time that it is declared until it is first associated with some target (other than another pointer which has an undefined association status). Thereafter it will always be either *associated* or *disassociated*. It is strongly recommended, therefore, that pointers should always be either associated with a target variable immediately after their declaration, or nullified, thereby ensuring that their status is disassociated:

```
    .
    .
    .
REAL, POINTER :: a,b,c
INTEGER, POINTER :: p,q,r
NULLIFY(a,b,c,p,q,r)
    .
    .
    .
```

There are two restrictions on the use of the pointer and target attributes, both of which are to be expected. The first of these is that a variable with the parameter attribute cannot have either the pointer or the target attribute, while the second is that a variable must not be given both the target attribute and the pointer attribute.

16.2 Using pointers in expressions

We can now begin to investigate how pointers are used in programs to provide additional capabilities that would not, otherwise be available. When using pointers, the first, and the most important, rule is that when a pointer appears in a situation where a value is expected (for example, as one of the operands of an operator) it is treated as if it were the associated target, i.e., the object being pointed to. This is sometimes called **dereferencing**. Consider, for example, the program fragment shown in Figure 16.4, overleaf. In this example, the two pointer assignment statements

```
p => i
q => j
```

first associate **p** with **i** and **q** with **j**. The next statement

```
p = q + 1
```

is a conventional assignment statement, and expects a variable name on the left of the assignment operator, and an expression on the right. The expression is analysed first and, since in the arithmetic expression **q+1** the plus operator expects **q** to have a value, the pointer **q** is dereferenced and the expression becomes equivalent to **j+1**; it will therefore have the value 3. The pointer **p** on the left-hand side of the assignment operator is also dereferenced, in this case to the variable **i**. Thus, the effect of the statement

```
p = q + 1
```

```
    .
    .
    .
INTEGER, POINTER :: p, q
INTEGER, TARGET :: i=1, j=2
p => i                          ! Pointer assignment;
                                ! p points to i
q => j                          ! Pointer assignment;
                                ! q points to j
p = q + 1                       ! Assignment (to i)
IF (p-1==q) p => j              ! Equality test and pointer
                                ! assignment
p = q + 1                       ! Assignment (to j)
    .
    .
    .
```

Figure 16.4 An example of an arithmetic expression involving a pointer.

is to set the value of **i** to 3; **p** is unchanged, and continues to point to **i**.

In the following statement, the expression **(p-1==q)** results in both **p** and **q** being dereferenced to the integers **i** and **j**, respectively. The statement is, therefore, testing to see if **i-1** is equal to **j**. Since this is true, the pointer assignment statement **p => j** is executed, with the result that both **p** and **q** point to the same integer variable, **j**.

In the final line of Figure 16.4 first **q**, and then **p**, are dereferenced to **j**, with the result that the statement is equivalent to **j** = **j** + 1, and **j** is consequently set to the value 4. The pointer **p** is unchanged.

Thus the fifth and seventh lines of the example, although they look identical, have different effects – the first modifying the value of **i** and the second modifying the value of **j**.

The value of an expression containing pointers, or the effect of an assignment to a pointer, can therefore be seen to depend on the current targets the pointers are associated with. The pointers themselves are unchanged, and continue pointing to their initial targets.

The point which these examples is making, and which must be clearly understood, is that there is a significant difference between the behaviour of pointers on the left-hand side of a pointer assignment statement and the behaviour of pointers in a value-demanding situation. To illustrate this difference in a slightly different way from the previous example, consider the statements

```
REAL, POINTER :: p, q
REAL, TARGET :: x=2.0, y=3.0
p => x                      ! p points to x
q => y                      ! q points to y
p = q                       ! Same as x = y; p is unchanged
p => q                      ! p points to y
```

In this example, the assignment statement **p** = **q** sets **x** to have the value 3.0 and leaves the value of **p** unaltered. On the other hand, the pointer assignment statement **p** => **q** sets **p** to point to **y** and leaves the value of **x** unaltered.

We are now able to illustrate how pointers can be used to improve the efficiency of work involving large objects. Suppose, for example, that we have a derived type **huge** that has many different fields, some of which are large arrays. Furthermore, let us suppose that we wish to interchange two objects **large_1** and **large_2** of type **huge**. This would conventionally be accomplished by statements such as

```
            .
            .
            .
    TYPE(huge) :: large_1, large_2, temp
            .
            .
            .
    temp = large_1
    large_1 = large_2
    large_2 = temp
```

However, this involves three copies of large amounts of data, and also involves the extra storage space for the variable **temp**. Using pointers will enable the same goal to be achieved considerably more efficiently:

```
            .
            .
            .
    TYPE(huge), TARGET :: large_1, large_2
    TYPE(huge), POINTER :: p1, p2
    p1 => large_1                ! p1 points to large_1
    p2 => large_2                ! p2 points to large_2
    ! Now work with p1 and p2 instead of large_1 and large_2
            .
            .
            .
    ! Interchange pointers so that p1 points to large_2
    ! and p2 points to large_1
    p1 => large_2                ! p1 points to large_2
    p2 => large_1                ! p2 points to large_1
```

In this version, no large objects are copied; instead only two pointers are reset. However, life is never perfect, and there is a small cost to be paid. In this case, every time that **large_1** is required we must write **p1**, before the exchange has taken place, or **p2**, after the exchange. This means that, when the program is being executed, an extra step is needed to go from **p1** to the object to which it is pointing. Generally, however, this cost is small compared to the saving made through not moving large objects.

Once a pointer has been associated with an object of intrinsic type, the pointer may be used in place of the target object in any context where an object of the type of the target is expected. In particular, the dereferencing of pointers to objects of derived type works in an identical manner to the dereferencing of pointers to intrinsic types, as can be seen from the following example:

```
.
.
.
TYPE point
   REAL :: x, y
END TYPE point

TYPE(point), TARGET :: pt1
TYPE(point), POINTER :: pt
pt => pt1
pt%x = 1.0                    ! Equivalent to pt1%x = 1.0
pt%y = 2.0                    ! Equivalent to pt1%y = 2.0
.
.
.
```

The other situation in which a pointer may occur, and in which it will be dereferenced before being used, is in an input or output statement. Pointers which are associated with a target may occur in the list of items specified in a read or write statement. The pointer is dereferenced, and it is the associated target that data is written from or read into. Thus, if the program extract shown above has a subsequent statement of the form

```
READ *,pt
```

the pointer variable **pt** will be dereferenced to the variable **pt1** of type **point**, as long as **pt** still points to **pt1**, and the **READ** statement will expect to read two real numbers, which will be read into the two components **pt1%x** and **pt1%y**.

16.3 Pointers and arrays

So far, we have only shown pointers that point to scalars. However, as we would expect, the target of a pointer can also be an array. As with scalars, the type declaration statement for an array pointer does not associate the variable with an array; its purpose is to define what sort of arrays the pointer can point to.

The type declaration statement for an array pointer specifies the type of arrays that it can point to, and also the rank of the arrays that it can point to. Note that only the rank is required, not the extents or array bounds.

The dimension attribute of a pointer array cannot specify an explicit-shape or an assumed-shape array, but must take the form of a deferred-shape array, in a similar manner to that used for an allocatable array (see Section 13.6). This does not mean that an array pointer cannot point to an explicit-shape or an assumed-shape array; it is merely a question of how the dimension attribute of an array pointer must be specified.

Although array pointers are similar to allocatable arrays, we shall see that they have more capabilities. The deferred-shape dimension attribute for an array pointer is, however, specified in the same way as that for allocatable arrays. The extent of each attribute must, therefore, be specified by a colon, and the total number of colons is the rank of the array.

Thus, the statement

```
REAL, DIMENSION(:), POINTER :: p_array
```

declares a pointer, **p_array**, which can point only to rank-one real arrays. Similarly, the statement

```
CHARACTER(LEN=5), DIMENSION(:,:,:), POINTER :: p_array2
```

declares a pointer, **p_array2**, which can only point to rank-three, character arrays whose length attribute is 5.

The array pointers **p_array** and **p_array2** may be associated with any arrays having matching type, type parameters and rank, and which have the target attribute. The extents and index bounds of the arrays can be of any magnitude.

The following example shows the use of pointer arrays, and there are several important points to observe.

```
    .
    .
    .
INTEGER :: n, u, v, w
REAL, DIMENSION(10), TARGET :: a
REAL, DIMENSION(n), TARGET :: b
CHARACTER(LEN=5), DIMENSION(u, v, w), TARGET :: d
CHARACTER(LEN=5), DIMENSION(v, 10, 20), TARGET :: e
CHARACTER(LEN=4), DIMENSION(v, 10, 20), TARGET :: f
REAL, DIMENSION(:), POINTER :: p
CHARACTER(LEN=5), DIMENSION(:,:,:), POINTER :: q
p => a                      ! Associate p with array a
p => b                      ! Associate p with array b
q => d                      ! Associate q with array d
q => e                      ! Associate q with array e
    .
    .
    .
```

```
        .
        .
        .
    REAL, POINTER :: p1, p2, p3
    REAL, TARGET, DIMENSION(10) :: a
    INTEGER, DIMENSION(3) :: u = (/14, 7, 1/)
    p1 => a                         ! Valid
    p2 => a(1:10:2)                 ! Valid
    p3 => a(u)                      ! INVALID!!
        .
        .
        .
```

Figure 16.5 Valid and invalid pointer assignments to array sections.

Note that **p** is associated at different times with arrays having different extents, as was **q**. This is allowed because it is only the rank that matters; the pointer **p** can point to *any* rank-one, default-real array; the extent of the array does not matter. Similarly, **q** is made to point to two differently shaped arrays, but their ranks are the same. Finally, note that **q** would not be allowed to point at the array **f** because, even though their type and rank are the same, the type parameters, specifically the length attribute, do not match.

Note, however, that whereas it is legitimate to associate an array pointer with an array section defined by a subscript triplet, it is not permitted to associate one with an array section defined by a vector subscript (see Section 13.9). Thus, in the program fragment shown in Figure 16.5 the first pointer assignment statement associates **p1** with **a**, and **p1(i)** is interpreted as **a(i)**. The second pointer assignment statement associates **p2** with the odd-numbered elements of **a**. Thus, **p2(1)** is **a(1)**, **p2(2)** is **a(3)**, and so on. The third pointer assignment statement is invalid because it attempts to associate **p3** with an array section having a vector subscript.

Whatever form of array is being used, once a pointer association has been made the pointer can be used in place of the target array in an expression in exactly the same way as for scalars.

The arrays being pointed to in the previous examples have already been declared in another declaration statement; however, one of the most powerful aspects of pointer arrays is their use as a means of dynamically creating space for an array when required, and releasing it when it is no longer required. This is carried out by use of the **ALLOCATE** statement in a similar fashion to the use of the **ALLOCATE** statement to create space for an allocatable array, as discussed in Section 13.6.

The statement takes the form

ALLOCATE (*pointer* (*dimension specification*))

or

ALLOCATE (*pointer* (*dimension specification*) , **STAT=***status*)

where *pointer* is a pointer array (that is, it has both the dimension and pointer attributes), *dimension specification* is the specification of the extents for each dimension, and *status* is an integer variable which will be assigned the value zero if the allocation is successful, and a processor-dependent positive value if there is an error, for example if there is not enough memory available. The statement will create an un-named array of the specified size, having the correct type, type parameters and rank, and with an implied target attribute. Because this array does not have a name it can only be referred to by means of a pointer.

After successful execution of the **ALLOCATE** statement, the allocation status of *pointer* will become *allocated*, and its association status will become *associated*. Note that, although the **STAT=** portion of the **ALLOCATE** statement can be omitted, an undetected allocation error will cause the program to terminate execution. Testing *status* produces more portable and informative code.

Note also that, unlike the situation with allocatable arrays, it is not an error to allocate an array pointer that is currently associated with a target. The effect is to set the pointer to point to the new object just allocated, and to break the connection with the previous target. However, care must be exercised if the first target was created by an allocate statement. This is because, unless another pointer has been set to point to the first target array, the space for the first array will become inaccessible to the program. Not only is this bad programming practice, but it results in the memory becoming cluttered up with unusable space:

```
.
.
.
INTEGER :: error, m, n
REAL, DIMENSION(:,:), POINTER :: p, q
! Calculate values of m and n.
.
.
.
ALLOCATE(p(m+n,m*n), STAT=error)        ! Allocate p
IF (error /= 0) THEN
   PRINT *, "Allocation Error"
   STOP
END IF
q => p                                  ! q points to the
                                        ! elements of p

ALLOCATE(p(10,n), STAT=error)           ! Allocate p again
IF (error /= 0) THEN
   PRINT *, "Allocation Error"
   STOP
END IF
```

In this code fragment the pointer **p** is first set to point to a dynamically created real array of size **m+n** by **m*n**. The pointer **q** is then set to point to the same array. Finally **p** is allocated again to dynamically create a new array of size 10 by n, and **p** now points to this new array, and the association of **p** with the first array is broken. The pointer **q**, however, is unaffected by the second allocation of **p** and continues to point at the first **m+n** by **m*n** array.

If the pointer assignment statement (**q => p**) were removed, however, the space for the first array would become completely inaccessible to the program. A second execution of the original **ALLOCATE** statement would not associate **p** with the first array, but would, instead, create another array of the same shape.

There is one other point to notice in this example. When **p** was allocated, the size expressions were not constants, as in the examples previously given for array pointer allocation, but were integer expressions using the variables **m** and **n**, which might, for example, have been procedure dummy arguments. The size expressions in an array pointer allocation statement can, in fact, be any scalar, integer expressions.

Note that, if the space for an array pointer is created by an **ALLOCATE** statement, and the pointer association status is subsequently set to disassociated by a **NULLIFY** statement, then the space for the elements of the array pointer is *not* deallocated. The space will, however, be inaccessible unless a second pointer has been set to point to it before the **NULLIFY** statement is executed.

To avoid the problems caused through such inaccessible space, the space for an array which was created by a pointer allocate statement can be released by means of a **DEALLOCATE** statement, which takes a similar form to that used to deallocate an allocatable array:

```
DEALLOCATE (pointer)
```

or

```
DEALLOCATE (pointer, STAT=status)
```

The following program uses both allocatable and pointer arrays to illustrate the similarities and the differences between these two forms of dynamic arrays:

```
PROGRAM space_pointer
   IMPLICIT NONE

   INTEGER, DIMENSION(:) ALLOCATABLE :: a
   REAL, DIMENSION(:,:), POINTER :: p
   INTEGER :: alloc_error, dealloc_error
   INTEGER :: i                       ! Loop control variable
   INTEGER :: n                       ! Size of diagonal

   ! Read input data
   OPEN (UNIT=1,FILE="diagonal",STATUS="OLD",ACTION="READ")
   READ (UNIT=1,FMT='(*)') n          ! Size of diagonal
```

```
      ALLOCATE(a(n),STAT=alloc_error)
      IF (alloc_error /= 0) THEN
         PRINT *, "Couldn't allocate space for a"
         STOP
      END IF
      READ (UNIT=1,FMT='(*)') a


      ! Allocate space for p.
      ALLOCATE(p(SIZE(a,1),SIZE(a,1),STAT=alloc_error))
      IF (alloc error /= 0) THEN
         PRINT *, "Couldn't allocate space for p"
         STOP
      END IF


      ! Space for p allocated
      p = 0.0                    ! Set elements of p to zero
      DO i=1, SIZE(a,1)          ! Set diagonal of p to the
         p(i,i) = a(i)           ! elements of a
      END DO


      ! Calculate using p
      .
      .
      .
      ! Deallocate a and p.
      DEALLOCATE(a,p,STAT=dealloc_error)
      IF (dealloc_error /= 0 ) THEN
         PRINT *, "Couldn't deallocate space for a and p"
         STOP
      END IF
      ! Other calculations
      .
      .
      .

END PROGRAM space_pointer
```

The program uses an allocatable array **a** to hold the elements of a rank-one real array. A real, square, rank-two array **p** is then created whose diagonal elements are the elements of **a** and whose other elements are zero; the array **p** is defined by a pointer variable whose element space is created by execution of an **ALLOCATE** statement. Once **p** is allocated, all of its elements are set to zero by a whole-array expression, and its diagonal elements are then set to the elements of **a** in a **DO** loop.

When the calculations are completed, the space for **a** and **p** is deallocated. Notice that it is permitted to deallocate allocatable arrays and pointers in the same statement; it is also permitted to allocate arrays of both types in the same statement where this is appropriate. When the space for **p** is deallocated, the pointer association status of **p** becomes disassociated.

Care must be taken when deallocating pointer arrays to ensure that they are not associated with an object that was not created by a pointer allocation statement. Thus, for example, if a program contains the following statements

```
REAL, ALLOCATABLE, DIMENSION(:,:), TARGET :: A
REAL, POINTER, DIMENSION(:,:) :: p
ALLOCATE (a(10,20))
p => a
```

and then subsequently attempts to obey the statement

```
DEALLOCATE(p)
```

an error will occur because the pointer deallocation statement will attempt to deallocate the space allocated to the allocatable array **a**. This can be corrected by first nullifying the pointer **p**

```
NULLIFY(p)
```

which breaks the association between **p** and **a**.

The general rule is that a pointer deallocate statement must not be used to deallocate any object, scalar or array, that was not allocated by a *pointer* allocate statement. Only objects dynamically created by a pointer allocate statement can be destroyed by a pointer deallocate statement.

Although we have shown how the space for the elements of an array pointer can be dynamically created and destroyed by use of the **ALLOCATE** and **DEALLOCATE** statements, they can, in fact, also be used to dynamically create and destroy scalar objects of any intrinsic or derived type. For example, in the following code fragment **any** could be of any derived type that is available to the program at this point, and the **ALLOCATE** statement dynamically creates an object of this type with **p** pointing to it. The pointer **p** will be dereferenced in any context expecting an object of type **any**, so that, for example, **p%c** will be interpreted as the **c** component of the object that **p** is pointing to.

```
    .
    .
    .
INTEGER :: error
TYPE(any), POINTER :: p,q
ALLOCATE(p,STAT=error)
IF (error/=0) THEN
   PRINT *,"Allocation Error"
   STOP
END IF
q => p
! Use p and q
    .
    .
    .
```

```
NULLIFY(q)
DEALLOCATE(p,STAT=error)
IF (error/=0) THEN
   PRINT *,"Deallocation Error"
   STOP
END IF
   .
   .
   .
```

The `NULLIFY` statement breaks the association between **q** and **p** and changes the pointer association status of **q** to disassociated. The status of **p** is unchanged. Note that if the pointer association status of **q** had not been set to disassociated before **p** was deallocated, **q** would have been left pointing to space which was no longer accessible to the program – a situation which, as we have already pointed out, is likely to lead to subsequent program errors.

The deallocate statement releases the space created for holding the object of type **any** and sets the pointer association status of **p** to disassociated.

16.4 Pointers as components of derived types

Before we start to use pointers in real programs, there is one other very important concept to be introduced. We have seen that pointers can point at objects of derived type in just the same way as they can point at objects of intrinsic type. However, a pointer can also be a component of a derived type. Such a pointer component of a derived type can point to an object of any intrinsic type or to any accessible derived type, *including the type being defined*. This has several very important implications.

We shall first, however, consider a derived type which contains a pointer component that does not refer to any objects of the same type, for example:

```
TYPE mine
   INTEGER :: i
   REAL, DIMENSION(:), POINTER :: p
END TYPE mine
```

This is quite straightforward, although it should be noted that objects of this type will need to have space allocated for their pointer component before they can be used in a useful fashion:

```
TYPE(mine) :: a,b
ALLOCATE (a%p(10),b%p(20))
a%i = 1
a%p = 0.0                 ! Fill all elements of a%p with 0
b%i = 2
```

```
b%p(1:19:2) = 0.0          ! Fill odd-numbered elements of
                           ! b%p with 0
b%p(2:20:2) = 1.0          ! Fill even-numbered elements of
                           ! b%p with 1
```

The ability to have array pointers as components permits us to improve the definition of the **vector** type that was defined in Example 12.2. In that example the derived type was defined as follows:

```
TYPE vector
   PRIVATE
   INTEGER :: length
   REAL, DIMENSION(max_length) :: elements
END TYPE vector
```

where **max_length** was a named constant which specified the maximum length of vector permitted. This meant that there was considerable wasted space due to the need for every vector to have an array component big enough to cater for the largest vector anticipated.

We can now define the derived type **vector** as:

```
TYPE vector
   PRIVATE
   INTEGER :: length
   REAL, DIMENSION(:), POINTER :: elements
END TYPE vector
```

Using this new type we could define vectors of length 1, 10 and 20 by code such as the following:

```
      .
      .
      .
INTEGER :: error
TYPE(vector) :: u, v, w
ALLOCATE (u%elements(1),v%elements(10), &
          w%elements(20), STAT = error)
IF (error == 0) THEN
   u%length = 1
   v%length = 10
   w%length = 20
ELSE
   PRINT *, "Vector allocation error"
   STOP
END IF
      .
      .
      .
```

Now, unlike the situation when using the earlier **vector** definition, there is no space wastage when creating space for the elements of a vector. Moreover, we can create vectors of any size we wish, subject only to the size of the computer's memory.

Finally, we shall consider the situation in which a derived type contains a pointer component which points to an object of the same type. Consider, for example, the following type definition:

```
TYPE node
   INTEGER :: i
   CHARACTER(LEN=3) :: id
   TYPE(node), POINTER :: p      ! p points to objects
                                 ! of type node
END TYPE node
```

With this style of derived type definition, objects can be made to point at each other, as can be seen in the following example:

```
TYPE(node), TARGET :: n1, n2, n3

! Make n1 point at n2
n1%i = 1
n1%id = 'E31'
n1%p => n2

! Make n2 point at n1
n2%i = 2
n2%id = 'AX4'
n2%p => n1

! Make n3 point at n2
n3%i = 3
n3%id = 'CC5'
n3%p => n2
```

Notice that in order to permit the pointers to be set correctly **n1**, **n2** and n3 had to be given the target attribute.

This ability to have pointer components that can point to variables of the same type allows the creation of structures in which the relationships between the data elements (usually called nodes) can be arbitrarily complex, as opposed to the entities in an array which always have a rectangular structure. One of the simplest examples of such a relationship structure is a **linked list**. These are lists in which each node points to a successor (or predecessor) node. Linked lists occur very commonly in applications such as artificial intelligence, compiler writing, simulation, modelling and neural networks. We shall examine this important area in more detail in Section 16.7.

■ **EXAMPLE 16.1**

1 Problem

In order to build up a database of professional contacts, a derived type is defined to contain the name, sex, telephone number and address of each contact. It is required to design and maintain this database in such a way that the contact details are always stored in alphabetic order of last names.

2 Analysis

This is, in principle, a simple sorting problem, but with records that may each involve a large number of fields. Sorting the file by any method which involves exchanging data items will, therefore, be inefficient and we should look to using a method that sorts pointers to the data, and not the data itself.

This implies a requirement for an array of pointers. Although this is a relatively common requirement, we have already stated that, because a pointer is an attribute and not a data type, it is impossible to create such an array. We must, therefore, proceed indirectly.

Objects that simulate arrays of pointers can easily be created by using a derived type containing a pointer of the desired type, and then creating an array of that derived type. For example, suppose an array of pointers to integers is required. The following statements will define a derived type **int_pointer** whose only component is a pointer to integers:

```
TYPE int_pointer
   INTEGER, POINTER :: p
END TYPE int_pointer
```

We can then define an array of variables of this type:

```
TYPE(int_pointer), DIMENSION(10) :: a
```

It is now possible to refer to the *i*th pointer by writing **a**(*i*)**%p**.

We can now return to our problem and define a suitable derived type for the contact data, for example:

```
TYPE contact
   CHARACTER(LEN=15) :: first_name, last_name
   CHARACTER(LEN=20) :: title
   CHARACTER(LEN=1)  :: sex
   CHARACTER(LEN=20) :: telephone
   CHARACTER(LEN=40) :: street
   CHARACTER(LEN=20) :: city
   CHARACTER(LEN=20) :: state
   CHARACTER(LEN=10) :: zip
END TYPE contact
```

Pointers as components of derived types

We shall use a naive sort algorithm called an injection sort. It is not one of the best sort algorithms known, but is an appropriate one for this problem, and also has the advantage that it does not obscure, by its complexity, the way in which we shall use pointers.

An injection sort starts with an empty list and adds items sequentially. When an item is added to the list, it is added so that it is in the correct position as defined by the ordering criteria. This is done by scanning sequentially down the list and, when the correct position is found, moving all the items already in the list, starting at that position, down one position. The new item is then inserted in the position just vacated. In an injection sort, therefore, the list of items processed so far is always in the correct order, which will avoid the need for any subsequent sorting; this is a major advantage, for this problem, over many other methods which are more efficient at sorting an existing list.

For reasons of clarity (and brevity!) we shall assume that there is already a set of contact data stored in a file, and will develop a program to sort this into order and then print the ordered list. The provision of an input procedure to, for example, create the initial file from data typed at the keyboard, and further development of the program to preserve the sorted list and to allow it to be subsequently updated are left as exercises for the reader.

The data design for this problem is quite straightforward, but lengthy, and will be omitted in this example; it can easily be deduced by studying the solution given below. We shall give a structure plan for the sort procedure, but will omit those for the main program and display procedure, as these are relatively trivial.

Subroutine sort

Structure plan

> **1** Set $p\_contacts(1)$ to point at $contacts(1)$
>
> **2** Repeat for i from 2 to n
>
>   **2.1** Repeat for j from 1 to $i - 1$
>
>   **2.1.1** If last_name of $contacts(i) <$ last_name of $p\_contacts(j)$
>
>   **2.1.1.1** Move $p\_contacts(j:)$ down one place
>
>   **2.1.1.2** Insert $contacts(i)$ at position j
>
>   **2.1.1.3** Cycle for next contact (at step 2)
>
>   **2.2** Insert $contacts(i)$ at end of list

③ Solution

```
MODULE storage
   IMPLICIT NONE

   ! Field lengths for contact data
   INTEGER, PARAMETER :: name_len = 15
   INTEGER, PARAMETER :: title_len = 20
   INTEGER, PARAMETER :: sex_len = 1
```

```
      INTEGER, PARAMETER :: phone_len = 20
      INTEGER, PARAMETER :: street_len = 40
      INTEGER, PARAMETER :: city_len = 20
      INTEGER, PARAMETER :: state_len = 20
      INTEGER, PARAMETER :: zip_len = 10

      ! Derived type for contact data
      TYPE contact
         CHARACTER(LEN=name_len) :: first_name, last_name
         CHARACTER(LEN=title_len) :: title
         CHARACTER(LEN=sex_len) :: sex
         CHARACTER(LEN=phone_len) :: telephone
         CHARACTER(LEN=street_len) :: street
         CHARACTER(LEN=city_len) :: city
         CHARACTER(LEN=state_len) :: state
         CHARACTER(LEN=zip_len) :: zip
      END TYPE contact

      ! Derived type to create an array of pointers to objects
      ! of type contact
      TYPE contact_pointer
         TYPE(contact), POINTER :: pointer_to_contact
      END TYPE contact_pointer

      ! Global data
      INTEGER :: n                   ! Number of data records

      ! Array of contacts
      TYPE(contact), ALLOCATABLE, DIMENSION(:), &
                  TARGET, SAVE :: contacts

      ! Array of pointers to array of contacts
      TYPE(contact_pointer), ALLOCATABLE, DIMENSION(:), &
                        SAVE :: p_contacts
END MODULE storage

PROGRAM sort_contacts
   USE storage
   IMPLICIT NONE
   ! This program sorts a list of contacts into alphabetic
   ! order and then prints the contacts in that order

   ! Declaration
   INTEGER :: error

   ! Open data file
   OPEN(UNIT=1,FILE="contact data",STATUS="OLD",ACTION="READ")

   ! Read number of data records
   READ (UNIT=1,FMT='(*)') n

   ! Allocate space for all records
   ALLOCATE (contacts(n),p_contacts(n),STAT=error)
```

```
   IF (error/=0) THEN
      PRINT *,"Allocation error"
      STOP
   END IF


   ! Read all contact data
   READ (UNIT=1,FMT=*) contacts
   CLOSE (UNIT=1)

   ! Sort data into order
   CALL sort

   ! Print sorted list
   CALL display

   ! Deallocate arrays before ending
   DEALLOCATE(contacts,p_contacts,STAT=error)
   IF (error/=0) THEN
      PRINT *,"Error deallocating contacts and p_contacts"
   END IF

END PROGRAM sort_contacts

SUBROUTINE sort
   USE storage
   IMPLICIT NONE
   ! This subroutine sorts the array p_contacts based on
   ! the alphabetic order of the last_name field of the array
   ! contacts using an injection sort

   ! Local variables
   INTEGER :: i,j                ! Loop control variables

   ! Initialize pointer list
   p_contacts(1)%pointer_to_contact => contacts(1)

   ! Main sorting loop
   main: DO i=2,n

      ! Check current contact against contacts in list so far
      DO j=1,i-1
         IF (contacts(i)%last_name < &
             p_contacts(j)%pointer_to_contact%last_name) THEN

            ! Shift last part of p_contacts array down
            p_contacts(j+1:i) = p_contacts(j:i-1)
            ! Insert current contact in list
            p_contacts(j)%pointer_to_contact => contacts(i)

            ! Return to find position for next contact
            CYCLE main
         END IF
      END DO
```

```
            ! Current contact comes after all items already in list
            ! Insert it at the end
            p_contacts(i)%pointer_to_contact => contacts(i)
      END DO main

END SUBROUTINE sort

SUBROUTINE display
   USE storage
   IMPLICIT NONE
   ! This subroutine prints the names of people in the contact
   ! list sorted by their last names

   ! Local variable
   INTEGER :: i                       ! Loop control variable

   ! Print alphabetical list of last names
   DO i=1,n
      PRINT '(5X,A,1X,A)',                                  &
            p_contacts(i)%pointer_to_contact%first_name,    &
            p_contacts(i)%pointer_to_contact%last_name
   END DO

END SUBROUTINE display
```

Note that at the end of the main program the allocatable array **contacts** and the array of pointers **p_contacts** were deallocated. It may be felt that this was unnecessary, since the program is going to end immediately after this anyway. The main reason is that it is good programming style to acquire a habit of always explicitly deallocating allocated arrays and pointers for the reasons discussed earlier; a secondary reason is that it will often detect programming errors such as might occur if a procedure had inadvertently deallocated an array prematurely.

There is one final point that should be made regarding the use of pointers as components in derived types, which relates to their occurrence in an input or output statement.

If a derived type ultimately contains a pointer, then an object of the type must not appear in the list of items specified in a read or write statement, since it is not possible to read or write the value of a pointer. Thus if, during the course of a program's execution, you have built up an elaborate structure of relationships by using derived types containing pointers (a linked list would be a simple example) and you wish to save the structure in a file before the program terminates, you *must* create a secondary storage scheme for the output that does not involve pointers, and copy the information to that secondary storage before executing the **WRITE** statement.

SELF-TEST EXERCISES 16.1

1   What is a pointer? What is a target?

2   What can a pointer point to?

3   What are the possible association states of a pointer?

4   What is a pointer assignment statement and what forms can it take?

5   How can the pointer association status of a pointer variable be set to disassociated?

6   How can the pointer association status of a pointer variable be determined?

7   What is dereferencing? Give several examples.

8   How do pointers and the input/output features of Fortran interact?

9   How can pointer variables be defined that can point to arrays?

10   How can the space for the elements of an array pointer be created dynamically? How can it be deallocated dynamically?

16.5 Pointers as arguments to procedures

It will be remembered that allocatable arrays cannot be used as dummy arguments of procedures (see Section 13.6). Pointers (and targets), on the other hand, are allowed to be procedure arguments, but only as long as the following conditions are adhered to:

- If a procedure has pointer or target dummy arguments, then the procedure must have an explicit interface.
- If a dummy argument is a pointer, then the actual argument must be a pointer with the same type, type parameters and rank.
- A pointer dummy argument cannot have the intent attribute.

A particularly important aspect of pointer arguments concerns their allocation and deallocation. In the examples of pointer allocation and deallocation shown so far, the allocation and deallocation has always occurred in the same program unit; however, this is not a necessity, as can be seen from the following program extract:

```
         .
         .
         .
    SUBROUTINE create
       IMPLICIT NONE
       INTERFACE                    ! Explicit interface required
          SUBROUTINE destroy(x)
             IMPLICIT NONE
             REAL, POINTER, DIMENSION(:) :: x
       END INTERFACE
       REAL, DIMENSION(:), POINTER :: p
       ALLOCATE (p(100))          ! Error checking omitted
          .                       ! for clarity
          .
          .
       CALL destroy(p)
    END SUBROUTINE create

    SUBROUTINE destroy(x)
       IMPLICIT NONE
       REAL, POINTER, DIMENSION(:) :: x
       ! Calculate using x
          .
          .
          .
       DEALLOCATE(x)                ! Error checking omitted
          .                        ! for clarity
          .
          .
    END SUBROUTINE destroy
          .
          .
          .
```

Note the use of an interface block in the subroutine **create** to provide an explicit interface for **destroy**. An alternative approach would, of course, be to place both procedures in a module.

The space for the elements of **p** is allocated in the subroutine **create**, which then calls the subroutine **destroy**. This associates the dummy pointer argument **x** with the actual pointer argument **p**. After using the array **x**, the subroutine **destroy** deallocates it. This also deallocates the actual argument **p** in subroutine **create** and sets the pointer association status of **p** to disassociated.

This flexibility is in strong contrast to the situation with allocatable arrays which cannot be used in derived-type definitions, as function results, or as dummy arguments, and must, therefore, be allocated and deallocated in the same program unit. However, this flexibility can bring its own problems if care is not taken. We strongly recommend, therefore, that the error checking provided by the **STAT** specifier should always be used, and that in complex programs full use be made of the **ASSOCIATED** and **ALLOCATED** intrinsic procedures to establish what is the status of pointers which are used in other procedures.

16.6 Pointer-valued functions

To complement the possibility of using a pointer as an argument to a procedure, it is also permitted for a function result to be a pointer. In this case, the keyword **RESULT** must be used in the definition of the function (see Chapter 10), and the result variable must be specified to be a pointer. For example

```
MODULE small
   IMPLICIT NONE
CONTAINS
   FUNCTION even_pointer(a) RESULT(p)
      REAL, DIMENSION(:), POINTER :: a
      REAL, DIMENSION(:), POINTER :: p
      ! The result of even_pointer is an array
      ! pointer to the even-numbered elements
      ! of the input array a.
      p => a(2 :: 2)       ! p points to an array section
   END FUNCTION even_pointer
END MODULE small
```

The function has been put in a module, because the interface to a pointer-valued function must be explicit when it is used. Putting the function in a module is frequently a more convenient way of achieving this than using an interface block.

In Section 16.1, where we first discussed pointer assignment statements, we stated that the form of a pointer assignment statement was

pointer => *target*

We can now generalize this to

pointer => *expr*

where *expr* is an expression delivering a pointer result. Figure 16.6 shows an example of this extended form of pointer assignment, using the pointer-valued function **even_pointer** shown above. The program first uses the function to set **p** to point to the even-numbered elements of the array **a** by use of the intermediate pointer array **pa**. Then **q** is set to point to the even-numbered elements of the array pointed to by **p** because, in this statement, **p** will be dereferenced as the array it is pointing to. As a result, **q** therefore points to the array consisting of **a(4)**, **a(8)** and **a(12)**. Finally, **r** is set to point to the even-numbered elements of **q**, and therefore points to the array consisting of the single element **a(8)**.

```
PROGRAM pointer_function
   USE small
   IMPLICIT NONE
   REAL, DIMENSION(15), TARGET :: a
   REAL, DIMENSION(:), POINTER :: pa, p, q, r
   .
   .
   .
   pa => a
   p => even_pointer(pa)  ! p points to even elements of a
   q => even_pointer(p)   ! q points to even elements of p
   r => even_pointer(q)   ! r points to even elements of q
   .
   .
   .
END PROGRAM pointer_function
```

Figure 16.6 Pointer assignment of the result of a pointer-valued function.

16.7 Linked lists and other dynamic data structures

One of the most common uses of pointers is to create what are called linked lists. These are lists of objects in which every object has a pointer to the next object in the list. In an array, by contrast, the items are stored sequentially, and the array, at some point in a program, must have a specific size defined for it. In a linked list, items that are *connected* are not necessarily stored contiguously. Moreover, items for the list can be created dynamically (that is, at execution time) and may be inserted at any position in the list. Likewise, they may be removed dynamically. Thus, the size of a list may grow to an arbitrary size as a program is executing, constrained only by the memory resources of the computer being used.

When analysing a problem which is to use linked lists it is frequently convenient to represent the list in diagrammatic form, as shown in Figure 16.7. Conventionally, the first item in the list is referred to as the **head** of the list, while the last item is called the **tail**.

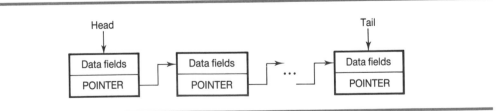

Figure 16.7 A linked list.

A linked list in Fortran typically consists of a derived type containing fields for the data plus a field that is a pointer to the next item in the list. The head and the tail will usually be represented by pointers to the appropriate list items. Example 16.2 illustrates how such a linked list can be used in the simulation of a real-time system, in which the underlying database is constantly changing.

■ EXAMPLE 16.2

1 Problem

We wish to model a national network of cash machines. In this example, however, we shall examine only that part of the program that handles the set of pending requests. We shall assume that requests are processed in the order in which they are received and that, therefore, the set of pending requests will be kept in order in such a way that a new request coming in is added at the end of the set and the next item to be processed comes from the front of the set.

2 Analysis

It would be inconvenient to keep such an ordered set, where elements are being added and deleted in an unpredictable order, in an array, and we shall therefore use a linked list. This will consist of a set of objects of a derived type that contains the request information. For this example we shall assume that these are the cash machine number, the customer's account number, the date and time of the request, and the amount of cash requested.

The derived type will also have one more field which will contain a pointer that can point to entities of the same derived type. During execution, this pointer will be set to point to the next request, in order of arrival. A new request arriving will be linked onto the end of the list; an order for the top-priority request will be satisfied by delivering the request at the front of the list and removing it from the list.

We can, therefore, represent the list of unsatisfied requests as shown in Figure 16.8.

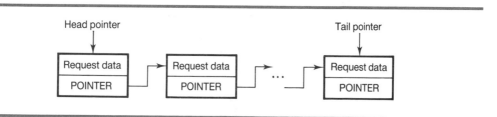

Figure 16.8 The list representing unsatisfied transaction requests.

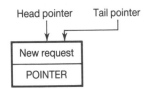

Figure 16.9 The list with only one entry.

The space for each request will be allocated dynamically when the request arrives. Initially, the list will be empty, and the head and tail pointers will be set to be disassociated.

There are two cases to consider when a new request is being added to the list. The first possibility is that the list is empty. In this case, the head and tail pointers will both be set to point to a new item when it arrives (see Figure 16.9).

If the list is not empty, then the new request can be added at the end of the list by adjusting two pointers. Before the new request is added, the end of the list will be as shown in Figure 16.10, while Figure 16.11 shows the situation after the new request has been added at the end.

When asked to provide the front item in the list, there are three possibilities. The first possibility is that the list is empty, in which case an indication that the list is empty must be returned. The second possibility is that there is only one item in the list, in which case that item should be delivered and the head and tail pointers set to disassociated. The third possibility is that the list contains at least two items, in which case that item should be delivered and the head pointer adjusted so that the second item is now the head of the list. Figure 16.12 shows the start of the list before the first item is delivered in this case, while Figure 16.13 shows how it has changed after the item has been delivered and the head pointer reset.

In this example, and in the next, we shall diverge from our normal practice and proceed directly to a sample solution without showing the data design and structure plan. This is because the code required to implement this model is essentially very straightforward, apart from the statements involved in manipulating the list. In this case, it will be more useful for the reader to examine the code carefully, with the aid of the comments provided, in order to see exactly how the various pointer statements work, than it would be to proceed with the more abstract analysis involved in a structure plan. Such an initial planning stage is, however, vital in writing such a program, as it is with all programming.

3 **Solution**

```
MODULE data_types
    IMPLICIT NONE
```

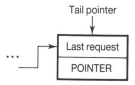

Figure 16.10 The end of the list before adding a new item.

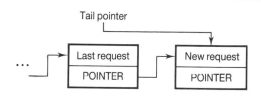

Figure 16.11 The end of the list after adding a new item.

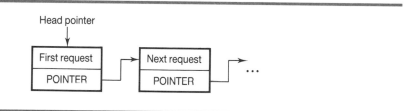

Figure 16.12 The start of the list before removing an item.

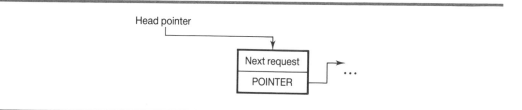

Figure 16.13 The start of the list after removing an item.

```
                    ! Derived type to record transaction data
                    TYPE request
                       INTEGER :: machine
                       INTEGER :: customer
                       CHARACTER(LEN=8) :: date
                       CHARACTER(LEN=4) :: time
                       REAL :: amount
                       TYPE(request), POINTER :: next
                    END TYPE request
                 END MODULE data_types

                 MODULE linked_list
                    USE data_types
                    IMPLICIT NONE
                    ! This module contains the procedures to manipulate the linked
                    ! list representing the outstanding transaction requests

                 CONTAINS
                    SUBROUTINE init(head,tail)
                       ! Initialize the empty list

                       ! Dummy arguments
                       TYPE(request), POINTER :: head, tail

                       NULLIFY(head,tail)          ! No successor
                    END SUBROUTINE init

                    SUBROUTINE add(new, head, tail)
                       ! Add a new item to the end of the list

                       ! Dummy arguments
                       TYPE(request), POINTER :: new, head, tail

                       ! Check to see if list is empty
                       IF (ASSOCIATED(head)) THEN
                          ! List is not empty
                          tail%next => new       ! Attach new request
                          NULLIFY(new%next)      ! at end of list
                          tail => new            ! Reset tail pointer
                       ELSE
                          ! List is empty
                          head => new            ! Start up list with new
                          tail => new
                          NULLIFY(tail%next)     ! No successor
                       END IF
                    END SUBROUTINE add

                    SUBROUTINE delete(head, tail, first)
                       ! Return a pointer to the first item in the linked
                       ! list, and remove it from the list

                       ! Dummy arguments
                       TYPE(request), POINTER :: head, tail, first
```

```fortran
    ! Check to see if list is empty
    IF (ASSOCIATED(head)) THEN
        ! List is not empty
        ! Check if more than one item in the list
        IF (ASSOCIATED(head%next)) THEN
            ! More than 1 item in the list
            first => head       ! Return pointer to first item
            head => head%next  ! Remove item from list

        ELSE
            ! Only 1 item in the list
            first => head       ! Return pointer to first item
            NULLIFY(head,tail) ! List is now empty
        END IF

    ELSE
        ! List is empty
        NULLIFY(first)          ! Return no element
    END IF
END SUBROUTINE delete

SUBROUTINE list(head)
    ! List the contents of the list

    ! Dummy argument
    TYPE(request), POINTER :: head

    ! Local variable
    TYPE(request), POINTER :: ptr

    PRINT *," "
    PRINT *,"Pending Request List"

    ! Check whether list is empty
    IF (.NOT. ASSOCIATED(head)) THEN
        ! List is empty - print message
        PRINT *,"List is Empty"

    ELSE
        ! List contains at least one item
        ! Set local pointer to head of list
        ptr => head

        ! Loop to print all items in the list
        DO
            ! Print details of this request item
            PRINT *,ptr%machine,ptr%customer,ptr%date,  &
                    ptr%time,ptr%amount

            ! Set pointer to next item
            ptr => ptr%next
            ! Exit loop if there are no more items in the list
            IF (.NOT.ASSOCIATED(ptr)) EXIT
        END DO
```

```fortran
            END IF
         END SUBROUTINE list
      END MODULE linked_list

      PROGRAM bank
         USE linked_list
         IMPLICIT NONE
         ! This program simulates the operation of the cash machines

         ! Declarations
         INTEGER :: i=1, j=1, m
         REAL :: x=100.0
         TYPE(request), POINTER :: head,tail
         TYPE(request), POINTER :: item,first

         ! Initialize empty list
         CALL init(head,tail)

         ! Loop to add four items to the list
         DO m = 1,4
            ! Create a transaction request
            CALL make(i,j,x,item)

            ! Add it to the list
            CALL add(item,head,tail)

            ! Print the current state of the list
            CALL list(head)
         END DO

         ! Loop to remove six items from the list
         DO m = 1, 6
            ! Remove item from head of list
            CALL delete(head,tail,first)

            ! Check to see if any item was removed
            IF (ASSOCIATED(first)) THEN
               ! An item was removed - print it
               PRINT *," "
               PRINT *,"Request to be processed is:"
               PRINT *,first%machine,first%customer,first%date,    &
                       first%time,first%amount
            END IF

            ! Print items remaining in list
            CALL list(head)
         END DO

      CONTAINS

         SUBROUTINE make(i,j,x,item)
            ! Subroutine for simulating input requests
```

```
! Dummy variables
INTEGER, INTENT(INOUT) :: i,j
REAL, INTENT(INOUT) :: x
TYPE(request), POINTER :: item

! Local variable
INTEGER :: err

! Create a new transaction record
ALLOCATE(item, STAT=err)
! Check that it was created successfully
IF (err /= 0) THEN
   ! Print error message and terminate processing
   PRINT *,"Machine out of memory"
   STOP
END IF

! Assign a value to each field of the new record
item%machine = i
item%customer = j
item%date = "06091993"
item%time = "1215"
item%amount = x
i = i+1
j = j+2
x = x+10
    END SUBROUTINE make
END PROGRAM bank
```

Note that modules have been used to encapsulate the **request** data type and the linked list procedures. A procedure to print the contents of the list of pending requests has also been added to the module so that the process can be checked. The main program uses an internal procedure to create a set of requests, and then removes these from the list to simulate the action of the cash machine network.

Figure 16.14 shows the results produced by executing this program.

```
Pending Request List
 1 1 060919931215   1.0000000E+02

Pending Request List
 1 1 060919931215   1.0000000E+02
 2 3 060919931215   1.1000000E+02

Pending Request List
 1 1 060919931215   1.0000000E+02
 2 3 060919931215   1.1000000E+02
 3 5 060919931215   1.2000000E+02
```

Figure 16.14

(continues)

(continued)

```
Pending Request List
1 1 060919931215   1.0000000E+02
2 3 060919931215   1.1000000E+02
3 5 060919931215   1.2000000E+02
4 7 060919931215   1.3000000E+02

Request to be processed is:
1 1 060919931215   1.0000000E+02

Pending Request List
2 3 060919931215   1.1000000E+02
3 5 060919931215   1.2000000E+02
4 7 060919931215   1.3000000E+02

Request to be processed is:
2 3 060919931215   1.1000000E+02

Pending Request List
3 5 060919931215   1.2000000E+02
4 7 060919931215   1.3000000E+02

Request to be processed is:
3 5 060919931215   1.2000000E+02

Pending Request List
4 7 060919931215   1.3000000E+02

Request to be processed is:
4 7 060919931215   1.3000000E+02

Pending Request List
List is Empty

Pending Request List
List is Empty

Pending Request List
List is Empty
```

Figure 16.14   The result of testing the banking simulation program.

Another dynamic data structure that can be created by using pointers is a **tree**. This is similar in concept to a linked list, except that each node of the tree has two or more pointer components. Figure 16.15 shows, diagrammatically, how a tree with two such components can be represented, and it can be seen that the tree is always represented as being upside-down! The single node from which the tree 'grows' is, nevertheless, conventionally referred to as the **root** of the tree, while each of the linked lists which make up the complete tree is referred to as a **branch**. A tree which splits into two branches at each node is called a **binary tree**, one which splits into three at each node is called a **ternary tree**, and so on.

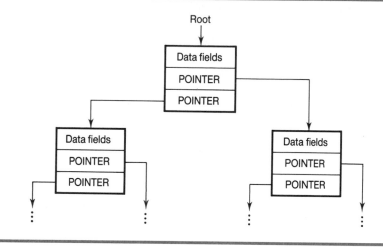

Figure 16.15 A binary tree.

Trees are very useful ways of representing many natural and artificial structures, and lend themselves, in particular, to recursive methods of traversing the branches of the tree in order to carry out various tasks upon the elements at its nodes. Example 16.3 shows how a binary tree can be used in this way to provide a much more efficient form of insertion sort than that presented in Example 16.1.

■ EXAMPLE 16.3

1 Problem

Example 16.1 used an injection sort to order and list a file of contact names and addresses. A much improved version can be developed by storing the contact data in a binary tree instead of in an array.

2 Analysis

We shall use the same derived type for the details of each contact as before, but will define a second derived type from which to create a binary tree, as shown in Figure 16.16.

We can see how the sorting algorithm will work most easily, as is usually the case when working with lists and trees, by expressing the sequence of operations diagrammatically. We shall illustrate how a sequence of names (and associated other data) would be placed in the tree so that a subsequent process can 'walk through' the tree in the correct order. Initially the tree will be empty, and so the first contact, Miles Ellis, will be placed at the root, as shown in Figure 16.17, where we have used a form of representation which, in order to simplify the diagram, only shows the name of the contact.

When the next contact is to be added the last name is compared with the last name of the contact at the root, and the contact placed on the right or left, as appropriate, as shown in Figure 16.18.

Each time a new contact is to be added in the tree a decision is first made whether to go to the left or right of the root, and then to the left or right of the next node on that branch, and so on until the end of a branch is reached. Figures 16.19–16.22 show how the authors of this book and their wives would be inserted using this approach.

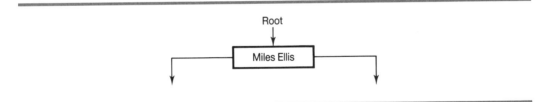

Figure 16.16 A node of a binary tree for a contact database.

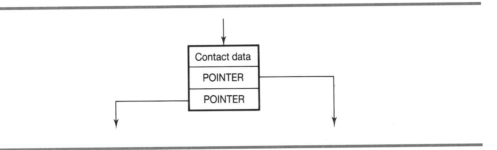

Figure 16.17 The tree after Miles Ellis has been added.

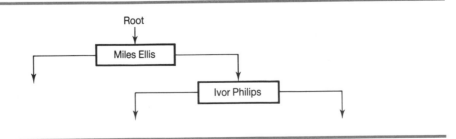

Figure 16.18 The tree after Ivor Philips has been added.

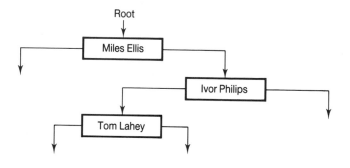

Figure 16.19 The tree after Tom Lahey has been added.

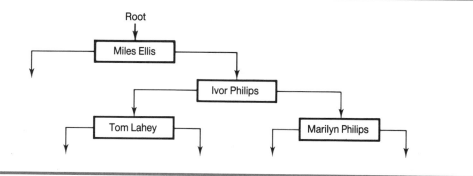

Figure 16.20 The tree after Marilyn Philips has been added.

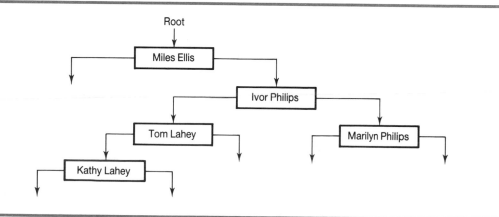

Figure 16.21 The tree after Kathy Lahey has been added.

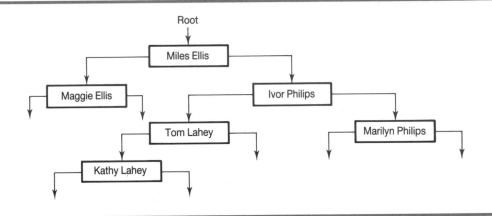

Figure 16.22 The tree after Maggie Ellis has been added.

When the data is drawn in this fashion it is clear that, since at each node the item on the left precedes the node alphabetically, and the one on the right succeeds it, the process of printing the names in alphabetic order is simply a question of traversing the tree in a logical fashion. The process is to first move down the leftmost branches of the tree until there are no more nodes; this will be the first item. After printing this name the printing procedure must move up one level and print that name. This is followed by moving to the right node and down any left branches from there, before repeating the same process.

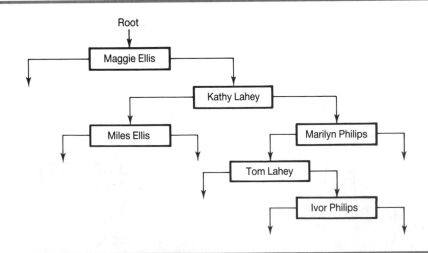

Figure 16.23 The tree if the names are entered in the reverse order.

Notice, incidentally, that the order in which the contacts are entered will significantly affect the structure of the tree. Figure 16.23 shows how the tree would look if the same six names were entered as before, but in the reverse order. However, despite the fact that it looks quite different it retains the same properties, and the process described above for 'walking through' the tree will result in exactly the same order.

It is clear from the above discussion, moreover, that both insertion and printing are recursive processes, as, indeed, are most processes carried out on tree-structured data. We shall place two recursive subroutines to carry out these actions in a module, together with the two derived type definitions. As in the previous example we shall omit the data design and structure plan, since the algorithm is almost trivially simple and it is the implementation of it using pointers that is of interest.

3 Solution

```
MODULE contact_database
   IMPLICIT NONE

   ! Field lengths for contact data
   INTEGER, PARAMETER :: name_len = 15
   INTEGER, PARAMETER :: title_len = 20
   INTEGER, PARAMETER :: sex_len = 1
   INTEGER, PARAMETER :: phone_len = 20
   INTEGER, PARAMETER :: street_len = 40
   INTEGER, PARAMETER :: city_len = 20
   INTEGER, PARAMETER :: state_len = 20
   INTEGER, PARAMETER :: zip_len = 10

   ! Derived type for contact data
   TYPE contact_data
      CHARACTER(LEN=name_len) :: first_name, last_name
      CHARACTER(LEN=title_len) :: title
      CHARACTER(LEN=sex_len) :: sex
      CHARACTER(LEN=phone_len) :: telephone
      CHARACTER(LEN=street_len) :: street
      CHARACTER(LEN=city_len) :: city
      CHARACTER(LEN=state_len) :: state
      CHARACTER(LEN=zip_len) :: zip
   END TYPE contact_data

   ! Derived type for binary tree containing contacts
   TYPE contact_tree
      TYPE (contact_data) :: data
      TYPE (contact_tree), POINTER :: left,right
   END TYPE contact_tree

CONTAINS
   RECURSIVE SUBROUTINE insert_contact(contact,database)
      ! This subroutine inserts a contact in the binary tree
```

```
      ! Dummy arguments
      TYPE (contact_data) :: contact
      TYPE (contact_tree), POINTER :: database

      ! Check if (sub)tree is empty
      IF (.NOT. ASSOCIATED(database)) THEN
         ! (sub)tree is empty, so insert contact at root
         ALLOCATE (database)
         database%data = contact
         NULLIFY (database%left)
         NULLIFY (database%right)

      ! Compare contact and the root of the (sub)tree
      ELSE IF ((contact%last_name<database%data%last_name)      &
         .OR. ((contact%last_name==database%data%last_name)      &
         .AND. (contact%first_name<database%data%first_name))) &
                                                             THEN
         ! Contact comes first, so insert it in the left branch
         CALL insert_contact(contact,database%left)

      ELSE
         ! Insert contact in the right branch
         CALL insert_contact(contact,database%right)
      END IF
   END SUBROUTINE insert_contact

   RECURSIVE SUBROUTINE print_names(database)
      ! This subroutine prints the (sub)tree elements in order

      ! Dummy argument
      TYPE (contact_tree), POINTER :: database

      IF (ASSOCIATED(database)) THEN
         CALL print_names(database%left)
         PRINT '(5X,A,1X,A)', database%data%first_name  &
                              database%data%last_name
         CALL print_names(database%right)
      END IF
   END SUBROUTINE Print_names

END MODULE contact_database

PROGRAM sort_contacts
   USE contact_database
   IMPLICIT NONE
   ! This program sorts a list of contacts into alphabetic
   ! order and then prints the contacts in that order

   ! Declarations
   TYPE (contact_data) :: contact_details
   TYPE (contact_tree), POINTER :: contacts        ! Database
   INTEGER :: ios
```

```
! Ensure that contact database tree is empty
NULLIFY(contacts)

! Open data file
OPEN(UNIT=1,FILE="contact data",STATUS="OLD",ACTION="READ")

! Loop to read contact details and insert them in the tree
DO
    READ (UNIT=1,FMT=*,IOSTAT=ios) contact_details
    ! Test for end of file
    IF (ios<0) THEN
       ! All data read and inserted
       CLOSE (UNIT=1)
       EXIT
    ELSE
       ! Insert this contact in the tree
       CALL insert_contact(contact_details,contacts)
    END IF
END DO

! All contacts now in database, so print names in order
CALL print_names(contacts)

END PROGRAM sort_contacts
```

As can be seen, the use of recursive data structures and recursive procedures provides an extremely elegant method of processing data. It is also worth pointing out that the sorting of contacts into alphabetical order, first by last name and then by first name, is almost trivially easy.

It must also be emphasized that this method is totally dynamic, and, subject to the size of memory available, will cater equally easily with any number of contacts.

In the last two examples we have demonstrated the use of two of the most common forms of dynamic data structures based on pointers. These are also two of the simplest forms of linked data structures, and more general structures than lists and trees are feasible, in which the connectivity between nodes can be arbitrarily complex. There is a considerable amount of literature in this area; for those wishing to pursue the topic further, Knuth (1969) provides a comprehensive summary of the topic.

SELF-TEST EXERCISES 16.2

1 What are the restrictions on pointers and targets being procedure dummy arguments?

2 How is the result of a function declared to be a pointer, and what is the restriction on the use of such a function?

3 How can pointers be made components of a derived type? What is such a capability useful for?

4 What is a linked list?

5 Give three advantages of linked lists over arrays.

6 What is a tree structure? What is a binary tree?

7 Give one situation when a list is preferable to a tree, and one where a tree is preferable to a list.

8 Why is recursion useful when working with lists and trees?

SUMMARY

- Being a pointer is an attribute of a variable.
- A pointer type declaration statement specifies what type of entity, scalar or array, implicit or derived type, a pointer can point to.
- A variable can only be pointed to if it has the target attribute.
- A pointer has an association status that can be either undefined, associated, or disassociated.
- A pointer can be associated with a target by a pointer assignment statement. The type, type parameters and rank of the pointer and target must agree.
- Once associated with a target, in any situation where the pointer occurs in which an entity of the type of the target is expected, the pointer is dereferenced to obtain the current value of the target.
- The association status of a pointer can be set to disassociated by the NULLIFY statement.
- The association status of a pointer can be determined by use of the intrinsic function ASSOCIATED.
- The space for the elements of an array pointer can be dynamically created and released by use of ALLOCATE and DEALLOCATE statements, respectively.
- Pointers and targets can be procedure dummy arguments.
- The result of a function can be a pointer.

- Pointers can be components of derived types.

- An array of pointers cannot be declared directly, but can be simulated by means of a derived type having a pointer component.

- A pointer component of a derived type can point at an object of the same type; this enables linked lists to be created.

- Linked lists and binary trees provide powerful data structuring capabilities, especially when used in recursive algorithms.

- Fortran 90 syntax introduced in Chapter 16:

Pointer assignment	*pointer_variable* => *pointer_target*
Pointer attribute	`POINTER`
Target attribute	`TARGET`
Allocate and dealocate statements	`ALLOCATE` (*pointer* (*dimension_specification*) *list*, `STAT=`*status*)
	`ALLOCATE` (*pointer* (*dimension_specification*) *list*)
	`ALLOCATE` (*pointer list*, `STAT=`*status*)
	`ALLOCATE` (*pointer list*)
	`DEALLOCATE` (*pointer list*, `STAT=`*status*)
	`DEALLOCATE` (*pointer list*)
Nullify statement	`NULLIFY` (*pointer*)

PROGRAMMING EXERCISES

16.1   Exercise 13.6 explained how to find prime numbers by using the Sieve of Eratosthenes. In that exercise you used an allocatable array in which to store the integers to be tested. Modify that program (or write a new one) to use a pointer instead of an allocatable array.

Which approach do you prefer?

*16.2   Write a program which asks the user for an integer between 5 and 20. The program should then read that number of real numbers and store them in real variables that have been created with pointers for this purpose. The program should then print the numbers with the largest and smallest absolute values, and the mean of all the numbers.

When you have thoroughly tested this program, modify it so that the data is stored in a pointer array.

16.3   Write a program which builds up a sentence from characters read from the keyboard in the following manner. Characters are read one at a time (use non-advancing input) and stored in a linked list. When a space or punctuation character is read then the characters read since the previous space or punctuation character are combined into a word and inserted in the list in place of the first character of the word, and the remaining characters removed from the list. When the terminating character of the sentence is read, the complete sentence should be printed. Thus the processing of the first word of the first sentence of this exercise would be as follows:

Current state of list   *Next character*

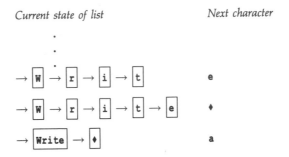

where, as usual, ♦ represents a space.

Note, incidentally, that this is a simplification of the way that many compilers, and similar programs, often build up a list of the symbols that make up a statement in a source language.

16.4   Write a function that has a rank-one, assumed-shape, real dummy argument. The function should, internally, create a rank-two, real pointer whose (i, j)th element is the ith element of the input array divided by the jth element of the input array. Your procedure should calculate the maximum value in the rank-two array, return it as the function result, and deallocate the space for the pointer array.

16.5   Put the definition for a vector given in Section 16.4 into a module and add procedures for allocating and deallocating space for the elements of a vector, associating the element space of a vector with a user-specified real array, returning a pointer to the element space of a vector (use a pointer-valued function), overloading the - and + operators to create vector subtraction and addition, overloading the ∗ operator to multiply a vector by a scalar, and overloading the assignment operator appropriately. Write a suitable program to test your module.

16.6   Devise a derived type to store sparse matrices. These are matrices in which the great majority of elements are zero. The structure need only contain the non-zero elements. Write procedures to create and print sparse matrices, by printing only the non-zero elements and their locations. Write a procedure to overload the + operator for sparse matrices.

16.7   A doubly linked list is one in which every data item has pointers to the predecessor element (if any) and the successor element (if any). Define a derived type whose single data field is an integer and whose other fields are for the forward and backward pointers.

Maintain the doubly linked list so that the nodes (the derived type objects) are kept in increasing numerical order. Keep a pointer to the head of the list (initially disassociated). Keep the predecessor pointer of the first node in the list and the successor pointer of the last node in the list disassociated.

Write procedures to add and delete nodes from the list and to print, in order, all elements of the list.

For efficiency, keep a pointer that points to the last node added to the list. Use this pointer to add and delete nodes efficiently from the list. If items tend to come in grouped clumps, then it will be more efficient to start a search from the last position a node was added, rather than always start from the head of the list.

16.8   Example 16.3 showed how a binary tree could be used to store data in a pre-sorted order. Using a similar technique, write a program that reads a list of words (from a file) and stores them in a data structure in such a way that they can easily be listed in (a) the order in which they were read, (b) the reverse of the order in which they were read, or (c) alphabetic order. (Hint: you will need several pointers for each element.)

16.9   A botanist investigating the habitat of various wild flowers divides the area to be surveyed into squares of approximately 3 ft × 3 ft. The botanist then starts at the south-east corner of the survey area and identifies each square by the number of rows west and the number of rows north of the base corner. For each square the number of flowers of each type is recorded by writing down the number of rows west and north, followed by the number and name of each flower in that square, for example:

        6W 19N 37 bluebells 16 snowdrops 1 foxglove
        7W 19N 13 bluebells 7 daffodils 19 snowdrops 4 dandelions
        etc.

Some areas were inaccessible, and for these the words 'not surveyed' were recorded after the two row numbers.

        Write a program to read the data and produce a list of the locations of the five most populous flowers in the survey in the form:

        The five most populous flowers were as follows:

        1   Bluebells (735 found)
            Locations were: 6W 19N (37), 7W 19N (13), ...

        2   Forget-me-not (692 found)
            Locations were: 12W 4N (81), 13W 3N (65), ...

Note that neither the range of west and north coordinates nor the number of different flowers can be known to the program until all the data has been read.

16.10   Modify the program you wrote for Exercise 16.9 so that the data structure created can be preserved in a file. A subsequent execution of the program can then read this file and use new data to extend the coverage of the survey. (Note that Section 16.4 pointed out that it is not possible to read or write pointer information, and that if a pointer-based data structure is to be written to a file it must first, therefore, be copied into another data structure which does not contain pointers.)

Global data through storage association

17

Large programs frequently require many of their procedures to have access to the same data. This is best achieved through the use of modules, but an alternative approach is through the use of COMMON blocks, which were the only means of providing global data access in earlier versions of Fortran.

COMMON blocks, and the related EQUIVALENCE facility, operate by specifying exactly how variables and arrays are to be stored in the memory of the computer – a concept known as storage association. Although this concept worked well on older computers it is less appropriate for modern computers, especially those utilizing various forms of parallel memory access, where the computer system will often wish to distribute variables and arrays between different processors in order to gain optimum speed and efficiency.

The description of these features is therefore provided in this chapter only because they will frequently be met in older Fortran programs. *The use of these features is not recommended in new programs.*

17.1 The FORTRAN 77 storage association concept versus Fortran 90 modules

Scalar and array variables which are declared in a program unit are local to that program unit, and are not accessible by another program unit unless they appear as arguments. This has important implications because it enables a subroutine or function subprogram to be written without any knowledge of the program unit from which it will be called, or indeed of any subprograms which it may use itself. All that is required is that the interface is known.

One effect of developing programs in a modular fashion is often that several subprograms are required to have a very large number of arguments in order to access a large number of common scalar and/or array variables. In these situations the fact that storage is local to a program unit can be a great hindrance, and gives rise to a requirement for a controlled form of **global storage** which can be accessed directly by more than one program unit.

In Fortran 90 this is best achieved by placing all the variables which are to be shared in a module which can then be accessed by a **USE** statement in each procedure that requires access to this common data area.

However, FORTRAN 77 did not have a module facility and so a quite different approach had to be used. This is known as **storage association** and relies upon the programmer instructing the compiler to store certain items of data in a defined relationship to each other. This was a practice which worked well on earlier computers, but modern computers frequently use multiple processors and multiple memory banks and the old FORTRAN 77 storage association methods can be inefficient in these situations. Moreover, the whole concept is intrinsically undesirable as it quite deliberately destroys much of the data security and integrity upon which modern programming languages place great emphasis.

We strongly recommend that storage association methods should not be used when writing new programs.

Nevertheless, most Fortran programmers will be involved at some time with programs which were written in the days before Fortran 90 was available, and such programs will almost certainly utilize storage association methods. This chapter, therefore, discusses these concepts and how they work so that the programmer will understand them and, hopefully, will be able to rewrite such programs to utilize the far more powerful, safer and useful Fortran 90 modules.

Note that, contrary to the practice elsewhere in this book, in the following examples only upper case is used, and only the old, obsolete, form of variable declarations. This is to emphasize that these methods should only be used when modifying existing, FORTRAN 77, code which was written in this way.

17.2 Global storage using COMMON blocks

In FORTRAN 77 the memory of a computer was thought of as consisting, conceptually, of a (large) number of storage units of two varieties. The first variety was a **numeric storage unit**, and was used to store integers, real numbers, logical values, double precision numbers and complex numbers – the last two each requiring two consecutive storage units. The other variety was a **character storage unit** which was used to store a single character; a character string of length *len* required *len* consecutive character storage units. There were no parameterized or derived data types in FORTRAN 77.

In the FORTRAN 77 model of a program unit, a *name* is used to identify a storage unit or, in the case of an array name or a character name, a block of consecutive storage units. These names, as we have seen, are *local* to the program unit and are for the programmer's convenience only. The compiler will refer to storage units by their *addresses* within the memory and will keep a list of names and their corresponding addresses only while it is compiling the program unit. (This is a slight over-simplification, but is sufficient for our present purpose.)

However, some names are preserved and have a *global* significance; for example, the names of any subprograms that are defined in the program, and the names of any subprograms that are invoked in one of the program units that constitute the program.

To provide a global storage facility, FORTRAN 77 allowed *blocks* of the memory (consisting of one or more consecutive storage units of the same variety) to be identified by a global name, and for the storage units contained within that block to be made available to any program unit that refers to the block by its global name. Such a block of consecutive storage units is called a **COMMON block**.

It is important to realize that the names of the individual scalar and array variables are not global names – the whole block is made available, not individual

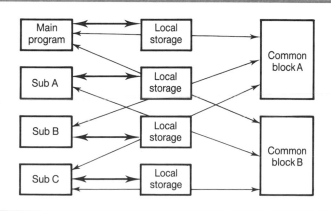

Figure 17.1 Local and COMMON storage.

storage units. This means that a program unit may call the items in a **COMMON** block by any name that it wishes (just as it can use any name for its dummy arguments); the type and order of the items within the block are fixed, not their names.

Figure 17.1 illustrates this structure in graphic form, and also shows how the various **COMMON** blocks may be accessed by different program units.

17.3 Named COMMON blocks

A named block of storage is defined by a statement of the form

```
COMMON/name/n1,n2,...
```

where *name* is the global name of the **COMMON** block and *n1,n2,...* is a list of local scalar variable names, array names or array declarators. Thus the statements

```
INTEGER NUM,AGE(50)
REAL MARK(50,6),AV(50),AVAGE
COMMON/EXAM/NUM,MARK,AV,AGE,AVAGE
```

define a **COMMON** block **EXAM** which consists of 402 numeric storage units. In this particular program unit the first of these is an integer **NUM**, the next 300 a rank-two real array **MARK**, the next 50 a real array **AV**, the next 50 an integer array **AGE**, and the last a real number **AVAGE**.

In the type of program which contains **COMMON** blocks a number of 'short-cuts' will often be found, such as implicitly declaring the types of variables, and combining the array declaration with the **COMMON** block declaration:

```
INTEGER AGE(50)
REAL MARK(50,6)
COMMON/EXAM/NUM,MARK,AV(50),AGE,AVAGE
```

This is legal Fortran, but is bad practice, and if it is essential to use **COMMON** blocks all the items in the block should be declared properly in type statements.

The **COMMON** statement is a specification statement and must, therefore, appear with other specification statements preceding any **DATA** or executable statements. Although not essential, it is good practice to immediately precede it by any type or array declaration statements which refer to items within the **COMMON** block, as has been done above.

Notice that, because the name of a **COMMON** block is a global name, it must be different from the names of any other **COMMON** blocks *or program units*. It is permitted for the name of a **COMMON** block to be the same as that of a local entity other than a named constant, an intrinsic procedure or the name of an external function, but it is strongly recommended that the names of **COMMON** blocks should not be used for anything else in the procedures in which they are referred to.

One consequence of the fact that only the COMMON block name is global is that different program units may refer to the individual storage units within a COMMON block in different ways. For example, the COMMON block EXAM referred to above could be defined in another program unit as

```
COMMON/EXAM/N,TOTAL(50,6),AV(50),NYRS(50),AVYRS
```

where different names have been used for two of the arrays and for both variables, or even as

```
COMMON/EXAM/N,SCORE(50,7),NAGE(50),AVAGE
```

where the two real arrays have been declared as a single array. The order of storage of array elements (see Section 13.2) means that those elements of SCORE whose second subscript is 7 occupy the last 50 storage units and thus correspond exactly to the array AV in the earlier COMMON block specifications. If the contents of a COMMON block are specified differently in different subprograms, however, it is essential that they should have the same length.

In FORTRAN 77 there was one important restriction concerning COMMON blocks. As mentioned in Section 17.2, there were two types of storage unit in FORTRAN 77, one for characters and one for everything else. The effect of this was that if a COMMON block contained any character variables or character arrays then it could not contain any variables or arrays of any other type. This restriction has been lifted in Fortran 90.

As we would expect, we can declare several COMMON blocks in a single statement; however, because of the format of the statement there are two ways of doing this

```
COMMON/name1/list1,/name2/list2,...
COMMON/name1/list1/name2/list2/name3/...
```

The second version (without any separating commas) is possible because of the 'slashes' which surround the names of the COMMON blocks. Thus we may write either

```
COMMON/EXAM/N,MARK,AV,AGE,AVAGE,/PUPILS/NAME
```

or

```
COMMON/EXAM/N,MARK,AV,AGE,AVAGE/PUPILS/NAME
```

although the first form is to be preferred, as its structure is clearer than the second form. Better still is to only declare one COMMON block in one statement and to write

```
COMMON/EXAM/N,MARK,AV,AGE,AVAGE
COMMON/PUPILS/NAME
```

A COMMON block will usually be specified in a single statement. This is not obligatory, however, and if the same COMMON block name appears in two (or more) COMMON statements in the same program unit then they are treated as though the two (or more) lists were combined into a single list. Thus the statements

```
COMMON/EXAM/NUM
COMMON/PUPILS/NAME,/EXAM/SCORE(50,6),AV(50)
COMMON/EXAM/NAGE(50),AVAGE
```

will have the same effect for the COMMON block EXAM as the statement

```
COMMON/EXAM/NUM,SCORE(50,6),AV(50),NAGE(50),AVAGE
```

The major use of COMMON storage is in large programs, where several subprograms need access to all, or part, of a **database** which consists of a number of arrays and variables. In such situations it would be both inelegant to write subprograms with large numbers of arguments, and also inefficient, since there is always an overhead involved during execution in the processing of the list of arguments on each call to a subroutine or function.

However, the situations in which COMMON blocks were valuable in FORTRAN 77 programs are not those which lend themselves to use as examples in a book such as this. The penultimate section of this chapter (Section 17.8), therefore, consists of a discussion of an extract from a very large computer-aided manufacturing program written in the 1960s, which makes very extensive use of COMMON blocks to organize its database. In a new version of this program it would be preferable to use modules for this purpose.

17.4 Initializing named COMMON blocks

We have seen in earlier chapters how initial values may be given to various types of data entities. These are, of course, *local* entities and the initializing statements, therefore, provide initial values for storage locations which can only be accessed by name from the program units in which the initializing statements occur.

The situation is potentially rather different with COMMON blocks, since the same storage locations are accessible from several different program units; that, after all, is the purpose of COMMON. This means that if an entity was given an initial value in one program unit then it could also be given a different initial value (presumably by accident) in another — which would lead to confusion and error. It would also cause extra problems for the compiler, which does not really know where the entities in a COMMON block are situated in the memory, but merely where they are relative to the start of the block; this is satisfactory for most purposes, but not for setting initial values.

BLOCK DATA *name*

.

.

.

Specification statements etc.

.

.

.

END

Figure 17.2 A block data program unit.

To get round these problems, the initializing of entities in **COMMON** blocks is forbidden, except in a special type of subprogram which is called a **block data program unit**. We mentioned this very briefly in Chapter 4 when discussing the structure of program units, and Figure 17.2 shows its overall structure (as already shown in Figure 4.7). Note that it contains *no executable statements*.

A block data program unit exists for the sole purpose of giving initial values to items contained in named **COMMON** blocks. It cannot be executed by means of a **CALL** or other reference, and any attempt to do so will cause an error. Similarly the presence of any type of statement other than a specification statement, a DATA statement, or a comment, between the initial **BLOCK DATA** and the final **END** statements will lead to an error.

The name of a block data program unit is a global name, like that of all other program units, and, although it cannot appear in a **CALL** statement, it *is* allowed to appear in an **EXTERNAL** statement; in some systems, for example, this might be required in order to ensure that it is loaded from a library. There may be one unnamed block data program unit in a program, and, since in many programs there is no need for more than one block data program unit, the need for a name is frequently absent.

17.5 Blank COMMON

The **COMMON** statement, as we have seen, allows us to define a block of storage of a fixed size and to identify it by means of a global name. Fortran also allows us to have one further block of storage that is available to any program unit that requires it and that has neither a name nor a fixed size. This is known as **blank COMMON** and is declared in a similar way to that used for named **COMMON** blocks, but without any reference to a **COMMON** block name:

```
COMMON X,Y,Z(-10:10)
```

Alternatively, or if the COMMON statement is also declaring a named COMMON block, we can represent the name of blank COMMON by two consecutive slashes:

```
COMMON/PLAYER/NAME,//X,Y,Z(-10:10)
```

There are three main differences between named COMMON blocks and blank COMMON (apart from the absence of a name for blank COMMON). The first is that, unlike a named COMMON block, the size of blank COMMON need not be the same in different program units. Thus, for example, the statement

```
COMMON N,INDEX(500)
```

could appear in a subprogram while the main program unit and the other subroutines could contain

```
INTEGER SCORE(500),INDEX(500)
COMMON N,INDEX,SCORE
```

The second difference between blank COMMON and named COMMON blocks is that blank COMMON cannot be initialized and thus cannot appear in a block data program unit. Any COMMON entities which require initial values must therefore be placed in named COMMON blocks.

We shall meet the other difference in the next section of this chapter.

Blank COMMON is usually appropriate where a number of variables and/or arrays are to be made available to all (or nearly all) of the program units in a

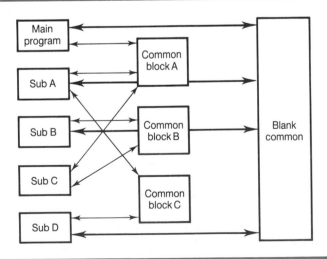

Figure 17.3 Blank and named COMMON.

program. Named blocks are more appropriate where such COMMON storage is only required by a few of the subprograms, or where it is more convenient to split the COMMON storage into several smaller units. Figure 17.3 illustrates this in graphic form.

17.6 Preserving values in COMMON blocks

We have already seen in earlier chapters that the values of any local variables become undefined when a return is made from a subprogram, unless they either have the **SAVE** attribute or appear in an initialization statement.

A similar situation exits with COMMON blocks. A COMMON block enables two or more program units to share a block of memory. It would clearly be nonsense if an exit from a subroutine always caused any COMMON blocks to which it referred to become undefined. However there is one situation, which is somewhat analogous to the case of local variables in a single subprogram, in which there would be no such conflict. Figure 17.4 illustrates this situation diagrammatically.

The program consists of five program units and three COMMON blocks; furthermore, the subroutines are called in a hierarchical way (for ease of explanation) such that the main program calls **SUBA**, which calls **SUBB**, which calls **SUBC**, which calls **SUBD**. The diagram also indicates which COMMON blocks each program unit refers to.

If we examine this diagram carefully we see that as control returns from **SUBD** back up to the main program, at certain stages there will no longer be any

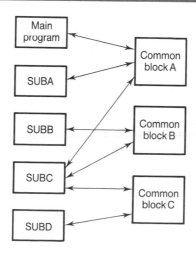

Figure 17.4 Defined and undefined COMMON blocks.

reference to some of the **COMMON** blocks. Thus when a return is made to **SUBB** we find that **COMMON** block **C** is no longer accessible, as it is only referred to by **SUBC** and **SUBD**. Similarly, **COMMON** block **B** is no longer referred to once a return has been made to **SUBA**. The third **COMMON** block (**A**) is referred to in the main program and will, therefore, always be accessible.

At those stages where an exit from a procedure means that a **COMMON** block is no longer referred to either by the program unit currently being executed or by any *higher level* program units, the contents of the **COMMON** block may become undefined in exactly the same way as do local variables on exit from a subprogram. If we do not wish this to happen, for example if we want to keep some or all of the **COMMON** values for use on the next entry to a subprogram (or group of subprograms), then we have two options.

The first is to use the **SAVE** statement. In Section 11.4 we stated that this took the form

```
SAVE name1,name2,...
```

where *name1* etc. were the names of local scalars or arrays. We can now extend this to include the global names of **COMMON** blocks (which are declared in the same program unit) enclosed in 'slashes'. Thus the statement

```
SAVE NAME,POS,/CB1/,SCORE
```

will save the three local variables **NAME**, **POS** and **SCORE** and *all* the contents of the **COMMON** block **CB1**.

If a **COMMON** block name appears in a **SAVE** statement in one subprogram, then it must appear in a **SAVE** statement in *every* subprogram that refers to that **COMMON** block.

The other way of preserving the values in a **COMMON** block (and probably the best way in many cases) is to declare the **COMMON** block in the main program. It is not necessary to use it there, but simply to include its name in a **COMMON** statement. As we saw in Figure 17.4, this will mean that there is always a program unit which refers to the **COMMON** block and it will never become undefined.

In a large program with several named **COMMON** blocks it is, in any event, good practice to declare *all* the **COMMON** blocks in the main program unit so that it is possible to see the whole global storage at one time. This will also have the effect of preserving the values of all items in these block for the duration of the program.

This leads to the third difference between blank **COMMON** and named **COMMON** blocks. Blank **COMMON** *never* becomes undefined; it is truly global and is always preserved throughout the entire execution of the program.

It should be mentioned at this point that, in practice, most Fortran systems always preserve *all* **COMMON** blocks for the duration of the program's execution. You should be aware, though, that a Fortran processor does not have to preserve a **COMMON** block on exit from a subprogram unless its name appears in a **SAVE** statement in that subprogram or it is referred to by a subprogram at a higher level, and you should never rely on them being preserved unless the actions described above have been taken.

17.7 Sharing storage locations

FORTRAN 77 also provided a concept which allowed the programmer to instruct the compiler to store two or more data entities in the same location. This was achieved by use of the **EQUIVALENCE** statement, which takes the form

```
EQUIVALENCE (nlist1) , (nlist2) , . . .
```

where each *nlist* is a list of scalar variable names, array element names, array names and character substring names. If one of the names in a list is of type **CHARACTER** then all the names in that list must be of type **CHARACTER**.

It is permitted to include entities of parameterized or derived types in an **EQUIVALENCE** statement, but it is very strongly recommended that this statement should only be used with data of default integer, real, complex, logical or character types, or with double precision types (the FORTRAN 77 data types), and then only in existing programs which already make use of **COMMON** and **EQUIVALENCE**.

The **EQUIVALENCE** statement specifies that storage of all the items whose names appear in a list must start at the same storage unit. In this statement, unusually, an array name is taken to refer to the first element of that array. Apart from the restriction regarding **CHARACTER** items, there are no restrictions on the type of the names in a list as long as only the six (FORTRAN 77) types referred to above are used and, for example, the statements

```
REAL R(2),RL,IM
COMPLEX C
EQUIVALENCE (R,RL,C),(R(2),IM)
```

will cause the real array **R**, the real variable **RL** and the complex variable **C** all to start at the same place, and will cause the real variable **IM** to start at the same place as **R(2)**. Figure 17.5 shows that this has the effect of making **RL** occupy the same storage unit as the real part of **C**, and **IM** the same storage unit as the imaginary part of **C**.

It is not necessary for arrays or character strings to match and it is possible to arrange for them to overlap, as is shown in Figures 17.6 and 17.7. In the first of these, the array elements **X(50)** and **Y(100)** are equivalenced, leading

	real(C)	imag(C)
Complex C:		
Real array R:	R(1)	R(2)
Real variable	RL	
Real variable		IM

Figure 17.5 The effect of equivalencing REAL and COMPLEX.

to the relationship shown in Figure 17.6. This could equally well have been achieved by writing

```
EQUIVALENCE (X,Y(51))
```

or a number of other variations.

Figure 17.7 shows a similar situation with characters, where we can refer to substrings as well as variable names, array names and array elements. Once again there are a number of ways of expressing the relationship and, for example, the shorter statement

```
EQUIVALENCE (A(6:),B,C(1)(2:))
```

would have done equally well, although reference to a substring of an array element should be avoided where possible, as it is slightly confusing at first sight.

EQUIVALENCE is usually used in large programs in association with COMMON blocks since it provides an easy way of identifying only those parts of the block which are relevant to a particular subprogram. For example, if a COMMON block contains 10 variables A0 to A9 and ten arrays B0 to B9, each of a different size, such that the total size of the block is 210 storage units, it might be defined as follows:

```
COMMON/BLK/A0,A1,A2,A3,A4,A5,A6,A7,A8,A9,
1        B0(5),B1(10),B2(3:9),B3(4,5),B4(8),B5(20),
2        B6(4,6),B7(-12:12),B8(7,9),B9(6,3)
```

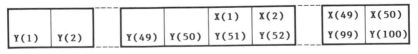

```
REAL X(50),Y(100)
EQUIVALENCE (X(50),Y(100))
```

Figure 17.6 Equivalencing arrays.

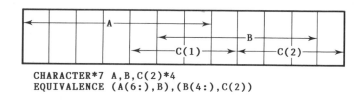

```
CHARACTER*7 A,B,C(2)*4
EQUIVALENCE (A(6:),B),(B(4:),C(2))
```

Figure 17.7 Equivalencing character strings.

However, if a particular subprogram needed to access only **A0**, **A7** and **B4** we could write

```
COMMON/BLK/BLK(210)
REAL B4(8)
EQUIVALENCE(A0,BLK),(A7,BLK(8)),(B4,BLK(53))
```

thereby avoiding the declaration of unnecessary variables and arrays. The next section shows the use of this technique in an extract from a very large (and very old!) real-life program.

17.8 An example from real life

The real benefits of **COMMON** and **EQUIVALENCE** (especially the latter) in programs written before Fortran 90 introduced modules cannot easily be demonstrated in a book such as this, because they do not become apparent in programs of the size that we can include as examples. This section, therefore, shows a (very) short extract from a real-life program as an illustration of how they can be used in practice.

The program concerned is called APT IV, where APT stands for Automatically Programmed Tools, and was developed under sponsorship from over 100 organizations (including IBM, Boeing, General Motors, Rolls-Royce, English Electric Computers, the US Air Force, etc.) at the Illinois Institute of Technology Research Institute in Chicago. The program, in fact, had its origins at MIT in the late 1950s and was under continuous development for over 20 years, first at MIT, then at IITRI, and finally at CAM-I (Computer Aided Manufacturing – International) at Arlington, Texas. The extract shown below dates from the central period of that development and was written in 1968. It predates Fortran 90 by over 20 years and yet is perfectly valid Fortran 25 years later – an eloquent tribute to the longevity of Fortran programs.

APT is a program which processes a high-level language so as to produce control information to drive a numerically controlled machine tool, and has been used in the manufacture of almost all modern airliners, motor cars, spacecraft and innumerable artefacts which require high-precision machining of some or all of their parts. One part of the program is a library of subroutines which are used in the analysis of the geometric surfaces defined by the user and in the calculation of the required motion on the machine tool. In 1968, at the time of the first release of APT IV, this library contained 78 geometric definition routines, 92 tool motion routines, and 75 other routines – a total of 245 subroutines! (This was by no means the whole program – merely a part of one of four major phases.)

Due to the nature of the problem, a considerable number of these subroutines need access to global information and the layout of the storage is of vital importance. There are, in fact, twelve named **COMMON** blocks, of which one is conceptually divided into 18 different areas, several of which overlap.

Figure 17.8 shows the first 70 or so lines of one subroutine from the library, APT030. Notice that most of the lines are comments. In a large program it is essential to document every aspect of the program fully, and the inclusion of detailed comments and a specification of each subprogram within that subprogram is a sure way of doing this. This subroutine is used to define a circle, given two tangent lines and its radius.

The subroutine starts with a definition of the **COMMON** block **TOTAL**, which is 'included in every program in the subroutine library'. This block consists of eight arrays, each of which will be equivalenced to other variables and/or arrays as appropriate for the particular subroutine.

Block 2 then contains a definition of arrays which are equivalenced to the array **DEF**.

Block 3 is a shared block, and in other routines *blocks 4, 5* and *6* are also equivalenced to the array **DSHARE** in completely different ways. Thus different groups of subroutines will use this part of the **COMMON** block **TOTAL** for their own purposes in a well-planned and consistent way.

This subroutine does not use those parts of the **COMMON** block which correspond to the arrays **FXCOR**, **HOLRTH** or **SV**, and the next set of statements defines *block 10*, which consists of a set of real variables equivalenced to the array **ZNUMBER**.

Subsequent *blocks* in this subroutine also define parts of the array **ISV**, which is actually defined in no fewer than eight ways, not all of which define the whole array.

Thus, each of the 245 subroutines in the library defines only those parts of the total data base which are relevant to its particular needs.

```
C.....FORTRAN SUBROUTINE            APT030...              3/1/68   GK
C
C                FORTRAN SUBROUTINE APT030
C
C PURPOSE        TO GENERATE THE CANONICAL FORM OF A CIRCLE DEFINED
C                AS TANGENT TO EACH OF TWO GIVEN LINES AND HAVING
C                A GIVEN RADIUS BY THE FOLLOWING APT STATEMENT
C                RESULT = CIRCLE/****, L1, ****, L2, RADIUS, RAD
C                **** = XLARGE, YLARGE, XSMALL, YSMALL
C
C LINKAGE        CALL APT030 (RESULT, M1, L1, M2, L2, RAD)
C ARGUMENTS      RESULT   ARRAY TO CONTAIN THE CANONICAL FORM OF
C                         THE RESULTING CIRCLE
C                M1       INTEGER EQUIVALENT OF THE FIRST MODIFIER
C                            1 = XLARGE       2 = YLARGE
C                            4 = XSMALL       5 = YSMALL
C                L1       ARRAY CONTAINING THE CANONICAL FORM OF
C                         THE FIRST INPUT LINE
C                M2       INTEGER EQUIVALENT OF THE SECOND MODIFIER
C                            1 = XLARGE       2 = YLARGE
C                            4 = XSMALL       5 = YSMALL
C                L2       ARRAY CONTAINING THE CANONICAL FORM OF
C                         THE SECOND INPUT LINE
C                RAD      REAL VARIABLE CONTAINING THE VALUE OF THE
C                         DESIRED RADIUS
C
C SUBSIDIARIES TYPE                 ENTRY
C                SUBROUTINE         APT003
C                SUBROUTINE         APT020
C                SUBROUTINE         APT078
      SUBROUTINE APT030 (RESULT,M1,L1,M2,L2,RAD)
      REAL L1,L2
      DIMENSION RESULT(7),L1(4),L2(4)
C
C
C
C... 1.MAIN CDE PACKAGE. INCLUDED IN EVERY PROGRAM IN THE SUBROUTINE
C...    LIBRARY.
C
      LOGICAL LDEF
      DIMENSION DEF(75),DSHARE(100),FXCOR(170),HOLRTH(20),SV(442),
     1         ZNUMBR(30),LDEF(15),ISV(379)
      DIMENSION IBRKPT(51),IDEF(20),IFXCOR(60),ISHARE(31),KNUMBR(51)
      COMMON/TOTAL/DEF,DSHARE,FXCOR,HOLRTH,SV,ZNUMBR,LDEF,ISV
      EQUIVALENCE(ISV(30),IBRKPT(1)),(ISV(110),KNUMBR(1)),
     1           (ISV(190),IDEF(1)),(ISV(210),ISHARE(1)),
     2           (ISV(279),IFXCOR(1))
C
C
C
```

Figure 17.8

(continues)

(continued)

```
C...  2.DEF BLOCK. REAL VARIABLES USED BY DEF. RED. ROUTINES WHICH MUST
C...     REMAIN INVIOLATE.
C
      REAL LN1
      DIMENSION     A(12,2),   AHOLD(2,4),     C1( 8),
     1              LN1( 5),      R(10),     REF(2,4),
C
      EQUIVALENCE (DEF(1),A(1,1)),(DEF(25),AHOLD(1,1)),(DEF(33),C(1)),
     +             (DEF(41),LN1(1)),  (DEF(46),R(1)), (DEF(56),REF(1,1))
C
C
C...  3. DSHARE DEF. RED. BLOCK. USED FOR REAL VARIABLES AND SHARED WITH
C...     ARELEM
C
      REAL L
      DIMENSION            C(100),  G(93),  L(83),
     +          P(79), SC(63),  T(47), T1(35),  V(23)
C
      EQUIVALENCE  (DSHARE(100),  C(100),  G(93),  L(83),
     +          P(79), SC(63),  T(47), T1(35),  V(23))
C
C...  10. ZNUMBR BLOCK. REAL LITERALS.
C
      EQUIVALENCE (ZNUMBR(1),Z0),  (ZNUMBR(2),Z1) ,  (ZNUMBR( 3),Z2)    ,
     1    (ZNUMBR( 4),Z3)    ,  (ZNUMBR( 5),Z5)    ,  (ZNUMBR( 6),Z10)   ,
     2    (ZNUMBR( 7),Z90)   ,  (ZNUMBR( 8),Z1E6)  ,  (ZNUMBR( 9),Z1E38) ,
     3    (ZNUMBR(10),Z5EM1) ,  (ZNUMBR(11),Z6EM1) ,  (ZNUMBR(12),Z9EM1) ,
     4    (ZNUMBR(13),Z11EM1),  (ZNUMBR(14),Z12EM1),  (ZNUMBR(15),Z1EM2) ,
     5    (ZNUMBR(16),Z1EM3) ,  (ZNUMBR(17),Z1EM5) ,  (ZNUMBR(18),Z5EM6) ,
     6    (ZNUMBR(19),Z1EM6) ,  (ZNUMBR(20),Z1EM7) ,  (ZNUMBR(21),Z1EM9) ,
     7    (ZNUMBR(22),Z1EM1) ,  (ZNUMBR(23),ZM1)   ,  (ZNUMBR(24),DEGRAD),
     8    (ZNUMBR(25),PI)
C
          .
          .
          .
```

Figure 17.8 An example of the use of COMMON and EQUIVALENCE in APT IV.

APT is a particularly good example of the use of **COMMON** and **EQUIVALENCE** due to the combination of its size and complexity with the overall modular structure of the program. As an example of how things can be improved by the use of modules, Figure 17.9 shows how the same subroutine might start if it were rewritten using the full capability of Fortran 90, although it must be emphasized that the way in which the **COMMON** blocks are used in the original version is being preserved only as an example; if it were really being rewritten there would be other, more significant, changes to be made to the global data structure as well.

```
      SUBROUTINE APT030(result,mod1,line1,mod2,line2,radius)

!  Fortran subroutine    APT030            28/3/93   TMRE

!  Purpose     To generate the canonical form of a circle defined
!              as tangent to each of two given lines and having a
!              given radius by the following APT statement:

!                RESULT = CIRCLE/****, L1, ****, L2, RADIUS, RAD


!              where **** = XLARGE, YLARGE, XSMALL or YSMALL
!  Linkage     CALL APT030(result,mod1,line1,mod2,line2,radius)

!  Arguments   result   array to contain the canonical form of the
!                       resulting circle
!              mod1     integer equivalent of the first modifier
!                         1 = XLARGE    2 = YLARGE
!                         4 = XSMALL    5 = YSMALL
!              line1    array containing the canonical form of the
!                       first input line
!              mod2     integer equivalent of the second modifier
!                         1 = XLARGE    2 = YLARGE
!                         4 = XSMALL    5 = YSMALL
!              line2    array containing the canonical form of the
!                       second input line
!              radius   real variable containing the value of the
!                       desired radius

!  Modules Used
!              Def      REAL a(12,2),ahold(2,4),c1(8),ln1(5),
!                       r(10),ref(2,4)
!              Dshare   REAL c,g,l,p,sc,t,t1,v
!              Znumber  REAL z0,z1,z2,z3,z5,z10,z90,z1e6,z1e38,
!                       z5em1,z6em1,z9em1,z11em1,z12em1,
!                       z1em2,z1em3, z1em5,z5em6,z1em6,
!                       z1em7,z1em9,z1em1,zm1,degrad,pi

!  Subsidiaries      Type            Name
!                    Subroutine      APT003
!                    Subroutine      APT020
!                    Subroutine      APT078
      USE Def
      USE Dshare
      USE Znumber
      IMPLICIT NONE

      INTEGER, INTENT(IN) :: mod1,mod2
      REAL, INTENT(IN) :: radius
      REAL, DIMENSION(4), INTENT(IN) :: line1, line2
      REAL, DIMENSION(7), INTENT(OUT) :: result
        .
        .
        .
```

Figure 17.9 A hypothetical APT IV example using modules.

17.9 Ensuring consistent COMMON block specifications

COMMON blocks are normally used in large programs and their specification will appear in a number of different program units. Although some programs deliberately declare the same COMMON block in different, but compatible, ways in different program units, as was done in the extract shown in Figure 17.8, it is usually preferable to use identical declarations in every program unit that requires access to the COMMON block in order to ensure that there are no mistakes as a result of incompatible COMMON block specifications.

Fortran 90 provides two methods for ensuring that COMMON blocks are specified and used in a consistent fashion. The first of these is to place the complete COMMON block specification in a module and then to USE that module in all the program units that require access to the COMMON block. Figure 17.10 shows how such a module might be written and used.

Although it is quite acceptable to specify several COMMON blocks in the same module, it is important to realize that it is not possible to use a statement of the form

```
USE Common_blocks, ONLY : BLOCK1
```

to make only the contents of a single COMMON block available to a particular program unit, since this form of statement will only make the name of the COMMON

```
MODULE Common_blocks
   IMPLICIT NONE
   SAVE

!  This module contains the definition of COMMON blocks used
!  in the program

   REAL, DIMENSION(100) :: A,B,C
   REAL :: X,Y,Z
   INTEGER :: N,M
   COMMON /BLOCK1/ A,B,C,X,Y,Z,N,M
      .
      .
      .

END MODULE Common_blocks

SUBROUTINE sub
   USE Common_blocks
      .
      .
      .

END SUBROUTINE sub
```

Figure 17.10 Using a module to ensure consistent COMMON block specifications.

block available but *not the names of the variables that make up the block*. It would, of course, be possible to list the names of all the entities in the block, but that would eliminate the advantage of placing the COMMON block in a module! If a program has several COMMON blocks, therefore, not all of which are required in all program units, it is preferable to place them in several modules so that only those which are required need be specified in individual program units:

```
SUBROUTINE sub
   USE Common_block_1
   USE Common_block_2
   USE Common_block_4
   .
   .
   .
END SUBROUTINE sub
```

An alternative approach is to use the Fortran 90 INCLUDE facility. This enables Fortran source text to be inserted into the program at a specified point during the compilation of the program. The INCLUDE line, which is *not* a Fortran statement, takes the form

INCLUDE *char-literal-constant*

where *char-literal-constant* is a character constant which, in a processor-dependent manner, indicates what the text to be inserted is, or where it is to be obtained from. Typically it will be the name of a file containing the source text to be inserted.

An INCLUDE line must be the only non-blank text on the line on which it appears, other than an optional trailing comment. Its effect is as though the text reference by the INCLUDE line physically replaces the INCLUDE line immediately before the line is processed by the Fortran processor. The included text may itself contain additional INCLUDE lines up to a limit defined by the processor.

The Fortran 90 INCLUDE facility is similar to INCLUDE facilities which were extensions to the language in almost all FORTRAN 77 processors, and was added in response to an overwhelming demand from certain sections of the Fortran community. However, it is defined in an intrinsically non-portable fashion and we do not recommend its use other than in certain very specific situations. The main reason for this type of facility in the past was to simplify the inclusion of COMMON blocks, and this is better done in Fortran 90 by use of modules. If the same sequence of statements is required in several different program units it is usually preferable to use the facilities of the source editor in the first instance or, if there is a long sequence of statements, to place them in a procedure.

SELF-TEST EXERCISES 17.1

1   What is the purpose of a **COMMON** block?

2   What are the three differences between blank **COMMON** and named **COMMON**?

3   Why should **COMMON** blocks not be used in new Fortran programs?

4   A FORTRAN 77 program contains a subroutine **TEST4A** which begins with the following statements:

```
SUBROUTINE TEST4A
INTEGER K1(20),K2(20),K3(20)
DOUBLE PRECISION D(15)
COMPLEX Q(5)
COMMON /TEST4/ K1,D,Q,K2,K3
K1(1) = 1
K1(11) = 11
K2(1) = 2
K2(11) = 21
K3(1) = 3
K3(11) = 31
D(1) = 12.0
Q(1) = (-3.0,-4.0)
   .
   .
   .
```

Another subroutine, **TEST4B**, begins as follows:

```
SUBROUTINE TEST4B
REAL X(20),Y(2,15),Z(2,10)
INTEGER M1(15),M2(15)
COMMON /TEST4/ X,Y,Z,M1,M2
CALL TEST4A
   .
   .
   .
```

After executing the call to **TEST4A** what are the values of the array elements X(1), Y(1,1), Z(1,1), M1(1), M1(15), M2(1), M2(15)?

5   What will be printed by the following (FORTRAN 77) program?

```
PROGRAM TEST5
CHARACTER*20 S
CHARACTER S1(5),S2(5),S3(5),S4(5),S5(5)
EQUIVALENCE (S2(2),S1(5)), (S2(3),S3(1),S(6:))
EQUIVALENCE (S4(1),S3(5)), (S4(5),S5(2))
S = 'My name is David'
PRINT *,S1(1)//S2(2)//S5(4)//S1(4)//S2(4)//S4(1)//S3(5)
END
```

SUMMARY

- A COMMON block is a contiguous block of memory in which the individual items are identified by their position within the block and only locally by their name.

- A COMMON block may have a global name.

- There may be at most one (unnamed) blank COMMON block in a program.

- Initial values can only be given to items in a named COMMON block, and then only in a special, non-executable, BLOCK DATA program unit.

- Named COMMON blocks may become undefined when no currently active program units refer to them, unless referred to in a SAVE statement.

- The EQUIVALENCE statement instructs the compiler to arrange the program's storage so that two or more items share the same location(s).

- Fortran 90 syntax introduced in Chapter 17:

COMMON block declaration	COMMON /name/ list of local names
	COMMON // list of local names
	COMMON list of local names
Initial statements	BLOCK DATA name
	BLOCK DATA
Saving COMMON blocks	SAVE /common_block_name/
Sharing storage	EQUIVALENCE (name1,name2, ...)
Inclusion of source text from another source	INCLUDE name

PROGRAMMING EXERCISES

We strongly recommend that you do not use any of the features described in this chapter in any new programs. Nevertheless, because you are bound to meet them in older FORTRAN 77 programs, we include a small number of exercises to help familiarize you with their use. To emphasize that these features should not be used in new Fortran 90 programs, all examples use the old FORTRAN 77 style.

17.1 Write an input subroutine, having no arguments, which reads up to 20 sets of data, where each set of data consists of the following information:

Columns 1–30	First name and last name, separated by one or more spaces
Column 32	Sex (M or F)
Columns 34–36	Age
Column 38	Marital status (S = single, M = married, W = widowed, D = divorced, C = co-habiting)

The subroutine should store the data in a COMMON block.

A second subroutine, having a single integer argument n, should print the details of the nth person in the set of data.

Write a main program which uses these two subroutines to read a set of data and print the name, sex, marital status and age of the oldest person in the data set. If there are two or more 'oldest people' then print the details of all of them.

17.2 Modify the program written for Exercise 17.1 by adding a third subroutine, having no arguments, which will sort the data into alphabetical order of last names (and first names if the last names are the same).

Your program should now read the data, print it out in alphabetic order, and print the name and age of the oldest person(s).

When you have tested this program, modify it so that it does not use any COMMON blocks but uses a module instead.

17.3 **(a)** Write a program to generate all the permutations of the numbers 1 to n, where n is read by the program. (Hint: as well as an array P to store the current permutation, it may be useful to generate related arrays, such as W, where W(P(I))=I for I=1 to n and to store them in COMMON storage if they are used in more than one program unit.)

(b) The distances by road between five towns A, B, C, D and E are as follows: A–B, 7 miles; A–C, 7 miles; A–D, 6 miles; A–E, 10 miles; B–C, 11 miles; B–D, 3 miles; B–E, 4 miles; C–D, 12 miles; C–E, 9 miles; D–E, 6 miles. A salesman has to visit each town once, starting and finishing at A. Write a program to calculate the distances for each possible route, and so to find the shortest possible distance.

17.4 Three one-dimensional arrays are declared with the following statements:

```
REAL A(3),B(3),C(3)
EQUIVALENCE (A,B)
```

Write a program containing these declarations which reads three values into each of the arrays A and B, and then stores the sums of corresponding elements of A and B in C. Finally the program should print the three arrays as three columns (A, B and C).

Were the results what you expected? If not, add extra PRINT statements at various points in your program to obtain intermediate values.

17.5 Use a BLOCK DATA subprogram to initialize two arrays NUMB1 and NUMB2 to the following values:

NUMB1(1) = 0	NUMB2(1) = 0
NUMB1(2) = 0	NUMB2(2) = 0
NUMB1(3) = 0	NUMB2(3) = 0
NUMB1(4) = 1	NUMB2(4) = 0
NUMB1(5) = 1	NUMB2(5) = 1
NUMB1(6) = 0	NUMB2(6) = 1
NUMB1(7) = 0	NUMB2(7) = 1
NUMB1(8) = 0	NUMB2(8) = 0

The arrays contain the binary numbers 11000 and 1110. Use a COMMON block to make these arrays available to two subroutines. The first subroutine should perform binary addition between the two numbers, and place the result in NUMB1, while the second should convert the binary number stored in NUMB1 to a decimal value. The result should then be displayed on the screen in the main program.

More about numerical methods

18

The preceding chapters have covered all of Fortran 90, apart from certain features which we do not recommend using that are described briefly in Appendix E. In this final chapter we return to the subject of numerical methods, which was first discussed in Chapter 10.

After a brief review of some of the limitations of numerical methods, the bulk of the chapter is taken up with a discussion of some of the most widely used numerical techniques relating to the solution of various types of equation, the fitting of curves through sets of data points, and the integration of functions by numerical quadrature. The exercises at the end of this chapter also briefly describe certain other techniques.

Although the descriptions given in this chapter give a sound basis for the understanding of these and other numerical methods, we cannot emphasize too strongly that this is a highly specialized area. If your programs are likely to involve much numerical work then you should either use one of the excellent libraries of numerical software that are widely available, or you should refer to one of the many books devoted to numerical methods, several of which are cited in this chapter.

18.1 Numerical methods and their limitations

In Chapter 10 we introduced some of the basic concepts involved in numerical computation and emphasized that, because of such effects as round-off, conditioning and stability, the choice of the numerical method to be used could substantially affect the result obtained in a particular case. It is not our intention to discuss these concepts any further in this book, but it is important that the programmer should be aware of the strengths and weaknesses of different methods before deciding which one to use in a particular situation. This is particularly relevant when using a sophisticated mathematical library such as the NAG library (NAG, 1988) or the IMSL library (Visual Numerics, 1992), where there are often a large number of subroutines which, to the uninitiated, will all carry out the same type of calculation. A well-documented mathematical subprogram library will explain which one of a choice of subprograms should be used in a particular circumstance.

When writing a program, we are generally trying to solve a problem to which there is an exact mathematical answer. Mathematics abounds with existence theorems which typically state that, given certain conditions, a solution to a specified problem exists. However, the proofs are often non-constructive – in the sense that they can imply an infinity of operations to obtain the desired solution or, even worse, do not even specify what set of operations is required to construct the solution. A second type of difficulty arises from the fact that many existence proofs show that some set of real (or complex) numbers is a solution to a specified problem. The set of real (or complex) numbers forms a continuum. However, on a computer, real or complex numbers can only be specified with a finite precision. For example, neither π nor $\sqrt{2}$ can be exactly represented numerically on a digital computer.

The field of numerical analysis is the design of algorithms that will approximate, to a specified precision, the mathematical solutions of problems. Moreover, it is a requirement that these algorithms execute efficiently; in other words, that they use as few operations as possible. Finally, it is required that they be robust; that is, that they perform reliably for a large range of inputs and detect and report when they are unable to solve a problem. This is the ideal. In practice, there are still many problems for which we have to settle for less.

In Chapter 10 we also discussed the use of parameterized real variables as a means of writing procedures whose precision was both portable and readily changeable. However, we pointed out that relying on increasing the precision of calculations would not always eliminate numerical difficulties. Understanding the underlying reasons for the numerical difficulties is important for their correct resolution.

Chapter 10 also introduced two simple, but widely used, techniques in numerical programming, namely the method of least squares for fitting a straight line as an approximation to a set of data points and the bisection method for the solution of a non-linear equation.

In this chapter we shall examine other, superior, methods of solution of non-linear equations, and will also consider the solution of a system of simultaneous linear equations. We shall also look at more sophisticated methods of interpolation and curve-fitting in which the data does not necessarily lie near a straight line. Finally, we shall briefly discuss methods of integration in order, for example, to find the area under a curve.

It is important to emphasize, however, that most of the subprograms developed in this chapter are only examples to illustrate the basic techniques. Some introductory textbooks on numerical analysis are by Dahlquist and Björck (1974), Scheid (1968), and Forsythe *et al.* (1977). A great deal of effort has been expended by many people over many years in refining algorithms for numerical computation, especially to deal with the difficult cases, and anyone who has a serious need in this area should normally consider using procedures from one of the established libraries (such as those produced by NAG and IMSL) and not write their own.

18.2 Solving quadratic equations

We start with what, on the surface, appears to be a simple problem, namely finding the roots of a quadratic equation. We shall, however, see that even such a simple problem involves subtle numerical issues if we are trying to produce robust software. This should instill a healthy caution in the reader when more complicated problems are being solved.

Everyone who studied algebra in high school learned that the quadratic equation

$$ax^2 + bx + c = 0$$

where $a \neq 0$, has two roots, given by the formula

$$\frac{-b \pm \sqrt{b^2 - 4ac}}{2a}$$

We shall now examine some of the difficulties which can occur when using this formula on a computer with six decimal digits of precision and an exponent range of 10^{40} (many workstations and PCs have single-precision hardware close to this situation).

Let us consider the equation

$$x^2 - 6x + 5 = 0$$

If we solve this on a computer by using the above formula we will obtain answers very close to 1 and 5 (which are the exact roots).

If we multiply the above equation by 10^{30}, we obtain the new equation

$$10^{30}x^2 - 6 \times 10^{30}x + 5 \times 10^{30} = 0$$

The roots of this equation are, of course, still 1 and 5.

Now, using the standard formula, we would calculate

$$\frac{6 \times 10^{30} \pm \sqrt{(6 \times 10^{30})^2 - 4 \times 10^{30} \times 5 \times 10^{30}}}{2 \times 10^{30}}$$

However, on our hypothetical computer, 10^{60} is not a representable number. Consequently, the program would abort with an overflow. Similarly, if the original equation was multiplied by 10^{-30}, we would either abort with a numeric underflow or, if the computer being used simply represents underflow as 0, would obtain the roots

$$\frac{6 \times 10^{-30} \pm \sqrt{(6 \times 10^{-30})^2 - 4 \times 10^{-30} \times 5 \times 10^{-30}}}{2 \times 10^{-30}}$$

$$= \frac{6 \times 10^{-30} \pm \sqrt{0}}{2 \times 10^{-30}}$$

$$= 3 \text{ and } 3$$

which are two very poor answers!

This type of difficulty can sometimes be reduced by scaling the equations before attempting to solve them. For example, we could divide the equation by $\max(|a|, |b|, |c|)$, so that all the coefficients lie in the range $[-1, 1]$. This, unfortunately, is not a complete solution to the scaling problem. Consider, for example, the equation

$$10^{-20}x^2 + 10^{20}x + 10^{20} = 0$$

This has one root near -1 and one root near -10^{40}. If we simply scale the equation by dividing by 10^{20}, we will either get an underflow error, or the coefficient of x^2 will become 0. In the latter case the equation becomes the linear equation

$$x + 1 = 0$$

This has only one root, $x = -1$, and we have lost the second, large negative, root of the original quadratic.

In situations like this, where one root is in the range of the floating-point numbers, we would like to obtain the representable root and indicate that the other root is too large in absolute value to be represented. In this case, we might resort to transforming the equation by scaling the roots or to using one of the methods for finding roots that are described in Sections 10.5 (bisection method), 18.3 (Newton's method) and 18.4 (secant method).

Next, let us consider the case where one root is much bigger, in absolute value, than the other. For example, the equation

$$x^2 - 10^6 x + 1 = 0$$

has, to six significant places, the roots 10^{-6} and 10^6. The application of the standard formula gives

$$\frac{10^6 \pm \sqrt{(10^6)^2 - 4}}{2}$$

Because of the round-off errors, since 4 will not significantly add to 10^{12}, this becomes

$$\frac{10^6 \pm \sqrt{10^{12}}}{2}$$

So the standard formula gives the roots 10^6 (which is good) and 0 (which is bad).

The usual way employed to solve this case is first to calculate the root in which the sign of $\sqrt{b^2 - 4ac}$ is the same as that of $-b$. This eliminates any round-off problems caused by subtracting two nearly equal numbers. In the above example, since $-(-10^6)$ is positive, we take the positive value of the square root. This will give one root as $(10^6 + 10^6)/2$, or 10^6, which is a good answer. To obtain the other root, we note that the product of the roots of the general quadratic equation is c/a. Therefore, once one root has been found accurately, we can obtain the other root by dividing c/a by the first root. In the above example, this would give a second root of $(1/1)/10^6$, or 10^{-6}, another good answer. Note that this technique eliminates the possibility of catastrophic cancellation when two nearly equal numbers are subtracted.

In order to reduce overflow problems during computation, we rewrite the standard formula in a different, but mathematically equivalent, way. Thus, the roots of the equation

$$ax^2 + bx + c = 0, \qquad a \neq 0$$

are the same as the roots of

$$rx^2 + sx + t = 0, \qquad r \neq 0$$

where

$$r = \frac{a}{\max(|a|, |b|, |c|)}$$

$$s = \frac{b}{\max(|a|, |b|, |c|)}$$

$$t = \frac{c}{\max(|a|, |b|, |c|)}$$

The roots of this equation are

$$\frac{-s \pm \sqrt{s^2 - 4rt}}{2r}$$

What we have accomplished by these manipulations is that the coefficients we are now working with (r, s, and t) are all in the interval $[-1, 1]$. Thus overflow problems are diminished.

We shall then use the preceding formula to obtain one root only by, as already discussed, taking the sign of the square root so as to match that of the first part of the numerator (that is, match the sign of $-s$). This is to minimize cancellation effects.

Finally, the second root is obtained by dividing c/a by the first root.

A subroutine to implement this algorithm is shown in Figure 18.1. Note that the module **library_constants** is assumed, amongst other things, to define the constant **lib_prec** as the kind type parameter for real values, for example

```
MODULE library_constants
   IMPLICIT NONE


   ! Define precision
   INTEGER, PARAMETER :: lib_prec = &
                         SELECTED_REAL_KIND(P=6)
   .
   .
   .

END MODULE library_constants
```

Using this subroutine to find the roots of the equation

$$x^2 - 10^6 x + 1 = 0$$

we obtain the roots 10^6 and 10^{-6}.

```
SUBROUTINE quad_roots(a,b,c,root1,root2,error)
  USE library_constants
  IMPLICIT NONE

  ! Dummy arguments
  REAL(KIND=lib_prec), INTENT(IN) :: a,b,c
  REAL(KIND=lib_prec), INTENT(OUT) :: root1,root2
  LOGICAL :: error

  ! Local variables
  REAL(KIND=lib_prec) :: f,r,s,t,d

  ! Check for a=0
  error = a==0.0_lib_prec
  IF (error) RETURN

  ! Calculate scaled coefficients
  f = MAX(ABS(a),ABS(b),ABS(c))
  r = a/f
  s = b/f
  t = c/f

  ! Solve modified equation for first root
  d = SQRT(s*s-4.0_lib_prec*r*t)
  IF (s>0.0_lib_prec) THEN
     root1 = (-s-d)/(r+r)
  ELSE
     root1 = (-s+d)/(r+r)
  END IF

  ! Calculate other root
  root2 = (t/r)/root1

END SUBROUTINE quad_roots
```

Figure 18.1   An improved procedure for finding the roots of a quadratic equation.

18.3 Newton's method for solving non-linear equations

The bisection method introduced in Section 10.5 has one major strength and one major weakness. The strength is that, because the interval is halved at each iteration, it is guaranteed to converge to a root after a finite, and predictable, number of iterations. The weakness of the method, however, is that it is slow to converge. One of the reasons for this is that the method does not use all the available information, since it uses the sign of $f(x)$ at the end-points of the interval, but not the value of $f(x)$ at those points. Another weakness is that, for the method to work at all, the initial two points must bracket a root. In this section and the next, we will show some other commonly used techniques that

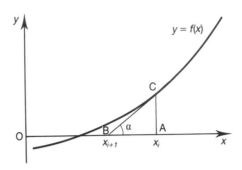

Figure 18.2 Newton's method of approximation.

usually converge considerably faster but have the defect that they sometimes fail to converge at all. Fast convergence is important, because each function evaluation can be expensive.

It is possible to combine interval-bisection with such faster methods and retain much of the best of both worlds, namely fast convergence and guaranteed convergence. This combination, however, would go beyond the scope of this book. It is described in Forsythe *et al.* (1977).

First we shall discuss **Newton's method**, sometimes known as the **Newton–Raphson method**. This method uses not only function values but also uses the first derivative, or **gradient**, of the curve to help find the next approximation. Figure 18.2 shows how, given the gradient at a point x_i, it is easy to obtain a new estimate for the root. In this method, we do not bracket a root by an interval but, instead, generate a sequence of approximations that (if successful) tend to the root.

From Figure 18.2 we can readily see that

$$
\begin{aligned}
x_{i+1} &= OB \\
&= OA - AB \\
&= x_i - AB \\
&= x_i - \frac{AC}{\tan \alpha} \\
&= x_i - \frac{f(x_i)}{f'(x_i)}
\end{aligned}
$$

where $f'(x_i)$ is the gradient of the curve at the point C, $(x_i, f(x_i))$, which is equal to $\tan \alpha$.

This formula

$$x_{i+1} = x_i - \frac{f(x_i)}{f'(x_i)}$$

is known as **Newton's iteration**, and is the basis for Newton's method of approximation to a root.

There will be situations in which the first derivative is not available, or would be very time-consuming to calculate, and in these situations Newton's method is not an appropriate one to choose (but see the description of the secant method in the next section). However, in many cases the derivative is readily available, and in these situations Newton's method will usually converge very rapidly.

It should be noted that Newton's method will converge slowly, sometimes more slowly than interval bisection, if the slope of the function is zero (or almost zero) in a region containing the zero of the function we are trying to find.

The only remaining problem is the determination of the form of convergence criterion to be used. In the bisection method, we used the size of the interval, which we showed to be related to the difference between the approximation to the root and the true value of that root. However, the Newton method does not bracket the root by an interval whose size tends to zero. The appropriate criterion for the Newton method is, therefore, to stop the iteration when a point x is found such that

$$|f(x)| \leqslant \epsilon$$

where ϵ is a user-specified tolerance. We are, by using this convergence criteria, not insisting that the Newton method find a root exactly. This is because the exact root may not be (indeed, for most functions, is not) a rational number and, therefore, cannot be expressed exactly as a floating-point number. Moreover, when a function is evaluated using floating-point arithmetic, it will not be evaluated exactly. Thus, even if there is a rational number X such that $f(X) = 0$, on a computer it is unlikely that $f(X) = 0$ exactly.

In choosing ϵ, the user must exercise some discretion. If f has a large derivative near a root, we should tolerate a relatively large value of $|f(x)|$ for x being accepted as a good approximation to a zero of f. On the other hand, if f has a small slope near the root, we should adopt a small value for ϵ. Otherwise, $|f(x)|$ may be small, but x could be a long way from the true zero. When working with a new function, some experimentation with the value of ϵ may be necessary.

■ **EXAMPLE 18.1**

1 Problem

Write a program to find a root of the equation $f(x) = 0$ using Newton's method. The program should use external functions to define the equation and its first derivative, and the user should input the accuracy required together with the x-coordinate of a point which can be used as the starting point for the interpolation.

2 Analysis

We have already discussed the mathematics involved in this method and so can proceed to the design of the program. We must, however, note that, generally, the closer the starting value is to the root, the better the convergence will be. Because the Newton method does not guarantee convergence, we shall specify an upper limit for the number of iterations permitted before terminating the process. The data design and structure plan are then quite straightforward:

Data design

	Purpose	Type	Name
A	Dummy arguments		
	Function whose root is required	REAL FUNCTION	f
	First derivative of f	REAL FUNCTION	f_prime
	Start point for interpolation	REAL	start
	Accuracy of result	REAL	epsilon
	Upper limit for iteration	INTEGER	max_iter
	Value of root	REAL	root
	Error/success condition	INTEGER	error
B	Local variables		
	Current value of f(x)	REAL	f_val
	Current value of f'(x)	REAL	f_der
	DO-loop control	INTEGER	i

Structure plan

> **1** If *epsilon* $\leq$ 0 then return with *error* $= -3$
>
> **2** Set *root* to initial approximation (*start*)
>
> **3** Repeat up to *max_iter* times
> > **3.1** Set *f_val* to *f*(*root*)
> > **3.2** If $|$ *f_val* $| \leq$ *epsilon* then
> > > **3.2.1** Process has converged, so return with *error* = 0
> > **3.3** Set *f_der* to *f'*(*root*)
> > **3.3** If *f_der* = 0 then
> > > **3.3.1** Iteration cannot proceed further, so return with *error* = −2
> > **3.4** Set *root* to *root* − *f_val*/*f_der*
>
> **4** Process has not converged after *max_iter* steps, so set *error* to −1

3 Solution

The main program is sufficiently similar to that given in Example 10.2 that we have not included it here. The subroutine which calculates the root is as follows:

```fortran
SUBROUTINE newton_raphson(f,f_prime,start,epsilon, &
                          max_iter,root,error)
   IMPLICIT NONE

   ! This subroutine finds a root of the equation f(x)=0
   ! using Newton-Raphson iteration.
   ! The function f-prime returns the value of the derivative of
   ! the function f(x).

   ! Dummy arguments
   REAL, EXTERNAL :: f,f_prime
   REAL, INTENT(IN) :: start,epsilon
   INTEGER, INTENT(IN) :: max_iter
   REAL, INTENT(OUT) :: root
   INTEGER, INTENT(OUT) :: error
      ! error indicates the result of the processing as follows:
      ! = 0   a root was found
      ! = -1  no root found after max_iter iterations
      ! = -2  the first derivative became zero, and so no further
      !       iterations were possible
      ! = -3  the value of epsilon supplied was negative or zero

   ! Local variables
   INTEGER :: i
   REAL :: f_val, f_der

   ! Check validity of epsilon
   IF (epsilon <= 0.0) THEN
      error = -3
      root = HUGE(root)
      RETURN
   END IF

   ! Begin the iteration at the specified value of x
   root = start

   ! Repeat the iteration up to the maximum number specified
   DO i=1, max_iter
      f_val =  f(root)
      ! Output latest estimate while testing
      PRINT '(2(A,E15.6))', "root = ",root," f(root) = ",f_val
      IF (ABS(f_val) <= epsilon) THEN
         ! A root has been found
         error = 0
         RETURN
      END IF
```

```
      f_der = f_prime(root)
      IF (f_der == 0.0) THEN
         ! f'(x)=0, so no more iterations are possible
         error = -2
         RETURN
      END IF


      ! Use Newton's iteration to obtain next approximation
      root = root - f_val/f_der
   END DO

   ! Process has not converged after max_iter iterations
   error = -1

END SUBROUTINE newton_raphson
```

Notice that if $\epsilon \leqslant 0$, we have set error to -3 *and* returned an answer of
HUGE(root). This is an example of double safety when an error in usage is
detected. If a user is so foolish as not to check error returns for problems, the
answer returned will be so absurd that a problem should be detected anyway. We
have also included a PRINT statement to show the progress of the iteration; this
would normally be removed when the subroutine has been verified to be working
correctly.

Figure 18.3 shows the result of running the program with three different
starting points using the same function f as was used in Example 10.2, namely
$f(x) = x + e^x$. A value of 10^{-6} was used for ϵ in each program execution. The
functions f and f_prime are extremely simple to write in this case:

```
REAL FUNCTION f( x )
   IMPLICIT NONE
   REAL, INTENT(IN) :: x
   f = x + EXP(x)
END FUNCTION f

REAL FUNCTION f_prime( x )
   IMPLICIT NONE
   REAL, INTENT(IN) :: x
   f_prime = 1.0 + EXP(x)
END FUNCTION f_prime
```

It will be noticed that although using a value of -10.0 or 0.0 as the initial
value produced extremely fast convergence (4 and 3 iterations, respectively),
using $+10.0$ produced a relatively slow convergence, which required 13
iterations. A moment's thought about the shape of the function will make the
reason for this difference quite clear – namely that for values of x greater than 2
or 3 the curve is almost parallel to the y-axis, with the result that Newton's
iteration does not work very well. Once again, this emphasizes the importance of

Starting at −10
```
root =    -0.100000E+02  f(root) =    -0.999995E+01
root =    -0.499725E-03  f(root) =     0.999001E+00
root =    -0.500125E+00  f(root) =     0.106330E+00
root =    -0.566314E+00  f(root) =     0.129968E-02
root =    -0.567143E+00  f(root) =     0.119209E-06
A root was found at x = -0.567143  f(x) =  0.119209E-06
```

Starting at 0
```
root =     0.000000E+00  f(root) =     0.100000E+01
root =    -0.500000E+00  f(root) =     0.106531E+00
root =    -0.566311E+00  f(root) =     0.130451E-02
root =    -0.567143E+00  f(root) =     0.238419E-06
A root was found at x = -0.567143  f(x) =  0.238419E-06
```

Starting at 10
```
root =     0.100000E+02  f(root) =     0.220365E+05
root =     0.899959E+01  f(root) =     0.810878E+04
root =     0.799860E+01  f(root) =     0.298480E+04
root =     0.699625E+01  f(root) =     0.109953E+04
root =     0.599077E+01  f(root) =     0.405713E+03
root =     0.497832E+01  f(root) =     0.150208E+03
root =     0.395111E+01  f(root) =     0.559442E+02
root =     0.289542E+01  f(root) =     0.209865E+02
root =     0.179614E+01  f(root) =     0.782247E+01
root =     0.682831E+00  f(root) =     0.266230E+01
root =    -0.210718E+00  f(root) =     0.599285E+00
root =    -0.541814E+00  f(root) =     0.398782E-01
root =    -0.567026E+00  f(root) =     0.183344E-03
root =    -0.567143E+00  f(root) =    -0.596046E-07
A root was found at x = -0.567143  f(x) = -0.596046E-07
```

Figure 18.3 Three solutions for $x + e^x = 0$ using the subroutine `newton_raphson`.

thinking about the method to be used *and* the range of values in which it should be used. In the next section we shall meet a third approach to solving this type of problem, and a comparison of the three methods will be shown in Figure 18.7.

Newton–Raphson iteration can be shown, under certain circumstances, to have superior convergence properties to interval bisection. Whereas the error in the bisection method is only halved at each iteration, the error in Newton's method is approximately proportional to the square of the error of the previous iterate. The mathematical analysis required to show this is beyond the scope of this book, but is discussed by Dahlquist and Björck (1974). However, the faster convergence comes at a cost, for Newton–Raphson iteration, unlike interval bisection, does not always converge to zero. Consider, for example, the case in which $f(x) = x^{1/3}$. The Newton–Raphson iteration in this case is

$$
\begin{aligned}
x_{n+1} &= x_n - \frac{x_n^{1/3}}{x_n^{-2/3}/3} \\
&= x_n - 3x_n \\
&= -2x_n
\end{aligned}
$$

So, if we start at the point x_0, we generate a sequence of iterates $x_0, -2x_0, 4x_0, -8x_0, 16x_0, \ldots$. Thus, if $x_0 \neq 0$, the sequence will oscillate with ever-increasing amplitude and will definitely not converge to 0 (the answer we are hoping to get) no matter how close to 0 we start the iteration. It will only converge to 0 if we start the iteration at 0 – which is not a very practical algorithm!

18.4 The secant method of solving non-linear equations

As we have seen, Newton's method for the solution of non-linear equations requires the values of the first derivative of the function as well as the values of the function itself. For many functions, calculating the derivative is expensive or impossible, and in these situations the **secant method** can be used. This method can be regarded as being derived from Newton's method by replacing the derivative by an estimate of the derivative obtained from the slope of the line joining the last two iterates, as shown in Figure 18.4.

The point where this line (called a secant – hence the name of the method) cuts the x-axis is taken to be the next iterate. Notice that, unlike Newton's

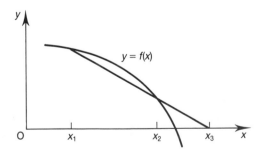

Figure 18.4   The secant method of approximation.

method, we now require two values of x to start the iteration. However, unlike the interval bisection method, the two values do not have to have opposite signs for the corresponding function values. It is thus easier to find two values to start the secant method than the interval bisection method.

The equation of the straight line joining the two end-points of the interval can easily be derived by noting that

$$\frac{y - f_1}{x - x_1} = \frac{f_2 - f_1}{x_2 - x_1}, \qquad \text{for } x_2 \neq x_1$$

where f_1 is the value of $f(x_1)$ and f_2 is the value of $f(x_2)$, and that the equation of the line is therefore

$$y = \frac{f_2 - f_1}{x_2 - x_1}(x - x_1) + f_1, \qquad x_2 \neq x_1$$

This line cuts the x-axis where $y = 0$. Thus x_3, the x-coordinate of the intersection, satisfies the equation

$$0 = \frac{f_2 - f_1}{x_2 - x_1}(x_3 - x_1) + f_1$$

and, therefore,

$$x_3 = x_1 - \frac{f_1(x_2 - x_1)}{f_2 - f_1}, \qquad f_2 \neq f_1$$

The next iterate x_3 is thus calculated as a correction to the end-point x_1. This is a good form from a computational viewpoint as it tends to minimize round-off errors. For the next iteration we therefore discard x_1 and replace it by x_3.

One potential problem is immediately apparent, namely the situation where f_1 and f_2 are the same, or very close to each other. This corresponds to the position shown in Figure 18.5, and clearly will cause the method to fail since the line joining the two end-points is either parallel to the x-axis, or almost parallel to it.

Although less intuitively obvious than the situation shown in Figure 18.5, there are other situations in which the secant method may not converge, and for which another method may be better. It is thus imperative that the DO loop used to control the iteration should have a sensible maximum iteration count, so that another method can be tried in the event that the secant method does not converge to a solution.

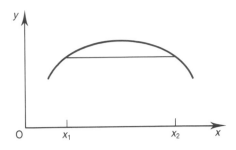

Figure 18.5 A failure position for the secant method.

As with Newton's method, the appropriate convergence criterion is that the iteration be stopped when a point x is found such that

$$|f(x)| \leqslant \epsilon$$

where ϵ is a user-specified tolerance. The considerations that go into choosing ϵ are the same as those already discussed for Newton's method.

■ **EXAMPLE 18.2**

1 Problem

Write a program to find a root of the equation $f(x) = 0$ using the secant method. The program should use an external function to define the equation, and the user should input the accuracy required and the x-coordinates of two points to be used as starting points for the iteration.

2 Analysis

As with Newton's method, the closer the two starting values are to the root, the better the convergence will generally be. We shall ensure that x_2 is the most recent approximation, and will rearrange the initial values, if necessary, so as to ensure that x_2 is the one apparently closest to a root, that is, $|f_2| \leqslant |f_1|$. Furthermore, as already discussed, because the secant method does not guarantee convergence, we shall specify an upper limit for the number of iterations permitted before terminating the process.

As with the very similar Example 18.1, the data design and structure plan are quite straightforward:

Data design

Purpose	Type	Name
A Dummy arguments		
Function whose root is required	REAL FUNCTION	f
Start points for interpolation	REAL	start1, start2
Accuracy of result	REAL	epsilon
Upper limit for iteration	INTEGER	max_iter
Value of root	REAL	root
Error/success condition	INTEGER	error
B Local variables		
Current values of end points	REAL	x1, x2
New end point	REAL	x3
Values of f(x) at x1, x2 and x3	REAL	f1, f2, f3
Temporay variables for use during swapping	REAL	tempx, tempf
DO loop control	INTEGER	i

Structure plan

1 If $x1 = x2$ then return with *error* $= -1$

2 If *epsilon* $\leqslant 0$ then return with *error* $= -2$

3 Set *f1* and *f2* to $f(x1)$ and $f(x2)$

4 If $|f1| < |f2|$ then interchange *x1* and *x2*, *f1* and *f2*

5 Repeat up to *max_iter* times

    5.1 If *f1* $=$ *f2* then

        5.1.1 Iteration cannot proceed further, so return with *error* $= -4$

    5.2 Calculate *x3* and *f3*

    5.3 If $|f3| \leq$ *epsilon* then

        5.3.1 Process has converged, return with *root* $= x3$, *error* $= 0$ otherwise

        5.3.2 Set $x1 = x2$, $f1 = f2$ and $x2 = x3$, $f2 = f3$

6 Process has not converged after *max_iter* steps, so set *error* to -3

[3] Solution

Once again, we shall not include the main program, since it is very similar to the one used in Example 10.2 (and to the one used in Example 18.1). The subroutine which calculates the root is as follows:

```
SUBROUTINE secant(f,start1,start2,epsilon,max_iter,    &
                root, error)
    IMPLICIT NONE

    ! This subroutine calculates a root of the equation f(x) = 0
    ! by use of the secant method
```

```fortran
! Dummy arguments
REAL, EXTERNAL :: f
REAL, INTENT(IN) :: start1,start2,epsilon
INTEGER, INTENT(IN) :: max_iter
REAL, INTENT(OUT) :: root
INTEGER, INTENT(OUT) :: error

! Local variables
REAL :: x1,x2,x3,f1,f2,f3,tempx,tempf
INTEGER :: i

! Check validity of initial points
IF (start1 == start2) THEN
   error = -1
   root = HUGE(root)              ! Largest number
   RETURN
END IF

! Check validity of epsilon
IF (epsilon <= 0.0) THEN
   error = -2
   root = HUGE(root)              ! Largest number
   RETURN
END IF

! Set up initial pair of points
x1 = start1
x2 = start2
f1 = f(x1)
f2 = f(x2)

! Choose the x with the best function value to be
! the most recent estimate
IF (ABS(f1) < ABS(f2)) THEN
   tempx = x1
   tempf = f1
   x1 = x2
   f1 = f2
   x2 = tempx
   f2 = tempf
END IF

! Repeat the iteration up to the maximum number specified
DO i = 1,max_iter
   IF (f1 == f2) THEN
      ! No further iterations possible
      error = -4
      root = x2
      RETURN
   END IF

   ! Calculate next approximation
   x3 = x1 - f1*(x2 - x1)/(f2 - f1)
   f3 = f(x3)
   ! Output latest approximation while testing
   PRINT '(2(A,E15.6))', "x3 = ",x3," f(x3) = ",f3
```

```
    IF (ABS(f3) <= epsilon) THEN
       ! A root has been found
       error = 0
       root = x3
       RETURN
    END IF

    ! Update points for next iteration
    x1 = x2
    f1 = f2
    x2 = x3
    f2 = f3
  END DO

  ! Process has not converged after max_iter steps
  error = -3
  root = x2

END SUBROUTINE secant
```

Initial bounds of −10 and 0

```
x3 =    -0.909095E+00  f(x3) =    -0.506206E+00
x3 =    -0.603566E+00  f(x3) =    -0.567080E-01
x3 =    -0.565021E+00  f(x3) =     0.332731E-02
x3 =    -0.567157E+00  f(x3) =    -0.218153E-04
x3 =    -0.567143E+00  f(x3) =    -0.596046E-07
A root was found at x = -0.567143   f(x) = -0.596046E-07
```

Initial bounds of 10 and 11

```
x3 =     0.941777E+01  f(x3) =     0.123146E+05
x3 =     0.868028E+01  f(x3) =     0.589436E+04
x3 =     0.800319E+01  f(x3) =     0.299847E+04
x3 =     0.730211E+01  f(x3) =     0.149073E+04
x3 =     0.660895E+01  f(x3) =     0.748309E+03
x3 =     0.591028E+01  f(x3) =     0.374720E+03
x3 =     0.520950E+01  f(x3) =     0.188212E+03
x3 =     0.450232E+01  f(x3) =     0.947283E+02
x3 =     0.378572E+01  f(x3) =     0.478531E+02
x3 =     0.305417E+01  f(x3) =     0.242578E+02
x3 =     0.230209E+01  f(x3) =     0.122971E+02
x3 =     0.152885E+01  f(x3) =     0.614171E+01
x3 =     0.757328E+00  f(x3) =     0.288990E+01
x3 =     0.716745E-01  f(x3) =     0.114598E+01
x3 =    -0.378889E+00  f(x3) =     0.305733E+00
x3 =    -0.542831E+00  f(x3) =     0.382697E-01
x3 =    -0.566289E+00  f(x3) =     0.133967E-02
x3 =    -0.567140E+00  f(x3) =     0.590086E-05
x3 =    -0.567143E+00  f(x3) =     0.596046E-07
A root was found at x = -0.567143   f(x) = 0.596046E-07
```

Figure 18.6 Two solutions for $x + e^x = 0$ using the subroutine **secant**.

Bisect	Secant	Newton–Raphson
-10.000000	-10.000000	-10.000000
-5.000000	-0.909095	-0.000500
-2.500000	-0.603566	-0.500125
-1.250000	-0.565021	-0.566314
-0.625000	-0.567157	-0.567143
-0.312500	-0.567143	
-0.468750		
-0.546875		
-0.585938		
-0.566406		
-0.576172		
-0.571289		
-0.568848		
-0.567627		
-0.567017		
-0.567322		
-0.567169		
-0.567093		
-0.567131		
-0.567150		
-0.567141		

Figure 18.7 A comparison of the bisection, secant and Newton–Raphson methods.

Note that once the function has been evaluated at a point, that value is saved so it never needs to be recalculated. Also note that we have included a **PRINT** statement so that we can see each new estimate of the value of the root. This print statement will normally be removed when we are sure that subroutine **secant** is working correctly. Figure 18.6 shows the result of running this program twice, using different initial intervals, with the same function subprogram to define the equation to be solved as was used in Example 18.1 (and in Example 10.2). In both cases a value of 10^{-6} was specified for ϵ, and a maximum iteration count of 20. The first example used the initial interval of -10 to 0, while the second used an initial interval of 10 to 11, which is similar to the case which caused some difficulty for Newton's method in Example 18.1. It is interesting to examine the actual iterations carried out in these two cases.

Figure 18.7 shows the successive iterates produced by the subroutines **bisect** (Example 10.2), **secant** (Example 18.2) and **newton_raphson** (Example 18.1) using similar starting situations, and it can be seen very clearly how the Newton–Raphson and secant methods are much more efficient in this case than the bisection method, which frequently moves away from the root in the latter stages because of its inability to recognize that one of its end-points is very close to the root.

As with Newton's method, it can be shown that, under certain circumstances, the secant method has superior convergence properties than the interval bisection method. The error in the secant method is approximately proportional to the 1.6th power of the error of the preceding iterate; see Dahlquist and Björck (1974) for the mathematical analysis. However, as with Newton's method, the cost of the improved performance is that the secant method does not always converge to a root. Note that the rate of convergence is not as good as the Newton method, but we have avoided the cost of the derivative evaluation required by the Newton method. The choice between using the secant method or Newton's method, therefore, depends on the cost of evaluating the derivative.

18.5 Solution of simultaneous linear equations by Gaussian elimination

The solution of a system of linear equations is perhaps the most common need in engineering and scientific problems, not only because, often, the solution of a physical problem directly results in the need to solve a system of linear equations, but also because many numerical techniques for solving problems that apparently have nothing to do with systems of linear equations work by making appropriate linear approximations internally that result in the need to solve such systems of linear equations.

The method that we shall demonstrate is appropriate for general dense systems of linear equations, where by *general* we mean that the matrix of coefficients of the system of equations has no particular structure. Many physical problems, however, result in matrices of coefficients that do have a special structure, and special numerical techniques have been devised for their solution; see, for example, Dahlquist and Björck (1974) and Golub and Van Loan (1991). By *dense* we mean that most of the elements of the matrix of coefficients of the system of equations are non-zero. In this context, we note that many times a system of equations is sparse (non-dense), and special techniques have been devised for their solution; see, for example, George and Liu (1981) and Duff *et al.* (1986). The numerical solution of sparse systems of linear equations, or those with a special structure, is completely beyond the scope of this book, except for the very special case of tridiagonal systems, which we shall discuss in Section 18.6.

The method that we shall use is known as **Gaussian elimination**, and we shall first illustrate the process by reference to a small 3×3 system of simultaneous linear equations:

$$x_1 + 2x_2 + x_3 = 9 \tag{1}$$
$$2x_1 + 3x_2 - 2x_3 = 7 \tag{2}$$
$$4x_1 + 4x_2 + x_3 = 18 \tag{3}$$

Subtracting 2 times equation (1) from equation (2), and then 4 times equation (1) from equation (3), we obtain the equivalent set of equations:

$$x_1 + 2x_2 + x_3 = 9 \tag{4}$$
$$- x_2 - 4x_3 = -11 \tag{5}$$
$$- 4x_2 - 3x_3 = -18 \tag{6}$$

Subtracting 4 times equation (5) from equation (6), we obtain a further equivalent set of equations:

$$x_1 + 2x_2 + x_3 = 9 \tag{7}$$
$$- x_2 - 4x_3 = -11 \tag{8}$$
$$13x_3 = 26 \tag{9}$$

This completes the Gaussian elimination step. We now perform the **backward substitution** step.

Using equation (9), we obtain

$$x_3 = 26/13 = 2$$

Substituting this value for x_3 in equation (8), we obtain

$$-x_2 - 4 \times 2 = -11$$

and hence

$$x_2 = 11 - 8 = 3$$

Substituting these values for x_2 and x_3 in equation (7), we obtain

$$x_1 + 2 \times 3 + 2 = 9$$

Therefore

$$x_1 = 9 - 6 - 2 = 1$$

The solution of the original system of equations is therefore $x_1 = 1$, $x_2 = 3$, $x_3 = 2$.

Having seen how Gaussian elimination operates in the context of a simple example, we shall now discuss the general case. Suppose we have a system of n linear equations in n unknowns:

$$a_{1,1}x_1 + a_{1,2}x_2 + \ldots + a_{1,n}x_n = b_1$$
$$a_{2,1}x_1 + a_{2,2}x_2 + \ldots + a_{2,n}x_n = b_2$$
$$\vdots$$
$$a_{n,1}x_1 + a_{n,2}x_2 + \ldots + a_{n,n}x_n = b_n$$

Gaussian elimination will turn this system of equations into an equivalent system of equations of the form

$$c_{1,1}x_1 + c_{1,2}x_2 + \ldots + c_{1,n}x_n = d_1$$
$$c_{2,2}x_2 + \ldots + c_{2,n}x_n = d_2$$
$$\vdots$$
$$c_{n,n}x_n = d_n$$

In this form, all the coefficients below the diagonal are zero, and the matrix of coefficients, for obvious reasons, is said to be **upper triangular**. As we shall see, in this form, the system of equations can be solved with no further manipulation.

Gaussian elimination works by subtracting multiples of the first equations from all the other equations below it in such a way that the resulting equations each have a coefficient of 0 for x_1. Thus, the initial system of equations becomes

$$a_{1,1}x_1 + a_{1,2}x_2 + \ldots + a_{1,n}x_n = b_1$$
$$a_{2,2}^{(1)}x_2 + \ldots + a_{2,n}^{(1)}x_n = b_2^{(1)}$$
$$a_{2,2}^{(2)}x_2 + \ldots + a_{2,n}^{(2)}x_n = b_2^{(2)}$$
$$\vdots$$
$$a_{n,2}^{(2)}x_2 + \ldots + a_{n,n}^{(1)}x_n = b_n^{(1)}$$

Specifically, for $j \geqslant 2$, the jth equation is obtained by subtracting the first equation, multiplied by $a_{j,1}/a_{1,1}$, from the original jth equation. The superscripts on the coefficients are used to denote that this is step i of the process. The solution of the second set of equations is the same as that of the original system of equations.

We now repeat the process again on the $(n-1) \times (n-1)$ system of equations consisting of the second to the nth equations. Subtracting appropriate multiples of the second equation from the equations below it, we obtain a system of equations in which all the equations after the second have zero for the coefficient of x_2.

Proceeding iteratively, after $n-1$ steps, we obtain a system of equations of the form

$$a_{1,1}x_1 + a_{1,2}x_2 + a_{1,3}x_3 + a_{1,4}x_4 + \ldots + a_{1,n-1}x_{n-1} + a_{1,n}x_n = b_1$$
$$a_{2,2}^{(1)}x_2 + a_{2,3}^{(1)}x_3 + a_{2,4}^{(1)}x_4 + \ldots + a_{2,n-1}^{(1)}x_{n-1} + a_{2,n}^{(1)}x_n = b_2^{(1)}$$
$$a_{3,3}^{(2)}x_3 + a_{3,4}^{(2)}x_4 + \ldots + a_{3,n-1}^{(2)}x_{n-1} + a_{3,n}^{(2)}x_n = b_3^{(2)}$$
$$a_{4,4}^{(3)}x_4 + \ldots + a_{4,n-1}^{(3)}x_{n-1} + a_{4,n}^{(3)}x_n = b_4^{(3)}$$
$$\vdots$$
$$a_{n-1,n-1}^{(n-2)}x_{n-1} + a_{n-1,n}^{(n-2)}x_n = b_{n-1}^{(n-2)}$$
$$a_{n,n}^{(n-1)}x_n = b_n^{(n-1)}$$

This process, as we have already seen, is called Gaussian elimination, and the $a_{i,i}^{(i-1)}$ (the elements along the diagonal) are called **pivots**.

Now the nth equation is solved for x_n by dividing by $a_{n,n}^{(n-1)}$. This value is then substituted into the $(n-1)$th equation, which can then be solved for x_{n-1}. The values for x_n and x_{n-1} are substituted in the $(n-2)$th equation, which is then solved for x_{n-2}. We proceed backwards through the set of equations in this way until we finally put the values determined for $x_n, x_{n-1}, \ldots, x_3, x_2$ into the first equation and solve it for x_1. This process, for obvious reasons, is called **back substitution**.

We can see that the Gaussian elimination process will fail if, at the ith step, the coefficient $a_{i,i}^{(i-1)}$ is 0. We would in this case be unable to make all the coefficients of x_i in the equations below it 0, since subtracting any multiple of 0 leaves a number unchanged. If this situation occurs, however, we could interchange the ith equation with one below it that does not have a 0 for the coefficient of x_i, and then proceed. If there is no such equation, then it can be proved that the original system either has no solution or an infinite set of solutions. Observe that changing the order of occurrence of the equations does not change their solution.

In fact, we can go somewhat beyond this interchange procedure. If a pivot element is small, then large multiples of the equation containing it must be used during the elimination process. This will multiply any errors (due to round-off effects) in the other coefficients of this equation. Intuitively, we can see that this is undesirable. So, for reasons of numerical stability, at the beginning of the ith step, we will reorder the equations from the ith one down, so that the one that has the largest absolute value for the coefficient of x_j becomes the ith equation. In books on numerical analysis, you will see this equation reordering process referred to as **partial pivoting**. Proving mathematically that this is a good choice for a stable algorithm would, however, go beyond the scope of this book.

■ EXAMPLE 18.3

1 Problem

Write a program to read the coefficients of a set of simultaneous linear equations, and to solve the equations using Gaussian elimination.

2 Analysis

We have already discussed the Gaussian elimination method in some detail, and so we can proceed to the design of the program. We shall write one procedure to carry out the Gaussian elimination, and a second to perform the back substitution. Both of these procedures will be used by a third procedure to actually solve a set of equations. Because we shall not want the two subsidiary procedures to be available on their own, we shall encapsulate all three procedures in a module, which will make only the solving procedure public.

An initial structure plan for the Gaussian elimination algorithm is as follows:

> **1** Repeat for i taking values from 1 to $n - 1$
> > **1.1** Rearrange the order of the ith, $(i + 1)$th, ..., nth equations so that the one with the largest absolute value for the coefficient of x_i becomes the ith equation
> > **1.2** If $a_{i,i} = 0$ then
> > > **1.2.1** Return an error message to indicate that no solution is possible
> >
> > otherwise
> > > **1.2.2** Subtract multiples of the ith equation from all subsequent equations so that the coefficients of x_i in the subsequent equations become 0

Now we can amplify the steps of this loop. The coefficient of x_i in equation i is $a_{i,i}$, and the coefficient of x_i in equation j is $a_{j,i}$. To make the coefficient of x_i in the jth equation zero, we must therefore subtract $a_{j,i}/a_{i,i}$ times the ith equation from the jth equation.

We shall store the coefficients of the system of equations (the $a_{i,j}$) in a real rank-two array **a** and the right-hand sides of the equations (the b_i) in a real rank-one array **b**. The revised structure plan for the Gaussian elimination algorithm then becomes:

---

1 Repeat for i from 1 to $n-1$
   1.1 Find the row k of array **a** that has the largest value for $|a(j,i)|$, for
        $j = 1, \ldots, n$
   1.2 If this largest absolute value is 0 then
       1.2.1 Return an error message
     otherwise
       1.2.2 Interchange row i and row k of the array **a**, and also
            interchange element i and element k of the array **b**
   1.3 Repeat for j from $i+1$ to n
       1.3.1 Subtract $a(j,i)/a(i,i)$ times equation i from equation j

---

We can now turn to implementing the algorithm for back substitution. When the Gaussian elimination step has been completed, the ith equation is of the form

$$\sum_{j=i}^{n} a_{i,j} x_j = b_i, \qquad i = 1, 2, \ldots, n$$

That is, the coefficients of x_1, $x_2, \ldots, x_{i-1}$ are zero in the ith equation. Consequently, we can easily solve the ith equation for x_i, expressing it in terms of x_{i+1}, $x_{i+2}, \ldots, x_n$. Specifically,

$$a_{i,i} x_i + \sum_{j=i+1}^{n} a_{i,j} x_j = b_i, \qquad i = 1, 2, \ldots, n$$

$$x_i = a_{i,i}^{-1} \left(b_i - \sum_{j=i+1}^{n} a_{i,j} x_j \right), \qquad i = 1, 2, \ldots, n$$

This formula is used first with $i = n$, then with $i = n - 1, \ldots$, then with $i = 2$, and finally with $i = 1$. Note that, because of the row interchanges in the Gaussian elimination step, $a_{i,i} \neq 0$, $i = 1, 2, \ldots, n$. Thus, it will always be possible to divide by $a_{i,i}$.

We also note that after b_i has been used to calculate x_i it does not appear in any subsequent formulae; the solution x_i can therefore be stored in b_i, once b_i has been used to calculate x_i.

An outline structure plan for the back substitution procedure is now very straightforward:

> 1   Repeat for i from n down to 1
>   **1.1**   Initialize sum to $b(i)$
>   **1.2**   Repeat for j from $i + 1$ to n
>   **1.2.1**   Subtract $a(i, j) \times b(j)$ from sum
>   **1.3**   Set $b(i)$ to sum$/a(i, i)$

We shall not proceed further with the design phase, which is quite straightforward, in order to save space, but will simply present the final solution.

3 Solution

We have already indicated that the two subroutines **gaussian_elimination** and **back_substitution** will be called by a third subroutine, which we shall call **gaussian_solve**. Because this subroutine will use assumed-shape dummy arguments, it must have an explicit interface in the main program. Furthermore, we do not want a user to be able to call **gaussian_elimination** or **back_substitution** directly. To accomplish both of these aims, all three subroutines will be put in a module called **linear_equations**, with only **gaussian_solve** being public.

```
MODULE linear_equations
   IMPLICIT NONE
   PRIVATE
   PUBLIC :: gaussian_solve

CONTAINS

   SUBROUTINE gaussian_solve(a,b,error)
      ! This subroutine solves the linear system Ax = b
      ! where the coefficients of A are stored in the array a
      ! The solution is put in the array b
      ! error indicates if errors are found

      ! Dummy arguments
      REAL, DIMENSION(:,:), INTENT(INOUT) :: a
      REAL, DIMENSION(:), INTENT(INOUT) :: b
      INTEGER, INTENT(OUT) :: error

      ! Reduce the equations by Gaussian elimination
      CALL gaussian_elimination(a,b,error)

      ! If reduction was successful, calculate solution by
      ! back substitution
      IF (error == 0) CALL back_substitution(a,b,error)
   END SUBROUTINE gaussian_solve

   SUBROUTINE gaussian_elimination(a,b,error)
      ! This subroutine performs Gaussian elimination on a
      ! system of linear equations
```

```fortran
! Dummy arguments
! a contains the coefficients
! b contains the right-hand side
REAL, DIMENSION(:,:), INTENT(INOUT) :: a
REAL, DIMENSION(:) :: b
INTEGER, INTENT(OUT) :: error


! Local variables
REAL, DIMENSION(SIZE(a,1)) :: temp_array  ! Automatic array
INTEGER, DIMENSION(1) :: ksave
INTEGER :: i,j,k,n
REAL :: temp,m


! Validity checks
n = SIZE(a,1)
IF (n == 0) THEN
   error = -1              ! There is no problem to solve
   RETURN
END IF
IF (n /= SIZE(a,2)) THEN
   error = -2              ! a is not square
   RETURN
END IF
IF (n /= SIZE(b)) THEN
   error = -3              ! Size of b does not match a
   RETURN
END IF


! Dimensions of arrays are OK, so go ahead with Gaussian
! elimination
error = 0
DO i=1, n-1
   ! Find row with largest value of |a(j,i)|, j=i, ..., n
   ksave = MAXLOC(ABS(a(i:n, i)))

   ! Check whether largest |a(j,i)| is zero
   k = ksave(1) + i - 1
   IF (ABS(a(k,i)) <= 1E-5) THEN
      error = -4           ! No solution possible
      RETURN
   END IF

   ! Interchange row i and row k, if necessary
   IF (k /= i) THEN
      temp_array = a(i,:)
      a(i,:) = a(k,:)
      a(k,:) = temp_array
      ! Interchange corresponding elements of b
      temp = b(i)
      b(i) = b(k)
      b(k) = temp
   END IF
```

```
      ! Subtract multiples of row i from subsequent rows to
      ! zero all subsequent coefficients of x sub i
      DO j = i+1,n
         m = a(j,i)/a(i,i)
         a(j,:) = a(j,:) - m*a(i,:)
         b(j) = b(j) - m*b(i)
      END DO
   END DO
END SUBROUTINE gaussian_elimination


SUBROUTINE back_substitution(a,b,error)
   ! This subroutine performs back substitution once a system
   ! of equations has been reduced by Gaussian elimination

   ! Dummy arguments
   ! The array a contains the coefficients
   ! The array b contains the right-hand side coefficients.
   ! and will contain the solution on exit
   ! error will be set non-zero if an error occurs
   REAL, DIMENSION(:,:), INTENT(IN) :: a
   REAL, DIMENSION(:), INTENT(INOUT) :: b
   INTEGER, INTENT(OUT) :: error

   ! Local variables
   REAL :: sum
   INTEGER :: i,j,n

   error = 0
   n = SIZE(b)

   ! Solve for each variable in turn
   DO i = n,1,-1
      ! Check for zero coefficient
      IF (ABS(a(i,i)) <= 1E-5) THEN
         error = -4
         RETURN
      END IF

      sum = b(i)
      DO j = i+1,n
         sum = sum - a(i,j)*b(j)
      END DO
      b(i) = sum/a(i,i)
   END DO
END SUBROUTINE back_substitution

END MODULE linear_equations
```

A suitable main program which will use the subroutine **gaussian_solve** to solve a system of linear equations is as follows:

```
PROGRAM test_gauss
   USE linear_equations
   IMPLICIT NONE
```

```
! This program defines the coefficients of a set of
! simultaneous linear equations, and solves them using the
! module procedure gaussian_solve

! Allocatable arrays for coefficients
REAL, ALLOCATABLE, DIMENSION(:,:) :: a
REAL, ALLOCATABLE, DIMENSION(:) :: b

! Size of arrays
INTEGER :: n

! Loop variables and error flag
INTEGER :: i,j,error

! Get size of problem
PRINT *,"How many equations are there?"
READ *,n

! Allocate arrays
ALLOCATE (a(n,n), b(n))

! Get coefficients
PRINT *,"Type coefficients for each equation in turn"
DO i=1,n
    READ *,(a(i,j),j=1,n),b(i)
END DO

! Attempt to solve system of equations
CALL gaussian_solve(a,b,error)

! Check to see if there were any errors
IF (error <= -1 .AND. error >= -3 ) THEN
    PRINT *,"Error in call to gaussian_solve"
ELSE IF (error == -4) THEN
    PRINT *,"System is degenerate"
ELSE
    PRINT *," "
    PRINT *,"Solution is"
    PRINT '(1X,"x(",I2,") = ",F6.2)', (i,b(i),i=1,n)
END IF

END PROGRAM test_gauss
```

Note that for large problems, this code can be made more efficient by use of pointers, in order to avoid exchanging of large numbers of arrays and array sections; Exercise 18.8 at the end of this chapter gives you the chance to make such an improvement.

```
How many equations are there?
4
Type coefficients for each equation in turn
2 3 -1 1 11
1 -1 2 -1 -4
-1 -1 5 2 -2
3 1 -3 3 19
Solution is
x( 1) =   2.00
x( 2) =   1.00
x( 3) =  -1.00
x( 4) =   3.00
```

Figure 18.8 Solving a set of simultaneous linear equations using **test_gauss**.

Figure 18.8 shows the results produced when this program was used to solve the following set of equations:

$$2x_1 + 3x_2 - x_3 + x_4 = 11$$
$$x_1 - x_2 + 2x_3 - x_4 = -4$$
$$-x_1 - x_2 + 5x_3 + 2x_4 = -2$$
$$3x_1 + x_2 - 3x_3 + 3x_4 = 19$$

18.6 Solving a tridiagonal system of equations

One form of sparse system which is particularly important is known as a **tridiagonal system**, for reasons which become obvious when we examine such a system:

$$a_{1,1}x_1 + a_{1,2}x_2 = b_1$$
$$a_{2,1}x_1 + a_{2,2}x_2 + a_{2,3}x_3 = b_2$$
$$a_{3,2}x_2 + a_{3,3}x_3 + a_{3,4}x_4 = b_3$$
$$\vdots$$
$$a_{n-1,n-2}x_{n-2} + a_{n-1,n-1}x_{n-1} + a_{n-1,n}x_n = b_{n-1}$$
$$a_{n,n-1}x_{n-1} + a_{n,n}x_n = b_n$$

Systems of equations of this type occur frequently in the solution of partial differential equations, and are also found in cubic and bicubic curve fitting, as we shall see in Section 18.7. In order to emphasize the form of such a system it is common practice to use a different terminology for the coefficients, namely

$$d_1 x_1 + c_1 x_2 \qquad\qquad\qquad\qquad = b_1$$
$$a_2 x_1 + d_2 x_2 + c_2 x_3 \qquad\qquad\qquad = b_2$$
$$a_3 x_2 + d_3 x_3 + c_3 x_4 \qquad\qquad = b_3$$
$$\ddots \qquad\qquad\qquad\qquad \vdots$$
$$a_{n-1} x_{n-2} + d_{n-1} x_{n-1} + c_{n-1} x_n = b_{n-1}$$
$$a_n x_{n-1} + d_n x_n \ = b_n$$

Clearly, the computation involved in solving a system of this nature should be much simpler than in the general case, since in each column there is only one element to be eliminated. Furthermore, and this is another reason why we have used a different terminology, considerable savings can be made in storage requirements by storing only these tridiagonal coefficients (as three one-dimensional arrays) and ignoring the zero elements which occupy the remainder of the matrix of coefficients.

We shall not give an exhaustive account of the mathematics involved in deriving a solution method, as it is similar to that used in the previous section when discussing Gaussian elimination, except that we only need to subtract the pivotal equation from the equation immediately below it in order to transform the original set of equations into a new, upper triangular set:

$$D_1 x_1 + c_1 x_2 \qquad\qquad\qquad\qquad = B_1$$
$$D_2 x_2 + c_2 x_3 \qquad\qquad\qquad = B_2$$
$$D_3 x_3 + c_3 x_4 \qquad\qquad = B_3$$
$$\ddots \qquad\qquad\qquad \vdots$$
$$D_{n-1} x_{n-1} + c_{n-1} x_n = B_{n-1}$$
$$D_n x_n \ = B_n$$

We can readily see that the c_i coefficients are unaltered by the transformation, and that

$$D_1 = d_1$$

and

$$B_1 = b_1$$

Furthermore, when processing the $(i + 1)$th equation in order to eliminate x_i we shall use a multiplier m_i which is equal to a_{i+1}/D_i to give a new equation:

$$D_{i+1}x_{i+1} + c_{i+1}x_{i+2} = B_{i+1}$$

where

$$D_{i+1} = d_{i+1} - m_i c_i$$

and

$$B_{i+1} = b_{i+1} - m_i B_i$$

It can be shown that in some situations pivoting can be eliminated. One example of such a situation is where the system of equations is diagonally dominant, i.e. for each row the absolute value of the diagonal term is greater than or equal to the sum of the absolute values of the other terms. Using our original notation, this requires that $|a_{i,i}| \geqslant |a_{i,i-1}| + |a_{i,i+1}|$, $i = 1, 2, \ldots, n$. Here, we interpret $a_{1,0}$ and $a_{n,n+1}$ as being zero. The proof that diagonal dominance eliminates the need for pivoting goes beyond the scope of this book.

A Fortran implementation of this method, in which no pivoting is performed, is shown in Figure 18.9, while Figure 18.10 shows a suitable back substitution procedure.

```
SUBROUTINE tri_gauss(a,d,c,b,error)
  IMPLICIT NONE

  ! This subroutine performs Gaussian elimination with no
  ! pivoting on a tridiagonal, diagonally dominant, system
  ! of linear equations

  ! Dummy arguments
  ! Array a holds the subdiagonal coefficients
  ! Array d holds the diagonal coefficients
  ! Array c holds the above-diagonal coefficients
  ! Array b holds the right-hand-side coefficients
  ! error is a variable that indicates success or failure
  REAL, DIMENSION(:), INTENT(IN) :: a,c
  REAL, DIMENSION(:), INTENT(INOUT) :: d,b
  INTEGER, INTENT(OUT) :: error

  ! Local variables
  REAL :: m
  INTEGER :: n,i
```

Figure 18.9

(continues)

(continued)
```
! Validity checks
n = SIZE(a)
IF (n <= 0) THEN
   ! There is no problem to solve
   error = -1
   RETURN
END IF
IF (n /= SIZE(d) .OR.                            &
    n /= SIZE(c) .OR.                            &
    n /= SIZE(b) ) THEN
   ! The arrays of coefficients do not have the same size
   error = -2
   RETURN
END IF

! Calculate new coefficients of upper diagonal system
DO i = 1,n-1
   m = a(i+1)/d(i)
   d(i+1) = d(i+1) - m*c(i)
   b(i+1) = b(i+1) - m*b(i)
END DO
error = 0
END SUBROUTINE tri_gauss
```

Figure 18.9 A subroutine for Gaussian elimination on a tridiagonal system.

```
SUBROUTINE back_tri_substitution(d,c,b)
   IMPLICIT NONE

   ! This subroutine performs back substitution to a
   ! tridiagonal system of linear equations that has been
   ! reduced to upper triangular form

   ! Dummy arguments
   ! d is the array of diagonal coefficients
   ! c is the array of above-diagonal coefficients
   ! b is the array of right-hand-side coefficients
   ! and will contain the solution on exit
   REAL, DIMENSION(:), INTENT(IN) :: d,c
   REAL, DIMENSION(:), INTENT(OUT) :: b

   ! Local variables
   INTEGER :: i,n

   n = SIZE(d)
   b(n) = b(n)/d(n)
   DO i = n-1,1,-1
      b(i) = (b(i) - c(i)*b(i+1))/d(i)
   END DO
END SUBROUTINE back_tri_substitution
```

Figure 18.10 A subroutine for back substitution on an upper triangular system.

We shall use these subroutines as part of a method for curve fitting in the next section. The development of a procedure for solving tridiagonal systems with pivoting is given as an exercise at the end of this chapter.

Since both the subroutines `tri_gauss` and `back_tri_substitution` use assumed-shape arrays, their interfaces must be explicit before they can be referenced. Accordingly, as in the similar case in Example 18.3, we shall put them in a module called `tridiagonal_systems`. We shall also, for the same reason, put `tri_solve`, the subroutine that solves a tridiagonal system by calling `tri_gauss` and then `back_tri_solve`, in the same module. Since only `tri_solve` is supposed to be directly called by a user, all entities in the module will be private except `tri_solve`. This module could be written as follows:

```
MODULE tridiagonal_systems
   IMPLICIT NONE
   PRIVATE
   PUBLIC :: tri_solve


CONTAINS


   SUBROUTINE tri_solve(a,d,c,b,error)
      ! This subroutine solves a diagonally dominant tridiagonal
      ! system by Gaussian elimination and back substitution


      ! Dummy arguments
      ! Array a holds the subdiagonal coefficients
      ! Array b holds the diagonal coefficients
      ! Array c holds the above-diagonal coefficients
      ! Array d holds the right-hand-side coefficients
      ! Array b will contain the solution on exit
      REAL, DIMENSION(:), INTENT(IN) :: a,c
      REAL, DIMENSION(:), INTENT(OUT) :: d,b
      INTEGER, INTENT(OUT) :: error
      CALL tri_gauss(a,d,c,b,error)
      IF (error == 0) CALL back_tri_substitution(d,c,b)
   END SUBROUTINE tri_solve


   SUBROUTINE tri_gauss ( . . . )
      .
      .
      .

   SUBROUTINE back_tri_substitution ( . . . )
      .
      .
      .


END MODULE tridiagonal_systems
```

18.7 Fitting a curve through a set of data points using a cubic spline

We have considered the solution of equations of various types at some length, because this is a very common requirement in scientific programming. However, another important application is the fitting of an equation to a set of (usually) experimental data with a view to using this equation to predict further results. In Chapter 10 we considered the simple case in which it was believed that the data satisfied a linear relationship. We shall now briefly examine a more general case.

As usual in numerical analysis, there are a number of different methods for fitting a curve to a set of discrete data points; however, by far the best known, and the most widely used, are those methods which are based on **splines**. A spline was an instrument once used by draughtsmen to enable them to draw a smooth curve through a set of points. It consisted of a flexible wooden (or sometimes metal) strip which was constrained (by pins) to pass through the data points. Because the spline would take up the shape which minimized its potential energy, the resulting curve was a smooth one.

Mathematically, splines are curves consisting of n polynomial pieces, each one of the same degree k, joined together such that the curve has $k - 1$ continuous derivatives at the join points, as shown in Figure 18.11.

Let us suppose we are given some finite interval $[a, b]$ and a set of points $x_0, x_1, \ldots, x_n$ in $[a, b]$ such that $a = x_0 \leqslant x_1 \leqslant x_2 \leqslant \ldots \leqslant x_n = b$. The points $x_0, x_1, \ldots, x_n$ are called **knots**.

Now, let $k \geqslant 0$ be a fixed integer, and P_i be a polynomial of degree k, $i = 1, 2, \ldots, n$. Then a spline s of degree k on $[a, b]$ is defined as

$$s(x) = \begin{cases} P_1(x) & \text{on} & [x_0, x_1] \\ P_2(x) & \text{on} & [x_1, x_2] \\ \vdots & & \\ P_n(x) & \text{on} & [x_{n-1}, x_n] \end{cases}$$

The polynomials must be such that at $x_1, x_2, \ldots, x_{n-1}$, $s(x)$ has $k - 1$ continuous derivatives.

Such a spline is said to be C^{k-1}, referring to the $k - 1$ continuous derivatives.

It might be asked why objects as complicated as splines are used when we could simply, given n points, fit a polynomial of degree $n - 1$ through them. The reason is that polynomials of degree more than 3 tend to oscillate considerably between the given data points, with the amount of oscillation tending to increase as the degree of the polynomial increases. Thus the intrinsic shape represented by a set of data points is usually badly represented by higher-degree polynomials. Splines, on the other hand, conform much better to the shape implied by the data, even though, in practice, they are rarely of degree higher than three.

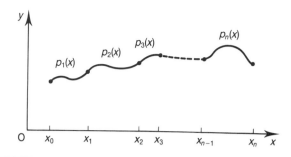

Figure 18.11   A spline curve.

In this section we shall concentrate on **cubic splines**. The cubic spline is the mathematical equivalent of the draughtsman's physical instrument and enables the construction of a smooth curve which passes through all the data points. Furthermore, as a measure of its smoothness, its first and second derivatives are continuous everywhere within the range of the data points. Thus, we shall analyse a C^2 cubic spline, and will show the simplest method for constructing such a spline. There are many other, more sophisticated methods based on what are known as basis functions. Dierckx (1993) gives an introduction to such methods for those who are interested in this subject.

A cubic spline actually consists of a set of cubic polynomials, one for each pair of data points. These polynomials are chosen so that they obey the following criteria:

(1) In each interval $[x_i, x_{i+1}]$, $i = 0, \ldots, n - 1$, the spline consists of a cubic polynomial $s_i(x)$.

(2) The spline passes through each data point, and so

$$s_i(x_i) = y_i \quad \text{and} \quad s_i(x_{i+1}) = y_{i+1}, \quad \text{for} \quad i = 0, \ldots, n - 1$$

(3) At each of the points where two sub-intervals join, the first and second derivatives must be continuous, so, for $i = 1, \ldots, n - 1$

$$s_{i-1}(x_i) = s_i(x_i)$$
$$s'_{i-1}(x_i) = s'_i(x_i)$$
$$s''_{i-1}(x_i) = s''_i(x_i)$$

For fairly obvious reasons, round-off errors will be less if we express the cubic polynomials as functions of $(x - x_i)$ rather than as functions of x, with the result that we shall require to find the coefficients of the equations

$$s_i(x) = a_i(x - x_i)^3 + b_i(x - x_i)^2 + c_i(x - x_i) + d_i, \tag{1}$$

for $i = 0, \ldots, n - 1$

We now consider, for $i = 0, 1, \ldots, n - 1$, how to find a_i, b_i, c_i and d_i. For a particular i, we have two conditions

$$s_i(x_i) = y_i$$
$$s_i(x_{i+1}) = y_{i+1}$$

We need two more conditions to fix a_i, b_i, c_i and d_i.

For the moment, suppose that we know the second derivatives at $x_0, x_1, \ldots, x_n$. We shall call these derivatives $\sigma_0, \sigma_1, \sigma_2, \ldots, \sigma_n$. Now, for $i = 0, 1, \ldots, n - 1$, we have the two extra conditions needed to determine a_i, b_i, c_i and d_i. At this stage, of course, we do not know what values to assign to the σ_i. We shall see later than the continuity conditions on the first and second derivatives we require at $x_0, x_1, \ldots, x_{n-1}$ will (with two extra conditions) determine the values of σ_i, and hence the values of a_i, b_i, c_i and d_i.

We now proceed with the analysis to determine a_i, b_i, c_i and d_i in terms of y_i, y_{i+1}, σ_i and σ_{i+1}. First, we let

$$h_i = x_{i+1} - x_i \qquad \text{for} \qquad i = 0, 1, \ldots, n - 1$$

The h_i are, therefore, the distances between successive pairs of data points.

For $i = 0, 1, \ldots, n - 1$, substituting x_i for x, and y_i for $s_i(x_i)$ in equation (1) and rearranging, we obtain

$$d_i = y_i \tag{2}$$

Substituting $x = x_{i+1}$ in equation (1), we obtain

$$y_{i+1} = a_i h_i^3 + b_i h_i^2 + c_i h_i + d_i$$

Using equation (2) and rearranging, we now obtain

$$c_i = \frac{y_{i+1} - y_i}{h_i} - a_i h_i^2 - b_i h_i \tag{3}$$

Now, differentiating equation (1) twice, we have

$$s_i''(x_i) = 6a_i(x - x_i) + 2b_i$$

Substituting $x = x_i$ and $x = x_{i+1}$ in this equation leads to

$$\sigma_i = 2b_i$$
$$\sigma_{i+1} = 6a_ih_i + 2b_i$$

Thus, from these two equations, we have

$$b_i = \frac{\sigma_i}{2} \tag{4}$$

$$a_i = \frac{\sigma_{i+1} - \sigma_i}{6h_i} \tag{5}$$

Substituting equations (4) and (5) in equation (3), we obtain

$$c_i = \frac{y_{i+1} - y_i}{h_i} - \frac{\sigma_{i+1} - \sigma_i}{6h_i} h_i^2 - \frac{\sigma_i}{2} h_i$$

$$= \frac{y_{i+1} - y_i}{h_i} - \frac{\sigma_{i+1} + 2\sigma_i}{6} h_i \tag{6}$$

Equations (2), (4), (5) and (6) thus determine a_i, b_i, c_i and d_i, for $i = 0$, $1, \ldots, n-1$, once we know the values of the σ_is. Our next step, therefore, will be to determine the values of the σ_is.

Recall that we required the spline to have a continuous first derivative at each x_i, for $i = 1, 2, \ldots, n-1$. This requirement, which we have not yet used, will determine σ_i.

Differentiating equation (1), we obtain

$$s_i'(x) = 3a_i(x - x_i)^2 + 2b_i(x - x_i) + c_i$$

Substituting $x = x_i$ and $x = x_{i+1}$ in this equation, we obtain

$$s_i'(x_i) = c_i \tag{7}$$

and

$$s_i'(x_{i+1}) = 3a_ih_i^2 + 2b_ih_i + c_i \tag{8}$$

For continuity of the first derivative at x_i, $i = 1, 2, \ldots, n-1$, we require

$$s_{i-1}'(x_i) = s_i'(x_i)$$

Substituting equations (7) and (8) into this equation, we obtain

$$3a_{i-1}h_{i-1}^2 + 2b_{i-1}h_{i-1} + c_{i-1} = c_i$$

Substituting equations (4), (5) and (6) into this equation, we have

$$\frac{3(\sigma_i - \sigma_{i-1})h_{i-1}^2}{6h_{i-1}} + \sigma_{i-1}h_{i-1} + \frac{y_i - y_{i-1}}{h_{i-1}} - \frac{(\sigma_i + 2\sigma_{i-1})h_{i-1}}{6}$$

$$= \frac{y_{i+1} - y_i}{h_i} - \frac{(\sigma_{i+1} + 2\sigma_i)h_i}{6}$$

Grouping terms together, we have

$$\sigma_{i-1}\left(-\frac{h_{i-1}}{2} + h_{i-1} - \frac{h_{i-1}}{3}\right) + \sigma_i\left(\frac{h_{i-1}}{2} - \frac{h_{i-1}}{6} + \frac{h_i}{3}\right) + \frac{\sigma_{i+1}h_i}{6}$$

$$= \frac{y_{i+1} - y_i}{h_i} - \frac{y_i - y_{i-1}}{h_{i-1}}$$

Thus, multiplying by 6, for $i = 1, \ldots, n - 1$,

$$h_{i-1}\sigma_{i-1} + 2(h_{i-1} + h_i)\sigma_i + h_i\sigma_{i+1} = 6\left(\frac{y_{i+1} - y_i}{h_i} - \frac{y_i - y_{i-1}}{h_{i-1}}\right) \qquad (9)$$

Equation (9) gives us $n - 1$ linear equations in the $n + 1$ unknowns $\sigma_0, \sigma_1, \ldots, \sigma_n$.

We therefore need two more equations to be able to calculate a unique solution, and, hence, a unique cubic interpolating function. This is achieved by applying some form of constraint to the spline at the end-points x_0 and x_n. This is desirable in any case, since extra constraints on a curve fit are frequently required at the end-points of an interval. In design work, for example, the curve may be required to blend into some existing curve. There are a number of possibilities, of which some common ones are:

- Force the second derivative of the spline to be zero at the end-points:

  $$\sigma_0 = \sigma_n = 0$$

- Force the third derivative of the spline to be continuous at the points adjacent to the end-points. This means that

  $$a_0 = a_1 \qquad \text{and} \qquad a_{n-1} = a_n$$

which leads to the two further equations

$$\sigma_0 h_1 - \sigma_1(h_0 + h_1) + \sigma_2 h_0 = 0$$
$$\sigma_{n-2} h_{n-1} - \sigma_{n-1}(h_{n-2} + h_{n-1}) + \sigma_n h_{n-2} = 0$$

- Force the first derivative (the gradient) at the end-points to be the same as that of the true curve $y = f(x)$; this assumes that further information is available about the gradient of this curve at these points. Thus

$$s_0'(x_0) = f_0' \qquad \text{and} \qquad s_{n-1}'(x_n) = f_n'$$

which leads to two further linear equations in σ_0 and σ_1, and in σ_{n-1} and σ_n, respectively.

Different treatment of the end-points will be appropriate for different situations, but it will be noticed by the observant reader that, in the first and third cases, we have tridiagonal systems of n equations in n unknowns. The second case also has n equations in n unknowns, but is not strictly tridiagonal; however, it is a trivial task to convert it to tridiagonal form.

We discussed the solution of a tridiagonal system in Section 18.6, and since the system of equations (9) is diagonally dominant (do you see why?), we can use the subroutines developed in that section in the calculation of the coefficients of a cubic spline. A subroutine which will calculate the values of the coefficients for a tridiagonal system of equations using the first of the above criteria for treatment of end-points ($\sigma_0 = \sigma_n = 0$) is shown below; it has been encapsulated in a module, which in turn uses the earlier module **tridiagonal_systems**, in order to ensure that its interface is always explicit.

```
MODULE spline
   USE tridiagonal_systems
   IMPLICIT NONE

CONTAINS

   SUBROUTINE cubic_spline(x,y,a,b,c,d,error)
      ! This subroutine calculates the coefficients of a
      ! cubic spline through the set of data points with
      ! x-coordinates in the array x and corresponding
      ! y-coordinates in the array y.
      ! The coefficients of the cubic polynomials will be
      ! put in arrays a, b, c, d
      ! error will indicate the success or failure of the fit

      ! Dummy arguments
      REAL, DIMENSION(0:), INTENT(IN) :: x,y
      REAL, DIMENSION(0:), INTENT(OUT) :: a,b,c,d
      INTEGER, INTENT(OUT) :: error
```

```fortran
! Local variables
INTEGER :: n,i
REAL, DIMENSION(0:SIZE(x,1)-2) :: h      ! Automatic array
! Automatic arrays for tridiagonal equations
REAL, DIMENSION(0:SIZE(x,1)-1) :: t,u,v,w


! Validity checks
n = SIZE(x) - 1
IF (n < 1) THEN
   ! There is no problem to solve
   error = -1
   RETURN
END IF
IF (n+1 /= SIZE(y) .OR.   &
      n /= SIZE(a) .OR.   &
      n /= SIZE(b) .OR.   &
      n /= SIZE(c) .OR.   &
      n /= SIZE(d)) THEN
   ! The array sizes don't correspond.
   error = -2
   RETURN
END IF


! Test that the x-coordinates are either strictly
! increasing or strictly decreasing
IF (x(0) < x(1)) THEN
   ! Test that x-coordinates are ordered increasingly
   DO i = 1,n-2
      IF (x(i) < x(i+1)) CYCLE
      ! x-coordinates aren't monotonically increasing
      error = -3
      RETURN
   END DO
ELSE IF (x(0) == x(1)) THEN
      ! x-coordinates aren't distinct.
      error = -3
      RETURN
ELSE
      ! Test that x-coordinates are ordered decreasingly
      DO i = 1,n-2
         IF (x(i) > x(i+1)) CYCLE
         ! x-coordinates aren't monotonically decreasing
         error = -3
         RETURN
      END DO
END IF


! Data is OK
error = 0
! Set h array to interval lengths
DO i = 0,n-1
   h(i) = x(i+1) - x(i)
END DO
```

```
! Fill up coefficient arrays for the tridiagonal system
DO i = 1,n-1
    t(i) = h(i-1)
    u(i) = 2.0*(h(i-1) + h(i))
    v(i) = h(i)
    w(i) = 6.0*((y(i+1)-y(i))/h(i) - (y(i)-y(i-1))/h(i-1))
END DO


! Set end-point conditions.
u(0) = 1.0
v(0) = 0.0
w(0) = 0.0
t(n) = 0.0
u(n) = 1.0
w(n) = 0.0


! Calculate the sigma values
CALL tri_solve(t,u,v,w,error)
IF (error /= 0) THEN
    PRINT *, "An 'IMPOSSIBLE' error has occurred - call &
            &consultant."
    STOP
END IF


! Calculate the spline coefficients from the sigmas
DO i = 0,n-1
    a(i) = (w(i+1)-w(i))/(6.0*h(i))
    b(i) = w(i)/2.0
    c(i) = (y(i+1)-y(i))/h(i) - (w(i+1)+2.0*w(i))*h(i)/6.0
    d(i) = y(i)
END DO
END SUBROUTINE cubic_spline

END MODULE spline
```

The subroutine **cubic_spline** can be used by any program which wishes to obtain a set of spline coefficients to fit a particular set of data, and which can then use these coefficients to create a mathematical model of the curve to use in whatever way is appropriate.

Figure 18.12 shows a program which uses this subroutine to fit a spline through 18 unevenly spaced points in the range $-3 \leqslant x \leqslant 3$, which lie on a curve defined by an external function **f**, and then to print out the values of the interpolated and actual functions at a series of intermediate values. The result of running this program using the function given below is shown in Figure 18.13.

```
REAL FUNCTION f(x)
    IMPLICIT NONE
    REAL, INTENT(IN) :: x
    f = EXP(-0.5*x*x)
END FUNCTION f
```

```
PROGRAM spline_test
  USE spline
  IMPLICIT NONE

  ! This program tests the subroutine cubic_spline

  ! Maximum coefficient for data points
  INTEGER, PARAMETER :: n = 17
  ! Defining external function
  REAL, EXTERNAL :: f

  ! Local variables
  INTEGER :: error,i,j
  REAL, DIMENSION(0:n) :: x =                              &
      (/ -2.95, -2.6, -2.1, -1.8, -1.4, -1.0, -0.75,  &
         -0.3, -0.05, 0.2, 0.55, 0.9, 1.25, 1.6, 1.7, &
         2.1, 2.4, 3.0 /)
  REAL, DIMENSION(0:n) :: y
  REAL, DIMENSION(0:n-1) :: a,b,c,d
  REAL :: z,zj,yz

  ! Calculate y-coordinates corresponding to data
  ! values of x
  DO i = 0, n
     y(i) = f(x(i))
  END DO

  ! Call cubic_spline to fit a set of n polynomials.
  CALL cubic_spline(x,y,a,b,c,d,error)
  IF (error /= 0) THEN
     PRINT *, 'Error ',error
     STOP
  END IF

  ! Now compare interpolated values with true ones, using
  ! an evenly spaced set of values between -2.8 and +2.8
  PRINT '(9X,"x      exp(-0.5x**2)    Spline value"/)'
  DO i = 0,14
     ! Calculate z (the value to be used)
     z = -2.8 + 0.4*i
     ! Find in which interval z lies
     DO j = 0,n-1
        IF (x(j) <= z .AND. z <= x(j+1)) EXIT
     END DO

     ! Calculate s(z) for x(j) <= z <= x(j+1)
     zj = z-x(j)
     yz = ((a(j)*zj + b(j))*zj + c(j))*zj + d(j)

     ! Print comparative results
     PRINT '(6X,F6.2,2E15.6)',z,f(z),yz
  END DO
END PROGRAM spline_test
```

Figure 18.12 A test program for the cubic spline subroutine `cubic_spline`.

x	exp(-0.5x**2)	Spline value
-2.80	0.198411E-01	0.204182E-01
-2.40	0.561348E-01	0.558913E-01
-2.00	0.135335E+00	0.135367E+00
-1.60	0.278037E+00	0.278160E+00
-1.20	0.486752E+00	0.486894E+00
-0.80	0.726149E+00	0.726171E+00
-0.40	0.923116E+00	0.922998E+00
0.00	0.100000E+01	0.999988E+00
0.40	0.923116E+00	0.922994E+00
0.80	0.726149E+00	0.726146E+00
1.20	0.486752E+00	0.486761E+00
1.60	0.278037E+00	0.278037E+00
2.00	0.135335E+00	0.135443E+00
2.40	0.561347E-01	0.561347E-01
2.80	0.198411E-01	0.209970E-01

Figure 18.13 Results produced by the test program spline_test.

In the above discussion, we have presented the spline method of fitting curves through a set of data points as a two-dimensional problem; however, the method can easily be extended to three or more dimensions, for example to calculate the equation of a surface, $z = f(x, y)$, through a set of points whose heights above some base plane have been measured on a rectangular grid. **Bicubic patches**, in three dimensions, exhibit the same continuity with adjacent patches at their common boundaries as do the two-dimensional cubic spline polynomials at their common points. Such **bicubic spline interpolation** is therefore often used to create mathematical models of surfaces using, for example, data obtained by remote sensing devices such as satellites or oceanic depth sounders; these mathematical models of the surface can then be used by a drawing program which will plot a graphical representation of the surface as viewed from any particular angle, or which will produce a contour map of the surface.

One final point to emphasize is that we have assumed throughout the foregoing discussion that the spline polynomials must pass through *all* the data points. However, just as in the case where a linear fit is expected (see Chapter 10), when the data is the result of experimentation it is likely that there may be small errors in that data. In these situations, therefore, we may require the spline to be a good fit to the data, but not necessarily to pass through all the data points. This involves a somewhat more complex mathematical treatment, and it is not intended to go into the matter here. It is sufficient to emphasize that some form of least squares approximation is normally used so that data points which will produce significant perturbations if an exact fit is used will have less effect when a least squares fit is used.

18.8 Integration and numerical quadrature

A common problem in science and engineering is the need to evaluate the definite integral of a function. That is, if the function is f, we want

$$I = \int_a^b f(x)dx$$

We shall, for simplicity, assume that $a < b$. There is no loss of generality, because

$$\int_a^b f(x)dx = -\int_b^a f(x)dx$$

In many practical problems the function f cannot be integrated analytically, and we cannot, therefore, find a known function F such that

$$F'(x) = f(x) \qquad \text{on } [a, b]$$

If we could, then $I = F(b) - F(a)$.

If we cannot find such an F then we must turn to numerical techniques. The process of numerically calculating the value of a definite integral is known as **numerical quadrature** (the term **integrate** is used for the numerical solution of differential equations). We shall present here a simple version of a method that demonstrates the algorithmic basis for more sophisticated methods.

We recall that a definite integral over a finite interval (we shall not deal with infinite intervals here) can be interpreted as the area lying between the curve $y = f(x)$ and the x-axis on the interval $[a, b]$. This is shown in Figure 18.14.

The integral I is equal to the area shaded in the figure. Consequently, it is clear that the area, and hence I, can be calculated by subdividing the interval $[a, b]$

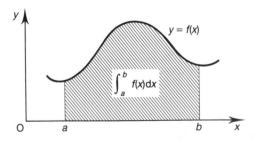

Figure 18.14 $\int_a^b f(x)dx$ interpreted as an area.

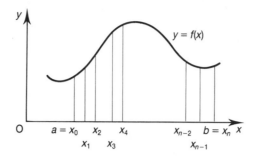

Figure 18.15 Calculating an area by subdividing it into smaller sub-areas.

into n sub-intervals and summing the areas of these sub-intervals, as shown in Figure 18.15. In this we have subdivided the interval $[a, b]$ by an increasing sequence of x_i, such that $a = x_0 < x_1 < x_2 < \ldots < x_{n-1} < x_n = b$.

Now let the length of the ith interval be h_i, so that $h_i = x_i - x_{i-1}$, $i = 1, 2, \ldots, n$. Note that we are not assuming that the x_i are uniformly spaced, so that h_is may be unequal.

We are going to estimate $\int_{x_{i-1}}^{x_i} f(x)dx$ by the area of the trapezium formed by joining the point $(x_{i-1}, f(x_{i-1}))$ to the point $(x_i, f(x_i))$ by a straight line. This is shown shaded in Figure 18.16. Since the area of the trapezium T_i is given by the formula

$$T_i = \frac{h_i \left(f(x_{i-1}) + f(x_i) \right)}{2}$$

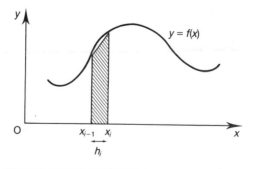

Figure 18.16 Estimating an area by use of a trapezium.

we can deduce that

$$I = \sum_{i=1}^{n} I_i$$

and

$$I_i \simeq \frac{1}{2} h_i(f(x_{i-1}) + f(x_i)), \qquad i = 1, 2, \ldots, n$$

It therefore follows that

$$I \simeq \sum_{i=1}^{n} \frac{1}{2} h_i(f(x_i) + f(x_{i+1}))$$

Before we examine the use of this formula to obtain an approximation to I, however, there are two questions that should be answered. The first concerns the accuracy of the approximation; ideally we would like to be able to specify an error tolerance and not have it exceeded. The second question concerns how many points are required to meet a specified error tolerance, and how they should be positioned. These two questions, as we shall see, are intimately related.

Before we begin the analysis, we note that, intuitively, the best way to position the x_i is to group them the most closely in regions where f is changing the most rapidly and to have them relatively sparse in regions where f is not changing very fast. Thus, as shown in Figure 18.17, we would group x_i and x_{i+1} close together in regions where the first derivative of f is high. We do not, however, wish to group the x_i closer than necessary, because this would result in the need for extra function evaluations, and it is the number of a function evaluations required that is the efficiency measure of a numerical quadrature algorithm.

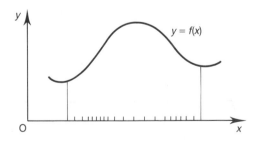

Figure 18.17 Uneven spacing of intervals to improve accuracy.

We now start to analyse how many x_i are needed and how to position them, by first estimating the error created by using the approximating trapeziums. Using Taylor's theorem, expanded about x_{i-1}, with three terms, we see that

$$
\begin{aligned}
I_i &= \int_{x_{i-1}}^{x_i} f(x)dx \\
&= \int_{x_{i-1}}^{x_i} \left(f(x_{i-1}) + (x - x_{i-1})f'(x_{i-1}) \right. \\
&\qquad \left. + \frac{1}{2}(x - x_{i-1})^2 f''(x_{i-1}) + \dots \right) dx \\
&= f(x_{i-1})\int_{x_{i-1}}^{x_i} dx + f'(x_{i-1})\int_{x_{i-1}}^{x_i}(x - x_{i-1})\,dx \\
&\qquad + \frac{1}{2}f''(x_{i-1})\int_{x_{i-1}}^{x_i}(x - x_{i-1})^2\,dx + \dots \\
&= f(x_{i-1})\left[x\right]_{x_{i-1}}^{x_i} + \frac{1}{2}f'(x_{i-1})\left[(x - x_{i-1})^2\right]_{x_{i-1}}^{x_i} \\
&\qquad + \frac{1}{6}f''(x_{i-1})\left[(x - x_{i-1})^3\right]_{x_{i-1}}^{x_i} + \dots \\
&= f(x_{i-1})(x_i - x_{i-1}) + \frac{1}{2}f'(x_{i-1})(x_i - x_{i-1})^2 \\
&\qquad + \frac{1}{6}f''(x_{i-1})(x_i - x_{i-1})^3 + \dots \\
&= h_i f(x_{i-1}) + \frac{1}{2}h_i^2 f'(x_{i-1}) + \frac{1}{6}h_i^3 f''(x_{i-1}) + \dots
\end{aligned}
$$

Since we are going to be dealing with h_is that are relatively small, and if the higher derivative of f are well-behaved, we can ignore the terms involving $h_i^4, h_i^5, \dots$ and commit no significant error. Thus, we have, effectively,

$$
I_i = h_i f(x_{i-1}) + \tfrac{1}{2}h_i^2 f'(x_{i-1}) + \tfrac{1}{6}h_i^3 f''(x_{i-1})
$$

Now, examining T_i, we have, using Taylor's theorem expanded about x_{i-1}:

$$
\begin{aligned}
T_i &= \frac{1}{2}h_i\left[f(x_{i-1}) + f(x_i)\right] \\
&= \frac{1}{2}h_i\left[f(x_{i-1}) + f(x_{i-1}) + (x_i - x_{i-1})f'(x_{i-1}) \right. \\
&\qquad \left. + \frac{1}{2}(x_i - x_{i-1})^2 f''(x_{i-1}) + \dots\right] \\
&= h_i f(x_i) + \frac{1}{2}h_i^2 f'(x_{i-1}) + \frac{1}{4}h_i^3 f''(x_{i-1}) + \dots
\end{aligned}
$$

Again, we commit no significant error by ignoring the terms h_i^4, h_i^5, ... and have, effectively,

$$T_i = h_i f(x_i) + \frac{1}{2} h_i^2 f'(x_{i-1}) + \frac{1}{4} h_i^3 f''(x_{i-1})$$

Therefore,

$$I_i - T_i = \left(\frac{1}{6} - \frac{1}{4}\right) h_i^3 f''(x_{i-1}) = -\frac{1}{12} h_i^3 f''(x_{i-1})$$

This, then, is the estimate we shall use for calculating the error caused by approximating the ith integral by the trapezoidal rule. We shall call the error E_i. Thus, $E_i = -\frac{1}{12} h_i^3 f''(x_{i-1})$. The total error E committed will thus be given by the equation

$$E = \sum_{i=1}^{n} E_i = -\frac{1}{12} \sum_{i=1}^{n} h_i^3 f''(x_{i-1})$$

It appears from this that we need to be able to evaluate the second derivative of f in order to calculate the error. Furthermore, we have, as yet, no method for determining how to choose the x_is. We shall now proceed to eliminate the need for explicit values of f'' and at the same time create an algorithm for choosing the x_is.

Consider the ith sub-interval $[x_{i-1}, x_i]$. Suppose we split it at the midpoint m_i into two sub-intervals J_1 and J_2 and apply the trapezoidal rule to each sub-interval. Let us assume that the trapezoidal rules give areas of J_i' and J_i'' with errors E_i' and E_i''. We shall denote $\int_{x_{i-1}}^{m_i} f(x)dx$ by I_i' and $\int_{m_i}^{x_i} f(x)dx$ by I_i''. This leads to

$$I_i - T_i = E_i = -\frac{1}{12} h_i^3 f''(x_{i-1}) \tag{1}$$

$$I_i' - J_i' = E_i' = -\frac{1}{12} \left(\frac{h_i}{2}\right)^3 f''(x_{i-1})$$

$$= -\frac{1}{96} h_i^3 f''(x_{i-1})$$

$$I_i'' - J_i'' = E_i'' = -\frac{1}{12}\left(\frac{h_i}{2}\right)^3 f''(x_{i-1})$$

$$= -\frac{1}{96}\, h_i^3\, f''(x_{i-1})$$

Note that we are assuming the interval is so small that, effectively, $f''(m_i) = f''(x_{i-1})$. Now, adding the last two equations we get

$$I_i' + I_i'' - (J_i' + J_i'') = -\frac{1}{48}\, h_i^3\, f''(x_{i-1}) = E_i' + E_i''$$

Now $I_i = I_i' + I_i''$, so

$$I_i - (J_i' + J_i'') = E_i' + E_i'' = -\frac{1}{48}\, h_i^3\, f''(x_{i-1}) = \frac{1}{4}\, E_i$$

What this equation tells us is that, if we split the ith interval up into two equal sub-intervals and use the trapezoidal rule on each piece, the error is reduced by a factor of 4.

For convenience, let $C_i = J_i' + J_i''$. Then,

$$I_i - C_i = \frac{1}{4}\, E_i \qquad\qquad (2)$$

Subtracting equation (2) from equation (1), we obtain

$$C_i - T_i = \frac{3}{4}\, E_i$$

and, therefore

$$E_i = \frac{4}{3}\, (C_i - T_i)$$

This equation tells us that we can obtain the value of the error committed by use of the trapezoidal rule on the ith interval by applying it three times, once to the whole interval and once to each half interval. By making the reasonable assumption that we are dealing with intervals so small that f'' can be regarded as effectively constant on the interval, we have eliminated the need to know values of f'' in calculating the error E_i.

Let us suppose that the integral is wanted with an error no greater than ϵ (specified by the user). We know that the total error E is given by

$$E = \sum_{i=1}^{n} E_i$$

Therefore, if $|E_i| \leq \epsilon h_i / (b - a)$ for each i, then

$$|E| E \leq \sum_{i=1}^{n} |E_i|$$

$$\leq \sum_{i=1}^{n} \frac{\epsilon h_i}{b - a} = \frac{\epsilon}{b - a} \sum_{i=1}^{n} h_i = \frac{\epsilon(b - a)}{b - a} = \epsilon$$

and the requirement is met.

A suitable algorithm will, therefore, start with the whole interval and test to see if the error is less than $\epsilon h_i / (b - a)$.

If not, then the interval is split into two equal sub-intervals and the process is repeated on each sub-interval until the criterion is met. To guard against the process failing to converge, the user should specify a limit on how small a sub-interval may become before the process is terminated as not converging.

We shall define the algorithm in the form of a structure plan, but before doing so we must note an important fact. Quadrature algorithms are judged by how many function evaluations are required to determine the integral. In the method outlined above, when an interval is split into two the values at the two end-points can be re-used as end-points of the two sub-intervals. The only additional function value required is at the mid-point of the original interval. We therefore have an economical algorithm in which no function evaluations are wasted.

We also note that the process we have described is naturally recursive. We shall therefore develop a subprogram **adaptive_quadrature** that will be called by the user. This subprogram will perform some validity checks and then calculate the initial function values to be used by a recursive subprogram **adap_quad**. This recursive subprogram will perform the numerical quadrature by calling itself as many times as are appropriate.

Let the left and right end-points be xl and xu, respectively, and let $fl = f(xl)$, where f is the function to be integrated, and let $fu = f(xu)$. A suitable structure plan is then as follows:

1   If the interval length h has become too small then
    1.1   Set an error flag and return
2   Calculate the mid-point xm of the interval, and the value fm of $f(xm)$

3 Calculate the value *t* of the trapezoidal estimate of integral over the whole interval

4 Calculate the value *c* of the sum of the trapezoidal rule applied to the two sub-intervals

5 Estimate the error $e = 4(c - t)/3$

6 If $|e| \leqslant \epsilon h/(b - a)$ then

   6.1 Return *c* as the value of the integral over $[xl, xu]$

   otherwise

   6.2 Split $[xl, xu]$ into two equal sub-intervals $[xl, xm]$ and $[xm, xu]$

   6.3 Call **adap_quad** using the sub-interval $[xl, xm]$

   6.4 Call **adap_quad** using the sub-interval $[xm, xl]$

   6.5 If no errors occur in either call, return the sum of the two values received as the value of the integral over $[xl, xb]$

     (Note that this is the recursive step.)

A module containing both subroutines is as follows:

```
MODULE numerical_quadrature
   IMPLICIT NONE
   PRIVATE
   PUBLIC :: adaptive_quadrature

CONTAINS

   SUBROUTINE adaptive_quadrature(f,a,b,epsilon,           &
                             subdivide_limit,answer,error)
      ! This subroutine integrates the function f from a to b
      ! using an adaptive method based on the trapezoidal rule.
      ! epsilon is the user-specified error tolerance.
      ! subdivide_limit is a user-specified smallest interval
      ! size to use.
      ! answer is the calculated answer success.

      ! Dummy arguments
      REAL, EXTERNAL :: f
      REAL, INTENT(IN) :: a,b,epsilon,subdivide_limit
      REAL, INTENT(OUT) :: answer
      INTEGER, INTENT(OUT) :: error

      ! Validity check
      IF (epsilon <= 0.0) THEN
         error = -1
         RETURN
      END IF
      IF (a < b) THEN
         call adap_quad(f,a,b,f(a),f(b),subdivide_limit,   &
                     epsilon/(b-a),answer,error)
```

```fortran
      ELSE IF (a > b) THEN
         call adap_quad(f,b,a,f(b),f(a),subdivide_limit,  &
                        epsilon/(a-b),answer,error)
         IF (error == 0) answer = -answer
      ELSE
         error = 0
         answer = 0.0
      END IF
END SUBROUTINE adaptive_quadrature


RECURSIVE SUBROUTINE adap_quad(f,xl,xu,fl,fu,              &
                               lower,delta,answer,error)
   ! This subroutine performs an adaptive numerical
   ! quadrature using the trapezoidal rule

   ! Dummy arguments
   REAL, EXTERNAL :: f
   REAL, INTENT(IN) :: xl,xu,fl,fu,lower,delta
   REAL, INTENT(OUT) :: answer
   INTEGER, INTENT(OUT) :: error

   ! Local variables
   REAL :: h,t,c,xm,fm,e,ans1,ans2

   h = xu - xl
   IF (ABS(h) < lower) THEN
      ! Interval has become too small
      error = -2
      answer = HUGE(answer)
      RETURN
   END IF
   t = h*(fl + fu)/2.0
   xm = xl + h/2.0
   fm = f(xm)
   c = h*(fl + 2.0*fm + fu)/4.0
   e = 4.0*(c - t)/3.0
   IF (ABS(e) <= delta*h) THEN
      ! Trapezoidal rule has achieved required accuracy
      ! The PRINT statement is only for during development
      ! It will be removed when code is certified as
      ! functional
      PRINT '(1X,''Interval Used ('',E12.4,'','',E12.4,'')'',  &
            3X,''h ='',E12.4)', xl, xu, xu - xl
      error = 0
      answer = t
   ELSE
      ! Subdivide the interval
      call adap_quad(f,xl,xm,fl,fm,lower,delta,  &
                     ans1,error)
      IF (error /= 0) RETURN
      call adap_quad(f,xm,xu,fm,fu,lower,delta,  &
                     ans2,error)
```

```
          IF (error /= 0) RETURN
          answer = ans1 + ans2
       END IF
    END SUBROUTINE adap_quad
END MODULE numerical_quadrature
```

We have put the two subprograms **adaptive_quadrature** and **adap_quad** into the module **numerical_quadrature** for several reasons. The first is because we believe in using modules as a packaging mechanism for related procedures. The second is to prevent the subprogram **adap_quad** being inadvertently called by the user; the use of the **PUBLIC** and **PRIVATE** statements in the module achieves this.

Finally, since the subroutine **adap_quad** is recursive, its interface must be explicit for the calling subroutine **adaptive_quadrature**. As in many other examples in this book, putting a procedure into a module is usually the best way of making its interface explicit.

We shall test this module by evaluating $\int_{0.1}^{1} (1/x)dx$ with an accuracy of 0.01 and by evaluating $\int_{0}^{\pi/2} \cos x dx$, also with an accuracy of 0.01, using the following functions:

```
REAL FUNCTION f(x)
   IMPLICIT NONE
   REAL, INTENT(IN) :: x
   f = 1.0/x
   RETURN
END FUNCTION f

REAL FUNCTION g(x)
   IMPLICIT NONE
   REAL, INTENT(IN) :: x
   g = cos(x)
   RETURN
END FUNCTION g
```

Note, incidentally, that

$$\int_{0.1}^{1} (1/x)dx = \left[\log_e(x)\right]_{0.1}^{1} = \log_e(1) - \log_e(0.1)$$

$$= 0 + 2.302\,585 = 2.302\,585$$

and

$$\int_{0}^{\pi/2} \cos x dx = \left[\sin x\right]_{0}^{\pi/2} = \sin(\pi/2) - \sin(0) = 1.0 - 0.0 = 1.0$$

A suitable test program is shown below:

```
PROGRAM test_quadrature
   USE numerical_quadrature
   IMPLICIT NONE
```

```
! Declarations
REAL, PARAMETER :: pi=3.1415926
REAL, EXTERNAL :: f, g

REAL :: a,b,accuracy_tolerance,value
REAL :: smallest_subdivision = 1.E-5
INTEGER :: error

! Calculate integral of f on [0.1,1.0]
a = 1.0E-1
b = 1.0
accuracy_tolerance = 1.0E-2
call adaptive_quadrature(f,a,b,accuracy_tolerance,        &
                         smallest_subdivision,value,error)

! Print result or error message, as appropriate
SELECT CASE (error)
CASE (0)
   PRINT '(//1X,''Value of integral of x**(-1) from '',E9.1, &
             '' to '',E9.1/                                  &
          1X,''with accuracy tolerance '',F14.6/             &
          1X,''is '',F14.6/                                  &
          1X,''Correct answer is '',F14.6//)',               &
          a,b,accuracy_tolerance,value,-log(a)
CASE (-2)
   PRINT *,''Failed to converge to a solution for first &
         &problem''
CASE (-1)
   PRINT *,''Epsilon was less than or equal to &
         &zero - should be impossible''
END SELECT

! Calculate integral of g on [0,pi/2]
a = 0.0
b = pi/2.0
accuracy_tolerance = 1.0E-2
call adaptive_quadrature(g,a,b,accuracy_tolerance,        &
                         smallest_subdivision,value,error)

! Print result or error message, as appropriate
SELECT CASE (error)
CASE (0)
   PRINT '(//1X,''Value of integral cos(x) from '',F5.1,    &
             ''to '',F10.6/                                 &
          1X,''with accuracy tolerance '',F14.6/            &
          1X,''is '', F14.6/                                &
          1X,''Correct answer is '',F14.6//)',              &
          a,b,accuracy_tolerance,value,1.0
CASE (-2)
   PRINT *,''Failed to converge to a solution for second &
         &problem''
CASE (-1)
   PRINT *,''Epsilon was less than or equal to &
         &zero - should be impossible''
END SELECT
END PROGRAM test_quadrature
```

```
Interval Used (  0.1000E+00,  0.1070E+00)   h =  0.7031E-02
Interval Used (  0.1070E+00,  0.1141E+00)   h =  0.7031E-02
Interval Used (  0.1141E+00,  0.1211E+00)   h =  0.7031E-02
Interval Used (  0.1211E+00,  0.1281E+00)   h =  0.7031E-02
Interval Used (  0.1281E+00,  0.1352E+00)   h =  0.7031E-02
Interval Used (  0.1352E+00,  0.1422E+00)   h =  0.7031E-02
Interval Used (  0.1422E+00,  0.1562E+00)   h =  0.1406E-01
Interval Used (  0.1562E+00,  0.1703E+00)   h =  0.1406E-01
Interval Used (  0.1703E+00,  0.1844E+00)   h =  0.1406E-01
Interval Used (  0.1844E+00,  0.1984E+00)   h =  0.1406E-01
Interval Used (  0.1984E+00,  0.2125E+00)   h =  0.1406E-01
Interval Used (  0.2125E+00,  0.2266E+00)   h =  0.1406E-01
Interval Used (  0.2266E+00,  0.2406E+00)   h =  0.1406E-01
Interval Used (  0.2406E+00,  0.2688E+00)   h =  0.2813E-01
Interval Used (  0.2688E+00,  0.2969E+00)   h =  0.2812E-01
Interval Used (  0.2969E+00,  0.3250E+00)   h =  0.2813E-01
Interval Used (  0.3250E+00,  0.3531E+00)   h =  0.2813E-01
Interval Used (  0.3531E+00,  0.3813E+00)   h =  0.2812E-01
Interval Used (  0.3813E+00,  0.4375E+00)   h =  0.5625E-01
Interval Used (  0.4375E+00,  0.4938E+00)   h =  0.5625E-01
Interval Used (  0.4938E+00,  0.5500E+00)   h =  0.5625E-01
Interval Used (  0.5500E+00,  0.6625E+00)   h =  0.1125E+00
Interval Used (  0.6625E+00,  0.7750E+00)   h =  0.1125E+00
Interval Used (  0.7750E+00,  0.8875E+00)   h =  0.1125E+00
Interval Used (  0.8875E+00,  0.1000E+01)   h =  0.1125E+00

Value of integral of x**(-1) from   0.1E+00 to   0.1E+01
with accuracy tolerance       0.010000
is       2.307365
Correct answer is        2.302585

Interval Used (  0.0000E+00,  0.1963E+00)   h =  0.1963E+00
Interval Used (  0.1963E+00,  0.3927E+00)   h =  0.1963E+00
Interval Used (  0.3927E+00,  0.5890E+00)   h =  0.1963E+00
Interval Used (  0.5890E+00,  0.7854E+00)   h =  0.1963E+00
Interval Used (  0.7854E+00,  0.9817E+00)   h =  0.1963E+00
Interval Used (  0.9817E+00,  0.1178E+01)   h =  0.1963E+00
Interval Used (  0.1178E+01,  0.1571E+01)   h =  0.3927E+00

Value of integral cos(x) from   0.0 to   1.570796
with accuracy tolerance       0.010000
is       0.996049
Correct answer is        1.000000
```

Figure 18.18   Results produced by the adaptive quadrature test program.

The results of running this program are shown in Figure 18.18. In the first case, we would expect the subdivision points to be clustered more closely as we move towards the origin, since the function x^{-1} becomes increasingly steep as we approach the origin. The printed output verifies this is happening. Also, $\cos(x)$

```
Value of integral of x**(-1) from   0.1E+00 to   0.1E+01
with accuracy tolerance          0.000100
is      2.302638
Correct answer is      2.302585

Value of integral cos(x) from   0.0 to   1.570796
with accuracy tolerance          0.000100
is      0.999938
Correct answer is      1.000000

Value of integral of x**(-1) from   0.1E+00 to   0.1E+01
with accuracy tolerance          0.000010
is      2.302591
Correct answer is      2.302585

Value of integral cos(x) from   0.0 to   1.570796
with accuracy tolerance          0.000010
is      0.999995
Correct answer is      1.000000

Failed to converge to a solution for first problem

Value of integral cos(x) from   0.0 to   1.570796
with accuracy tolerance          0.000001
is      0.999999
Correct answer is      1.000000
```

Figure 18.19 More accurate results produced by `test_quadrature`.

becomes flatter near $\pi/2$, so we would expect longer steps to be taken in that vicinity. The printed output verifies this expectation also.

In the above example a relatively low accuracy tolerance of 10^{-2} was used. To illustrate that life is not always straightforward, however, Figure 18.19 shows the result of repeating the same calculations with tolerances set to 10^{-4}, 10^{-5} and 10^{-6}. The PRINT statement has been removed from the subroutine `adap_quad` in order not to produce too much output.

Note that the required accuracies were obtained except when we requested an accuracy of 10^{-6} for $\int_{0.1}^{1} (1/x)dx$. What do you think went wrong, and how would you fix it?

We must caution the user that, while the principle of adaptively changing the step size and using the subdivision results to estimate errors is frequently employed, more sophisticated approximations than the trapezoidal rule are often used. We have used the trapezoidal rule to keep the mathematics as simple as possible so that we could concentrate on principles.

We finish our discussion of numerical quadrature on a faint note of gloom. Any numerical quadrature process will require the evaluation of the given function f at a finite number of points $x_1, x_2, \ldots, x_p$.

Consider, for example, the function

$$\phi(x) = f(x) - k(x - x_1)^2 (x - x_2)^2 \ldots (x - x_p)^2$$

For $i = 1, 2, \ldots, p, \phi(x_p) = f(x_p)$, because the term we have subtracted from f will be 0 at each x_i. So, to the numerical quadrature procedure

$$\int_a^b \phi(x)dx = \int_a^b f(x)dx$$

while, mathematically

$$\int_a^b \phi(x)dx + k \int_a^b (x - x_1)^2 \ldots (x - x_p)^2 dx = \int_a^b f(x)dx$$

Clearly, by making k large enough, the difference between $\int_a^b f(x)dx$ and $\int_a^b \phi(x)dx$ can be made as large as we please! This fact puts a note of uncertainty into all numerical quadrature algorithms. However, for most practical problems, it is not significant.

SELF-TEST EXERCISES 18.1

1   What are the advantages and disadvantages of each of the three methods introduced for solving non-linear equations (bisection method, Newton's method and secant method)?

2   What is partial pivoting? Why is it important in Gaussian elimination?

3   What is the major difference between a cubic spline curve-fitting algorithm and one using a polynomial? What are the advantages of each method?

4   What is adaptive quadrature? Why is caution necessary in accepting the result of any numerical quadrature?

PROGRAMMING EXERCISES

This chapter has presented sample programs for a number of the most common types of numerical problems. However, the choice of the best method for the numerical solution of mathematical problems is far from easy in many cases, and you are advised to use one of the major numerical libraries, such as the NAG Library (NAG, 1988) or the IMSL Library (Visual Numerics, 1992), wherever possible.

Most of the following examples use the procedures developed in this chapter as a means of experimentation with their accuracy and usefulness. However, the opportunity is also taken to introduce several further techniques in the form of programming exercises. For more details concerning these, and other, numerical methods you should consult an appropriate numerical analysis text.

18.1 In Exercise 10.4 you wrote a program to solve a polynomial equation using the bisection method, and then used it again in Exercise 10.5 to find those roots of the following polynomials which lie in the range $-10 \leqslant x \leqslant 10$. Modify your program, if necessary, to print the number of iterations taken and use it to find the roots again, saving the roots and the number of iterations in a file.

(a) $10x^3 - x^2 - 69x + 72$
(b) $20x^3 - 52x^2 + 17x + 24$
(c) $5x^3 - x^2 - 80x + 16$
(d) $10x^4 + 13x^3 - 163x^2 - 208x + 48$
(e) $x^4 + 2x^3 - 23x^2 - 24x + 144$
(f) $9x^4 - 42x^3 - 1040x^2 + 5082x - 5929$

Now replace the subroutine that uses the bisection method by one that uses Newton's method and run the program again, taking care that you do not overwrite the results saved in a file by the previous program.

Finally, repeat the process using the secant method.

Now write another program to list the three sets of results in a form suitable for comparing the effectiveness of the three methods.

18.2 Use the programs you wrote for Exercise 18.1 to produce a similar comparison for the following functions:

(a) $\sin(3x + \pi/4)$
(b) $\sin 3x \cos x$
(c) $\sin 5x + 5 \cos x$
(d) $2 - e^{\sin x}$
(e) $\tan(x + \pi/6)$
(f) $\sin(e^{x/3})$

18.3 Use Newton's method to calculate the following values:

(a) the square root of 5;
(b) the cube root of 7;
(c) the seventh root of 2000

*18.4 Use the Gaussian elimination method, described in Section 18.5, to solve the following systems of simultaneous linear equations:

(a) $\begin{aligned} 2x + 3y + z &= 4 \\ x - 2y - z &= 3 \\ -2x + y + 3z &= 4 \end{aligned}$

(b) $2x + y - z = 1$

   $4x - y - 3z = -3$

   $x + 3y + z = 4$

(c) $-2x - y + 4z = 4$

   $x + 2y - 2z = 1$

   $3x + 4y - 6z = -1$

(d) $x - 2y - z + w = 3$

   $3x + y + z - 2w = 3$

   $-2x - 3y + 2z - w = 4$

   $x + y - z + w = 0$

(e) $x \qquad\qquad + t = 1$

   $2y - z \qquad\qquad = 5$

   $2x \qquad - w \qquad = 1$

   $2z + w \qquad = -3$

   $y \qquad - 2t = 3$

How did your program deal with systems (c) and (e)?

18.5   Use the Gaussian elimination method, described in Section 18.5, to solve the following system of simultaneous linear equations:

   $10x + 7y + 8z + 7w = 32$

   $7x + 5y + 6z + 5w = 23$

   $8x + 6y + 10z + 9w = 33$

   $7x + 5y + 9z + 10w = 31$

If the coefficients had been obtained by experimental means, or as the result of some earlier calculation, there could be some slight errors in them. In order to test the effect of this, change the coefficients on the right-hand side of the equations by one in the fourth significant figure (about 0.03%) to 32.01, 22.99, 32.99, and 31.01, and run the program again to find a new solution. Did the result surprise you?

   Now change the same coefficients by one in the third significant figure to 32.1, 22.9, 32.9 and 31.1, and run it again.

   This example (which is due to T.S. Wilson) illustrates the problem of ill-conditioned systems, which was first mentioned in Chapter 10.

18.6   Modify the module `tridiagonal_systems` that was developed in Section 18.6 so that partial pivoting is performed when solving tridiagonal systems, and test it with a suitable tridiagonal system.

18.7 The subroutine `gaussian_elimination`, in Example 18.3, subtracts a multiple of the whole of row i from row j. This is unnecessary, because elements 1 to $i - 1$ of row i are zero, and element i of row j will become zero after the subtraction. Modify the subroutine to be more efficient.

Test both your modified subroutine and the original one in a program that uses the computer's clock (or some other means) to measure the time taken for solution by each version of a 10 × 10 system of equations.

18.8 Modify the subroutine `gaussian_elimination` written in Example 18.3, or the modified one produced for Exercise 18.7, to use pointers to eliminate the actual interchange of rows of the coefficient matrix. Modify the subroutine `back_substitution` accordingly. Test this new version on a 10 × 10 system of equations. What were the run times compared with the original version?

18.9 In order to simplify usage and, generally, make programming simpler and safer for those solving linear systems of equations, create a derived type `square_matrix` and a derived type **vector**. Rewrite the module that was developed in Example 18.3 to use these derived types. Test your module using the various sets of equations that were solved in Exercise 18.4.

18.10 In Section 18.5 it was mentioned that iterative methods were sometimes more suitable than Gaussian elimination for the solution of simultaneous equations, especially when many of the coefficients are zero. One of the best-known iterative methods is the Gauss–Seidel method, which can be summarized as follows.

In the discussion in Section 18.5 we considered the set of simultaneous equations

$$a_{11}x_1 + a_{12}x_2 + \ldots + a_{1n}x_n = b_1$$
$$a_{21}x_1 + a_{22}x_2 + \ldots + a_{2n}x_n = b_2$$

$$\vdots$$

$$a_{n1}x_1 + a_{n2}x_2 + \ldots + a_{nn}x_n = b_n$$

We shall obtain a sequence of vectors which converge to the correct solution vector to the system of equations. We will call these successive approximations $x^{(0)}$, $x^{(1)}$, $x^{(2)}$, ..., and will let

$$x^{(i)} = \begin{bmatrix} x_1^{(i)} \\ x_2^{(i)} \\ \vdots \\ x_n^{(i)} \end{bmatrix}$$

where the superscripts denote which approximate solution is being referred to. The Gauss–Seidel method gives an iteration to obtain $x^{(i+1)}$ from $x^{(i)}$.

We proceed by first rearranging the system of equations, by row interchanges, so that the diagonal elements are all non-zero. If we cannot achieve this, the system of equations is degenerate. After this rearrangement, for $i = 1, 2, \ldots, n$, we divide the ith equation by a_{ii}. This means each diagonal coefficient of the system of equations is 1. We shall use primes to denote the coefficients of the resulting system.

In this system, we can rearrange the equations as

$$x_1 = b'_1 - (a'_{12}x_2 + a'_{13}x_3 + \ldots + a'_{1n}x_n)$$
$$x_2 = b'_2 - (a'_{21}x_1 + a'_{23}x_3 + \ldots + a'_{2n}x_n)$$

$$\vdots$$

$$x_n = b'_n - (a'_{n1}x_1 + a'_{n2}x_2 + \ldots + a'_{n,n-1}x_{n-1})$$

We can now use $x_2^{(i)}, x_3^{(i)}, \ldots, x_n^{(i)}$ on the right-hand side of the first equation, to obtain $x_1^{(i+1)}$. We then use $x_1^{(i+1)}, x_3^{(i)}, x_4^{(i)}, \ldots, x_n^{(i)}$, the right-hand side of the second equation, to obtain $x_2^{(i+1)}$. Note that we immediately use $x_1^{(i+1)}$ in obtaining $x_2^{(i+1)}$. We then use $x_1^{(i+1)}, x_2^{(i+1)}, x_4^{(i)}, x_5^{(i)}, \ldots, x_n^{(i)}$, on the right-hand side of the third equation, to obtain $x_3^{(i+1)}$. Again, notice that we immediately use $x_1^{(i+1)}$ and $x_2^{(i+1)}$ in obtaining $x_3^{(i+1)}$. Formally:

$$x_j^{i+1} = b'_j - \sum_{k=1}^{j-1} a'_{jk} x_k^{(i+1)} - \sum_{k=j+1}^{n} a'_{jk} x_k^{(i)} \qquad \text{for } j = 1, \ldots, n$$

The conditions under which this process is guaranteed to converge to the solution vector go beyond the scope of this book.

A suitable convergence criterion will be the third type described in Section 10.5, namely that the difference between successive approximations should be less than a small value. This can be expressed in this context as

$$|x_j^{(i+1)} - x_j^{(i)}| < e, \qquad \text{for all } j$$

Write a subroutine to implement the Gauss–Seidel method, and modify your existing program for the solution of simultaneous equations (or the one in Section 18.5) to use this subroutine. Use this new program to solve the five systems of simultaneous equations given in Exercise 18.4.

Which method proved to be most suitable for each system?

18.11 A solid shape is formed by rotating the curve $y = f(x)$ about the x-axis. The volume of such a shape is

$$A = \int_a^b \pi f(x)^2 dx$$

where a and b are the start and end of the curve. Write a subroutine that has a function name **f** and the limits **a** and **b** as arguments, and returns the volume of the corresponding solid shape by evaluating the above integral. Use the adaptive quadrature method described in Section 18.8.

Confirm that for $f(x) = x^{1/2}$, $a = 1$ and $b = 3$, the volume contained is 4π units.

18.12 Investigate how the number of function evaluations required by the subroutine **adaptive_quadrature** to calculate $\int_{0.1}^{1} \frac{dx}{x}$ varies as the precision requirements are increased.

18.13 Using the subroutine `adaptive_quadrature`, calculate π to 4, 5 and 6 decimal places by integrating the equation for a circle of radius 1 with its centre at the origin over the range 0 to 1. How many function evaluations were required?

18.14 Using the subroutine `adaptive_quadrature`, calculate π to 4, 5 and 6 decimal places by evaluating $\int_0^1 1/(1 + x^2)dx$. How many function evaluations were required?

18.15 Modify the subroutine `adaptive_quadrature` so that it additionally returns its estimate of the error. Repeat Exercises 18.13 and 18.14 using your modified algorithm.

18.16 Modify the subroutine `adaptive_quadrature` to use parameterized real numbers so that you can repeat Exercises 18.13 and 18.14 to obtain π to 12 decimal places. How many function evaluations were required?

18.17 Write a program, or programs, to perform the following actions:

(**1**) Calculate a set of values of $f(x)$, for x within a specified range (for instance, $x = -10$ to $x = +10$ in steps of 0.5), and tabulate these.
(**2**) Use these tabulated values to interpolate a set of splines, or other approximating curves, through these points.
(**3**) Use the subroutine `adaptive_quadrature` to find the definite integral of the original function between two specified values of x, and also of the interpolated curves between the same values.
(**4**) Display the difference between the two integrals as one measure of the goodness of fit.

Test your program(s) on the following functions:

(**a**) x^2
(**b**) $x^2 + 3x - 5$
(**c**) x^3
(**d**) $2x^3 - 3x^2 - 6x + 4$
(**e**) x^4
(**f**) $3x^4 + 5x^3 - 2x^2 + 7x - 9$
(**g**) $\sin 2x$
(**h**) $\sin(x/2 + \pi/3)\cos x$
(**i**) $e^{x^2/2}$

18.18 Exercises 10.8 and 10.9 showed how the Newton quotient could be used to calculate the first derivative of a function, but also showed how the choice of h in the formula for the quotient

$$f'(x) = \frac{f(x + h) - f(x)}{h}$$

where h is small, was critical to the accuracy of the calculation. Euler's method for the solution of first-order differential equations of the form

$$\frac{dy}{dx} = g(x, y)$$

where $y = y_0$ when $x = x_0$, uses the Newton quotient to replace the derivative on the left-hand side of the equation:

$$\frac{f(x + h) - f(x)}{h} = g(x, y)$$

or

$$f(x + h) = f(x) + hg(x, y)$$

If we know the value of $f(x)$ for some initial value of x (for instance $x = 0$), then we can calculate the value at $x + h$, then at $x + 2h$, and so on. However, our experience in Exercises 10.8 and 10.9 might lead us to suppose that the choice of h will be critical, and this supposition is normally correct.

Euler's method usually requires h to be so small that it is frequently impractical and other methods have to be employed. However, it can be modified, by techniques similar to that used for creating the adaptive quadrature subroutine of Section 18.8, to make it more practical. Such modifications are beyond the scope of this book. Consult Dahlquist and Björck (1974) for an introduction to such techniques.

Use Euler's method in a program to solve the following problem. It is well-known that in a vacuum a steel ball and a feather will fall at the same speed under the influence of gravity. However, in practice there is always some air resistance, which will lead to the steel ball hitting the ground first. This retarding force is normally assumed to be proportional to the square of the velocity, leading to the following equation (from Newton's second law):

$$ma = mg - cv^2$$

where m is the mass of the ball, a is its downward acceleration, g is the acceleration due to gravity, v is the velocity of the ball, and c is some constant. This, in turn, leads us to the first-order differential equation

$$\frac{dv}{dt} = a = g - kv^2$$

where $k = c/m$.

Assuming that for a steel ball of mass 1 kg the value of k is 0.001, write a program to tabulate the downward velocity of a 1 kg steel ball dropped from a stationary hot-air balloon at a great height, and hence calculate the terminal velocity of the ball (the maximum speed that can be attained, which will be achieved when the retarding force due to air resistance equals the accelerating force due to gravity).

Run your program for a range of values for h in order to determine what is the best value (the time interval between 'samplings' in this case).

18.19 Use the program you wrote for Exercise 18.18 to find the terminal velocity of a person jumping from the balloon. Assume the person's mass to be 100 kg and k to be 0.004.

When the person has reached terminal velocity, a parachute opens, with the result that k becomes 0.3. Modify your program to find how this affects the parachutist's speed. (Hint: you may need to alter h again.)

18.20 Radioactive elements decay into other elements at a rate given by the equation

$$\frac{dm}{dt} = -rm$$

where m is the mass of the original material still present at time t and r is a constant property of the element known as the decay rate.

Analytical solution of this equation leads, among other things, to the conclusion that the mass of the original material is reduced by one half in a time T, known as the half-life of the substance, where $T = (\log_e 0.5)/r$ ($\approx 0.693/r$).

Use Euler's method to calculate the mass remaining, over a period of 500 years, of an initial 10 kg radioactive substance whose half-life is 200 years. Experiment with different values of h, starting with $h = 20$ years.

18.21 In your program for Exercise 18.20 you calculated the change in mass of an element due to radioactive decay. In general, the amount of this mass lost in energy is infinitesimal compared with that converted into another element, and can be ignored. It is simple, therefore, to calculate the mass of the new element, given the initial mass present, after a given time.

However, in many cases, this new element itself decays into a third element. In this situation, clearly, a pair of simultaneous differential equations are required to describe the process.

An example of this process is the decay of strontium 92 (with a half-life of about 162 minutes) into yttrium 92 (with a half-life of about 327 minutes), which in turn decays into zirconium.

Write a program which will use Euler's method to calculate how many atoms there will be of each element at 15 minute intervals over a 10 hour period, assuming that there were 10^{20} atoms of pure strontium 92 at the start of the experiment.

Run your program again using time intervals of 5, 10 and 20 minutes.

AFTERWORD –
Seven golden rules

This book is called *Fortran 90 Programming*, and we hope that we have made it clear that there is much more to programming than simply writing the code. Indeed, we have emphasized that coding will often represent little more than 20–25% of the total effort involved, with some 30–35% being spent on the design, and the remainder being spent in testing and debugging. We shall sum up our philosophy, therefore, in what we call the *Seven Golden Rules of Programming*.

(1) *Always plan ahead*   It is invariably a mistake to start to write a program without having first drawn up a program design plan which shows the structure of the program and the various levels of detail.

(2) *Develop in stages*   In a program of any size it is essential to tackle each part of the program separately, so that the scale and scope of each new part of the program is of manageable proportions.

(3) *Modularize*   The use of procedures and modules, which can be written and tested independently, is a major factor in the successful development of large programs, and is closely related to the staged development of the programs.

(4) *Keep it simple*   A complicated program is usually both inefficient and error-prone. Fortran 90 contains many features which can greatly simplify the design of code and data structures.

(5) *Test thoroughly*   Always test your programs thoroughly at every stage, and cater for as many situations (both valid and invalid) as possible. Keep your test data for reuse if (when) your program is modified in the future.

(6) *Document all programs*   There is nothing worse than returning to an undocumented program after an absence of any significant time. Most programs can be adequately documented by the use of meaningful names, and by the inclusion of plenty of comments, but additional documentation should be produced if necessary to explain things that cannot be covered in the code itself. A program has to be written only once – but it will be read many times, so effort expended on self-documenting comments will be more than repaid later.

(7) *Enjoy your programming*   Writing computer programs, and getting them to work correctly, is a challenging and intellectually stimulating activity. It should also be enjoyable. There is an enormous satisfaction to be obtained from getting a well-designed program to perform the activities that it is supposed to perform. It is not always easy, but it should be fun!

Happy programming!

APPENDIX A
Intrinsic procedures

Fortran 90 includes a rich set of intrinsic procedures, both subroutines and functions, which are intended to facilitate the solution of scientific, statistical, mathematical and other problems. These intrinsic procedures are part of the Fortran language because it is only with a complete set of tools that a solution to a problem is 'easy' and elegant. This appendix describes all the intrinsic procedures contained within the Fortran 90 language.

Section A.1 consists mainly of a complete table of all specific and generic names of intrinsic procedures, in alphabetical order, showing their class, whether a function may be referenced by a generic name, the function type, whether the name may be used as an argument, and the name of the function with its calling sequence.

Section A.2 explains how the detailed descriptions of the intrinsic procedures are arranged, following which, the remaining sections group the procedures according to their function, and within each section briefly describe the purpose of the procedures, together with their argument and result types. (Note that Fortran 90 processors may, and usually will, provide additional intrinsic procedures; for details of these, for more details about the standard intrinsic procedures, and any other processor-dependent details, you should refer to the language manual of the Fortran 90 system you are using.)

A.1 Alphabetical list of the intrinsic procedures

Table A.1 lists every intrinsic procedure defined in Fortran 90. It is a merger of three alphabetically ordered lists, namely the specific names of those intrinsic functions that have specific names, the generic names of all the intrinsic functions and the names of all the intrinsic subroutines.

The table is arranged as follows:

- The first column, *Specific name*, identifies those specific names (carried forward from FORTRAN 77) which may appear in an **INTRINSIC** statement (see Section 11.3) and may be used as actual arguments in calls to other procedures. The corresponding dummy argument may only reference the specific name with scalar arguments of default type. Those specific names prefixed with * must *not* be used as actual arguments. The column 4 section reference is for the corresponding generic function; there are no descriptions of the specific name functions *per se*.

Argument names for the specific functions are shown in lower case letters to differentiate them from argument keywords and to indicate their default type:

d	Double precision real
i, j	Integer
s	Character
x, y	Single precision real
z	Complex (single precision)

- The second column, *Generic name and calling sequence*, gives the generic name and the argument keywords in upper case. A generic function is one whose resultant type depends on the *type* of the argument. Usually, the type and kind of the generic function result is the same as the type and kind of the argument(s). The argument keywords are indicative of their usage; keywords printed in a lighter font (for instance, OPTIONAL), indicate that the argument is optional. A keyword is required if a preceding optional argument is omitted, or if the arguments are supplied in a different order from that specified (see Section 11.3). For example, a reference to **INDEX** may be written in either of the following forms:

```
INDEX('find me','d m')
INDEX(SUBSTRING='d m',STRING='find me')
```

The type (any kind is possible) of the argument keywords is as follows:

A	Any
BACK	Logical
DIM	Integer
I	Integer
KIND	Integer
MASK	Logical
STRING	Character
X, Y	Numeric
Z	Complex

Note that the numeric types are integer, real and complex. For details of the type corresponding to other argument keywords, reference should be made to the description of the procedure later in this appendix.

- The third column, *Function type*, specifies the type of the generic function, in the case of a function, or the word 'subroutine' otherwise. Entries in this column and their meanings are:

Argument type	The type and kind of the generic function agree with the type and kind of the principal argument.
Character	If *1 is not specified, the length is either the length of the principal argument (for example, **ADJUSTL**), or is based on how the function modifies the principal argument (for example, **REPEAT**).
Complex	The type and kind of the principal argument are preserved, or the result has the kind of the real argument(s).

Logical   Except for the function **LOGICAL**, the result has default kind.

Real   Except for the function **REAL**, the kind of the result is the kind of the argument(s).

- The final column, *Section*, identifies where in the appendix the named procedure (generic function or subroutine) is described in detail.

For example, the second and third items in Table A.1 are as follows:

	ACHAR(I)	Character*1	A.7
ACOS(x)	**ACOS(X)**	Argument type	A.6

The first of these two entries indicates that **ACHAR(I)** does not have a specific name and, therefore, may not be used as an actual argument; that it takes a single integer argument (of any kind) and returns a character*1 result; and that it is described in more detail in Section A.7.

The next entry indicates that **ACOS(X)** may be used as an actual argument; that the result of the generic function agrees with the type of its argument, and that, as a consequence, the specific name, **ACOS(x)**, returns a real result; and that the generic procedure is described in more detail in Section A.6.

Table A.1 Specific and generic names of all Fortran 90's intrinsic procedures.

Specific name	Generic name and calling sequence	Function type	Section
ABS(x)	**ABS(A)** — If **A** is Complex, **ABS** is Real	Argument type	A.6
	ACHAR(I)	Character*1	A.7
ACOS(x)	**ACOS(X)**	Argument type	A.6
	ADJUSTL(STRING)	Character	A.7
	ADJUSTR(STRING)	Character	A.7
AIMAG(z)	**AIMAG(Z)**	Real	A.6
AINT(x)	**AINT(A,**KIND**)**	Real	A.6
	ALL(MASK,DIM**)**	Logical	A.8
	ALLOCATED(ARRAY)	Logical	A.9
ALOG(x)	**LOG(X)**	Argument type	A.6
ALOG10(x)	**LOG10(X)**	Argument type	A.6
*AMAX0(i,j,...)	**REAL(MAX(A1,A2,**A3**,...))**	Real	A.6
*AMAX1(x,y,...)	**MAX(A1,A2,**A3**,...)**	Real	A.6
*AMIN0(i,j,...)	**REAL(MIN(A1,A2,**A3**,...))**	Real	A.6
*AMIN1(x,y,...)	**MIN(A1,A2,**A3**,...)**	Real	A.6
AMOD(x,y)	**MOD(A,P)**	Real	A.6
ANINT(x)	**ANINT(A,**KIND**)**	Real	A.6
	ANY(MASK,DIM**)**	Logical	A.8
ASIN(x)	**ASIN(X)**	Real	A.6
	ASSOCIATED(POINTER,TARGET**)**	Logical	A.9
ATAN(x)	**ATAN(X)**	Real	A.6
ATAN2(y,x)	**ATAN2(Y,X)**	Real	A.6
	BIT_SIZE(I)	Integer	A.4
	BTEST(I,POS)	Logical	A.5
CABS(z)	**ABS(A)**	Argument type	A.6
CCOS(z)	**COS(X)**	Argument type	A.6
	CEILING(A)	Integer	A.6

Table A.1 *(cont.)* Specific and generic names of all Fortran 90's intrinsic procedures.

Specific name	Generic name and calling sequence	Function type	Section
CEXP(z)	EXP(X)	Argument type	A.6
	CHAR(I,KIND)	Character*1	A.7
CLOG(z)	LOG(X)	Argument type	A.6
	CMPLX(X,Y,KIND)	Complex	A.4
CONJG(z)	CONJG(X)	Complex	A.6
COS(x)	COS(X)	Argument type	A.6
COSH(x)	COSH(X)	Argument type	A.6
	COUNT(MASK,DIM)	Integer	A.8
	CSHIFT(ARRAY,SHIFT,DIM)	**ARRAY** type	A.8
CSIN(z)	SIN(X)	Argument type	A.6
CSQRT(z)	SQRT(X)	Argument type	A.6
DABS(d)	ABS(A)	Argument type	A.6
DACOS(d)	ACOS(X)	DP Real	A.6
DASIN(d)	ASIN(X)	DP Real	A.6
DATAN(d)	ATAN(X)	DP Real	A.6
DATAN2(d2,d1)	ATAN2(Y,X)	DP Real	A.6
	DATE_AND_TIME(DATE,TIME,ZONE, VALUES)	Subroutine	A.3
	DBLE(A)	DP Real	A.4
DCOS(d)	COS(X)	DP Real	A.6
DCOSH(d)	COSH(X)	DP Real	A.6
DDIM(d1,d2)	DIM(X,Y)	DP Real	A.6
DEXP(d)	EXP(X)	DP Real	A.6
	DIGITS(X)	Integer	A.4
DIM(x,y)	DIM(X,Y)	Argument type	A.6
DINT(d)	AINT(A)	Argument type	A.6
DLOG(d)	LOG(X)	Argument type	A.6
DLOG10(d)	LOG10(X)	DP Real	A.6
*DMAX1(d1,d2,...)	MAX(A1,A2,A3,...)	DP Real	A.6
*DMIN1(d1,d2,...)	MIN(A1,A2,A3,...)	DP Real	A.6
DMOD(d1,d2)	MOD(A,P)	DP Real	A.6
DNINT(d)	ANINT(A)	DP Real	A.6
	DOT_PRODUCT(VECTOR_A,VECTOR_B)	Argument type	A.6
DPROD(x,y)	DPROD(X,Y)	DP Real	A.6
DSIGN(d1,d2)	SIGN(X,Y)	DP Real	A.6
DSIN(d)	SIN(X)	DP Real	A.6
DSINH(d)	SINH(X)	DP Real	A.6
DSQRT(d)	SQRT(X)	DP Real	A.6
DTAN(d)	TAN(X)	DP Real	A.6
DTANH(d)	TANH(X)	DP Real	A.6
	EOSHIFT(ARRAY,SHIFT,BOUNDARY,DIM)	**ARRAY** type	A.8
	EPSILON(X)	Real	A.4
EXP(x)	EXP(X)	Argument type	A.6
	EXPONENT(X)	Integer	A.4
*FLOAT(i)	REAL(A)	Real	A.4
	FLOOR(A)	Integer	A.6
	FRACTION(X)	Real	A.6
	HUGE(X)	Argument type	A.4
IABS(i)	ABS(A)	Integer	A.6
	IACHAR(C)	Integer	A.7
	IAND(I,J)	Integer	A.5

Table A.1 *(cont.)* Specific and generic names of all Fortran 90's intrinsic procedures.

Specific name	Generic name and calling sequence	Function type	Section
	IBCLR(I,POS)	Argument type	A.5
	IBITS(I,POS,LEN)	Argument type	A.5
	IBSET(I,POS)	Argument type	A.5
	ICHAR(C)	Integer	A.7
IDIM(i,j)	DIM(X,Y)	Integer	A.6
*IDINT(i)	INT(A)	Integer	A.4
IDNINT(i)	NINT(A)	Integer	A.6
	IEOR(I,J)	Argument type	A.5
*IFIX(x)	INT(A)	Integer	A.4
INDEX(s1,s2)	INDEX(STRING,SUBSTRING,BACK)	Integer	A.7
	INT(A,KIND)	Integer	A.4
	IOR(I,J)	Argument type	A.5
	ISHFT(I,SHIFT)	Argument type	A.5
	ISHFTC(I,SHIFT,SIZE)	Argument type	A.5
ISIGN(i,j)	SIGN(A,B)	Integer	A.6
	KIND(X)	Integer	A.4
	LBOUND(ARRAY,DIM)	Integer	A.8
LEN(s)	LEN(STRING)	Integer	A.7
	LEN_TRIM(STRING)	Integer	A.7
	LGE(STRING_A,STRING_B)	Logical	A.7
	LGT(STRING_A,STRING_B)	Logical	A.7
	LLE(STRING_A,STRING_B)	Logical	A.7
	LLT(STRING_A,STRING_B)	Logical	A.7
	LOG(X)	Argument type	A.6
	LOG10(X)	Argument type	A.6
	LOGICAL(L,KIND)	Logical	A.4
	MATMUL(MATRIX_A,MATRIX_B)	Argument type	A.6
*MAX0(i,j,...)	MAX(A1,A2,A3,...)	Argument type	A.6
*MAX1(x,y,...)	INT(MAX(A1,A2,A3,...))	Integer	A.6
	MAXEXPONENT(X)	Integer	A.4
	MAXLOC(ARRAY,MASK)	Integer	A.8
	MAXVAL(ARRAY,DIM,MASK)	Argument type	A.8
	MERGE(TSOURCE,FSOURCE,MASK)	Argument type	A.8
*MIN0(i,j,...)	MIN(A1,A2,A3,...)	Argument type	A.6
*MIN1(x,y,...)	INT(MIN(A1,A2,A3,...))	Integer	A.6
	MINEXPONENT(X)	Integer	A.4
	MINLOC(ARRAY,MASK)	Integer	A.8
	MINVAL(ARRAY,DIM,MASK)	Argument type	A.8
MOD(i,j)	MOD(A,P)	Integer	A.6
	MODULO(A,P)	Argument type	A.6
	MVBITS(FROM,FROMPOS,LEN,TO,TOPOS)	Subroutine	A.5
	NEAREST(X,S)	Real	A.6
NINT(x)	NINT(A,KIND)	Integer	A.6
	NOT(I)	Argument type	A.5
	PACK(ARRAY,MASK,VECTOR)	Argument type	A.8
	PRECISION(X)	Integer	A.4
	PRESENT(A)	Logical	A.9
	PRODUCT(ARRAY,DIM,MASK)	Argument type	A.8
	RADIX(X)	Integer	A.4
	RANDOM_NUMBER(HARVEST)	Subroutine	A.6
	RANDOM_SEED(SIZE,PUT,GET)	Subroutine	A.6

Table A.1 *(cont.)* Specific and generic names of all Fortran 90's intrinsic procedures.

Specific name	Generic name and calling sequence	Function type	Section
	`RANGE(X)`	Integer	A.4
	`REAL(A,`KIND`)`	Real	A.4
	`REPEAT(STRING,NCOPIES)`	Character	A.7
	`RESHAPE(SOURCE,SHAPE,`PAD,ORDER`)`	Argument type	A.8
	`RRSPACING(X)`	Argument type	A.4
	`SCALE(X,I)`	Argument type	A.4
	`SCAN(STRING,SET,`BACK`)`	Integer	A.7
	`SELECTED_INT_KIND(R)`	Integer	A.4
	`SELECTED_REAL_KIND(`P,R`)` — at least one of P and R is required	Integer	A.4
	`SET_EXPONENT(X,I)`	Argument type	A.4
	`SHAPE(SOURCE)`	Integer	A.8
`SIGN(x,y)`	`SIGN(A,B)`	Argument type	A.6
`SIN(x)`	`SIN(X)`	Argument type	A.6
`SINH(x)`	`SINH(X)`	Argument type	A.6
	`SIZE(ARRAY,`DIM`)`	Integer	A.8
`*SNGL(d)`	`REAL(A)`	Real	A.4
	`SPACING(X)`	Argument type	A.4
	`SPREAD(SOURCE,DIM,NCOPIES)`	Argument type	A.8
`SQRT(x)`	`SQRT(X)`	Argument type	A.6
	`SUM(ARRAY,`DIM,MASK`)`	Argument type	A.8
	`SYSTEM_CLOCK(`COUNT,COUNT_RATE, COUNT_MAX`)`	Subroutine	A.3
`TAN(x)`	`TAN(X)`	Argument type	A.6
`TANH(x)`	`TANH(X)`	Argument type	A.6
	`TINY(X)`	Real	A.4
	`TRANSFER(SOURCE,MOLD,`SIZE`)`	Argument type	A.8
	`TRANSPOSE(MATRIX)`	Argument type	A.8
	`TRIM(STRING)`	Character	A.7
	`UBOUND(ARRAY,`DIM`)`	Integer	A.8
	`UNPACK(VECTOR,MASK,FIELD)`	Argument type	A.8
	`VERIFY(STRING,SET,`BACK`)`	Integer	A.7

A.2 Intrinsic procedure classes and their descriptions in this appendix

In addition to the intrinsic subroutines, one of which is elemental, there are three classes of intrinsic functions: elemental, inquiry and transformational.

An elemental procedure is one that is specified for scalar arguments, but may also be applied to array arguments.

In a reference to an elemental intrinsic function:

- If the arguments are all scalar, the result is scalar. If an argument is an array, the shape of the result is the shape of the array; if there is more than one argument, they must be conformable.

- The elements of the result have the same values as would have been obtained if the scalar-valued function had been applied separately, in any order, to corresponding elements of each argument.
- When the KIND argument is present, it must be a scalar integer initialization expression (only integer is noted in the descriptions) and must specify a representation method for the function result that exists on the processor.

An inquiry function (Sections A.4 and A.9) is one whose value depends on the properties of its principal argument; in most cases the argument *value* need not be defined.

The third and last group of intrinsic functions are transformational functions (Sections A.6 and A.8) which all have one or more array-valued arguments or an array-valued result.

In the remaining sections of this appendix each procedure is described in a consistent format in which the name of the procedure and its calling sequence appear on the first line. This is followed by three or four bulleted items.

The first of these is the classification of the procedure and, in the case of a function, the type of the result. The second is the purpose of the procedure, and the third is a list of the arguments and their type (and their **INTENT** in the case of a subroutine), together with any explanatory comments that may be necessary. Finally, in the case of some of the more complicated procedures, a fourth section explains more details about the procedure's operation.

A consistent set of rules is used to describe the intrinsic procedures in a concise manner. These rules are:

- All intrinsic functions arguments are **INTENT(IN)**; the **INTENT** of the intrinsic subroutine arguments is indicated in the description.
- In calling sequences, optional arguments are printed in a lighter font, for instance OPTIONAL.
- When a function has a KIND dummy argument, then the result is of the kind specified by that argument if KIND is present, or of the appropriate default type otherwise.
- When *kind* appears in textual context (as opposed to the name of an argument), it is to be read as *kind type parameter*.
- When describing the type of arguments and function results, type, length and dimension data are all given in a shorthand, as shown in the following examples:

    Integer(8) means the corresponding item must be declared as

    ```
    INTEGER, DIMENSION(8) :: ...
    ```

    Character*8(n) means that the corresponding item must be declared as:

    ```
    CHARACTER(LEN=8), DIMENSION(n) :: ...
    ```

Furthermore, Integer(k, ...) means that the corresponding item is an integer array with rank one or more.

Unless otherwise specified, a reference to one entity as being of the same type as another implies that both entities have the same kind of parameter.

A.3 Date and time intrinsic subroutines

DATE_AND_TIME(DATE,TIME,ZONE,VALUES)

- Subroutine.
- Returns current date and time.
- DATE   Character*8   **OUT**   Set to the form CCYYMMDD, where CC represents the century, YY the year, MM the month and DD the day.

  TIME   Character*10   **OUT**   Set to the form hhmmss.sss, where hh represents the hour, mm the minute and ss.sss the second and millisecond.

  ZONE   Character*5   **OUT**   Set to + or − hhmm, where hh (hour) and mm (minutes) are the time difference with respect to Coordinated Universal Time (UTC, also known as Greenwich Mean Time).

  VALUES   Integer(8)   **OUT**   See the table below for element definitions.

If a value is not available for DATE, TIME or ZONE it is set to blanks.
The following integers are returned in VALUES when the information is available:

VALUES(1): Year
VALUES(2): Month
VALUES(3): Day
VALUES(4): Minutes difference from Coordinated Universal Time (UTC)
VALUES(5): Hour, in the range 0 to 23
VALUES(6): Minutes, in the range 0 to 59
VALUES(7): Seconds, in the range 0 to 60 (to allow astronomers to adjust the length of the earth's year)
VALUES(8): Milliseconds, in the range 0 to 999

An array element is set to **-HUGE(0)** if the corresponding value is not available on the system.

SYSTEM_CLOCK(COUNT,COUNT_RATE,COUNT_MAX)

- Subroutine.
- Returns integer data from a real-time clock; the integer is incremented by one for each clock count until COUNT_MAX is reached, then it is reset to 0 at the next count; that is, the integer lies in the range 0 to COUNT_MAX.
- COUNT   Integer   **OUT**   COUNT is set to a value based on the current value of the system clock.

- COUNT_RATE   Integer   **OUT**   COUNT_RATE is set to the number of processor clock counts per second, or to 0 if there is no clock.

- COUNT_MAX   Integer   **OUT**   COUNT_MAX is set to the maximum value that COUNT can have.

If there is no clock, COUNT and COUNT_RATE are set to **-HUGE(0)** and COUNT_MAX is set to 0.

A.4 Kind, numeric processor and conversion intrinsic functions

BIT_SIZE(I)
- Integer inquiry function.
- Returns the number of bits in the integer **I**.
- I   Integer

CMPLX(X,Y,KIND)
- Complex elemental function.
- Returns a complex value. If **X** is non-complex the result has a real part of **X** and an imaginary part of Y if Y is present, or an imaginary part of 0.0 if Y is not present; if **X** is complex then Y must not be present.
- X   Numeric
  Y   Integer or real
  KIND   Integer

DBLE(A)
- Double precision real elemental function.
- Returns **A** converted, if necessary, to double precision real. If **A** is complex, **DBLE(A)** becomes **REAL(A,KIND(0.D))**.
- A   Numeric

DIGITS(X)
- Integer inquiry function.
- Returns the number of significant digits in **X**.
- X   Integer or real

EPSILON(X)
- Inquiry function of same type as **X**.
- Returns a positive number that is almost negligible compared to 1.0 of the same type and kind as **X**.
- X   Real

EXPONENT(X)
- Integer elemental function.
- Returns the exponent part of **X**. **EXPONENT(0.0)** has the value 0; for **X** non-zero, the result is one plus the integer part of the log to the base 2 of X.
- X   Real

HUGE(X)
- Inquiry function of the same type as **X**.
- Returns the largest number of the same type and kind as **X**.
- X   Integer or real

INT(A,KIND)
- Integer elemental function.
- Returns non-integer **A** truncated and converted to integer type of KIND; if **A** is integer, **INT** converts it to a different kind.
- A   Numeric
  KIND   Integer

KIND(X)
- Integer inquiry function.
- Returns the kind value of an intrinsic type item **X**.
- **X**   Any intrinsic type

LOGICAL(L,KIND)
- Logical elemental function.
- Returns a logical value converted from the kind of **L** to KIND. If KIND is not present, the result has default logical kind.
- **L**   Logical

  KIND   Integer

MAXEXPONENT(X)
- Integer inquiry function.
- Returns the maximum exponent of the same type and kind as **X**.
- **X**   Real

MINEXPONENT(X)
- Integer inquiry function.
- Returns the minimum exponent of the same type and kind as **X**.
- **X**   Real

PRECISION(X)
- Integer inquiry function.
- Returns the decimal precision of real values with the same kind as **X**.
- **X**   Real or complex

RADIX(X)
- Integer inquiry function.
- Returns the base of the mathematical model for values of the same type and kind as **X**.
- **X**   Integer or real

RANGE(X)
- Integer inquiry function.
- Returns the decimal exponent range for integer or real numbers with the same kind as **X**.
- **X**   Numeric

REAL(A,KIND)
- Real elemental function.
- Returns integer **A** converted to real; converts non-integer **A** to the different real kind.
- **A**   Numeric

  KIND   Integer

RRSPACING(X)
- Elemental function of the same type as **X**.
- Returns the reciprocal of the relative spacing of numbers near **X**.
- **X**   Real

SCALE(X,I)

- Elemental function of the same type as **X**.
- Returns **X*(b**I)** where **b** is the base in the representation of **X**.
- **X**   Real
  I   Integer

SELECTED_INT_KIND(R)

- Integer transformation function.
- Returns a processor-dependent kind value that represents all integers n such that **ABS**(n) **< 10**R**.
- **R**   Integer
- Note that if there is more than one such kind, the value returned is the one with the smallest decimal exponent range. If there are several such kinds, the smallest is returned. If no such kind is available the result is -1.

SELECTED_REAL_KIND(P,R)

- Integer transformational function.
- Returns a processor-dependent kind value for a real with decimal precision of at least P digits (see **PRECISION**) and a decimal exponent range of at least R (see **RANGE**).
- P   Integer
- R   Integer

  At least one of P and R must be present.
- If more than one kind meets the criteria, the value returned is the one with the smallest decimal precision, unless there are several such values, in which case the smallest kind is returned. If no such kind is available, the result is -1 if the precision requested is not available, -2 if the exponent range is not available, and -3 if neither is available.

SET_EXPONENT(X,I)

- Elemental function of the same type as **X**.
- Returns the number whose fractional part is the fractional part of the representation of **X** and whose exponent part is **I**; if **X**$=0$ then the result has the value 0.
- **X**   Real
  I   Integer

SPACING(X)

- Elemental function of the same type as **X**.
- Returns the absolute spacing of numbers near **X** in the mathematical model used for real numbers if this is within range, otherwise the result is the same as **TINY(X)**.
- **X**   Real

TINY(X)

- Inquiry function of the same type as **X**.
- Returns the smallest positive number of the same type and kind as **X**.
- **X**   Real

A.5 Bit intrinsic procedures

For the purposes of the bit procedures, the model used effectively defines an object to consist of s consecutive bits numbered from 0 to $s - 1$; on a PC, s is 32.

BTEST(I,POS)
- Logical elemental function.
- Returns *true* if bit **POS** of **I** is 1; otherwise *false*.
- **I**   Integer
  POS   Integer, non-negative, $<$ **BIT_SIZE(I)**

IAND(I,J)
- Elemental function of the same type as **I**.
- Returns the logical AND of the integers **I** and **J**.
- **I**   Integer
- **J**   Same as I

IBCLR(I,POS)
- Elemental function of the same type as **I**.
- Returns **I** with bit **POS** set to zero.
- **I**   Integer
  POS   Integer, non-negative, $<$ **BIT_SIZE(I)**

IBITS(I,POS,LEN)
- Elemental function of the same type as **I**.
- Returns a right-adjusted sequence of bits extracted from **I** of length **LEN** beginning at bit **POS**; all other bits are 0.
- **I**   Integer
  POS   Integer, non-negative, **POS+LEN <= BIT_SIZE(I)**
  LEN   Integer, non-negative

IBSET(I,POS)
- Elemental function of the same type as **I**.
- Returns **I** with the **POS** bit set to one.
- **I**   Integer
  POS   Integer, non-negative, $<$ **BIT_SIZE(I)**

IEOR(I,J)
- Elemental function of the same type as **I**.
- Returns the exclusive OR, bit-by-bit, of **I** and **J**.
- **I**   Integer
  J   Same as I

IOR(I,J)
- Elemental function of the same type as **I**.
- Returns the inclusive OR, bit-by-bit, of **I** and **J**.
- **I**   Integer
  J   Same as I

ISHFT(I,SHIFT)
- Elemental function of the same type as **I**.
- Returns **I** logically shifted right (**SHIFT** negative) or left (**SHIFT** positive); zeros are used to fill the vacated positions.
- **I**   Integer
  SHIFT   Integer, **ABS(SHIFT) <= BIT_SIZE(I)**

ISHFTC(I,SHIFT,SIZE)
- Elemental function of the same type as **I**.
- Returns the value of **I** with its SIZE rightmost bits circularly shifted **SHIFT** right (**SHIFT** negative) or left (**SHIFT** positive); if SIZE is absent, the effect is as though it were present with the value **BIT_SIZE(I)**.
- **I**   Integer
  SHIFT   Integer, **ABS(SHIFT) <= SIZE**
  SIZE   Integer, positive, ⩽ **BIT_SIZE(I)**

MVBITS(FROM,FROMPOS,LEN,TO,TOPOS)
- Subroutine.
- Copies a sequence of bits from **FROM** to **TO**.
FROM	Integer	**IN**	The object from which the bits are to be moved
FROMPOS	Integer	**IN**	Non-negative
LEN	Integer	**IN**	Non-negative; **FROMPOS+LEN <= BIT_SIZE(FROM)**
TO	Integer	**INOUT**	Same kind as **FROM**, may be the same variable as **FROM**. **TO** is set by copying the sequence of bits of length **LEN**, starting at position **FROMPOS** of **FROM** to position **TOPOS** of **TO**; the other bits of **TO** are unaltered.
TOPOS	Integer	**IN**	Non-negative; **TOPOS+LEN <= BIT_SIZE(TO)**

NOT(I)
- Elemental function of the same type as **I**.
- Returns the logical complement of the bits of **I**.
- **I**   Integer

A.6   Numeric and mathematical intrinsic procedures

ABS(A)
- Elemental function of the same type as **A**, or real if **A** is complex.
- Returns the absolute value of **A**. For **A** complex, **ABS(A)** returns the real square root of the sum of the squares of the real and imaginary parts.
- **A**   Numeric

ACOS(X)
- Real elemental function.
- Returns the arccosine of **X** in the range $0 \leqslant$ **ACOS(X)** $\leqslant \pi$, where $|$**X**$| \leqslant 1.0$.
- **X**   Real

AIMAG(Z)
- Real elemental function.
- Returns the imaginary part of complex **Z**, that is, **AIMAG(CMPLX(X,Y))** has the value **Y**.
- **Z**   Complex

AINT(A,KIND**)**
- Real elemental function.
- Returns **A** truncated to a whole number. **AINT(A)** has the value of the largest integer that does not exceed the magnitude of **A** and whose sign is the same as the sign of **A**.
- **A**   Real
  KIND   Integer

ANINT(A,KIND**)**
- Real elemental function.
- Returns the nearest whole number to **A**. If **A** is positive, **ANINT(A)** has the value **AINT(A+0.5)**; otherwise **ANINT(A)** has the value **AINT(A-0.5)**.
- **A**   Real
  KIND   Integer

ASIN(X)
- Real elemental function.
- Returns the arcsine of **X** in the range $-\pi/2 \leqslant$ **ASIN(X)** $\leqslant \pi/2$, where $|$**X**$| \leqslant 1.0$.
- **X**   Real

ATAN(X)
- Real elemental function.
- Returns the arctangent of **X** in the range $-\pi/2 \leqslant$ **ATAN(X)** $\leqslant \pi/2$.
- **X**   Real

ATAN2(Y,X)
- Real elemental function.
- Returns the arctangent of **Y/X** in the range $-\pi <$ **ATAN(X)** $\leqslant \pi$.
- **Y**   Real
  X   Same as **Y**
- Both **X** and **Y** cannot be 0, and the following rules also apply:
        if **Y** $= 0$ the result is 0.0 if **X** >0
        if **Y** $= 0$ the result is π if **X** <0
        if **Y** >0 the result is positive
        if **Y** <0 the result is negative
        if **X** $= 0$ the absolute value of the result is $\pi/2$

CEILING(A)
- Integer elemental function.
- Returns the least integer greater than or equal to **A**.
- **A**   Real

CONJG(Z)
- Complex elemental function.
- Returns the conjugate of **Z**.
- **Z**　　　　　Complex

COS(X)
- Elemental function of the same type as **X**.
- Returns the cosine of **X**.
- **X**　　　　　Real or complex

COSH(X)
- Real elemental function.
- Returns the hyperbolic cosine of **X**.
- **X**　　　　　Real

DIM(X,Y)
- Elemental function of the same type as **X**.
- Returns the difference **X-Y** if the difference is positive; otherwise 0.
- **X**　　　　　Integer or real
  Y　　　　　Same as **X**

DOT_PRODUCT(VECTOR_A,VECTOR_B)
- Transformational function.
- Returns the dot product of numeric or logical vectors. If the arguments are numeric then the result type is the same as the type of the expression **VECTOR_A*VECTOR_B**; if they are logical the result type is logical.
- **VECTOR_A**　　Numeric(n) or logical(n)
  VECTOR_B　　Numeric(n) if **VECTOR_A** is numeric, logical(n) if **VECTOR_A** is logical
- If the vectors have zero size then the result is 0 or *false*, as appropriate.

DPROD(X,Y)
- Double precision real elemental function.
- Returns the double precision real product of **X** and **Y**.
- **X**　　　　　Default real
  Y　　　　　Same as **X**

EXP(X)
- Elemental function of the same type as **X**.
- Returns e raised to the power **X**.
- **X**　　　　　Real or complex

FLOOR(A)
- Integer elemental function.
- Returns the greatest default integer less than or equal to **A**.
- **A**　　　　　Real

FRACTION(X)
- Real elemental function.
- Returns the fractional part of **X**.
- **X**　　　　　Real

LOG(X)
- Elemental function of the same type as **X**.
- Returns the natural logarithm of **X**.
- **X**   Real, positive or complex, non-zero

LOG10(X)
- Real elemental function.
- Returns the logarithm of **X** to base 10.
- **X**   Real, positive

MATMUL(MATRIX_A,MATRIX_B)
- Transformational function.
- Returns the matrix product of numeric or logical matrices. If the arguments are numeric then the result type is the same as the type of the expression **MATRIX_A*MATRIX_B**; if they are logical the result type is logical.
- **MATRIX_A**   Numeric or logical of rank one or two.
  MATRIX_B   Numeric if **MATRIX_A** is numeric, logical if **MATRIX_A** is logical. It must be of rank two if **MATRIX_A** is of rank one, and of rank one if **MATRIX_A** is of rank two; its first (or only) dimension must equal the size of the last (or only) dimension of **MATRIX_A**.

MAX(A1,A2,A3,...)
- Elemental function of the same type as its arguments.
- Returns the maximum value of **A1**, **A2**, A3, ...
- **A1**   Integer or real
  A2   Same as **A1**
  A3   Same as **A1**
- For example, **MAX((/-9.0,7.0/),(/2.0,0.3/))** has the value (/2.0,7.0/).

MIN(A1,A2,A3,...)
- Elemental function of the same type as its arguments.
- Returns the minimum value of **A1**, **A2**, A3, ...
- **A1**   Integer or real
  A2   Same as **A1**
  A3   Same as **A1**

MOD(A,P)
- Elemental function of the same type as **A**.
- Returns **A - P*INT(A/P)**; if **P** = 0, the result is processor-dependent.
- **A**   Integer or real
  P   Same as **A**
- For example, **MOD(3.0,2.0)** has the value 1.0, **MOD(8,5)** has the value 3, **MOD(-8,5)** has the value −3, **MOD(8,-5)** has the value 3 and **MOD(-8,-5)** has the value −3.

MODULO(A,P)
- Elemental function of the same type as **A**.
- Returns the modulo of **A** with respect to **P**; if **P** = 0, the result is processor-dependent.
- **A**   Integer or real
  P   Same as **A**

- For **A** integer, the result **R** is such that **A = Q*P + R**, where **Q** is an integer and the signs of **P** and **R** agree, and the inequalities $0 \leqslant$ **ABS(R)<ABS(P)** hold. For **A** real, the result **R** is such that **R = A - FLOOR(A/P)*P**.
- For example, **MODULO(8,5)** has the value 3, **MODULO(-8,5)** has the value 2, **MODULO(8,-5)** has the value -2 and **MODULO(-3.0,-2.0)** has the value -1.0.

NEAREST(X,S)

- Real elemental function.
- Returns the nearest machine representable number different from **X** in the direction of **S**.
- **X**   Real
  S   Real, non-zero

NINT(A,KIND)

- Integer elemental function.
- Returns integer nearest to **A**; if **A**>0, **NINT(A)** has the value **INT(A+0.5)**; otherwise **NINT(A)** has the value **INT(A-0.5)**.
- **A**   Real
  KIND   Integer

RANDOM_NUMBER(HARVEST)

- Subroutine.
- Returns pseudo-random number(s) from the uniform distribution over the range $0 \leqslant$ **HARVEST**<1.0.
- **HARVEST**   Real   **OUT**   **HARVEST** may be either a scalar or an array.

RANDOM_SEED(SIZE,PUT,GET)

- Subroutine.
- Either restarts the pseudo-random number generator used by **RANDOM_NUMBER** or returns generator parameters.

SIZE	Integer	**OUT**	SIZE is set to the number of integers the processor uses to hold the value of the seed (n).
PUT	Integer(m)	**IN**	$m \geqslant n$; the seed is set to the value of PUT.
GET	Integer(m)	**OUT**	$m \geqslant n$; GET is set to the current value of the seed.

- There must either be no arguments, in which case the subroutine sets the seed to a processor-dependent value, or there must be exactly one argument – which is used as described above.

SIGN(A,B)

- Elemental function of the same type as **A**.
- Returns the absolute value of **A** set to the same sign as **B**.
- **A**   Integer or real
  B   Same as **A**

SIN(X)

- Elemental function of the same type as **X**.
- Returns the sine of **X**.
- **X**   Real or complex

SINH(X)
- Real elemental function.
- Returns the hyperbolic sine of **X**.
- **X**   Real

SQRT(X)
- Elemental function of the same type as **X**.
- Returns the square root of **X**. For **X** real, **X** must be non-negative. For **X** complex, **SQRT(X)** has the real part non-negative; if the real part of **SQRT(X)** is 0, the imaginary part is non-negative.
- **X**   Real or complex

TAN(X)
- Real elemental function.
- Returns the tangent of **X**.
- **X**   Real

TANH(X)
- Real elemental function.
- Returns the hyperbolic tangent of **X**.
- **X**   Real

A.7   Character intrinsic functions

ACHAR(I)
- Character*1 elemental function.
- Returns the character in a specified position in the ASCII collating sequence.
- **I**   Integer
- For **I** positive, < 128, the result is the **I**th character of the ASCII collating sequence; otherwise, the result is processor-dependent. **ACHAR(IACHAR(C))** has the value **C** for any character **C** capable of representation in the processor; that is, **ACHAR** and **IACHAR** are inverse functions.

ADJUSTL(STRING)
- Character elemental function.
- Returns a character value with the leading blanks of **STRING** removed and the same number of trailing blanks added at the end.
- **STRING**   Character

ADJUSTR(STRING)
- Character elemental function.
- Returns a character value with the trailing blanks of **STRING** removed and the same number of leading blanks added at the beginning.
- **STRING**   Character

CHAR(I,KIND)
- Character*1 elemental function.
- Returns the character in a specified position in the processor collating sequence associated with the specified kind.

- **I**   Integer
  KIND   Integer
- **I** must have a non-negative value less than the number of characters in the collating sequence associated with the specified kind. **CHAR** is the inverse of the intrinsic function **ICHAR**.

IACHAR(C)

- Integer elemental function.
- Returns the position of a character in the ASCII collating sequence; a processor-dependent value is returned if **C** is not in the ASCII collating sequence.
- **C**   Character*1
- Note that if **LLE(C,D)** is *true* then **IACHAR(C)<=IACHAR(D)** is *true*, where **C** and **D** are any two characters, and similarly for **LGE**, **LGT** and **LLT**.

ICHAR(C)

- Integer elemental function.
- Returns the position of a character in the processor collating sequence associated with the kind of the character.
- **C**   Character*1
- The result is non-negative and less than the number of characters in the processor collation sequence. **ICHAR** is the inverse of the intrinsic function **CHAR**.

INDEX(STRING,SUBSTRING,BACK)

- Integer elemental function.
- Returns the starting position of a substring within a string.
- **STRING**   Character
  SUBSTRING   Character of the same kind as **STRING**
  BACK   Logical
- If **LEN(STRING)<LEN(SUBSTRING)** the result is 0; if **LEN(SUBSTRING)** = 0 the result is 1. If BACK is absent, or present with the value *false*, the result is the lowest value of **I** such that **STRING(I:I+LEN(SUBSTRING)-1)** = **SUBSTRING**, or 0 if there is no such value.

  If BACK is *true*, the result is the maximum **I** less than or equal to **LEN(STRING)-LEN(SUBSTRING)** such that **STRING(I:I+LEN(SUBSTRING)-1)** = **SUBSTRING**, or 0 if no such **I** exists. A result of 0 is also returned if **LEN(STRING)<LEN(SUBSTRING)**. **LEN(STRING)+1** is returned if **LEN(SUBSTRING)** = 0.

LEN(STRING)

- Integer inquiry function.
- Returns the length of **STRING**.
- **STRING**   Character

LEN_TRIM(STRING)

- Integer elemental function.
- Returns the length of **STRING** without counting any trailing blank characters; if **STRING** is all blanks, the result is 0.
- **STRING**   Character

LGE (STRING_A, STRING_B)

- Logical elemental function.
- Returns *true* if **STRING_A** $\geqslant$ **STRING_B** in the ASCII collating sequence; otherwise *false*. If both **STRING_A** and **STRING_B** have zero length then the result is *true*.
- **STRING_A**   Default character
  STRING_B   Default character
- If necessary, the shorter string is first extended on the right with blanks in order to make the strings equal length. If either string contains a character not in the ASCII character set, the result is processor-dependent. The result is *true* if the strings satisfy the comparison; otherwise *false*.

LGT (STRING_A, STRING_B)

- Logical elemental function.
- Returns *true* if **STRING_A** > **STRING_B** in the ASCII collating sequence; otherwise *false*.
- **STRING_A**   Default character
  STRING_B   Default character
- If necessary, the shorter string is first extended on the right with blanks in order to make the strings equal length. If either string contains a character not in the ASCII character set, the result is processor-dependent. The result is *true* if the strings satisfy the comparison; otherwise *false*.

LLE (STRING_A, STRING_B)

- Logical elemental function.
- Returns *true* if **STRING_A** $\leqslant$ **STRING_B** in the ASCII collating sequence; otherwise *false*. The result is *true* if the strings satisfy the comparison; otherwise *false*.
- **STRING_A**   Default character
  STRING_B   Default character
- If necessary, the shorter string is first extended on the right with blanks in order to make the strings equal length. If either string contains a character not in the ASCII character set, the result is processor-dependent. The result is *true* if the strings satisfy the comparison; otherwise *false*.

LLT (STRING_A, STRING_B)

- Logical elemental function.
- Returns *true* if **STRING_A** < **STRING_B** in the ASCII collating sequence; otherwise *false*.
- **STRING_A**   Default character
  STRING_B   Default character
- If necessary, the shorter string is first extended on the right with blanks in order to make the strings equal length. If either string contains a character not in the ASCII character set, the result is processor-dependent. The result is *true* if the strings satisfy the comparison; otherwise *false*.

REPEAT (STRING, NCOPIES)

- Character transformational function.
- Returns a character value which is produced by concatenating **NCOPIES** copies of **STRING**. If either **STRING** is zero length or **NCOPIES** is 0, the result is a zero length string.
- **STRING**   Character
  NCOPIES   Integer, non-negative

SCAN(STRING,SET,BACK)

- Integer elemental function.
- Scans a string for any one of the characters in a specified set of characters.
- **STRING**   Character
  SET   Character of the same kind as **STRING**
  BACK   Logical
- The function returns an integer which is the first instance of a member of the characters in **SET** that appears in **STRING**, counting from the left. If BACK is *true*, the search is from the right, but the count is still from the left. If no character of **STRING** is in **SET**, or if the length of **STRING** or **SET** is 0, the result is 0.

TRIM(STRING)

- Character transformational function.
- Returns **STRING** with any trailing blanks removed. If **STRING** contains no non-blank characters, the result has zero length.
- **STRING**   Character

VERIFY(STRING,SET,BACK)

- Integer elemental function.
- Returns 0 if every character in **STRING** is also in **SET** or if **STRING** has zero length. If a character in **STRING** is not in set, the result is its position in **STRING**. If BACK is *true*, then the search is from the right.
- **STRING**   Character
  SET   Character
  BACK   Logical

A.8 Array and pointer intrinsic functions

The availability of a considerable number of the intrinsic procedures for use in array processing was discussed in Chapters 7 and 13, especially the latter, and the most important of them were described in detail there. This section contains a complete summary of all 23 array intrinsics.

In the following descriptions many of the procedures follow similar conventions:

- The optional logical argument MASK is used by some of the functions to select the elements of one or more of the arguments to be operated on by the function.
- When referring to the rank of the (primary) array argument, an italicized *r* is used.
- A scalar is defined as an array of rank 0.
- The term *positive* always means *strictly positive*, that is, greater than 0.

Furthermore, in the functions **ALL**, **ANY**, **LBOUND**, **MAXVAL**, **MINVAL**, **PRODUCT**, **SUM** and **UBOUND**, but not **CSHIFT**, **EOSHIFT**, **SIZE** and **SPREAD**, the optional argument DIM, when present, requires that the corresponding actual argument is not an optional dummy argument of the calling program unit. This is because the functions in the first list all return either a scalar or an array based on the presence or absence of DIM, and the function must, therefore, be able to determine the presence or absence of DIM from the list of actual arguments.

ALL (MASK,DIM)
- Logical transformational function.
- Returns *true* if all **MASK** values are *true* along dimension DIM or if **MASK** has zero size; otherwise *false*.
- **MASK**   Logical(n, ...)
  DIM   Integer, positive, less than $r + 1$. The corresponding actual argument must not be an optional dummy argument.
- Note that the result is scalar if DIM is absent; otherwise it has rank $r - 1$ and shape $(\mathtt{d(1)}, \mathtt{d(2)}, \dots, \mathtt{d(DIM-1)}, \mathtt{d(DIM+1)}, \dots, \mathtt{d}(r))$, where $(\mathtt{d(1)}, \mathtt{d(2)}, \dots, \mathtt{d}(r))$ is the shape of **MASK**. The value of element $(\mathtt{s(1)}, \mathtt{s(2)}, \dots, \mathtt{s(DIM-1)}, \mathtt{s(DIM+1)}, \dots, \mathtt{s}(r))$ of **ALL(MASK,DIM)** is **ALL(MASK($\mathtt{s(1)}, \mathtt{s(2)}, \dots, \mathtt{s(DIM-1)}, :, \mathtt{s(DIM+1)}, \dots, \mathtt{s}(r)$))**.

ANY (MASK,DIM)
- Logical transformational function.
- Returns *true* if any **MASK** value is *true* along dimension DIM; otherwise *false* (including the case in which **MASK** has zero size).
- **MASK**   Logical($n, \dots$).
  DIM   Integer, positive, less than $r + 1$. The corresponding actual argument must not be an optional dummy argument.
- Note that the result is scalar if DIM is absent; otherwise it has rank $r - 1$ and shape $(\mathtt{d(1)}, \mathtt{d(2)}, \dots, \mathtt{d(DIM-1)}, \mathtt{d(DIM+1)}, \dots, \mathtt{d}(r))$, where $(\mathtt{d(1)}, \mathtt{d(2)}, \dots, \mathtt{d}(r))$ is the shape of **MASK**. The value of element $(\mathtt{s(1)}, \mathtt{s(2)}, \dots, \mathtt{s(DIM-1)}, \mathtt{s(DIM+1)}, \dots, \mathtt{s}(r))$ of **ANY(MASK,DIM)** is **ANY(MASK($\mathtt{s(1)}, \mathtt{s(2)}, \dots, \mathtt{s(DIM-1)}, :, \mathtt{s(DIM+1)}, \dots, \mathtt{s}(r)$))**.

COUNT (MASK,DIM)
- Integer transformational function.
- Returns the number of *true* elements of **MASK** along dimension DIM; returns 0 if **MASK** has zero size.
- **MASK**   Logical($n, \dots$).
  DIM   Integer, positive, less than $r + 1$. The corresponding actual argument must not be an optional dummy argument.
- Note that the result is scalar if DIM is absent; otherwise it has rank $r - 1$ and shape $(\mathtt{d(1)}, \mathtt{d(2)}, \dots, \mathtt{d(DIM-1)}, \mathtt{d(DIM+1)}, \dots, \mathtt{d}(r))$, where $(\mathtt{d(1)}, \mathtt{d(2)}, \dots, \mathtt{d}(r))$ is the shape of **MASK**. The value of element $(\mathtt{s(1)}, \mathtt{s(2)}, \dots, \mathtt{s(DIM-1)}, \mathtt{s(DIM+1)}, \dots, \mathtt{s}(r))$ of **COUNT(MASK,DIM)** is **COUNT(MASK($\mathtt{s(1)}, \mathtt{s(2)}, \dots, \mathtt{s(DIM-1)}, :, \mathtt{s(DIM+1)}, \dots, \mathtt{s}(r)$))**.

CSHIFT (ARRAY,SHIFT,DIM)
- Transformational function of the same type as **ARRAY**.
- Performs a circular shift on an array expression of rank one or circular shifts on all the complete rank one sections along a given dimension of an array expression of rank two or greater. Elements shifted out at one end of a section are shifted in at the other end. Different sections may be shifted by different amounts and in different directions.

- **ARRAY**   Any(n).
  SHIFT   Integer. It must be a scalar if **ARRAY** has rank one, otherwise it must have rank $r - 1$ and shape $(\mathtt{d(1)}, \mathtt{d(2)}, \ldots, \mathtt{d(DIM-1)}, \mathtt{d(DIM+1)}, \ldots, \mathtt{d(r)})$, where $(\mathtt{d(1)}, \mathtt{d(2)}, \ldots, \mathtt{d(r)})$ is the shape of **ARRAY**.
  DIM   Integer, positive, less than $r + 1$. If DIM is omitted, a value of 1 is assumed.

EOSHIFT(ARRAY,SHIFT,BOUNDARY,DIM**)**

- Transformational function of the same type as **ARRAY**.
- Performs an end-off shift on an array expression of rank one or end-off shifts on all the complete rank-one sections along a given dimension of an array expression of rank two or greater. Elements are shifted off at one end of a section and copies of a boundary value are shifted in at the other end. Different sections may have different boundary values and may be shifted by different amounts and in different directions.
- **ARRAY**   Any(n)
  SHIFT   Integer, rank $r - 1$ and shape $(\mathtt{d(1)}, \mathtt{d(2)}, \ldots, \mathtt{d(DIM-1)}, \mathtt{d(DIM+1)}, \ldots, \mathtt{d(r)})$, where $(\mathtt{d(1)}, \mathtt{d(2)}, \ldots, \mathtt{d(r)})$ is the shape of **ARRAY**.
  BOUNDARY   Same as **ARRAY**, rank $r - 1$ and of shape $(\mathtt{d(1)}, \mathtt{d(2)}, \ldots, \mathtt{d(DIM-1)}, \mathtt{d(DIM+1)}, \ldots, \mathtt{d(r)})$. If BOUNDARY is omitted, it is treated as if it were present with the scalar value shown:

Type of **ARRAY**	Value of BOUNDARY
Numeric	0 of the appropriate type and kind
Logical	*false*
Character(*len*)	*len* blanks

  DIM   Integer, positive, less than $r + 1$; if omitted, it is as if it were present with the value 1.

LBOUND(ARRAY,DIM**)**

- Integer inquiry function.
- Returns all the lower bounds or a specified lower bound of **ARRAY**.
- **ARRAY**   Any($n, \ldots$); it must not be a pointer that is not associated or an allocatable array that is not allocated.
  DIM   Integer, positive, less than $r + 1$. The corresponding actual argument must not be an optional dummy argument.
- Note that if DIM is present then the result is scalar and takes the value 1 for an array section or for an array expression, other than a whole array or array structure component; otherwise it is the lower bound for subscript DIM of **ARRAY** if dimension DIM of **ARRAY** does not have zero size, and has the value 1 if dimension DIM has zero size. If DIM is not present then the result is an array whose ith element is **LBOUND(ARRAY,**i**)**, for $i = 1, 2, \ldots, r$.

MAXLOC(ARRAY,MASK**)**

- Integer transformational function, returning a rank-one array of size r.
- Returns the location of the first element of **ARRAY** having the maximum value of the elements identified by MASK.
- **ARRAY**   Integer($n, \ldots$) or real($n, \ldots$)
  MASK   Logical($n, \ldots$), conformable with **ARRAY**

- If MASK is not present, each element of the result is the subscript corresponding to the element of **ARRAY** having the maximum value in that dimension; if there is more than one such element then the value returned is the first such subscript in array element order. The ith subscript of the rank-one array returned is positive and less than or equal to the extent of the ith dimension of **ARRAY**. If MASK is present then the result is based only upon those elements of **ARRAY** which correspond to *true* elements of MASK. If **ARRAY** has zero size, or every element of MASK is *false*, the result is processor-dependent.

MAXVAL (**ARRAY**,DIM,MASK)

- Transformational function of the same type as **ARRAY**.
- Returns the maximum value of the elements of **ARRAY** along dimension DIM (if present) corresponding to the true elements of MASK (if present). If **ARRAY** has zero size, or if every element of MASK is *false*, the result is the negative number of largest magnitude of the type and kind of **ARRAY**.
- **ARRAY**   Integer$(n, \dots)$ or real$(n, \dots)$
  DIM   Integer, positive, less than $r + 1$. The corresponding actual argument must not be an optional dummy argument.
  MASK   Logical$(n, \dots)$, conformable with **ARRAY**.
- Note that if DIM is absent then the result is scalar; otherwise the result has rank $r - 1$ and shape $(\mathbf{d(1)}, \mathbf{d(2)}, \dots, \mathbf{d(DIM-1)}, \mathbf{d(DIM+1)}, \dots, \mathbf{d(r)})$, where $(\mathbf{d(1)}, \mathbf{d(2)}, \dots, \mathbf{d(r)})$ is the shape of **ARRAY**.

MERGE (**TSOURCE**,**FSOURCE**,**MASK**)

- Elemental function of the same type as **TSOURCE**.
- Selects one of two alternative values according to **MASK**. If **MASK** (or an element of **MASK**) is *true* then the result is **TSOURCE** (or an element of **TSOURCE**), otherwise it is **FSOURCE** (or an element of **FSOURCE**).
- **TSOURCE**   Any
  FSOURCE   Same as **TSOURCE**
  MASK   Logical
- For example, **MERGE((/1.0,1.0/),(/0.0,0.0/),(/.TRUE.,.FALSE./))** has the value **((/1.0,0.0/))**.

MINLOC (**ARRAY**,MASK)

- Integer transformational function, returning a rank-one array of size r.
- Returns the location of the first element of **ARRAY** having the minimum value of the elements identified by MASK.
- **ARRAY**   Integer$(n, \dots)$ or real$(n, \dots)$.
  MASK   Logical$(n, \dots)$, conformable with **ARRAY**.
- If MASK is not present, each element of the result is the subscript corresponding to the element of **ARRAY** having the minimum value in that dimension; if there is more than one such element then the value returned is the first such subscript in array element order. The ith subscript of the rank-one array returned is positive and less than or equal to the extent of the ith dimension of **ARRAY**. If MASK is present then the result is based only upon those elements of **ARRAY** which correspond to *true* elements of MASK. If **ARRAY** has zero size, or every element of MASK is *false*, the result is processor-dependent.

MINVAL (ARRAY,DIM,MASK**)**

- Transformational function of the same type as **ARRAY**.
- Returns the minimum value of the elements of **ARRAY** along dimension DIM (if present) corresponding to the true elements of MASK (if present). If **ARRAY** has zero size, or if every element of MASK is *false*, the result is the positive number of largest magnitude of the type and kind of **ARRAY**.
- **ARRAY**   Integer$(n, \ldots)$ or real$(n, \ldots)$
  DIM   Integer, positive, less than $r + 1$. The corresponding actual argument must not be an optional dummy argument.
  MASK   Logical$(n, \ldots)$, conformable with **ARRAY**.
- Note that if DIM is absent then the result is scalar; otherwise the result has rank $r - 1$ and shape **(d(1),d(2),...,d(DIM-1),d(DIM+1),...,d(r))**, where **(d(1), d(2),...,d(r))** is the shape of **ARRAY**.

PACK (ARRAY,MASK,VECTOR**)**

- Transformational function of the same type as **ARRAY**.
- Packs an array into an array of rank one under the control of a mask.
- **ARRAY**   Any$(n, \ldots)$.
  MASK   Logical$(n, \ldots)$, conformable with **ARRAY**.
  VECTOR   Same as **ARRAY**, rank-one, must have at least as many elements as there are *true* elements in **MASK**; if **MASK** is a scalar with the value *true*, VECTOR must have at least as many elements as **ARRAY**.
- If VECTOR is present, the size of the result is the same as the size of VECTOR; otherwise the result size is the number of *true* elements in **MASK** unless **MASK** is scalar with the value *true*, in which case the result size is the size of **ARRAY**. Element i of the result is the element of **ARRAY** that corresponds to the ith *true* element of **MASK**, taking elements in array-element order, for $i = 1, \ldots, t$. If VECTOR is present and has size $n > t$, element i of the result has the value VECTOR(i), for $i = t + 1, \ldots, n$. The result can be unpacked by the intrinsic function **UNPACK**.

PRODUCT (ARRAY,DIM,MASK**)**

- Transformational function of the same type as **ARRAY**.
- Returns the product of the elements of **ARRAY** along dimension DIM (if present) corresponding to the *true* elements of MASK (if present); if **ARRAY** has zero size or if MASK has no *true* elements the result has the value one.
- **ARRAY**   Numeric$(n, \ldots)$.
  DIM   Integer, positive, less than $r + 1$. The corresponding actual argument must not be an optional dummy argument.
  MASK   Logical$(n, \ldots)$, conformable with **ARRAY**.
- The result is scalar if DIM is absent or if **ARRAY** has rank one; otherwise it has rank $r - 1$ and shape **(d(1),d(2),...,d(DIM-1),d(DIM+1),...,d(r))**, where **(d(1), d(2),...,d(r))** is the shape of **ARRAY**.

RESHAPE (SOURCE,SHAPE,PAD,ORDER**)**

- Transformational function of the same type as **SOURCE**.
- Constructs an array of a specified shape from the elements of another array.

- **SOURCE**   Any(k, ...).
  SHAPE   Integer(m), where m is a positive constant less than 8.
  PAD   Same as **SOURCE**, must be an array.
  ORDER   Integer(m), same shape as **SHAPE**; its value must be a permutation of $(1, 2, \ldots, n)$, where n is the size of **SHAPE**.
- The result is an array of shape **SHAPE** constructed from the elements of **SOURCE**. The elements of the result, taken in permuted subscript order ORDER(1), ..., ORDER(n) if ORDER is present or in order $1, \ldots, n$ if it is absent, are those of **SOURCE** in array-element order followed, if necessary, by the elements of PAD in array-element order, followed, if necessary, by additional copies of PAD in array-element order.

SHAPE(SOURCE)

- Integer inquiry function.
- Returns the shape of **SOURCE** as a rank-one array whose size is r and whose elements are the extents of the corresponding dimensions of **SOURCE**.
- **SOURCE**   Any, array or scalar; must not be a pointer that is disassociated, an allocatable array that is not allocated, or an assumed-size array.

SIZE(ARRAY,DIM)

- Integer inquiry function.
- Returns either the extent of **ARRAY** along a specified dimension (if DIM is present) or the total number of elements in the array.
- **ARRAY**   Any(n, ...); must not be a pointer that is disassociated or an allocatable array that is not allocated.
  DIM   Integer, positive, less than $r + 1$; if **ARRAY** is an assumed-size array, then DIM must be present with a value less than r.

SPREAD(SOURCE,DIM,NCOPIES)

- Transformational function of the same type as **SOURCE**.
- Returns an array of rank $r + 1$ by copying **SOURCE** along a specified dimension (as in making a book from copies of a single page).
- **SOURCE**   Any, $0 \leqslant r < 7$
  DIM   Integer, positive, less than $r + 2$
  NCOPIES   Integer
- If **SOURCE** is scalar, the shape of the result is (**MAX(NCOPIES,0)**), and each element of the result has a value equal to **SOURCE**.
  If **SOURCE** is an array with shape (d(1),d(2),...,d(r)) the shape of the result is (d(1),d(2),..., d(DIM-1),**MAX(NCOPIES,0)**,d(DIM),...,d(r)), and the element of the result with subscripts ($s_1, s_2, \ldots, s_{r+1}$) has the value SOURCE($s_1, s_2, \ldots, s_{DIM-1}, s_{DIM+1}, \ldots, s_{r+1}$).

SUM(ARRAY,DIM,MASK)

- Transformational function of the same type as **ARRAY**.
- Returns the sum of the elements of **ARRAY** along dimension DIM (if present) corresponding to the *true* elements of MASK (if present); if **ARRAY** has zero size or if MASK has no *true* elements the result has the value one.

- **ARRAY**   Numeric($n, \ldots$)
  DIM   Integer, positive, less than $r + 1$. The corresponding actual argument must not be an optional dummy argument.
  MASK   Logical($n, \ldots$), conformable with **ARRAY**.
- The result is scalar if DIM is absent or if **ARRAY** has rank one; otherwise it has rank $r - 1$ and shape $(\mathtt{d(1)}, \mathtt{d(2)}, \ldots, \mathtt{d(DIM-1)}, \mathtt{d(DIM+1)}, \ldots, \mathtt{d}(r))$, where $(\mathtt{d(1)}, \mathtt{d(2)}, \ldots, \mathtt{d}(r))$ is the shape of **ARRAY**.

TRANSFER(SOURCE,MOLD,SIZE)

- Transformational function of the same type as **MOLD**.
- Returns either a scalar or a rank-one array with a physical representation identical to that of **SOURCE** but interpreted with the type and kind of **MOLD**.
- **SOURCE**   Any; scalar or array.
  MOLD   Any; scalar or array.
  SIZE   Integer. The corresponding actual argument must not be an optional dummy argument.
- If **MOLD** is a scalar and SIZE is absent, the result is a scalar; if **MOLD** is an array and SIZE is absent, the result has a size as small as possible such that its physical representation is not shorter than that of **SOURCE**; if SIZE is present, the result is a rank-one array of size SIZE.
  If the lengths of the physical representations of the result and **SOURCE** are not the same then the effect is as though the physical representation of **SOURCE** had either been truncated or extended in an undefined manner, as appropriate.

TRANSPOSE(MATRIX)

- Transformational function of the same type as **MATRIX**.
- Transposes an array of rank two; element (i, j) of the result has the value **MATRIX**(j, i).
- **MATRIX**   Any(m, n)

UBOUND(ARRAY,DIM)

- Integer inquiry function.
- Returns all the upper bounds or a specified upper bound of **ARRAY**.
- **ARRAY**   Any($n, \ldots$); it must not be a pointer that is not associated or an allocatable array that is not allocated.
  DIM   Integer, positive, less than $r + 1$. The corresponding actual argument must not be an optional dummy argument.
- Note that if DIM is present then the result is scalar and takes a value equal to the number of elements in the given dimension for an array section or for an array expression, other than a whole array or array structure component; otherwise it is the upper bound for subscript DIM of **ARRAY** if dimension DIM of ARRAY does not have zero size, and has the value 0 if dimension DIM has zero size. If DIM is not present then the result is an array whose ith element is **UBOUND**(ARRAY,i), for $i = 1, 2, \ldots, r$.

UNPACK(VECTOR,MASK,FIELD)

- Transformational function of the same type as **VECTOR**.
- Unpacks a rank-one array into an array under the control of a mask.

- **VECTOR**   Any(n).
  MASK   Logical($m, \ldots$).
  FIELD   Same as **VECTOR**, conformable with **MASK**.
- The element of the result that corresponds to the ith *true* element of **MASK**, in array-element order, has the value **VECTOR**(i) for $i = 1, 2, \ldots, t$, where t is the number of *true* values in **MASK**. The other result elements have either the corresponding array element of **FIELD**, if **FIELD** is array-valued, or the scalar value of **FIELD** if it is a scalar. The inverse operation of packing an array into a rank-one array is performed by the intrinsic function **PACK**.

A9   Miscellaneous inquiry functions

ALLOCATED (ARRAY)
- Logical inquiry function.
- Returns *true* if **ARRAY** is currently allocated; otherwise *false*. The result is undefined if the allocation status of **ARRAY** is undefined.
- **ARRAY**   Any type, but must have the allocatable attribute.

ASSOCIATED (POINTER, TARGET)
- Logical inquiry function.
- Returns *true* if **POINTER** is associated with a target and TARGET is not present, or if TARGET is the target that **POINTER** is associated with; otherwise *false*. The result is also *false* if either **POINTER** or TARGET is disassociated.
- **POINTER**   Any type, but must have the pointer attribute. Its pointer association status must not be undefined.
  TARGET   Pointer or target; if it is a pointer, its pointer association status must be defined.

PRESENT (A)
- Logical inquiry function.
- Returns *true* if **A** is present, where **A** is an optional argument of the procedure in which the reference to **PRESENT** occurs; otherwise *false*.
- **A**   Any

APPENDIX B
The rules for host and USE association

B.1 USE association

Any scoping unit may gain access to named data objects, derived types, interface blocks, procedures, generic identifiers and namelist groups in a module by means of a USE statement, as a result of which the entities in the scoping unit are said to be USE associated with the entities in the module, and have the attributes specified in the module. A USE statement may restrict the public entities in the module which are available in the scoping unit by USE association by means of an ONLY qualifier, and may rename any of the USE associated entities.

More than one USE statement for a given module may appear in a scoping unit. If all such statements contain ONLY qualifiers then only those public entities of the module which appear in one or more ONLY lists are accessible; the effect is as though a single USE statement were present with an ONLY qualifier containing a concatenation of all the ONLY lists. If at least one of the USE statements does not have an ONLY qualifier then all public entities in the module are accessible, and the effect is as if all the ONLY lists and all the rename lists were concatenated into a single *rename* list.

If two or more generic interfaces that are accessible in the scoping unit have the same name, the same operator, or are both assignments, they are interpreted as a single generic interface. Other than this case, two or more accessible entities may not have the same name unless no entity is referenced by this name in the scoping unit. Thus, it is not necessary to rename a public entity of the module to avoid a name clash if that name is not used within the scoping unit to reference either the module entity or some other entity.

The local name of an entity made accessible by USE association cannot appear in any other specification statement that would respecify any of the attributes of that entity in the scoping unit, except that its accessibility may be altered by means of a PUBLIC or PRIVATE statement.

B.2 Host association

An internal subprogram, a module subprogram or a derived type definition has access to the named entities from its host via host association. These entities may be variables, constants, procedures, interfaces, derived types, type parameters, derived type components

- A type name in a derived type definition
- A function name in a **FUNCTION** statement, in a type declaration statement or in a statement function statement
- A subroutine name in a **SUBROUTINE** statement
- An entry name in an **ENTRY** statement
- An object name in a type declaration statement, in a **POINTER** statement, in a **SAVE** statement or in a **TARGET** statement
- A named constant in its defining **PARAMETER** statement
- An array name in an **ALLOCATABLE** statement or in a **DIMENSION** statement
- A variable name in a common block in a **COMMON** statement
- The name of a variable that is wholly or partially initialized in a **DATA** statement
- The name of an object that appears in an **EQUIVALENCE** statement
- A dummy argument name in a **FUNCTION** statement, in a **SUBROUTINE** statement, in an **ENTRY** statement or in a statement function statement
- A result name in a **FUNCTION** statement or in an **ENTRY** statement
- An intrinsic procedure name in an **INTRINSIC** statement
- A namelist group name in a **NAMELIST** statement
- A generic name in a generic **INTERFACE** statement

Figure B.1 Local entities which hide entities of the same name in the host.

or namelist groups, and are known by the same name, and have the same attributes as in the host.

There are, however, a number of situations in which entities in the host are not available for access by host association because they are *hidden* by the availability of another entity of the same non-generic name within the same scoping unit. These fall into three groups, as follows:

- An entity accessed by **USE** association makes a host entity of the same non-generic name inaccessible.
- A name that appears in an **EXTERNAL** statement, or which is declared with the **EXTERNAL** attribute is a global name and makes a host entity of the same non-generic name inaccessible.
- A name that appears in the scoping unit in one of the categories shown in Figure B.1 is a local name and makes a host entity of the same non-generic name inaccessible.

Note that an interface body does not access any entities in its host by host association, but it may access entities by **USE** association.

APPENDIX C
Statement order in Fortran 90

Fortran 90 programs consist of one or more program units, each of which contains two or more statements from the complete set of legal Fortran statements. These statements can be grouped into 17 different categories:

(1) Initial statements (**PROGRAM, FUNCTION, SUBROUTINE, MODULE** and **BLOCK DATA**)
(2) Comments
(3) **USE** statements
(4) **IMPLICIT NONE** statement
(5) Other **IMPLICIT** statements
(6) **PARAMETER** statements
(7) **DATA** statements
(8) Derived type definitions
(9) Type declaration statements
(10) Interface blocks
(11) Statement function statements
(12) Other specification statements
(13) **FORMAT** statements
(14) **ENTRY** statements
(15) Executable constructs
(16) **CONTAINS** statement
(17) **END** statements

Strictly speaking, a comment is not a statement, but we can consider it to be such from an informal and practical viewpoint.

Every program unit must start with an initial statement and end with an **END** statement. Within the body of each program unit, however, there are several constraints on the ordering. Figure C.1 illustrates these in a diagrammatic form in which the horizontal lines separate groups of statement categories which cannot be interspersed, and which must appear in the order shown, while vertical lines are for convenience only, and have no significance as regards the allowable ordering. Comments have been omitted, but can appear anywhere.

In addition to the constraints on the order of statements within a program unit, there are also constraints on which categories of statements are allowed within different kinds of scoping units. Figure C.2, therefore, shows which categories of statements can appear in each of the various different kinds of scoping unit. The categories are listed in

PROGRAM, FUNCTION, SUBROUTINE, MODULE or **BLOCK DATA** statement					
USE statements					
FORMAT and **ENTRY** statements	**IMPLICIT NONE** statement				
	PARAMETER statements	**IMPLICIT statements**			
	PARAMETER and **DATA** statements	Derived type definitions, Interface blocks, Type declaration statements, Statement function statements, and Specification statements			
	DATA statements	Executable constructs			
CONTAINS statement					
Internal subprograms or module subprograms					
END statement					

Figure C.1 Requirements on statement ordering in Fortran 90 program units.

the same order as above, except that the heading *Other specifications* has been used to group together **IMPLICIT** statements, **PARAMETER** statements, type declarations and other specification statements not explicitly mentioned.

Note, incidentally, that the scoping unit of a module does not include any module subprograms that the module may contain.

Kind of scoping unit	*MP*	*M*	*BD*	*ES*	*MS*	*IS*	*IB*
USE statement	Y	Y	Y	Y	Y	Y	Y
DATA statement	Y	Y	Y	Y	Y	Y	N
Derived type definition	Y	Y	Y	Y	Y	Y	Y
Interface block	Y	Y	N	Y	Y	Y	Y
Statement function	Y	N	N	Y	Y	Y	N
Other specifications	Y	Y	Y	Y	Y	Y	Y
FORMAT statement	Y	N	N	Y	Y	Y	N
ENTRY statement	N	N	N	Y	Y	N	Y
Executable statement	Y	N	N	Y	Y	Y	N
CONTAINS	Y	Y	N	Y	Y	N	N

Key: *MP* Main program unit *M* Module
      BD Block data program unit *ES* External subprogram
      MS Module subprogram *IS* Internal subprogram
      IB Interface body

Figure C.2 Categories of statements allowed in scoping units.

APPENDIX D
The ASCII character set

Character information which is to be stored in the memory of a computer must first be converted into a coded form. In the past, this coded form almost always consisted of 7 or 8 bits, giving a total of 128 or 256 possible characters; however, recent developments mean that in the future most computers are likely to adopt a 16 bit coded form, providing a total of 65536 characters, or even a 24 or 32 bit coding, giving almost unimaginable numbers of possible characters.

	0	1	2	3	4	5	6	7
0			sp	0	@	P	`	p
1			!	1	A	Q	a	q
2			"	2	B	R	b	r
3			#	3	C	S	c	s
4			$	4	D	T	d	t
5			%	5	E	U	e	u
6			&	6	F	V	f	v
7			'	7	G	W	g	w
8			(	8	H	X	h	x
9			)	9	I	Y	i	y
10			*	:	J	Z	j	z
11			+	;	K	[	k	{
12			,	<	L	\	l	|
13			–	=	M	]	m	}
14			.	>	N	^	n	~
15			/	?	O	_	o	

Notes: (1) **sp** indicates the space, or blank, character
(2) character position 2/3 (#) may sometimes be represented as £
(3) character position 2/4 ($) may sometimes be represented as ¤
(4) character positions 4/0, 5/11, 5/12, 5/13, 5/14, 6/0, 7/11, 7/12, 7/13 and 7/14 are reserved for national use and may appear quite differently in different countries

Figure D.1 The ASCII (or ISO 646) coded character set.

The actual coding system does not matter for most purposes, although it may affect the range of characters available. However, a program which contains extensive character manipulation may run into difficulties when transferred to another computer which uses a different character code. Most of the problems concerned with the ordering of characters can be avoided by the use of the **LGT**, **LGE**, **LLE** and **LLT** intrinsic functions for character comparisons (see Section 5.5), since these will always compare characters according to their order in the ASCII code.

This code was originally an American standard code, but also forms the basis for the widely used international standard coding system known as ISO 646. Unfortunately, this code allows certain character codes to be used for specific national characters (for instance Å or ö) which can cause problems when programs are moved from one country to another. Figure D.1 shows the ASCII code which is used to define the ASCII collating sequence used by the four intrinsic functions referred to above; those characters which may differ in certain national versions are, however, indicated in the table.

The table is laid out in a *hexadecimal* fashion, as is conventional for such tables, corresponding to the actual pattern of bits in the coded character representation. The order of characters in this table thus runs from the top to the bottom of the first column, and then from the top to the bottom of the next column to the right, and so on. To find the decimal value corresponding to a particular character you should multiply the column number by 16 and then add the row number; thus **A** corresponds to 65 $(4 \times 16 + 1)$, while } corresponds to 125 $(7 \times 16 + 13)$ − although it should be noted that this character occupies one of the code positions reserved for national use and so may have a different graphic representation in different countries.

APPENDIX E
Older and obsolescent features of Fortran 90

Fortran 90 is a large language which has evolved to its present state over a period of almost 40 years. During that time there have been a great many changes in the way in which programmers write programs and, even more importantly, in the way in which software designers plan and design their programs. These changes have been reflected in the many new features which each version of Fortran has added to the language, and in the consequent changes in relative importance of older features.

In this book we have concentrated on a *core language*, and have identified other, less desirable, features of the language by printing them in a smaller typeface. This appendix briefly summarizes all of these older, redundant, features of the language, as well as mentioning a number of even older features which are totally obsolete in modern programming.

The appendix is divided into six sections each covering one area of the language. Within each section the redundant features are very briefly described and a reference provided to a more detailed description, either in this book or in its predecessor textbook on FORTRAN 77 programming (Ellis, 1990). A reference to a description in this book is in the form (*cc.ss*), while a reference to a description in Ellis (1990) is in the form [77/*cc.ss*], where, in both cases, *cc.ss* is the section number within chapter *cc* of the appropriate book. At the end of each section is a list of those features which are believed to be totally obsolete and, in most cases, a reference to where a further description can be found in Ellis (1990) – although that description is usually in a chapter on obsolescent features of FORTRAN 77!

None of the features mentioned in the appendix should be used in new programs; they are mentioned here solely for reference, and for completeness.

E.1 Redundant source form

All versions of Fortran prior to Fortran 90 used a fixed-form source, based on the layout of a punched card, in which statement labels used the first five columns of a line and the statement itself occupied columns 7–72; column 6 was reserved for a *continuation marker*, and columns 73 onwards were not used (although 73–80 could be used for sequence numbers on cards in the days when programs were input to the computer on punched cards). Fortran 90 introduced a new, free-form, way of writing programs, and this has been used throughout this book. Although the new source form should be used for all new programs, the older form will be met for some time to come in older programs. It is described in (2.6) and [77/2.1].

E.2 Redundant data type

Fortran has always been used primarily for scientific and technological programming, and numerical calculations have always been of great importance. In FORTRAN 77, and earlier versions of the language, there were two forms of real variables and constants, known as **REAL** and **DOUBLE PRECISION**, with the latter providing greater precision than the former — although not necessarily exactly double. This concept was inherently non-portable, since different computers have always had different hardware precisions for floating-point arithmetic, and has been replaced by the far superior concept of parameterized data types in Fortran 90. **DOUBLE PRECISION** should, therefore, never be used in new programs; it will, however, be frequently met in older programs. It is described in (10.6) and, in rather more detail, in [F77/11.2].

E.3 Redundant and obsolete specification statements

- When FORTRAN was first invented there were only two data types, namely **REAL** and **INTEGER**, and the creators of the language decided that the need to declare variables could be minimized by determining the type of a variable from the first letter of its name — if it was in the range I–N it represented an integer, otherwise it was real. This concept of *implicit typing* is still in Fortran (see (3.2) and [77/2.1,2.2]), but is extremely dangerous and all variables should be properly declared. The use of the **IMPLICIT NONE** statement at the beginning of every program unit will ensure that any variables which are not declared will cause a compilation error, rather than being implicitly declared as real or integer variables.
- Earlier versions of Fortran did not allow the declaration of attributes for variables, and the type declaration took one of the following forms (3.8):

  REAL *list of real variables*
  INTEGER *list of integer variables*
  DOUBLE PRECISION *list of double precision real variables*
  COMPLEX *list of complex variables*
  LOGICAL *list of logical variables*
  CHARACTER *list of character variables*
  CHARACTER∗*len list of character variables*

  It is recommended that the new form with a double colon between the type (and any attributes) and the list of variables is always used in new programs, even when no attributes are being specified.
- FORTRAN 77 introduced the concept of a named constant to Fortran for the first time. Such a constant was declared by means of a **PARAMETER** statement, which took the form

  PARAMETER (*name1=value1 , name2=value2 , . . .*)

  This statement has been superseded in Fortran 90 by the **PARAMETER** attribute in a type declaration statement and should not be used in new programs. It is described in [77/3.2].

- Fortran 90 also introduced the concept of an initialization expression in a type declaration statement. Prior to Fortran 90 such initialization was carried out by means of **DATA** statements, which took the form

  DATA *list of names/list of values/, list of names/list of values/, . . .*

  The number of values in each list must match the number of names in the immediately preceding list; if the same value was to be repeated several times then it could be preceded by a repeat count (for example, **5*1.0** has the same effect as **1.0,1.0,1.0,1.0,1.0**). In the case of arrays, the unsubscripted array name represents all the elements of the array in array element order. An implied **DO**, similar to that used in array constructors in Fortran 90, can also be used to select specific elements of an array. **DATA** statements are no longer required in Fortran 90, but will usually be met in older Fortran programs; they are described in [77/3.6, 6.5, 15.5].

- One of the major developments in Fortran 90 is its handling of arrays. In FORTRAN 77 the only form of adjustable size array was the *assumed-size array*, whereby the extent of the last dimension of a dummy array was represented by an asterisk. This has been superseded by the assumed-shape array in Fortran 90, which should always be used in new programs. Assumed-size arrays are briefly described in (7.7, 13.5), and in more detail in [77/6.4, 14.2].

- The following specification statements are obsolete and should never be used:
  — The **IMPLICIT** statement allows implicit type declaration (see above) to use a user-defined rule instead of the default rule (I–N are integers, others are real). It therefore makes a dangerous and undesirable feature of the language even more dangerous and undesirable! [77/19.5].

    Note that **IMPLICIT** should not be confused with its close relative **IMPLICIT NONE**, which it is strongly recommended should appear at the start of every program unit.
  — The **DIMENSION** statement specifies the dimensions of an array, whose type is declared elsewhere. The inclusion of this information, together with any other attributes, in the type declaration statement is much to be preferred. It is discussed in [77/6.2].
  — The **SEQUENCE** attribute was only introduced in Fortran 90, after considerable controversy; we recommend that it should never be used. It is a means of permitting components of objects of derived type to be used in **COMMON** and **EQUIVALENCE** statements, thus resulting in programs with complicated, and usually dangerous, storage association aspects. It will not be described here.

E.4   Redundant and obsolete control statements

- Earlier versions of Fortran did not contain an **END DO** statement, and used a statement label in the **DO** statement to identify the last statement in the loop. This type of **DO** loop took the form

  DO *label, loop-var=start,end* [*,inc*]
  .
  .
  .
  label   *terminating statement*

where the *terminating statement* was a normal Fortran statement, although some types of statement are not allowed. The block `DO` construct of Fortran 90 is far superior, and should always be used in new programs. The older, non-block, structure will always be met in older programs, however; it is described in detail in [77/5.2–5.5].

- In order to avoid problems with the restrictions on the terminating statement of a non-block `DO` loop, most FORTRAN 77 programmers always ended their loops with a dummy statement that does nothing, but can be labelled. This statement is

      CONTINUE

  Its use is not restricted to `DO` loops, and some programmers adopted a convention that the only statements which would have a statement label, to which a `GOTO`, or other, statement might jump, would be `CONTINUE` statements, thus reducing the possibility of inadvertently introducing errors when modifying programs at a later date. It will be met in older programs, but is no longer required in Fortran 90.

- Fortran 90 also introduced another form of `DO` loop control, in which the initial statement of the loop takes the form

      DO WHILE (*logical expression*)

  This provides no increased functionality, and similar constructs in other languages have sometimes caused confusion as to exactly when the check on the value of the logical expression takes place. It is briefly described in (6.6), but we do not recommend its use.

- The powerful `CASE` construct was only introduced in Fortran 90. In earlier versions of Fortran it was necessary to use either the block `IF` construct for all forms of selection or the computed `GOTO` statement. The computed `GOTO` was the only possibility prior to FORTRAN 77, and uses the value of an integer expression to perform an unconditional `GOTO` to one of a list of statement labels. Although it was a useful feature in its day, it can very easily lead to very complicated and potentially error-prone code, and its use has not been recommended since the advent of FORTRAN 77. It is briefly described in [77/ 19.1].

- The following control statements and concepts are obsolete and should never be used:
  — FORTRAN 77 allowed a real variable to be used as a `DO` variable. This was a disastrous extension because round-off errors mean that it is impossible to be certain how many times the loop will be executed without taking special precautions! It has been flagged for removal from the Fortran Standard in the not-too-distant future, but, meanwhile, should never be used in any new programs [77/19.3].
  — Early versions of Fortran contained a form of `IF` statement, known as an arithmetic `IF`, which caused a jump to one of three labelled statements, depending upon whether the value of an integer expression was negative, zero or positive. The introduction of the logical `IF` statement over 25 years ago largely eliminated the need for this statement, and the block `IF` and `CASE` constructs have now totally superseded it [77/19.1].
  — The `ASSIGN` statement, and the related assigned `GOTO`, provided a means of storing the value of a statement label in an integer variable, and then using this to jump to a different part of the program dependent upon the value of

that variable. This concept is so inherently dangerous that its use has long been deplored by most Fortran programmers and educators. It is likely to be removed from the Fortran Standard in the not-too-distant future, and is not described in this book or in Ellis (1990).

— The **PAUSE** statement is a relic from the past, when a programmer might wish to temporarily suspend execution of a program in order that the computer's operator might take some action before resuming the program. Operators of large, multi-user, computer systems have not been able to provide this type of interaction for many years, and a far preferable method where such interaction is possible is to print a message on the console with a **PRINT** statement, followed by a **READ** which will wait until the user (or operator) types an appropriate reply. It is not described in this book or in Ellis (1990).

E.5   Redundant and obsolete features of input and output

- There are two ways of dealing with exceptional conditions in input and output. The recommended way is to use an **IOSTAT** specifier. An alternative approach is to use **END**, **EOR** or **ERR**, as appropriate, to cause a branch to a specified labelled statement if an end-of-file, end-of-record or error condition occurs during the input/output statement. This approach, however, suffers from two major disadvantages. The first is that the use of this style of branching to statements always leads to badly structured programs, and all of the statements that use this approach have been replaced by more appropriate statements in Fortran 90. The second is that the **IOSTAT** specifier can, potentially, provide more information than simply that the operation has failed, which is not available if the **ERR** specifier is used. These three specifiers are briefly described in (15.1, 15.3).

- Fortran 90 contains a large number of edit descriptors for use in formatted input and output. Most of these have been described in Chapters 8 and 15, but there are five whose use is no longer recommended in Fortran programs.

  — The **BN** and **BZ** edit descriptors allow control over the interpretation of blanks in numeric fields on input. **BN** specifies that any blank characters in subsequent numeric fields input under the control of this format will be treated as null characters. **BZ**, on the other hand, specifies that any such blank characters will be treated as zeros. This was an important issue in the days of punched cards, but is less relevant nowadays; in any event, the **BLANK** specifier provides a better way of dealing with the problem. A more detailed description will be found in [77/17.3].

  — The **D** edit descriptor remains in Fortran for purely historical reasons and has been totally superseded by the **E** edit descriptor (15.2).

  — The **H** edit descriptor was the only way of specifying character strings in an output format prior to FORTRAN 77. It takes the form

    *n*H*exactly_n_characters*

  and has been totally superseded by the character constant edit descriptor, which is both more natural and less prone to error; there can be few, if any, older Fortran programmers whose programs have not failed because they miscounted the number of characters in an **H** edit descriptor. It is briefly described in [77/9.5].

— The **P** edit descriptor allows numeric data to be scaled on either input or output. It was a convenient feature when data was normally punched on cards, and re-punching was time-consuming, but is not very useful in the days of files and editors with global edit commands. It is quite a complicated process, moreover and, especially on output, can lead to confusion for many users. Its use is not recommended, but a description can be found in [77/19.4].

- The following input/output concept is obsolete and should never be used:
  — As well as its use in connection with an assigned **GOTO**, the **ASSIGN** statement allows the label of a **FORMAT** statement to be assigned to a variable, which is then used in a formatted input or output statement. There are better ways of achieving this effect, for example by storing the format expressions in character variables, and this concept, like all others relating to the **ASSIGN** statement, should never be used. It is not described in this book or in Ellis (1990).

E.6   Redundant and obsolete procedure statements and concepts

- Prior to Fortran 90 the only form of internal procedure was a one line function known as a statement function. This has been totally superseded by the concept of an internal procedure. It is, however, described in detail in [77/16.3].

- The concept of a generic function was first introduced in FORTRAN 77, and prior to that all intrinsic functions were known by their specific names. With the introduction of generic functions in FORTRAN 77 the need for multiple names for the same function (such as **IABS**, **CABS**, **DABS**, **ABS**) largely disappeared, and the use of generic names is strongly recommended in all cases. The only place where specific names are required in Fortran 90 is when the name of an intrinsic function is being used as an actual argument — which is a somewhat artificial situation, in general. Specific names of all generic intrinsic functions will be found in (A.1).

- The following statements for use with procedures are obsolete and should never be used:
  — The **ENTRY** statement allows a procedure to have more than one entry point. There are a number of difficulties with this concept, and its use is not recommended. It is described in [77/19.6].
  — The alternate **RETURN** allows a procedure to return to one of several labelled statements in the calling program unit, dependent upon the value of an integer variable. This has all the disadvantages of other, similar, branching instructions, such as the computed **GOTO** and arithmetic **IF**, with the added complication that the branching takes place in a different program unit from the one in which the decision about which path to follow is taken. Its use is not recommended, but it is briefly described in [77/19.2].

Glossary

Note that the number in parentheses following most items in this glossary refers to the section of the book where more detailed information may be found. Further details of italicized words can be found elsewhere in this glossary.

actual argument   A *variable* or an *expression* used in a procedure *invocation* to pass information to the *procedure*, the name of a procedure which appears in a procedure reference, or the name of a variable used in a *subroutine call* to receive results from the subroutine. (4.5, 11.3)

allocatable array   An *array* which is declared with the **ALLOCATABLE** *attribute*, but whose *shape* and *size* are not determined until space is created for the array by means of an *allocation statement*. (13.6)

allocation statement   (a) A statement which allocates space to an *allocatable array* (13.6); (b) a statement which allocates space to a *pointer array*. (16.3)

allocation status   A *logical* indication of whether an *allocatable array* is currently allocated, which can be examined using the **ALLOCATED** *intrinsic function*. (13.6)

argument   An *actual argument* or a *dummy argument*.

arithmetic unit   That part of the *CPU* which carries out arithmetic and other types of operation on items of *data*. (1.2)

array   A set of items of the same *type* which are referred to by the same collective name. (7.1)

array constructor   An *array-valued constant*. (7.3)

array element   A single item from the set of items which make up an *array*, and which is identified by means of integer *subscripts* which follow the array name in parentheses. (7.1)

array element order   The order in which the *elements* of an *array* are conceptually stored. Note that the physical arrangement within the computer's *memory* may not follow this order, but any attempt to access array elements in sequence will do so. (13.2)

array processing   The feature of Fortran 90 that allows arrays to appear in expressions and assignments as single objects. (7.5, 13.7)

array section   Part of an *array* which can be used as an array in its own right. (13.9)

array specification   A means of defining the *shape* and *size* of an *array* by following its name in a *type declaration* statement by the relevant information; see also *dimension attribute*. (7.2)

array variable   An *array-valued variable*.

array-valued Having the property of being an *array*.

array-valued function A *function* whose result is an *array*. (7.8)

ASCII The American Standard Code for Information Interchange (ANSI X3.4 1977) – a widely used internal character coding set; also known as ISO 646 (International Reference Version).

ASCII collating sequence The *collating sequence* which results from the use of the *ASCII* character code; used by the **LLT**, **LLE**, **LGE** and **LGT** *intrinsic functions*. (5.5)

assembly language A form of programming a computer which is specific to a particular computer and which (usually) utilizes a symbolic form of the electronic instructions which are contained within the computer's circuitry. (1.3)

assignment The action of storing the value of an *expression* in a variable. (3.3, 7.5)

assignment statement A Fortran statement which causes the value of an *expression* to be *assigned* to a variable. (3.3, 7.5)

association status A *logical* indication of whether a *pointer* is currently associated with a *target*, which can be examined using the **ASSOCIATED** *intrinsic function*. (16.1)

assumed length character declaration The declaration of a *character dummy argument* with an asterisk for its *length*, the actual length being obtained from the corresponding *actual argument* when the *procedure* is *invoked*. (4.5)

assumed-shape array An *array-valued dummy argument* whose *upper bounds* in each *dimension* are represented by colons, the actual bounds being obtained from the corresponding *actual argument* when the *procedure* is invoked. (7.7)

assumed-size array A FORTRAN 77 concept, whereby the *upper bound* of the last *dimension* of an *array-valued dummy argument* is represented by an asterisk; it has been superseded by the *assumed-shape array*. (7.7)

attribute A property of a *variable* or a *constant* that may be specified in a *type declaration statement*.

automatic array An *explicit-shape array* in a *procedure*, which is not a *dummy argument*, some or all of whose *bounds* are provided when the procedure is *invoked*, thus allowing the array to have a different *size* and *shape* every time the procedure is invoked. (7.7)

back substitution The procedure in which, during a *Gaussian elimination*, the solution for one variable is substituted into another equation in order to obtain a solution for another variable. (18.5)

back-up The process of making an additional copy of a *file* for security against errors. (15.4)

batch working A mode of using a computer in which programs are run under the control of the *operating system* without any intervention by the user. (2.3)

bicubic patch A three-dimensional equivalent of a section of a *cubic spline* which is used for surface interpolation. (18.7)

bicubic spline interpolation The process of calculating a *bicubic patch*. (18.7)

binary digit A 0 or a 1, as used in the binary arithmetic notation. (1.3)

binary operator An arithmetic, or other, *operator* which is written between two *operands*. (3.3)

binary tree A *tree* structure which splits into two *branches* at each *node*. (16.7)

bisection method An *iterative method* for finding the roots of a polynomial equation; cf. *secant method* and *Newton's method*. (10.5)

bit A *binary digit*. (1.3)

blank COMMON A **COMMON block** which has no name; there may only be one blank **COMMON** block in a program. (17.5)

block data program unit   A *program unit* which contains no executable statements and is used to give initial values to *variables* in `COMMON blocks`. (17.4)

block IF construct   A program structure in which the execution of one or more blocks of statements are controlled by a *block* `IF` *statement*, or by a block `IF` statement and one or more `ELSE IF` *statements*. (5.3)

block IF statement   A form of `IF` *statement* in which a *logical expression* is used to determine whether or not a block of statements is obeyed. (5.3)

bottom-up development   The process of developing a program by writing and testing individual *procedures* or *modules*, and then bringing them together to form the complete program (cf. *top-down design*). (2.1)

bound   A *lower bound* or an *upper bound*.

branch   (a) A *transfer of control* within a single program unit; (b) a *linked list* which forms part of a *tree*. (16.7)

central processing unit   The part of a computer which carries out the main processing of data. (1.2)

character   A letter, a digit or some other representable symbol. (3.5)

character constant edit descriptor   An *edit descriptor* which takes the form of a *character constant* in an *output format*, and causes the value of the character constant to be output starting at the next character position. (8.5)

character context   *Characters* that form part of a *character literal constant* or a *character constant edit descriptor*. (3.5, 8.5)

character repertoire   A collection of *characters* that form a usable subset of the set of all known characters, for instance those used in a particular language or culture; not necessarily related to a particular *coded character set*. (14.5)

character storage unit   The type of *memory location* used for the storage of a single *character* value. (3.5)

character string   A sequence of one or more *characters*.

character variable   A *variable* which consists of a sequence of one or more *character storage units* and which may be assigned one or more characters. (3.5)

close   The process of terminating the link between a *file* and an *input/output unit*. (15.1)

coded character set   A defined set of *characters* for which a specific set of codes have been defined to represent them, for example, the *ASCII* coded character set. (14.5)

collating sequence   The order in which a set of *characters* is sorted by default. (5.5)

comment   Explanatory text in a *program unit* which is ignored by a *compiler*, other than for listing purposes. (2.2)

COMMON block   An area of the *memory* which is accessible to more than one *program unit* for the storage of *variables*, and in which the variables are identified by their position and not by their name. (17.2)

compilation error   An error in a *program* which is detected by the *compiler*. (2.4)

compiler   A computer *program* which translates a program written in a *high-level programming language*, such as Fortran, into the *machine code* of the computer. (1.3)

compiling   The process by which a *compiler* converts a *program* written in a *high-level programming language* into *machine code*. (1.3)

complex   An *intrinsic data type* used to represent *complex numbers*. (14.7)

complex arithmetic   A form of arithmetic using *complex numbers*.

complex number   A number, consisting of a *real part* and an *imaginary part*, which obeys the rules of *complex arithmetic*; it is represented by a pair of *real numbers*, corresponding to the real and imaginary parts. (3.7, 14.7)

component (a) One of the elements that constitute a *derived type* (3.7); (b) a part of a programming problem which can be analysed and coded independently of the rest of the program; a key element in *modular program development*. (4.6)

concatenation The process of joining two character strings by use of the *concatenation operator*. (3.5)

concatenation operator An operator which combines two character strings to form a single character string. (3.5)

conditioning A measure of the sensitivity of a numerical problem to changes in the values of its parameters. (10.3)

conformable Two *arrays* are conformable if they have the same *shape*; a *scalar* is conformable with any array. All *intrinsic operations* are defined between conformable objects. (7.5)

connecting The process of associating a specified *input* or *output unit* to a *file*, prior to carrying out input or output on the file. (9.3)

constant A *data object* whose value is unchanged throughout the execution of a program. (1.2, 3.6)

constant expression An *expression* containing no *variables*, and whose value, therefore, can be determined prior to execution. (3.6)

continuation line A line which forms part of a Fortran statement, but which is not the first line of that statement. (2.2)

control information list The list of *specifiers* used in a **READ** or **WRITE** statement. (8.6)

control unit That part of the *CPU* which fetches instructions, decodes them and initiates appropriate action. (1.2)

convergence criteria The criteria for determining when to terminate an *iterative process*. (10.5)

count-controlled DO loop A *loop* whose repetition is controlled by counting how many times it has been obeyed, normally in a **DO** *loop*. (6.2)

CPU The *central processing unit* of a computer. (1.2)

creation See *file creation*.

cubic spline A set of cubic polynomials which together constitute a function which passes through a set of data points, and has continuous first and second derivatives at each of these points. (18.7)

data Information to be processed by a computer program. (1.2)

data abstraction The ability to create new *data types*, together with associated operators, and to hide the internal structure and operations from the user, thus allowing the new data type to be used in an analogous fashion to intrinsic data types. (12.5)

data hiding The concept that some items in a *module* may not be accessible to a user of that module; a key element of *data abstraction*. (12.3)

data object A *variable* or a *constant*.

data structure (a) An arrangement of variables and/or arrays to suit the requirements of a specific problem; (b) the totality of the *data objects* used by a program. (4.10)

data type A named category of data which is characterized by a set of values and a set of operations that can be used to manipulate those values. (3.2)

database A collection of variables and constants containing information which is used by a number of different subprograms. (4.7, 17.3)

deallocation statement A statement which releases space that has been previously allocated to an *allocatable array* or a *pointer array*. (13.6, 16.3)

declaration statement A statement which specifies the *type* and, optionally, *attributes* of one or more *variables* or *constants*. (3.2, 3.5, 3.6, 3.7)

default character set   The set of characters available for use by programs, on the particular processor being used, without any specific action being taken; the default character set always includes the *Fortran Character Set*. (3.5)

default input unit   The *input unit* which is identified by an asterisk in a **READ** statement. (8.6)

default kind   The *kind type parameter* which is used for a particular intrinsic data type if it is not explicitly specified. (14.1)

default output unit   The *output unit* which is identified by an asterisk in a **WRITE** statement, and which is used by a **PRINT** statement. (8.6)

default real   The *real data type* having *default kind*. (10.2)

default type   A *data type* having *default kind*. (14.2)

deferred-shape array   An *allocatable array* or a *pointer array*.

defined assignment   A user-defined assignment in which either the left-hand side or the right-hand side, or both, is of a *derived type*. (12.4)

defined operation   A user-defined operation which either extends an intrinsic operation for data types for which it is not defined or defines a user-specified name for an operation between two *data objects*. (12.4)

dereferencing   The interpretation of a *pointer* as the *target* to which it is pointing, when the context requires it. (16.2)

derived type   A user-defined data type, which supplements the *intrinsic data types*. (3.7)

diagnostic   Information provided by a compiler, or during the execution of a program, to inform the programmer of errors. (1.3)

dimension   The means of specifying one of the *subscripts* of an array, and the various attributes of that subscript such as its *bounds* and its *extent*. (7.2)

dimension attribute   A means of defining the *shape* and *size* of the arrays in a *type declaration* statement; see also *array specification*. (7.2)

direct access   A form of file in which each record has the same length and is written to a specified part of the file, so that the records may be written and read in any order. (15.4)

disconnection   The process of cancelling the *connection* between an *input* or *output unit* and a *file*; carried out by the **CLOSE** statement. (15.1)

diskette   An exchangeable *magnetic disk*, usually either $5\frac{1}{4}''$ or $3\frac{1}{2}''$ in diameter; see also *floppy disk*.

DO construct   A *loop* which is initiated by a **DO** *statement* and terminated by an **END DO** *statement*. (6.1)

DO loop   A *loop* which is controlled by a **DO** *statement*. (6.1)

DO statement   A statement which initiates a **DO** *loop*. (6.1)

DO variable   The variable which is used to control the number of iterations in a *count-controlled* **DO** *loop*. (6.2)

double-precision   (a) One of the two hardware representations of *floating-point* numbers on most computers, providing more accuracy than the default *single-precision* representation; (b) an obsolete method of storing real values which uses two *numeric storage units* for each value, instead of one, in order to provide approximately twice as many significant digits of accuracy; it has been superseded in Fortran 90 by *parameterized real variables*. (10.7)

dummy argument   The argument used in a procedure definition which will be associated with the *actual argument* when the procedure is *invoked*. (4.5, 11.3)

edit descriptor   An item in a *format* which specifies the conversion between internal (computer) and external (human-readable) forms. (8.2)

editing (a) The use of an *editor* to create or modify text files (2.4); (b) the process of converting values between internal and external forms during input or output. (8.2)

editor A program which is used to create or modify text files, including program files. (2.4)

element See *array element*.

elemental An *operation, assignment* or *procedure invocation* that is applied independently to *elements* of an *array*, or of a set of *conformable* arrays and *scalars*.

elemental intrinsic procedure An *intrinsic procedure* which can accept an array-valued argument or arguments and will deliver an array-valued result obtained by applying the procedure to corresponding elements of the argument array(s) in turn. (7.6)

ELSE IF statement A statement that introduces an alternative block of statements in a *block IF construct*. (5.3)

embedded format A format which is expressed as a character expression, and is incorporated within an input/output statement. (8.2)

END DO statement The statement which marks the end of a **DO** *loop*. (6.1)

end-of-file condition A condition set when an *endfile record* is read, and which can be detected by an **IOSTAT** specifier (or an **EOF** specifier) in a **READ** statement. (9.2)

endfile record A special type of record which can only occur as the last record of a sequential file and is written by an **ENDFILE** statement. (9.2)

executable statement A statement which causes the computer to carry out a specified action during the execution of the program. (4.2)

execution error An error which occurs during the execution of a program. (2.4)

exist A *file* exists if it is *connected* to a program. (9.3)

explicit interface A procedure *interface* which is known to a program unit which may invoke the procedure. (11.2)

explicit-shape array An *array* which is declared with explicit *bounds* in every *dimension*. (7.2)

exponent (a) The power of ten by which the *mantissa* of a *real number* expressed in *exponent form* must be multiplied to give the required value (3.3); (b) the power of two by which the *mantissa* of a *floating-point* number must be multiplied to give the required value. (3.1, 10.2)

exponent form A way of writing a *literal constant* as a *mantissa* and an *exponent*. (3.3)

expression A sequence of *operands* and *operators* and, optionally, parentheses, where the operands may be *variables, constants* or *function references*.

extent The number of *elements* in a particular *dimension* of an array. (7.2)

external file A *file* which is stored on some external medium. (9.1)

external function A function which is not an *intrinsic function*. (4.3)

external subprogram A *function subprogram* or a *subroutine subprogram*.

fail-safe mechanism A program structure in which an error will not lead to a catastrophic failure, but will result in appropriate remedial action being taken. (6.3)

field width The number of character positions occupied by an item of input data or required for the representation of an output item. (8.3, 8.5)

file (a) A sequence of *records* (9.1); (b) a single unit of program or data which is held on some external medium outside the memory of the computer. (1.2)

file creation The act of *connecting* a *file* to an *input/output unit*. (9.3)

file store The set of all *files* which are available for use by a computer. (1.2, 9.1)

file store device A piece of equipment by means of which a computer writes information to a *magnetic disk*, or to such other forms of permanent storage as are used for the *file store*, and by means of which it also reads information from the disk or other storage medium; a file store device is both an *input device* and an *output device*.

fixed disk   A *magnetic disk* which is a permanent part of a computer and cannot be removed; it is usually of much greater capacity and speed than an exchangeable *diskette*.

fixed form   An obsolete method of writing Fortran programs in which certain columns were reserved for specific purposes; see also *free form*. (2.6)

floating-point   A method of storing numbers as a *mantissa* and an *exponent*. (3.1)

floppy disk   A *magnetic disk* made of a flexible material enclosed in a rigid case; a *diskette*.

format   A sequence of *edit descriptors* which determine the interpretation of a line, or *record*, of input data, or the form of representation of an output record. (8.2)

format specifier   A specifier which specifies the *format* to be used. (8.2)

FORMAT statement   A labelled statement which defines a *format*. (8.4)

formatted input statement   A *formatted* **READ** statement or a **PRINT** statement.

formatted input/output statement   A *formatted input statement* or a *formatted output statement*.

formatted output statement   A *formatted* **WRITE** *statement*.

formatted READ statement   A **READ** statement which includes a *format specifier*.

formatted record   A record consisting of a sequence of characters selected from those which can be represented by the processor being used, and which has been written by a *formatted output statement*, by a *list-directed output statement*, or by some means other than a Fortran program (for example, by being typed at a keyboard). (9.2)

formatted WRITE statement   A **WRITE** statement which includes a *format specifier*.

Fortran Character Set   The 58 characters which may be used to write a Fortran program. (3.5)

free form   The recommended method of writing Fortran programs in which all character positions in a line may be used for any purpose; see also *fixed form*. (2.6)

function   A *subprogram* which returns a single result which can be used in an *expression* in which a *reference* to the function occurs. (4.3)

function reference   The use of a function name in an *expression* to generate a *transfer of control* to the function to carry out some action and return a value which is used in the evaluation of the expression. (4.3)

function subprogram   A self-contained part of a Fortran program which implements an *external function*. (4.3)

function value   The value which is returned by the execution of a *function*. (4.3)

Gaussian elimination   A method for the solution of a set of simultaneous linear equations. (18.5)

general-purpose language   A *programming language* which is intended for use in a wide variety of different problem areas. (1.3)

generalized edit descriptor   An *edit descriptor* which can be used with any of the *intrinsic data types*, the exact form of editing used being dependent upon the value being input or output. (15.2)

generic function   A *function* which can be called with different types of arguments, generally, but not always, returning corresponding types of results. (4.1)

generic interface block   A form of *interface block* which is used to define a *generic name* for a set of procedures. (11.6)

generic name   A name which is used to identify two or more procedures, the required procedure being determined by the types of the non-optional arguments in the procedure invocation. (4.1, 11.6)

global accessibility   The possibility of directly accessing data and derived type definitions from any program unit; provided in Fortran 90 by means of *modules*. (4.7)

global entity   An entity whose *scope* is that of the whole program. (11.7)

global storage   A block of memory which is accessible from any program unit; largely made redundant in Fortran 90 by *global accessibility* through *modules*. (17.1)

goodness of fit   A measure of how closely an interpolating function passes through the original data points. (10.4)

gradient   The first derivative of the equation of a curve.

grandfather–father–son   A safety system used when updating files in which the oldest of a three-file cycle is used for the latest update. (15.4)

hard disk   A *magnetic disk* made from a rigid material; normally a *fixed disk*. (9.1)

hardware   The mechanical, electrical and optical devices which constitute a computer; cf. the *software* which causes the computer to perform particular actions. (1.1)

hash table   An array into which data is entered in a semi-random order by use of a *hashing technique* in order to speed up insertion and retrieval of such data. (15.4)

hashing technique   A technique used to create a *hash table*, in which the array element in which an item is to be stored is determined by converting some feature of the item, such as a related name, into an integer in a given range (that is, the size of the hash table). (15.4)

head   The first item in a *linked list*. (16.7)

high-level programming language   A form of programming a computer which uses English-like words to express the operations required of the computer. (1.3)

host   See *host scoping unit*.

host association   The means by which entities in a *host* are made available to an inner *scoping unit*. (11.8)

host scoping unit   A *scoping unit* which surrounds another scoping unit. (11.7)

IF statement   A *block* **IF** *statement* or a *logical* **IF** *statement*.

ill-conditioned problem   A problem whose answer is highly sensitive to changes in the values of its parameters. (10.3)

imaginary part   The second of the two numbers which make up a *complex number*. (14.7)

implicit declaration   The determination of the *type* of a *variable* by the initial letter of its name. (3.2, E.3)

implicit interface   A *procedure interface* which is not fully known to a *program unit* which invokes the procedure. (11.2)

implied DO   A shorthand notation for a list of *array elements* in an *input/output list*, in an *array constructor*, or in a **DATA** statement, in which an *implied* **DO** *variable* is used to specify elements of an array (or arrays) whose *subscript(s)* depend on the implied **DO** variable. (7.3)

implied DO variable   The *variable* which is used to control the iterations in an *implied* **DO**.

index array   An *array* containing the indexes, or *subscripts*, to other arrays; often used in sorting in order to avoid extensive data swapping. (7.7)

infinite loop   A *loop* whose terminating condition never occurs, and which therefore never terminates. (6.3)

information engineering   The discipline of using computers to solve problems and to process information. (Preface)

initial statement   The first statement of a *program unit*; a **PROGRAM, SUBROUTINE, FUNCTION, MODULE** or **BLOCK DATA** statement. (4.2)

initialization expression   A restricted form of *constant expression* which can appear as an initial value in a declaration statement. (14.2)

input device   A piece of equipment by means of which a computer receives information from the outside world, such as a keyboard, a disk drive or an optical character reader. (1.2)

input format A *format* used in a *formatted input statement*. (8.3)

input list The list of *variable, array* and/or *array element* names in a **READ** statement into which data is to be read. (3.4, 7.4)

input statement A **READ** or **PRINT** statement.

input unit An *input device*.

input/output list An *input list* or an *output list*.

input/output statement An *input statement* or an *output statement*.

input/output unit An *input unit* or an *output unit*.

instance A single *invocation* of a *procedure*. (11.4)

integer (a) A whole number (3.1); (b) an *intrinsic data type* used to represent whole numbers. (3.2)

integer division Division of one *integer* value by another, in which any fractional part of the result is lost. (3.3)

integrate The numerical solution of a differential equation. (18.8)

interactive working A mode of using a computer in which the user controls the execution of a program from a terminal, with input coming from the keyboard and output going to the screen. (2.3)

interactive system A computer system whose users control the execution of their programs directly from a terminal, with input coming from the keyboard and output going to the screen.

interface The name of a *procedure*, whether it is a *subroutine* or a *function*, the names and characteristics of its *dummy arguments* and, in the case of a function, the characteristics of the *result variable*. (11.2)

interface block (a) A means of making the *interface* of a procedure *explicit* (11.2); (b) a means of defining a *generic procedure* or *operator* name. (11.6, 12.4)

internal file A *character variable* which can be processed as though it were an *external file* by the normal Fortran formatted **READ** and **WRITE** statements. (15.5)

internal procedure A *procedure* which is contained within another *program unit*, and which can only be invoked from within that program unit. (11.8)

internal variable A *local variable*.

intrinsic data type One of the six data types defined in the Fortran language – *integer*, *real*, double precision, complex, *logical* and *character*.

intrinsic function An *intrinsic procedure* which is a *function*.

intrinsic procedure A *procedure* whose definition is part of the Fortran language, and which must be provided by a standard-conforming Fortran processor (4.1, Appendix A).

intrinsic subroutine An *intrinsic procedure* which is a *subroutine*.

invoke To **CALL** a *subroutine* or *reference* a *function*.

iteration count The number of times that a *count-controlled* **DO** *loop* is to be obeyed. (6.2)

iterative method A method of calculating a solution to a problem by calculating successive approximations until the approximations have *converged* to the solution. (10.5)

iterative process A numerical solution to a problem which uses an *iterative method*.

job control language A form of *programming language* which is used to instruct the computer's *operating system* how to execute a particular *program*, or sequence of programs. (2.3)

keyword A word, or name, which has a defined meaning in the Fortran language. (2.2)

keyword argument A method of specifying an *actual argument* in which the value is preceded by the name of the corresponding *dummy argument*; particularly important in connection with *optional arguments*. (11.3)

kind   All *intrinsic data types*, other than DOUBLE PRECISION, may have more than one, processor-dependent, representation; each representation is known as a different kind of that type. (14.1)

kind selector   The means of specifying the *kind type parameter* of a *variable*. (14.2)

kind type parameter   An *integer* value used to identify the *kind* of an *intrinsic data type*. (14.1)

language extension   The ability to use features of a language itself to extend that language; see also *data abstraction*. (12.5)

least squares   A method of data fitting in which the sum of the squares of the *residuals* is minimized. (10.4)

length   (a) The number of *characters* that can be stored in a *character variable* (3.5); (b) the number of characters in a *formatted input* or *output record* (15.2, 15.4); (c) the number of processor-defined units, normally *bytes* or *words*, in an *unformatted input* or *output record*. (15.4, 15.6)

library   A collection of *procedures*, often for use in a particular application area, which are made available for use by a program in that application area; in Fortran 90 a procedure library is usually provided as a *module*.

link   The process of combining compiled *program units* to form an executable *program*.

linked list   A *data structure* in which each element identifies its predecessor or successor by some form of *pointer*. (16.7)

list-directed formatting   The *format* used during *list-directed input* or *list-directed output*, and which is determined by the processor by reference to the *input* or *output list*; it is represented in an *input/output statement* by an asterisk. (3.4, 3.5)

list-directed input   A special type of *formatted input* in which the *format* used for the interpretation of the data is selected by the processor according to the *type* of each of the items in the *input list*. (3.4, 3.5)

list-directed input/output statement   An *input* or *output statement* which uses *list-directed formatting*.

list-directed output   A special type of *formatted output* in which the *format* used for the display of the results is selected by the processor according to the *type* of each of the items in the *output list*, and its value. (3.4, 3.5)

literal constant   The representation of a *constant* by writing its value directly (or literally) in the program. (3.3)

local entity   An entity whose *scope* is that of a *scoping unit*. (11.7)

local variable   A *variable* declared in a *program unit*, and which is not in a COMMON block; see also *local entity*. (4.5)

locality of variables   The concept that the *variables* declared in a *program unit* are only known to that program unit. (4.5)

logical   An entity which can only represent a *logical value*.

logical constant   A *constant* whose value is a *logical value*.

logical expression   An *expression* containing only *logical variables*, *logical constants*, *logical operators* and *relational operators*, and whose value is one of the two logical values *true* or *false*. (5.2)

logical IF statement   A statement in which the value of a *logical expression* determines whether the rest of the statement is obeyed. (5.4)

logical operator   An *operator* whose *operands* are *logical expressions*. (5.2)

logical value   One of the two values *true* or *false*. (5.2)

LOGICAL variable   A *variable* of the *intrinsic logical type*. (5.2)

look-up table   A *rank-one array* which can be used to determine an index to other arrays. (15.4)

loop   A sequence of statements which is repeated a number of times; in Fortran a loop is usually controlled by a **DO** *statement*. (6.1)

lower bound   The minimum value permitted for a *subscript* of an array. (7.2, 13.2)

machine code   The sequence of *bits* which causes the electronic circuitry of a computer to perform a specified operation. (1.3)

magnetic disk   A rapidly rotating disk covered with a magnetic coating on which information may be stored by altering the magnetization of very small parts of its surface; the almost universal form of permanent storage of information in computer systems; see also *floppy disk, hard disk.*

main program   The *main program unit.*

main program unit   A *program unit* which starts with a **PROGRAM** statement, and which is where the program will start executing; a program must have exactly one main program unit. (4.2)

maintainability   The ease, or otherwise, with which a program can be maintained subsequent to its having been written and thoroughly tested; the need for such maintenance may arise from both undetected errors and changes to the original specification. (2.5)

mantissa   (a) The significant digits of a number in *exponent form* which when multiplied by ten a given number of times will result in the required value (3.3); (b) the significant *bits* of a number in *floating-point* form which when multiplied by two a given number of times will result in the required value. (3.1, 10.2)

many–one array section   An *array section* defined by a *vector subscript* which has at least two elements with the same value; a many–one array section may not appear on the left-hand side of an *assignment* or in an *input list*. (13.9)

mask   (a) A *logical expression* which is used to control *assignment* in a *masked array assignment* (13.8); (b) a *logical argument* in several of the *array intrinsic functions* which determines to which *array elements* the function is to be applied. (A.8)

masked array assignment   A form of array assignment in which a logical *mask* determines which elements are to be assigned; implemented by a **WHERE** *statement* or a **WHERE** *construct.* (13.8)

massively parallel computers   A form of computer in which thousands of processors are arranged in such a way that they can operate on certain types of data in parallel, thus providing a massive speed increase for parts of a program.

memory   The electronic circuits which enable a computer to store information for subsequent use during the execution of a program; such storage is transient, and for permanent storage the information must be saved in a *file.*

memory location   A part of the *memory* of a computer in which a single value may be stored.

microcomputer   A small, yet powerful, computer whose processor and memory is contained within a small box capable of being placed on an office desk.

mixed-mode expression   An arithmetic *expression* in which all the *operands* are not of the same *type.* (3.3)

modular program development   A method of programming in which different parts of the program are developed and tested independently, before being brought together to form the complete program; see also *top-down design, bottom-up development.* (4.6)

module   A *program unit* which allows other program units to access *variables, derived type* definitions and *procedures* declared within it by **USE** *association.* (4.7, Chapter 12)

module procedure   A *procedure* which is contained within a *module*. (12.1)

multiprogramming   A method of utilizing the speed of a computer's central processor so that it can appear to be executing several programs at once, when it is actually giving each program a small slice of processor time in turn. (2.3)

name-value subsequence   The means by which data is represented for **NAMELIST** *input* or *output*. (15.7)

named constant   A *constant* which has been given a name by means of a *parameter attribute* in a *declaration statement*, or in a **PARAMETER** statement. (3.6)

NAMELIST input/output   A form of input or output in which the values in the data or results are accompanied by the names of the corresponding *variables*, thus eliminating the need for an *input/output list*. (15.7)

nested   The inclusion of a program construct as part of another program construct of the same type; especially applied to **DO** *loops*. (6.2)

Newton's iteration   The iterative approximation which forms the basis for *Newton's method* for solving non-linear equations. (18.3)

Newton's method   An *iterative method* for finding the roots of a non-linear equation, cf. *bisection method* and *secant method*. (18.3)

Newton–Raphson method   Another name for Newton's method. (18.3)

node   An element in a *linked list*. (16.7)

non-advancing input/output   A method of *formatted input/output* in which each **READ**, **WRITE** or **PRINT** statement does not necessarily begin a new *record*. (15.3)

normalized binary floating-point form   The form of *floating-point* representation of numbers used by most computers, in which the most significant *bit* of the *mantissa* is 1; cf. *normalized decimal floating-point form*. (10.1)

normalized decimal floating-point form   A representation of decimal numbers in *floating-point* form in which the most significant digit of the *mantissa* is non-zero; cf. *normalized binary floating-point form*. (10.1)

notebook computer   A *microcomputer* in which processor, memory, disk drive(s), screen and keyboard are all integrated in a box whose dimensions are of the same order as an A4 pad of paper around $1-1\frac{1}{2}''$ thick; notebook computers contain their own, rechargeable, batteries, or may run from a mains power supply.

null value   The 'value' input by a *list-directed* input statement when it encounters two consecutive *value separators*; its effect is to leave the value of the corresponding input list item unchanged. (3.4, 8.1)

numeric storage unit   The type of memory location used for storage of *integer*, *real*, *double precision*, *complex* and *logical* values of default kind. (3.5, 17.2)

numerical quadrature   The process of calculating the value of a definite integral by numerical means. (18.8)

object-oriented programming   A style of programming in which objects are defined, together with various actions and attributes appropriate to the use of those objects; widely used, in particular, for graphical programming.

octal   The system of counting to base 8 which is particularly convenient on a binary computer, since each octal number consists of three *bits*.

operand   An *expression* that precedes or succeeds an *operator*.

operating system   A program which controls the operation of a computer system, including the loading and execution of programs and the storage and retrieval of information in files. (2.3)

operation   A computation involving one or two *operands*.

operator   A *character*, or sequence of characters, that defines an *operation*.

optional argument   A *dummy argument* which need not have a corresponding *actual argument* when the *procedure* in which it appears is *invoked*. (11.3)

output device   A piece of equipment by means of which a computer communicates with the outside world, such as a display, a printer or a disk drive. (1.2)

output format   A *format* used in a *formatted output statement*. (8.5, 8.7)

output list   The list of *expressions* in a **WRITE** or **PRINT** statement whose values are to be output. (3.4)

output statement   A **WRITE** statement or a **PRINT** statement.

output unit   An *output device*.

overflow   An error condition arising from an attempt to store a value which is too large for the storage location specified; typically caused by an attempt to divide by zero, or by an extremely small number. (10.1)

parameter attribute   A means of specifying that the entities declared in a *type declaration statement* are to represent *constants*, not *variables*. (3.6)

parameterize   Explicitly specify the *kind* of a *variable* or *constant*. (10.2, Chapter 14)

parameterized variable   A *variable* whose *kind* is explicitly specified. (10.2, Chapter 14)

partial pivoting   An essential technique in a *Gaussian elimination* to ensure that the multipliers at each stage are as small as possible; it improves the *stability* of the solution process. (18.5)

peripheral device   An *input device*, an *output device* or a *file store device*.

pivot   The first coefficient of each equation after reduction by *Gaussian elimination*. (18.5)

pointer   A *variable* which has the *pointer attribute*. (16.1)

pointer array   An *array* which is declared with the *pointer attribute*, but whose *shape* and *size* are not determined until space is created for the array by means of an *allocation statement*. (16.3)

pointer assignment statement   A statement which associates a *pointer* with a *target*. (16.1)

pointer attribute   A means of specifying that the entities declared in a *type declaration statement* will contain pointers to other *variables* rather than data values. (16.1)

portability   The ability of a program written on one computer system to be *compiled* and executed on another type of computer system with little or no alteration. (2.5)

portable programs   Programs which can be moved from one computer system to another with little or no alteration. (2.5)

preconnected   An *input* or *output unit* which is automatically connected to the program and does not require an **OPEN** statement; typically the *default input* and *output units*. (9.3)

printer control character   The first character of each line, or *record*, sent to a printer which is not printed but is used to determine the vertical movement of the paper before the printing of the rest of the line takes place. (8.6)

private   An entity in a *module*, or a *component* of a *derived type* definition in a module, which has been made private is not accessible through **USE** *association*. (12.3)

procedure   A *subroutine* or a *function*.

program   A sequence of instructions to a computer which causes the computer to carry out the actions required for the solution of a specified problem. (1.2, 2.1)

program unit   A sequence of statements and comment lines, starting with a **PROGRAM**, **SUBROUTINE**, **FUNCTION**, **MODULE** or **BLOCK DATA** statement and ending with an **END**, **END PROGRAM**, **END SUBROUTINE**, **END FUNCTION** or **END MODULE** statement, which is the fundamental component part of an executable Fortran program. (4.2)

programming language   A means of representing the instructions that make up a program in human-readable form. (1.3)

public   An entity in a *module* which is not *private*.

punched card An obsolete form of input to a computer in which characters were represented by holes punched in a rectangular card. (2.6)

quadrature See *numerical quadrature*.

random access Another name for *direct access*.

range The statements between a **DO** *statement* and the corresponding **END DO** *statement*, inclusive, are known as the range of the **DO** loop.

rank The number of permissible *subscripts* for an *array*. (7.2, 13.2)

rank-*n* array An *array* with *n dimensions*.

real An *intrinsic data type* used to represent numbers using a *floating-point* representation. (3.2)

real number A number of the *real intrinsic data type*.

real part The first of the two numbers which make up a *complex number*. (14.7)

record A defined sequence of *characters*, or of values. (9.1)

record number The index number of a *record* in a *direct access file*. (15.4)

recursion The *invocation* of a *procedure*, either directly or indirectly, by itself; not allowed in Fortran unless the procedure is declared to be **RECURSIVE**. (11.5)

reference See *function reference*.

register A special part of the memory, usually capable of higher speeds of storage and retrieval than the rest of the memory, which is used for arithmetic and other key operations. (10.1)

relational expression A *logical expression* in which two *operands* are compared by a *relational operator* to give a *logical value* for the *expression*. (5.2)

relational operator An *operator* which compares two values, and returns either the value *true* or the value *false*. (5.2)

repeat count A number placed before an *edit descriptor*, or a group of edit descriptors enclosed in parentheses, which defines how many times the descriptor, or group of descriptors, is to be repeated. (8.5)

repertoire See *character repertoire*.

residual The difference between the calculated value y and the original data value y when attempting to fit a function through a set of data points. (10.4)

residual sum The sum of the squares of the *residuals*. (10.4)

result variable A variable in a *function subprogram* whose value on exit from the function will be the result of the *function reference*. (4.3, 11.5)

root (a) A value of x for which a function $f(x)$ has the value zero; see also *zero*; (b) the *node* of a *tree* from which the tree 'grows'. (16.7)

round-off error The cumulative error that occurs during *floating-point* arithmetic operations. (10.1)

save attribute The value of a *local entity* in a *procedure* will only be preserved on exit from the procedure if it has the save attribute. (11.4)

scalar variable A *variable* which is not an *array variable*.

scope The part of a program in which a name or entity has a specified interpretation; see also *scoping unit*. (11.7)

scoping unit A *derived type* definition; an *interface* body, excluding any derived type definitions or interface bodies contained within it; a *program unit* or *subprogram*, excluding any derived-type definitions, interface bodies or subprograms contained within it. (11.7)

secant method An *iterative method* for finding the roots of a polynomial equation; cf. *bisection method* and *Newton's method*. (18.4)

sequential A form of *file* in which each *record* is written after the previously written record, so that the normal way of reading the records is in the same order as they were written. (9.1, 9.3)

shape The *rank* and *extent* of an *array* in each of its *dimensions*; can be stored in a rank-one array. (7.2, 13.2)

single-precision One of the two hardware representations of *floating-point* numbers on most computers, providing less accuracy than *double-precision*. (10.2)

size The total number of *elements* in an *array*. (7.2, 13.2)

slice The unit of time allocated to a program in a *time-sharing* system. (2.3)

software Programs that can be executed on a computer, cf. *hardware*. (1.1)

source form The way in which a Fortran program is written — either *free form* or *fixed form*. (2.6)

specification expression A restricted form of *scalar integer constant expression* which can appear as a *bound* in an *array declaration* or as the *length* in a *character declaration*. (3.5, 13.5)

specification statement A non-executable statement which precedes the executable statements in a *program unit* and provides information for use by the *compiler*. (4.2)

specifier An item in a *control information list* which provides additional information for the *input/output statement* in which it appears. (8.6)

spline A set of polynomials, each of the same degree k, which are joined together to form a single curve which has $k - 1$ continuous derivatives at each join point; see also *cubic spline*. (18.7)

stability A measure of the sensitivity of a numerical process to small changes in its data, including *round-off errors* and *truncation errors*; see also *stable* and *unstable processes*. (10.3)

stable process A numerical process whose result is the mathematically exact answer to a problem that is only slightly different from the one given. (10.3)

statement entity An entity whose *scope* is that of a single statement, or part of a statement, for example an *implied* **DO** *variable*. (11.7)

statement label A number preceding a statement, by means of which the statement can be referred to in another statement. (6.5, 8.4)

storage association A method of associating two or more *variables* or *arrays* by aligning their physical storage in the computer's *memory*; used by **COMMON** and **EQUIVALENCE**, but not recommended in new programs. (17.1)

stored-program computer The formal name for a computer which is capable of executing different programs (which it stores in its *memory* during their execution). (1.2)

straight selection A simple, and moderately efficient, method of sorting the elements of an array into either increasing or decreasing order. (7.7)

stride The increment used in a *subscript triplet*. (13.9)

structure constructor A *derived type literal constant*. (3.7)

structure plan An English-language aid to good program design; used throughout this book. (2.1)

subprogram A *function subprogram* or a *subroutine subprogram*. (4.2)

subroutine A *subprogram* which may only return any results through its *arguments* and is invoked by a **CALL** statement. (4.4)

subroutine subprogram A self-contained part of a Fortran program which implements a *subroutine*. (4.4)

subscript The value of the *subscript expression* which follows an *array* name in parentheses in order to identify a particular *element* of the array. (7.1, 13.1)

subscript expression   An *integer expression* whose value is used as a *subscript* to an *array*. (7.1, 13.1)

subscript triplet   A method of specifying an *array section* by means of the initial and final *subscript* values and a *stride* (or increment). (13.9)

substring   A contiguous part of a *character string*. (3.5)

tail   The last item in a *linked list*. (16.7)

target   A *variable* that has the **TARGET** *attribute*.

TARGET attribute   A means of specifying that the entities declared in a *type declaration statement* may be pointed to by a *pointer*. (16.1)

ternary tree   A *tree* structure which splits into three *branches* at each *node*. (16.7)

time-sharing   A method of utilizing the speed of a computer's central processor in an *interactive system* in which each user is given a small *slice* of the processor's time in turn. (2.3)

top-down design   The process of analysing a problem by starting with the major steps, and successively refining each step until the individual steps are all readily soluble, cf. *bottom-up development*. (2.1)

track   A circular band on the surface of a *magnetic disk* on which information is recorded; a single surface will contain many tracks. (9.1)

transfer of control   The interruption of the normal sequential execution of Fortran statements as a result of executing a **CALL** to a *subroutine*, a *reference* to a *function*, or a **GOTO** statement.

translation   The process of converting a *program* into *machine code*; see also *compiling*. (1.3)

tree   A form of *linked list* in which each *node* points to at least two other nodes, thus creating a flexible and dynamic structure. (19.7)

tridiagonal system   A sparse system of simultaneous linear equations in which only those elements in the matrix of coefficients which are on the diagonal or immediately above or below it are non-zero. (18.6)

truncate   (a) The process in which the fractional part of a number is discarded before the number is *assigned* to an *integer variable* (3.3); (b) the process in which excess *characters* are removed from the right-hand end of a *character string* before it is assigned to a *character variable* of a shorter *length*. (3.5)

truncation error   The error caused by terminating an iterative calculation before it is mathematically correct. (10.3)

type   An *intrinsic data type* or a *derived type*.

type declaration statement   See *declaration statement*.

unary operator   An *operator* which has only one *operand*. (3.3)

undefined   A *data object* which does not have a defined value.

underflow   An error condition in which a number is too close to zero to be distinguished from zero in the *floating-point* representation being used; many computers will not report this form of error, and will store the number as zero. (10.1)

unformatted input statement   An *unformatted* **READ** *statement*.

unformatted output statement   An *unformatted* **WRITE** *statement*.

unformatted READ statement   A **READ** statement which does not include a *format specifier*.

unformatted record   A *record* consisting of a sequence of values (in a processor-dependent form) which is, essentially, a copy of some part, or parts, of the *memory*; it can only be produced by an *unformatted output statement*. (9.2)

unformatted WRITE statement A WRITE statement which does not include a *format specifier*.

unit An *input unit* or an *output unit*.

unit specifier A *specifier* which specifies the *unit* on which input or output is to occur. (8.6)

unstable process A numerical process whose result is the mathematically exact answer to a problem substantially different from the one given. (10.3)

upper bound The maximum value permitted for a *subscript* of an array. (7.2, 13.2)

upper triangular matrix A square matrix in which all the elements below the diagonal are zero.

USE association The means by which entities in a *module* are made available to a *program unit*. (4.7)

USE statement A statement which references a *module*, some of whose entities are to be made available by USE *association*. (4.7)

value separator A comma, a space, a slash or an end of *record* which separates two data values in *listed-directed input*. (3.4, 8.1)

variable A *data object* whose value may be changed during the execution of a program. (1.2)

variable declaration The *declaration* of the *type* of a *variable* together with, optionally, one or more *attributes* of that variable. (3.2, 3.7, 3.9, 14.2)

varying string A form of *character data type* whose *length* is not fixed at the time of the *declaration* of a variable of that type, but may vary during the execution of the program; not available in Fortran 90, but the subject of an auxiliary Fortran standard. (12.5)

vector subscript A method of specifying an *array section* by means of a *rank-one array* containing the *subscripts* of the *elements* of the parent *array* that are to constitute the array section; see also *many-one array section*. (13.9)

well-conditioned problem A numerical process which is relatively insensitive to changes in the values of its parameters. (10.3)

WHERE construct The construct used in a *masked array assignment* where one of two alternative *assignments* takes place on an *elemental* basis. (13.8)

WHERE statement The statement used in a *masked array assignment* where a single *assignment* either takes place, or does not, on an *elemental* basis. (13.8)

word-processing A computer application for typing, manipulating and printing text; possibly the most widely used of all computer applications.

work array A temporary *array* used for the storage of intermediate results during processing; frequently implemented as an *automatic array* in Fortran 90.

zero A value of x for which the function $f(x)$ has the value zero; see also *root*. (16.7)

Bibliography

ANSI (1966). *American National Standard Programming Language FORTRAN. (ANSI X3.9-1966)*. New York: American National Standards Institute

ANSI (1978). *American National Standard Programming Language FORTRAN. (ANSI X3.9-1978)*. New York: American National Standards Institute

Atkinson L.V., Harley P.J. and Hudson J.D. (1988). *Numerical Methods with FORTRAN 77: A Practical Introduction*. Wokingham: Addison-Wesley

Cipra B.A. (1988). PCs factor a 'most wanted' number. *Science*, **242**, 1634–5

Dahlquist G. and Björck A. (1974). *Numerical Methods*. Englewood Cliffs, NJ: Prentice-Hall

Dierckx P. (1993). *Curve and Surface Fitting With Splines*. Oxford: Clarendon Press

Duff I.S., Erisman A.M. and Reid J.K. (1986). *Direct Methods for Sparse Matrices*. Oxford: Clarendon Press

Ellis T.M.R. (1990). *FORTRAN 77 Programming*, 2nd edn. Wokingham: Addison-Wesley

Forsythe G.E., Malcolm M.A. and Moler C.B. (1977). *Computer Methods for Mathematical Computations*. Englewood Cliffs, NJ: Prentice-Hall

George A. and Liu J.W. (1981). *Computer Solution of Large Sparse Positive Definite Systems*. Englewood Cliffs, NJ: Prentice-Hall

Gerver J.L. (1983). Factoring large numbers with a quadratic sieve. *Mathematics of Computation*, **42/163**, 287–94

Golub G.H. and Van Loan C.F. (1991). *Matrix Computations*, 2nd edn. Baltimore, MD: Johns Hopkins University Press

Gries D. (1991). *The Science of Computer Programming*. Berlin: Springer

Hopkins T. and Phillips C. (1988). *Numerical Methods in Practice: Using the NAG Library*. Wokingham: Addison-Wesley

ISO/IEC (1991). *Information Technology – Programming Languages – Fortran. (ISO/IEC 1539 : 1991 (E)*. Geneva: ISO/IEC Copyright Office

Knuth D.E. (1969). *The Art of Computer Programming, Volume 1 – Fundamental Algorithms*. Reading, MA: Addison-Wesley

NAG Ltd (1988). *The NAG Fortran Library Manual – Mark 13*. Oxford: NAG Ltd

Richards I. (1982). The invisible prime number. *American Scientist*, **70**, 176–9

Scheid F. (1968). *Theory and Problems of Numerical Analysis*. New York: McGraw-Hill

SPSS Inc. (1988). *SPSS-X User's Guide*, 3rd edn. Chicago: SPSS Inc.

Visual Numerics Inc. (1992). *IMSL Fortran Numerical Libraries, Version 2.0*. Houston, TX: Visual Numerics Inc.

Wilkinson J.H. (1963). *Rounding Errors in Algebraic Processes*. Englewood Cliffs, NJ: Prentice-Hall

Answers to self-test exercises

Self-test exercises 2.1 (page 24)

1 • Specifying the problem.
   • Analysing the problem, and breaking it down into its main components.
   • Writing the code to solve the problem.

2   The most difficult part of the whole process is usually the testing, and the elimination of errors (usually referred to as *debugging*). The next most difficult is the analysis of the problem and the design of the program (step 2, above).

3 • They must begin with a letter.
   • They must contain only letters, digits and the underscore character, _.
   • They must contain between 1 and 31 characters.
   • Upper case and lower case letters are treated as being equivalent, so that the following all represent the same name: **NAME**, **Name**, **name**, **NaMe**, etc.

4   The first statement must be a **PROGRAM** statement, and the last must be an **END** statement. (This is an oversimplification, as we shall see in Chapter 4, but is accurate for the types of programs that we can write until then.)

5   If the last non-blank character of a line is an ampersand (&), then the statement is continued on the next line.

       If the ampersand appears in a character context (that is, in the middle of a character string enclosed in quotation marks or apostrophes) then the first non-blank character of the next line must also be an ampersand, and the character string continues from immediately after that ampersand.

       If the ampersand at the end of the first line is not in a character context then the statement is continued either from the first character after an ampersand, if that is the first non-blank character on the line, or from the start of the next line, if the first non-blank character is not an ampersand.

6   Programs are usually read many times, often by several different people, over their lifetime. Comments provide explanations of what is happening, and why, where this is not immediately obvious from the code itself, and thus make the program easier to understand by anyone who is reading it.

```
! A comment may be a line whose first non-blank character
! is an exclamation mark
a = 1     ! or it may be a trailing comment following
b = 2     ! any program statement, in which case the
c = 3     ! first non-blank character after the end of
d = 4     ! the statement must be an exclamation mark
```

Self-test exercises 2.2 (page 34)

1   A syntactic error is an error in the syntax, or *grammar*, of a statement. A semantic error is an error in the logic of the program; that is, it does not do what it was intended to do.

Compilation errors (errors detected during the compilation process) are usually the result of syntactic errors, although some semantic errors may also be detected. Execution errors (errors that occur during the execution of the compiled program) are always the result of semantic errors in the program.

2   ● A well-designed program is easier to test.
   ● A well-designed program is easier to maintain.
   ● A well-designed program is easier to port to other computer systems.

3   ● Ensure that the purpose of the program is fully understood.
   ● Ensure that the data requirements (the inputs) and the reporting requirements (the outputs) are fully understood and specified.
   ● Divide the overall problem into smaller, more manageable, sub-problems.
   ● Check to see if some, or all, of the functionality required in your program already exists in procedure libraries.

4   ● Ensure that your program carries out as many checks on the validity of the data it reads as is possible (and realistic). A program that attempts to process invalid data will never produce a meaningful answer!
   ● Carry out internal validity checks at critical points in the calculations.
   ● Check that a reasonable number of iterations are being made while trying to converge to a solution.
   ● Test each part of your program thoroughly before testing the complete program.

5   A line may contain up to 132 characters. (The older, fixed form, layout only allows 72 characters, of which the first six are reserved for special purposes.)

6   A statement may consist of up to 40 lines (20 in fixed form).

7   There is no limit to the number of statements that may appear on a single line, other than that imposed by the limit on the number of characters per line, and the number of continuation lines. Statements on a single line are separated by semi-colons.

Self-test exercises 3.1 (page 57)

1   An integer is a whole number, and has no fractional part. A real number does have a fractional (or decimal) part.

2   Integers are stored exactly in the memory of a computer, and all operations using only integers result in exact answers. Real numbers are stored as (very accurate) approximations to their 'true' values, and operations involving real numbers result in approximations to the mathematically correct answer.

3   ● Real numbers encompass a very much wider range than integers – typically between -10^{38} and $+10^{38}$ on a 32-bit computer, as compared with between -2×10^9 and $+2 \times 10^9$ on the same computer for integers.
   ● Most arithmetic calculations involve numbers with fractional parts, and only real numbers can represent such values.

4   A declaration statement is a statement that identifies a name that will be used to represent a variable, and which also specifies the *type* of information (such as real or integer numbers) that will be stored in that variable.

5   (a)   `INTEGER :: men,women,children`
            `REAL :: adults_to_children`

        (b)   `INTEGER :: l_ft,l_ins,  & ! Length in ft and ins`
                        `h_ft,h_ins,  & ! Height in ft and ins`
                        `d_ft,d_ins     ! Depth in ft and ins`

Note that the above declaration assumes that measurements are to the nearest inch. If fractions of an inch are required then the three variables `l_ins`, `h_ins` and `d_ins` should be real.

        (c)   `REAL :: length,height,depth`

The same approach could be used as for (b), but since the metric system is a decimal one, it is more natural to use real numbers and extract the centimetres when required.

        (d)   `REAL :: time`
                `INTEGER :: photons`

It is reasonable to assume that the time will be measured to a greater accuracy than the nearest second. The number of photons must be a whole number, however.

6   An implicit declaration is one in which a variable does not appear in a type declaration statement, but takes its type from the first letter of its name.

    An **IMPLICIT NONE** statement at the beginning of the program, immediately after the **PROGRAM** statement, prevents implicit declaration and results in an error if a variable is used without first being declared. Implicit declaration is very dangerous, and can lead to many types of program errors, for example as a result of a mistyped name not being detected or a variable accidentally being of the wrong type.

7   An assignment statement causes the result of an expression to be assigned to a variable; that is, to be stored in the memory location identified by the variable name.

8   In order of decreasing precedence (priority) the operators are:
    `**` (exponentiation)
    `*` (multiplication) and `/` (division)
    `+` (addition) and `-` (subtraction)

9   `REAL :: a,b,av`
    `av = (a+b)/2.0`

10   `6.5000    10.0000    0.6500`
        `6    10    0`

The exact spacing of the numbers, and the number of decimal places for the real values may vary from computer to computer, but will follow essentially the same layout as shown above. Note that it is possible that the second number on the second line will be printed as 9 if the result of multiplying 2.5 by 4.0 resulted in a value of, for example, 9.999 999 9 as a result of round-off errors during the calculation.

11 • 1.2 3.456 7.89 42.0
   • 1.2,3.456,7.89,42.0
   • 1.2
      3.456
      7.89
      42.0
   • 1.2 / 3.456 / 7.89 / 42

Self-test exercises 3.2 (page 65)

1   The Fortran character set consists of the 26 alphabetic characters of the Latin alphabet (with no distinction being made between upper and lower case letters), the 10 decimal digits, the underscore character, and 21 other specified characters. Only these characters may appear in Fortran statements, other than comments or character constants.

      The default character set is that set of characters which a particular processor supports.

2   The declaration of a character variable includes a length specification.

3
```
CHARACTER(LEN=20) :: a,b,c,d
CHARACTER :: x
CHARACTER(LEN=9) :: month   ! September is the longest
```

4
```
CHARACTER(LEN=20) :: a,b,c,d,x*1,month*9
```

5
```
A small step for a man
A giant leap for mankind
```

Self-test exercises 3.3 (page 74)

1   An entity which is given an initial value in its declaration statement can have that value changed later in the program. An entity with the **PARAMETER** attribute is a constant, and its value cannot subsequently be changed.

2   A derived type is a user-defined data type. It consists of one or more components each of which is either of an intrinsic type or of another derived type. A derived type is, therefore, ultimately derived from entities of intrinsic types.

3   Derived types allow data types to be created which reflect the nature of the problem being solved and the data that it uses.

4   (a)
```
TYPE uk_address
    CHARACTER(LEN=50) :: house_name
    INTEGER :: number
    CHARACTER(LEN=30) :: street,village,town,county
    CHARACTER(10) :: post_code
END TYPE uk_address
```

        (b)
```
TYPE us_address
    INTEGER :: number
    CHARACTER(LEN=30) :: street,city
    CHARACTER(LEN=2) :: state
    INTEGER :: zip_code
END TYPE us_address
```

```
5    (a)  TYPE(uk_address) :: my_uk_home
          my_uk_home =                              &
              uk_address("The Old Manor House",     &
                          3,"High Street",          &
                          "Little Uffington",       &
                          "Wokingham",              &
                          "Berks.","RG26 9QZ")

     (b)  TYPE(us_address) :: my_us_home
          my_us_home =                              &
              us_address(19725,"Main Street"        &
                          "Chicago"                 &
                          "IL",60689)

6    TYPE person
         CHARACTER(LEN=20) :: first_name,last_name
         TYPE(us_address) :: address
     END TYPE PERSON
     TYPE(person) :: individual
     PRINT *,"Please type name and address in the order"
     PRINT *,"first name, last name, number and street,"
     PRINT *,"city, state (2 letters), zip code"
     READ *,individual
```

Note that it would also be possible to read the data by specifying each component, as shown below, but this is not necessary:

```
     READ *,individual%first_name,individual%last_name,  &
            individual%address%number,                   &
            individual%address%street,                   &
            individual%address%city,                     &
            individual%address%state,                    &
            individual%address%zip_code
```

Self-test exercises 4.1 (page 108)

1   Breaking a program up into a main program and a set of procedures enables the top-down design approach to be carried through into the structure of the code, so that each procedure carries out a single, well-defined task. This also means that each procedure can be tested independently of the rest of the program.

2   A function returns a single result through the result variable, which has the same name and type as the function itself. A function's arguments are only used to provide information to the function; that is, they are **INTENT(IN)**. A function is referenced by its name appearing as part of an expression.

A subroutine uses its arguments both to provide information to the subroutine and to return results to the calling program unit. A subroutine is called by means of a **CALL** statement.

3   An intrinsic procedure is one which is defined as a part of the Fortran language, and which is provided by the Fortran processor.

4   A generic function is a function which exists in several versions to carry out the same function on arguments of different types. For example, if **int_var** and **real_var** are integer and real variables, respectively, **ABS(int_var)** will calculate the absolute value of **int_var** and return the result as an integer value, while **ABS(real_var)** will calculate the absolute value of **real_var** and return the result as a real value.

5   A dummy argument declared as `INTENT(INOUT)` may be used both to provide information to the procedure and to return results from the procedure; it may be used freely throughout the procedure. A dummy argument declared as `INTENT(OUT)`, on the other hand, is used only to return results from the procedure, and is undefined on entry to the procedure; it must therefore be given a value in an assignment statement, or by some other means, before being used in an expression.

6

(a)
```
INTEGER FUNCTION count(char,string)
    IMPLICIT NONE
    CHARACTER, INTENT(IN) :: char
    CHARACTER(LEN=*), INTENT(IN) :: string
```

(b)
```
SUBROUTINE quadratic(a,b,c,root1,root2)
    IMPLICIT NONE
    REAL, INTENT(IN) :: a,b,c
    REAL, INTENT(OUT) :: root1,root2
```

(c)
```
INTEGER FUNCTION prime(n)
    IMPLICIT NONE
    INTEGER, INTENT(IN) :: n
    ! The function will return a factor, or zero if
    ! the number n is a prime
```

(d)
```
CHARACTER(LEN=*) FUNCTION reverse(string)
    IMPLICIT NONE
    CHARACTER(LEN=*), INTENT(IN) :: string
```

or, alternatively

```
SUBROUTINE reverse(string)
    IMPLICIT NONE
    CHARACTER(LEN=*), INTENT(INOUT) :: string
```

(e)
```
SUBROUTINE error(error_num)
    IMPLICIT NONE
    INTEGER, INTENT(IN) :: error_num
```

(f)
```
INTEGER FUNCTION get_number()
    IMPLICIT NONE
```

or, alternatively

```
SUBROUTINE get_number(n)
    IMPLICIT NONE
    INTEGER, INTENT(OUT) :: n
```

Self-test exercises 4.2 (page 122)

1   A module is a means of packaging various entities in such a way that they can have global accessibility; that is, they can be accessed by any procedure that wishes to do so.

2   `USE` association associates a name in a procedure with an entity in a module having the same name, thereby making the entity in the module available in the procedure.

3   A derived type cannot be passed to a procedure as an argument and, as a result, an object of that derived type cannot be passed as an argument because the procedure cannot know about that type. (Simply repeating the derived type definition in the procedure creates a different, albeit identical, derived type.) Placing the derived type definition in a module, and making it available to all program units by `USE` association means that they all have access to the *same* derived type definition and eliminates the problem.

4   If a procedure has an explicit interface at the point where it is referenced then the number and type of its arguments are known, and the actual arguments (and result, in the case of a function) can be checked against the interface details. If a procedure has an implicit interface, then nothing is known about the procedure apart from its name, and the calling program unit can only *assume* that the actual argument matches the requirements of the procedure.

5 ● To provide global availability of certain variables, thus avoiding the need for long argument lists.
   ● When using derived types, in order that they can be used as arguments to procedures.
   ● To provide explicit interfaces for procedures.

Self-test exercises 5.1 (page 150)

1   A logical operator has one or two logical operands; a relational operator has two numeric, or two character, operands. Both give a logical result.

2   (a) *false*
       (b) *true*
       (c) *true*
       (d) Because of possible round-off errors in the evaluation of the expression (0.1+0.3) it is not possible to predict with absolute certainty what the result will be.
       (e) *true*
       (f) *false*
       (g) *true*
       (h) *true*

3   A block **IF** construct is used either to choose one of several alternative blocks of statements or to determine whether a single block of statements is executed.

4   A logical **IF** statement only controls whether a single statement is executed; a block **IF** controls the execution of as many statements as required.

5 ● The 26 upper case letters are collated in alphabetic order.
   ● The 26 lower case letters are collated in alphabetic order.
   ● The 10 digits are collated in increasing numerical order.
   ● Digits are either all collated before A, or all after Z.
   ● Digits are either all collated before a, or all after z.
   ● Space (blank) is collated before both letters and digits.

6   (a) *true*
       (b) Not defined
       (c) *true*
       (d) Not defined
       (e) *true* (blank comes before ? in the ASCII code; see Appendix D)

Self-test exercises 5.2 (page 162)

1 The order of the blocks, and their preceding **IF, ELSE IF** or **ELSE** statements matters with a block **IF** construct, because each test is carried out in sequence. The order does not matter in a **CASE** construct, because the case selectors cannot overlap.

2 The case expression must be integer, character or logical. It cannot be a real expression.

3 The case selector may take any of the following forms, unless it is a logical value, in which case only the first form is permitted:

```
value
low_value:high_value
low_value:
:high_value
```

4 Overflow occurs when a calculation gives rise to a value which is too large to be represented by the type being used.

5 A **CASE** construct is the more appropriate when there is no overlap between the criteria for making the choice, and the basis for making the choice is, or can easily be, one of the three discrete intrinsic data types (integer, character and logical). A block **IF** construct is the more appropriate if there is an overlap between the criteria (and hence the order in which the tests are made may matter), or if the decision must be made using real values.

Self-test exercises 6.1 (page 186)

1 A **DO** loop is a means of specifying that a sequence of statements (between the **DO** statement and the corresponding **END DO** statement) is to be repeated a number of times.

2 There are no restrictions on the statements that may appear within a **DO** loop.

3 A count-controlled **DO** loop contains the information necessary to determine how many times the loop is to be repeated as part of the **DO** statement; other forms of **DO** loop decide when to stop repeating the loop on the basis of a condition that occurs during the execution of the loop.

A count-controlled loop is most appropriate if the nature of the problem requires that the loop be repeated a pre-defined number of times, regardless of the results of the loop repetition. A count-controlled loop is also appropriate in situations where some other means is expected to determine the exit condition, in order to provide a *fail-safe* mechanism in case the exit condition never occurs.

4 The **DO** variable is the integer variable specified in a count-controlled **DO** statement which is incremented at the end of each pass through the loop. It is not permitted to alter the value of the **DO** variable during the execution of the loop.

5 The iteration count is the count of the number of times a count-controlled **DO** loop is to be obeyed. It is calculated before the start of execution of the loop as the maximum of $(final - initial + inc)/inc$ and zero.

6   (a)   11 times
      (b)   6 times
      (c)   3 times
      (d)   0 times (the loop will not be obeyed at all)
      (e)   17 times
      (f)   once

7   What it would have been on the *next* pass through the loop, if there had been one.

8   (a)   10   8   2   8   0   0

      Since 1 is greater than m, and k is positive, the second loop is never obeyed; however, the DO variable j, is given its initial value before this decision is made. The two innermost loops are never obeyed either, therefore. The outermost loop has an iteration count of one, but its DO variable, i, is set to the value it would have had on the second pass, had there been one.

      (b)   10   -2   9   9   64   0

      The only difference between this program and the previous one is that k is set to -i at the start of the outermost loop, thus causing the second loop to count down from 8 to 0 in steps of -2. On the first pass through this loop the third loop is obeyed once, but on subsequent passes it is not obeyed at all as n is less than 1.

9   An infinite loop is one which never reaches an exit condition. It can be avoided by always using a count-controlled loop to place an upper limit on the number of times a loop is executed.

10   An **EXIT** statement is used to provide a means of terminating the execution of a loop when some condition occurs; it causes an immediate branch to the statement immediately after the **END DO** statement of the innermost loop currently being executed.

11   A **CYCLE** statement is used to end the processing of the statements in a loop *for this iteration*; it causes an immediate branch to the start of the loop in an identical fashion to that which occurs when the **END DO** statement is executed.

Self-test exercises 6.2 (page 193)

1   A block **DO** construct is named so that an **EXIT** or **CYCLE** statement in a nested block **DO** can exit from more than the innermost loop, or cycle to the start of other than the innermost loop. The name, which follows the normal rules for Fortran names, must precede the **DO** statement, separated from the **DO** by a colon, *and* follow the corresponding **END DO** statement.

2   The names on a block **IF** or **CASE** construct are only for the benefit of the human reader in the case of complicated or nested structures. They are not used during the execution of the program, but will be checked by the compiler to ensure that they match correctly.

3   A **RETURN** statement provides a means of returning from a procedure to the calling program unit in the same way as occurs when execution of the procedure reaches the **END** statement. It is useful in an exceptional situation where there is no requirement to execute the remainder of the procedure, for example if an error has occurred.

4   A **STOP** statement terminates processing of the program in the same way as occurs when execution reaches the **END** statement of the main program unit. It is normally only used after a catastrophic error has meant that no further processing is meaningful.

5   A **GOTO** statement causes an immediate transfer of control to the statement whose label is given in the **GOTO** statement. It should never be used except in certain exceptional situations, for example after some types of errors, when it is the only way to get to the part of the procedure which will restore normal processing. Always ask yourself 'is this really necessary?' before using a **GOTO**.

6   A statement label is a whole number, in the range 1 to 99999, which may be used to identify a statement, for example so that a **GOTO** statement may branch to it. Statement labels are not usually required in Fortran 90 programs.

Self-test exercises 7.1 (page 212)

1   An array is an ordered set of variables having the same name and type. An array element is one of the individual variables that forms part of the array.

2   An array variable occupies several memory locations, each of which can be independently accessed and may contain a separate value. A scalar variable occupies a single memory location and contains a single value.

3   An array specification consists of the name of the array, followed by the lower and upper bounds for its subscript(s), separated by a colon, enclosed in parentheses, or simply by the upper bound, in which case the lower bound is one. It appears in the variable list of a declaration statement:

```
REAL :: arr1(10:50), arr2(25)
```

A dimension attribute consists of the word **DIMENSION** followed by the lower and upper bounds for the array subscript(s), separated by a colon, enclosed in parentheses, or simply by the upper bound, in which case the lower bound is one. It appears as an attribute in a declaration statement:

```
REAL, DIMENSION(10:50) :: arr1,arr3
REAL, DIMENSION(25) :: arr2
```

4   A subscript expression must be an integer expression.

5 ● The rank of an array is the number of permissible subscripts for the array; each subscript refers to one of the dimensions of the array.
 ● The extent of a dimension of an array is the number of elements in that dimension.
 ● The size of an array is the total number of elements in the array.
 ● The shape of an array consists of the rank of the array and its extent in each dimension; it can be represented by a rank-one array in which the value of each element is the extent of the array in the corresponding dimension.

6   (a)
```
INTEGER, PARAMETER :: max_gamblers=100
REAL, DIMENSION(max_gamblers) ::      &
                  wages,av_loss,max_win,max_loss
INTEGER, DIMENSION(max_gamblers) ::   &
                  gambles_per_week,num_weeks_addict
```

An alternative approach would be to define a suitable derived type:

```
TYPE gambler
   REAL :: wages
   INTEGER :: gambles_per_week
   REAL :: av_loss,max_win,max_loss
   INTEGER :: num_weeks_addict
END TYPE gambler
INTEGER, PARAMETER :: max_gamblers=100
TYPE(gambler), DIMENSION(max_gamblers) :: gambler_anon
```

(b)
```
INTEGER, PARAMETER :: max_tests=20
REAL, DIMENSION(max_tests) :: mass,height
INTEGER, DIMENSION(max_tests) :: num_blows
```

or, using a derived type:

```
TYPE exp_data
   REAL :: mass,height
   INTEGER :: num_blows
END TYPE exp_data
INTEGER, PARAMETER :: max_tests=20
TYPE(exp_data), DIMENSION(max_tests) :: experiment
```

(c)
```
INTEGER, PARAMETER :: max_points=50
REAL, DIMENSION(max_points) :: x,y,z
```

(d)
```
REAL, DIMENSION(366) :: temp_6am,temp_noon,  &
                        temp_6pm,temp_midnight
INTEGER, DIMENSION(-11:31) :: noon_temp
```

The first four arrays have subscripts from 1 to 366, to allow for an entry for every day of the year, including a leap year. The last array uses subscripts from -10 to 30 to accumulate the count of days on which the noon temperature is equal to the subscript value, with **noon_temp(-11)** being used for temperatures less than $-10°$C and **noon_temp(31)** being used for temperatures over 30°C.

7   An array constructor is an array-valued constant.

8   An implied **DO** is a means of using the count control part of the **DO** loop syntax to control stepping through a list of values or a list of array elements. It is used in an array constructor to avoid the need for repeated values or repeated sequences of values.

9   The occurrence of a scalar variable in an input or output list causes the input or output of a single value. The occurrence of an array variable in an input or output list, on the other hand, causes the input or output of the same number of values as the size of the array. An implied **DO** may also be used with an array in order to read or write a subset only of the array elements in the array.

10   The controlling values of the implied **DO** in an array constructor must be constants, whereas they may be variables in an input/output statement.

11   Two arrays are conformable if they have the same shape.

12   Whole array operations are possible between two conformable objects; that is, all intrinsic operations are defined between conformable objects. Note that a scalar is conformable with any array, and is treated as an array of the same shape, every element of which has the value of the scalar.

13   Arrays can be used in expressions in the same way as scalars, as long as all the objects in the expression are conformable.

14   An elemental procedure is a procedure whose arguments may be scalar or array-valued, and will return a scalar result if the actual arguments are scalar and an array-valued result if they are arrays. In the latter case each element of the result is obtained by applying the procedure to the corresponding element(s) of the input argument(s).

Self-test exercises 7.2 (page 229)

1   An assumed-shape array is a dummy argument whose rank is specified but whose shape is not known, but is assumed from the corresponding actual argument. An assumed-shape array is used in a procedure which is designed to accept actual array arguments of different sizes.

2   An assumed-shape array will be as large or as small as required each time the procedure is executed. An explicit-shape dummy array with bounds passed as arguments, or by some other means such as in a module, will also be as large or as small as required. The advantage of the assumed-shape array is primarily that it avoids the need to make this information explicitly available, and thus makes the program less cluttered.

   The disadvantage of an assumed-shape array is that the procedure that it is declared in must have an explicit interface in any program unit that references it – although this is no problem if procedures are packaged in modules.

3   An automatic array is an explicit-shape array, which is not a dummy argument, whose bounds are variables which are either dummy arguments, or whose values are available on entry to the procedure by some other means, such as from a module.

4   An explicit-shape array may have non-constant bounds if
   - the array is a dummy argument
   - the array is an automatic array
   - the array is a function result

5   The type of an array-valued function is declared in a type declaration statement in the body of the function. The result of an array-valued function cannot be an assumed-size array.

6   An array-valued component of a derived type must be an explicit-shape array with constant bounds. (It may also be a deferred-shape array, as we shall see in Chapter 13.)

Self-test exercises 8.1 (page 257)

1   A value separator is a character which is used to determine the end of one input item (and the start of the next).

2   Value separators during list-directed input are a comma, a slash, a blank or the end of record, ignoring any blanks before or after the value separator.

3   A character string which is contained within a single line, does not contain any value separators, in which the first character is not a quotation mark or an apostrophe, and which does not begin with a number followed by an asterisk, may be input without delimiting quotation marks or apostrophes.

4   An embedded format is a list of edit descriptors, enclosed in parentheses, and further enclosed in apostrophes or quotation marks, which is included as part of an input or output statement.

A **FORMAT** statement consists of the word **FORMAT** followed by a list of edit descriptors, enclosed in parentheses. A **FORMAT** statement is always labelled.

5   If the same format is to be used by several input or output statements it is preferable to use a **FORMAT** statement to avoid repetition, and to ensure that a change to the format for one input/output statement is made to all the others using the same format. An embedded format is preferable in all other cases.

6   An edit descriptor is a specification of how a sequence of characters on the external medium is to be converted to a value in the computer system, or vice versa.

7   ♦♦♦♦♦6789 minus 4567 is 2222♦♦♦♦234.50 minus 12.34 is 222.160

where ♦ represents a space.

8   ♦♦♦♦♦♦♦345678♦♦♦♦♦1234♦♦♦♦♦123456
         ♦♦♦♦♦345678♦♦♦♦♦1234♦♦♦♦♦♦♦123456

Self-test exercises 8.2 (page 271)

2   A **PRINT** statement always sends its output to the default output unit (normally the computer's printer). A **WRITE** statement sends its output to the unit specified in the statement.

3   To obtain information about the success, or otherwise, of the input/output operation.

4   A printer control character is the first character of an output record being sent to an output unit designated as a printer. It controls vertical movement of the paper before the rest of the record is printed. The printer control character is not, itself, printed.

space	print on the next line
0	print on the next line but one; that is, leave a blank line
+	print on the same line; that is, do not move the paper
1	print at the top of the next page

5   A format is repeated when all the edit descriptors have been used and there are still items in the input or output list which have not been processed.

6   The formats will be repeated from the place identified by an arrow below:

(a)   (3I8,2F8.2)
         ↑

(b)   (3I8,2(3X,F5.2))
            ↑

(c)   (3(3X,I5),2F8.2)
         ↑

(d)   (3(3X,I5),2(3X,F5.2))
                ↑

(e)   (3I8/2F8.2)
         ↑

(f)   (3I8/2(3X,F5.2))
            ↑

7   (a)   `READ '(3(F4.2,4X))', height,width,depth`

The three input list items **height**, **width** and **depth** are assumed to be real variables.

    (b)   `PRINT '(2(F4.2," * "),F4.2," (= ",F7.2," cubic metres)")', &`
            `height,width,depth`

    (c)   `READ '(3(I2,1X,I2,5X))', height_ft,height_ins, &`
            `width_ft,width_ins,depth_ft,depth_ins`

The six input list items are assumed to be integer variables.

    (d)   `PRINT '(2(I2,"'"",I2,"""""," * "),I2,"'"",I2,""" (= ", &`
            `F9.2," cubic feet)")', height_ft,height_ins, &`
            `width_ft,width_ins,depth_ft,depth_ins`

Note the double apostrophes and double quotation marks in the format, because of the requirement to include both characters in the output text.

Self-test exercises 9.1 (page 299)

1   A formatted record is produced by a formatted output statement, or by some external means, and consists of a sequence of characters. An unformatted record is produced by an unformatted output statement, i.e. one with no format specifier, and consists of a sequence of values.

Formatted records should be used if the file is to be transferred to another type of computer, or if it is required to subsequently list the file. Unformatted records should be used if the information written to the file is to be subsequently read by the same program, or by another program on the same type of computer.

2   A formatted **READ** or **WRITE** statement must include a format specifier, and each statement may process several records, as defined by the format. An unformatted **READ** or **WRITE** statement must not include a format specifier, and always processes exactly one record.

3   An endfile is a special record, of no defined length, which is written by an **ENDFILE** statement. If a **READ** statement reads an endfile record it will result in an execution error unless it is detected by means of an **IOSTAT** specifier (or an **END** specifier), and appropriate action taken.

4   A file must be connected to a program so that the program knows on which logical unit the input or output is to take place. The connection is carried out by an **OPEN** statement.

5   (a)   `OPEN (UNIT=7,FILE="Payroll_Data",STATUS="OLD", &`
            `ACTION="READ",IOSTAT=open_status)`

Note that the file will be formatted by default, so it is not necessary to specify this.

    (b)   `OPEN (UNIT=11,FILE="Intermediate_results_1", &`
            `STATUS="OLD",FORM="UNFORMATTED", &`
            `ACTION="READ",IOSTAT=open_status)`

    (c)   `OPEN (UNIT=8,FILE="Intermediate_results_2", &`
            `FORM="UNFORMATTED",ACTION="READWRITE", &`
            `IOSTAT=open_status)`

No status is specified, as it is not clear whether the file already exists.

(d) OPEN (UNIT=10,FILE="Results",STATUS="OLD", &
                ACTION="READWRITE",POSITION="APPEND", &
                IOSTAT=open_status)

(e) OPEN (UNIT=9,STATUS="SCRATCH",FORM="UNFORMATTED", &
                IOSTAT=open_status)

Scratch files are always opened for both reading and writing, as they would not be much use otherwise!

(f) OPEN (UNIT=10,FILE=file_name,ACTION="WRITE", &
                IOSTAT=open_status)

As the name of the file is not specified it has been included as a variable, which can either be given a value in the program or from the keyboard.

Self-test exercises 10.1 (page 326)

1   For floating-point numbers, overflow occurs when an attempt is made to create a number whose value is larger than possible for the computer being used. This is always fatal. Similarly, underflow occurs when an attempt is made to create a number with a value that is too small. On some computers, the result will be zero. On others, it will be fatal.

     For integers, overflow occurs if an attempt is made to calculate a number that is larger than possible for the computer being used. Similarly, underflow occurs when an attempt is made to calculate a number that is too small. In either case, the attempt is fatal.

2   **(a)** $(a + b)*(a - b)$ is preferable because a^2 and b^2 are more likely to overflow or underflow than $a - b$ or $a + b$.
     (b) $(a - b)/c$ is preferable because it involves one less division and hence is likely to be more accurate in the case when a and b are almost equal.
     (c) This is really the same as (b), since either a or b could be positive or negative. Therefore the form $(a + b)/c$ is preferable.
     (d) $a + b + c + d + e$ is preferable because adding numbers in increasing order of magnitude minimizes round-off errors.
     (e) $a/b - c/d$ is preferable because it involves no multiplications and is consequently less prone to round-off errors. There is also the possibility that $a*d$, $b*c$ or $b*d$ might overflow or underflow.

3   Real variables are parameterized by specifying a kind type parameter in their declaration:

REAL(KIND=*n*), ... :: *list of variable names*

4   Default real is the kind of real used if no kind type is specified in a real declaration statement.

5   The intrinsic procedure **SELECTED_REAL_KIND** may be used to determine the correct kind type parameter for a particular precision and/or exponent range, to improve portability. Thus the statement

REAL(KIND=SELECTED_REAL_KIND(P=6,R=30))):: **x**

defines **x** to be a floating point variable with at least 6 decimal digits of precision and a decimal exponent range of at least 30.

If a program is to be executed on a variety of machines it is generally preferable to explicitly specify a kind having the precision and/or exponent range required to avoid numeric portability problems; this is particularly true when more than normal precision is required.

6   Program `test_10b` will usually give more accurate results. Program `test_10a` is requesting that the variables **x**, **y** and **z** have at least 3 decimal digits of precision. The compiler will therefore select single-precision computer memory locations to store them and will correspondingly use single-precision registers to perform arithmetic operations on them. Program `test_10b` is requesting at least 12 decimal digits of accuracy. Most computers will use more than one word in memory to store the variables **x**, **y** and **z** and will use double-precision hardware registers to perform arithmetic operations.

Note that the compiler is permitted to use double-precision storage and registers for both programs (in which case, there would be no accuracy differences in the answers obtained) since minimum precision requirements are being specified. However, a reasonable compiler is most unlikely to do this.

7   The accuracy of a calculation is determined by the conditioning of the problem (how sensitive the answer is to small changes in the input), and by the stability of the algorithm employed (whether it gives a mathematically correct answer to a problem that differs only slightly from that specified). If either condition is not satisfied the answer must be regarded with suspicion.

8   The stability of an algorithm is affected by round-off effects (caused by the use of finite-precision floating-point arithmetic) and by truncation errors (the terminating of a process before it is mathematically correct). Since many mathematical processes imply an infinite number of operations, some level of truncation error is often unavoidable.

9   A well-conditioned problem is one in which the answer only changes slightly when the problem changes slightly. An ill-conditioned problem is one in which a small change in the problem causes a large change in the answer. If you have an ill-conditioned problem it is worthwhile seeing if it can be reformulated to be well-conditioned.

10   A well-conditioned (or stable) numerical process is one that gives the mathematically correct answer to a problem that is only slightly different from the one specified. An ill-conditioned (or unstable) process is one in which the answer given is the mathematically correct answer to one that is substantially different from the one specified. If you have created such a process it is worthwhile reprogramming it to be stable. Round-off error, which introduces errors at each stage of a numerical calculation, is the prime cause of unstable algorithms. Stable algorithms are designed so that these errors do not grow substantially as a calculation proceeds.

Self-test exercises 10.2 (page 341)

1 ● The magnitude of some quantity related to the process becomes less than some specified value. For example, the value of a function whose root you are trying to find becomes, in absolute value, acceptably small.

   ● The magnitude of the difference between two successive approximations becomes less than some specified tolerance. When this occurs we conclude that, since the process is not changing much between iterations, we have probably converged to an answer. Sometimes this is not true.

- The magnitude of the difference between the calculated answer and the mathematically correct answer is acceptably small. It is rare to be able to use this criterion since we usually cannot mathematically bound the answer.

2 The residual, at a point, is the difference between the calculated value (determined from the least squares fit) and the specified value at that point. The residual sum is the square root of the sum of the squares of all the residuals.

3 The residual sum provides a measure of how good the fit is to the whole data set. The smaller the residual sum the better the overall fit. Since it involves the squares of the residuals, it is unaffected by whether the fit passes above or below the data points.

4 The bisection method requires that it is provided initially with two points at which the function takes opposite signs. If this cannot be done then the process cannot start. Notice that this is a stronger requirement than just knowing an interval that contains a root.

A second, possibly harmless, problem is that an interval containing the function sign change may have more than one function root. The interval bisection method will only find one of the roots. It will not even indicate that other roots are present.

Self-test exercises 11.1 (page 370)

1 Invoking a procedure means calling a subroutine or referencing a function, as appropriate.

2 A procedure's interface consists of the name of the procedure, whether it is a subroutine or a function, the names and characteristics of its dummy arguments, and the name and characteristics of the result variable if it is a function.

The interface of a procedure is explicit if all the above information is available at the point at which it is invoked; it is implicit if some of this information is not available at that point. An explicit interface is required when using certain features of Fortran 90 such as assumed-shape array dummy arguments, and optional or keyword arguments.

3 An interface block is a means of providing an explicit interface for a procedure.

4　(a)　
```
INTERFACE
    SUBROUTINE demo(a,b,c,d,x)
        IMPLICIT NONE
        REAL, INTENT(INOUT) :: a,b,c,d
        INTEGER, OPTIONAL, INTENT(IN) :: x
    END SUBROUTINE demo
END INTERFACE
```

　(b)　
```
INTERFACE
    REAL FUNCTION mean(a)
        IMPLICIT NONE
        INTEGER, DIMENSION(:) :: a
    END FUNCTION mean
END INTERFACE
```

　(c)　
```
INTERFACE
    SUBROUTINE input(num_pts,points)
        USE geometric_data
        IMPLICIT NONE
        INTEGER, INTENT(OUT) :: num_pts
        TYPE(point), DIMENSION(:), INTENT(OUT) :: points
    END SUBROUTINE input
END INTERFACE
```

5   A function must be declared with the **EXTERNAL** attribute if its name is used as either a dummy argument or an actual argument. If a subroutine name is to be used in either of these situations then it must appear in an **EXTERNAL** statement.

6   The specific name of an intrinsic function must be declared with the **INTRINSIC** attribute if its name is used as an actual argument. Note, however, that the specific names of some intrinsic procedures are not allowed to appear as an argument – see Appendix A.

7   A positional actual argument corresponds with a dummy argument through its position in the list of arguments. A keyword actual argument includes the name of the corresponding dummy argument and may appear anywhere in the list of actual arguments; note, however, that once a keyword argument has appeared, then all subsequent actual arguments must be keyword arguments.

8   When using positional actual arguments, each actual argument corresponds to the dummy argument in the same position in the list of arguments. If any optional arguments are omitted from the list of actual arguments then all subsequent arguments must also be omitted.

When using keyword arguments, each actual argument corresponds to the dummy argument whose name precedes the actual argument, separated from it by an equals sign. Such actual arguments may be in any order.

If both positional and keyword arguments appear in a procedure invocation, then all actual arguments after the first keyword argument must be keyword arguments.

9   An optional dummy argument is declared with the **OPTIONAL** attribute.

The intrinsic procedure **PRESENT** can be used to determine whether an actual argument was supplied to correspond with any specified optional dummy argument.

10   Any local variables which are given an initial value are saved between invocations of the procedure, as are any variables which are explicitly given the **SAVE** attribute.

11   Any local variable in a procedure that has the **SAVE** attribute retains its value on exit from the procedure, and has the same value when the procedure is next entered. It can be given explicitly, or implicitly by the variable being initialized in its declaration.

12   A recursive procedure may invoke itself, both directly and indirectly. A non-recursive procedure may not invoke itself, either directly or indirectly.

A recursive procedure's initial statement has the keyword **RECURSIVE** before **FUNCTION** or **SUBROUTINE**, as appropriate. The absence of the **RECURSIVE** qualifier means that the procedure is non-recursive.

Self-test exercises 11.2 (page 384)

1   A generic interface block specifies that all the procedures whose interfaces form part of the block may be invoked by means of the same generic name. It is distinguished from a non-generic interface block by the appearance of the generic name after the word **INTERFACE** at the start of the interface block.

2   A **MODULE PROCEDURE** statement is used to include the names of module procedures as specific names in a generic interface block. It is required because the interfaces of module procedures are not permitted in an interface block as they already have an explicit interface anywhere that they are accessible by USE association, and a duplicate interface is not permitted.

3 • All the procedures specified in a generic interface block must be functions, or they must all be subroutines.
• Any two procedures in a generic interface block must be distinguishable by reference to their non-optional dummy arguments, at least one of which must be different, whether considered as positional arguments or as keyword arguments.

4 There are seven scoping units, as shown below:

```
SUBROUTINE scoping_test         ! 1 - program unit
   IMPLICIT NONE                ! 1
   INTERFACE                    ! 1
      SUBROUTINE sub_1          ! 2 - interface body
         TYPE my_type           ! 3 - derived type defn.
            .                   ! 3
            .                   ! 3
            .                   ! 3
         END TYPE my_type       ! 3
         .                      ! 2
         .                      ! 2
         .                      ! 2
      END SUBROUTINE sub_1      ! 2
      SUBROUTINE sub_2          ! 4 - interface body
         .                      ! 4
         .                      ! 4
         .                      ! 4
      END SUBROUTINE sub_2      ! 4
   END INTERFACE                ! 1
   TYPE my_type                 ! 5 - derived type defn.
      .                         ! 5
      .                         ! 5
      .                         ! 5
   END TYPE my_type             ! 5
   .                            ! 1
   .                            ! 1
   .                            ! 1
CONTAINS                        ! 1
   SUBROUTINE sub_3             ! 6 - internal subprogram
      TYPE my_type              ! 7 - derived type defn.
         .                      ! 7
         .                      ! 7
         .                      ! 7
      END TYPE my_type          ! 7
      .                         ! 6
      .                         ! 6
      .                         ! 6
   END SUBROUTINE sub_3         ! 6
END SUBROUTINE scope_test       ! 1
```

5 Host association is the result of a scoping unit having access to entities from an enclosing scoping unit. USE association is the result of a scoping unit having access to entities in a module by means of a USE statement.

6 An internal subprogram is either an internal function procedure or an internal subroutine procedure; it is not permitted to have any other form of internal subprogram.

An internal procedure is the same as an external procedure except that:

- the name of an internal procedure is not global, and the procedure may, therefore, only be invoked by the host program unit;
- the name of an internal procedure may not be used as an actual argument;
- an internal procedure has access to entities of its host by host association.

7   An entity in a host scoping unit is not accessible by host association in a nested scoping unit if it has the same name as a local name in the nested scoping unit.

Self-test exercises 12.1 (page 406)

1   The **ONLY** qualifier in a **USE** statement causes only those entities listed after the **ONLY** qualifier to be accessible by **USE** association.

2   If a local name is the same as a name made available through **USE** association an error will result (unlike the situation with host association). The module entity can be renamed in the **USE** statement to avoid this problem.

3   Making the components of a derived type private means that only the type, and not its internal structure, is accessible elsewhere in the program.

4   A derived type definition must be in a module for its components to be made private. There are no other restrictions.

5   If the components of a derived type in a module are made private, then only the type itself is available outside the module; inside the module, however, the components are available in the normal way. This means that the author of the module can ensure that the components of the derived type can only be accessed in an approved fashion, for example through procedures which are also defined in the module, thus avoiding the danger of a program inadvertently corrupting the inner form of variables of that type.

6   The private components of a derived type entity can be accessed from within the module in the normal way, as if the components were not specified as being private. In other words, the privacy only applies outside the module in which the derived type definition appears.

7   Making the components of a derived type private means that a program unit which has access to the module in which the derived type definition appears has access to the type, and can declare and use variables of that type, but cannot access the components directly. Making the definition of the derived type private means that it is not accessible at all outside the module, and is only, therefore, for use by procedures which are part of that module.

8   Data hiding is the principle of only allowing access to a restricted set of entities within a module, namely those which the using program units need to know about. It allows the writer of a module to improve the security of programs by controlling the way in which programs, for example, access the data, or parts of the data, on which their program is operating.

9   It is strongly recommended that the default accessibility of all modules be changed to **PRIVATE**, and that only those entities that are required by the user of the module be given explicit **PUBLIC** accessibility.

Self-test exercises 12.2 (page 420)

1   A defined operation is a unary or binary operator which either extends the meaning of an intrinsic operator, for use with operands of types for which the intrinsic operator is not defined, or defines a new operator for use with any specified types of operands.

A defined operation is defined by means of a variation of a generic interface block, and a function which defines the actions to be taken.

2 ● It is not permitted to change the meaning of an intrinsic operator, but only to extend it. It must, therefore, be possible to distinguish any new meanings from the intrinsic meanings solely by reference to the types of its operands.
  ● The number of arguments in the defining function must be consistent with the intrinsic uses of the operator.
  ● Extending the meaning of the relational operators (<, <=, etc.) also extends the meaning of the alternative way of writing the same operators (.LT., .LE., etc.).

3 ● The function `TOM` has two integer arguments, which means that it cannot be distinguished by reference to its arguments from one of the intrinsic meanings of the < operator.
  ● The function **reduce** only has one argument, which is inconsistent with the intrinsic use of the < operator, which always has two operands.

Neither of the two extensions to the meaning of the < operator is, therefore, valid.

4   Defined assignment is an extension of the meaning of the assignment operator when used with derived types. It is defined by means of another variation on the generic interface block, together with a subroutine having exactly two non-optional arguments, the first, `INTENT(OUT)`, corresponding to the object on the left of the assignment operator and the second, `INTENT(IN)`, corresponding to the expression on the right of the assignment operator.

5   Data abstraction encompasses the ability to define new types, procedures and operators, including generic ones, and to encapsulate them in a module in such a manner that only the highest level of detail is available to the user of the module. This allows the user to concentrate on the problem without having to worry about the underlying detail of these application-oriented extensions to the Fortran language.

Self-test exercises 13.1 (page 448)

1   The index bounds of an array are, for each dimension, the lower and upper bounds the index for that dimension is permitted to take in specifying an array element. They are integers and may be positive, negative or zero. The extents are, for each dimension, the number of index values permitted. The size is the total number of elements in the array.

2   The shape of an array is the rank (the number of dimensions) and the extents along each dimension. Since, for an n-dimensional array, the shape is specified by n positive (or possibly zero) numbers, the shape may be represent by a rank-one array of size n whose elements are the extents for each dimension.

3 The array element order is:

```
wow(1,1,1),   wow(2,1,1),   wow(1,2,1),   wow(2,2,1),
wow(1,3,1),   wow(2,3,1),   wow(1,1,2),   wow(2,1,2),
wow(1,2,2),   wow(2,2,2),   wow(1,3,2),   wow(2,3,2),
wow(1,1,3),   wow(2,1,3),   wow(1,2,3),   wow(2,2,3),
wow(1,3,3),   wow(2,3,3),   wow(1,1,4),   wow(2,1,4),
wow(1,2,4),   wow(2,2,4),   wow(1,3,4),   wow(2,3,4)
```

4 Notice that the elements of **wow** are in reversed array element order. The read statement is:

```
READ *, (((wow(i,j,k), k=1,4), j=1,3), i=1,2)
```

5 The **RESHAPE** function takes a rank-one array as input and constructs from it an array of any shape, taking the elements of the rank-one array in array-element order.

6 An explicit-shape array is one in which the bounds for each dimension of the array are explicitly given. The bounds may be expressions as well as constants. In a main program the bounds of an explicit-shape array must be constant.

7 An assumed-shape array is a dummy argument array that takes its shape from the actual argument array. Its extents are specified using colons.

Assumed-shape arrays cannot be specified in the main program since they must be dummy argument arrays. There are no other restrictions on the use of assumed-shape arrays.

8 The intrinsic functions **LBOUND** and **UBOUND** return the lower index bounds of an array and the upper index bounds of an array, respectively.

9 Automatic arrays can only occur in procedures. They are arrays that are not dummy arguments but whose index bounds are non-constant and depend on the procedure's dummy arguments. Automatic arrays are useful when a procedure needs some temporary work space whose size depends on the input arguments.

Self-test exercises 13.2 (page 470)

1
```
INTEGER, ALLOCATABLE(:,:) :: A, B
```

2
```
INTEGER :: error
ALLOCATE(A(3,4), B(m,n), STAT=error)
IF (error /= 0) THEN
   ! Error processing
   ...
END IF
! Arrays were successfully allocated
...
```

3 After the array has been successfully allocated it, or its elements, may be used in the normal manner. Before it is allocated, however, the array may still be used as an argument to the intrinsic function **ALLOCATED** (which returns the allocation status of an allocatable array).

4   The allocation status of an array defines whether or not it has been allocated. There are three possible states:

> **(a)** Not currently allocated. All allocatable arrays have this status at the beginning of an executable program. An allocatable array also has this status after the successful execution of a **DEALLOCATE** statement.
>
> **(b)** Currently allocated. This is the status of an allocatable array after the successful execution of an **ALLOCATE** statement.
>
> **(c)** Undefined. An allocatable array (without the save attribute) has this status if it is not deallocated prior to exit from a procedure. This is bad programming practice because such an array cannot be subsequently employed in any useful way.

5   By executing a **DEALLOCATE** statement before executing a **RETURN** or **END** statement in the procedure in which the allocatable array was defined.

6   The allocation status of an allocatable array (that does not have undefined status) is determined by use of the intrinsic function **ALLOCATED**. This function returns *true* if its argument is allocated and *false* if it is not.

7   An automatic array has index bounds that are functions of the dummy arguments. This is not necessary for an allocatable array. The space for an automatic array is created when a procedure is entered and removed upon exit from the procedure. By contrast, the space for an automatic array is allocatable and deallocatable anywhere in a procedure. An allocatable array may have the save attribute, while an automatic array may not.

8   Operators in a whole array expression are applied element-wise to each element position in the arrays comprising the expression.

9   All intrinsic functions that are elemental may be used in a whole-array expression. They are applied element-wise to each element position of their array arguments.

10   Whole-array expressions greatly simplify code and therefore make it considerably more readable and maintainable.

11   A masked array assignment permits detailed control over the assignment of one array to another by using a logical mask to control how the assignment is to proceed, on an element-wise basis. For example:

```
REAL, DIMENSION(m,n) :: x
...
WHERE (x < 0.0) x = 2.0*x
```

has the effect of replacing every negative element in **x** by twice its value and leaving the positive elements unaltered.

12   An array section is extracted from an array by a specified pattern. An array section is itself an array. Array sections may be used in a similar manner to any other array.

13 ●   A subscript triplet specifies an array section according to a rectangular pattern. For example, in the following extract the last line specifies an array section that is a rank-one array consisting of the elements **x(3,2,1)**, **x(5,2,1)** and **x(7,2,1)**:

```
INTEGER, DIMENSION(9,4,10) :: x
...
x(3:7:2,2,1) = ...
```

- A vector subscript, on the other hand, can be used to define an array section extracted in an irregular manner from its parent array. For example, in the following extract the array **hold** will contain the values of **x(3,4,1)**, **x(2,4,1)**, **x(3,4,1)** and **x(1,4,1)**:

```
INTEGER, DIMENSION(5,4,10) :: x
INTEGER, DIMENSION(4) :: extract = (/3,2,3,1/)
INTEGER, DIMENSION(4) :: hold
...
hold = x(extract,4,1)
```

From the above discussion it is clear that a subscript triplet should be used whenever the extraction pattern can be expressed in a rectangular pattern, whereas a vector subscript should be used when the extraction pattern is irregular.

Self-test exercises 14.1 (page 491)

1   All of the intrinsic data types of Fortran are parameterized. In other words, they have associated with them subsidiary information that further specifies the data type. These parameters are called kind type parameters. In the case of integers, for example, the kind type parameter specifies the range of integers that a variable of that type of integer can store.

Kind type parameters are important because, in the case of numeric variables, they permit the portable specification of precision and range requirements. In the case of character variables they specify what character repertoires are to be used.

2   Explicit kind type parameters for variables are specified by adding kind type specifiers to the type declaration statements. For example:

```
REAL(KIND=SELECTED_REAL_KIND(P=6)) :: x
CHARACTER(KIND=3), DIMENSION(9) :: arr
```

3   Explicit kind type parameters for numeric and logical constants are specified by appending an underscore and the value of the kind type parameter to the constant; for character constants the value of the kind type parameter and an underscore precede the constant:

```
13.2E2_high
greek_"αβγ"
```

where **high** and **greek** are integer constants.

4   If no kind type parameter is explicitly specified for a **REAL** variable or constant a machine-dependent default value is assigned, and the type is said to be default **REAL**.

If no kind type parameter is explicitly specified for a **CHARACTER** variable or constant then a default value is assigned which is that for the ASCII character set on that particular computer, and the type is said to be default **CHARACTER**.

5   For **INTEGER** variables the intrinsic function **SELECTED_INT_KIND(R)** returns the kind type value, for the current computer, of a kind type that can represent all integers in the range $[-10^R, 10^R]$.

For **REAL** variables the intrinsic function **SELECTED_REAL_KIND(P,R)** returns the kind type value, for the current computer, of a real data type that can represent all numbers in the range $[-10^R, 10^R]$, with at least **P** decimal digits of accuracy. The second argument, **R**, is optional.

Kind type values are machine-dependent. Therefore, the above functions should be used to specify minimal accuracy and range requirements in a portable manner. For example, the declaration

```
REAL(KIND=SELECTED_REAL_KIND(P=12)) :: x
```

declares **x** to be a real variable with at least 12 decimal digits of precision.

6   If an impossible **INTEGER** range or **REAL** precision is requested the functions **SELECTED_INT_KIND** and **SELECTED_REAL_KIND** will return negative integer results. This will cause a compilation error if they are used to set the **KIND** value for an **INTEGER** or **REAL** variable or constant.

7   The kind type parameter of the expression is that of the **REAL** variable **x**. This is processor-dependent, since **x** is a default real. The constant **1234567_2** is, therefore, converted to a **REAL** value with a processor-dependent kind type before the addition is performed. This may, on some processors, result in a loss of precision.

Specifying that the integer is of kind type 2 may, therefore, in some circumstances, be irrelevant. Writing such expressions is poor programming practice.

8   Fortran specifies no meaning for the kind type parameter values for **LOGICAL** variables or constants. Therefore, each compiler is free to attach any meaning to them it wishes. Consequently, using other than default logical entities can only result in non-portable code, and their use should be avoided.

Self-test exercises 14.2 (page 502)

1   The Fortran standard states that a compiler must at least meet the specifications (if it can). A compiler is free, therefore, to satisfy precision and range requirements by exceeding them.

The underlying reality of the hardware for most computers is that only two precisions and exponent ranges are provided, and all precision and range requests are mapped onto those two choices in the best manner possible.

2   A **COMPLEX** variable or constant is stored as two consecutive **REAL** numbers, with the real part coming first.

3   In a similar manner to **REAL** variables, a **COMPLEX** variable may have its kind type explicitly declared, or may be allowed to default. The kind type parameter for the two **REAL** components of a **COMPLEX** variable is the same as the kind type parameter of the **COMPLEX** variable.

4
```
( 1.000, 2.000)  ( 3.000, 4.000) 5.000
( 4.000, 6.000)  ( -2.000, -2.000) ( 6.000, 2.000)
( -5.000, 10.000) ( 15.000, 20.000) ( 0.440, 0.080)
( 0.200, 0.400)  ( 1.000, -2.000) ( 1.000, 2.000)
```
The exact layout and number of decimal places printed will be processor-dependent.

5   The kind type of (**1.0,7.0_4**) is the kind type of the component with the greatest precision; if both components have the same precision the processor is free to choose the kind type of either component. Now the real part is a default **REAL** and, therefore, its kind type is processor-dependent. However, **7.0_4** is of kind type 4. The kind type parameter of the complex number is, therefore, processor-dependent, which could result in unpredictability in expressions involving this complex number.

Self-test exercises 15.1 (page 524)

1   You should normally always use the **BLANK** specifier when opening a file where blank characters in numeric fields need special attention. Only if the treatment of different records in the same file is to be different in this regard (an unlikely situation!) should you use the **BN** or **BZ** edit descriptors.

2   A **CLOSE** statement will disconnect a file which has been connected by means of an **OPEN** statement.
     Although files are automatically closed when a program's execution ends, a **CLOSE** statement is required if it is required to use the same unit for a different file later in the program or if it is required to specify that the closing status of the file be changed from the default.

3
1	000001	000001	000001	000001	1
2	000002	000010	000002	000002	2
4	000004	000100	000004	000004	4
8	000008	001000	000010	000008	8
16	000016	010000	000020	000010	16
32	000032	100000	000040	000020	32
64	000064	1000000	000100	000040	64

4
80000000.000	0.800E+08	80.000E+06	8.000E+07	0.800E+08
16000.000	0.160E+05	16.000E+03	1.600E+04	0.160E+05
3.200	0.320E+01	3.200E+00	3.200E+00	3.200
0.001	0.640E-03	640.000E-06	6.400E-04	0.640E-03
0.000	0.128E-06	128.000E-09	1.280E-07	0.128E-06

5   An advancing input statement (the default) always starts reading from the beginning of a new record. A non-advancing input statement will start reading the same record as was read by the last read statement, beginning immediately after the last character read, unless the previous read statement attempted to read beyond the end of the record, or the previous read statement gave rise to an error or end-of-file condition, or the file position has been changed, in which case it will start at the beginning of the next record.
     Non-advancing input should be used if it is necessary to read part of an input record before reading the rest of it – for example, if its content cannot be determined until the first item, or items, have been read. Otherwise, advancing input should normally be used.

6   An advancing output statement (the default) will always start writing a new record. A non-advancing output statement will write to the same record as the last output statement, beginning immediately after the last character written, unless the previous write gave rise to an error, in which case the writing will start at the beginning of a new record.
     Non-advancing output should be used if it is required to output a record in two, or more, stages. Otherwise, advancing output should normally be used.

Self-test exercises 15.2 (page 549)

1   A **RECL** specifier for a sequential file specifies the maximum length of a record in the file. A **RECL** specifier for a direct-access file specifies that all the records in the file will have the specified length. In both cases the length is measured in characters if the file is formatted, and in processor-defined units if it is unformatted.

2   Yes. As long as it is first closed and then re-opened for sequential access.

3   No. One of the reasons is that every record in a direct-access file must have the same length, whereas there is no guarantee that this is the case for a sequential file.

4   Direct-access input and output may not use list-directed formatting or namelist formatting, nor may it use non-advancing input or output.

5   A hash table is a table in which data is entered in a random order in such a way that it can be quickly found again. In its simplest form, an appropriate algorithm is used to convert the value to be stored into an integer key which lies in exactly the same range as the permissible subscripts of the table. This key is then used to identify the first place to look, and if this place is full (on entry) or contains the wrong value (on retrieval) then a further algorithm defines where to look next – for example in the next element of the array.

A hash table normally consists of several tables, implemented as a single rank-two array or as several related rank-one arrays, with one containing the identifying data (such as a name), and the others containing additional data that can be extracted from the table once the correct subscript has been found.

The major disadvantage of a hash table is that removing an item requires re-organization of the entire table.

6
```
One  One  One  One  One   One  One   One   One  One
One  Two  Three Four Five  Six  Seven Eight Nine Ten
```
The rather surprising result of the first **PRINT** statement is because each time the **READ** statement in the loop is obeyed it starts at the beginning of the internal file **line1**, even though that file contains 10 records. When the internal file is read by a single **READ** statement each element of **line2** requires a new record from the internal file, and so all ten words are correctly read.

7   The following program will provide the length of the record:
```
PROGRAM record_length_inquiry
   IMPLICIT NONE
   REAL :: p,q
   REAL, DIMENSION(7) :: x
   REAL(KIND=SELECTED_REAL_KIND(12,30)) :: y,z
   INTEGER :: record_length
   INQUIRE (IOLENGTH=record_length) p,q,x,y,z
   PRINT *,"The record length is ",record_length
END PROGRAM record_length_inquiry
```

Self-test exercises 16.1 (page 581)

1   A pointer is a variable that, instead of containing data itself, points to another variable where the data is stored.

A variable can only be pointed at if it has the **TARGET** attribute. This is to permit the compiler to generate efficient code.

2   A pointer can only be made to point to objects of the type specified in its type declaration statement that have the **TARGET** attribute.

3 • Undefined: this is the status when it is initially specified in a type declaration statement.
  • Associated: this is the status when a pointer is associated with a specific target.
  • Disassociated: this is the status when a pointer has been associated with a target and the association has subsequently been broken (by a **NULLIFY** statement).

4   A pointer assignment statement associates a pointer with a target. There are two forms:

(a)   Where the object on the right-hand side of the assignment statement is a variable with the **TARGET** attribute:

```
REAL, POINTER :: p
REAL, TARGET :: a
p => a
```

This associates the pointer **p** with the target **a**.

(b)   Where the object on the right-hand side of the assignment statement is a pointer, pointing to variables of the same type and attributes:

```
REAL, POINTER :: p,q
REAL, TARGET :: a,b
p => a
q => p
```

The second pointer assignment statement makes **q** point to **a** (not to **p**, because pointers cannot be pointed at).

5   The pointer association status of a pointer variable can be set to disassociated by use of the **NULLIFY** statement. For example, using the pointers of the preceding question, the statement

```
NULLIFY(p,q)
```

breaks the association of **p** with **a** and **q** with **a**.

6   The pointer association status of a pointer variable is determined by use of the intrinsic function **ASSOCIATED**, which returns *true* if the pointer supplied as its actual argument is associated with a target, and *false* if it is not. Note that the actual argument pointer association status must not be undefined.

7   When a pointer occurs in an expression where a value is expected, the value of the target the pointer is associated with is used. This is called dereferencing. For example, if the variables **p** and **a** are defined as

```
INTEGER, POINTER :: p
INTEGER, TARGET :: a = 1
p => a
```

then the following assignment statements all have the same effect:

```
a = a + 1
a = p + 1
p = a + 1
p = p + 1
```

Note that in the last two examples **p** is unaltered.

8   It is not possible to read or write a pointer. Consequently, a variable of a derived type that contains a pointer cannot occur in an input or output statement. Otherwise, a pointer in an input or output statement is dereferenced to its associated target.

9   The pointer **p** in the following example can point to any rank-three array of integers:

```
INTEGER, DIMENSION(:,:,:), POINTER :: p
INTEGER, DIMENSION(4,3,2), TARGET :: a
p => a
```

The pointer assignment statement associates **p** with the rank-three integer array **a**.

10   The space for the elements of an array pointer can be allocated and deallocated dynamically by means of the **ALLOCATE** and **DEALLOCATE** statements.

Self-test exercises 16.2 (page 599)

1   If a procedure has a pointer or target dummy arguments, then:
- The procedure must have an explicit interface in any program unit that references it.
- An actual argument corresponding to a pointer dummy argument must be a pointer with the same type, type parameters and rank.
- A pointer dummy argument cannot have the **INTENT** attribute.

2   To permit a function to return a pointer as its result the keyword **RESULT** must be used in defining the function and the result variable must be defined to be a pointer:

```
FUNCTION ours(a) RESULT(p)
  IMPLICIT NONE
  INTEGER, INTENT(IN) :: a
  REAL, DIMENSION(:), POINTER :: p
  ...
  p => ...
END FUNCTION ours
```

The interface to a pointer-valued function must be explicit in any program unit that references it.

3   A pointer can be a component of a derived type in the same way as any other type of entity:

```
TYPE other
  INTEGER :: i
  INTEGER, DIMENSION(:), POINTER :: point
  TYPE(other), POINTER :: node
END TYPE other
```

This derived type contains two pointers – one to a rank-one array of integers and the other to an object of the same derived type.

Derived types with pointer components are very useful for creating linked lists.

4   A linked list, in its simplest form, is a data structure in which each element of the structure consists of data and a pointer to the next element of the list.

5   The advantages of linked lists over arrays are:
- A linked list is superior for data structures in which the elements are added to the list in random order. It is easy to add an element to its position in the list by adjusting pointers – the element itself does not have to be moved (a considerable time saving if the element is large). It is also possible for elements to be shared between different linked lists without duplicating the element.
- The size of a linked list does not have to be predefined – elements can be added freely at any time during execution. Thus, space can be used efficiently.
- The elements of a linked list can be freely deleted during execution of a program, thus easily releasing space during program execution for use by other parts of the program.

6   A tree structure is a set of connected data elements (called nodes) in which each node of the list has at most one parent (node pointing to it) and only one node (the root) has no parent.

A more formal definition is that a tree is a finite set of nodes with a distinguished node, called the root, and where the non-root nodes are themselves disjoint (that is, having no elements in common) trees. The non-root nodes are called subtrees.

A binary tree is one in which each node has a maximum of two subtrees (or branches).

7   A list is preferable to a tree when each node has only one predecessor and one successor. For example, the children of one set of parents may be kept as a list in order of their ages.

A tree is preferable to a list when each node can have more than one successor node associated with it. For example, a family tree (note the common usage) showing the parental structure is best kept as a tree structure.

8   Recursion is useful in dealing with lists and trees because formal definitions of lists and trees are best done recursively. Using recursion to write programs involving lists and trees usually results in simpler programs because the structure of the algorithms now matches naturally the structure of the data.

Self-test exercises 17.1 (page 624)

1   A COMMON block is a means of enabling several program units to have access to the same area of memory, and hence to the variables stored in that area of memory. Note that it is only the memory area, or block, which is globally accessible — not the names of the individual variables stored there.

2   • A named COMMON block must be declared with the same length in every program unit that uses it (although most compilers do not enforce this restriction); blank COMMON may be declared with different lengths in different program units.
   • Named COMMON blocks may be initialized in a block data subprogram; blank COMMON may not be initialized.
   • Blank COMMON remains in existence throughout the execution of the program; named COMMON blocks may cease to exist unless they are explicitly given the save attribute (although most compilers preserve named COMMON blocks throughout execution).

3   COMMON blocks rely on a particular arrangement of variables within the memory, defined by the programmer, which may be sub-optimal on many modern computer architectures, especially those with multiple processors. Moreover, the fact that only the name of the COMMON block is global means that there is very great scope for errors as a result of different program units specifying the same block in different ways.

Modules provide a far more flexible, powerful, safer and usable alternative for global data access, and provide many additional features as well.

4   X(1) will cause an error if it is accessed because it corresponds to K(1) in the subroutine TEST4A, where it was assigned the integer value 1, and since this will not be a valid floating-point number any attempt to use the value of X(1) will cause an error.

Y(1,1) will also cause an error if accessed. In this case the array Y corresponds to the double precision array D, and so Y(1,1) corresponds to the first half of D(1), which will not take the correct form of a floating-point number, with the result that any attempt to use the value of Y(1,1) will cause an error.

$Z(1,1)$ has the value -3.0, since the first half of the array Z occupies the same space as the complex array Q, and $Z(1,1)$ therefore occupies the same space as the real part of $Q(1)$.

$M1(1)$ has the value 21, since the array $M1$ occupies the same space as the second half of $K2$ and the first five elements of $K3$. $M1(1)$, therefore, occupies the same memory location as $K2(11)$, which is also an integer.

$M1(15)$ is undefined from the information given, since it corresponds to $K3(5)$ which has not been given a value, and nor has $M1(15)$ itself.

$M2(1)$ and $M2(15)$ are both undefined from the information given, for the same reason as $M1(15)$.

5   The **EQUIVALENCE** statements result in the following mappings of the six character variables:

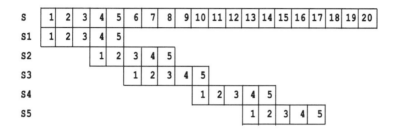

If the assignment statement

    `S = "My name is David"`

is applied to this diagram it will readily be seen that the result of the **PRINT** statement will be the message

    Madness

Self-test exercises 18.1 (page 685)

1   The bisection method has the advantage that it is guaranteed to converge to a root to within a specified tolerance. It has the disadvantages that it can only be started when an interval with a function sign change is known, and it converges relatively slowly because it only uses information about the sign of the function – not its magnitude.

Newton's method has the advantage that, when it converges, it converges rapidly. It has the disadvantages that it must be started close to a root to guarantee convergence (sometimes even this is insufficient) and that the derivative of the function must be calculated.

The secant method also has the advantages that, when it converges, it converges rapidly (but not as fast as Newton's method) and does not require derivatives to be evaluated. It has the same disadvantage as Newton's method, namely that convergence is not always guaranteed.

Consequently, the best root-finding algorithms use a blend of methods to achieve a guaranteed convergence that is faster than interval bisection.

2   Partial pivoting is the name giving to the process in Gaussian elimination in which the current pivot row is exchanged with the row having the largest element in absolute value in the column below the current pivot.

It is important to perform partial pivoting in order to have a stable algorithm.

3   The major difference between a cubic spline curve fit and one using a polynomial is that the cubic spline uses a set of cubic polynomial pieces (one for each data sub-interval), whereas a polynomial fit will involve one high-degree polynomial over the entire range of the data set.

The cubic spline will almost always produce a superior fit because high-degree (and we mean degree greater than 5) polynomials tend to oscillate badly between the points at which they interpolate the given data. A polynomial fit will be slightly faster to evaluate than a cubic spline fit. However, this is almost never a good reason to choose a polynomial fit over a spline fit.

4   Adaptive quadrature is a method of calculating the values of definite integrals. It does it by splitting the entire interval of integration up into sub-intervals using more (and smaller) sub-intervals where the function being integrated is varying most rapidly.

Caution is necessary in accepting the result of any numerical quadrature process because two different functions may have the same values at the points employed by the numerical quadrature process to estimate the numerical value of the definite integral.

Answers to selected programming exercises

Note that the programs shown in this section are only sample solutions. There are a large number of possible programs that could be written to solve almost any programming problem, and those that are shown here are our solutions. There is no such thing as a single 'best' solution, since different situations may attach different priorities to such factors as speed of execution, memory requirements, volume of comments in the code etc. However, if your solution should differ in any significant fashion from the sample solution shown here, you should very carefully examine the differences in order to establish why there is a difference and why, in all probability, our solution is, in some way, better than yours!

2.2   There are a total of 14 errors which will be detected by a compiler, and one probable error which will not be detected in this program, as follows:

line 1   A space, or blank, character is not allowed in a name in free source form — although one is allowed in the obsolete fixed source form.

A period is not allowed in a name.

line 3   There should be two colons in the declaration statement.

Although not an error, the indentation of this line, and the following two, is confusing.

line 4   The use of the ampersand to mean 'and' is treated as a continuation marker because it is the last non-blank character in the line; however, a comment line cannot be continued.

line 5   This line is a comment, but without an initial exclamation mark.

line 6   It is not permitted to have a trailing comment when a character context is being continued.

line 7   This line is a character context continuation and should therefore either end with a closing quotation mark or with another continuation marker — which is obviously what is missing here. In this case, the trailing comment is not allowed since a character context is being continued.

line 8   This line is intended to be a character context continuation and should therefore either end with a closing quotation mark or with another continuation marker; in this case a closing quotation mark is obviously what is missing.

line 10 The variable name, **number**, should not be enclosed in quotation marks.

line 11 The asterisk, and following comma, have been omitted from the **PRINT** statement.

line 12 This line is a character context continuation, and will therefore include a number of redundant blanks unless an ampersand is inserted just before the start of the text. Note that this is not a syntax error, but just bad programming – or an error of omission by the programmer which does not result in any formal error.

It would also be desirable to include a space after the character string to ensure that it is separated from the number following, regardless of the size of that number.

A comma has been omitted between the end of the character string and the variable name.

line 13 If a name is included on an **END** statement it must match the name on the **PROGRAM** statement. Furthermore, the word **PROGRAM** must follow **END** if a name is included.

The corrected program is as follows:

```
PROGRAM exercise_2_2
   IMPLICIT NONE
   REAL :: number
   ! This program used to contain a number of errors and
   ! is not a good example of Fortran 90 at all!
   PRINT *,"This &
           &is a silly &
           &program"
   PRINT *,"Type a number"
   READ *,number
   PRINT *,"Thank you.  &
           &Your number was ",number
END PROGRAM exercise_2_2
```

2.3 The four errors are as follows:

lines 2, 3 A comment line cannot be continued.

line 4 The character string should be enclosed between quotation marks or apostrophes.

line 5 There should be a comma after the asterisk.

lines 5, 6 One of the variables **numbr** and **number** has been mistyped. This error will not be detected by a compiler, as both variables will be implicitly declared to be integer variables.

The three other mistakes are as follows:

- *All* programs should include an **IMPLICIT NONE** statement immediately after the **PROGRAM** statement, in order to prevent any implicit declarations being allowed.
- *All* variables should be declared in a type declaration statement.
- Every **END** statement should include the name of the program.

If only those errors detected by the compiler are corrected the mistyping of one of the variable names will not be detected, and so the variable **number** will not have had any value assigned to it when its value is printed in line 6; this will probably result in an error, but may result in either zero, or some special value being printed – or possibly even a random value. The inclusion of an **IMPLICIT NONE** will prevent this type of error, since it will mean that the use of any variable names which have not been declared will be flagged as an error.

The corrected program is as follows:

```
PROGRAM test
   IMPLICIT NONE
```

```
      ! This program used to contain four major errors
      ! and three examples of bad programming style
      REAL :: number
      PRINT *,"Please type a number"
      READ *,number
      PRINT *,"The number you typed was ",number
END PROGRAM test
```

3.1   ```
PROGRAM exercise_3_1
      IMPLICIT NONE

      ! Variable declarations
      REAL :: x1,x2,x3,x4,x5,x6,x7,x8,x9,x10,sum

      PRINT *,"Please type ten numbers"
      READ *,x1,x2,x3,x4,x5,x6,x7,x8,x9,x10
      sum = x1+x2+x3+x4+x5+x6+x7+x8+x9+x10
      PRINT *,"The sum of these numbers is ",sum
END PROGRAM exercise_3_1
```

If you tried running your program with the set of numbers suggested you will almost certainly not get the correct answer of $-1.000\,01$, because the ninth data item $(3951.448\,99)$ cannot be stored to the necessary accuracy of nine significant figures — even though the result only requires six significant figures, which your computer should be capable of dealing with.

3.5     ```
PROGRAM exercise_3_5
      IMPLICIT NONE
      ! This program prints the internal representations of
      ! the characters which make up the Fortran Character Set

      ! Use the intrinsic function ICHAR to find the internal
      ! representation of each character
      PRINT *,"A ",ICHAR("A")
      PRINT *,"B ",ICHAR("B")
      .                              ! letters C-Y
      .
      .
      PRINT *,"Z ",ICHAR("Z")
      PRINT *,"0 ",ICHAR("0")
      .                       ! digits 1-9
      .                       ! special characters sp-?
      PRINT *."$ ",ICHAR("$")
END PROGRAM exercise_3_5
```

4.1   ```
SUBROUTINE distances(x1,y1,x2,y2,dist_orig_p1, &
                        dist_orig_p2,dist_p1_p2)
      IMPLICIT NONE
      ! This subroutine calculates the distances of two points
      ! from the origin and from each other

      ! Dummy arguments
      REAL, INTENT(IN) :: x1,y1,x2,y2
      REAL, INTENT(OUT) :: dist_orig_p1,dist_orig_p2, &
                        dist_p1_p2

      ! Calculate distances
      dist_orig_p1 = SQRT(x1**2 + y1**2)
      dist_orig_p2 = SQRT(x2**2 + y2**2)
      dist_p1_p2 = SQRT((x2-x1)**2 + (y2-y1)**2)
END SUBROUTINE distances
```
```

A suitable program to test this subroutine is:

```
PROGRAM exercise_4_1
   IMPLICIT NONE
   ! This program tests the subroutine distances

   ! Variable declarations
   REAL :: x1,y1,x2,y2,d1,d2,d1_2

   ! Get coordinates of points
   PRINT *,"Please type the coordinates of the first point"
   READ *,x1,y1
   PRINT *,"Now type the coordinates of the second point"
   READ *,x2,y2

   ! Calculate the required distances
   CALL distances(x1,y1,x2,y2,d1,d2,d1_2)

   ! Print calculated results for checking
   PRINT *,"The distance of the point (",x1,",",y1, &
           ") from the origin is ",d1
   PRINT *,"The distance of the point (",x2,",",y2, &
           ") from the origin is ",d2
   PRINT *,"The distance between the points is ",d1_2
END PROGRAM exercise_4_1
```

4.4
```
MODULE global_data
   IMPLICIT NONE
   INTEGER :: first,second,third,sum
END MODULE global_data

PROGRAM exercise_4_4
   USE global_data
   IMPLICIT NONE
   CALL input
   CALL calculate
   CALL output
END PROGRAM exercise_4_4

SUBROUTINE input
   USE global_data
   IMPLICIT NONE

   ! Read data into global variables
   PRINT *,"Please type three integers"
   READ *,first,second,third
END SUBROUTINE input

SUBROUTINE calculate
   USE global_data
   IMPLICIT NONE

   ! Calculate sum
   sum = first + second + third
END SUBROUTINE calculate

SUBROUTINE output
   USE global_data
   IMPLICIT NONE

   ! Print sum of input values
   PRINT *,"The sum of these three numbers is ", sum
END SUBROUTINE output
```

5.1 (a) Using a block **IF** construct:
```
PROGRAM exercise_5_1_a
   IMPLICIT NONE
   INTEGER :: number
```

```
            PRINT *,"Please type a negative, zero or positive &
                   &integer"
            READ *,number
            IF (number<0) THEN
               PRINT *,"The number you typed is negative"
            ELSE IF (number>0) THEN
               PRINT *,"The number you typed is positive"
            ELSE
               PRINT *,"The number you typed is zero"
            END IF
         END PROGRAM exercise_5_1_a
```

(b) Using a **CASE** construct:

```
         PROGRAM exercise_5_1_b
            IMPLICIT NONE
            INTEGER :: number

            PRINT *,"Please type a negative, zero or positive &
                   &integer"
            READ *,number
            SELECT CASE (number)
            CASE (:-1)
               PRINT *,"The number you typed is negative"
            CASE (1:)
               PRINT *,"The number you typed is positive"
            CASE DEFAULT
               PRINT *,"The number you typed is zero"
            END SELECT
         END PROGRAM exercise_5_1_b
```

5.10
```
      PROGRAM exercise_5_10
         IMPLICIT NONE
         ! This program calculates the nett cost for watch orders
         ! after applying a variable quantity discount

         ! Variable declarations
         INTEGER :: num_watches
         REAL :: gross_cost,discount_rate,discount,net_cost

         ! Input number of watches required
         PRINT *,"How many watches are required?"
         READ *,num_watches

         ! Calculate discount rate
         SELECT CASE (num_watches)
         CASE (300:)
            discount_rate = 0.3
         CASE (100:299)
            discount_rate = 0.25
         CASE (30:99)
            discount_rate = 0.2
         CASE (10:29)
            discount_rate = 0.15
         CASE (5:9)
            discount_rate = 0.1
         CASE (2:4)
            discount_rate = 0.05
         CASE DEFAULT
            discount_rate = 0.0
         END SELECT
```

```
                        ! Calculate and print gross cost, discount and net cost
                        gross_cost = 15*num_watches
                        discount = discount_rate*gross_cost
                        net_cost = gross_cost - discount
                        PRINT *,"The gross cost of ",num_watches,    &
                                " watches is $",gross_cost
                        PRINT *,"A discount of $",discount," applies"
                        PRINT *,"The net cost is $",net_cost
                      END PROGRAM exercise_5_10
```

6.4   ```
       PROGRAM exercise_6_4
         IMPLICIT NONE
         ! This program prints a table showing all the characters
         ! in the default character set

         ! Parameter to specify the number of characters in the
         ! default character set for the processor being used
         INTEGER, PARAMETER :: num_chars=128

         ! Variable declaration
         INTEGER :: i

         ! Print heading
         PRINT *,"The following table shows the character &
                 &representation of values from 0 to ",   &
                 num_chars-1

         ! Loop to print table
         DO i=0,num_chars-1
            PRINT *,i,CHAR(i)
         END DO
       END PROGRAM exercise_6_4
       ```

6.14   ```
       PROGRAM exercise_6_14
         IMPLICIT NONE
         ! This program calculates at what temperature a can of
         ! carbonated drink will explode

         ! Constant declaration
         REAL, PARAMETER :: explode_pressure=3.2

         ! Variable declarations
         INTEGER :: temp=15
         REAL :: pressure

         ! Loop to calculate pressure as temperature increases
         DO
            pressure = 0.00105*temp**2 + 0.0042*temp + 1.352
            PRINT *,"At ",temp," degrees C the pressure is ",   &
                    pressure," atm"
            temp = temp + 1
            IF (pressure >= explode_pressure) EXIT
         END DO

         ! Pressure has exceeded that required to explode the can
         PRINT *,"The can has exploded!!"
       END PROGRAM exercise_6_14
       ```

7.4   ```
       SUBROUTINE array_of_sines(angle,low,high)
         IMPLICIT NONE

         ! This subroutine calculates and prints the sines of
         ! the angles supplied as its argument

         ! Dummy arguments
         INTEGER, INTENT(IN) :: low,high
         REAL, DIMENSION(low:high), INTENT(IN) :: angle
       ```
       ```

```
   ! Local variables
   REAL, DIMENSION(low:high) :: sine    ! Automatic array
   INTEGER :: i

   ! Calculate sines
   sine = SIN(angle)

   ! Print table of sines
   DO i=low,high
      PRINT *,"sin(",angle(i),") = ",sine(i)
   END DO
END SUBROUTINE array_of_sines
```

Note that using an implied DO for the printing, such as

```
   PRINT *,(angle(i),sine(i),i=low,high)
```

would not be appropriate here, as it would not start a new line for each angle. We shall see how to deal with this in the next chapter.

A suitable test program might be as follows:

```
PROGRAM exercise_7_4
   IMPLICIT NONE

   ! This program tests the subroutine "array_of_sines"

   ! Declaration of array of angles
   REAL, PARAMETER :: pi=3.1415927
   INTEGER, PARAMETER :: low_bound=1, high_bound=12
   REAL, DIMENSION(low_bound,high_bound) :: angles = &
      (/ -pi/2.0, -pi/3.0, -pi/4.0, -pi/6.0, 0.0, pi/6.0, &
         pi/4.0, pi/3.0, pi/2.0, 2.0*pi/3.0, 5.0*pi/6.0, pi /)

   ! Calculate and print sines of angles
   CALL array_of_sines(angles,low_bound,high_bound)
END PROGRAM exercise_7_4
```

To use an assumed-shape array in the subroutine, the initial statement should be changed to

```
   SUBROUTINE array_of_sines(angle)
```

and the declarations of the two arrays to

```
   REAL, DIMENSION(:), INTENT(IN) :: angle
```

and

```
   REAL, DIMENSION(LBOUND(angle,1):UBOUND(angle,1)) :: sine
```

In addition, the DO statement will need to be changed to

```
   DO i=LBOUND(angle,1),UBOUND(angle,1)
```

If preferred, the values of the lower and upper bounds of the dummy argument array **angle** could be preserved in variables, such as **low** and **high**, and these can be used in the DO statement, as before.

The CALL statement in the main program will also need an appropriate alteration, of course.

```
7.12   INTEGER FUNCTION bin_to_dec(binary)
          IMPLICIT NONE

          ! This function converts a binary number to decimal
          ! The binary number is stored in an integer array

          ! Dummy argument
          INTEGER, DIMENSION(8), INTENT(IN) :: binary

          ! Local variables
          INTEGER :: i,temp
```

```
      ! Use a loop to accumulate the number in temp
      temp = 0
      DO i=1,8
         temp = 2*temp + binary(i)
      END DO
      bin_to_dec = temp
   END FUNCTION bin_to_dec

   FUNCTION dec_to_bin(number)
      IMPLICIT NONE

      ! This function converts a decimal number to binary,
      ! returning the result in an integer array

      ! Dummy argument and result variable
      INTEGER, INTENT(IN) :: number
      INTEGER, DIMENSION(8) :: dec_to_bin

      ! Local variables
      INTEGER :: i,temp

      ! Determine each bit by successively dividing the
      ! number by two and taking the remainder

      temp = number
      DO i=8,1,-1
         dec_to_bin(i) = MOD(temp,2)
         temp = temp/2
      END DO
   END FUNCTION dec_to_bin
```

Note that the function **dec_to_bin** does not check to see if the number is too big to be stored in 8 bits. This can easily be done by checking that the value of **temp** is zero on exit from the loop. Some means of indicating that an error has occurred must then be established.

Note also that, since the function **dec_to_bin** is array-valued, its interface must be explicit. Placing both functions in a module will ensure that this requirement is satisfied.

A suitable test program is as follows:

```
PROGRAM exercise_7_12
   USE binary_procedures
   IMPLICIT NONE

   ! This program tests the two functions "bin_to_dec"
   ! and "dec_to_bin" stored in the module binary_procedures

   ! Variable declarations
   CHARACTER(LEN=8) :: bin_num_1,bin_num_2,bin_num_3
   INTEGER, DIMENSION(8) :: bin1,bin2,bin3
   INTEGER :: sum,i

   ! Read two binary numbers
   PRINT *,"Please type two binary numbers in the range &
           &00000000 to 11111111"
   PRINT *,"separated by a space or a comma"
   READ *,bin_num_1,bin_num_2

   ! Convert them to integer arrays
   DO i=1,8
      IF (bin_num_1(i:i)=="1") THEN
         bin1(i) = 1
      ELSE
         bin1(i) = 0
      END IF
```

```
           IF (bin_num_2(i:i)=="1") THEN
              bin2(i) = 1
           ELSE
              bin2(i) = 0
           END IF
        END DO

        ! Add them together
        sum = bin_to_dec(bin1) + bin_to_dec(bin2)

        ! Convert result back to binary
        bin3 = dec_to_bin(sum)

        ! Convert binary sum to characters and print it
        DO i=1,8
           IF (bin3(i)==1) THEN
              bin_num_3(i:i) = "1"
           ELSE
              bin_num_3(i:i) = "0"
           END IF
        END DO
        PRINT *,"The sum of ",bin_num_1," and ",bin_num_2,  &
                " is ",bin_num_3
     END PROGRAM exercise_7_12
```

8.6   PROGRAM exercise_8_6
```
        IMPLICIT NONE

        ! This program is an exercise in output formatting

        ! Variable declaration
        INTEGER, DIMENSION(12) :: number =          &
           (/ 12345,23456,34567,45678,56789,67890,  &
              78901,89012,90123,10123,10234,10345 /)

        ! Print the array in three ways
        PRINT '(I6)',number              ! One number per line
        PRINT '(3I6)',number             ! Three numbers per line
        PRINT '(12I6)',number            ! Twelve numbers per line
     END PROGRAM exercise_8_6
```

The second part of this question requires some lateral thinking! In Section 8.2 we stated that one of the forms of the **READ** statement was

     READ *ch_var,input_list*

where *ch_var* is a character constant, character variable, character array, character array element or other character expression. In all the examples we have shown it has been a character expression, but this is a situation where a character variable is appropriate, as shown in the following modified version of the above program:

```
     PROGRAM exercise_8_6a
        IMPLICIT NONE

        ! This program is an exercise in output formatting

        ! Variable declarations
        INTEGER, DIMENSION(12) :: number =          &
           (/ 12345,23456,34567,45678,56789,67890,  &
              78901,89012,90123,10123,10234,10345 /)
        CHARACTER(LEN=6) :: output_format
        INTEGER :: numbers_per_line
```

```
         ! Ask how many numbers per line
         PRINT *,"How many numbers do you require to be &
              &printed per line?"

         ! Use a DO loop and a CASE structure to select the
         ! appropriate format and to keep repeating the query
         ! until a valid response is typed
         DO
            PRINT *,"Type 1, 3 or 12"
            READ *,numbers_per_line
            SELECT CASE (numbers_per_line)
            CASE (1)
               output_format = "(I6)"
               EXIT
            CASE (3)
               output_format = "(3I6)"
               EXIT
            CASE (12)
               output_format = "(12I6)"
               EXIT
            END SELECT
         END DO

         ! Print the array in the requested way
         PRINT output_format,number
      END PROGRAM exercise_8_6a


8.13   MODULE geology
          IMPLICIT NONE
          TYPE seismic_data
             INTEGER :: degrees_long,minutes_long
             CHARACTER :: ew_long
             INTEGER :: degrees_lat,minutes_lat
             CHARACTER :: ew_lat
             REAL :: richter_strength
          END TYPE seismic_data
       END MODULE geology

       PROGRAM exercise_8_13
          USE geology
          IMPLICIT NONE

          ! This program records and lists seismic measurements

          ! Variable and constant declarations
          INTEGER, PARAMETER :: max_centres = 100
          TYPE(seismic_data), DIMENSION(max_centres) :: &
             earthquake_data
          TYPE(seismic_data) :: centre
          CHARACTER(LEN=30) :: epicentre
          INTEGER :: i,count

          ! Read data
          PRINT *,"Where was the earthquake?"
          READ *,epicentre
          PRINT *,"Please type longtitude, latitude and Richter &
                 &scale reading for each seismic centre"
          PRINT *,"Data should be terminated by a line of five zeros"
          DO count=1,max_centres
             READ *,centre%degrees_long,centre%minutes_long, &
                    centre%degrees_lat,centre%minutes_lat,   &
                    centre%richter_strength
```

```
            ! Check for end of data
            IF (centre%degrees_long==0 .AND.   &
                centre%minutes_long==0 .AND.   &
                centre%degrees_lat==0  .AND.   &
                centre%minutes_lat==0  .AND.   &
                centre%richter_strength==0.0) EXIT

            ! Set E/W as appropriate for longtitude and latitude
            IF (centre%degrees_long<0) THEN
              centre%degrees_long = -centre%degrees_long
              centre%ew_long = "W"
            ELSE
              centre%ew_long = "E"
            END IF
            IF (centre%degrees_lat>0) THEN
              centre%degrees_lat = -centre%degrees_lat
              centre%ew_lat = "W"
            ELSE
              centre%ew_lat = "E"
            END IF
            earthquake_data(count) = centre
        END DO

        ! Adjust count for terminating record
        count = count-1

        ! Print table of measurements
        PRINT '("Seismic measurements recorded after ",A,     &
                " earthquake"//                                &
                T6,"Recording Station",T33,"Richter"/          &
                T6,"Longtitude",T20,"Latitude",                &
                T33,"Strength"//)',TRIM(epicentre)
        DO i=1,count
            PRINT '(T6,I2,"O",I2,"''",A2,T20,I3,"O",I2,"''",    &
                    A2,T33,F6.2)', earthquake_data(i)
        END DO
    END PROGRAM exercise_8_13
```

Note that the above program does not check that the number of sets of data is less than or equal to the maximum number of centres specified by the constant **max_centres**. This is easily done by checking the value of the DO variable on exit from the input loop.

Also note that the statement that prints the seismic measurements contains the character º to signify degrees, which is not in the Fortran character set but is available on most computers as part of the default character set, and is thus acceptable in a character string. Furthermore, the character ' to signify minutes has been doubled because of the apostrophe delimiters surrounding the embedded format.

9.2
```
    PROGRAM exercise_9_2
        IMPLICIT NONE

        ! This program copies data in a file in reverse order

        ! Variable declarations
        CHARACTER(LEN=20) :: infile,outfile
        INTEGER, DIMENSION(10) :: number
        INTEGER :: ios,i

        ! Get names of files
        PRINT *,"What is the name of the input file?"
        READ *,infile
        PRINT *,"What is the name of the output file?"
        READ *,outfile
```

```
! Open files
OPEN (UNIT=7,FILE=infile,STATUS="OLD",IOSTAT=ios)
IF (ios/=0) THEN
   PRINT '("Error number ",I3," during opening of ",  &
           A)',ios,infile
   STOP
END IF
OPEN (UNIT=8,FILE=outfile,STATUS="NEW",IOSTAT=ios)
IF (ios/=0) THEN
   PRINT '("Error number ",I3," during opening of ",  &
           A)',ios,outfile
   STOP
END IF

! Read numbers from input file
DO i=1,10
   READ (UNIT=7,FMT=*,IOSTAT=ios) number(i)
   IF (ios/=0) THEN
      PRINT '("Error number ",I3," while reading &
              &record ",I2," of ",A)',ios,i,infile
      STOP
   END IF
END DO

! Write numbers to output file in reverse order
DO i=1,10
   WRITE (UNIT=8,FMT=*,IOSTAT=ios) number(11-i)
   IF (ios/=0) THEN
      PRINT '("Error number ",I3," while writing &
              &record ",I2," of ",A)',ios,i,outfile
      STOP
   END IF
END DO

! Write end-of-file record after last record
ENDFILE (UNIT=8,IOSTAT=ios)
IF (ios/=0) THEN
   PRINT '("Error number ",I3," while writing &
           &end-of-file record to ",A)',ios,outfile
END IF
END PROGRAM exercise_9_2
```

9.10   ```
PROGRAM exercise_9_10
   IMPLICIT NONE

   ! This program searches a file for a specified name

   ! Variable declarations
   CHARACTER(LEN=20) :: data_file,first_name,last_name, &
                        area_code,phone_number,first,last
   CHARACTER(LEN=5) :: search_type
   INTEGER :: ios
   LOGICAL :: found

   ! Get file name
   PRINT *,"Please type the name of the data file"
   READ *,data_file
   ! Open data file
   OPEN (UNIT=7,FILE=data_file,STATUS="OLD",IOSTAT=ios)
   IF (ios/=0) THEN
      PRINT '("Error number ",I3," during opening of ", &
              A)',ios,data_file
      STOP
   END IF
```
```

```
PRINT *,"Type first and last names of each person     &
        &whose telephone number is required"
PRINT *,"If all people with a given last name are     &
        &required, type * for first name"
PRINT *,"If all people with a given first name are    &
        &required, type * for last name"
PRINT *,"If no more numbers are required, type two    &
        &asterisks separated by a space"

! Loop to get names
DO
   READ *,first,last
   IF (first=="*" .AND. last=="*") EXIT
   IF (first=="*") THEN
      search_type = "LAST"
   ELSE IF (last=="*") THEN
      search_type = "FIRST"
   ELSE
      search_type = "BOTH"
   END IF

   ! Search for name in file
   REWIND (UNIT=7,IOSTAT=ios)
   IF (ios/=0) THEN
      PRINT '("Error number ",I3," during rewinding  &
            &of ",A)',ios,data_file
      STOP
   END IF

   ! Set flag for recording if a match was found
   found = .FALSE.

   DO
      READ (UNIT=7,FMT=*,IOSTAT=ios)                  &
         first_name,last_name,area_code,phone_number
      IF (ios<0) THEN
         ! End-of-file
         EXIT
      ELSE IF (ios>0)
         PRINT '("Error number ",I3," during reading &
               &from ",A)',ios,data_file
         STOP
      END IF

      ! Check if this is the required record
      SELECT CASE (search_type)
      CASE ("LAST")
         IF (last_name==last) THEN
            PRINT '(A,1X,A,3X,A,1X,A)',first_name,  &
               last_name,area_code,phone_number
            found = .TRUE.
         END IF
      CASE ("FIRST")
         IF (first_name==first) THEN
            PRINT '(A,1X,A,3X,A,1X,A)',first_name,  &
               last_name,area_code,phone_number
            found = .TRUE.
         END IF
      CASE DEFAULT
         IF (first_name==first .AND.                &
            last_name==last) THEN
```

```
                   PRINT '(A,1X,A,3X,A,1X,A)',first_name,  &
                         last_name,area_code,phone_number
                   found = .TRUE.
               END IF
           END SELECT
       END DO

       ! All records searched - check if a match was found
       IF (.NOT.found) PRINT *,"No match found!"
   END DO
END PROGRAM exercise_9_10
```

10.3   The major difficulty in this problem is that the answer will be very large – too large even for many computers to represent as a floating-point number in any of the hardware representations available (it is actually around 8×10^{374}). However, by using logs we need never use the number itself, although we shall retain more precision than is provided by default **REAL** numbers by specifying a precision of at least 12 digits.

```
PROGRAM exercise_10_3
   IMPLICIT NONE

   ! This program calculates factorial 200

   ! Variable and constant declarations
   INTEGER, PARAMETER :: kind12 = SELECTED_REAL_KIND(P=12)
   REAL(KIND=kind12) :: log_factorial,mantissa,stirling, &
                        log_stirling
   INTEGER :: exponent,i

   ! Loop to calculate 200! by adding logarithms
   log_factorial = 0.0
   DO i=1,200
      log_factorial = log_factorial + LOG10(REAL(i,kind12))
   END DO

   ! Obtain exponent and mantissa from logarithm and print
   exponent = INT(log_factorial)
   mantissa = FRACTION(log_factorial)
   PRINT *,"200! is ",mantissa," times 10 to the power &
           &of ",exponent

   ! Now calculate it using Stirling's approximation
   twopi=2.0_kind12*ATAN(1.0_kind12)
   stirling = 200.5_kind12*LOG(200.0_kind12) -   &
              200.0_kind12 + 0.5_kind12*LOG(twopi)

   ! Convert from log to base e to log to base 10
   log_stirling = stirling/LOG(10.0_kind12)

   ! Obtain exponent and mantissa from logarithm and print
   exponent = INT(log_stirling)
   mantissa = FRACTION(log_stirling)
   PRINT *,"Stirling's formula for 200! gives ",mantissa, &
           " times 10 to the power of ",exponent
END PROGRAM exercise_10_3
```

10.5   **(a)**   All three roots lie in the specified range, at $x = -3.0$, $x = 1.5$ and $x = 1.6$. If your initial tabulation did not give changes of sign between, for example, $x = 1$ and $x = 2$ then you should have noticed that the values of x were falling as x increased from 0 to 1, but increasing as it increased from 2 to 3, indicating a minimum somewhere in this area.

(b)   The three roots are at $x = -0.5$, $x = 1.5$ and $x = 1.6$.

(c)   The three roots are at $x = -4.0$, $x = 0.2$ and $x = 4.0$.

(d) The four roots are at $x = -4.0$, $x = -1.5$, $x = 0.2$ and $x = 4.0$.

(e) The four roots are at $x = -4.0$ (twice) and $x = 3.0$ (twice). Your program probably did not find these, because the value of the polynomial *never* falls below zero. However, examination of the tabulation should have indicated what was happening (that there were two minimums) and more detailed tabulation should have solved the equation.

(f) There are only two roots in the specified range, both at $x = 2.333\,33$. If your program did not find them, see the comments in (e) above.

Note that, in Example 10.2, we stated that if $f(x\_mid) = 0$ then we should not immediately accept this as a root because we should not mix convergence criteria. This was to keep the algorithm as simple, mathematically, as possible, and because, for almost all real problems, such a situation will not occur. However, for artificial cases, such as finding a root of the equation $x - 1 = 0$ in the interval $[0, 2]$, this situation can occur, and the algorithm will not function correctly. Can you see what the problem is, and how to fix it?

```
11.1   CHARACTER FUNCTION next_char()
         IMPLICIT NONE

         ! This function returns the next character from a
         ! buffer, refilling the buffer from the keyboard
         ! when necessary

         ! Local variables
         CHARACTER(LEN=80), SAVE :: buffer=" "
         INTEGER, SAVE :: len,chars_left = 0
         INTEGER :: char_pos

         ! Test to see if any characters left
         IF (chars_left==0) THEN
            ! No characters left - refill buffer
            PRINT *,"? "
            READ (UNIT=*,FMT='(A)') buffer

            ! Set len to length without any trailing blanks
            len = LEN_TRIM(buffer)
            chars_left = len
         END IF

         ! Return next character in buffer
         char_pos = len-chars_left+1
         next_char = buffer(char_pos:char_pos)
         chars_left = chars_left-1
       END FUNCTION next_char
```

Note that, because both **buffer** and **chars_left** are initialized as part of their declaration, they have the save attribute; nevertheless, the situation is clearer to the reader if this is also explicitly stated in the relevant declaration statements.

A suitable test program is as follows:

```
PROGRAM exercise_11_1
   IMPLICIT NONE

   ! This program uses the function next_char to read
   ! a character string from the keyboard

   ! Function declaration
   CHARACTER, EXTERNAL :: next_char

   ! Variable declarations
   CHARACTER(LEN=500) :: message
   INTEGER :: i,pos=1
```

```
        PRINT *,"Please type a sentence of no more than 500 &
                &characters terminated by a period."
        PRINT *,"Type one line at a time when prompted by a ?"

        ! Loop to read the sentence
        DO
           message(pos:pos) = next_char()

           ! Check if this was the terminating character
           IF (message(pos:pos)==".") EXIT
           pos = pos + 1
        END DO

        ! Print message
        PRINT '("The sentence you typed was:"/(A60))', &
           (message(i:MIN(i+60,pos)),i=1,pos,60)
     END PROGRAM exercise_11_1
```

Note the use of an implied DO in the PRINT statement to print the message in lines of 60 characters, and the use of the MIN intrinsic function in the subscript expression to prevent any elements of the buffer which have not had data read into them being printed.

11.10 The first encoded message can be decoded by the program written for Exercise 11.5, and reads as follows, after removing the trailing filler characters at the very end:

> modify the program that you wrote for exercise eleven point five so that instead of using the keyword for encoding and decoding each block it is used only for the first block semicolon thereafter the previous coded block is used to encode or decode the next one stop

The second encoded message can only be decoded with this modified program!

```
12.4    MODULE complex_arithmetic
        IMPLICIT NONE
        PRIVATE
        PUBLIC complex_number,OPERATOR(+),OPERATOR(-), &
               OPERATOR(*),OPERATOR(/)

        ! This module defines a complex number derived type and
        ! extends the four intrinsic operators +, -, * and / to
        ! have complex operands

        TYPE complex_number
           REAL :: real_part,imag_part
        END TYPE complex_number

        INTERFACE OPERATOR(+)
           MODULE PROCEDURE c_add
        END INTERFACE

        INTERFACE OPERATOR(-)
           MODULE PROCEDURE c_sub
        END INTERFACE

        INTERFACE OPERATOR(*)
           MODULE PROCEDURE c_mult
        END INTERFACE

        INTERFACE OPERATOR(/)
           MODULE PROCEDURE c_div
        END INTERFACE

     CONTAINS
```

```
FUNCTION c_add(z1,z2)

   ! Function result and dummy arguments
   TYPE(complex_number) :: c_add
   TYPE(complex_number), INTENT(IN) :: z1,z2

   ! Calculate function result
   c_add%real_part = z1%real_part + z2%real_part
   c_add%imag_part = z1%imag_part + z2%imag_part
END FUNCTION c_add

FUNCTION c_sub(z1,z2)

   ! Function result and dummy arguments
   TYPE(complex_number) :: c_sub
   TYPE(complex_number), INTENT(IN) :: z1,z2

   ! Calculate function result
   c_sub%real_part = z1%real_part - z2%real_part
   c_sub%imag_part = z1%imag_part - z2%imag_part
END FUNCTION c_sub

FUNCTION c_mult(z1,z2)

   ! Function result and dummy arguments
   TYPE(complex_number) :: c_mult
   TYPE(complex_number), INTENT(IN) :: z1,z2

   ! Calculate function result
   c_mult%real_part = z1%real_part*z2%real_part - &
                      z1%imag_part*z2%imag_part
   c_mult%imag_part = z1%real_part*z2%imag_part + &
                      z1%imag_part*z2%real_part

END FUNCTION c_mult

FUNCTION c_div(z1,z2)

   ! Function result and dummy arguments
   TYPE(complex_number) :: c_div
   TYPE(complex_number), INTENT(IN) :: z1,z2

   ! Local variable to save calculating denominator twice
   REAL :: denom

   ! Calculate function result
   denom = z2%real_part**2 + z2%imag_part**2
   c_div%real_part = (z1%real_part*z2%real_part + &
                      z1%imag_part*z2%imag_part)/denom
   c_div%imag_part = (z2%real_part*z1%imag_part - &
                      z1%real_part*z2%imag_part)/denom
END FUNCTION c_div

END MODULE complex_arithmetic
```

Note that the components of the derived type **complex_number** have not been made private. Ideally, they should be private, but that would require additional procedures to create a complex number from the values of the real and imaginary parts, and to extract these two values from a complex number. Give yourself a bonus mark if you did this! (Deduct several marks, however, if you made the components private without providing the means to access the components, for example, for input and output!)

12.6 If it is not already there, add the following type definition to the module:

```
TYPE circle
   TYPE(point) :: centre
   REAL :: radius
END TYPE circle
```

Add the following interface blocks to the specification part of the module:

```
INTERFACE OPERATOR(.centre.)
    MODULE PROCEDURE centre_of_circle
END INTERFACE

INTERFACE OPERATOR(.intersects.)
    MODULE PROCEDURE point_two_lines
END INTERFACE
```

and add the corresponding procedures to the procedures part of the module:

```
FUNCTION centre_of_circle(cir)

    ! This function returns the point at the centre of
    ! the circle supplied as an argument

    ! Function result and dummy argument
    TYPE(point) :: centre_of_circle
    TYPE(circle), INTENT(IN) :: cir

    centre_of_circle = cir%centre
END FUNCTION centre_of_circle

FUNCTION point_two_lines(line1,line2)

    ! This function returns the point of intersection of
    ! two lines supplied as arguments. If the lines are
    ! parallel the x and y coordinates of the result are
    ! set to HUGE(0.0) and -HUGE(0.0), respectively

    ! Function result and dummy arguments
    TYPE(point) :: point_two_lines
    TYPE(line), INTENT(IN) :: line1,line2

    ! Local constant and variable
    REAL, PARAMETER :: epsilon=1E-6
    REAL :: denom
    denom = line1%a*line2%b - line2%a*line1%b

    ! If denom is zero lines are parallel
    IF (ABS(denom)<epsilon) THEN
        ! Lines are parallel - return special values
        point_two_lines%x = HUGE(0.0)
        point_two_lines%y = -HUGE(0.0)

    ELSE
        ! Lines intersect - return point of intersection
        point_two_lines%x = &
                (line1%b*line2%c - line2%b*line1%c)/denom
        point_two_lines%y = &
                (line1%c*line2%a - line2%c*line1%a)/denom
    END IF
END FUNCTION point_two_lines
```

13.1
```
PROGRAM exercise_13_1
    IMPLICIT NONE

    ! This program is an exercise in array manipulation

    ! Declarations and initialization of array
    INTEGER :: i,j
    INTEGER, DIMENSION(4,5) :: array = &
        RESHAPE ((/ ((10*i+j, i=1,4),j=1,5) /),(/ 4,5 /))

    ! Print the array in a rectangular pattern
    PRINT '(4I6)',array
END PROGRAM exercise_13_1
```

In the above program the values are placed in the array by means of an array constructor and the **RESHAPE** function, and the rectangular nature of the data represented in the output by using a format which prints four numbers per line. In order to print the array rotated through 90° it is necessary to replace the **PRINT** statement by the following statement, in which the implied **DO** alters the order in which the array elements are printed:

```
PRINT '(5I6)',((array(i,j), j=1,5),i=1,4)
```

13.7
```
FUNCTION reverse(array)
    IMPLICIT NONE

    ! This function reverses the order of the elements of
    ! the array supplied as the argument

    ! Function type and dummy argument
    INTEGER, DIMENSION(SIZE(array)) :: reverse
    INTEGER, DIMENSION(:), INTENT(IN) :: array

    ! Automatic (vector subscript) array
    INTEGER :: i
    INTEGER, DIMENSION(SIZE(array)) :: v_sub

    ! Create the vector subscript
    DO i=1,SIZE(array)
        v_sub(i) = SIZE(array)-i+1
    END DO

    ! Copy array elements in reverse order by using v_sub
    ! as a vector subscript
    reverse = array(v_sub)
END FUNCTION reverse
```

The following program uses the above function to reverse the elements of one row of a rank-two array:

```
PROGRAM exercise_13_7
    USE reverse_fun    ! Needs explicit interface
    IMPLICIT NONE

    ! This program tests the function reverse

    ! Declarations
    INTEGER :: i,j,row
    INTEGER, DIMENSION(6,7) :: array = &
        RESHAPE ((/ ((10*i+j, i=1,6),j=1,7) /),(/ 6,7 /))

    ! Ask which row to reverse
    PRINT *,"Which row is to be reversed (in range 1-7)?"
    READ *,row

    ! Deal with invalid replies
    SELECT CASE (row)
    CASE (:0)
        row = 1
        PRINT *,"Out of range - row 1 will be reversed"
    CASE (8:)
        row = 7
        PRINT *,"Out of range - row 7 will be reversed"
    END SELECT

    ! Use function to reverse the appropriate array section
    array(row,:) = reverse(array(row,:))

    ! Print the array in a rectangular pattern
    PRINT '(7I6)',((array(i,j),j=1,7),i=1,6)
END PROGRAM exercise_13_7
```

Note that the function **reverse** must have an explicit interface because it is array-valued. The above program assumes that it has been placed in a module, **reverse_fun**, in order to make its interface explicit.

14.3
```
PROGRAM exercise_14_3
   IMPLICIT NONE

   ! This program calculates 1/n!

   ! Declarations
   REAL, PARAMETER :: one=1.0
   REAL :: n=one, reciprocal_factorial=one

   ! Loop until 1/n! is indistinguishable from zero
   DO
      n = n+one
      reciprocal_factorial = reciprocal_factorial/n
      PRINT *,n,reciprocal_factorial
      IF (reciprocal_factorial==0) EXIT
   END DO

   PRINT *,"The value of 1/n! was indistinguishable from &
            &zero when n = ",n
END PROGRAM exercise_14_3
```

Note that this program deliberately does something that has always been warned against, namely comparing two real values. In this case, however, that is the whole point of the program!

The program should now be altered so that the two declaration statements include a **KIND** parameter, for example:
```
REAL(KIND=4), PARAMETER :: one=1.0_4
REAL(KIND=4) :: n=one, reciprocal_factorial=one
```

The program should be run with each value for real kinds that is supported by your processor.

This will show you which kind value corresponds to default real and that different kind values will give a result indistinguishable from zero at different values of n, because of the different degrees of precision being used.

14.7   Fortran 90 contains all the facilities to carry out the specified calculations, either as operators or as intrinsic functions. It is not necessary to write any of these yourself:
```
PROGRAM exercise_14_7
   IMPLICIT NONE

   ! This program is an exercise in complex arithmetic

   ! Declarations
   COMPLEX :: w,z,q

   ! Get numbers
   PRINT *,"Please type two complex numbers as pairs of &
            &real numbers,"
   PRINT *,"representing the real and imaginary parts"
   READ *,w,z

   ! Calculate and print the required functions
   q = w+z
   PRINT *,"w+z = (",REAL(q),",",AIMAG(q),")"

   q = CONJG(z)
   PRINT *,"z(bar) = (",REAL(q),",",AIMAG(q),")"

   q = CONJG(w)
   PRINT *,"w(bar) = (",REAL(q),",",AIMAG(q),")"
```

```fortran
      q = z**2
      PRINT *,"z**2 = (",REAL(q),",",AIMAG(q),")"

      q = z*CONJG(z)
      PRINT *,"z*z(bar) = (",REAL(q),",",AIMAG(q),")"

END PROGRAM exercise_14_7
```

15.4   PROGRAM exercise_15_4
```fortran
      IMPLICIT NONE

      ! This program is an exercise in using INQUIRE

      ! Declarations
      CHARACTER, DIMENSION(26) :: alphabet = &
         (/ "A","B","C","D","E","F","G","H","I","J","K", &
            "L","M","N","O","P","Q","R","S","T","U","V", &
            "W","X","Y","Z" /)
      CHARACTER(LEN=20) :: filename
      INTEGER :: ios,i
      LOGICAL :: file_exists

      ! Ask for name of file
      PRINT *,"What is the name for the output file?"
      DO
         READ '(A)',filename
         ! Check to see if file already exists
         INQUIRE(FILE=filename,EXIST=file_exists)
         IF (.NOT.file_exists) EXIT

         ! File exists already - ask for another
         PRINT '("The file ",A," already exists. Please &
                 &give another name for the output file")', &
                 filename
      END DO

      ! Open the file
      OPEN (UNIT=7,FILE=filename,STATUS="NEW",IOSTAT=ios)
      IF (ios/=0) THEN
         PRINT '("Error ",I5," while opening ",A)', filename
         STOP
      END IF

      ! Write alphabet array to file
      WRITE (UNIT=7,FMT='(A)',IOSTAT=ios) (alphabet(i),i=1,26)
      IF (ios/=0) THEN
         PRINT '("Error ",I5," while writing to ",A)', filename
      END IF
END PROGRAM exercise_15_4
```

15.5   PROGRAM exercise_15_5
```fortran
      IMPLICIT NONE

      ! This program is an exercise in using an internal file

      ! Declarations
      REAL, DIMENSION(5,4) :: matrix
      REAL, DIMENSION(4) :: mean
      CHARACTER(LEN=50) :: record
      CHARACTER(LEN=20) :: filename
      INTEGER :: ios,i,j

      ! Get name of file
      PRINT *,"What is the name of the file?"
      READ '(A)',filename
```

```
      ! Open file
      OPEN (UNIT=7,FILE=filename,STATUS="OLD",IOSTAT=ios)
      IF (ios/=0) THEN
         PRINT '("Error ",I5," while opening ",A)', filename
         STOP
      END IF

      ! Read each record in turn from the file
      DO i=1,5
         READ (UNIT=7,FMT='(A50)',IOSTAT=ios) record
         IF (ios/=0) THEN
            PRINT '("Error ",I5," while reading ",A)', filename
            STOP
         END IF
         ! Now read the record as an internal file
         READ (UNIT=record,FMT=*) (matrix(i,j),j=1,4)
      END DO

      ! Calculate and print the mean of each column
      mean = SUM(matrix,1)/5.0
      PRINT *,"The means of the four columns are: ",mean
   END PROGRAM exercise_15_5
```

Note the use of the intrinsic function **SUM** to create an array containing the sums of the four columns of the matrix. Since a scalar is conformable with any array, the result of the reference to **SUM** can be divided by 5.0, with the resulting array of means being stored in **mean**. Alternatively, the expression **SUM(matrix,1)/5.0** could have appeared in the output list of the following **PRINT** statement, thus avoiding the need to save the means.

16.2   ```
PROGRAM exercise_16_2
   IMPLICIT NONE

   ! This program is an exercise in using an array of
   ! pointers

   ! Declarations
   REAL :: max_abs=0,min_abs=HUGE(0.0),total=0.0,mean
   INTEGER :: n,i,alloc_err
   TYPE real_ptr   ! This type will be used
      REAL, POINTER :: ptr   ! to simulate an array
   END TYPE real_ptr   ! of pointers to reals
   TYPE(real_ptr), DIMENSION(:), ALLOCATABLE :: x

   ! Get number of numbers
   PRINT *,"How many numbers are there? (between 5 and 20)"
   DO
      READ *,n
      IF (5<=n .AND. n<=20) EXIT
      PRINT *,"Between 5 and 20 please. Try again!"
   END DO

   ! Create an array of pointers
   ALLOCATE(x(n),STAT=alloc_err)
   IF (alloc_err/=0) THEN
      PRINT *,"Allocation error ",alloc_err," when trying &
              &to allocate space for array of pointers"
      STOP
   END IF
```
```

```
! Create n real variables and read numbers into them
DO i=1,n
   ALLOCATE(x(i)%ptr,STAT=alloc_err)
   IF (alloc_err/=0) THEN
      PRINT *,"Allocation error ",alloc_err," when &
              &trying to allocate space for variable ",i
      STOP
   END IF

   PRINT *,"Next number: "
   READ *,x(i)%ptr

   ! Update total, max_abs and min_abs
   total = total + x(i)%ptr
   IF (ABS(x(i)%ptr) > max_abs) max_abs = ABS(x(i)%ptr)
   IF (ABS(x(i)%ptr) < min_abs) min_abs = ABS(x(i)%ptr)
END DO

! Calculate mean
mean = total/n

! Print results
PRINT *,"Largest absolute value is ",max_abs
PRINT *,"Smallest absolute value is ",min_abs
PRINT *,"Mean of all the numbers is ",mean
END PROGRAM exercise_16_2
```

Note that it is not permissible to allocate all the real variables in a single statement, such as

```
ALLOCATE(x%ptr,STAT=alloc_err)
```

since **ptr** is a component of each *element* of the array **x**, not of the array itself. The following program shows how the program can be modified to use a pointer array instead of an array of pointers:

```
PROGRAM exercise_16_2a
   IMPLICIT NONE

   ! This program is an exercise in using a pointer array

   ! Declarations
   REAL :: max_abs,min_abs,mean
   INTEGER :: n,i,alloc_err
   REAL, DIMENSION(:), POINTER :: x

   ! Get number of numbers
   PRINT *,"How many numbers are there? (between 5 and 20)"
   DO
      READ *,n
      IF (5<=n .AND. n<=20) EXIT
      PRINT *,"Between 5 and 20 please. Try again!"
   END DO

   ! Create pointer array
   ALLOCATE(x(n),STAT=alloc_err)
   IF (alloc_err/=0) THEN
      PRINT *,"Allocation error ",alloc_err," when &
              &trying to allocate space for pointer array"
      STOP
   END IF

   ! Read data
   PRINT *,"Type ",n," numbers"
   READ *,(x(i),i=1,n)
```

```
          ! Calculate required values
          max_abs = MAXVAL(ABS(x))
          min_abs = MINVAL(ABS(x))
          mean = SUM(x)/n
          ! Print results
          PRINT *,"Largest absolute value is ",max_abs
          PRINT *,"Smallest absolute value is ",min_abs
          PRINT *,"Mean of all the numbers is ",mean
      END PROGRAM exercise_16_2a
```

18.4   The solutions to the sets of equations are as shown below:

(a) $x = 3.0$ $y = -2.0$ $z = 4.0$

(b) $x = -1.0$ $y = 2.0$ $z = -1.0$

(c) $y = -2.0$ and $x = 2z - 3$.

The problem here is that the equations are not independent. This can easily be seen by adding twice the second equation to the first equation, which leads to the conclusion that $y = 2$, and then substituting this value for y into all three equations, resulting in the following equations:

$$-2x + 4z = 6$$
$$x - 2z = -3$$
$$3x - 6z = -9$$

These are clearly all the same equation, thus showing that the system of equations has no unique solution.

In this situation the back-substitution step will fail. Ideally, you should check for this possibility, but the method for doing this is beyond the scope of this book – though not particularly difficult.

(d) $x = 2.0$ $y = -1.0$ $z = 4.0$ $w = 3.0$

(e) $x = 2.0$ $y = 1.0$ $z = -3.0$ $w = 3.0$ $t = -1.0$

This is a rather sparse system, but it should not cause any problems.

Index to programs and procedures

This book contains almost 200 complete programs and procedures, all of which have been fully tested. This index details all of these programs, as well as most of the modules that have been developed in the book. It also contains a reference to various operators and generic procedure names that are defined by means of interface blocks. Those entries preceded by an asterisk refer to programs, procedures and modules which are included as sample solutions to certain of the programming exercises, and in these cases the number of the exercise is included in parentheses.

The first section of this index lists all complete programs, while the second and third parts list all complete procedures, including those which form part of a larger program; operator and generic procedure definitions also appear in these two parts. The final part of this index lists all modules, other than those which simply contain a small number of constants for use in a program.

Many of these programs and procedures are specific to the problem being solved, and should be treated simply as examples of how to write Fortran 90 programs, but a number of them can be used with little or no modification in other programs. Particular examples of this latter category are those concerned with sorting and with the implementation of various numerical methods (but remember that it is always preferable to use procedures from a good numerical library).

Complete programs

Modules

Index

In the worked examples throughout this book, those features of the Fortran 90 language which have been introduced in the same chapter as the example program are printed in blue. In this index references to these instances are enclosed in brackets to distinguish them from references to the text of the book. Where both would refer to the same page only the reference to the text is shown. It should also be noted that only those intrinsic procedures that are important to the use of a language feature are shown in the main index, although all those referred to in the body of the book are listed under the *intrinsic procedures* heading; full details of all intrinsic procedures will be found in Appendix A, pages 695–722. Finally, the Glossary on pages 735–51 contains brief explanations of 412 Fortran terms and expressions; these are not included in this index.